## SECOND EDITION

# Competing for Advantage

D0776703

**Robert E. Hoskisson**
Arizona State University

**Michael A. Hitt**
Texas A&M University

**R. Duane Ireland**
Texas A&M University

**Jeffrey S. Harrison**
University of Richmond

THOMSON

SOUTH-WESTERN

Australia · Brazil · Canada · Mexico · Singapore · Spain · United Kingdom · United States

## THOMSON ™

## SOUTH-WESTERN

Australia · Brazil · Canada · Mexico · Singapore · Spain · United Kingdom · United States

*Competing for Advantage, Second Edition*

Robert E. Hoskisson, Michael A. Hitt, R. Duane Ireland, Jeffrey S. Harrison

**VP/Editorial Director:** Jack W. Calhoun
**Editor-in-Chief:** Melissa Acuña
**Senior Acquisitions Editor:** Michele Rhoades
**Developmental Editor:** Rebecca von Gillern, Bookworm Editorial Services
**Marketing Manager:** Clint Kernen
**Manager, Editorial Media:** John Barans
**Technology Project Manager:** Kristen Meere
**Associate Content Project Manager:** Joanna Grote

**Senior Frontlist Buyer:** Doug Wilke
**Production House:** Newgen–Austin
**Senior Art Director:** Tippy McIntosh
**Cover and Internal Designer:** Craig Ramsdell, Ramsdell Design
**Cover Images:** Stephen Johnson, Stone/Getty Images
**Printer:** Edwards Brothers, Ann Arbor, MI

Printed in the United States of America
1 2 3 4 5 10 09 08 07

Student Edition (Package) ISBN 13:
978-0-324-31661-2
Student Edition (Package) ISBN 10:
0-324-31661-5
Student Edition (Book) ISBN 13:
978-0-324-31666-7
Student Edition (Book) ISBN 10:
0-324-31666-6

For permission to use material from this text or product, submit a request online at http://www.thomsonrights.com.

Library of Congress Control Number:
2007926819

For more information about our products, contact us at:
Thomson Learning Academic Resource Center
1-800-423-0563

**Thomson Higher Education**
5191 Natorp Boulevard
Mason, OH 45040
USA

To my father, Claude W. Hoskisson, a great example of honesty and hard work.

*Robert E. Hoskisson*

To my family. I love each and every one of you.

*Michael, Dad, Papa Hitt, and PaPa*

To my loving wife Mary Ann. Over the years, you have given so much of yourself to me and to our children. We are blessed by your grace and kindness. I love you.

*R. Duane Ireland*

To Marie for her pure heart and her willingness to give me a place in it.

*Jeffrey S. Harrison*

# About the Authors

## Robert E. Hoskisson

Robert E. Hoskisson is the W. P. Carey Chair and Professor of Management in the W. P. Carey School of Business at Arizona State University. He received his Ph.D. from the University of California–Irvine. Professor Hoskisson's research topics focus on corporate governance, acquisitions and divestitures, international diversification, privatization, and cooperative strategy. Professor Hoskisson has served on several editorial boards for such publications as the *Academy of Management Journal* (consulting editor and guest editor of a special issue), *Strategic Management Journal* (currently associate editor), *Journal of Management* (associate editor), *Journal of International Business Studies* (currently consulting editor), *Journal of Management Studies* (guest editor of a special issue), and *Organization Science*.

He has co-authored several books including *Strategic Management: Competitiveness and Globalization*, 8th edition (forthcoming from Thomson/South-Western), *Understanding Business Strategy* (Thomson/South-Western), and *Downscoping: How to Tame the Diversified Form* (Oxford University Press). He is also a consulting editor for a series of graduate-level texts on strategic management topics for Oxford University Press. Professor Hoskisson's research has appeared in numerous publications including the *Academy of Management Journal, Academy of Management Review, Strategic Management Journal, Organization Science, Journal of Management, Journal of Management Studies, Academy of Management Executive,* and *California Management Review*.

Professor Hoskisson is a Fellow of the Academy of Management and a charter member of the Academy of Management Journal's Hall of Fame. In 1998, he received an award for Outstanding Academic Contributions to Competitiveness from the American Society for Competitiveness. He also received the William G. Dyer Distinguished Alumni Award given at the Marriott School of Management, Brigham Young University. He recently completed three years of service as a representative at large on the Board of Governors of the Academy of Management and currently is on the Board of Directors of the Strategic Management Society.

## Michael A. Hitt

Michael A. Hitt is a Distinguished Professor of Management and holds the Joe B. Foster Chair in Business Leadership at Texas A&M University. He received his Ph.D. from the University of Colorado. He has authored or co-authored several books and book chapters.

His recent publications include four books: *Downscoping: How to Tame the Diversified Firm* (Oxford University Press), *Strategic Management: Competitiveness and Globalization* (Thomson/South-Western), *Understanding Business Strategy* (Thomson/South-Western), and *Mergers and Acquisitions: Creating Value for Stakeholders* (Oxford University Press).

His numerous journal articles have appeared in such publications as the *Academy of Management Journal, Academy of Management Review, Strategic Management Journal, Journal of Applied Psychology, Organization Science, Journal of Management Studies,* and *Journal of Management,* among others. He has also served on the editorial review boards of several journals, including *Academy of Management Journal, Academy of Management Executive, Journal of Applied Psychology, Journal of World Business,* and *Journal of Applied Behavioral Sciences.* Furthermore, Professor Hitt served as consulting editor (1988–1990) and editor (1991–1993) of *Academy of Management Journal.* He has been a co-editor for special issues of *Strategic Management Journal, Academy of Management Review, Journal of Engineering and Technology Management,* and *Academy of Management Executive.* He is currently co-editor of the *Strategic Entrepreneurship Journal.*

Professor Hitt is a past president of the Academy of Management and is the current president of the Strategic Management Society. He received the 1996 Award for Outstanding Academic Contributions to Competitiveness and the 1999 Award for Outstanding Intellectual Contributions to Competitiveness Research, both awarded by the American Society for Competitiveness. He is a member of the Academy of Management Journals Hall of Fame and a Fellow of the Academy of Management and of the Strategic Management Society. He received an honorary doctorate (Doctor Honoris Causa) from the Universidad Carlos III de Madrid for his contributions to the field.

## R. Duane Ireland

R. Duane Ireland holds the Foreman R. and Ruby S. Bennett Chair in Business and is a Professor of Management in the Mays Business School at Texas A&M University, where he previously served as head of the management department. He received his Ph.D. from Texas Tech University. Prior to joining Texas A&M University, he held positions at University of Richmond, Baylor University, and Oklahoma State University.

He is interested in research questions related to both the entrepreneurship and strategic management disciplines. He is co-author of nearly a dozen books, including *Strategic Management: Competitiveness and Globalization* (8th edition, forthcoming), *Entrepreneurship: Successfully Launching New Ventures* (2nd edition), and *Understanding Business Strategy.* His work has been published in a range of journals, including *Academy of Management Review, Academy of Management Journal, Administrative Science Quarterly, Strategic Management Journal, Academy of Management Executive, Journal of Management, Journal of Management Studies, Decision Sciences, Human Relations, Business Horizons, British Journal of Management, Journal of Business Venturing,* and *Entrepreneurship: Theory & Practice.* Working with colleagues, he has served as a guest editor for special issues of *Academy of Management Review, Academy of Management Executive, Strategic Management Journal, Journal of Business Venturing,* and *Journal of Engineering and Technology Management.* He has also served in various editorial capacities including terms as a member of the editorial review boards for *Academy of Management Review, Academy of Management Journal, Academy of Management Executive, Journal of Management, Journal of Business Venturing,* and *Entrepreneurship: Theory & Practice.* Additionally, he previously completed terms as an associate editor for *Academy of Management Executive,* as consulting editor for *Entrepreneurship: Theory & Practice,* and as an associate editor for *Academy of Management Journal.* Currently, he is the editor elect for *Academy of Management Journal.* He also has served as a member of the Academy of Management's Board of Governors.

He received the 1999 award for Outstanding Intellectual Contribution to Competitiveness Research from the American Society for Competitiveness. He is a Fellow of the Academy of Management. Two of his papers received Best Paper awards from *Academy of Management Journal* (2000) and *Academy of Management Executive* (1999).

## Jeffrey S. Harrison

Jeffrey S. Harrison is the W. David Robbins Chair of Strategic Management in the Robins School of Business at the University of Richmond. Prior to his current appointment, he served as the Fred G. Peelen Professor of Global Hospitality Strategy at Cornell University. He has served on several review boards, including the *Academy of Management Journal* and the *Academy of Management Executive.*

Dr. Harrison's research interests include strategic management and business ethics, with particular expertise in the areas of mergers and acquisitions, diversification, strategic alliances, and stakeholder management. Much of his work has been published in prestigious academic journals such as *Academy of Management Journal, Strategic Management Journal,* and *Journal of Business Ethics.* He has authored or co-authored numerous books, including *Foundations of Strategic Management* (4th edition), *Strategic Management of Organizations and Stakeholders,* and *Mergers and Acquisitions: A Guide to Creating Value for Stakeholders.* Dr. Harrison has also provided consulting and executive training services to many companies on a wide range of strategic, entrepreneurial, and other business issues.

# Brief Contents

# Contents

# Part 3: Creating Competitive Advantage    127

## Chapter 5: Business-Level Strategy    128

## Chapter 6: Competitive Rivalry and Competitive Dynamics    158

## Chapter 7: Cooperative Strategy     183

## Chapter 8: Corporate-Level Strategy     211

## Chapter 9: Acquisition and Restructuring Strategies — 243

## Chapter 10: International Strategy — 267

# Part 4: Monitoring and Creating Entrepreneurial Opportunities     301

## Chapter 11: Corporate Governance     302

# Preface

## Purpose of the Book

The purpose of this book is to provide a comprehensive yet concise description of the core concepts of strategic management that firms need to use to meet the challenge of competing in the current fast-paced and globally competitive environment. Written to meet the educational needs of full-time and part-time MBA students as well as those pursuing an Executive MBA degree, this book will also serve the practicing manager, consultant, or corporate trainer whose firms or clients are faced with global economic challenges in achieving competitive advantage over their rivals. CEOs, line managers, and especially executives charged with developing and implementing strategic initiatives will find much to challenge their thinking and put to prescriptive use while reading and studying this book.

Our examination of strategic management is distinctive in several important ways. The book contains a detailed treatment of multiple perspectives, including traditional industrial organization economics, the resource-based view, and the stakeholder perspective. These three perspectives form the foundation upon which other important ideas and tools for developing strategy are built. The net effect is an integrated approach that demonstrates how firms can simultaneously be ethical and efficient, socially responsible and profitable, responsive to multiple stakeholders and capable of sustaining high financial performance over the long term.

Another distinguishing feature of this book is that strategies and methods for implementing them are treated within the same chapters. For example, the organizational structures required for implementing each of the business-level strategies are discussed in the chapter on business strategies. This approach provides students with a more complete understanding of the organizational implications of selecting a particular strategy. We also describe patterns of competitive rivalry and competitive dynamics, because these phenomena occur as firms implement business strategies to compete in their chosen markets. The chapter in which these important topics are considered discusses concisely yet thoroughly the competitive dynamics in slow-cycle, fast-cycle, and standard-cycle markets.

To ensure that our descriptions of the core concepts of strategic management are accurate and up-to-date, we draw extensively from both current and classic academic research, using as guides the literature in economics, finance, marketing, business ethics, entrepreneurship, and social psychology in addition to strategic management. Also, to fulfill our purpose of providing contemporary insights and analysis, we use numerous current examples from the business press to illustrate how companies make use of the concepts presented here to achieve multiple goals and especially to improve firm performance. We tackle the critical issues of the day: strategic leadership, corporate governance, business ethics, competitive rivalry and competitive dynamics, strategic entrepreneurship, and real options. In fact, this is the only leading MBA-level strategic management text with separate chapters on corporate governance, strategic entrepreneurship, and real options analysis.

This book also fully incorporates concepts of globalization and technological change. Increasing globalization and rapid technological change in the 21st century make the strategic management process highly challenging for managers. These trends create a high level of complexity and turbulence during the strategy development process and also increase the need for speed in making strategic decisions. We integrate issues associated with globalization and technological change in the chapters throughout the book. To emphasize their importance, we also discuss globalization and technological change in a separate chapter on international strategy.

Additionally, because the strategic management process is most effective when grounded in ethical practices, ethics questions are presented at the end of each chapter. These questions challenge readers to place chapter-specific strategic management practices within an ethical context.

## Parts of the Strategic Management Process

**Strategic Thinking** is the foundation for the effective use of strategic management; as such, it is the first of this book's themes. We then focus on the principles and techniques of **Strategic Analysis** in Part 2. In Part 3 we examine the topic of **Creating Competitive Advantage.** This discussion shows how firms create competitive advantage by developing and implementing effective business-level, cooperative, corporate-level, and international strategies. In Part 4, **Monitoring and Creating Entrepreneurial Opportunities,** we emphasize the important trend toward increased corporate governance that emerged in the post-Enron era. Because more intensive corporate governance tends to make firms more conservative, we integrate a discussion of strategic entrepreneurship into this section. We end with a chapter on real options that flows naturally from strategic entrepreneurship. Integrating these topics allows us to show how increased governance can in turn create a need for firms to actively identify and exploit entrepreneurial opportunities.

### Part 1—Strategic Thinking

Strategic thinking and the strategic leadership resulting from it are critical inputs to an effective strategic management process. In Chapter 1, we discuss strategic thinking and its link with effective strategic management. This relationship is more critical in the current competitive environment, which is characterized by globalization and increased technological change. Chapter 1 also examines the emergence of Strategic Management as a discipline. Some of the important early work in the field is reviewed, as are prominent contemporary ideas in the field.

Three major perspectives that influence strategic thinking are introduced in Chapter 1. The Industrial Organization (IO) model of value creation, which is based in industrial organization economics, focuses on how competitive forces in the firm's external environment shape the firm's strategy. The resource-based model of value creation focuses on how strategy is shaped by the firm's idiosyncratic and valuable resources, capabilities, and core competencies. The stakeholder model of responsible firm behavior and firm performance envisions the firm at the center of a network of stakeholders. According to this model, firms that recognize the needs of stakeholders and that effectively manage relationships with a broad group of stakeholders are more likely to achieve high performance over the long term. The first chapter closes with a discussion of the key elements of strategic thinking and how it can be effectively integrated into the strategic management process. This process is described in detail, and the strategic management model described in Chapter 1 serves as an outline for the rest of the book.

Because of the important role of managers in the strategic management process, Chapter 2 uses a comprehensive model to describe how managers, as strategic leaders, foster better strategic thinking throughout the organization. This chapter opens with a discussion of individual strategic leaders, their decision-making styles, and factors that influence their strategic decisions. The chapter then broadens to a discussion of top management teams, including the influence of team heterogeneity, team power, and executive succession processes. The rest of the chapter explains key strategic leadership responsibilities and actions, which include ensuring that the firm is well positioned economically, managing strategic resources, managing relationships with external stakeholders, determining strategic direction, overseeing formulation and implementation of specific strategies, and establishing balanced controls.

## Part 2—Strategic Analysis

In Part 2 of the book, we focus on how firms analyze their external environment and internal organization. After managers are oriented toward strategic thinking and understand principles of effective strategic leadership, the results of these analyses provide the information and knowledge needed to achieve competitive advantages by selecting and using particular strategies.

Chapter 3 examines the different tools the firm uses to analyze the three parts (the general environment, the industry environment, and competitors) of its external environment. By studying its general environment, the firm can identify opportunities and threats. The IO model provides the foundation that firms use to study industries. The primary purpose of examining this part of the external environment is to determine the profitability potential of an industry or a segment of it. Competitor analysis, the final part of the firm's external environment, yields information that allows the firm to know more about its competitors and about the actions and responses each competitor might take while competing in different markets.

The emphasis in Chapter 4 is on internal analysis, and the purpose is to identify the resources, capabilities, and core competencies that can help a firm to achieve competitive advantages. Whereas Chapter 3 focused on what a firm *might do* as suggested by the external environment, this chapter focuses on what a firm *can do* as suggested by its resources, capabilities, and core competencies.

The resource-based view of the firm is the underlying theoretical framework for Chapter 4's discussions. Four criteria that firms use to identify core competencies—value, rarity, imperfect imitability, and nonsubstitutability—are described. In addition, we examine the value chain in terms of primary and support activities to show how firms determine those activities with which they can or cannot create value. This analysis also provides information suggesting when a firm should outsource an activity in the value chain to a supplier. Finally, firms are cautioned to remain flexible so that core competencies do not become core rigidities. An understanding derived from strategic analysis is the foundation needed to focus on the strategies firms can use to create competitive advantages.

Chapter 4 concludes with a detailed examination of firm performance from multiple perspectives. The demands and needs of multiple stakeholders, as well as their power to influence the firm, are described. Multiple measures of firm performance are introduced, including both financial and nonfinancial measures. The chapter closes with a discussion of sustainable performance.

## Part 3—Creating Competitive Advantage

In Part 3's chapters we simultaneously discuss formulation and implementation, components of the strategic management process that are examined separately in other books. Our joint treatment of formulation and implementation actions is comprehensive and integrated. For example, our study of business-level strategies in Chapter 5 includes analyses of cost leadership, differentiation, focused cost leadership, focused differentiation, and integrated cost leadership/differentiation strategies. After explaining the characteristics of each strategy, we describe the unique organizational structure that firms match to each type of business-level strategy. In this manner, we link formulation (i.e., the selection of a business-level strategy) with implementation (i.e., the appropriate organizational structure matched with individual business-level strategies). This important and unique pattern of linking strategy with structure is followed in the remaining chapters of Part 3.

Chapter 6 also focuses on business-level strategy in describing patterns of competitive rivalry between individual firms as well as patterns of competitive dynamics among all firms that compete within an industry. An important reason for the firm to understand competitive rivalry and competitive dynamics is to learn how to predict the actions that competitors might take against it as well as how the competitor might respond in retaliation against the focal firm's competitive action. The chapter examines factors that are important to competitive rivalry (e.g., awareness, motivation, and ability as drivers of a firm's competitive behavior) and the dimensions of competitive dynamics (e.g., the effects of varying rates of competitive speed in different markets). Thus, in total, the chapter's analysis of rivalry and dynamics highlights their influences on firms' competitive actions and competitive responses.

We focus on cooperative strategies in Chapter 7. Cooperative strategies such as strategic alliances, joint ventures, and network strategies have become increasingly important in the 21st-century competitive landscape. A key reason for this importance is that few if any firms have the resources necessary to either internally develop or acquire from external sources all of the resources needed to create value. Cooperative strategy is another path that firms follow when gaining access to and developing new resources and capabilities as well as exploiting current ones. This chapter examines strategies that have evolved in response to the challenges and opportunities created by increasing globalization and technological change. The chapter also explains the risks associated with cooperative strategies, including inadequate contracts, opportunism, and misrepresentation of competencies by partners. Dominant approaches for managing strategic alliances are also explored to explain how risk is managed when the firm cooperates with others to create value.

Chapter 8 begins our discussion of corporate-level strategy. Concerned with the businesses in which the diversified firm intends to compete—and with how it will manage its portfolio of businesses—we discuss four major corporate-level strategies in this chapter. These strategies range from one with relatively little diversification (single business) to one with substantial diversification (unrelated diversification). In addition, the unique organizational structures required to successfully implement each corporate-level strategy are described.

The analysis of corporate-level strategy and diversification is extended in Chapter 9, where we discuss mergers and acquisitions. Mergers and acquisitions have been popular for many decades, and recent trends suggest that their popularity is unlikely to decline much in the next few years. Although many mergers and acquisitions fail, some do succeed. Chapter 9 presents reasons that account for failure as well as those that contribute to merger and acquisition success. The dominant approaches to restructuring (downsizing, downscoping, and leveraged buyouts) are also discussed in this chapter. Successful firms restructure their portfolio of businesses as necessary. Restructuring can be initiated to deal with merger and acquisition failures or to adjust the firm's portfolio of businesses in response to emerging opportunities in its external environment.

Chapter 10 explores both corporate-level and business-level international strategies. As in the previous chapters in Part 3, we describe the organizational structures necessary to implement each of the corporate-level strategies. We also discuss some of the implications of implementing business-level strategies in a particular country. After selecting an international strategy, a firm must decide which mode of entry to pursue when implementing the chosen strategy. Exporting, licensing, strategic alliances, acquisitions, and establishing a new wholly owned subsidiary are entry modes that firms consider when entering markets. We also discuss outcomes of international diversification and the attendant political and economic risks.

## Part 4—Monitoring and Creating Entrepreneurial Opportunities

Corporate governance, strategic entrepreneurship, and real options analysis are examined in Part 4, the book's final section. Corporate governance, given the post-Enron environment and the challenges many firms experience, is a critically important topic warranting a separate chapter. Therefore, Chapter 11 describes major corporate governance mechanisms and how they can be effectively used to ensure that the actions of the firm's agents (key decision makers) are aligned with the principals' (owners') best interests. The chapter examines large institutional investors, boards of directors, and executive compensation as dominant governance mechanisms and indicates how they can be effectively used in the current business environment. In addition, we discuss trends in international corporate governance along with the need for continuous displays of ethical behavior by top-level managers and members of the firm's board of directors.

Combining Chapter 11's examination of effective corporate governance mechanisms with Chapter 2's study of successful strategic leadership practices yields a comprehensive treatment of how the strategic management process can be used to ethically achieve a competitive advantage. In addition to grounding the analysis of effective corporate governance and strategic leadership in current research, we provide several company-specific examples to enhance understanding of how these principles can be successfully applied in today's business organizations.

Although corporate governance is important, increasingly stringent governance can create a more conservative strategic management process, particularly in the selection and implementation of the firm's strategies. A highly conservative approach to the strategic management process increases the need for firms to pursue aggressively the identification and exploitation of entrepreneurial opportunities. Accordingly, Chapter 12 emphasizes actions that firms can take to create entrepreneurial opportunities and to manage them strategically in order to gain and sustain a competitive advantage. Entrepreneurship is commonly practiced in existing firms to renew current competitive advantages while simultaneously enhancing the firm's ability to create new competitive advantages for future success. Furthermore, we examine how cooperative strategies and merger and acquisition strategies can be used in a more entrepreneurial manner to create competitive advantages.

The final chapter focuses on how to manage entrepreneurial opportunities in an uncertain environment using real options tools. This chapter, which is new to this edition of *Competing for Advantage*, is of significant value for readers interested in understanding all aspects the strategic management process. Contributed by Jeff Reuer and edited by the authors, this new chapter provides up-to-date methods for planning and calculating the value of potential entrepreneurial projects. Successful use of these methods increases the firm's flexibility when making decisions within the context of uncertain technological, product, and market environments.

## Summary

This book offers comprehensive yet concise coverage of the core concepts in strategic management as well as an explanation of the strategic management process that professional managers and those pursuing an MBA or EMBA degree will find useful. The book is comprehensive in that it examines traditional strategic management topics (e.g., industry analysis) along with other important topics (e.g., corporate governance, strategic leadership, competitive rivalry and competitive dynamics, strategic entrepreneurship, and real options) to help prepare students for a successful managerial career. The book's four themes—Strategic Thinking, Strategic Analysis, Creating Competitive Advantage, and Monitoring and Creating Entrepreneurial Opportunities—are the foundation for providing readers with an integrated traditional and contemporary analysis of an effective strategic management process. We hope that all readers—instructors, students, and managers—will find the book helpful in understanding and successfully using strategic management concepts. We wish you well with your careers and with your use of the strategic management process.

## Tools for Teaching and Learning
### Instructor's Resource CD-ROM

(ISBN 0-324-654979) Key ancillaries—**Instructor's Manual, Test Bank,** and **PowerPoint**®—are provided on CD-ROM for easy customization in files formatted for Microsoft Office's core word processor, Microsoft Word, and its core presentation graphics program, PowerPoint. The Instructor's Manual contains outlines, sample syllabi, and discussion prompts. Test questions are provided in several formats: true/false, multiple-choice, essay, and case scenarios (problem-solving application questions). PowerPoint slides for each chapter of the text provide a complete chapter overview combined with figures and tables from the text.

### *Competing for Advantage* Website

(www.thomsonedu.com/management/hoskison) Broad online support is provided on the text's dedicated Website, including a map to relevant Harvard Business School cases.

## Business & Company Resource Center (BCRC)

BCRC puts a complete business library at your students' fingertips. BCRC is a premier online business research tool that allows students to seamlessly search thousands of periodicals, journals, references, financial information sources, market share reports, company histories, and much more.

## TextChoice: Management Exercises and Cases

TextChoice is the home of Thomson Learning's online digital content. TextChoice provides the fastest, easiest way for you to create your own learning materials. Thomson's Management Exercises and Cases database includes a variety of experiential exercises, classroom activities, exercises, and cases to enhance any management course. Choose as many exercises as you like, or add your own material to create a supplement tailor-fitted to your course. Contact your South-Western/Thomson Learning sales representative for more information.

---

## Acknowledgments

We are grateful to the team at Thomson for working diligently on this project and to our students and colleagues (including many reviewers) who have provided valuable insights helping us to improve the overall quality of the book. We are especially appreciative of our families for giving us support and encouragement and to our academic institutions for allowing us to pursue this and other book projects. We would be remiss if we did not also thank the many hundreds of authors we have cited in this volume for adding so much to the field through their thoughtful observations and rigorous research. In particular, we are grateful to Jeffrey Reuer for his insights on real options. This book reflects the work of numerous scholars with a common purpose of discovering and disseminating valuable research findings that help foster understanding and improve the strategic management process. We sincerely hope that we have presented the material in a way that is useful to graduate business students and others who are interested in learning how to help a firm "Compete for Advantage."

*Robert E. Hoskisson*
*Michael A. Hitt*
*R. Duane Ireland*
*Jeffrey S. Harrison*

# Strategic Thinking

# Introduction to Strategic Management

**KNOWLEDGE OBJECTIVES**
*Studying this chapter should provide you with the strategic management knowledge needed to:*

1. Describe the 21st-century competitive landscape and explain how globalization and technological changes shape it.
2. Use the industrial organization (I/O) model to explain how firms can earn above-average returns.
3. Use the resource-based model to explain how firms can earn above-average returns.
4. Explain the stakeholder perspective and how effective management of stakeholders can lead to high firm performance and responsible firm behavior.
5. Define strategic thinking and explain how it is used to guide decision making during the strategic management process.
6. Describe the strategic management process.

Business executives face a world that is increasingly complex and ever changing. Rapidly advancing technologies in areas such as communications and transportation have led to unprecedented levels of global trade and awareness. These trends, combined with dramatic economic, social, and political changes in Asia, Eastern Europe, Latin America, the Middle East, Africa, and elsewhere, have created a globally interconnected marketplace characterized by intense competition. Strategic management is a discipline that has emerged in response to the need for mental models and strategic planning tools to help executives guide their firms in this challenging global business environment. It is concerned primarily with the actions organizations take to achieve competitive advantage and create value for the organization and its stakeholders.

**Competitive advantage** comes from successful formulation and execution of strategies that are different from and create more value than the strategies of competitors.[1] When a firm is able to achieve a competitive advantage, that advantage normally can be sustained only for a limited period.[2] A **sustainable competitive advantage** (hereafter called *competitive advantage*) is possible only after competitors' efforts to duplicate the value-creating strategy have ceased or failed. The speed with which competitors are able to acquire the skills needed to duplicate the benefits of a firm's value-creating strategy determines how long the competitive advantage will last.[3] Firms must understand how to exploit a competitive advantage if they intend to create more value than competitors, which can then lead to higher returns for those who have invested money and other resources in the firm.[4] When a firm earns returns that are higher than those of competitors, it is an indication that the strategies the firm is pursuing are leading to competitive advantage.

The **strategic management process** (as illustrated later in the chapter; see Figure 1.6) is the full set of commitments, decisions, and actions required for a firm to create value and earn returns that are higher than those of competitors.[5] In its simplest form, the process involves analyzing the firm and its environment, and then using the information to formulate and implement strategies that lead to competitive advantage. Thus, the strategic management process is used to match the conditions of an ever-changing market and competitive structure with a firm's continuously evolving resources, capabilities, and competencies. Strategic leaders guide the strategy-creation process, help the organization acquire and develop needed resources, manage relationships with key organizational stakeholders, and develop adequate organizational controls to ensure that the process is successful in leading to desired firm outcomes. The responsibilities of effective strategic leaders are discussed in Chapter 2.

This chapter introduces several topics. First, we examine some of the major characteristics of the 21st-century competitive landscape that form the context in which strategies are created and executed. We then relate a brief history of the major events and central ideas that played a prominent role in the creation of the field now called strategic management. The early ideas lay the groundwork for a discussion of three prominent models that suggest the strategic inputs needed to select strategic actions necessary to create value. The first model (industrial organization) suggests that the external environment is the primary determinant of a firm's strategies. The key to this model is identifying and competing successfully in an attractive (i.e., profitable) industry.[6] The second model (resource based) proposes that a firm's unique resources and capabilities are the critical link to value creation.[7] The third model (stakeholder) suggests that long-term competitive advantage is a function of the strength of a firm's relationships with stakeholders and how those relationships are managed.[8] Comprehensive explanations in this chapter and the next three chapters show that through the combined use of these models, firms obtain the strategic inputs they need to successfully formulate and implement strategies.

The final section of this chapter begins with an examination of the characteristics of strategic thinking and how strategic leaders can encourage this sort of thinking within their firms. *Strategic thinking* describes the more creative aspects of strategic management.[9] The strategic management process, as it will be examined in this book, is then described in detail. Effective strategic actions taken in the context of carefully integrated strategy formulation and implementation plans result in desired firm performance.[10]

## The Competitive Landscape

Business failure is rather common. In the United States, the number of businesses that filed for bankruptcy averaged more than 41,000 per year in the decade ending in 2005.[11] Furthermore, because data about business start-ups and failures tend to be incomplete, the actual number of companies closing their doors may actually exceed this count. Thomas J. Watson Jr., formerly IBM's chairman, once cautioned people to remember that "corporations are expendable and that success—at best—is an impermanent achievement which can always slip out of hand."[12]

Even more common than businesses that fail completely are those that have become uncompetitive because of an inability to make the changes that are necessary for continued success. The automobile industry is an example of the way in which changes in the global environment have influenced businesses. After World War II the big three U.S. automakers—General Motors (GM), Ford, and Chrysler—enjoyed a dominant position in the industry. However, increases in gas prices in the early 1970s helped fuel a trend toward smaller, more efficient automobiles in the United States.[13] This trend was accompanied by a dramatic increase in the quality of Japanese-made automobiles from companies such as Toyota, Honda, and Datsun (now called Nissan).[14]

The three U.S. automakers were slow to respond to these changes, resulting in dramatic reductions in their market shares. In an effort to catch up, they engaged in a number of joint ventures with Japanese and other foreign auto companies. Now, joint ventures are common among all the major automobile companies around the world.[15] Several rounds of shakeups in top management and boards of directors have also occurred, with one of the earliest major board revolts happening at GM.[16] Chrysler, under the leadership of Lee Iacocca, returned from the brink of bankruptcy and ultimately merged with the German company Daimler-Benz.[17] Meanwhile, new entrants came into the large U.S. market and other markets with successful brands such as Korean Hundai and Kia. The major Japanese companies also launched brands to compete with higher-end automobiles such as BMW, Cadillac, and Mercedes Benz. Lexus, Acura, and Infiniti are now major brands in the United States and elsewhere.[18] In addition, companies such as BMW, Toyota, Honda, and others have established a major manufacturing presence in the United States, and U.S. companies have likewise expanded their manufacturing operations around the globe, including large operations in Latin America, Asia, and elsewhere.

Global forces in the industry have taken an enormous toll on the performance of the large U.S. manufacturers. With bloated inventories, the Chrysler division of Daimler-Chrysler suffered a loss of approximately $1.5 billion in the third quarter of 2006.[19] Under increasing pressure from the board for a rapid turnaround, the company launched a program to try to cut $1,000 in costs from every vehicle it produces.[20] Ford also had a poor quarter, posting a $5.8 billion loss, even as management warned of worse performance in the future. Newly appointed Ford CEO Alan Mulally said he was not surprised by the bad news and that he was approaching the problem with his "eyes wide open."[21] GM's loss of only $115 million for the third quarter was trumpeted by CEO Rick Wagoner as "significant progress" and evidence that the company was recovering, despite concerns from analysts regarding employee healthcare costs, liquidity, and increased debt.[22] Meanwhile, Toyota was reporting increases in sales and profits in North America, and Kia broke ground on a $1 billion manufacturing facility in Georgia.[23]

Changes in the automobile industry are, in part, a result of globalization and rapid changes in technology. U.S. firms, in particular, have been unable to keep up with either of these trends. They have been slow to adopt a global mind-set, and they have been unable to make all of the technological changes needed to stay competitive. We will now examine these trends toward globalization and rapid technological change.

## Globalization of Markets and Industries

The fundamental nature of competition in many of the world's industries is changing.[24] One of the most important of these changes is the continuous increase in the globalization of the world's markets.[25] **Globalization** can be defined as increasing economic interdependence among countries as reflected in the flow of goods and services, financial capital, and knowledge across country borders.[26] Relatively unfettered by artificial constraints, such as tariffs, the global economy significantly expands and complicates a firm's competitive environment.[27] For instance, in 2008 the value of goods imported into the United States is expected to be greater than the value of all revenues collected by the federal government.[28] In global markets and industries, financial capital might be obtained in one national market and used to buy raw materials in another. Manufacturing equipment bought from a third national market can then be used to produce products that are sold in yet a fourth market. Thus, globalization increases the range of opportunities for companies competing in the 21st century[29] and is a fundamental driver of the business economies in today's competitive

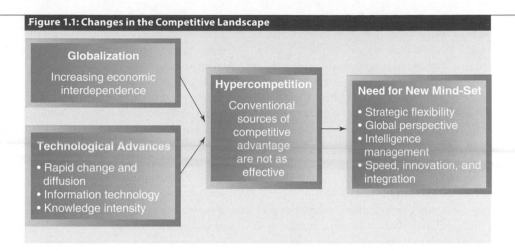

**Figure 1.1: Changes in the Competitive Landscape**

**Globalization**

Increasing economic interdependence

**Technological Advances**

- Rapid change and diffusion
- Information technology
- Knowledge intensity

**Hypercompetition**

Conventional sources of competitive advantage are not as effective

**Need for New Mind-Set**

- Strategic flexibility
- Global perspective
- Intelligence management
- Speed, innovation, and integration

landscape.[30] Although most large U.S. firms compete in international markets to some degree, not all of them are aggressively responding to global market opportunities.[31]

Globalization has contributed to **hypercompetition,** or extremely intense rivalry among firms. The term often is used to capture the realities of the 21st-century competitive landscape. As shown in Figure 1.1, hypercompetition results from the dynamics of strategic maneuvering among global and innovative combatants. It is a condition of rapidly escalating competition based on price-quality positioning, competition to create new know-how and establish first-mover advantage, and competition to protect or invade established product or geographic markets.[32] In a hypercompetitive market, firms often aggressively challenge their competitors in the hopes of improving their competitive position and ultimately their performance.[33]

Partly because of globalization and hypercompetition, it is becoming difficult for firms even to recognize or determine an industry's boundaries. Consider, for example, how advances in interactive computer networks and telecommunications are blurring the definition of the television industry. The near future may find traditional television companies such as ABC, CBS, NBC, and HBO competing not only among themselves but also with companies involved primarily with telephone (AT&T), cable (Cox), satellite (DirectTV), computer software (Microsoft), consumer electronics (Sony), and others.

## Technological Advances

In addition to globalization, rapid technological change is also associated with hypercompetition.[34] Three categories of technological trends are significantly altering the nature of competition. The first is the increasing rate of technological change and diffusion. Both the rate of change of technology and the speed at which new technologies become available have increased substantially over the past 15 to 20 years. Consider, for instance, that it took the telephone industry 35 years to get into 25 percent of all homes in the United States, compared with 26 years for television, 22 years for radio, 16 years for personal computers, and only seven years for the Internet.[35] Some evidence suggests that it takes only 12 to 18 months for firms to gather information about their competitors' research and development and subsequent product decisions.[36] The shorter product life cycles resulting from rapid diffusions of new technologies place a competitive premium on a firm's being able to quickly introduce new goods and services into the marketplace. In fact, when products become somewhat indistinguishable because of the widespread and rapid diffusion of technologies, speed to market may be the primary source of competitive advantage.[37] For instance, approximately 75 percent of the product-life gross margins for a typical personal computer are earned within the first 90 days of sales.[38]

Another factor associated with rapid technological change is the development of disruptive technologies that destroy the value of existing technology and create new markets.[39] Some have referred to this concept as Schumpeterian innovation, from the work of the famous economist Joseph A. Schumpeter. He suggested that such innovation emerged from a process of creative destruction, in which existing technologies are replaced by new ones. Others refer to this outcome as radical or breakthrough innovation.[40] The development and use of the Internet for commerce is an example of a disruptive technology.[41]

A second category of technological trends that are influencing competition is the dramatic changes in information technology that have occurred in recent years. Personal computers, cellular phones, artificial intelligence, virtual reality, and massive databases (e.g., Lexis/Nexis) are examples of how information is used differently as a result of technological developments. An important outcome of these changes is that the ability to effectively and efficiently access and use information has become a significant source of competitive advantage in virtually all industries.[42] Companies are building electronic networks that link them to customers, employees, vendors, and suppliers.[43] The Internet provides an infrastructure that allows the delivery of information to computers in any location.[44] Access to significant quantities of relatively inexpensive information yields strategic opportunities for a range of industries and companies. Retailers, for example, use the Internet to provide abundant shopping privileges to customers in multiple locations. The pervasive influence of e-business is creating a new culture, referred to as e-culture, that affects the way managers lead, organize, and think as well as develop and implement strategies.[45]

Finally, increasing knowledge intensity is dramatically influencing the competitive environment. Knowledge (information, intelligence, and expertise) is the basis of technology and its application. In the 21st-century competitive landscape, knowledge is a critical organizational resource and is increasingly a valuable source of competitive advantage.[46] As a result, many companies now strive to transmute the accumulated knowledge of individual employees into a corporate asset. Some argue that the value of intangible assets, including knowledge, is growing as a proportion of total shareholder value.[47] The probability of a firm achieving value creation in today's business environment is enhanced for the firm which is aware that its survival depends on the ability to capture intelligence, transform it into usable knowledge, and diffuse it rapidly throughout the company.[48] Firms accepting this challenge shift their focus from merely obtaining information to exploiting that information to gain a competitive advantage over rival firms.[49] We discuss this trend toward increased rivalry more fully in Chapter 6.

Many implications are associated with the hypercompetitive environment resulting from globalization and technological advances. For instance, traditional ways of looking at competitiveness are unlikely to lead to competitive advantage.[50] Conventional sources of competitive advantage, such as economies of scale and huge advertising budgets, are not as effective as they once were.[51] Managers must adopt a new mind-set that values speed, innovation, and integration along with the challenges that evolve from constantly changing conditions.[52] Global competition has increased performance standards in many dimensions, including quality, cost, productivity, product introduction time, and operational efficiency.[53] Moreover, these standards are not static; they are exacting, requiring continuous improvement from a firm and its employees. As they accept the challenges posed by these increasing standards, companies improve their capabilities and individual workers sharpen their skills. Thus, in the 21st-century competitive landscape, only firms capable of meeting, if not exceeding, global standards typically develop competitive advantage.[54]

Also, to achieve high performance, firms must be able to adapt quickly to changes in their competitive landscape. Such adaptation requires that firms develop strategic flexibility. **Strategic flexibility** is a set of capabilities used to respond to various demands and opportunities existing in a dynamic and uncertain competitive environment (managing strategic flexibility is addressed more fully in Chapter 13). Thus, strategically flexible firms know how to cope with uncertainty and its accompanying risks.[55] In the words of John Browne, former CEO of British Petroleum, "In order to generate extraordinary value for shareholders, a company has to learn better than its competitors and apply that knowledge throughout its businesses faster and more widely than they do."[56] Continuous learning provides the firm with new and up-to-date sets of skills, which allow it to adapt to its environment as it encounters changes.[57] Strategic thinking, described later in this chapter, can help a firm remain strategically flexible. Effective strategic leadership, the topic of Chapter 2, is essential to both strategic thinking and flexibility.

The changes described in this section did not occur all at once. The strategic landscape of today emerged from several decades of dramatic economic, social, technological, and political changes. The field of strategic management was born of the need for managers to effectively deal with such changes. A brief history of the intellectual emergence of the field is presented in the next section. This history will serve as a conceptual foundation for the development of strategic management concepts found in this and other chapters.

## The Emergence of Strategic Management as a Business Discipline

Many of the competitive trends and influences that were described in the last section began to take shape right after World War II. Specifically, the era brought with it management challenges associated with dramatic advances in technology, especially in communications and transportation, as well as increasing national and global competition. Rapid economic, social, technological, and political changes created a turbulent business environment. In addition, the sheer size and complexity of business firms made them difficult to manage. Scholars and consulting firms recognized that organizational success depended on the organization successfully navigating an increasingly difficult external environment.[58]

By the middle of the last century, many business schools were offering a course called business policy, a capstone course that was intended to help students examine complicated, high-level business problems through integration of knowledge obtained from the various functional disciplines of business.[59] Eventually, the American Assembly of Collegiate Schools of Business (now called the Association to Advance Collegiate Schools of Business) made the business policy course a requirement for accreditation. Also, the major academic management society, the Academy of Management, formed a Business Policy and Planning Division to support academic research and teaching on the subject. The business policy course, as it was typically taught, used business cases to challenge students to develop policies that would solve business problems through an integrated, multifunctional approach. However, business policy was considered as more of a course than a field of study.[60] Outside the academic arena, consulting firms such as the Boston Consulting Group were developing tools to help top managers guide their firms.

## Early Influences on the Strategy Concept

In 1962 Alfred Chandler, a business historian, published a book that was among the most influential in guiding early business policy scholarship. Chandler defined strategy as "determination of the basic long-term goals and objectives of an enterprise, and the adoption of courses of action and the allocation of resources necessary for carrying out these goals."[61] His definition embraced the notion that a firm should establish goals, strategies to achieve them, and an implementation (allocation) plan, but it did not address the essential role strategy plays in linking the firm to its environment. Shortly thereafter, Igor Ansoff discussed strategy in terms of product-market scope, growth vector, competitive advantage, and synergy.[62] Ansoff's definition, with its treatment of market factors, is more oriented toward the external environment. He also advanced the idea that the objectives of the firm should attempt to balance the conflicting claims of various internal and external stakeholders, including stockholders, managers, employees, suppliers, and vendors. He divided objectives into two categories, economic and social, with the social objectives acting as constraints on the economic objectives.

Around the same time (1965), Edmund Learned, C. Ronald Christensen, Kenneth Andrews, and William Guth published what would become a classic book on the strategic management process. They defined strategy as "the pattern of objectives, purposes, or goals and major policies and plans for achieving these goals, stated in such a way as to define what business the company is in or is to be in and the kind of company it is or is to be."[63] They identified the four components of strategy development as "(1) market opportunity, (2) corporate competences and resources, (3) personal values and aspirations, and (4) acknowledged obligations to segments of society other than stockholders."[64] This treatment of the strategy concept foreshadowed the importance of an economic approach to strategy formulation (market opportunity), as well as the importance of resources and capabilities and an acknowledgement of firm obligations to broad groups of stakeholders. As we will discuss later in this chapter, industrial organization economics, the resource-based view, and the stakeholder perspective serve as theoretical foundations for this book. Also, their third component, personal values and aspirations, is incorporated into our discussion of strategic leadership in Chapter 2.

Several other concepts were also important to the development of the foundational literature of modern strategic management. One of the most important is recognition that organizations are systems that depend on their external environments for survival.[65] Dependence comes from the need for transactions with external stakeholders in order for resources such as raw materials, supplies, machinery, sales dollars, and long-term capital to be obtained. As I. C. MacMillan writes, "Thus, all organizations are dependent upon the environment for the provision of certain inputs; which the organization then transforms into outputs; which it, in turn, uses to get more inputs."[66] Jeffrey Pfeffer and Gerald Salancik observed that firm dependence on external stakeholders also gives those stakeholders a certain amount of control over the firm.[67] Associated with the systems perspective and resource dependence is recognition that strategy formulation contains both rational-deductive and political processes.[68] Consequently, in addition to economically based strategies, firms should develop political strategies to deal with stakeholders—such as shareholders, employee groups and unions, competitors, and suppliers—that can facilitate achievement of firm goals.[69]

The ideas of Henry Mintzberg also significantly affected the business policy field.[70] Defining strategy as "a pattern in a stream of decisions," he challenged the underlying assumption that strategies are always a reflection of deliberate plans conceived in advance of particular organizational decisions.[71] Instead, he argued that organizations learn from a process of trial and error. This perspective is consistent with the view that firms can and should learn from their external stakeholders. The importance of organizational learning processes to strategic success has been widely acknowledged.

In another important work, Michael Jensen and William Meckling contributed to the perspective that managers serve as agents for the owners or shareholders.[72] **Agency theory** argues that agency problems exist when managers take actions that are in their own best interests rather than those of the shareholders. The popularity of agency theory seems to have influenced strategic management scholars and business executives to keep their focus on shareholder returns as a primary criterion for firm success.

Another major advance came from Oliver Williamson, who examined the efficiency of economic activity within and between markets and organizational hierarchies.[73] **Transaction cost economics** suggests that firms are better off purchasing required resources through a market transaction unless particular conditions exist that make creating them internally more efficient.[74] If there are a lot of potential suppliers of a resource a firm needs, then a market mechanism can be used. But when there are only a small number of suppliers, there is a much larger risk that they will try to take maximum advantage of their situation. This situation can lead to a firm foregoing a market transaction in favor of internalizing the supplier organization through vertical integration.

## Modern Strategic Management

The early work in the field of business policy was fragmented. By the late 1970s, interest in the topic was growing, and the term *strategic management* began to replace *business policy*. The new title was broader in its scope and implied that a focus on simply establishing business policies to integrate functional strategies was not a sufficient solution to the strategic challenges executives were facing.[75] In May of 1977 scholars and practitioners who were experts on the topic gathered at the University of Pittsburgh to share ideas. At that meeting, Dan Schendel and Charles Hofer, the conference organizers, presented a model of the fundamental activities in the strategic management process.[76] It included organizational goal formulation, environmental analysis, strategy formulation, strategy evaluation, strategy implementation, and strategic control. The general premise underlying their model was that the most effective firm strategies were those that best "fit" the environmental situation. The **deterministic perspective** of strategy formulation argues that firms should adapt to their environments because characteristics of the environment determine which strategies will succeed.[77]

Environmental determinism was challenged by Jay Bourgeois, who stated that "the strategy of a firm cannot be predicted, nor is it predestined; the strategic decisions made by managers cannot be assumed to be the product of deterministic forces in their environments . . . On the contrary, the very nature of the concept of strategy assumes a human agent who is able to take actions that attempt to distinguish one's firm from the competitors."[78] The principle of **enactment** means that firms do not have to entirely submit to environmental forces because they can, in part, create their own environments through strategic actions.[79] These actions might include forming alliances and joint ventures with stakeholders, investing in leading technologies, advertising, or political lobbying.[80] The truth is that adaptation and enactment are both important to strategy formulation. A firm should attempt to predict and adapt to trends and influences over which it has no control or that would be too expensive to influence. On the other hand, firms can also influence their environments in ways that make them better suited to organizational success.

The early advances in strategic management are all incorporated into this book. Our model of the strategic management process is comprehensive, in that it includes all of the activities that were identified as important in the significant early work, such as goal setting, external orientation, development and management of internal resources, formulation and implementation of specific strategies, political strategies, transaction costs, agency theory, the importance and role of external stakeholders, and organizational learning.

## Three Perspectives on Value Creation

Beginning in the 1980s, as the field of strategic management began to grow and develop, three perspectives gained momentum as comprehensive ways to organize the central ideas and activities associated with strategic management. They are industrial organization (I/O) economics, the resource-based view, and the stakeholder approach. These three perspectives serve as a foundation for much of what is found in this book.

### The I/O Model of Above-Average Returns

The strategic management process is dynamic, as ever-changing markets and competitive structures must be coordinated with a firm's continuously evolving strategic inputs.[81] From the 1960s through the 1980s, the external environment was thought to be the primary determinant of strategies that firms selected to be successful.[82] Consistent with this deterministic view, the industrial organization (I/O) model of above-average returns explains the dominant influence of the external environment on a firm's strategic actions. The model specifies that the industry in which a firm chooses to compete has a stronger influence on the firm's performance than do the choices managers make inside their organizations.[83] The firm's performance is believed to be determined primarily by a range of industry properties, including economies of scale, barriers to market entry, product differentiation, and the degree of concentration of firms in the industry.[84] We examine these industry characteristics in Chapter 3 more fully.

Grounded in economics, the I/O model has four underlying assumptions. First, the external environment is assumed to impose pressures and constraints that determine the strategies that would result in above-average returns. Second, most firms competing within a particular industry or industry segment are assumed to control similar strategically relevant resources and to pursue similar strategies in light of those resources. Third, resources used to implement strategies are assumed to be highly mobile across firms. Because of resource mobility, any resource differences that might develop between firms will be short lived. Fourth, organizational decision makers are assumed to be rational and committed to acting in the firm's best interests, as shown by their profit-maximizing behaviors.[85] The I/O model challenges firms to locate the most attractive industry in which to compete.[86] Because most firms are assumed to have similar strategically relevant resources that are mobile across companies, competitiveness generally can be increased only when firms find the industry with the highest profit potential and learn how to use their resources to implement the strategy required by the industry's structural characteristics.[87]

In the 1980s, the work of Michael Porter captured a lot of attention from strategic management scholars and practitioners.[88] Porter's work reinforced the importance of the economic theory upon which much of the field of strategic management was already based.[89] The early stage of development of strategic management is reflected in one of his early books, *Competitive Strategy:* "Competitive strategy is an area of primary concern to managers, depending on a subtle understanding of industries and competitors. Yet the strategy field has offered few analytical techniques for gaining this understanding, and those that have emerged lack breadth and comprehensiveness."[90]

Porter's books and articles helped to fill the void. He provided a description of the forces that determine the nature and level of competition in an industry, as well as suggestions for how to use this information to develop competitive advantage. The five forces model (explained in Chapter 3) suggests that an industry's profitability (i.e., its rate of return on invested capital relative to its cost of capital) is a function of interactions among suppliers, buyers, competitive rivalry among firms currently in the industry, product substitutes, and potential entrants to the industry.[91] Using this tool, a firm is challenged to understand an industry's profit potential and the strategy necessary to establish a defensible competitive position, given the industry's structural characteristics. Typically, the model suggests that firms can earn above-average returns by manufacturing standardized products or producing standardized services at costs below those of competitors (a cost-leadership strategy) or by manufacturing differentiated products for which customers are willing to pay a price premium (a differentiation strategy, described in depth in Chapter 5).

As shown in Figure 1.2, the I/O model suggests that above-average returns are earned when firms implement the strategy dictated by the characteristics of the general, industry, and competitor environments. Companies that develop or acquire the internal skills needed to implement strategies required by the external environment are likely to succeed, while those that do not are likely to fail. Hence, this model suggests that external characteristics rather than the firm's unique internal resources and capabilities primarily determine returns.

Research findings support the I/O model. They show that approximately 20 percent of a firm's profitability is determined by the industry or industries in which it chooses to operate. This research also shows, however, that 36 percent of the variance in profitability could be attributed to the firm's characteristics and actions.[92] The results of the research suggest that both the environment and the firm's characteristics play a role in determining the firm's profitability. Thus, there is likely a reciprocal relationship between the environment and the firm's strategy that affects the firm's performance.[93] As the research suggests, successful competition mandates that a firm build a unique set of resources and capabilities within an industry or industries in which the firm competes.

## The Resource-Based Model of Above-Average Returns

In a general sense, the central question of strategic management is why some firms outperform other firms. Before the I/O model and other economic approaches became the favored answers to this question, as noted above, much of the early effort focused on firm competencies.[94] Distinctive competencies are firm attributes that allow it to pursue a strategy better than other firms.[95] One of the first competencies identified as a source of persistent performance was general management capability.[96] Because of their influence on the decisions of the firm, high-quality general managers tended to be associated with higher firm performance.[97] Much of the early work was devoted to determining how to define a high-quality manager.

Around the same time, Edith Penrose published a book in which she argued that firms could be understood both as an administrative framework that links and coordinates the activities of numerous groups and individuals and as a collection of resources.[98] The ad-

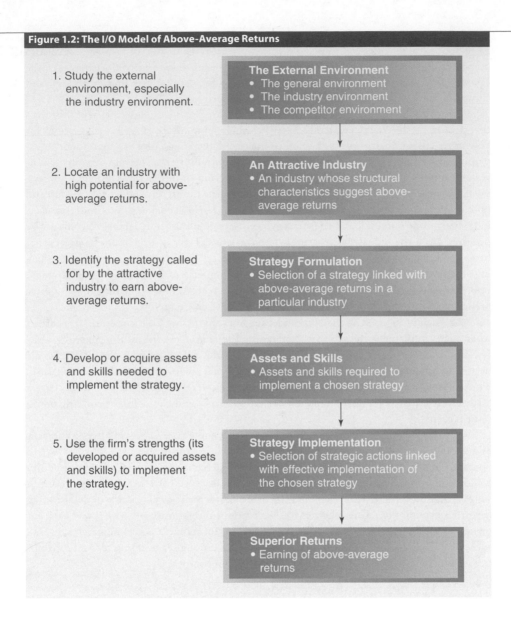

**Figure 1.2: The I/O Model of Above-Average Returns**

1. Study the external environment, especially the industry environment.

**The External Environment**
- The general environment
- The industry environment
- The competitor environment

2. Locate an industry with high potential for above-average returns.

**An Attractive Industry**
- An industry whose structural characteristics suggest above-average returns

3. Identify the strategy called for by the attractive industry to earn above-average returns.

**Strategy Formulation**
- Selection of a strategy linked with above-average returns in a particular industry

4. Develop or acquire assets and skills needed to implement the strategy.

**Assets and Skills**
- Assets and skills required to implement a chosen strategy

5. Use the firm's strengths (its developed or acquired assets and skills) to implement the strategy.

**Strategy Implementation**
- Selection of strategic actions linked with effective implementation of the chosen strategy

**Superior Returns**
- Earning of above-average returns

ministrative framework foreshadowed the importance of the stakeholder perspective that will be discussed in the next section. Her second perspective, the resource-based view, has become even more important in the strategic management field.[99] It is closely linked to the distinctive competencies approach because resources serve as the foundation for the establishment of competencies. Another early contribution to this literature envisioned resources as important because of their ability to facilitate implementation of a product market strategy, consistent with the I/O perspective.[100]

The resource-based model assumes that an individual firm's unique collection of resources and capabilities, rather than the structural characteristics of the industry in which it competes, is the primary influence on the selection and use of its strategy or strategies.[101]

Capabilities evolve and must be managed dynamically in pursuit of value creation.[102] The model also assumes that across time, firms acquire different resources and develop unique capabilities. Therefore, not all firms competing within a particular industry possess the same resources and capabilities. Additionally, *the model assumes that resources may not be highly mobile across firms* and that the differences in resources are the basis of competitive advantage.[103]

**Resources** are inputs into a firm's production process, such as capital equipment, the skills of individual employees, patents, finances, and talented managers. In general, a firm's resources can be classified into three categories: physical, human, and organizational capital. Described fully in Chapter 4, resources may be either tangible or intangible in nature.

Individual resources alone may not yield a competitive advantage.[104] In general, competitive advantages are formed through the combination and integration of sets of resources. A **capability** comes from resources that allow a firm to perform a task or an activity in an integrative manner. Capabilities evolve over time and must be managed dynamically in pursuit of higher firm performance.[105] Through the firm's continued use, capabilities become stronger and more difficult for competitors to understand and imitate. As a source of competitive advantage, a capability "should be neither so simple that it is highly imitable, nor so complex that it defies internal steering and control."[106]

Figure 1.3 shows the resource-based model of superior returns. Instead of focusing on the accumulation of resources necessary to successfully use the strategy dictated by conditions and constraints in the external environment (I/O model), the resource-based view suggests that a firm's unique resources and capabilities provide the basis for a strategy. The strategy chosen should allow the firm to effectively use its competitive advantages to exploit opportunities in its external environment.

Not all of a firm's resources and capabilities have the potential to be a competitive advantage. This potential is realized when resources and capabilities are valuable, rare, costly to imitate, and nonsubstitutable.[107] Resources are *valuable* when they allow a firm to take advantage of opportunities or neutralize threats in its external environment. They are *rare* when possessed by few, if any, current and potential competitors. Resources are *costly to imitate* when other firms either cannot obtain them or are at a cost disadvantage in obtaining them compared with the firm that already possesses them. And, they are *nonsubstitutable* when they have no structural equivalents.

When these four criteria are met, resources and capabilities become core competencies. **Core competencies** are resources and capabilities that serve as a source of competitive advantage for a firm over its rivals. Often related to a firm's skills in terms of organizational functions (e.g., Wal-Mart's distribution skills are superior to those of its competitors), core competencies, when developed, nurtured, and applied throughout a firm, contribute to the earning of above-average returns.

Managerial competencies are important in most firms.[108] For example, they have been shown to be critically important to successful entry into foreign markets.[109] Such competencies may include the capability to effectively organize and govern complex and diverse operations and the capability to create and communicate a strategic vision.[110] Managerial capabilities are important in a firm's ability to take advantage of its resources. For example, the Palo Alto Research Center developed by Xerox in the 1970s was the birthplace of the personal computer (PC), the laser printer, and the Ethernet, all technologies subsequently exploited by other firms. Because Xerox managers did not foresee the value-creating potential of these technologies, they did not make efforts to commercially exploit them. The

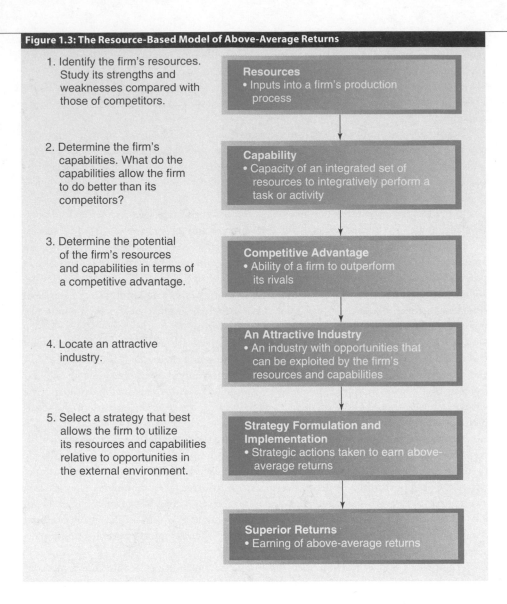

**Figure 1.3: The Resource-Based Model of Above-Average Returns**

1. Identify the firm's resources. Study its strengths and weaknesses compared with those of competitors.

**Resources**
- Inputs into a firm's production process

2. Determine the firm's capabilities. What do the capabilities allow the firm to do better than its competitors?

**Capability**
- Capacity of an integrated set of resources to integratively perform a task or activity

3. Determine the potential of the firm's resources and capabilities in terms of a competitive advantage.

**Competitive Advantage**
- Ability of a firm to outperform its rivals

4. Locate an attractive industry.

**An Attractive Industry**
- An industry with opportunities that can be exploited by the firm's resources and capabilities

5. Select a strategy that best allows the firm to utilize its resources and capabilities relative to opportunities in the external environment.

**Strategy Formulation and Implementation**
- Strategic actions taken to earn above-average returns

**Superior Returns**
- Earning of above-average returns

effects of this lack of foresight are suggested by the fact that the Hewlett-Packard division that makes and sells laser printers has more total revenue than all of Xerox.[111]

Another set of important competencies is product related, such as a firm's capability to develop innovative new products and to reengineer existing products to satisfy changing consumer tastes.[112] Firms must also continuously develop their competencies to keep them up-to-date. This development requires a systematic program for updating old skills and introducing new ones. Such programs are especially important in rapidly changing environments, such as those that exist in high-technology industries. Thus, the resource-based model suggests that core competencies are the basis for a firm's competitive advantage and its ability to earn above-average returns.

As noted previously, research shows that both the industry environment and a firm's internal resources affect a firm's performance over time.[113] The industry is composed of stakeholders such as customers, suppliers, and competitors that influence the nature and level of competition. A firm's internal resources are influenced by relationships with those external stakeholders and are also directly linked to internal stakeholders such as employees and managers. The most important competencies largely reside in people—the knowledge they possess and the systems they manage—rather than inanimate objects. The stakeholder perspective provides a framework for understanding how firms can simultaneously manage relationships with internal and external stakeholders to create and sustain competitive advantage. It is well-suited to the morally turbulent times in which we live because it is based on a moral as well as an economic foundation.

## The Stakeholder Model of Responsible Firm Behavior and Firm Performance

In 1984, Edward Freeman advanced a process for strategic management that addressed many of the concerns that scholars had identified as important at the time. Called the stakeholder approach, it embraced external analysis as a way to help firms deal with an increasingly turbulent environment. According to Freeman, "The business environment of the 1980s and beyond is complex, to say the least. If the corporation is to successfully meet the challenges posed by this environment, it must begin to adapt integrative strategic management processes which focus the attention of management externally as a matter of routine."[114]

From a stakeholder perspective, the firm can be envisioned as a nexus of formal and social contracts with its stakeholders.[115] **Stakeholders** are the individuals and groups who can affect, and are affected by, the strategic outcomes a firm achieves and who have enforceable claims on a firm's performance.[116] Claims on a firm's performance are enforced through the stakeholders' ability to withhold participation essential to the organization's survival, competitiveness, and profitability.[117] Firm dependence on external stakeholders is consistent with a systems perspective of the firm.[118] However, stakeholder theory also suggests that firms can alter their environments through effective management of relationships with external stakeholders.[119] In this sense, the stakeholder perspective integrates political and economic strategy-making processes.[120] In addition, the stakeholder approach is consistent with the perspective that organizations can learn from their environments.[121]

As illustrated in Figure 1.4, stakeholders of primary interest to the firm can be separated into at least three groups: the capital market stakeholders (shareholders and the major suppliers of a firm's capital), the product market stakeholders (the firm's primary customers, suppliers, host communities, and unions representing the workforce), and the organizational stakeholders (all of a firm's employees, including both nonmanagerial and managerial personnel). Outside of these primary stakeholders, other stakeholders may be important depending on the industry and situation of the firm. They may include an assortment of federal, state, or regional government entities and administrators as well as various secondary stakeholders, such as activists, advocacy groups, religious organizations, or other nongovernmental organizations.[122] Secondary stakeholders should not be ignored, but unless their objectives are closely tied to a firm's operations or objectives, they probably should not be given as much importance in the strategic planning process.[123]

A stakeholder approach to strategic management is highly pertinent to one of the central problems that management is facing today—a general lack of trust of corporations and their managers.[124] Corporate scandals have reduced trust among stakeholders and in society in general and have simultaneously led to increased government legislation and regulation such as the Sarbanes–Oxley Act in the United States.[125] Societies throughout the

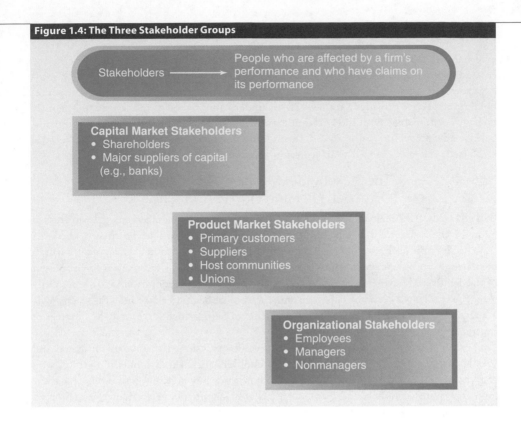

**Figure 1.4: The Three Stakeholder Groups**

Stakeholders → People who are affected by a firm's performance and who have claims on its performance

**Capital Market Stakeholders**
- Shareholders
- Major suppliers of capital (e.g., banks)

**Product Market Stakeholders**
- Primary customers
- Suppliers
- Host communities
- Unions

**Organizational Stakeholders**
- Employees
- Managers
- Nonmanagers

world are demanding better ethical performance, and the stakeholder perspective has a moral component.[126] It recognizes that firms have obligations to a broad group of constituencies and that they should treat all of their stakeholders in a trustworthy fashion.[127] However, it does not go so far as to say that all stakeholders should be given the same priority, attention, or consideration in strategic decisions.[128] Furthermore, it was not originally intended to be a model of social responsibility. From its inception, the stakeholder perspective is about effective and efficient management of the business enterprise.[129]

Research supports the idea that firms that effectively manage stakeholder relationships outperform those that do not.[130] This research implies that stakeholder relationships can be managed in such a way as to create competitive advantage (see Figure 1.5). Competitive advantage may come from a variety of sources.[131] A firm that has excellent stakeholder relationships based on trust and mutual satisfaction of goals is more likely to obtain knowledge from them that can be used to make better strategic decisions.[132] A firm's ability to create value and earn high returns is compromised when strategic leaders fail to respond appropriately and quickly to changes in the complex global competitive environment.[133] Also, **strategic intelligence,** the information firms collect from their network of stakeholders, can be used to help a firm deal with diverse and cognitively complex competitive situations.[134]

Evidence suggests that trust can be a source of competitive advantage, thereby supporting an organizational commitment to treat stakeholders fairly and with respect.[135] Firms with trustworthy reputations draw customers, suppliers, and business partners to them.[136]

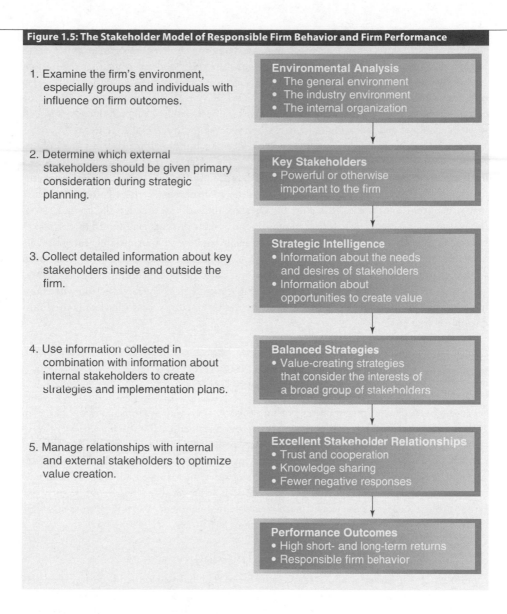

**Figure 1.5: The Stakeholder Model of Responsible Firm Behavior and Firm Performance**

1. Examine the firm's environment, especially groups and individuals with influence on firm outcomes.

**Environmental Analysis**
- The general environment
- The industry environment
- The internal organization

2. Determine which external stakeholders should be given primary consideration during strategic planning.

**Key Stakeholders**
- Powerful or otherwise important to the firm

3. Collect detailed information about key stakeholders inside and outside the firm.

**Strategic Intelligence**
- Information about the needs and desires of stakeholders
- Information about opportunities to create value

4. Use information collected in combination with information about internal stakeholders to create strategies and implementation plans.

**Balanced Strategies**
- Value-creating strategies that consider the interests of a broad group of stakeholders

5. Manage relationships with internal and external stakeholders to optimize value creation.

**Excellent Stakeholder Relationships**
- Trust and cooperation
- Knowledge sharing
- Fewer negative responses

**Performance Outcomes**
- High short- and long-term returns
- Responsible firm behavior

This can enhance firm performance by increasing the number of attractive business transactions from which a firm can select. Consequently, the firm may find it easier to acquire or develop competitive resources. For instance, investors may be more likely to buy shares in a company with a trustworthy reputation.[137] In addition, workers may be attracted to employers who are known to treat their employees well.[138] In addition to the resource advantages, the transaction costs associated with making and enforcing agreements are reduced because there is less need for elaborate contractual safeguards and contingencies.[139] Of course, excellent stakeholder relationships also can enhance implementation of strategies because people are more committed to a course of action when they believe they have had some influence on the decision to pursue it, even if it is not exactly what they wanted the firm to do.[140]

Responsible behavior with regard to stakeholders such as government regulators, consumers, and employees can lead to intangible assets that buffer and protect a firm from negative actions such as adverse regulation, legal suits and penalties, consumer retaliation, strikes, walkouts, and bad press.[141] Avoiding such outcomes reduces expenses, but it also reduces risks associated with variations in returns. Risk reduction may enhance the value of a firm's securities because, in an efficient market, investors are expected to consider both future cash flows and risk simultaneously when assessing the value of a security.[142]

In a comprehensive sense, a firm can be viewed as a bundle of market activities, a bundle of resources, or a network of relationships.[143] The three perspectives we have examined in this section have reflected each of these different approaches. Market activities are understood through the application of the I/O model. The development and effective use of a firm's resources, capabilities, and competencies are understood through the application of the resource-based model. Effective management of relationships is reflected by the stakeholder model. The most successful organizations learn how to appropriately integrate the information and knowledge gained by using each model. In turn, appropriate integration of the outcomes from using each model is the foundation for determining the firm's strategic direction and for selecting and implementing its strategies. The next section will examine strategic thinking and outline the strategic management process that forms the foundation for this book.

## Strategic Thinking and the Strategic Management Process

Strategic management incorporates both a process and a way of thinking about the firm and its environment. The term "strategic thinking" has been used in such a variety of ways that it has almost lost its meaning. Sometimes people use it to mean "long-term thinking" while others may think it means simply "thinking about strategy." In this book, we will associate the term with the more creative aspects of strategic management that result in new strategies and organizational changes. Elements of strategic thinking should be incorporated into the processes associated with strategic management. We will discuss strategic thinking first, followed by the strategic management process.

### Strategic Thinking

One of the most essential characteristics of firms that have sustained high levels of performance is their ability to innovate and make the changes in their structures, systems, technologies, and products and services so that they continue to stay ahead of their competitors. Toyota in the automobile industry, Intel in microprocessors, Nucor in steel, Southwest Airlines, and even the British conglomerate Virgin Group continue to be successful because of their ability to innovate and change. This is not to say that these companies do not have tough times or make mistakes, but they seem to have an amazing ability to rebound again and again. Their top managers think strategically. Strategic thinking is intent focused, comprehensive, and opportunistic; considers multiple time horizons; and is hypothesis driven.[144]

The organizational term used for a dream that challenges and energizes a company is *strategic intent*.[145] Strategic leaders have opportunities to dream and to act, and the most effective ones provide a vision (the strategic intent) to effectively elicit the help of others in creating a firm's competitive advantage. **Strategic intent** is the leveraging of a firm's resources, capabilities, and core competencies to accomplish the firm's goals in the competitive environment.[146] Strategic intent exists when all employees and levels of a firm are committed to the pursuit of a specific (and significant) performance criterion. Strategic intent has been effectively formed when employees believe fervently in their company's product (good or service) and when they are focused totally on their firm's ability to outperform its competitors. A company's success may also be grounded in a keen and deep understanding of the strategic intent of customers, suppliers, partners, and competitors as the firm attempts to position itself relative to these stakeholders.[147]

Strategic thinking is also comprehensive in that it envisions the firm as a system that is part of a larger system.[148] Decision makers make decisions fully recognizing and understanding the interdependencies of the firm's parts and how they interface with parts of their external environment. In this context, strategic thinking calls for recognizing that a strategy can be effectively used only when the actions of all parts of the firm are carefully integrated to support pursuit of the previously chosen strategic intent.

Opportunism, as it relates to strategic thinking, means that a firm takes advantage of unanticipated opportunities as they arise. Virgin Group, under the leadership of Richard Branson, is well-known for supporting an opportunistic culture in its companies. Such thinking has taken the group into credit cards, cell phones, "lifestyle" electronics, and soft drinks. The group opened the first ever vehicle department store. Within its core transportation businesses, Virgin has embraced innovations such as extra-wide seats (double suites) that essentially become double beds for upper-class airline passengers who are traveling together and the introduction of a new high-tech passenger train called the Pendolino in England.[149]

When people consider strategic thinking, they frequently think about the long term. Managers, especially in the United States, are often accused of being too focused on the short term.[150] Strategic thinking does include long-term thinking, which is characterized by an understanding that success today does not guarantee success in the future in that all competitive advantages can eventually be imitated (this point is further discussed in Chapter 4). However, strategic thinking does not ignore the past or the present. In addition to exploring sources of competitive advantage that can lead to value creation in the future, it is oriented toward learning from the past and determining what the firm should do now to exploit its current competitive advantages.[151] In short, it addresses past, present, and future.

Finally, strategic thinking is a sequential process in which creative ideas are generated, carefully evaluated, and, if they then appear reasonable, implemented. Hypothesis testing occurs initially at two stages. First, during early evaluation of an idea, a firm gathers information from inside the organization, from external stakeholders, and from analysis of environmental forces. If the idea is for a new product or service, marketing professionals may do research to test how the market will accept it. In addition, finance specialists may conduct analyses to determine the net present value or internal rate of return the idea might generate. Real options analysis, discussed in Chapter 13, may also be a part of the evaluation process. All of this information is then used to test the idea to see whether it makes sense from a strategic perspective. The second stage of hypothesis testing involves actually implementing the idea. Frequently, firms will try something on a smaller scale to see whether it works before launching into a full organizational implementation. The Virgin Group, for example, frequently tries ideas on a limited scale before investing a lot of resources in them. In fact, Virgin's credit card business began in only one business area and has now spread around the world.[152]

Firms can encourage strategic thinking in a number of ways. First, top managers need to be champions of change rather than protectors of the status quo.[153] Innovations frequently bubble up from the operating areas of an organization rather than coming from an "innovation" department.[154] Consequently, the second way a firm can encourage strategic thinking is to have systems and processes in place so that this "bubble up" can be captured when it happens. Highly successful companies like the arc welder manufacturer Lincoln Electric or the entertainment arm of Disney sometimes use simple processes such as collecting and considering suggestions from employees. On the other hand, Target and Procter & Gamble are using high-tech tools such as specialized maps of their innovation networks to foster strategic thinking. Based on social networks analysis and cartography, these maps allow them to visualize who is in their customer base, their supply chain, and under the sphere of their influence.[155]

Firms may also train their managers and employees in methods and processes associated with strategic thinking.[156] Sometimes they use retreats or consultant interventions and training to accomplish this purpose. In addition, it is important for strategic leaders to foster a climate that allows or even encourages risk taking. All of these ideas are associated with strategic leadership and fostering an innovative culture, which is the topic of Chapter 2. Firms must also provide enough flexibility in their strategic management process to allow incorporation of new ideas with high potential as they are introduced.[157] Chapter 12 on strategic entrepreneurship also provides ways of capturing new ideas.

## The Strategic Management Process

The strategic management process is a logical approach for helping a firm effectively respond to the challenges of the 21st-century competitive landscape. Figure 1.6, which outlines the process, also provides a road map for the topics examined in this book. Strategic thinking, as discussed, is the decision-making medium through which the firm uses the strategic management process to shape its present and influence its future while pursuing value creation and high financial returns.[158]

As strategic thinkers, strategic leaders are responsible for establishing and using an effective strategic management process in their firms.[159] Because strategic leaders are the engines driving the development and subsequent use of the strategic management process, Chapter 2 examines strategic leadership, as well as strategic direction because it is so closely associated with strategic leadership. Strategic direction is reflected in the firm's vision, mission, purpose, and long-term goals. The discussions in the first two chapters provide the foundation for a detailed treatment of the strategic management process—a treatment that begins with Part 2 of the book.

The two key sources of information-based inputs to the strategic management process are discussed in Part 2. As shown in Figure 1.6, these inputs are derived from an analysis of the firm's external environment (Chapter 3) and its internal organization (Chapter 4). These analyses identify the external environment's opportunities and threats and the resources, capabilities, and core competencies that collectively form or constitute the firm's internal organization. With knowledge about opportunities and threats and competitive advantages, the firm is prepared to develop its strategic direction, as well as the specific strategies it will use to create competitive advantage (see Figure 1.6).

The different strategies firms use to create competitive advantage are discussed in Part 3. First, we examine business-level strategies (Chapter 5). The central focus of business-level strategy is determining the competitive advantages the firm will use to effectively compete in specific product markets. A diversified firm competing in multiple product

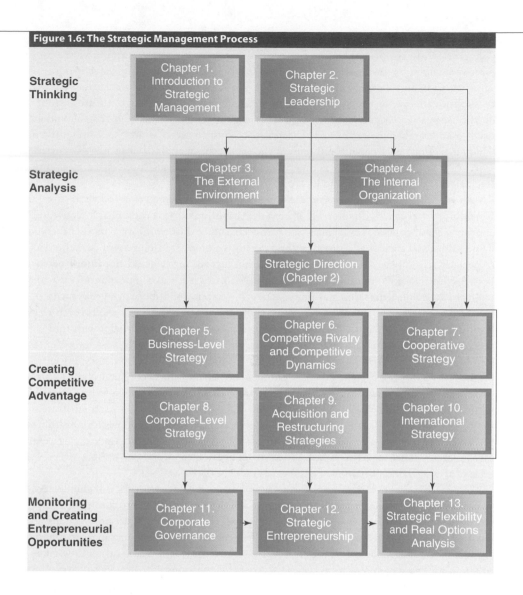

**Figure 1.6: The Strategic Management Process**

**Strategic Thinking**
- Chapter 1. Introduction to Strategic Management
- Chapter 2. Strategic Leadership

**Strategic Analysis**
- Chapter 3. The External Environment
- Chapter 4. The Internal Organization

Strategic Direction (Chapter 2)

**Creating Competitive Advantage**
- Chapter 5. Business-Level Strategy
- Chapter 6. Competitive Rivalry and Competitive Dynamics
- Chapter 7. Cooperative Strategy
- Chapter 8. Corporate-Level Strategy
- Chapter 9. Acquisition and Restructuring Strategies
- Chapter 10. International Strategy

**Monitoring and Creating Entrepreneurial Opportunities**
- Chapter 11. Corporate Governance
- Chapter 12. Strategic Entrepreneurship
- Chapter 13. Strategic Flexibility and Real Options Analysis

markets and businesses has a business-level strategy for each distinct product market area. A company competing in a single product market has only one business-level strategy. In all instances, a business-level strategy describes a firm's actions that are designed to exploit its competitive advantage over rivals. In the course of competition, competitors respond to each other's actions and reactions. Indeed, competitors respond to and try to anticipate each other's actions. Thus, the dynamics of competition are an important input when a firm selects and uses strategies.[160] Competitive rivalry and competitive dynamics are discussed in Chapter 6. Cooperative strategies, examined in Chapter 7, are also important to competitive dynamics. The trend toward cooperation reflects the increasing importance of forming partnerships to both share and develop competitive resources.[161]

Used in diversified organizations, corporate-level strategy (Chapter 8) is concerned with determining the businesses in which the company intends to compete as well as how resources are to be allocated among those businesses. Merger and acquisition strategies (Chapter 9) are the primary means diversified firms use to create corporate-level competitive advantages. International strategies (Chapter 10) also are used as the source of value creation and above-average returns. The various organizational structures required to support the use of the strategies examined in Chapters 5 through 10 are included in the respective chapters. Thus, individual organizational structures that should be used to effectively support the use of each unique business-level strategy are presented in Chapter 5. Chapters 6 through 10 present the same type of analysis of strategy–structure matches that firms use to create competitive advantage when using cooperative, corporate-level, merger and acquisition, and international strategies.

As with all organizational actions, strategies must be monitored to assess their success. Corporate governance (Chapter 11) is concerned with making certain that effective and appropriate strategic decisions and actions are occurring in the firm. Governance reflects the firm's values and is used to ensure that the company's actions are aligned with stakeholders' (especially stockholders') interests. With stakeholders voicing demands for improved corporate governance,[162] organizations are challenged to satisfy stakeholders' interests while trying to accomplish the strategic outcomes of value creation and above-average returns.

Although very important, governance of the firm may result in cautious, even risk-avoiding strategic decisions. Because strict governance may constrain efforts to find entrepreneurial opportunities, a natural tension exists between the firm's need for order (as represented by governance) and some chaos (which commonly results from pursuing entrepreneurial opportunities). Chapter 12 examines the need for the firm to continuously seek entrepreneurial opportunities—ones that the firm can pursue in its efforts to be successful while competing in its chosen markets. Chapter 13 contains a tool that is useful in evaluating new ventures as well as maintaining strategic flexibility. Real options analysis examines the real choices firms are given subsequent to making the decision to pursue a particular investment.[163] They have the right but not the obligation to pursue the option, which increases strategic flexibility in the future while reducing perceived risks.[164]

Primarily because they are related to how a firm interacts with its stakeholders, almost all strategic decisions have ethical dimensions.[165] Especially in the turbulent and often ambiguous 21st-century competitive landscape, those making strategic decisions are challenged to recognize how their decisions affect capital market, product market, and organizational stakeholders. Consequently, each of the chapters provides "Ethics Questions" to stimulate discussion of ethical issues. Most of the questions have no clear answers, but they should facilitate examination of the ethical dimensions of strategic topics.

## Summary

■ Strategic management has emerged in response to the need for mental models and planning tools to help executives guide their firms in this challenging global business environment. It is concerned primarily with the actions organizations take to achieve competitive advantage and create value for the organization and its stakeholders.

■ The competitive environment is characterized by globalization and rapid changes in technology. Globalization can be defined as the increasing economic interdependence among countries as reflected in the flow of goods and services, financial capital, and knowledge across country borders. The three categories of technological trends that are

PART 1 / STRATEGIC THINKING

altering the nature of competition are increases in the rate of technological change and diffusion, changes in information technology, and increases in knowledge intensity.

- The industrial organization (I/O) model of above-average returns explains the dominant influence of the external environment on a firm's strategic actions. The model specifies that the industry in which a firm chooses to compete has a stronger influence on the firm's performance than do the choices managers make inside their organizations.

- The resource-based model assumes that an individual firm's unique collection of resources and capabilities is the primary influence on the selection and use of its strategy or strategies. Resources are inputs into a firm's production process, such as capital equipment, the skills of individual employees, patents, finances, and talented managers. Resources and capabilities realize their competitive potential when they are valuable, rare, costly to imitate, and nonsubstitutable.

- From a stakeholder perspective, the firm can be envisioned as a nexus of formal and social contracts with its stakeholders. Stakeholders are the individuals and groups who can affect, and are affected by, the strategic outcomes a firm achieves and who have enforceable claims on a firm's performance. The stakeholder perspective posits that stakeholder relationships can be managed in such a way as to create competitive advantage.

- Strategic thinking is associated with the more creative aspects of strategic management. It is intent focused, comprehensive, and opportunistic; considers multiple time horizons; and is hypothesis driven. Strategic thinking is the decision-making medium through which the firm uses the strategic management process to shape its present and influence its future while pursuing value creation and high financial returns.

- The strategic management process is the full set of commitments, decisions, and actions required for a firm to create value and earn returns that are higher than those of competitors. In its simplest form, it involves analyzing the firm and its environment and then using the information to formulate and implement strategies that lead to competitive advantage. Thus, the strategic management process is used to match the conditions of an ever-changing market and competitive structure with a firm's continuously evolving resources, capabilities, and competencies.

# Ethics Questions

1. What is the relationship between ethics and the firm's stakeholders? For example, from an ethical perspective, how much information should the firm reveal to each of its stakeholders, and how does that vary among stakeholders?
2. Do firms face ethical challenges, perhaps even ethical dilemmas, when trying to satisfy both the short-term and long-term expectations of capital market stakeholders?
3. What types of ethical issues and challenges do firms encounter when competing internationally?
4. What ethical responsibilities does the firm have when it earns above-average returns? Who should make decisions regarding this issue, and why?
5. How should ethical considerations be included in analyses of the firm's external environment and its internal organization?
6. What should top-level managers do to ensure that a firm's strategic management process leads to outcomes that are consistent with the firm's values?

# Notes

1  D. G. Sirmon, M. A. Hitt, & R. D. Ireland, 2007, Managing firm resources in dynamic environments to create value: Looking inside the black box, *Academy of Management Review*, in press; J. B. Barney & T. B. Mackey, 2005, Testing resource-based theory, in D. J. Ketchen Jr. & D. D. Bergh (eds.), *Research Methodology in Strategy and Management*, 2nd ed., London: Elsevier, 1–13.

2  D. Lei & J. W. Slocum, 2005, Strategic and organizational requirements for competitive advantage, *Academy of Management Executive*, 19(1): 31–45; T. J. Douglas & J. A. Ryman, 2003, Understanding competitive advantage in the general hospital industry: Evaluating strategic competencies, *Strategic Management Journal*, 24: 333–347.

3  K. Shimizu & M. A. Hitt, 2004, Strategic flexibility: Organizational preparedness to reverse ineffective strategic decisions, *Academy of Management Executive*, 18(4): 44–59; D. J. Teece, G. Pisano, & A. Shuen, 1997, Dynamic capabilities and strategic management, *Strategic Management Journal*, 18: 509–533; E. Bonabeau & C. Meyer, 2001, Swarm intelligence, *Harvard Business Review*, 79(5): 107–114; D. Abell, 1999, Competing today while preparing for tomorrow, *Sloan Management Review*, 40(3): 73–81.

4  A. M. McGahan & M. E. Porter, 2003, The emergence and sustainability of abnormal profits, *Strategic Organization*, 1: 79–108; T. C. Powell, 2002, The philosophy of strategy, *Strategic Management Journal*, 23: 873–880; T. C. Powell, 2001, Competitive advantage: Logical and philosophical considerations, *Strategic Management Journal*, 22: 875–888.

5  R. P. Rumelt, D. E. Schendel, & D. J. Teece (eds.), 1994, *Fundamental Issues in Strategy*, Boston: Harvard Business School Press, 527–530.

6  M. Song, R. J. Calantone, & C. Anthony, 2002, Competitive forces and strategic choice decisions: An experimental investigation in the United States and Japan, *Strategic Management Journal*, 23: 969–978; A. Nair & S. Kotha, 2001, Does group membership matter? Evidence from the Japanese steel industry, *Strategic Management Journal*, 22: 221–235; A. M. McGahan & M. E. Porter, 1997, How much does industry matter, really? *Strategic Management Journal*, 18(summer special issue): 15–30.

7  D. G. Sirmon & M. A. Hitt, 2003, Managing resources: Linking unique resources, management and wealth creation in family firms, *Entrepreneurship Theory and Practice*, 27(4): 339–358; J. B. Barney, 2002, Strategic management: From informed conversation to academic discipline, *Academy of Management Executive*, 16(2): 53–57; J. B. Barney, 2001, Is the resource based "view" a useful perspective for strategic management research? Yes, *Academy of Management Review*, 26: 41–56.

8  J. P. Walsh, 2005, Taking stock of stakeholder management, *Academy of Management Review*, 30: 426–438; R. E. Freeman & J. McVea, 2001, A stakeholder approach to strategic management, in M. A. Hitt, R. E. Freeman, & J. R. Harrison (eds.), *Handbook of Strategic Management*, Oxford, UK: Blackwell Publishers, 189–207; J. E. Post, L. E. Preston, & S. Sachs, 2002, *Redefining the Corporation: Stakeholder Management and Organizational Wealth*, Stanford, CA: Stanford University Press.

9  J. M. Liedtka, 2001, Strategy formulation: The roles of conversation and design, in M. A. Hitt, R. E. Freeman, & J. R. Harrison (eds.), *Handbook of Strategic Management*, Oxford, UK: Blackwell Publishers, 70–94.

10  M. C. Mankins & R. Steele, 2005, Turning great strategy into great performance, *Harvard Business Review*, 83(7): 64–72; M. J. Epstein & R. A. Westbrook, 2001, Linking actions to profits in strategic decision making, *Sloan Management Review*, 42(3): 39–49.

11  2006, American Bankruptcy Institute, Filing statistics, http://www.abiworld.org/AM, December 20.

12  C. J. Loomis, 1993, Dinosaurs, *Fortune*, May 3, 36–46.

13  A. Chozick, 2006. Toyota lifts profit outlook, invests in fuel efficiency, *Wall Street Journal*, November 8, A3.

14  2001, BBC News, From Datsun to Nissan, http://news.bbc.co.uk/1/hi/business/1136490.stm, January 25.

15  B. Segrestin, 2005, Partnering to explore: The Renault–Nissan alliance as a forerunner of new cooperative patterns, *Research Policy*, 34: 657–677; M. Zineldin & M. Dodurova, 2005, Motivation, achievements and failure of strategic alliances: The case of Swedish auto manufacturers in Russia, *European Business Review*, 17: 460–470; E. K. Briody, S. T. Cavusgil, & S. R. Miller, 2004, Turning three sides into a Delta at General Motors: Enhancing partnership integration on corporate ventures, *Long Range Planning*, 37(5): 421–430.

16  J. B. Treece, 1992, The board revolt, *Business Week*, April 20, 31–36.

17  P. Bansal, D. Airey, A. Gepp, C. Harris, & Y. Menard, 2003, DaimlerChrysler: Post-merger news. London: Richard Ivey School of Business Case Collection, September 25.

18  S. A. Webster, 2006, New models position Lincoln to chase Cadillac, *Knight Ridder Tribune Business News*, January 9: 1.

19  N. E. Boudette, 2006, Chrysler sees '07 gain in U. S. share, *Wall Street Journal*, October 17*, A10.

20  N. E. Boudette & S. Power, 2006, Chrysler enlists Mercedes officials in bid to cut manufacturing costs, *Wall Street Journal*, October 20, A3.

21  J. McCracken, 2006, Ford posts $5.8 billion loss, warns of more woes, *Wall Street Journal*, October 24, A3.

22  J. D. Stoll, S. Power, & A. Chozick, Pressure mounts as car makers continue to bleed, *Wall Street Journal*, October 26, A3.

23  G. Chon, 2006, Kia's new U.S. plant advances sales push in North America, *Wall Street Journal*, October 23, B2; A. Chozick, 2006, Toyota lifts profit outlook, *Wall Street Journal*, November 8, A3.

24  R. Belderbos & L. Sleuwaegen, 2005, Competitive drivers and international plant configuration strategies: A product-level test, *Strategic Management Journal*, 26: 577–593; G. J. Castrogiovanni, 2002, Organization task environments: Have they changed fundamentally over time? *Journal of Management*, 28: 129–150; D. Tapscott, 2001, Rethinking strategy in a networked world, *Strategy & Business*, 24(third quarter): 34–41.

25  A. K. Gupta & V. Govindarajan, 2002, Cultivating a global mindset, *Academy of Management Executive*, 16(1): 116–126.

26  V. Govindarajan & A. K. Gupta, 2001, *The Quest for Global Dominance*, San Francisco: Jossey-Bass.

27  S. J. Chang & S. Park, 2005, Types of firms generating network externalities and MNCs' co-location decisions, *Strategic Management Journal*, 26: 595–615; S. C. Voelpel, M. Dous, & T. H. Davenport, 2005, Five steps to creating global knowledge-sharing systems: Siemens' ShareNet, *Academy of Management Executive*, 19(2): 9–23; A. Seth, K. P. Song, & R. R. Pettit, 2002, Value creation and destruction in cross-border acquisitions: An empirical analysis of foreign acquisitions of U.S. firms, *Strategic Management Journal*, 23: 921–940; D. G. McKendrick, 2001, Global strategy and population level learning: The case of hard disk drives, *Strategic Management Journal*, 22: 307–334.

28  M. Mandel, 2006, Can anyone steer this economy? *Business Week*, November 20, 56–62.

29  T. Khanna, K. G. Palepu, & J. Sinha, 2005, Strategies that fit emerging markets, *Harvard Business Review*, 83(6): 63–76; R. J. Trent & R. M. Monczka, 2002, Pursuing competitive advantage through integrated global sourcing, *Academy of Management Executive*, 16(2): 66–80.

30  K. M. Eisenhardt, 2002, Has strategy changed? *MIT Sloan Management Review*, 43(2): 88–91.

31  M. A. Carpenter & J. W. Fredrickson, 2001, Top management teams, global strategic posture, and the moderating role of uncertainty, *Academy of Management Journal*, 44: 533–545.

32  G. McNamara, P. M. Vaaler, & C. Devers, 2003, Same as it ever was: The search for evidence of increasing hypercompetition, *Strategic Management Journal*, 24: 261–278; R. A. D'Aveni, 1995, Coping with hypercompetition: Utilizing the new 7S's framework, *Academy of Management Executive*, 9(3): 46.

33  W. J. Ferrier, 2001, Navigating the competitive landscape: The drivers and consequences of competitive aggressiveness, *Academy of Management Journal*, 44: 858–877.

34  R. A. D'Aveni, 2004, Corporate spheres of influence, *MIT Sloan Management Review*, 45(4): 38–46; Ferrier, Navigating the competitive landscape; M. A. Hitt, B. W. Keats, & S. M. DeMarie, 1998, Navigating in the new competitive landscape: Building competitive advantage and strategic flexibility in the 21st century, *Academy of Management Executive*, 12(4): 22–42; R. A. Bettis & M. A. Hitt, 1995, The new competitive landscape, *Strategic Management Journal*, 16(special summer issue): 7–19.

35  K. H. Hammonds, 2001, What is the state of the new economy? *Fast Company*, September, 101–104.

36  C. W. L. Hill, 1997, Establishing a standard: Competitive strategy and technological standards in winner-take-all industries, *Academy of Management Executive*, 11(2): 7–25.

37  K. H. Hammonds, 2001, How do fast companies work now? *Fast Company*, September, 134–142; K. M. Eisenhardt, 1999, Strategy as strategic decision making, *Sloan Management Review*, 40(3): 65–72.

38  R. Karlgaard, 1999, Digital rules, *Forbes*, July 5, 43.

39  C. Gilbert, 2003, The disruptive opportunity, *MIT Sloan Management Review*, 44(4): 27–32; C. M. Christensen, M. W. Johnson, & D. K. Rigby, 2002, Foundations for growth: How to identify and build disruptive new businesses, *MIT Sloan Management Review*, 43(3): 22–31; C. M. Christensen, 1997, *The Innovator's Dilemma*, Boston: Harvard Business School Press.

40  G. Ahuja & C. M. Lampert, 2001, Entrepreneurship in the large corporation: A longitudinal study of how established firms create breakthrough inventions, *Strategic Management Journal*, 22(special issue): 521–543.

41  P. Anderson & E. Anderson, 2002, The new e-commerce intermediaries, *MIT Sloan Management Review*, 43(4): 53–62.

42  G. Ferguson, S. Mathur, & B. Shah, 2005, Evolving from information to insight, *MIT Sloan Management Review*, 46(2): 51–58.

43  R. Amit & C. Zott, 2001, Value creation in e-business, *Strategic Management Journal*, 22(summer special issue): 493–520.

44  B. Einhorn, B. Elgin, R. D. Hof, & T. Mullaney, 2005, The great Internet race, *Business Week*, June 13, 54–56.

45  R. M. Kanter, 2001, *e volve: Succeeding in the Digital Culture of Tomorrow*, Boston: Harvard Business School Press.

46  A. C. Inkpen & E. W. K. Tsang, 2005, Social capital, networks, and knowledge transfer, *Academy of Management Review*, 30: 146–165; A. S. DeNisi, M. A. Hitt, & S. E. Jackson, 2003, The knowledge-based approach to sustainable competitive advantage, in S. E. Jackson, M. A. Hitt, & A. S. DeNisi (eds.), *Managing Knowledge for Sustained Competitive Advantage*, San Francisco: Jossey-Bass, 3–33.

47  K. G. Smith, C. J. Collins, & K. D. Clark, 2005, Existing knowledge, knowledge creation capability, and the rate of new product introduction in high technology firms, *Academy of Management Journal*, 48: 346–357; F. Warner, 2001, The drills for knowledge, *Fast Company*, September, 186–191; B. L. Simonin, 1999, Ambiguity and the process of knowledge transfer in strategic alliances, *Strategic Management Journal*, 20: 595–624.

48  S. K. Ethiraj, P. Kale, M. S. Krishnan, & J. V. Singh, 2005, Where do capabilities come from and how do they matter? *Strategic Management Journal*, 26: 25–45; V. Anand, W. H. Glick, & C. C. Manz, 2002, Thriving on the knowledge of outsiders: Tapping organizational social capital, *Academy of Management Executive*, 16(1): 87–101; L. Rosenkopf & A. Nerkar, 2001, Beyond local search: Boundary-spanning, exploration, and impact on the optical disk industry, *Strategic Management Journal*, 22: 287–306.

49  D. F. Kuratko, R. D. Ireland, & J. S. Hornsby, 2001, Improving firm performance through entrepreneurial actions: Insights from Acordia Inc.'s corporate entrepreneurship strategy, *Academy of Management Executive*, 15(4): 60–71; T. K. Kayworth & R. D. Ireland, 1998, The use of corporate IT standards as a means of implementing the cost leadership strategy, *Journal of Information Technology Management*, IX(4): 13–42.

50  G. Probst & S. Raisch, 2005, Organizational crisis: The logic of failure, *Academy of Management Executive*, 19(1): 90–105.

51  J. D. Wolpert, 2002, Breaking out of the innovation box, *Harvard Business Review*, 80(8): 77–83.

52  L. Yu, 2005, Does knowledge sharing payoff? *MIT Sloan Management Review*, 46(3): 5; L. Valikangas & M. Gibbert, 2005, Boundary-setting strategies for escaping innovation traps, *MIT Sloan Management Review*, 46(3): 58–65.

53  J. Santos, Y. Doz, & P. Williamson, 2004, Is your innovation process global? *MIT Sloan Management Review*, 45(4): 31–37.

54  J. A. Robins, S. Tallman, & K. Fladmoe-Lindquist, 2002, Autonomy and dependence of international cooperative ventures: An exploration of the strategic performance of

U.S. ventures in Mexico, *Strategic Management Journal*, 23: 881–901; M. Subramaniam & N. Venkatraman, 2001, Determinants of transnational new product development capability: Testing the influence of transferring and deploying tacit overseas knowledge, *Strategic Management Journal*, 22: 359–378.

55   K. R. Harrigan, 2001, Strategic flexibility in old and new economies, in M. A. Hitt, R. E. Freeman, & J. R. Harrison (eds.), *Handbook of Strategic Management*, Oxford, UK: Blackwell Publishers, 97–123.

56   L. Gratton & S. Ghoshal, 2005, Beyond best practice, *MIT Sloan Management Review*, 46(3): 49–55.

57   K. Uhlenbruck, K. E. Meyer, & M. A. Hitt, 2003, Organizational transformation in transition economies: Resource-based and organizational learning perspectives, *Journal of Management Studies*, 40: 257–282.

58   D. E. Schendel & C. W. Hofer, 1979, *Strategic Management: A New View of Business Policy and Planning*, Boston: Little, Brown and Company.

59   R. A. Gordon & J. E. Howell, 1959, *Higher Education for Business*, New York: Columbia University Press, 206.

60   R. E. Hoskisson, M. A. Hitt, W. P. Wan, & D. Yiu, 1999, Swings of a pendulum: Theory and research in strategic management, *Journal of Management*, 25: 417–456.

61   A. D. Chandler, 1962, *Strategy and Structure: Chapters in the History of the American Industrial Enterprise*, Cambridge, MA: MIT Press, 16.

62   H. I. Ansoff, 1965, *Corporate Strategy: An Analytic Approach to Business for Growth and Expansion*, New York: McGraw-Hill.

63   E. P. Learned, C. R. Christensen, K. R. Andrews, & W. D. Guth, 1965, *Business Policy: Text and Cases*, Homewood, IL: Irwin, 17.

64   Ibid., 21.

65   R. Ackoff, 1974, *Redesigning the Future*, New York: Wiley; J. March & H. Simon, 1958, *Organizations*, New York: Wiley; C. I. Barnard, 1938, *Functions of the Executive*, Cambridge, MA: Harvard University Press.

66   I. C. MacMillan, 1978, *Strategy Formulation: Political Concepts*, St. Paul, MN: West Publishing Co., 66.

67   J. Pfeffer & G. R. Salancik, 1978, *The External Control of Organizations: A Resource Dependence Perspective*, New York: Harper & Row.

68   Ibid; D. Katz & R. L. Kahn, 1978, *The Social Psychology of Organizations*, 2nd ed., New York: Wiley; J. D. Thompson, 1967, *Organizations in Action*, New York: McGraw-Hill.

69   MacMillan, *Strategy Formulation*, 110.

70   H. Mintzberg, 1978, Managerial work: Analysis from observation. *Management Science*, 18: B97–B110; H. Mintzberg, 1971, Patterns in strategy formation, *Management Science*, 24: 934–948.

71   Mintzberg, Managerial work, B110.

72   M. Jensen & W. Meckling, 1976, Theory of the firm: Managerial behavior, agency costs and capital structure, *Journal of Financial Economics*, 3: 305–360.

73   O. E. Williamson, 1975, *Markets and Hierarchies: Analysis and Antitrust Implications*, New York: The Free Press.

74   E. W. K. Tsang, 2006, Behavioral assumptions and theory development: The case of transaction cost economics, *Strategic Management Journal*, 27: 999–1011.

75   Schendel & Hofer, *Strategic Management*.

76   Ibid.; C. W. Hofer & D. E. Schendel, 1978, *Strategy Formulation: Analytical Concepts*, St. Paul: West Publishing Co.

77   L. G. Hrebiniak & W. F. Joyce, 1985, Organizational adaptation: Strategic choice and environmental determinism. *Administrative Science Quarterly*, 30: 336–349.

78   L. J. Bourgeois III, 1984, Strategic management and determinism, *Academy of Management Review*, 9: 589.

79   L. Smirchich & C. Stubbart, 1985, Strategic management in an enacted world, *Academy of Management Review*, 10: 724–736.

80   J. S. Harrison & C. H. St. John, 1996, Managing and partnering with external stakeholders, *Academy of Management Executive*, 10(2): 46–60.

81   R. D. Ireland & C. C. Miller, 2004, Decision-making and firm success, *Academy of Management Executive*, 18(4): 8–12.

82   N. Argyres & A. M. McGahan, 2002, An interview with Michael Porter, *Academy of Management Executive*, 16(2): 43–52; Hoskisson, Hitt, Wan, & Yiu, Swings of a pendulum.

83   E. H. Bowman & C. E. Helfat, 2001, Does corporate strategy matter? *Strategic Management Journal*, 22: 1–23.

84   J. Shamsie, 2003, The context of dominance: An industry-driven framework for exploiting reputation, *Strategic Management Journal*, 24: 199–215; A. Seth & H. Thomas, 1994, Theories of the firm: Implications for strategy research, *Journal of Management Studies*, 31: 165–191.

85   Shamsie, The context of dominance.

86   J. W. Backmann, 2002, Competitive strategy: It's O.K. to be different, *Academy of Management Executive*, 16(2): 61–65.

87   L. F. Feldman, C. G. Brush, & T. Manolova, 2005, Co-alignment in the resource-performance relationship: Strategy as mediator, *Journal of Business Venturing*, 20: 359–383.

88   M. E. Porter, Competitive Advantage, New York: The Free Press; M. E. Porter, The contributions of industrial organization to strategic management, *Academy of Management Review*, 6: 609–620.

89   Schendel & Hofer, *Strategic Management*; Christensen, Berg, Bower, Hamermesh, & Porter, *Business Policy*.

90   M. E. Porter, 1980, *Competitive Strategy*, New York: The Free Press, ix.

91   Porter, *Competitive Advantage*.

92   A. M. McGahan, 1999, Competition, strategy and business performance, *California Management Review*, 41(3): 74–101; McGahan & Porter, How much does industry matter? 15–30.

93   R. Henderson & W. Mitchell, 1997, The interactions of organizational and competitive influences on strategy and performance, *Strategic Management Journal*, 18(summer special issue): 5–14; C. Oliver, 1997, Sustainable competitive advantage: Combining institutional and resource-based views, *Strategic Management Journal*, 18: 697–713; J. L. Stimpert & I. M. Duhaime, 1997, Seeing the big picture: The influence of industry, diversification, and business strategy on performance, *Academy of Management Journal*, 40: 560–583.

[94] J. B. Barney & A. M. Arikan, 2001, The resource-based view: Origins and implications, in M. A. Hitt, R. E. Freeman, & J. S. Harrison (eds.), *Handbook of Strategic Management*, Oxford, UK: Blackwell Publishers, 124–188.

[95] M. A. Hitt & R. D. Ireland, 1985, Corporate distinctive competence, strategy, industry and performance, *Strategic Management Journal*, 6: 273–293.

[96] R. A. Gordon & J. E. Howell, 1959, *Higher Education for Business*, New York: Columbia University Press.

[97] W. G. Bennis & R. J. Thomas, 2002, Crucibles of leadership, *Harvard Business Review*, 80(9): 39–45.

[98] E. T. Penrose, 1959, *The Theory of the Growth of the Firm*, New York: Wiley.

[99] F. J. Acedo, C. Barroso, & J. L. Galan, 2006, The resource-based theory: Dissemination and main trends, *Strategic Management Journal*, 27: 621–636; Barney & Arikan, The resource-based view.

[100] B. Wernerfelt, 1984, A resource-based view of the firm, *Strategic Management Journal*, 5: 171–180.

[101] B.-S. Teng & J. L. Cummings, 2002, Trade-offs in managing resources and capabilities, *Academy of Management Executive*, 16(2): 81–91.

[102] C. Lee, K. Lee, & J. M. Pennings, 2001, Internal capabilities, external networks, and performance: A study on technology-based ventures, *Strategic Management Journal*, 22(special issue): 615–640; C. C. Markides, 1999, A dynamic view of strategy, *Sloan Management Review*, 40(3): 55–72; Abell, Competing today while preparing for tomorrow.

[103] P. Bansal, 2005, Evolving sustainability: A longitudinal study of corporate sustainable development, *Strategic Management Journal*, 26: 197–218.

[104] R. L. Priem & J. E. Butler, 2001, Is the resource-based "view" a useful perspective for strategic management research? *Academy of Management Review*, 26: 22–40.

[105] S. Winter, 2003, Understanding dynamic capabilities, *Strategic Management Journal*, 10: 991–995; M. Blyler & R. W. Coff, 2003, Dynamic capabilities, social capital, and rent appropriation: Ties that split pies, *Strategic Management Review*, 24: 677–686.

[106] P. J. H. Schoemaker & R. Amit, 1994, Investment in strategic assets: Industry and firm-level perspectives, in P. Shrivastava, A. Huff, & J. Dutton (eds.), *Advances in Strategic Management*, Greenwich, CT: JAI Press, 9.

[107] A. A. Lado, N. G. Boyd, P. Wright, & M. Kroll, 2006, Paradox and theorizing within the resource-based view, *Academy of Management Review*, 31: 115–131; D. M. De Carolis, 2003, Competencies and imitability in the pharmaceutical industry: An analysis of their relationship with firm performance, *Journal of Management*, 29: 27–50; Barney, Is the resource-based "view" a useful perspective?; J. B. Barney, 1995, Looking inside for competitive advantage, *Academy of Management Executive*, 9(4): 56.

[108] R. D. Ireland, M. A. Hitt, & D. Vaidyanath, 2002, Alliance management as a source of competitive advantage, *Journal of Management*, 28: 413–446; P. M. Wright & W. R. Boswell, 2002, Desegregating HRM: A review and synthesis of micro and macro human resource management research, *Journal of Management*, 28: 247–276.

[109] A. Madhok, 1997, Cost, value and foreign market entry mode: The transaction and the firm, *Strategic Management Journal*, 18: 39–61.

[110] W. Kuemmerle, 2001, Go global—or not? *Harvard Business Review*, 79(6): 37–49.

[111] 2002, Xerox, Standard & Poor's Stock Report, http://www.standardandpoors.com, September 21; 2001, Xerox CEO Mulcahy says company still seeks profitability in 4th period, *Wall Street Journal Interactive*, http://www.wsj.com/articles, August 21.

[112] Ahuja & Lampert, Entrepreneurship in the large corporation; A. Arora & A. Gambardella, 1997, Domestic markets and international competitiveness: Generic and product specific competencies in the engineering sector, *Strategic Management Journal*, 18(summer special issue): 53–74.

[113] G. Hawawini, V. Subramanian, & P. Verdin, 2003, Is performance driven by industry- or firm-specific factors? A new look at the evidence, *Strategic Management Journal*, 24: 1–16.

[114] R. E. Freeman, 1984, *Strategic Management: A Stakeholder Approach*. Boston: Pitman Publishing, 249.

[115] M. C. Jensen & W. H. Meckling, 1976, Theory of the firm: Managerial behavior, agency costs and ownership structure. *Journal of Financial Economics*, 3: 305–360.

[116] T. M. Jones & A. C. Wicks, 1999, Convergent stakeholder theory, *Academy of Management Review*, 24: 206–221; Freeman, Strategic Management, 53–54.

[117] S. Sharma & I. Henriques, 2005, Stakeholder influences on sustainability practices in the Canadian Forest products industry, *Strategic Management Journal*, 26: 159–180; G. Donaldson & J. W. Lorsch, 1983, *Decision Making at the Top: The Shaping of Strategic Direction*, New York: Basic Books, 37–40.

[118] Ackoff, *Redesigning the Future*; March & Simon, *Organizations*; Barnard, *Functions of the Executive*.

[119] Freeman, *Strategic Management*.

[120] A. Hillman & M. A. Hitt, 1999, Corporate political strategy formulation: A model of approach, participation, and strategy decisions, *Academy of Management Review*, 24: 825–842; MacMillan, Strategy Formulation.

[121] Mintzberg, Managerial work.

[122] C. Eesley & M. J. Lenox, 2006, Firm responses to secondary stakeholder action, *Strategic Management Journal*, 27: 765–781.

[123] Walsh, Taking stock of stakeholder management.

[124] S. A. Waddock, C. Bodwell, & S. B. Graves, 2002, Responsibility: The new business imperative, *Academy of Management Executive*, 16(2): 132–148.

[125] R. Marden & R. Edwards, 2005, The Sarbanes–Oxley 'axe,' *CPA Journal*, April, 6–10.

[126] R. Phillips, R. E. Freeman, & A. C. Wicks, 2003, What stakeholder theory is not. *Business Ethics Quarterly*, 13: 481.

[127] R. E. Freeman, 2006, The Wal-Mart effect and business, ethics, and society, *Academy of Management Perspectives*, 20(3): 38–40; C. W. L. Hill & T. M. Jones, 1992, Stakeholder-agency theory, *Journal of Management Studies*, 29: 131–154.

[128] Phillips, Freeman, & Wicks, What stakeholder theory is not.

[129] Walsh, Taking stock of stakeholder management; Post, Preston, & Sachs, *Redefining the Corporation*.

[130] A. J. Hillman & G. D. Keim, 2001, Shareholder value, stakeholder management, and social issues: What's the bottom line? *Strategic Management Journal*, 22: 125–139; S. L. Berman, A. C. Wicks, S. Kotha, & T. M. Jones, 1999,

Does stakeholder orientation matter? The relationship between stakeholder management models and firm financial performance, *Academy of Management Journal*, 42(5): 488–506; S. Waddock & S. B. Graves, 1997, The corporate social performance-financial performance link, *Strategic Management Journal*, 18: 303–319; L. E. Preston & H. J. Sapienza, 1990, Stakeholder management and corporate performance, *Journal of Behavioral Economics*, 19: 361–375.

[131] T. M. Jones, 1995, Instrumental stakeholder theory: A synthesis of ethics and economics, *Academy of Management Review*, 20: 404–437; T. Donaldson & L. E. Preston, 1995, The stakeholder theory of the corporation: Concepts, evidence, and implications, *Academy of Management Review*, 20: 65–91.

[132] P. A. Argenti, R. A. Howell, & K. A. Beck, 2005, The strategic communication imperative, MIT Sloan Management Review, 46(3): 83–89; S. L. Hart & S. Sharma, 2004, Engaging fringe stakeholders for competitive imagination, *Academy of Management Executive*, 18(1): 7–18.

[133] J. T. Mahoney & A. M. McGahan, 2007, The field of strategic management within the evolving science of strategic organization, *Strategic Organization*, 5(1): 1–21.

[134] P. Nutt, 2004, Expanding the search for alternatives during strategic decision-making, *Academy of Management Executive*, 18(4): 13–28; M. Maccoby, 2001, Successful leaders employ strategic intelligence, *Research Technology Management*, 44(3): 58–60.

[135] M. H. Hansen, R. E. Hoskisson, & J. B. Barney, 2007, Competitive advantage in alliance governance: Resolving the opportunism minimization-gain maximization paradox, *Managerial and Decision Economics*, forthcoming; J. H. Davis, F. D. Schoorman, R. C. Mayer, & H. H. Tau, 2000, The trusted general manager and business unit performance: Empirical evidence of a competitive advantage, *Strategic Management Journal*, 21: 563–576.

[136] V. P. Rindova, I. O. Williamson, A. P. Petkova, & J. M. Sever, 2005, Being good or being known: An empirical examination of the dimensions, antecedents, and consequences of organizational reputation, *Academy of Management Journal*, 48: 1033–1049; C. J. Fombrun, 2001, Corporate reputations as economic assets, in M. A. Hitt, R. E. Freeman, & J. S. Harrison (eds.), *Handbook of Strategic Management*, Oxford, UK: Blackwell Publishers: 289–312; B. R. Barringer & J. S. Harrison, 2000, Walking a tightrope: Creating value through interorgnizational relationships, *Journal of Management*, 26: 367–403.

[137] M. L. Barnett & R. M. Salomon, 2006 {CE: Year missing}Beyond dichotomy: The curvilinear relationship between social responsibility and financial performance, *Strategic Management Journal*, 27: 1101–1122.

[138] T. M. Gardner, 2005, Interfirm competition for human resources: Evidence from the software industry, *Academy of Management Journal*, 48: 237–256; D. B. Turban & D. W. Greening, 1996, Corporate social performance and organizational attractiveness to prospective employees, *Academy of Management Journal*, 40: 658–672.

[139] Hansen, Hoskisson, & Barney, Competitive advantage in alliance governance; Williamson, *Markets and Hierarchies*.

[140] F. Stinglhamber, D. De Cremer, & L. F. Mercken, 2006, Support as a mediator of the relationship between justice and trust, *Group and Organization Management*, 31, 442–468; K. A. Hegtvedt, 2005, Doing justice to the group: Examining the roles of the group in justice research, *Annual Review of Sociology*, 31: 25–45; C. C. Chen, Y.-R. Chen, & K. Xin, 2004, Guanxi practices and trust in management: A procedural justice perspective, *Organization Science*, 15: 200–209.

[141] N. A. Gardberg, 2006, Corporate citizenship: Creating intangible assets across institutional environments, *Academy of Management Review*, 31: 329–346; Harrison & St. John, Managing and partnering with external stakeholders; B. Cornell & A. C. Shapiro, 1987, Corporate stakeholders and corporate finance, *Financial Management*, 16: 5–14.

[142] A. Mackey, T. B. Mackey, & J. B. Barney, 2007, Corporate social responsibility and firm performance: Investor preferences and corporate strategies, *Academy of Management Journal*, forthcoming; P. Bromiley, K. D. Miller, & D. Rau, 2001, Risk in strategic management research, in M. A. Hitt, R. E. Freeman, & J. S. Harrison (eds.), *Handbook of Strategic Management*, Oxford, UK: Blackwell Publishers, 259–288; S. B. Graves & S. A. Waddock, 1994, Institutional owners and corporate social performance, *Academy of Management Journal*, 37: 1035–1046.

[143] D. Lavie, 2006, The competitive advantage of interconnected firms: An extension of the resource-based view, *Academy of Management Review*, 31: 638–658; M. Makhija, 2003, Comparing the resource-based and market-based views of the firm: Empirical evidence from Czech privatization, *Strategic Management Journal*, 24: 433–451; T. J. Douglas & J. A. Ryman, 2003, Understanding competitive advantage in the general hospital industry: Evaluating strategic competencies, *Strategic Management Journal*, 24: 333–347; Harrison & St. John, Managing and partnering with external stakeholders.

[144] J. M. Leidtka, 2001, Strategy formulation: The roles of conversation and design, in M. A. Hitt, R. E. Freeman, & J. S. Harrison (eds.), *Handbook of Strategic Management*, Oxford, UK: Blackwell Publishers, 70–93.

[145] G. Hamel & C. K. Prahalad, 1994, *Competing for the Future*, Boston: Harvard Business School Press, 129.

[146] G. Hamel & C. K. Prahalad, 1989, Strategic intent, *Harvard Business Review*, 67(3): 63–76.

[147] M. A. Hitt, D. Park, C. Hardee, & B. B. Tyler, 1995, Understanding strategic intent in the global marketplace, *Academy of Management Executive*, 9(2): 12–19.

[148] Ackoff, *Redesigning the Future*.

[149] 2006, About Virgin, http://www.virgin.com/aboutvirgin/allaboutvirgin/thewholestory, December 23.

[150] J. S. Harrison & J. O. Fiet, 1999, New CEOs pursue their own interests by sacrificing stakeholder value, *Journal of Business Ethics*, 19: 301–308.

[151] R. Neustadt & E. May, 1986. *Thinking in Time: The Uses of History for Decision Makers*, New York: The Free Press, 251.

[152] About Virgin.

[153] G. Lundquist, 2004, The missing ingredients in corporate innovation, *Research Technology Management*, 47(5): 11–12.

[154] G. Hamel, 2000, *Leading the Revolution*, Boston: Harvard Business School Press.

[155] R. Zolli, 2006, Recognizing tomorrow's hot ideas today, *Business Week*, September 25, 12.

[156] Lundquist, The missing ingredients.

[157] J. Chen, Z. Zhou, & W. Anquan, 2005, A system model for corporate entrepreneurship, *International Journal of Manpower*, 26: 529–536.

[158] I. Bonn, 2005, Improving strategic thinking: A multilevel approach, *Leadership and Organizational Development Journal*, 26: 336–354.

[159] T. Hutzschenreuter & I. Kleindienst, 2006, Strategy-process research: What have we learned and what is still to be explored, *Journal of Management*, 32: 673–721; M. A. Hitt & R. D. Ireland, 2002, The essence of strategic leadership: Managing human and social capital, *Journal of Leadership and Organization Studies*, 9(1): 3–14.

[160] D. J. Ketchen, C. C. Snow, & V. L. Street, 2004, Improving firm performance by matching strategic decision-making processes to competitive dynamics, *Academy of Management Executive*, 18(4): 29–43.

[161] P. Evans & B. Wolf, 2005, Collaboration rules, *Harvard Business Review*, 83(7): 96–104.

[162] R. F. Felton & M. Watson, 2002, Change across the board, *McKinsey Quarterly*, http://www.mckinseyquarterly.com, September; J. A. Sonnenfeld, 2002, What makes great boards great, *Harvard Business Review*, 80(9): 106–113.

[163] L. Trigeorgis, 1997, *Real Options*, Cambridge, MA: MIT Press.

[164] J. J. Reuer & M. J. Leiblein, 2000, Downside risk implications of multinationality and international joint ventures, *Academy of Management Journal*, 43: 203–214.

[165] J. R. Ehrenfeld, 2005, The roots of sustainability, MIT Sloan Management Review, 46(2): 23–25; L. K. Trevino & G. R. Weaver, 2003, *Managing Ethics in Business Organizations*, Stanford, CA: Stanford University Press.

# CHAPTER 2

# Strategic Leadership

**KNOWLEDGE OBJECTIVES**

*Studying this chapter should provide you with the strategic management knowledge needed to:*

1. Define strategic leadership and describe the importance of top-level managers as resources.

2. Discuss the characteristics of effective strategic leaders and the factors that influence their ability to make effective strategic decisions, including managerial discretion and decision biases.

3. Define top management teams and explain their effects on firm performance.

4. Describe the factors that influence the ability of top managers to be effective strategic leaders.

5. Describe the processes associated with ensuring that a firm is well-positioned economically and identify the characteristics of a well-defined strategy.

6. Explain how strategic leaders acquire, develop, and manage firm resources to create one or more competitive advantages.

7. Describe how strategic leaders manage relationships with external stakeholders in order to reduce uncertainty and enhance value creation.

8. Discuss the roles of strategic leadership in determining and communicating the firm's strategic direction.

9. Discuss the importance and use of organizational controls.

Strategic leaders can profoundly influence firm performance.[1] Legendary business chief executive officers (CEOs) such as Jack Welch at General Electric, Sam Walton at Wal-Mart, and Akio Morita at Sony led their organizations to greater success than any of their many formidable competitors, yet they were very different in their approaches. Jack Welch was notorious for creating difficult targets for his subordinates and penalizing them when they did not perform. He drove managers to high levels of success or facilitated their departure from the firm, figuring that he was doing them a favor by helping them find some other situation in which they could excel.[2] Sam Walton took a positive and caring approach to the retailing business, treating customers as royalty and calling employees "associates." He also took an unconventional approach to the market by placing huge stores in rural areas and stocking them from warehouses that were centrally located near groups of stores. Although we now consider these features business-as-usual, they were anything but normal in the early days of Wal-Mart.[3] Akio Morita pushed hard on innovation and adopted a forward-looking, global perspective. He is heralded as a diplomat whose broad vision of Japan's role in the world economy helped Sony and other Japanese companies achieve high levels of success in international markets.[4]

Despite these different approaches, all of these leaders were visionaries, or transformational leaders: they established a clear view of what they wanted to accomplish. They were also agents of change, leading others to make their vision a reality. Effective strategic leadership is a requirement for successful strategic management. **Strategic leadership** is the ability to anticipate, envision, maintain flexibility, and empower others to create strategic change as necessary. Multifunctional in nature, strategic leadership involves managing through others, managing an entire enterprise rather than a functional subunit, and coping with change. Because of this landscape's complexity and global nature, strategic leaders must learn how to effectively influence human behavior in an uncertain environment. By word and/or by personal example, and through their ability to envision the future, effective strategic leaders meaningfully influence the behaviors, thoughts, and feelings of those with whom they work.[5] Transformational leadership entails motivating followers to do more than is expected, to continuously enrich their capabilities, and to place the organization's interests above their own.[6]

This chapter begins by focusing on individual strategic leaders—the personal characteristics that make them effective and the influences on their abilities to make effective strategic decisions. Then we examine top management teams and their influence on organizations, as well as factors associated with executive succession. The rest of the chapter discusses six key components of effective strategic leadership: ensuring that the firm is well-positioned economically, managing key resources, developing and maintaining effective relationships with key stakeholders, determining a strategic direction, overseeing the formulation and implementation of specific strategies, and establishing balanced organizational control systems. These activities influence the amount of value a firm creates and its economic performance.

## Individual Strategic Leaders and Influences on Their Decisions

Not all managers have the capacity to become effective strategic leaders. Furthermore, it may be that strategic leadership skills fall into a hierarchy, where managers must master lower-level skills before they fine-tune higher-level skills, as seen in the following chart from *Good to Great* by Jim Collins (see Figure 2.1).[7]

- ■ *Level 1: Highly Capable Individual.* The most basic skills for becoming a capable individual are developing skills and a strong work ethic.
- ■ *Level 2: Contributing Team Member.* Next, a person must be able to work effectively in teams and make useful contributions to the achievement of team goals.
- ■ *Level 3: Competent Manager.* Once the two lower-level skills are mastered, competent management comes from the ability to organize people and resources so as to achieve organizational objectives.
- ■ *Level 4: Effective Leader.* Not all competent managers are effective leaders. Leadership entails the ability to articulate a clear strategic intent and motivate followers to high levels of performance.
- ■ *Level 5: Level 5 Executive.* These are people with unwavering resolve to lead their companies to greatness. Frequently they are humble, attributing success to the team they have assembled rather than focusing on their own personal achievements. A Level 5 leader might also be called a transformational leader.

The concept of a skills hierarchy is appealing. People will not be able to contribute well to a team until they have attained a certain level of personal competence. Also, both of the

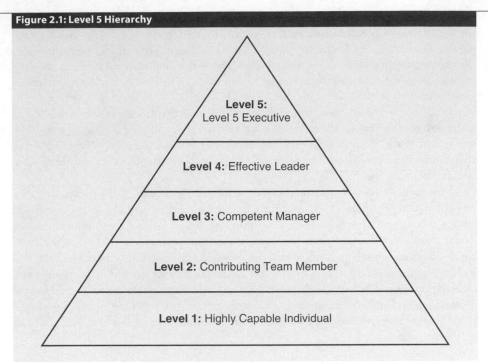

Level 5:
Level 5 Executive

**Level 4:** Effective Leader

**Level 3:** Competent Manager

**Level 2:** Contributing Team Member

**Level 1:** Highly Capable Individual

SOURCE: Adapted from J. Collins, 2001, *Good to Great: Why Some Companies Make the Leap . . . and Others Don't,* New York: Harper Business.

lower-level skills seem essential to becoming an excellent manager or leader. Furthermore, since competent management is defined as an ability to organize people and resources to achieve objectives, it seems reasonable that effective leaders also need these skills. Notice that the lower-level skill boxes in Figure 2.1 are larger than those at the top. This is a reflection of the numbers of people who possess those skills. Capable individuals are common compared with the number of Level 5 Executives.

One CEO who might justifiably be called a Level 5 Executive is Doug Conant of the Campbell Soup Company. In six years he transformed the company from a sleepy old brand to one of the industry's top performers, increasing the price of the company's stock 100 percent. He focused on reinvigorating the workforce as well as cutting costs and pursuing innovation. He deflects praise and admits mistakes by simply saying, "I can do better." During his tenure at Campbell, he has sent more than 16,000 handwritten thank-you notes, based on a philosophy that people should celebrate what is right rather than always finding fault. Says Campbell's chairman: "He's an extraordinary leader who behaves with the utmost integrity. People follow him and believe in him."[8]

## Strategic Leadership Style

Strategic leaders differ in the way they direct the strategic management process. The CEO sets the tone for the amount of management participation in strategic decisions and the way the decisions are implemented.[9] Some CEOs apply a very traditional "commander" approach, using meetings with top management team members to collect information but then individually deciding on strategies and directing subordinates to carry them out. A more collaborative style entails jointly arriving at strategies and implementation plans with members of the top management team. In other organizations, the CEO may delegate most strategy-making responsibilities to subordinates, allocating resources to them and giving them responsibility for utilizing them effectively.[10] The appropriateness of various decision-making styles tends to vary depending on the competitive situation. In situations in which rapid decisions are required, such as emergencies or unexpected shifts in the business environment, a more directive approach may be more appropriate. However, in general, a more participative style will lead to better decisions because managers share and consider a larger amount of relevant information.[11] Also, implementation may be easier and more successful because managers feel that they are a part of the decisions they are working to implement.[12]

The cultural and functional backgrounds of top managers may also influence the way strategic decisions are made.[13] An ongoing debate exists regarding whether it is appropriate to try to match the backgrounds of managers with the competitive situation in which they will lead. For instance, it may be appropriate for managers with production–operations backgrounds to run businesses that try to achieve low cost positions because of the internal focus on efficiency and engineering.[14] Alternatively, businesses that are seeking to differentiate their products may need someone with training in marketing or research and development (R&D) because of the need for innovation and market awareness. Growth strategies, in general, may call for a person with a strong marketing background, a willingness to take risks, and a high tolerance for ambiguity.[15] Nevertheless, these same characteristics may be inappropriate in turnaround situations. Some evidence also exists that strategic change and innovation are more likely when a manager is younger and has less time in the organization but is well-educated.[16] There is no absolute formula for matching a strategic leader to a competitive situation. The point to understand is that the effectiveness of strategic leadership may depend, in part, on how well the background and skills of a particular leader fit with the challenges the firm is facing.

## Managerial Discretion and Decision Biases

Managerial discretion and decision biases can also influence the effectiveness of strategic decisions. Because strategic decisions are intended to help a firm develop one or more competitive advantages, how managers exercise discretion (latitude for action) is critical to the firm's success.[17] Managers often use their discretion when making strategic decisions, including those associated with implementation of strategies.[18] Top executives must be action oriented; thus, the decisions that they make should spur the company to action. However, they are constrained by a number of factors that influence the level of discretion they have when making decisions. Some of these factors are associated with the external environment, such as the industry structure, the rate of market growth in the firm's primary industry, and the degree to which products can be differentiated. Consider, for example, that managers in a firm that produces a basic commodity are fairly limited in determining how they might alter their product to make it more appealing to the market. Characteristics of the organization, including its size, age, resources, and culture, can also influence discretion. For instance, strong organizational cultures can have a strong effect on the decisions that are made. Finally, discretion is influenced by individual characteristics of the manager, including commitment to the firm and its strategic outcomes, tolerance for ambiguity, skills in working with different people, and aspiration levels (see Figure 2.2).

In addition to managerial discretion, decision-making biases can have a large effect on strategic decisions.[19] Strategic managers tend to rely on a limited set of heuristics, or "rules of thumb," when they make strategic decisions.[20] These heuristics help managers

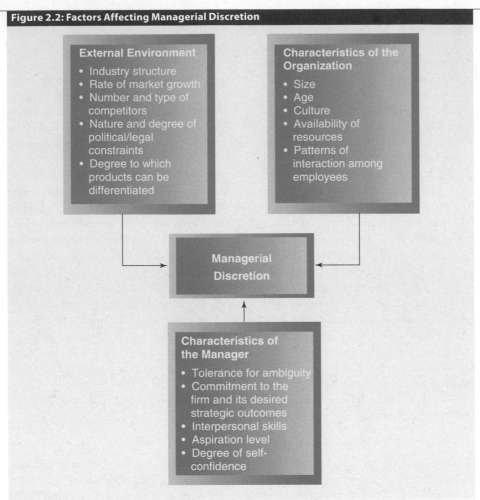

**Figure 2.2: Factors Affecting Managerial Discretion**

**External Environment**
- Industry structure
- Rate of market growth
- Number and type of competitors
- Nature and degree of political/legal constraints
- Degree to which products can be differentiated

**Characteristics of the Organization**
- Size
- Age
- Culture
- Availability of resources
- Patterns of interaction among employees

**Managerial Discretion**

**Characteristics of the Manager**
- Tolerance for ambiguity
- Commitment to the firm and its desired strategic outcomes
- Interpersonal skills
- Aspiration level
- Degree of self-confidence

SOURCE: Adapted from S. Finkelstein & D. C. Hambrick, 1996, *Strategic Leadership: Top Executives and Their Effects on Organizations*, St. Paul, MN: West Publishing Company.

simplify what might otherwise be an overwhelmingly complicated and uncertain decision environment. However, heuristics also can lead to suboptimal decisions.[21] Although dozens of potential decision-making biases have been described in the research literature,[22] five seem to have the most potential for influencing strategic decisions:[23]

- *Reliance on Previously Formed Beliefs.* Executives bring a number of preconceived ideas into any decision process. Some of them are a function of the executives' past experiences, while others are based on things they may have read or heard about, regardless of whether they have any actual empirical validity. Especially important to strategic decisions are beliefs about causality—that is, how the salient decision variables fit together. For instance, executives may believe that particular strategic actions will bring particular firm results. Clearly, experience is a valuable executive resource; however, preconceived ideas may cause decision makers to overlook information that could lead to different conclusions.[24] Stereotypes also fit into this category—that is, when executives hold preconceived notions about the abilities or potential behavior of individuals based on variables such as gender, nationality, religion, or race. Holding a stereotype can result in an executive ignoring the individual skills, background, and performance of a person who is being considered for a strategic position and thereby potentially choosing an individual who will not lead as effectively.

- *Focus on Limited Objectives.* Executives also tend to focus on a limited number of firm targets instead of thinking broadly about other worthwhile objectives.[25] For instance, a primary focus on budgetary controls may lead managers to focus on selected critical performance targets.[26] Too much of a focus on financial objectives, such as shareholder returns or return-on-equity, can lead to short-sighted decisions, where the firm takes actions with immediate financial benefits while damaging its longer-term performance.[27] It can also lead to neglect of and less favorable relationships with stakeholders that are important to firm competitiveness, such as customers, suppliers, the communities in which firms operate, or even employees.[28]

- *Exposure to Limited Decision Alternatives.* In an effort to simplify decision processes, executives tend to limit the number of alternatives for achieving a particular goal.[29] Instead, they rely on intuition to supplement rationality.[30] The problem is that in an effort to speed up decision processes, they may overlook viable or even potentially more successful alternatives.

- *Insensitivity to Outcome Probabilities.* Frequently, decision makers do not understand, trust, or use outcome probabilities to guide decision processes; that is, they tend to be more influenced by the magnitude of potential decision outcomes rather than the probability that they will occur.[31] They may also consider decision situations as unique and therefore discount information that might otherwise help them assess the probability of success.[32] The obvious danger associated with this bias is that, on the basis of the high potential returns that might accrue, strategic leaders will guide their firms into situations that are unlikely to be successful.

- *Illusion of Control.* As decision makers approach a particular decision situation, they may believe that they have more control over the outcomes from that decision than they actually do have.[33] This bias manifests itself in executives assessing lower probabilities of failure, which is related to the previous bias. However, it also results in a feeling among decision makers that they can use their professional skills to fix problems that occur as a decision is implemented.[34] This problem is linked to overconfidence or overoptimism.[35] Consequently, this bias can lead to poor decisions at the outset and inadequate planning for implementation of those decisions.

**Hubris,** which can be defined as excessive pride, leading to a feeling of invincibility, can magnify the effects of each of these potential biases.[36] CEOs tend to garner a lot of media, and they may win awards and gain other types of public recognition.[37] Research has shown that when CEOs begin to believe the glowing press accounts and to feel that they are unlikely to make errors, they are more likely to make poor strategic decisions.[38] Top executives need to have self-confidence, but they must also guard against allowing it to reach the point of hubris. Perhaps that is why some of the greatest business leaders of our day exhibit an unusual degree of humility.[39]

Awareness of decision-making biases can help strategic leaders at least partially overcome them. For instance, leaders can provide an open decision-making environment that invites new perspectives and challenges existing assumptions and strategies. Also, problems associated with the neglect of prior probabilities can be addressed through real options analysis (see Chapter 13). In addition, strategic leaders can address problems associated with decision biases by surrounding themselves with a top management team composed of individuals who have divergent views and varying backgrounds.

## Top Management Teams

In most firms, complex organizational challenges and the need for substantial information, knowledge, and skills to address these challenges result in a need for teams of executives to provide strategic leadership. The quality of strategic thinking and subsequent strategic decisions made by a top management team affect the firm's ability to innovate and engage in effective strategic change.[40] Top-level managers are an important resource for firms seeking to successfully use the strategic management process.[41]

A **top management team** is composed of the CEO and other key managers who are responsible for setting the direction of the firm and formulating and implementing its strategies. For instance, a team may include a chief operating officer (COO) and an assortment of other high-ranking officials typically representing the major businesses and/or functional areas of the firm, as well as members of the board of directors.[42] The decisions resulting from strategic thinking that top-level managers engage in influence how the firm is designed, the nature of its strategies, and whether it will achieve its goals. Thus, a critical element of organizational success is having a top management team with superior managerial and decision-making skills.[43]

Several factors influence the ability of top management teams to exercise effective strategic leadership, including team heterogeneity, team power, and executive succession processes.

### Top Management Team Heterogeneity

The job of top-level executives is complex and requires a broad knowledge of the firm's operations, as well as the three key parts of the firm's external environment—the general, industry, and competitor environments. (Chapter 3 explores these environments in depth.) The overwhelming complexity and strength of environmental forces, as well as the need to manage a wide variety of stakeholder relationships, require formation of a fairly diverse top management team with a wide variety of strengths, capabilities, and knowledge.[44] This normally requires a **heterogeneous top management team** composed of individuals with different functional backgrounds, experience, and education. The more heterogeneous a top management team is—the more varied the expertise and knowledge within the team—the more capacity it has to provide effective strategic leadership in formulating strategy.

In anticipation of his departure from Microsoft, Bill Gates assembled a team of leaders to retool and reinvigorate the company.[45] CEO Steven Ballmer has vowed that Microsoft will trade out its historical competency, writing time-consuming packaged software, for more flexibility in its products, including more use of a Web-based approach in all of its software. A heterogeneous team of senior managers is working with Ballmer, among them J. Allard, corporate vice president for design and development. Allard is described as an "edgy thinker" who is looking well beyond Windows for the company's next major innovation. For instance, he led the creation of the Zune music player, which took only eight months to develop and bring to market. Steven Sinofsky, senior vice president of Windows, is a detail-oriented computer whiz who recently spent a fall in Beijing, China, working on projects in marketing and R&D. Craig Mundie, chief research and strategy officer, began his career by developing operating systems at Systems Equipment Corporation. He continues to serve on national committees dealing with technology issues and spent time working directly with Bill Gates on research and incubation projects before Mundie left his former employer. Lisa Brummel, senior vice president of human resources, has made sweeping changes in response to employee discontent. In all, 21 managers make up the senior management team at Microsoft, a reflection of the size and diversity of the company and its products.[46]

Members of a heterogeneous top management team benefit from discussing the different perspectives that team members advance. In many cases, these discussions increase the quality of the team's decisions, especially when a synthesis emerges from the diverse perspectives that is superior to any one individual perspective.[47] Having members with substantive expertise in the firm's core functions and businesses is also important to a top management team's effectiveness. In a high-technology industry, it may be critical for a firm's top management team to have R&D expertise, particularly when growth strategies are being implemented.[48] Heterogeneous top management teams have sometimes demonstrated a propensity to take stronger competitive actions and reactions than more homogeneous teams.[49]

More heterogeneity in top management teams is also positively associated with innovation and strategic change.[50] Team heterogeneity may encourage members to "think outside the box" and thus be more creative in making decisions.[51] In essence, thinking outside the box means "thinking beyond the common mental models that shape the way people see the world."[52] Therefore, firms that need to change their strategies are more likely to do so if they have top management teams with diverse backgrounds and expertise. A team with various areas of expertise is more likely to identify environmental changes (opportunities and threats) or changes within the firms that require a different strategic direction.[53] Research also shows that more heterogeneity among top management team members promotes debate, which often leads to better strategic decisions. In turn, better strategic decisions produce higher firm performance.[54]

Once a decision is made, the next challenge is to create a level of cohesion among team members that will facilitate effective implementation of the change. One of the great challenges facing strategic leaders is integrating the diverse opinions and behavior of a heterogeneous team into a common way of thinking and behaving.[55] In general, the more heterogeneous and larger the top management team is, the more difficult it is for the team to effectively implement strategies.[56] Comprehensive and long-term strategic plans can be inhibited by communication difficulties among top executives who have different backgrounds and different cognitive skills.[57] As a result, a group of top executives with diverse backgrounds may inhibit the process of decision making if it is not effectively managed. In these cases, top management teams may fail to comprehensively examine threats and opportunities, leading to suboptimal strategic decisions.

CEO Daniel Vasella, chairman of Novartis, formed through the merger of Swiss drugmakers Sandoz and Ciba-Geigy in 1996, runs one of the largest pharmaceutical companies in the world.[58] Vasella, formerly a practicing physician, has transformed the once stodgy Swiss conglomerate into an aggressive innovator, partly by putting together an energetic but diverse top management team. One analyst noted: "Although the top executives at Novartis contain a diversity of strong personalities, their oft-used term 'alignment' rings true in their teamwork. . . . Yet, each team member carries a different charge and perspective."[59]

## The CEO and Top Management Team Power

Chapter 11 discusses the board of directors as a governance mechanism for monitoring a firm's strategic direction and for representing stakeholders' interests, especially those of shareholders.[60] Here, we focus on the characteristics that give the CEO and top management team power relative to the board and the influence these characteristics can have on the amount of strategic leadership the board provides. An underlying premise is that higher performance normally is achieved when the board of directors is more directly involved in shaping a firm's strategic direction.[61] However, directors may find it difficult to direct the strategic actions of powerful CEOs and top management teams.[62] Their relative power is at least partially a function of social or business ties with directors and their tenure as members of the team.

It is not uncommon for a powerful CEO to appoint a number of sympathetic outside board members such as friends, family members, or principals in companies with which the firm conducts business. CEOs may also appoint board members who are on the top management team and report directly to the CEO.[63] In either case, the CEO may have significant control over the board's actions. Westphal and Zajac have asked the "central question" of "whether boards are an effective management control mechanism . . . or whether they are a 'management tool,' . . . a rubber stamp for management initiatives . . . and often surrender to management their major domain of decision-making authority, which includes the right to hire, fire, and compensate top management."[64]

Xerox is an example of an industry giant that stumbled, at least in part, because of an ineffective board. A few years ago, amid lackluster financial results, rapid CEO turnover, and charges of accounting irregularities, the company's board was criticized for being "asleep at the wheel."[65] In response, the company has made dramatic changes, with more than half of its eleven board members appointed between 2003 and 2006.[66] The board now includes three women (including CEO Anne Mulcahy), two minority members, a business school dean, and representatives from a wide range of industries.

Despite the highly visible examples of poor governance in low-performing firms, close ties between board members and CEOs do not always lead to less board member involvement in strategic decisions. In fact, research shows that social ties between the CEO and board members may actually increase board members' involvement in strategic decisions. Thus, strong relationships between the CEO and the board of directors may result in positive or negative outcomes for firms, depending on how those relationships are managed.[67] The important point is to recognize and safeguard against the risks.

Another way for a CEO to achieve power relative to the board is to serve as chair of the board.[68] This practice, called **CEO duality,** has become more common in the United States. Although it varies across industries, duality occurs most often in the largest firms. Increased shareholder activism, however, has brought CEO duality under scrutiny and attack in both U.S. and European firms. Duality has been criticized for causing poor performance and slow response to change in a number of firms.[69]

Historically, an **independent board leadership structure,** in which different people held the positions of CEO and board chair, was believed to enhance a board's ability to monitor top-level managers' decisions and actions, particularly in terms of the firm's financial performance.[70] Consistent with this view, the two jobs are always separate in Britain. However, the British model can also lead to problems, particularly to power struggles and confusion regarding firm leadership.[71] Also, **stewardship theory** suggests that top managers want to do the right thing for the firm's shareholders and that reducing the amount of interference with their actions will increase the profit potential of the firm.[72] From this perspective, CEO duality would be expected to facilitate effective decisions and actions. In these instances, the increased effectiveness gained through CEO duality accrues from the individual who wants to perform effectively and desires to be the best possible steward of the firm's assets. Because of this person's positive orientation and actions, extra governance and the coordination costs resulting from an independent board leadership structure would be unnecessary. These arguments demonstrate that there is no clear answer regarding the influence of CEO duality on strategic decision making.

An additional influence on the power of the CEO and other top management team members is their tenure in the organization. CEOs with long tenure—on the team and in the organization—have a greater influence on board decisions.[73] And it follows that CEOs with greater influence may take actions in their own best interests, the outcomes of which increase their compensation from the company.[74] Long tenure is known to restrict the breadth of an executive's knowledge base. With the limited perspectives associated with a restricted knowledge base, long-tenured top executives typically develop fewer alternatives to evaluate in making strategic decisions.[75] However, long-tenured managers also may be able to exercise more effective strategic control, thereby obviating the need for board members' involvement because effective strategic control generally produces higher performance.[76]

To strengthen the firm, boards of directors should develop an effective relationship with the firm's top management team that makes sense in a particular competitive situation.[77] Specifically, the relative degree of power held by the board and top management team members should be examined in light of the situation. The abundance of resources in a firm's external environment and the volatility of that environment may affect the ideal balance of power between boards and top management teams.[78] For instance, a volatile and uncertain environment may create a situation in which a powerful CEO is needed to move quickly, and a diverse top management team could create less cohesion among team members and prevent or stall a necessary strategic move.[79] By developing effective working relationships, boards, CEOs, and other top management team members are able to serve the best interests of the firm's stakeholders.[80]

## Executive Succession Processes

The choice of top executives, especially CEOs, is a critical organizational decision with important implications for the firm's performance.[81] Many companies use leadership screening systems to identify individuals with managerial and strategic leadership potential. The most effective of these systems assess people within the firm and gain valuable information about the capabilities of other companies' managers, particularly their strategic leaders.[82] Based on the results of these assessments, training and development programs are provided for current managers in an attempt to preselect and shape the skills of people who may become tomorrow's leaders. The "ten-step talent" management development program at General Electric, for example, is considered one of the most effective in the world.[83]

Organizations select strategic leaders from two types of managerial labor markets: internal and external.[84] An *internal managerial labor market* consists of the opportunities for managerial positions within a firm, and an *external managerial labor market* consists of career opportunities for managers in organizations other than the one for which they work currently.

In the past, companies have strongly preferred that insiders fill top management positions because of a desire for continuity and a continuing commitment to the firm's current vision, mission, and chosen strategies.[85] In fact, some think that outside succession to the CEO position is "an extraordinary event for business firms [and] is usually seen as a stark indicator that the board of directors wants change."[86] Several benefits are thought to accrue to firms when insiders are selected as new CEOs. Because of their experience with the firm and the industry environment in which it competes, insiders are familiar with company products, markets, technologies, and operating procedures. Also, internal hiring produces lower turnover among existing personnel, many of whom possess valuable firm-specific knowledge. Also known as *private knowledge* and often a source of competitive advantage, firm-specific knowledge includes items such as the company's "unique routines, processes, documentation, or trade secrets."[87]

Thus, when the firm is performing well, internal succession is favored because it is assumed that hiring from inside keeps within the firm the important knowledge necessary to sustain the high performance. For an inside move to the top to occur successfully, however, firms must develop and implement effective succession management programs, which help develop managers so that one will eventually be prepared to ascend to the top.[88]

Given the impressive success of General Electric over the past 20-plus years and its highly effective management development program, an insider, Jeffrey Immelt, was chosen to succeed Jack Welch.[89] Similarly, at IBM, Samuel Palmisano, also an insider, was selected to replace Louis Gerstner, who, interestingly, was an outsider when he was chosen to be CEO. Gerstner was selected to change the strategic direction of the firm, which was suffering at the time of his hire. Since IBM's performance was improving, investors did not want a significant change in strategic direction, even in light of the firm's less-than-stellar performance at year-end 2002. Addressing the firm's performance at the time, new CEO Palmisano noted that it was a "tough, tough year." He also stated, though, that IBM's technical leadership would be the foundation for expected improvements in 2003 and beyond. Palmisano's statement was reinforced by the fact that IBM was leading the world in new patent awards at the time of his appointment.[90]

Because of changing competitive landscapes and varying levels of performance, an increasing number of boards of directors have been turning to outsiders to succeed CEOs.[91] Firms often hire an executive recruitment firm, or "headhunter," to help identify and recruit strong candidates. Valid reasons often exist for selecting an outsider. For example, research suggests that executives who have spent their entire careers with a particular firm may become "stale in the saddle."[92] Long tenure with a firm seems to reduce the number of innovative ideas top executives are able to develop to cope with conditions their firm faces. Given the importance of innovation for a firm's success in today's competitive landscape, an inability to innovate or to create conditions that stimulate innovation throughout a firm is a liability in a strategic leader. The diverse knowledge base and social networks they have developed while working for other organizations is another reason to hire from the external managerial labor market.[93] Unique combinations of diverse knowledge sets might create synergy as the foundation for developing new competitive advantages.

Figure 2.3 shows how the composition of the top management team and CEO succession (managerial labor market) may interact to affect strategy. For example, when the top management team is homogeneous (its members have similar functional experiences and educational backgrounds) and a new CEO is selected from inside the firm, the firm's current strategy is unlikely to change. On the other hand, when a new CEO is selected from outside the firm and the top management team is heterogeneous, there is a high probability that strategy will change. When the new CEO is from inside the firm and a heterogeneous top management team is in place, the strategy may not change, but innovation is likely to

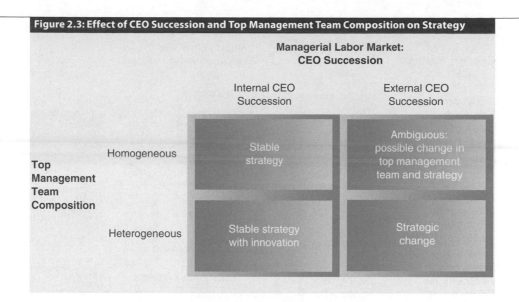

**Figure 2.3: Effect of CEO Succession and Top Management Team Composition on Strategy**

| | Managerial Labor Market: CEO Succession | | |
| --- | --- | --- | --- |
| | | Internal CEO Succession | External CEO Succession |
| **Top Management Team Composition** | Homogeneous | Stable strategy | Ambiguous: possible change in top management team and strategy |
| | Heterogeneous | Stable strategy with innovation | Strategic change |

continue. An external CEO succession with a homogeneous team creates a more ambiguous situation.

Given the need for diverse managerial perspectives in an increasingly competitive marketplace, it is unfortunate that some firms are still reluctant to fill their top jobs with individuals who might bring a different view to the table.[94] In particular, minority groups and especially women are underrepresented in the top positions of major for-profit organizations.[95] From a resource-based perspective, this is unfortunate because it signals that some firms are not taking full advantage of the resources they possess. The stakeholder view also would suggest that a firm that creates a "glass ceiling" for some of its members with regard to their promotion potential is missing opportunities to foster relationships with diverse segments of society.

Nevertheless, women are making slow but steady progress in terms of receiving more appointments in upper-level positions in for-profit firms, particularly in certain industries.[96] For instance, in the entertainment industry women occupy about a third of the higher executive slots at film studios.[97] This phenomenon makes sense from a strategic perspective because women make up approximately half the audience for films. In other industries, Xerox CEO Anne Mulcahy, Sara Lee CEO Brenda Barnes, and eBay CEO Meg Whitman are examples of women who have broken through the gender barrier. Additionally, organizations are beginning to utilize women's potential managerial talents through memberships on corporate boards of directors. These additional appointments suggest that women's ability to represent stakeholders' and especially shareholders' best interests in for-profit companies at the level of the board of directors is being more broadly recognized.

## Key Strategic Leadership Responsibilities and Actions

The primary responsibility for strategic thinking, and the effective strategic leadership that can result from it, rests with the top management team and, in particular, with the CEO. Strategic leadership is an extremely complex, but critical, form of leadership. Strategies

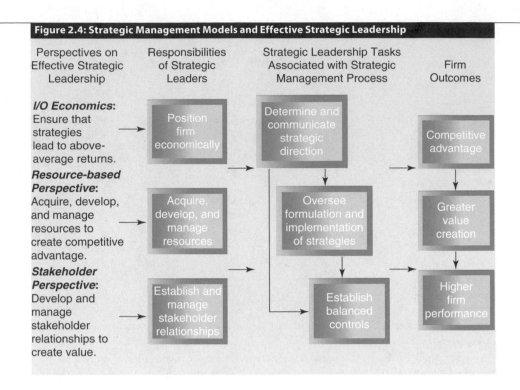

**Figure 2.4: Strategic Management Models and Effective Strategic Leadership**

| Perspectives on Effective Strategic Leadership | Responsibilities of Strategic Leaders | Strategic Leadership Tasks Associated with Strategic Management Process | Firm Outcomes |
|---|---|---|---|
| **I/O Economics:** Ensure that strategies lead to above-average returns. | Position firm economically | Determine and communicate strategic direction | Competitive advantage |
| **Resource-based Perspective:** Acquire, develop, and manage resources to create competitive advantage. | Acquire, develop, and manage resources | Oversee formulation and implementation of strategies | Greater value creation |
| **Stakeholder Perspective:** Develop and manage stakeholder relationships to create value. | Establish and manage stakeholder relationships | Establish balanced controls | Higher firm performance |

cannot be formulated and implemented to achieve above-average returns unless strategic leaders successfully fulfill several important responsibilities.

As described in Chapter 1, the I/O economic, resource-based, and stakeholder perspectives envision the strategic management process from different points of view. The three perspectives also provide different views regarding the primary responsibilities of strategic leaders. From an economic perspective, top managers have the primary responsibility for ensuring that firm strategies will lead to above-average economic performance by monitoring the external environment and positioning the firm optimally in terms of its strategic direction, strategies, and implementation plans.[98] According to the resource-based view, top managers are primarily responsible for making sure their organizations acquire, develop, and utilize resources that lead to achieving competitive advantage.[99] Finally, the stakeholder perspective gives top managers primary responsibility for managing relationships with important constituencies to facilitate the creation of value.[100]

These three perspectives reflect the varied responsibilities and tasks associated with strategic leadership. They emphasize different aspects of a strategic leader's job, but in reality top managers have all of the responsibilities outlined by each of the perspectives, although they may give them a different priority. As illustrated in Figure 2.4, the responsibilities of strategic leaders are translated into specific tasks associated with the strategic management process. These tasks include determining and communicating strategic direction, facilitating and overseeing the formulation and implementation of specific strategies, and establishing balanced controls to ensure that the firm is accomplishing what it needs to in order to move in the desired direction. When executed properly, these actions result in the establishment of competitive advantage, creation of greater value for the firm and its stakeholders, and, ultimately, above-average financial performance.

Strategic leaders have substantial decision-making responsibilities that cannot be delegated.[101] The rest of this chapter discusses some of the most important of these, using the responsibilities and tasks found in Figure 2.4 as an outline.

## Ensure That the Firm Is Well Positioned Economically

The I/O economic model is based on the idea that economic performance is determined by a firm's general, industry, and competitor environments and by how well the firm implements the strategy dictated by those environments (see Chapter 1). Consequently, strategic leadership involves selecting industries and industry segments in which to compete and responding to changes that occur in those environments. Effective strategic leaders engage in strategic thinking that leads to the firm and its environment being continuously aligned.[102] Individual judgment plays an important part in learning about and analyzing the firm's external conditions.[103] As Dan DiMicco, CEO of the steel giant Nucor, put it, "What I get paid for is not looking at yesterday, but looking at the future."[104]

Another way to envision the positioning responsibility of strategic leaders is to say that they should clearly define a firm's strategy, which is a manifestation of strategic intent. Strategic intent was defined in the first chapter as the way a firm leverages its resources, capabilities, and core competencies to accomplish its goals in the competitive environment.[105] Unfortunately, the term "strategy" has taken on so many meanings that it can be used to mean almost anything. For instance, some firms may define their strategy in terms of how they treat people, while others may talk about particular markets or products. Hambrick and Fredrickson suggest that strategy is "the central, integrated, externally oriented concept of how we will achieve our objectives."[106] Their view is consistent with our definition in Chapter 1 that strategy is an integrated and coordinated set of commitments and actions designed to exploit core competencies and gain a competitive advantage. A firm's fundamental purposes, reflected in its mission and goals, are treated separately from a firm's strategy. Instead, the strategy becomes a vehicle to achieve the firm's purposes. Organizational arrangements such as structures, processes, rewards systems, and functional policies also support, but do not define, strategy. Strategic leaders use the tools of strategic analysis, including analysis of industries, markets, competitors, and internal strengths and weaknesses, to help them determine firm strategy.[107]

Five important elements that identify a firm's strategy are arenas, growth vehicles, differentiators, staging, and the economic logic that ties all the elements together (see Figure 2.5). *Arenas* have to do with a firm's **scope,** which is the breadth of a firm's activities across products, markets, geographic regions, core technologies, and value creation stages. Defining the business is a critical starting point for all strategic planning and management.[108] Firms like Siemens AG, Sony, and General Electric have broad scope because of their involvement in a wide range of industries throughout the world. On the other hand, Frontier Airlines focuses its efforts exclusively on airline transportation in the western United States. McDonald's has wide geographic scope, but most of its revenues come from a particular technology—fast food preparation and delivery.

*Growth vehicles* also are important to understanding a firm's strategy. Some of the commonly used vehicles are internal development, joint ventures, licensing, franchising, and acquisitions. General Electric has historically engaged in frequent acquisitions to increase the scope of its businesses, as well as many joint ventures to enter new markets (such as China). However, now the company's focus is more on internal growth through innovation.[109] Quiznos used franchising to become one of the fastest growing restaurant chains in

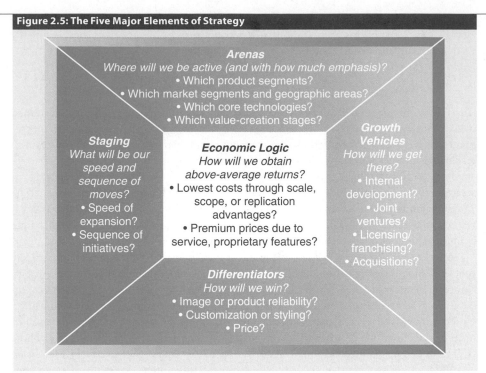

**Figure 2.5: The Five Major Elements of Strategy**

**Arenas**
Where will we be active (and with how much emphasis)?
• Which product segments?
• Which market segments and geographic areas?
• Which core technologies?
• Which value-creation stages?

**Staging**
What will be our speed and sequence of moves?
• Speed of expansion?
• Sequence of initiatives?

**Economic Logic**
How will we obtain above-average returns?
• Lowest costs through scale, scope, or replication advantages?
• Premium prices due to service, proprietary features?

**Growth Vehicles**
How will we get there?
• Internal development?
• Joint ventures?
• Licensing/ franchising?
• Acquisitions?

**Differentiators**
How will we win?
• Image or product reliability?
• Customization or styling?
• Price?

SOURCE: Adapted from D. C. Hambrick & J. W. Fredrickson, 2005, Are you sure you have a strategy? *Academy of Management Executive,* 19(4): 54, reprinted from 15(4).

the country.[110] On the other hand, Starbucks has grown rapidly through internal development rather than franchising.

*Differentiators* help a firm determine how it is expected to win customers in the marketplace. Southwest Airlines attracts customers through rock-bottom prices and by staying on schedule. McDonald's draws people in by offering them dependable quality and convenient locations. A company like General Electric has a more difficult problem in defining a consistent differentiator for its multitude of businesses. In fact, in diversified firms it is probably a better idea to allow the top management team of each distinct business to determine how it will win customers. However, even firms as highly diversified as General Electric may try to establish core competencies that differentiate several businesses in similar ways. For instance, General Electric stresses finding innovative ways to satisfy customer needs. According to CEO Jeffrey Immelt: "For GE, imagination at work is more than a slogan or tagline. It is a reason for being."[111]

*Staging* has to do with the timing of strategy and the sequence of moves the firm will take to carry it out. It is especially important because of the speed with which the competitive environment is changing.[112] For instance, Microsoft has been criticized because it is sometimes slow to respond to changes in its markets.[113] However, being fast to market is not a guarantee of success either. Consider that Yahoo! Inc. was an early entrant in the Chinese market, but through a series of missteps, the company now struggles to survive in that market.[114] Strategic leaders must make sure that everything is in place as they execute a strategy. As an example, Boeing had to work out problems with its unions before building its 787 Dreamliner, which required major changes to the firm's manufacturing processes.[115]

The *economic logic* of a strategy pulls together the other four elements. From an economic perspective, a strategy is unsuccessful unless its elements lead to above-average returns. Sun Microsystems was highly regarded for its innovation, but it lost money for years.[116] On the other hand, Michael Dell made his computer company the largest seller of personal computers through a focus on direct-to-consumer sales of low-cost machines combined with highly efficient manufacturing processes.[117] When everything comes together, the results can be outstanding. The Dell case, however, also illustrates one of the major themes of this book—the need for constant reassessment of strategy in an ever-changing external environment. As consumers demanded cutting-edge products and better service, Dell lost its number one slot to rival Hewlett-Packard.

## Acquire, Develop, and Manage Key Resources

The resource-based perspective focuses attention on the value of organizational resources in achieving competitive advantage. Strategic leaders are primarily responsible for ensuring that their firms acquire and develop the resources they need to achieve competitive success. Briefly mentioned in Chapter 1, *core competencies* are resources and capabilities that serve as a source of competitive advantage for a firm over its rivals. Firms develop and exploit core competencies in many different functional areas. Strategic leaders must verify that the firm's competencies are emphasized in strategy implementation efforts. Intel, for example, has core competencies of *competitive agility* (an ability to act in a variety of competitively relevant ways) and *competitive speed* (an ability to act quickly when facing environmental and competitive pressures).[118] Other firms have developed excellent capabilities to ascertain and satisfy the needs of their customers.[119] Firms with core competencies in R&D tend to be rewarded in the market because of the critical nature of innovation in many industries.[120]

Much of Chapter 4 deals with organizational resources and their potential as sources of competitive advantage. However, two resources—human capital and organizational culture—are so closely related to strategic leadership that we discuss them briefly here.

**Manage Human Capital.** The ability to manage human capital, or the knowledge and skills of a firm's entire workforce, may be the most critical of the strategic leader's skills.[121] In the 21st century, intellectual capital, including the ability to manage knowledge and create and commercialize innovation, affects a strategic leader's success.[122] Competent strategic leaders also establish the context through which stakeholders (such as employees, customers, and suppliers) can perform at peak efficiency.[123] Carey and Ogden point out that "when a public company is left with a void in leadership, for whatever reason, the ripple effects are widely felt both within and outside the organization. Internally, a company is likely to suffer a crisis of morale, confidence and productivity among employees and, similarly, stockholders may panic when a company is left rudderless and worry about the safety and future of their investment."[124] The crux of strategic leadership is the ability to manage the firm's operations and employees effectively in order to sustain high performance over time.[125]

From the perspective of human capital, employees are viewed as a capital resource that requires investment.[126] These investments are productive, in that much of the development of U.S. industry can be attributed to the effectiveness of its human capital,[127] leading to the conviction in many business firms today that "as the dynamics of competition accelerate, people are perhaps the only truly sustainable source of competitive advantage."[128] Human capital's increasing importance suggests a significant role for the firm's human resource management activities.[129] As a support activity (see Chapter 4), human resource management practices facilitate people's efforts to successfully select and especially to use the firm's strategies.[130]

Finding the human capital necessary to run an organization effectively is a challenge that many firms attempt to solve by using temporary employees. Other firms try to improve their recruiting and selection techniques. Solving the problem, however, requires more than hiring temporary employees; it requires building effective commitments to organizational goals as well. Hiring star players is also insufficient; rather, a strategic leader needs to build an effective organizational team committed to achieving the company's strategic intent.[131]

Increasingly, international experience has become essential to the development necessary for strategic leaders.[132] Because nearly every industry is targeting fast-growing foreign markets, more companies are requiring "global competency" among their top managers.[133] Thus, companies trying to learn how to compete successfully in the global economy should find opportunities for their future strategic leaders to work in locations outside of their home nation.[134] When multinational corporations invest in emerging economies, they are also wise to invest in human capital in foreign subsidiaries.[135] Furthermore, because international management capabilities are becoming important, managing "inpatriation" (the process of transferring host-country or third-country national managers into the domestic market of multinational firms) has become an important means of building global core competencies.[136]

Effective training and development programs increase the probability that a manager will be a successful strategic leader. These programs have grown progressively important as knowledge has become more integral to gaining and sustaining a competitive advantage.[137] Additionally, such programs build knowledge and skills, inculcate a common set of core values, and offer a systematic view of the organization, thus promoting the firm's strategic vision and organizational cohesion. The programs also contribute to the development of core competencies.[138] Furthermore, they help strategic leaders improve skills that are critical to completing other tasks associated with effective strategic leadership, such as determining the firm's strategic direction, exploiting and maintaining the firm's core competencies, and developing an organizational culture that supports ethical practices. Thus, building human capital is vital to the effective execution of strategic leadership.[139]

Strategic leaders must acquire the skills necessary to help develop human capital in their areas of responsibility. This challenge is important, given that most strategic leaders need to enhance their human resource management abilities.[140] For example, firms that value human resources and have effective reward plans for employees have obtained higher returns on their initial public offerings.[141] When human capital investments are successful, the result is a workforce capable of learning continuously. Continuous learning and leveraging the firm's expanding knowledge base are linked with strategic success.[142]

Programs that achieve outstanding results in the training of future strategic leaders become a competitive advantage for a firm. General Electric's system of training and development of future strategic leaders is comprehensive and thought to be among the best.[143] Accordingly, it may be a source of competitive advantage for the firm.

**Ensure an Effective Organizational Culture.** An **organizational culture** consists of a complex set of ideologies, symbols, and core values that is shared throughout the firm and influences the way business is conducted. Evidence suggests that a firm can develop core competencies in terms of both the capabilities it possesses and the way the capabilities are used to produce strategic actions. In other words, because the organizational culture influences how the firm conducts its business and helps regulate and control employees' behavior, it can be a source of competitive advantage.[144] Thus, shaping the context within which the firm formulates and implements its strategies—that is, shaping the organizational culture—is a central task of strategic leaders.[145]

An organizational culture often encourages (or discourages) the pursuit of entrepreneurial opportunities, especially in large firms.[146] Entrepreneurial opportunities are an important source of growth and innovation;[147] therefore, a key role of strategic leaders is to encourage and promote innovation by pursuing entrepreneurial opportunities.[148] One way to do this is to invest in opportunities as real options—that is, opportunities that provide options to make additional worthwhile investments in the future, if the situation calls for it.[149] For example, a firm may purchase property now because it wants the option to build on it in the future. Chapter 12 describes how large firms use strategic entrepreneurship to pursue entrepreneurial opportunities and to gain first-mover advantages. Chapter 13 covers the real options approach. Medium and small firms also rely on strategic entrepreneurship when trying to develop innovations as the foundation for earning above-average returns. In firms of all sizes, strategic entrepreneurship is more likely to be successful when employees have an entrepreneurial orientation. Five dimensions characterize a firm's entrepreneurial orientation: autonomy, innovativeness, risk taking, proactiveness, and competitive aggressiveness.[150] In combination, these dimensions influence the actions a firm takes in efforts to be innovative and launch new ventures.

*Autonomy* allows employees to take actions that are free of organizational constraints and permits individuals and groups to be self-directed. *Innovativeness* "reflects a firm's tendency to engage in and support new ideas, novelty, experimentation, and creative processes that may result in new products, services, or technological processes."[151] Cultures with a tendency toward innovativeness encourage employees to think beyond existing knowledge, technologies, and parameters in efforts to find creative ways to add value. *Risk taking* reflects a willingness by employees and their firm to accept risks when pursuing entrepreneurial opportunities. These risks can include assuming significant levels of debt and allocating large amounts of other resources (e.g., people) to projects that may not be completed. *Proactiveness* describes a firm's ability to be a market leader rather than a follower. Proactive organizational cultures constantly use processes to anticipate future market needs and to satisfy them before competitors learn how to do so. Finally, *competitive aggressiveness* is a firm's propensity to take actions that allow it to consistently and substantially outperform its rivals.[152]

Changing a firm's organizational culture is more difficult than maintaining it, but effective strategic leaders recognize when change is needed. Incremental changes to the firm's culture typically are used to implement strategies.[153] More significant and sometimes even radical changes to organizational culture are used to support the selection of strategies that differ from those the firm has implemented historically. Regardless of the reasons for change, shaping and reinforcing a new culture require effective communication and problem solving, along with the selection of the right people (those who have the values desired for the organization), effective performance appraisals (establishing goals and measuring individual performance toward goals that fit in with the new core values), and appropriate reward systems (rewarding the desired behaviors that reflect the new core values).[154]

Evidence suggests that cultural changes succeed only when the firm's CEO, other key top management team members, and middle-level managers actively support them.[155] Chief executive Myron "Mike" Ullman III led J.C. Penney in a successful turnaround strategy despite increased competition in department store retailing.[156] At the heart of the strategy was a "Winning Together" program that included fostering a culture of honesty, open communication, creative thinking, and risk taking. A two-day leadership conference in Dallas included all of the store managers in the company, who were encouraged to think of themselves as CEOs for their own stores. Other marketing and operating changes reinforced a set of guiding principles. Having achieved financial results that were the "envy of competitors," Ullman's team then developed "a Long Range Plan to move Penney from a position of 'turnaround' to a company focused on growth—with the aim of achieving retail industry leadership in five years."[157] In this example we see evidence of successfully changing an organization's culture linked to efforts to develop human capital. These two aspects of strategic leadership are essential to developing competitive advantage. Also important is managing relationships with key stakeholders outside the organization.

## Develop and Manage Relationships with External Stakeholders

One of the influential early writers on the topic of executive leadership, Henry Mintzberg, once followed around CEOs from a variety of industries to observe what they do.[158] From his observations, he determined that top executives perform a variety of roles in organizations (see Table 2.1). Some of the roles he identified, such as the leadership role of motivating and directing subordinates, the informational role of disseminating information to managers, or the decision-making role of allocating resources, are focused primarily on the internal organization. Here, we discuss roles associated with managing relationships with key external stakeholders.

From a stakeholder perspective, what is striking about Mintzberg's list is that most of the roles can be applied directly to developing and managing relationships with external stakeholders. For instance, as a figurehead, the top manager serves as a legal and symbolic leader for the firm, appearing at public events and signing important documents such as major contracts or other joint venture agreements. As a liaison, the strategic leader sits at the center of a network of stakeholders, with responsibility for maintaining excellent relationships with those stakeholders that are most influential in determining the firm's competitive success.[159]

Most of the information management and decision-making roles also can be applied directly to effective stakeholder management. Top managers who have fostered excellent relationships with external stakeholders can be more effective as monitors of significant

---

**Table 2.1: Mintzberg's Managerial Roles**

Interpersonal
- Figurehead—legal and symbolic leader
- Leader—motivates and directs subordinates
- Liaison—sits at the center of a network of contacts

Informational
- Monitor—collects strategically relevant information
- Spokesperson—communicates with external stakeholders
- Disseminator—communicates with internal stakeholders

Decisional
- Entrepreneur—makes decisions concerning innovations
- Disturbance Handler—resolves crises
- Resource Allocator—provides adequate resources to key areas
- Negotiator—forms agreements with stakeholders

SOURCE: Based on H. Mintzberg, 1973, *The Nature of Managerial Work*, New York: Harper & Row.

events in the external environment.[160] The information gathered from stakeholders can assist strategic leaders in making decisions about a firm's strategies and the innovations that will propel it into a successful future.[161] As a spokesperson, a strategic leader communicates with external stakeholders such as customers, suppliers, and the community. Strategic leaders also help negotiate agreements with stakeholders and potential stakeholders. For instance, it is typical for a CEO to be involved in the development of major contracts or in negotiations leading to an acquisition.

Many of the benefits associated with effective stakeholder management (as outlined in Chapter 1) depend on the actions and attitudes of the top management team, and especially the CEO. A CEO who fosters excellent relationships with key stakeholders can help the organization acquire timely and more accurate information about the external environment, which can enhance planning and decision making.[162] Furthermore, firms that have better reputations because of excellent stakeholder relationships may have the advantage of attracting customers and business partners, giving them more and better strategic options from which to select.[163] Also, a relationship of trust between top managers and external stakeholders can help to facilitate acquisition of valuable resources and reduce transaction costs associated with elaborate contractual safeguards and contingencies that might otherwise be necessary.[164] As the business world continues to increase in complexity and businesses become more interdependent, the leadership role of managing external stakeholders takes on even more strategic importance.[165]

This section emphasizes the responsibilities of top managers in creating and managing relationships with external stakeholders. The last section, based on the resource-based view, emphasized the strategic role top managers play in acquiring, developing, and managing internal resources, especially human capital and organizational culture. Although discussed separately, these two perspectives overlap, as do the roles strategic leaders play. For instance, from a resource-based perspective, stakeholder relationships *are* strategic resources that can help a firm acquire other resources and develop competitive advantage.[166] Also, the stakeholder perspective includes management of both external *and* internal stakeholders.

Economic positioning also is conceptually linked to the other two perspectives. For instance, external stakeholder management is closely associated with the monitoring that occurs as strategic leaders position their firms in their industries. Also, possession of particular resources and skills positions a firm relative to its competitors. Responsibilities associated with all three of the perspectives result in strategic direction and formulation and implementation of specific strategies (see Figure 2.4).

## Determine and Communicate Strategic Direction

The **strategic direction** of a firm defines its image and character over time, framed within the context of the conditions in which it operates. Like a firm's strategy, it grows out of strategic intent and is a function of the resources and capabilities a firm possesses or wishes to possess, as well as what the firm wants to do for its stakeholders. The CEO is the chief architect of strategic direction, although most top executives obtain input from many people inside and outside the organization.[167] Research has shown that having an effective strategic direction and properly reinforcing it can positively affect performance as measured by growth in sales, profits, employment, and net worth.[168]

Strategic direction is reflected in the firm's mission, vision, purpose, long-term goals, and values, which tend to be interconnected. In fact, sometimes a mission statement includes many of these things, such as Novartis' mission statement found in Table 2.2.

**Table 2.2: Mission of Novartis**

**Purpose**
We want to discover, develop and successfully market innovative products to cure diseases, to ease suffering, and to enhance the quality of life. We also want to provide a shareholder return that reflects outstanding performance and to adequately reward those who invest ideas and work in our company.

**Aspirations**
We want to be recognized for having a positive impact on people's lives with our products, meeting needs and even surpassing external expectations. We strive to create sustainable earnings growth, ranking in the top quartile of the industry and securing long-term business success. We want to build a reputation for an exciting workplace in which people can realize their professional ambitions. We strive for a motivating environment where creativity and effectiveness are encouraged and where cutting-edge technologies are applied. In addition, we want to contribute to society through our economic contribution, through the positive environmental and social benefits of our products, and through open dialogue with our stakeholders.

SOURCE: http://www.novartis.com/about_novartis/en/our_mission.shtml, visited on December 6, 2006.

Novartis has four divisions representing pharmaceuticals, generic drugs, vaccines and diagnostics, and consumer health.

A carefully constructed strategic mission should help the firm define the scope of its operations as well as its unique purposes.[169] With regard to scope, Novartis has defined its businesses in terms of customer functions. Specifically, the company's products and services cure diseases, ease suffering, and enhance the quality of life. Typically, purposes are defined in terms of what a firm intends to do for particular stakeholders. For instance, a firm may want to achieve high returns for shareholders or provide a motivating environment for employees. In the Novartis example, in addition to what the company intends to do for its customers, it aspires to help employees realize professional ambitions and to contribute to society and the environment. The company values of openness, innovation, and financial success are also found in the mission statement. Notice also that Novartis has included the concept of sustainability in its mission statement. **Sustainable development,** the concept that a firm can and should operate without adversely influencing its environment, has been gaining strategic importance in recent years.[170]

The ideal long-term vision has two parts: a core ideology and an envisioned future. The core ideology motivates employees through the company's heritage, and the envisioned future encourages employees to stretch beyond their comfort zones.[171] "Stretch goals" promote higher levels of personal and organizational performance.[172] The vision of Novartis is reflected by a desire to be recognized for having a positive effect on the lives of customers, employees, the environment, and society. This vision is built on a long history of success in the health sciences. Novartis also wants to remain in the top quartile of its industry based on growth in earnings. Achieving this goal over the long term will require a very high level of motivation among managers and employees. The company will have to continue to innovate and change in order to remain competitive in its volatile and highly competitive industry.

Although the Novartis example is particularly comprehensive, it is not unusual to find many of the components of strategic direction in a strategic mission statement. On the other hand, sometimes strategic direction is not found in a written statement, or it is divided into an assortment of statements with different names and purposes. Also, labels are used in a variety of different ways. What is most important is that the firm has a well-defined strategic direction and that it communicates the direction to internal and, to some extent, external stakeholders. Annual reports, speeches, press releases, training sessions, meetings, interpersonal communication, and comments from executives are all vehicles for communicating strategic direction.[173]

Internal stakeholders, including executives, managers, and employees, need to know the strategic direction so that it can guide them in their decision making. The firm can also communicate certain elements of its strategic direction to external stakeholders to help them know what to expect from the organization. Obviously, investors use such information to help them predict the firm's future performance. However, customers, communities, suppliers, venture partners, special interest groups, and regulators can benefit from understanding what the firm values and how it conducts business. In the wake of recent corporate scandals, this element of strategic direction has been receiving significantly more attention.

**Establish Values and Ethical Practices.** Mission statements often refer to values associated with ethical practices. In addition, codes of ethics frequently are created to reinforce those values. For instance, United Technologies has a twenty-four-page code of ethics based on the values of trust, respect, and integrity.[174] Nevertheless, values statements and codes of ethics are not a guarantee that managers and employees will act ethically.[175] The infamous sixty-four-page "Code of Ethics" allegedly published by Enron Corporation begins with a statement from CEO Kenneth Lay: "As officers and employees of Enron, Corp., its subsidiaries, and its affiliated companies, we are responsible for conducting the business affairs of the companies in accordance with all applicable laws and in a moral and honest manner."[176] Managerial opportunism may explain the behavior and decisions of key executives at Enron, where stockholders lost almost all the value in their Enron stock during the firm's bankruptcy proceeding. The bankruptcy was precipitated by off-balance-sheet partnerships formed by Enron managers.[177] The reputation of Arthur Andersen, Enron's auditor, was also damaged beyond repair, resulting ultimately in the company surrendering its license to practice as certified public accountants.[178] More recently, a massive money-laundering and bribery scandal at the German conglomerate Siemens AG has hurt the ability of its CEO Klaus Kleinfeld to restructure the company.[179]

Ethical companies encourage and enable people at all organizational levels to act ethically when doing what is necessary to implement the firm's strategies. In turn, ethical practices and the judgment on which they are based create "social capital" in the organization in that "goodwill available to individuals and groups" in the organization increases.[180] Thus, while "money motivates, it does not inspire" as social capital can.[181] Alternately, when unethical practices evolve in an organization, they become like a contagious disease.[182] Firms that have been reported to have poor ethical behavior, such as practicing fraud or having to restate financial results, see their overall corporate value in the stock market drop precipitously.[183]

To properly influence employees' judgment and behavior, ethical practices must shape the firm's decision-making process and be an integral part of an organization's culture. In fact, research has found that a value-based culture is the most effective means of ensuring that employees comply with the firm's ethical requirements.[184] Evidence also suggests that managers' values are critical in shaping a firm's cultural values.[185] Consequently, firms should employ ethical strategic leaders—leaders who include ethical practices as part of their long-term vision for the firm, who desire to do the right thing, and for whom honesty, trust, and integrity are important.[186] Strategic leaders who consistently display these qualities inspire employees as they work with others to develop and support an organizational culture in which ethical practices are the expected behavioral norms.[187] In addition to being a good example, top managers may also institute a formal program to manage ethics. Operating much like control systems, these programs help inculcate values throughout the organization.[188]

Additional actions strategic leaders can take to develop an ethical organizational culture include (1) establishing and communicating specific goals to describe the firm's ethical standards (e.g., developing and disseminating a code of conduct); (2) continuously revising and updating the code of conduct on the basis of input from people throughout the firm and from other stakeholders (e.g., customers and suppliers); (3) disseminating the code of conduct to all stakeholders to inform them of the firm's ethical standards and practices; (4) developing and implementing methods and procedures to use in achieving the firm's ethical standards (e.g., using internal auditing practices that are consistent with the standards); (5) creating and using explicit reward systems that recognize acts of courage (e.g., rewarding those who use proper channels and procedures to report observed wrongdoing); and (6) creating a work environment in which all people are treated with dignity.[189] The effectiveness of these actions increases when they are taken simultaneously, thereby making them mutually supportive.

## Oversee Formulation and Implementation of Specific Strategies

Strategic leaders are responsible for ensuring that appropriate strategies are both formulated and successfully implemented. Earlier in this chapter we outlined the responsibilities of strategic leaders from three perspectives. Each of these perspectives results in a slightly different but interrelated view of strategy formulation and implementation. I/O economics suggests that strategy is based on evaluation of the external environment and positioning the firm optimally in that environment. Implementation involves developing structures, systems, and programs to reinforce the position.[190] The resource-based view focuses on the acquisition and development of uniquely valuable resources and capabilities that are hard for competitors to imitate, thus leading to competitive advantage. Implementation plans involve making optimal use of and supporting those resources and capabilities.[191] The stakeholder perspective leads to strategies that attempt to make optimal use of relationships with stakeholders to create value. Implementation involves activities such as collecting information from stakeholders, assessing their needs and desires, integrating this knowledge into strategic decisions, effectively managing internal stakeholders, and forming interorganizational relationships with external stakeholders.[192] Chapters 5 through 10 discuss the specific nature of these strategies and how they are implemented.

Strategic direction also influences a firm's specific strategies. For instance, a firm's mission defines its basic approach to corporate-level strategy and may contain clues regarding the resources and skills that form the base for its business-level strategies. In addition, strategic direction serves as a guide to many aspects of a firm's strategy implementation process, including motivation, leadership, employee empowerment, and organizational design.[193] In the case of Novartis, the company is supporting its mission by transforming its headquarters in Basel, Switzerland, into an ultramodern, high-performance workplace that facilitates research and fosters communication and collaboration.[194]

Once strategic leaders have guided the establishment of the firm's strategic direction, strategies, and implementation plans, their final responsibility is to establish organizational control systems to ensure that the plans are actually executed and to measure their success.

## Establish Balanced Controls

Organizational controls have long been viewed as an important part of strategy implementation processes. Controls are necessary to help ensure that firms achieve their desired outcomes.[195] Defined as the "formal, information-based . . . procedures used by managers to maintain or alter patterns in organizational activities," controls help strategic leaders build credibility, demonstrate the value of strategies to the firm's stakeholders, and promote and support strategic change.[196] Most critically, controls provide the parameters within which strategies are to be implemented, as well as corrective actions to be taken when implementation-related adjustments are required.

Chapter 11 on corporate governance discusses organizational controls in greater detail, but here we look briefly at financial and strategic controls because strategic leaders are responsible for their development and effective use. Financial control focuses on short-term financial outcomes. In contrast, *strategic control* focuses on the content of strategic actions, rather than their outcomes. Some strategic actions can be correct, but poor financial outcomes may still result because of external conditions, such as a recession in the economy, unexpected domestic or foreign government actions, or natural disasters.[197] Therefore, an emphasis on financial control often produces more short-term and risk-averse managerial decisions because financial outcomes may be caused by events beyond managers' direct control. Alternatively, strategic control encourages lower-level managers to make decisions that incorporate moderate and acceptable levels of risk because outcomes are shared between the business-level executives making strategic proposals and the corporate-level executives evaluating them.

**The Balanced Scorecard.** The **balanced scorecard** is a framework that strategic leaders can use to verify that they have established both financial controls and strategic controls to assess their firm's performance.[198] This technique is most appropriate for use when dealing with business-level strategies but can also apply to corporate-level strategies.

The underlying premise of the balanced scorecard is that firms jeopardize their future performance possibilities when financial controls are emphasized at the expense of strategic controls,[199] in that financial controls provide feedback about outcomes achieved from past actions but do not communicate the drivers of the firm's future performance.[200] Thus, an overemphasis on financial controls could promote organizational behavior that has a net effect of sacrificing the firm's long-term, value-creating potential for short-term performance gains.[201] An appropriate balance of financial controls and strategic controls, rather than an overemphasis on either, allows firms to effectively monitor their performance.

Four perspectives are integrated to form the balanced scorecard framework (see Figure 2.6): *financial* (concerned with growth, profitability, and risk from the shareholders' perspective), *customer* (concerned with the amount of value that customers perceive was created by the firm's products), *internal business processes* (with a focus on the priorities for various business processes that create customer and shareholder satisfaction), and *learning and growth* (concerned with the firm's effort to create a climate that supports change, innovation, and growth). Thus, using the balanced scorecard's framework allows the firm to understand how it looks to shareholders (financial perspective), how customers view it (customer perspective), the processes it must emphasize to successfully use its competitive advantage (internal perspective), and what it can do to improve its performance in order to grow (learning and growth perspective).[202] Porsche used a balanced-scorecard approach to promote

**Figure 2.6: Strategic Controls and Financial Controls in a Balanced Scorecard Framework**

| Perspectives | Criteria |
| --- | --- |
| Financial | • Cash flow<br>• Return on equity<br>• Return on assets |
| Customer | • Assessment of ability to anticipate customers' needs<br>• Effectiveness of customer service practices<br>• Percentage of repeat business<br>• Quality of communications with customers |
| Internal Business Processes | • Asset utilization improvements<br>• Improvements in employee morale<br>• Changes in turnover rates |
| Learning and Growth | • Improvements in innovation ability<br>• Number of new products compared to competitors'<br>• Increases in employees' skills |

learning and continuous improvement while maintaining a market-leading position among sports car manufacturers.[203]

Firms use different criteria to measure their standing relative to the scorecard's four perspectives (see Figure 2.6). These criteria should be established on the basis of what the firm is trying to accomplish and its strategic direction. The firm should select the number of criteria that will allow it to have both a strategic understanding and a financial understanding of its performance without becoming immersed in too many details.[204] Several performance criteria, such as those associated with financial and customer as well as purely internal perspectives, will be discussed in Chapter 4. Of course, the criteria frequently are interrelated.[205]

Strategic leaders play an important role in determining a proper balance between strategic controls and financial controls for their firm. This is true in single business firms as well as in diversified corporations. A proper balance between controls is important in that "Wealth creation for organizations where strategic leadership is exercised is possible because these leaders make appropriate investments for future viability [through strategic control], while maintaining an appropriate level of financial stability in the present [through financial control]."[206] In fact, most corporate restructuring is designed to refocus the firm on its core businesses, thereby allowing top executives to reestablish strategic control of their separate business units.[207] Thus, both strategic controls and financial controls support effective use of the firm's corporate-level strategy.

# Summary

- Effective strategic leadership is a prerequisite to successful use of the strategic management process. Strategic leadership entails the ability to anticipate events, envision possibilities, maintain flexibility, and empower others to create strategic change.

- Strategic leadership skills fall into a hierarchy, where managers must master lower-level skills before they fine-tune higher-level skills. Level 5 Executives have mastered all the skills.

- Strategic leaders differ in the way they direct the strategic management process. A traditional "commander" approach limits manager participation in strategic decisions, whereas a more collaborative style entails jointly arriving at strategies and implementation plans with members of the top management team. The appropriate style depends on the nature of the competitive situation.

- Top managers are constrained by a number of factors that influence the level of discretion they have when making decisions. Some of these factors are associated with the external environment, such as the industry structure, the rate of market growth in the firm's primary industry, and the degree to which products can be differentiated.

- Strategic managers sometimes rely on heuristics, or "rules of thumb," when they make strategic decisions. These heuristics help managers simplify what might otherwise be an overwhelmingly complicated and uncertain decision environment, but they also can lead to suboptimal decisions. Awareness of decision-making biases, use of real options analysis, and formation of a heterogeneous top management team can help strategic decision makers reduce the ill effects of decision biases.

- A top management team is composed of the chief executive officer and other key managers who are responsible for setting the direction of the firm and formulating and implementing its strategies. The quality of strategic thinking and subsequent strategic decisions made by a top management team affect the firm's ability to innovate and engage in effective strategic change.

- The overwhelming complexity and strength of environmental forces, as well as the need to manage a wide variety of stakeholder relationships, require formation of a heterogeneous top management team composed of individuals with different functional backgrounds, experience, and education. The more heterogeneous a top management team is, with varied expertise and knowledge, the more capacity it has to provide effective strategic leadership in formulating strategy.

- Higher firm performance normally is achieved when the board of directors is more directly involved in shaping a firm's strategic direction. However, directors may find it difficult to direct the strategic actions of powerful CEOs and top management teams. The relative power of top managers is at least partially a function of social or business ties with directors, their tenure as members of the top management team, and whether the CEO also serves as chair of the board.

- Organizations select strategic leaders from two types of managerial labor markets—internal and external. Use of the internal or external market depends, in part, on the need for change in the organization.

- Six key components of effective strategic leadership include ensuring that the firm is well-positioned economically, managing key resources, developing and maintaining effective relationships with key stakeholders, determining a strategic direction (which includes establishing values and ethical practices), overseeing the formulation and implementation of specific strategies, and establishing balanced organizational control systems.

- Strategic direction is reflected in the firm's mission, vision, purpose, long-term goals, and values, which tend to be interconnected. There are several vehicles, such as annual reports, speeches, and press releases, for communicating strategic direction.

- An effective balance between strategic and financial controls allows for the flexible use of core competencies, but within the parameters indicated by the firm's financial position. The balanced scorecard is a tool that strategic leaders use to develop an appropriate balance between the firm's strategic and financial controls.

## Ethics Questions

1. What are the ethical issues influencing managerial discretion? Has the current business environment changed the influence of ethics on managerial discretion? If so, how?

2. Is there a difference between stakeholders' current view of an ethical strategic leader and the early 1990s' perspective of an ethical strategic leader? If so, describe the differences between the two views.

3. What should a newly appointed CEO from the external managerial labor market do to understand a firm's ethical climate? How important are the CEO's efforts to understand this climate?

4. Are ethical strategic leaders more effective than unethical strategic leaders? If so, why? If not, why not?

5. Assume that you are working in an organization that you believe has an unethical culture. What actions could you take to change that culture to make it more ethical?

6. Is corporate downsizing ethical? If not, why not? If corporate downsizing is ethical, what can strategic leaders do to mitigate the negative effects associated with reducing the size of their firm's labor force?

## Notes

[1] D. A. Ready, 2002, How storytelling builds next-generation leaders, *MIT Sloan Management Review*, 43(4): 63–69.

[2] 2006, Leadership styles at GE and Canon, *Strategic Direction*, 22(1): 15–20; R. Barnes, 2004, Executives who didn't survive Jack Welch's GE are now running 3M, Home Depot, *Knight Ridder Tribune Business News*, April 24, 1.

[3] C. H. Tong & L-I. Tong, 2006, Exploring the cornerstones of Wal-Mart's success and competitiveness, *Competitiveness Review*, 16(2): 143–149.

[4] J. Greco, 1999, Akio Morita: A founder of Japan, Inc., *The Journal of Business Strategy*, 20(5): 38–39.

[5] S. Green, F. Hassan, J. Immelt, M. Marks, & D. Meiland, 2003, In search of global leaders, *Harvard Business Review*, 81(8): 38–45; T. J. Peters, 2001, Leadership: Sad

facts and silver linings, *Harvard Business Review*, 79(11): 121–128.

[6] M. A. Hitt, C. C. Miller, & A. Colella, 2008, *Organizational Behavior: A Strategic Approach*, 2nd ed., New York: Wiley; D. Vera & M. Crossan, 2004, Strategic leadership and organizational learning, *Academy of Management Review*, 29: 222–240.

[7] J. Collins, 2001, *Good to Great: Why Some Companies Make the Leap . . . and Others Don't*, New York: Harper Business.

[8] A. Carter, 2006, Lighting a fire under Campbell: How Doug Conant's quiet, cerebral style got things bubbling again, *Business Week*, December 4, 96.

[9] L. J. Bourgeois III & D. R. Brodwin, 1984, Strategic implementation: Five approaches to an elusive phenomenon, *Strategic Management Journal*, 5: 241–264.

10  M. Carpenter & J. Fredrickson, 2001, Top management teams, global strategic posture, and the moderating role of uncertainty, *Academy of Management Journal*, 44: 533–545; S. F. Slater, 1989, The influence of style on business unit performance, *Journal of Management* 15: 441–455.

11  L. Markoczy, 2001, Consensus formation during strategic change, *Strategic Management Journal*, 22: 1013–1031; D. Knight, C. L. Pearce, K. G. Smith, J. D. Olian, H. P. Sims, K. A. Smith, & P. Flood, 1999, Top management team diversity, group process, and strategic consensus, *Strategic Management Journal*, 20: 446–465.

12  H. Chen, R.-R. Duh, & J. C. Lin, 2006, The determinants of implementation stages of balanced scorecard, *International Journal of Management and Decision Making*, 7(4): 1; I. M. Taplin, 2006, Strategic change and organizational restructuring: How managers negotiate change initiatives, *Journal of International Management*, 12: 284–301.

13  M. A. Hitt, M. T. Dacin, B. B. Tyler, & D. Park, 1997, Understanding the differences in Korean and U.S. executives' strategic orientations, *Strategic Management Journal*, 18: 159–167; J. G. Michel & D. C. Hambrick, 1992, Diversification posture and top management team characteristics, *Academy of Management Journal*, 35: 9–37; S. F. Slater, 1989, The influence of style on business unit performance, *Journal of Management*, 15: 441–455; A. S. Thomas, R. J. Litschert, & K. Ramaswamy, 1991, The performance impact of strategy–manager co-alignment: An empirical examination, *Strategic Management Journal*, 12: 509–522.

14  V. Govindarajan, 1989, Implementing competitive strategies at the business unit level: Implications of matching managers to strategies, *Strategic Management Journal*, 10: 251–269.

15  A. K. Gupta & V. Govindarajan, 1984, Business unit strategy, managerial characteristics, and business unit effectiveness at strategy implementation, *Academy of Management Journal*, 27: 25–41.

16  M. F. Wiersema & K. A. Bantel, 1992, Top management team demography and corporate strategic change, *Academy of Management Journal*, 35: 91–121; K. A. Bantel & S. E. Jackson, 1989, Top management and innovations in banking: Does the composition of the top team make a difference? *Strategic Management Journal*, 10: 107–124; C. M. Grimm & K. G. Smith, 1991, Management and organizational change: A note on the railroad industry, *Strategic Management Journal*, 12: 557–562.

17  W. Rowe, 2001, Creating wealth in organizations: The role of strategic leadership, *Academy of Management Executive*, 15(1): 81–94; S. Finkelstein & D. C. Hambrick, 1996, *Strategic Leadership: Top Executives and Their Effects on Organizations*, St. Paul, MN: West Publishing Co., 26–34, D. C. Hambrick & E. Abrahamson, 1995, Assessing managerial discretion across industries: A multimethod approach, *Academy of Management Journal*, 38: 1427–1441; D. C. Hambrick & S. Finkelstein, 1987, Managerial discretion: A bridge between polar views of organizational outcomes, in B. Staw & L. L. Cummings (eds.), *Research in Organizational Behavior*, Greenwich, CT: JAI Press, 369–406.

18  R. Whittington, 2003, The work of strategizing and organizing: For a practice perspective, *Strategic Organization*, 1: 117–125; M. Wright, R. E. Hoskisson, L. W. Busenitz, & J. Dial, 2000, Entrepreneurial growth through privatization: The upside of management buyouts, *Academy of Management Review*, 25: 591–601; M. J. Waller, G. P. Huber, & W. H. Glick, 1995,

Functional background as a determinant of executives' selective perception, *Academy of Management Journal*, 38: 943–974; N. Rajagopalan, A. M. Rasheed, & D. K. Datta, 1993, Strategic decision processes: Critical review and future directions, *Journal of Management*, 19: 349–384.

19  T. K. Das & B.-S. Teng, 1999, Cognitive biases and strategic decision processes: An integrative perspective, *Journal of Management Studies*, 36: 757–778. C. R. Schwenk, 1995, Strategic decision making, *Journal of Management*, 21: 471–493.

20  D. Kahneman, P. Slovic, & A. Tversky (eds.), 1982, *Judgment under Uncertainty: Heuristics and Biases*, New York: Cambridge University Press; A. Tversky & D. Kahneman, 1974, Judgment under uncertainty: Heuristics and biases, *Science*, 185: 1124–1131.

21  Kahneman, Slovic, & Tversky, *Judgment under Uncertainty*.

22  M. H. Bazerman, 1994. *Judgment in Managerial Decision Making*, 3rd ed., New York: Wiley; R. M. Hogarth, 1980, *Judgment and Choice: The Psychology of Decision*, Chichester, UK: Wiley.

23  Das & Teng, Cognitive biases and strategic decision processes; J. G. March & Z. Shapira, 1987, Managerial perspectives on risk and risk taking, *Management Science*, 33: 1404–1418.

24  C. R. Schwenk, 1984, Cognitive simplification processes in strategic decision-making, *Strategic Management Journal*, 5: 111–128.

25  March & Shapira, Managerial perspectives.

26  R. E. Hoskisson, M. A. Hitt, & C. W. L. Hill, 1991, Managerial risk taking in diversified firms: An evolutionary perspective, *Organization Science*, 2: 296–314.

27  J. Devan, K. Millan, & P. Shirke, 2005, Balancing short- and long-term performance, *McKinsey Quarterly*, (1): 31–33.

28  J. P. Walsh & W. R. Nord, 2005, Taking stock of stakeholder management, *Academy of Management Review*, 30: 426–438; J. E. Post, L. E. Preston, & S. Sauter-Sachs, 2002, *Redefining the Corporation: Stakeholder Management and Organizational Wealth*, Stanford, CA: Stanford University Press.

29  March & Shapira, Managerial perspectives; J. W. Fredrickson, 1984, The comprehensiveness of strategic decision processes: Extension, observations, future directions, *Academy of Management Journal*, 27: 445–466.

30  J. W. Fredrickson, 1986, An exploratory approach to measuring perceptions of strategic decision constructs, *Strategic Management Journal*, 7: 473–483.

31  Z. Shapira, 1995, *Risk Taking: A Managerial Perspective*, New York: Russell Sage Foundation.

32  D. Kahneman & D. Lovallo, 1993, Timid choices and bold forecasts: A cognitive perspective on risk taking, *Management Science*, 39: 17–31.

33  R. Durand, 2003, Predicting a firm's forecasting ability: The roles of organizational illusion of control and organizational attention, *Strategic Management Journal*, 9: 821–838; E. J. Langer, 1975, Illusion of control, *Journal of Personality and Social Psychology*, 32: 311–328.

34  Shapira, *Risk Taking*; C. Vlek & P. J. Stallen, 1980, Rational and personal aspects of risk, *Acta Psychologica*, 45: 273–300.

35  D. García, F. Sangiorgi, & B. Urošević, 2007, Overconfidence and market efficiency with

heterogeneous assets, *Economic Theory*, 30: 313–336; R. A. Lowe & A. Arvids, 2006, Overoptimism and the performance of entrepreneurial firms, *Management Science*, 52: 173–186.

36  N. J. Hiller & D. C. Hambrick, 2005, Conceptualizing executive hubris: The role of (hyper-) core self-evaluations in strategic decision making, *Strategic Management Journal*, 26: 297–319.

37  J. B. Wade, J. F. Porac, T. G. Pollock, & S. D. Graffin, 2006, The burden of celebrity: The impact of CEO certification contests on CEO pay and performance, *Academy of Management Journal*, 49: 643–660.

38  M. L. A. Hayward, V. P. Rindova, & T. G. Pollock, 2004, Believing one's own press: The causes and consequences of CEO celebrity, *Strategic Management Journal*, 25: 637–653.

39  Collins, *Good to Great.*

40  Markoczy, Consensus formation; A. L. Iaquito & J. W. Fredrickson, 1997, Top management team agreement about the strategic decision process: A test of some of its determinants and consequences, *Strategic Management Journal*, 18: 63–75.

41  R. Castanias & C. Helfat, 2001, The managerial rents model: Theory and empirical analysis, *Journal of Management*, 27: 661–678; H. P. Gunz & R. M. Jalland, 1996, Managerial careers and business strategy, *Academy of Management Review*, 21: 718–756.

42  I. Goll, R. Sambharya, & L. Tucci, 2001, Top management team composition, corporate ideology, and firm performance, *Management International Review*, 41(2): 109–129.

43  M. Beer & R. Eisenstat, 2000, The silent killers of strategy implementation and learning, *Sloan Management Review*, 41(4): 29–40; C. M. Christensen, 1997, Making strategy: Learning by doing, *Harvard Business Review*, 75(6): 141–156; M. A. Hitt, B. W. Keats, H. E. Harback, & R. D. Nixon, 1994, Rightsizing: Building and maintaining strategic leadership and long-term competitiveness, *Organizational Dynamics*, 23: 18–32.

44  M. A. Cusumano & A. Gawer, 2002, The elements of platform leadership, *MIT Sloan Management Review*, 43(3): 51–58; C. Pegels, Y. Song, & B. Yang, 2000, Management heterogeneity, competitive interaction groups, and firm performance, *Strategic Management Journal*, 21: 911–923; N. Athanassiou & D. Nigh, 1999, The impact of U.S. company internationalization on top management team advice networks: A tacit knowledge perspective, *Strategic Management Journal*, 20: 83–92.

45  J. Green, 2006, The soul of a new Microsoft, *Business Week*, December 4, 57–66.

46  2006, Microsoft Senior Leadership Team, http://www.microsoft.com/presspass/exec/leadership/default.mspx, December 12.

47  Markoczy, Consensus formation; D. Knight, C. L. Pearce, K. G. Smith, J. D. Olian, H. P. Sims, K. A. Smith, & P. Flood, 1999, Top management team diversity, group process, and strategic consensus, *Strategic Management Journal*, 20: 446–465.

48  J. Bunderson, 2003, Team member functional background and involvement in management teams: Direct effects and the moderating role of power and centralization, *Academy of Management Journal*, 46: 458–474; Markoczy, Consensus formation; U. Daellenbach, A. McCarthy, & T. Schoenecker, 1999, Commitment to innovation: The impact of top management team characteristics, *R&D Management*,

29(3): 199–208; D. K. Datta & J. P. Guthrie, 1994, Executive succession: Organizational antecedents of CEO characteristics, *Strategic Management Journal*, 15: 569–577.

49  D. C. Hambrick, T. S. Cho, & M. J. Chen, 1996, The influence of top management team heterogeneity on firms' competitive moves, *Administrative Science Quarterly*, 41: 659–684.

50  W. B. Werther, 2003, Strategic change and leader-follower alignment, *Organizational Dynamics*, 32: 32–45; S. Wally & M. Becerra, 2001, Top management team characteristics and strategic changes in international diversification: The case of U.S. multinationals in the European community, *Group & Organization Management*, 26: 165–188; W. Boeker, 1997, Strategic change: The influence of managerial characteristics and organizational growth, *Academy of Management Journal*, 40: 152–170.

51  A. Tomie, 2000, Fast Pack 2000, *Fast Company* online, http://www.fastcompany.com, March 1.

52  J. Magretta, 2002, The behavior behind the buzzwords, *MIT Sloan Management Review*, 43(4): 90.

53  Wally & Becerra, Top management team characteristics; L. Tihanyi, C. Daily, D. Dalton, & A. Ellstrand, 2000, Composition of the top management team and firm international diversification, *Journal of Management*, 26: 1157–1178; M. F. Wiersema & K. Bantel, 1992, Top management team demography and corporate strategic change, *Academy of Management Journal*, 35: 91–121; Bantel & Jackson, Top management and innovations in banking.

54  J. J. Distefano & M. L. Maznevski, 2000, Creating value with diverse teams in global management, *Organizational Dynamics*, 29(1): 45–63; T. Simons, L. H. Pelled, & K. A. Smith, 1999, Making use of difference, diversity, debate, and decision comprehensiveness in top management teams, *Academy of Management Journal*, 42: 662–673.

55  Z. Simsek, J. F. Veiga, M. H. Lubatkin, & R. H. Dino, 2005, Modeling the multilevel determinants of top management team behavioral integration, *Academy of Management Journal*, 48: 69–84.

56  Finkelstein & Hambrick, *Strategic Leadership*, 148.

57  S. Barsade, A. Ward, J. Turner, & J. Sonnenfeld, 2000, To your heart's content: A model of affective diversity in top management teams, *Administrative Science Quarterly*, 45: 802–836; C. C. Miller, L. M. Burke, & W. H. Glick, 1998, Cognitive diversity among upper-echelon executives: Implications for strategic decision processes, *Strategic Management Journal*, 19: 39–58.

58  2006, Novartis, http://www.novartis.com/about _novartis/en/structure.shtml, November 18; 2002, The top 25 managers: Daniel Vasella, *Business Week*, January 14, 58.

59  W. Koberstein, 2001, Executive profile: Novartis inside out, *Pharmaceutical Executive*, November, 36–50.

60  I. Filatotchev & K. Bishop, 2002, Board composition, share ownership, and "underpricing" of U.K. IPO firms, *Strategic Management Journal*, 23: 941–955.

61  L. Tihanyi, R. A. Johnson, R. E. Hoskisson, & M. A. Hitt, 2003, Institutional ownership and international diversification: The effects of boards of directors and technological opportunity, *Academy of Management Journal*, 46: 195–211; B. Taylor, 2001, From corporate governance to corporate entrepreneurship, *Journal of Change Management*, 2(2): 128–147; W. Q. Judge Jr.

& C. P. Zeithaml, 1992, Institutional and strategic choice perspectives on board involvement in the strategic decision process, *Academy of Management Journal*, 35: 766–794; J. A. Pearce II & S. A. Zahra, 1991, The relative power of CEOs and boards of directors: Associations with corporate performance, *Strategic Management Journal*, 12: 135–154.

62  G. Kassinis & N. Vafeas, 2002, Corporate boards and outside stakeholders as determinants of environmental litigation, *Strategic Management Journal*, 23: 399–415; B. R. Golden & E. J. Zajac, 2001, When will boards influence strategy? Inclination times power equals strategic change, *Strategic Management Journal*, 22: 1087–1111.

63  M. Carpenter & J. Westphal, 2001, Strategic context of external network ties: Examining the impact of director appointments on board involvement in strategic decision making, *Academy of Management Journal*, 44: 639–660.

64  J. D. Westphal & E. J. Zajac, 1995, Who shall govern? CEO/board power, demographic similarity, and new director selection, *Administrative Science Quarterly*, 40: 60.

65  M. Boyle, 2001, The dirty half-dozen: America's worst boards, *Fortune*, May 14, 249–252; see also L. Lavelle, 2002, The Best & Worst Boards, *Business Week* online, http://www.businessweek.com, October 7.

66  2006, Xerox board members, http://www.xerox.com, December 6.

67  J. D. Westphal, 1999, Collaboration in the boardroom: Behavioral and performance consequences of CEO-board social ties, *Academy of Management Journal*, 42: 7–24.

68  Ibid.; J. Roberts & P. Stiles, 1999, The relationship between chairmen and chief executives: Competitive or complementary roles? *Long Range Planning*, 32(1): 36–48.

69  J. Coles, N. Sen, & V. McWilliams, 2001, An examination of the relationship of governance mechanisms to performance, *Journal of Management*, 27: 23–50; J. Coles & W. Hesterly, 2000, Independence of the chairman and board composition: Firm choices and shareholder value, *Journal of Management*, 26: 195–214; B. K. Boyd, 1995, CEO duality and firm performance: A contingency model, *Strategic Management Journal*, 16: 301.

70  C. M. Daily & D. R. Dalton, 1995, CEO and director turnover in failing firms: An illusion of change? *Strategic Management Journal*, 16: 393–400.

71  J. W. Lorsch & A. Zelleke, 2005, Should the CEO be the chairman? *Sloan Management Review*, 46(2): 71–81.

72  R. Albanese, M. T. Dacin, & I. C. Harris, 1997, Agents as stewards, *Academy of Management Review*, 22: 609–611; J. H. Davis, F. D. Schoorman, & L. Donaldson, 1997, Toward a stewardship theory of management, *Academy of Management Review*, 22: 20–47.

73  M. A. Carpenter, 2002, The implications of strategy and social context for the relationship between top management team heterogeneity and firm performance, *Strategic Management Journal*, 23: 275–284; J. D. Westphal & E. J. Zajac, 1997, Defections from the inner circle: Social exchange, reciprocity and diffusion of board independence in U.S. corporations, *Administrative Science Quarterly*, 161–183.

74  J. G. Combs & M. S. Skill, 2003, Managerialist and human capital explanations for key executive pay premiums: A contingency perspective, *Academy of Management Journal*, 46: 63–73.

75  N. Rajagopalan & D. K. Datta, 1996, CEO characteristics: Does industry matter? *Academy of Management Journal*, 39: 197–215.

76  R. A. Johnson, R. E. Hoskisson, & M. A. Hitt, 1993, Board involvement in restructuring: The effect of board versus managerial controls and characteristics, *Strategic Management Journal*, 14(summer special issue): 33–50.

77  E. E. Lawler III, D. Finegold, G. Benson, & J. Conger, 2002, Adding value in the boardroom, *MIT Sloan Management Review*, 43(2): 92–93.

78  Boyd, CEO duality and firm performance.

79  M. Carpenter & J. Fredrickson, 2001, Top management teams, global strategic posture, and the moderating role of uncertainty, *Academy of Management Journal*, 44: 533–545.

80  M. Schneider, 2002, A stakeholder model of organizational leadership, *Organization Science*, 13: 209–220.

81  M. Sorcher & J. Brant, 2002, Are you picking the right leaders? *Harvard Business Review*, 80(2): 78–85; D. A. Waldman, G. G. Ramirez, R. J. House, & P. Puranam, 2001, Does leadership matter? CEO leadership attributes and profitability under conditions of perceived environmental uncertainty, *Academy of Management Journal*, 44: 134–143; R. Charan & G. Colvin, 2000, The right fit, *Fortune*, April 17, 226–238.

82  A. Kakabadse & N. Kakabadse, 2001, Dynamics of executive succession, *Corporate Governance*, 1(3): 9–14.

83  R. Charan, 2000, GE's ten-step talent plan, *Fortune*, April 17, 232.

84  R. E. Hoskisson, D. Yiu, & H. Kim, 2000, Capital and labor market congruence and corporate governance: Effects on corporate innovation and global competitiveness, in S. S. Cohen & G. Boyd (eds.), *Corporate Governance and Globalization*, Northampton, MA: Edward Elgar, 129–154.

85  W. Shen & A. A. Cannella, 2003, Will succession planning increase shareholder wealth? Evidence from investor reactions to relay CEO successions, *Strategic Management Journal*, 24: 191–198.

86  Finkelstein & Hambrick, *Strategic Leadership*, 180–181.

87  S. F. Matusik, 2002, An empirical investigation of firm public and private knowledge, *Strategic Management Journal*, 23: 457–467.

88  D. C. Carey & D. Ogden, 2000, *CEO Succession: A Window on How Boards Can Get It Right When Choosing a New Chief Executive*, New York: Oxford University Press.

89  S. B. Shepard, 2002, A Talk with Jeff Immelt: Jack Welch's successor charts a course for GE in the 21st century, *Business Week*, January 28, 102–104.

90  2002, Speeches, IBM's annual stockholders meeting, http://www.ibm.com, April 30.

91  L. Greiner, T. Cummings, & A. Bhambri, 2002, When new CEOs succeed and fail: 4-D theory of strategic transformation, *Organizational Dynamics*, 32: 1–16.

92  D. Miller, 1991, Stale in the saddle: CEO tenure and the match between organization and environment, *Management Science*, 37: 34–52.

93  V. Anand, W. H. Glick, & C. C. Manz, 2002, Thriving on the knowledge of outsiders: Tapping organizational social capital, *Academy of Management Executive*, 16(1): 87–101.

94 N. A. Ashkanasy, C. E. J. Hartel, & C. S. Daus, 2002, Diversity and emotion: The new frontiers in organizational behavior research, *Journal of Management*, 28: 307–338.

95 G. N. Powell, D. A. Butterfield, & J. D. Parent, 2002, Gender and managerial stereotypes: Have the times changed? *Journal of Management*, 28: 177–193; S. Foley, D. L. Kidder, & G. N. Powell, 2002, The perceived glass ceiling and justice perceptions: An investigation of Hispanic law associates, *Journal of Management*, 28: 471–496.

96 C. E. Helfat, D. Harris, & P. J. Wolfson, The pipeline to the top: Women and men in the top executive ranks of U.S. corporations, *Academy of Management Perspectives*, 20(4): 42–64; A. Stanley, 2002, For women, to soar is rare, to fall is human, *New York Times*, http://www .nytimes.com, January 13.

97 E. A. Ensher, S. E. Murphy, & S. E. Sullivan, 2002, Reel women: Lessons from female TV executives on managing work and real life, *Academy of Management Executive*, 16(2): 106–120.

98 R. D. Ireland & M. A. Hitt, 2005, Achieving and maintaining strategic competitiveness in the 21st century: The role of strategic leadership, *Academy of Management Executive*, 19(4): 63–77, originally published in 12(1): 43–57; A. Cannella Jr., A. Pettigrew, & D. Hambrick, 2001, Upper echelons: Donald Hambrick on executives and strategy, *Academy of Management Executive*, 15(3): 36–52; D. Lei, M. A. Hitt, & R. Bettis, 1996, Dynamic core competencies through meta-learning and strategic context, *Journal of Management*, 22: 547–567.

99 S. Gove, D. Sirmon, & M. A. Hitt, 2003, Relative resource advantages: The effect of resources and resource management on organizational performance, paper presented at the Strategic Management Society Conference, Baltimore, MD.

100 J. S. Harrison, 2003, *Strategic Management of Resources and Relationships*, New York: Wiley; R. E. Freeman, *Strategic Management: A Stakeholder Approach*, Boston: Pittman.

101 Finkelstein & Hambrick, *Strategic Leadership*, 2.

102 M. Farjoun, 2002, Towards an organic perspective on strategy, *Strategic Management Journal*, 23: 561–594.

103 C. L. Shook, R. L. Priem, & J. E. McGee, 2003, Venture creation and the enterprising individual: A review and synthesis, *Journal of Management*, 29: 379–399.

104 S. Berfield, 2006, Most inspiring steel boss, *Business Week*, December 18, 61.

105 G. Hamel & C. K. Prahalad, 1989, Strategic intent, *Harvard Business Review*, 67(3): 63–76.

106 D. C. Hambrick & J. W. Fredrickson, 2005, Are you sure you have a strategy? *Academy of Management Executive*, 19(4): 51–62, reprinted from 15(4).

107 Ibid.

108 D. F. Abell, 1980, *Defining the Business: The Starting Point of Strategic Planning*, Englewood Cliffs, NJ: Prentice Hall.

109 2006, GE, http://www.ge.com/en/product/, December 13.

110 2006, *Nation's Restaurant News*, June, 1.

111 2006, GE, http://cwcdn.geimaginationatwork.com/ @v=092520050111@/imaginationatwork/flash.html, December 13.

112 K. M. Eisenhardt & S. L. Brown, 1998, Time pacing: Competing in markets that won't stand still, *Harvard Business Review*, March–April: 59–69.

113 Green, The soul of a new Microsoft.

114 B. Einhorn, 2006, How Yahoo missed out on the mainland, *Business Week*, December 18, 54.

115 S. Holmes, 2006, Boeing and labor: Frayed relations, *Business Week*, December 18, 124–125.

116 2006, Most unlikely turnaround, *Business Week*, December 18, 69.

117 2006, Worst reaction time, *Business Week*, December 18, 76.

118 R. A. Burgelman, 2001, *Strategy Is Destiny: How Strategy-Making Shapes a Company's Future*, New York: The Free Press.

119 S. K. Ethiraj, P. Kale, M. S. Krishnan, & J. V. Singh, 2005, Where do capabilities come from and how do they matter? A study in the software services industry, *Strategic Management Journal*, 26: 25–45.

120 S. Dutta, O. Narasimhan, & S. Rajiv, 2005, Conceptualizing and measuring capabilities: Methodology and empirical application, *Strategic Management Journal*, 26: 277–285.

121 Hitt, Miller, & Colella, *Organizational Behavior*; M. A. Hitt & R. D. Ireland, 2002, The essence of strategic leadership: Managing human and social capital, *Journal of Leadership and Organizational Studies*, 9: 3–14. J. A. Oxman, 2002, The hidden leverage of human capital, *MIT Sloan Management Review*, 43(4): 79–83.

122 A. S. DeNisi, M. A. Hitt, & S. E. Jackson, 2003, The knowledge-based approach to sustainable competitive advantage, in S. E. Jackson, M. A. Hitt, & A. S. DeNisi (eds.), *Managing Knowledge for Sustained Competitive Advantage*, San Francisco: Jossey-Bass, 3–33; D. J. Teece, 2000, *Managing Intellectual Capital: Organizational, Strategic and Policy Dimensions*, Oxford, UK: Oxford University Press.

123 J. E. Post, L. E. Preston, & S. Sachs, 2002, Managing the extended enterprise: The new stakeholder view, *California Management Review*, 45(1): 6–28; M. F. R. Kets de Vries, 1995, *Life and Death in the Executive Fast Lane*, San Francisco: Jossey-Bass.

124 Carey & Ogden, *CEO Succession*.

125 C. M. Daily, P. P. McDougall, J. G. Covin, & D. R. Dalton, 2002, Governance and strategic leadership in entrepreneurial firms, *Journal of Management*, 28: 387–412; M. Maccoby, 2001, Making sense of the leadership literature, *Research Technology Management*, 44(5): 58–60.

126 C. A. Lengnick-Hall & J. A. Wolff, 1999, Similarities and contradictions in the core logic of three strategy research streams, *Strategic Management Journal*, 20: 1109–1132.

127 M. A. Hitt, L. Bierman, K. Shimizu, & R. Kochhar, 2001, Direct and moderating effects of human capital on strategy and performance in professional service firms: A resource-based perspective, *Academy of Management Journal*, 44: 13–28.

128 S. A. Snell & M. A. Youndt, 1995, Human resource management and firm performance: Testing a contingency model of executive controls, *Journal of Management*, 21: 711–737.

129 W. Watson, W. H. Stewart, & A. Barnir, 2003, The effects of human capital, organizational demography, and interpersonal processes on venture partner perceptions of firm profit and growth, *Journal of Business Venturing*, 18: 145–164; P. Caligiuri & V. Di Santo, 2001, Global competence: What is it, and can it be developed through

global assignments? *Human Resource Planning*, 24(3): 27–35; D. Ulrich, 1998, A new mandate for human resources, *Harvard Business Review*, 76(1): 124–134.

[130] A. McWilliams, D. D. Van Fleet, & P. M. Wright, 2001, Strategic management of human resources for global competitive advantage, *Journal of Business Strategies*, 18(1): 1–24; J. Pfeffer, 1994, *Competitive Advantage through People*, Cambridge, MA: Harvard Business School Press, 4.

[131] L. Gratton, 2001, *Living Strategy: Putting People at the Heart of Corporate Purpose*, London: Financial Times/ Prentice Hall.

[132] A. Yan, G. Zhu, & D. T. Hall, 2002, International assignments for career building: A model of agency relationships and psychological contracts, *Academy of Management Review*, 27: 373–391.

[133] Caligiuri & Di Santo, Global competence.

[134] M. W. McCall & G. P. Hollenbeck, 2001, *Developing Global Executives: The Lessons of International Experience*, Boston: Harvard Business School Press.

[135] C. F. Fey & I. Bjorkman, 2001, The effect of human resource management practices on MNC subsidiary performance in Russia, *Journal of International Business Studies*, 32: 59–75.

[136] M. G. Harvey & M. M. Novicevic, 2000, The influences of inpatriation practices on the strategic orientation of a global organization, *International Journal of Management*, 17: 362–371; M. G. Harvey & M. R. Buckley, 1997, Managing inpatriates: Building a global core competency, *Journal of World Business*, 32(1): 35–52.

[137] R. A. Noe, J. A. Colquitt, M. J. Simmering, & S. A. Alvarez, 2003, Knowledge management: Developing intellectual and social capital, in S. E. Jackson, M. A. Hitt, & A. S. DeNisi (eds.), *Managing Knowledge for Sustained Competitive Advantage: Designing Strategies for Effective Human Resource Management*, Oxford, UK: Elsevier Science, 209–242; C. A. Bartlett & S. Ghoshal, 2002, Building competitive advantage through people, *MIT Sloan Management Review*, 43(2): 34–41; D. M. De Carolis & D. L. Deeds, 1999, The impact of stocks and flows of organizational knowledge on firm performance: An empirical investigation of the biotechnology industry, *Strategic Management Journal*, 20: 953–968.

[138] G. P. Hollenbeck & M. W. McCall Jr., 2003, Competence, not competencies: Making a global executive development work, in W. H. Mobley & P. W. Dorfman (eds.), *Advances in Global Leadership*, Oxford, UK: Elsevier Science, 101–119; J. Sandberg, 2000, Understanding human competence at work: An interpretative approach, *Academy of Management Journal*, 43: 9–25.

[139] M. A. Hitt, B. W. Keats, & E. Yucel, 2003, Strategic leadership in global business organizations, in W. H. Mobley & P. W. Dorfman (eds.), *Advances in Global Leadership*, Oxford, UK: Elsevier Science, 9–35; J. Lee & D. Miller, 1999, People matter: Commitment to employees, strategy and performance in Korean firms, *Strategic Management Journal*, 20: 579–593.

[140] R. Cross & L. Prusak, 2002, The people who make organizations go—or stop, *Harvard Business Review*, 80(6): 105–112.

[141] T. M. Welbourne & L. A. Cyr, 1999, The human resource executive effect in initial public offering firms, *Academy of Management Journal*, 42: 616–629; J. Pfeffer & J. F. Veiga, 1999, Putting people first for organizational success, *Academy of Management Executive*, 13(2): 37–48.

[142] Bartlett & Ghoshal, Building competitive advantage through people.

[143] H. Collingwood & D. L. Coutu, 2002, Jack on Jack, *Harvard Business Review*, 80(2): 88–94.

[144] A. K. Gupta & V. Govindarajan, 2000, Knowledge management's social dimension: Lessons from Nucor steel, *Sloan Management Review*, 42(1): 71–80; C. M. Fiol, 1991, Managing culture as a competitive resource: An identity-based view of sustainable competitive advantage, *Journal of Management*, 17: 191–211; J. B. Barney, 1986, Organizational culture: Can it be a source of sustained competitive advantage? *Academy of Management Review*, 11: 656–665.

[145] V. Govindarajan & A. K. Gupta, 2001, Building an effective global business team, *Sloan Management Review*, 42(4): 63–71; S. Ghoshal & C. A. Bartlett, 1994, Linking organizational context and managerial action: The dimensions of quality of management, *Strategic Management Journal*, 15: 91–112.

[146] A. Ardichvilli, R. Cardoza, & S. Ray, 2003, A theory of entrepreneurial opportunity identification and development, *Journal of Business Venturing*, 18: 105–123; D. F. Kuratko, R. D. Ireland, & J. S. Hornsby, 2001, Improving firm performance through entrepreneurial actions: Acordia's corporate entrepreneurship strategy, *Academy of Management Executive*, 15(4): 60–71.

[147] T. E. Brown, P. Davidsson, & J. Wiklund, 2001, An operationalization of Stevenson's conceptualization of entrepreneurship as opportunity-based firm behavior, *Strategic Management Journal*, 22: 953–968.

[148] D. S. Elenkov, W. Judge, & P. Wright, 2005, Strategic leadership and executive innovation influence: An international multi-cluster comparative study, *Strategic Management Journal*, 26: 665–682.

[149] R. G. McGrath, W. J. Ferrier, & A. L. Mendelow, 2004, Real options as engines of choice and heterogeneity, *Academy of Management Review*, 29: 86–101; R. S. Vassolo, J. Anand, & T. B. Folta, 2004, Non-additivity in portfolios of exploration activities: A real options analysis of equity alliances in biotechnology, *Strategic Management Journal*, 25: 1045–1061.

[150] G. T. Lumpkin & G. G. Dess, 1996, Clarifying the entrepreneurial orientation construct and linking it to performance, *Academy of Management Review*, 21: 135–172.

[151] Ibid., 142.

[152] Ibid., 137.

[153] R. R. Sims, 2000, Changing an organization's culture under new leadership, *Journal of Business Ethics*, 25: 65–78.

[154] R. A. Burgelman & Y. L. Doz, 2001, The power of strategic integration, *Sloan Management Review*, 42(3): 28–38; P. H. Fuchs, K. E. Mifflin, D. Miller, & J. O. Whitney, 2000, Strategic integration: Competing in the age of capabilities, *California Management Review*, 42(3): 118–147.

[155] R. Goffee & G. Jones, 2006, Getting personal on the topic of leadership: Authentic self-expression works for those at the top, *Human Resource Management International Digest*, 14(4): 32; B. Axelrod, H. Handfield-Jones, & E. Michaels, 2002, A new game plan for C players, *Harvard Business Review*, 80(1): 80–88; J. S. Hornsby, D. F. Kuratko, & S. A. Zahra, 2002, Middle managers' perception of the internal environment for corporate entrepreneurship: Assessing a measurement scale, *Journal of Business Venturing*, 17: 253–273; J. E. Dutton, S. J. Ashford, R. M. O'Neill, E. Hayes, & E. E. Wierba,

1997, Reading the wind: How middle managers assess the context for selling issues to top managers, *Strategic Management Journal*, 18: 407–425.

156 2006, Best retail revival, *Business Week*, December 18, 64.

157 M. E. Ullman III, 2005, To our shareholders, *J.C. Penney, Inc. Annual Report*, 3.

158 H. Mintzberg, 1973, *The Nature of Managerial Work*, New York: Harper & Row.

159 Freeman, *Strategic Management*.

160 M. Farjoun, 2002, Towards an organic perspective on strategy, *Strategic Management Journal*, 23: 561–594.

161 V. H. Fried, G. D. Bruton, & D. Kern, 2006, The entrepreneurial CEO as "coach/player," *Journal of Private Equity*, 9(3): 35–41; S. Kaplan & E. D. Beinhocker, 2003, The real value of strategic planning, *MIT Sloan Management Review*, 44(2): 71–76.

162 R. E. Freeman & W. M. Evan, 1990, Corporate governance: A stakeholder interpretation, *The Journal of Behavioral Economics*, 19: 337–359.

163 C. J. Fombrun, 2001, Corporate reputations as economic assets, in M.A. Hitt, R.E. Freeman, & J. S. Harrison, *Handbook of Strategic Management*, Oxford, UK: Blackwell Publishers, 289–312; C. Fombrun & M. Shanley, 1990, What's in a name? Reputation building and corporate strategy, *Academy of Management Journal*, 33: 233–258.

164 O. E. Williamson, 1975, *Markets and Hierarchies: Analysis and Antitrust Implications*, New York: The Free Press.

165 J. S. Harrison & C. H. St. John, 2004, *Foundations of Strategic Management*, 3rd ed., Mason, OH: Thomson/South-Western.

166 D. Lavie, 2006, The competitive advantage of interconnected firm: An extension of the resource-based view, *Academy of Management Review*, 31: 638–658.

167 R. C. Ford, 2002, Darden restaurants CEO Joe Lee on the importance of core values: Integrity and fairness, *Academy of Management Executive*, 16(1): 31–36; P. W. Beamish, 1999, Sony's Yoshihide Nakamura on structure and decision making, *Academy of Management Executive*, 13(4): 12–16; R. M. Hodgetts, 1999, Dow Chemical's CEO William Stavropoulos on structure and decision making, *Academy of Management Executive*, 13(4): 29–35.

168 J. R. Baum, E. A. Locke, & S. A. Kirkpatrick, 1998, A longitudinal study of the relation of vision and vision communication to venture growth in entrepreneurial firms, *Journal of Applied Psychology*, 83: 43–54.

169 R. D. Ireland & M. A. Hitt, 1992, Mission statements: Importance, challenge, and recommendations for development, *Business Horizons*, 35(3): 34–42.

170 G. Kassinis & N. Vafeas, 2006, Stakeholder pressures and environmental performance, *Academy of Management Journal*, 49: 145–159.

171 I. M. Levin, 2000, Vision revisited, *Journal of Applied Behavioral Science*, 36: 91–107; J. C. Collins & J. I. Porras, 1996, Building your company's vision, *Harvard Business Review*, 74(5): 65–77.

172 S. Kerr & S. Landauer, 2004, Using stretch goals to promote organizational effectiveness and personal growth, *Academy of Management Executive*, 18(4): 134–138; Hitt & Ireland, The essence of strategic leadership; R. D. Ireland, M. A. Hitt, S. M. Camp, & D. L. Sexton, 2001, Integrating entrepreneurship and strategic management actions to create firm wealth,

*Academy of Management Executive*, 15(1): 49–63; K. R. Thompson, W. A. Hochwarter, & N. J. Mathys, 1997, Stretch targets: What makes them effective? *Academy of Management Executive*, 11(3): 48–59.

173 R. Goffee & G. Jones, 2006, Getting personal on the topic of leadership: Authentic self-expression works for those at the top, *Human Resource Management International Digest*, 14(4): 32–40.

174 2006, *Code of Ethics*, Hartford, CT: United Technologies.

175 J. M. Stevens, H. K. Steensma, D. A. Harrison, & P. L. Cochran, 2005, Symbolic or substantive document? Influence of ethics codes on financial executives' decisions, *Strategic Management Journal*, 26: 181–195.

176 2006, *Enron Code of Ethics July 2000*, The Smoking Gun, http://www.thesmokinggun.com/graphics/packageart/enron/enron.pdf, December 15.

177 S. Forest, W. Zellner, & H. Timmons, 2001, The Enron debacle, *Business Week*, November 12, 106–110.

178 E. Feldman, 2006, A basic quantification of the competitive implications of the demise of Arthur Andersen, *Review of Industrial Organization*, 29: 193–212.

179 M. Esterl, 2006, Corruption scandal at Siemens may derail restructuring drive, *Wall Street Journal*, December 18, A1, A14.

180 P. S. Adler & S.-W. Kwon, 2002, Social capital: Prospects for a new concept, *Academy of Management Review*, 27: 17–40.

181 T. A. Stewart, 2001, Right now the only capital that matters is social capital, *Business 2.0*, December, 128–130.

182 V. Anand, B. E. Ashforth, & M. Joshi, 2005, Business as usual: The acceptance and perpetuation of corruption in organizations, *Academy of Management Executive*, 19(4): 9–23, reprinted from 18(3); D. J. Brass, K. D. Butterfield, & B. C. Skaggs, 1998, Relationships and unethical behavior: A social network perspective, *Academy of Management Review*, 23: 14–31.

183 W. Wallace, 2000, The value relevance of accounting: The rest of the story, *European Management Journal*, 18(6): 675–682.

184 L. K. Trevino, G. R. Weaver, D. G. Toffler, & B. Ley, 1999, Managing ethics and legal compliance: What works and what hurts, *California Management Review*, 41(2): 131–151.

185 J. A. Petrick & J. F. Quinn, 2001, The challenge of leadership accountability for integrity capacity as a strategic asset, *Journal of Business Ethics*, 34: 331–343; R. C. Mayer, J. H. Davis, & F. D. Schoorman, 1995, An integrative model of organizational trust, *Academy of Management Review*, 20: 709–734.

186 C. J. Robertson & W. F. Crittenden, 2003, Mapping moral philosophies: Strategic implications for multinational firms, *Strategic Management Journal*, 24: 385–392; E. Soule, 2002, Managerial moral strategies: In search of a few good principles, *Academy of Management Review*, 27: 114–124; J. Milton-Smith, 1995, Ethics as excellence: A strategic management perspective, *Journal of Business Ethics*, 14: 683–693.

187 L. M. Leinicke, J. A. Ostrosky, & W. M. Rexroad, 2000, Quality financial reporting: Back to the basics, *CPA Journal*, August, 69–71.

188 J. R. Cohen, L. W. Pant, & D. J. Sharp, 2001, An examination of differences in ethical decision-making between Canadian business students and accounting

professionals, *Journal of Business Ethics*, 30: 319–336;
G. R. Weaver, L. K. Trevino, & P. L. Cochran, 1999,
Corporate ethics programs as control systems: Influences
of executive commitment and environmental factors,
*Academy of Management Journal*, 42: 41–57.

[189] P. E. Murphy, 1995, Corporate ethics statements:
Current status and future prospects, *Journal of Business
Ethics*, 14: 727–740.

[190] L. G. Hrebiniak & W. F. Joyce, 2001, Implementing
strategy: An appraisal and agenda for future research,
in M. A. Hitt, R. E. Freeman, & J. S. Harrison (eds.),
*Handbook of Strategic Management*, Oxford, UK:
Blackwell Publishers, 433–463.

[191] J.B. Barney, 1995, Looking inside for competitive
advantage, *Academy of Management Executive*, November,
49–61.

[192] B. R. Barringer & J. S. Harrison, 2000, Walking a
tightrope: Creating value through interorganizational
relationships, *Journal of Management*, 26: 367–404.

[193] J. Crotts, D. R. Dickson, & R. C. Ford, 2005, Aligning
organizational processes with mission: The case of
service excellence, *Academy of Management Executive*,
19(3): 54–68.

[194] 2006, Novartis, Basel campus project, http://www
.novartis.com/about_novartis/en/campus.shtml,
November 18.

[195] J. H. Gittell, 2000, Paradox of coordination and control,
*California Management Review*, 42(3): 101–117;
L. J. Kirsch, 1996, The management of complex tasks
in organizations: Controlling the systems development
process, *Organization Science*, 7: 1–21.

[196] M. D. Shields, F. J. Deng, & Y. Kato, 2000, The design
and effects of control systems: Tests of direct- and
indirect-effects models, *Accounting, Organizations and
Society*, 25: 185–202; R. Simons, 1994, How new top
managers use control systems as levers of strategic
renewal, *Strategic Management Journal*, 15: 170–171.

[197] K. J. Laverty, 1996, Economic "short-termism": The
debate, the unresolved issues, and the implications for

management practice and research, *Academy
of Management Review*, 21: 825–860.

[198] R. S. Kaplan & D. P. Norton, 2001, The strategy-focused
organization, *Strategy & Leadership*, 29(3): 41–42; R.
S. Kaplan & D. P. Norton, 2000, *The Strategy-Focused
Organization: How Balanced Scorecard Companies Thrive
in the New Business Environment*, Boston: Harvard
Business School Press.

[199] B. E. Becker, M. A. Huselid, & D. Ulrich, 2001, *The
HR Scorecard: Linking People, Strategy, and Performance*,
Boston: Harvard Business School Press, 21.

[200] Kaplan & Norton, *The Strategy-Focused Organization*.

[201] R. S. Kaplan & D. P. Norton, 2001, Transforming the
balanced scorecard from performance measurement to
strategic management: Part I, *Accounting Horizons*, 15(1):
87–104.

[202] R. S. Kaplan & D. P. Norton, 1992, The balanced
scorecard—measures that drive performance, *Harvard
Business Review*, 70(1): 71–79.

[203] J. D. Gunkel & G. Probst, 2003, Implementation of the
balanced scorecard as a means of corporate learning:
The Porsche case, Cranfield, UK: European Case
Clearing House.

[204] M. A. Mische, 2001, *Strategic Renewal: Becoming a
High-Performance Organization*, Upper Saddle River, NJ:
Prentice Hall, 181.

[205] H.-J. Cho & V. Pucik, 2005, Relationship between
innovativeness, quality, growth, profitability and
market value, *Strategic Management Journal*, 26:
555–575.

[206] Rowe, Creating wealth in organizations.

[207] R. E. Hoskisson, R. A. Johnson, D. Yiu, & W. P. Wan,
2001, Restructuring strategies of diversified business
groups: Differences associated with country institutional
environments; R. A. Johnson, 1996, Antecedents
and outcomes of corporate refocusing, *Journal of
Management*, 22: 437–481; R. E. Hoskisson &
M. A. Hitt, 1994, *Downscoping: How to Tame the
Diversified Firm*, New York: Oxford University Press.

# CHAPTER 3

# The External Environment: Opportunities, Threats, Industry Competition, and Competitor Analysis

## KNOWLEDGE OBJECTIVES

*Studying this chapter should provide you with the strategic management knowledge needed to:*

1. Explain the importance of analyzing and understanding the firm's external environment.
2. Define and describe the general environment and the industry environment.
3. Discuss the four activities of the external environmental analysis process.
4. Name and describe the general environment's six segments.
5. Identify the five competitive forces and explain how they determine an industry's profit potential.
6. Define strategic groups and describe their influence on the firm.
7. Describe what firms need to know about their competitors and different methods used to collect intelligence about them.

The *external environment* of a firm profoundly influences the firm's growth and profitability.[1] Major events such as a war, economic cycles, and the emergence of new technologies are a few conditions in the external environment that affect firms in the United States and other countries throughout the world. External environmental conditions such as these create threats to and opportunities for firms that, in turn, have major effects on firms' strategic actions.[2]

This chapter focuses on what firms do to analyze and understand the external environment. The external environment influences the firm's strategic options, as well as the decisions made in light of them. The firm's understanding of the external environment is matched with knowledge about its internal organization (discussed in Chapter 4) to form its strategic direction, and to take strategic actions that result in value creation and above-average returns.

As noted in Chapter 1, the environmental conditions in the current global economy differ from those that firms previously faced. Technological changes and the continuing growth of information gathering and processing capabilities demand more timely and effective competitive actions and responses.[3] The rapid sociological changes occurring in many countries affect labor practices and the nature of products demanded by increasingly diverse consumers. Governmental policies and laws also affect where and how firms choose to compete.[4] Deregulation and changes in local government, such as those in the global electric utilities industry, affect not only the general competitive environment, but also the strategic decisions made by companies competing globally. To achieve value creation, firms must be aware of and understand the various dimensions of the external environment.

Firms understand the external environment by acquiring information about competitors, customers, and other stakeholders to build their own base of knowledge and capabilities.[5] Firms may use this base to imitate the capabilities of their strongest competitors (and even may imitate successful firms in other industries), and they may use it to build new knowledge and capabilities to achieve a competitive advantage. On the basis of the new information, knowledge, and capabilities, firms can take actions to buffer themselves against environmental effects or to build relationships with stakeholders in their environment.[6] To build their knowledge and capabilities and to take actions that buffer or build bridges to external stakeholders, organizations must effectively analyze the external environment.

## The General, Industry, and Competitor Environments

An integrated understanding of the external and internal environments is essential for firms to understand the present and predict the future.[7] A firm's external environment includes the general environment and industry and competitor environments.

The **general environment** is composed of dimensions in the broader society that influence an industry and the firms within it.[8] We group these dimensions into six environmental *segments*: demographic, economic, political/legal, sociocultural, technological, and global (see Figure 3.1). Table 3.1 includes examples of *elements* analyzed in each of these segments. Firms cannot directly control the general environment's segments and elements. Accordingly, successful companies gather the information they need to understand each segment and its implications for selecting and implementing appropriate strategies. For example, the terrorist attacks in the United States on September 11, 2001, surprised most businesses throughout the world and had substantial effects on the U.S. economy. Although individual firms were affected differently, none could control the U.S. economy.

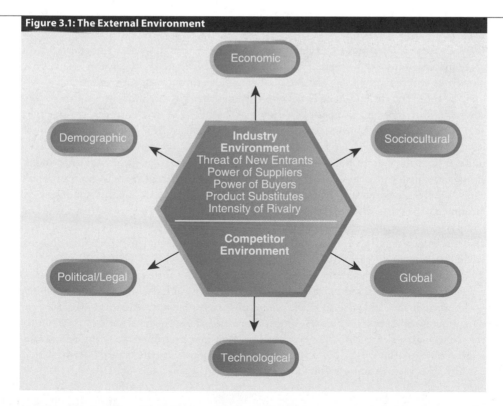

**Figure 3.1: The External Environment**

**Table 3.1: The General Environment: Segments and Elements**

| Demographic Segment | • Population size<br>• Age structure<br>• Geographic distribution | • Ethnic mix<br>• Income distribution |
|---|---|---|
| Economic Segment | • Inflation rates<br>• Interest rates<br>• Trade deficits or surpluses<br>• Budget deficits or surpluses | • Personal savings rate<br>• Business savings rates<br>• Gross domestic product |
| Political/Legal Segment | • Antitrust laws<br>• Taxation laws<br>• Deregulation philosophies | • Labor training laws<br>• Educational philosophies and policies |
| Sociocultural Segment | • Women in the workforce<br>• Workforce diversity<br>• Attitudes about the quality of work life | • Concerns about the environment<br>• Shifts in work and career preferences<br>• Shifts in preferences regarding product and service characteristics |
| Technological Segment | • Product innovations<br>• Applications of knowledge | • Focus of private and government-supported R&D expenditures<br>• New communication technologies |
| Global Segment | • Important political events<br>• Critical global markets | • Newly industrialized countries<br>• Different cultural and institutional attributes |

Instead, companies around the globe were challenged to understand the effects of the economy's decline on their current and future strategies. Similarly, the war in Iraq has had numerous economic, political, and social repercussions throughout the world.

The **industry environment** is the set of factors that directly influences a firm and its competitive actions and competitive responses: the threat of new entrants, the power of suppliers, the power of buyers, the threat of product substitutes, and the intensity of rivalry among competitors (see Figure 3.1). The interactions among these five factors determine an industry's profit potential. The challenge is to locate a position within an industry where a firm can favorably influence those factors or where it can successfully defend against their influence. The greater a firm's capacity to favorably influence its industry environment, the greater is the likelihood that the firm will earn above-average returns. How companies gather and interpret information about their competitors is called *competitor analysis*. Understanding the firm's **competitor environment** complements the insights provided by studying the general and industry environments.

Analysis of the general environment is focused on the future; analysis of the industry environment is focused on the factors and conditions influencing a firm's profitability within its industry; and analysis of the competitor environment is focused on predicting the dynamics of competitors' actions, responses, and intentions. In combination, the results of the three analyses of the firm's external environment influence its strategic intent and strategic actions. Although we discuss each analysis separately, performance improves when the firm integrates the insights provided by all three analyses.

# External Environmental Analysis

Most firms face external environments that are highly turbulent, complex, and global—conditions that make interpreting them increasingly difficult.[9] To cope with what are often ambiguous and incomplete environmental data and to increase their understanding of the general environment, firms engage in a process called *external environmental analysis*. The continuous process includes four activities: scanning, monitoring, forecasting, and assessing (see Table 3.2). Completing this analysis is a difficult, yet significant, activity.[10]

An important objective of studying the external environment is identifying opportunities and threats. An **opportunity** is a condition in the external environment that, if exploited, helps a company achieve value creation. For instance, Wal-Mart sees an excellent opportunity for growth by opening banks in Mexico.[11] IBM, recognizing tremendous opportunities in India, plans to triple its investment in that country.[12] Also, the fact that more than one billion of the world's total population of six billion has cheap access to a telephone is a huge opportunity for global telecommunications companies.[13]

A **threat** is a condition in the general environment that may hinder a company's efforts to achieve value creation.[14] The once revered firm Polaroid can attest to the seriousness of external threats. At one time, Polaroid was a leader in its industry and considered one of the top 50 firms in the United States. However, the company failed to respond quickly enough to the threat from digital photography, and eventually the company had to file for bankruptcy protection. It exists today only as an administrative shell. U.S. trucking companies face a different kind of threat. Rather than innovation causing them stress, they have a hard time competing when energy prices rise. Some experts estimate that for every 10-cent increase in fuel cost, approximately 1,000 trucking companies fail.[15] As these examples indicate, opportunities suggest competitive possibilities, whereas threats are potential constraints.

Several sources can be used to analyze the general environment, including a variety of printed materials (such as trade publications, newspapers, business publications, and the results of academic research and public polls); trade shows; and suppliers, customers, and employees of public-sector organizations.[16] External network contacts can be particularly rich sources of information on the environment.[17] Much information can be obtained by people in the firm's "boundary-spanning" positions. Salespeople, purchasing managers, public relations directors, and customer service representatives, each of whom interacts with external constituents, are examples of individuals in boundary-spanning positions.[18]

| Table 3.2: Components of the External Environmental Analysis | |
| --- | --- |
| Scanning | • Identifying early signals of environmental changes and trends |
| Monitoring | • Detecting meaning through ongoing observations of environmental changes and trends |
| Forecasting | • Developing projections of anticipated outcomes based on monitored changes and trends |
| Assessing | • Determining the timing and importance of environmental changes and trends for firms' strategies and their management |

## Scanning

**Scanning** entails the study of all segments in the general environment. Through scanning, firms identify early signals of potential changes in the general environment and detect changes that are already under way.[19] When scanning, the firm often deals with ambiguous, incomplete, or unconnected data and information. Environmental scanning is critically important for firms competing in highly volatile environments.[20] In addition, scanning activities must be aligned with the organizational context; a scanning system designed for a volatile environment is inappropriate for a firm in a stable environment.[21]

Some analysts expect the pressure brought to bear by the trend toward early retirement on countries such as the United States, France, Germany, and Japan to be significant and challenging. Governments in these countries appear to be offering state-funded pensions to their future elderly populations—but the costs of those pensions cannot be met with the present taxes and social security contribution rates.[22] Firms selling financial planning services and options should analyze this trend to determine whether it represents an opportunity for them to help governments find ways to meet their responsibilities.

Many firms use special software to help them identify events that are taking place in the environment and announced in public sources. For example, news event detection procedures use information-based systems to categorize text and reduce the trade-off between an important missed event and false alarms.[23] The Internet provides multiple opportunities for scanning. For example, Amazon.com records significant information about individuals visiting its Website, particularly if a purchase is made. Amazon then welcomes them by name when they visit the Website again. The firm even sends messages to them about specials and new products similar to those purchased in previous visits.

Additionally, many Websites and advertisers on the Internet obtain information from those who visit their sites using files called "cookies." These files are saved to the visitors' hard drives, allowing customers to connect more quickly to the Website, but also allowing the firm to solicit a variety of information about them. Because cookies are often placed without customers' knowledge, their use can be considered a questionable practice. The U.S. Congress is considering legislation that would ban spyware-enabling cookies.[24]

## Monitoring

When **monitoring,** analysts observe environmental changes to identify important emerging trends from among those spotted by scanning.[25] Critical to successful monitoring is the firm's ability to detect meaning in different environmental events and trends. For example, the size of the middle class of African Americans continues to grow in the United States. With increasing wealth, this group of citizens is beginning to pursue investment options more aggressively.[26] Companies in the financial planning sector could monitor this change in the economic segment to determine the degree to which competitively important trends and business opportunities are emerging. By monitoring trends, firms can be better prepared to introduce new goods and services at the appropriate time to take advantage of the opportunities these trends provide.[27]

Effective monitoring requires the firm to identify important stakeholders. Because the importance of different stakeholders can vary over a firm's life cycle, careful attention must be given to the firm's needs and its stakeholder groups over time.[28] Scanning and monitoring are particularly important when a firm competes in an industry with high technological uncertainty.[29] Scanning and monitoring not only can provide the firm with information, they also serve as a means of importing new knowledge about markets and about how to successfully commercialize new technologies that the firm has developed.[30]

## Forecasting

Scanning and monitoring are concerned with events and trends in the general environment at a point in time. When **forecasting,** analysts develop feasible projections of potential events, and how quickly they may occur, as a result of the changes and trends detected through scanning and monitoring.[31] For example, analysts might forecast the time that will be required for a new technology to reach the marketplace, the length of time before different corporate training procedures are required to deal with anticipated changes in the composition of the workforce, or how much time will elapse before changes in governmental taxation policies affect consumers' purchasing patterns.

Forecasting events and outcomes accurately is a significant challenge. For instance, in early 2006 Texas Instruments, the largest manufacturer of computer chips for cellular phones, increased its earnings forecast because of higher-than-expected demand for its chips.[32] Later in that same year, however, the company reduced its earnings forecast, citing lower-than-expected chip revenue.[33] Forecasting problems such as these make efficient manufacturing and inventory management difficult.

## Assessing

The objective of **assessing** is to determine the timing and significance of the effects of environmental changes and trends on the strategic management of the firm.[34] Through scanning, monitoring, and forecasting, analysts are able to understand the general environment. Going a step further, the intent of assessing is to specify the implications of that understanding for the organization. Without assessment, the firm is left with data that may be interesting but are of unknown competitive relevance.

For example, in the cellular phone market, small video screens have become increasingly popular. However, the effect of this trend for cell phone manufacturers is uncertain. Many competitors, including media producers such as Disney, cell phone manufacturers such as Motorola, and cell phone service operators such as Verizon, are trying to maximize profits from this trend. But it is uncertain which direction the trend will take and how to tap its potential. Will the cell phone eventually substitute for music players like Apple's iPod? Will they become miniature laptops that compete head-on with the BlackBerry phone/organizer/browser? How will new products combine communications, information such as weather forecasts, and entertainment such as television shows and movies? Getting the strategy right will depend on the accuracy of the assessment.[35]

---

# Segments of the General Environment

The general environment is composed of segments (and their individual elements) that are external to the firm (see Table 3.1). Although the degree of impact varies, these environmental segments affect each industry and its firms. The challenge to the firm is to scan, monitor, forecast, and assess those elements in each segment that are of the greatest importance. Resulting from these efforts should be a recognition of environmental changes, trends, opportunities, and threats. Opportunities are then matched with a firm's core competencies (the matching process is discussed further in Chapter 4).

# The Demographic Segment

The **demographic segment** is concerned with a population's size, age structure, geographic distribution, ethnic mix, and income distribution.[36] Demographic segments are analyzed on a global basis because of their potential effects across countries' borders and because many firms compete in global markets.

**Population Size.** Only a little more than one-sixth of the world's population lives in developed countries, while the rest of the world's population lives in developing nations. World population, currently around 6.5 billion, is expected to exceed nine billion by 2050. India and China, with 1.5 billion projected inhabitants, are expected to be the most populous countries.[37]

Observing demographic changes in populations highlights the importance of this environmental segment. For example, some advanced nations have a negative population growth, after discounting the effects of immigration. In some countries, including the United States and several European nations, couples are averaging fewer than two children. This birthrate will reduce populations in some countries over time, although immigration is still producing an increase in population in the United States, which now has more than 300 million residents.[38] In the United States, one person is born every eight seconds, one person dies every 11 seconds, and one international migrant becomes a resident every 31 seconds, for a net gain of one person every 14 seconds.[39] These projections suggest major 21st-century challenges and business opportunities in this country.

**Age Structure.** In some countries, the population's average age is increasing. In the United States, for example, the age-65-and-older population increased by a smaller percentage than the under-65 population in the 1990s. However, in the period 2010–2020, the population aged 65 and older is projected to grow by 35.3 percent.[40] As with the U.S. labor force, other countries also are witnessing a trend toward an older workforce. By 2030, the proportion of the total labor force of 45- to 59-year-olds of countries in the Organisation for Economic Co-operation and Development (OECD) (industrialized countries) is projected to increase from 25.6 to 31.8 percent; the share of workers aged 60 and older is expected to increase from 4.7 to 7.8 percent.[41] Contributing to this growth are increasing life expectancies.

The aging trend suggests numerous opportunities for firms to develop goods and services to meet the needs of an increasingly older population. For example, the elderly use a lot of prescription drugs, so Wal-Mart began a program to sell hundreds of generic drugs for only four dollars. In so doing, the firm is able to increase its sales and provide an important service to a population that might not be able to afford the drugs otherwise. Meanwhile, some observers expect the action to have a ripple effect on the entire healthcare industry.[42]

It has been projected that up to one-half of the females and one-third of the males born at the end of the 1990s in developed countries could live to be 100 years old, with some of them possibly living to be 200 or more.[43] If these life spans become a reality, a host of interesting business opportunities and societal issues will emerge. For example, the effect on individuals' pension plans will be significant and will create potential opportunities for financial institutions, as well as possible threats to government-sponsored retirement and health plans. There are also ramifications regarding the workforce. Because a labor force can be critical to competitive success, firms across the globe must learn to work effectively with older labor forces. Also, countries with increasing life expectancies need to ensure that there are enough workers to support the entire population and promote economic growth. In Japan, the government is providing incentives to encourage people to work longer.[44]

**Geographic Distribution.** For decades, the U.S. population has been shifting from the north and east to the west and south.[45] Similarly, the trend of relocating from metropolitan to nonmetropolitan areas continues and may well accelerate, given the terrorist attacks in New York City and Washington, D.C. These trends are changing local and state governments' tax bases. In turn, business firms' decisions regarding location are influenced by the degree of support that different taxing agencies offer.

The geographic distribution of populations throughout the world is also affected by the capabilities resulting from advances in communications technology. Through computer technologies, for example, people can remain in their homes while communicating with others in remote locations to complete their work.

**Ethnic Mix.** The ethnic mix of populations continues to change. Within the United States, the ethnicity of states and their cities varies significantly. Firms are challenged to be sensitive to these changes. Through careful study, companies can develop and market products that satisfy the unique needs of different ethnic groups. Si TV, a 24-hour cable channel for young Latinos, was launched in 2004 and almost immediately gained 10 million viewers. Its motto is "Speak English. Live Latin."[46]

Changes in ethnic mix also affect a workforce's composition. In the United States, for example, the population and labor force will continue to diversify, as immigration accounts for a sizable part of growth. Projections are that Hispanics and Asians will account for 19 percent of the U.S. population in 2020.[47] Effective management of a culturally diverse workforce can produce a competitive advantage. For example, heterogeneous work teams have been shown to produce more effective strategic analyses, more creativity and innovation, and higher-quality decisions than homogeneous work teams.[48] However, evidence also suggests that diverse work teams are difficult to manage to achieve these outcomes.[49]

**Income Distribution.** Understanding how income is distributed within and across populations informs firms of the purchasing power and discretionary income of different groups. Studies of income distributions suggest that although living standards have improved over time, variations exist within and between nations.[50] Of interest to firms are the average incomes of households and individuals. For instance, the increase in dual-career couples has had a notable effect on average incomes in the United States. Although real income has been declining in general, the income of dual-career couples has increased. These figures yield strategically relevant information for firms.

Another example of a change in income distributions is occurring in China. Rapid economic growth, especially in the coastal region, has created a rising generation of young and wealthy Chinese. These trend-conscious individuals buy coffee at Starbucks and shop online at Tiffany and Co. Procter & Gamble has taken advantage of this development by setting up sites to market its beauty brands Olay, SK-II, and Hugo Boss. General Motors held an online contest to choose the Chinese name for one of its new cars. It gave one of the cars, called the Lova, to the winner.[51]

## The Economic Segment

The health of a nation's economy affects individual firms and industries. Because of this, companies study the economic environment to identify changes, trends, and their strategic implications.

The **economic environment** refers to the nature and direction of the economy in which a firm competes or may compete.[52] Aspects of the economy that deserve ongoing attention include factors such as growth in gross national product (GNP), interest rates, inflation, foreign exchange rates, and trade balances. Growth in GNP, often reported per capita or adjusted for inflation, is a general indication of the strength of the economy. It influences and is influenced by the other factors.

Interest rates and inflation are interconnected. Low interest rates encourage new investment, which leads to higher GNP.[53] However, the increased production increases the demand for supplies, which can increase inflationary pressures. The U.S. Federal Reserve sets the interest rate at which banks borrow money from the U.S. government, which then influences other interest rates. Consequently, when the Federal Reserve is concerned about inflation, it raises interest rates, and when the economy is slowing down its growth in GNP, it lowers interest rates.

Because nations are interconnected as a result of the global economy, firms must scan, monitor, forecast, and assess the health of economies outside their host nations. For example, many nations throughout the world are affected by the U.S. economy, which is the largest consumer of oil, automobiles, and many other goods. To keep up with consumer demand, the United States imports more goods than it exports.[54] This influence means that foreign countries have substantial surplus dollars to invest in the United States. Foreign investment has grown tremendously in recent years, with many foreign firms building factories or buying companies.[55] This trend extends beyond the United States. For example, Indian companies are extending their reach well beyond their national borders. In late 2006 India's Tata Steel bought the British-Dutch company Corus in the biggest-ever foreign acquisition by an Indian company.[56] The move is a part of a trend that is facilitated by India's high volume of exports.

Both inflation and trade surpluses are among the influences on foreign exchange rates.[57] Foreign exchange rates affect whether firms that make investments in other countries are able to withdraw the earnings on those investments successfully. For instance, if a foreign country has very high inflation and exchange rates have changed dramatically since an investment was made, a firm might actually lose money if it tries to convert its earnings from that investment back into its home currency.

Although this discussion of economic forces is oversimplified, it illustrates the importance to firms of staying abreast of economic trends as they formulate and implement strategies, including international strategies.

## The Political/Legal Segment

Economic issues are intertwined with the realities of the external environment's political/legal segment. For instance, Japan plans to toughen regulations on foreign acquisitions of Japanese companies because it is concerned that its technology is being used overseas in military applications.[58] The **political/legal segment** is the arena in which organizations and interest groups compete for attention, resources, and a voice of overseeing the body of laws and regulations guiding the interactions among nations.[59] Essentially, this segment represents how organizations try to influence government and how governments influence them. Constantly changing, the segment influences the nature of competition through laws, regulations, and policies (see Table 3.1). Sometimes the penalties for inadequately responding to these forces can be harsh. For instance, the European Union (EU) fined Microsoft €280.5 million for defying antitrust orders.[60]

Firms must carefully analyze a new political administration's business-related policies and philosophies. Antitrust laws, taxation laws, industries chosen for deregulation, labor training laws, and the degree of commitment to educational institutions are areas in which an administration's policies can affect the operations and profitability of industries and individual firms. Often, firms develop a political strategy to influence governmental policies and actions that might affect them. The effects of global governmental policies on a firm's competitive position increase the importance of forming an effective political strategy.[61] For instance, Pfizer won a major victory when a Beijing court backed the company's patent protection for its drug Viagra.[62]

Business firms across the globe must confront an interesting array of political/legal questions and issues. For example, the debate continues over trade policies. Some believe that a nation should erect trade barriers to protect products manufactured by its companies. Others argue that free trade across nations serves the best interests of individual countries and their citizens. The International Monetary Fund (IMF) classifies trade barriers as restrictive when tariffs total at least 25 percent of a product's price. At the other extreme, the IMF stipulates that a nation has open trade when its tariffs are between 0 and 9 percent.[63] Although controversial, a number of countries (including the United States, nations in the European Union, Japan, Australia, Canada, Chile, Singapore, and Mexico) are cooperating in an effort to reduce or eventually eliminate trade barriers. The North American Free Trade Agreement (NAFTA) is one example of this trend. The treaty has had a large effect on trade, with U.S. shipments to Mexico up 18 percent between 2000 and 2005, while shipments to Canada increased 23 percent.[64]

The regulations related to pharmaceuticals and telecommunications, along with the approval or disapproval of major acquisitions, show the power of government entities. This power also suggests how important it is for firms to have a political strategy.

## The Sociocultural Segment

The **sociocultural segment** is concerned with a society's attitudes and cultural values. Because attitudes and values form the cornerstone of a society, they often drive demographic, economic, political/legal, and technological conditions and changes.

Sociocultural segments differ across countries. For example, in the United States, 13.1 percent of the nation's GDP is spent on health care. This is the highest percentage of any OECD country. Germany allocates 10.4 percent of GDP to health care, and Switzerland only 10.2 percent. Interestingly, the U.S. rate of citizens' access to health care is below that of these and other countries.[65]

The reverse is true for retirement planning. A study in 15 countries indicated that retirement planning in the United States starts earlier than in other countries: "Americans are involved in retirement issues to a greater extent than other countries, particularly in Western Europe where the Social Security and pensions systems provide a much higher percentage of income in retirement."[66] U.S. residents start planning for retirement in their 30s, whereas people in Portugal, Spain, Italy, and Japan start in their 40s and 50s. Attitudes regarding saving for retirement affect a nation's economic and political/legal segments.

As already mentioned, a significant trend in many countries is increased workforce diversity. This diversity includes female workers, who are a valuable source of highly productive employees. Women now account for about half the workforce in the United States and Sweden, with many other countries close behind.[67] An increasing number of women are also starting and managing their own businesses. Using data from the U.S. Census Bureau, the Center for Women's Business Research estimates that about half (47.7 percent) of the privately owned firms in the United States are majority owned by women. The number of new businesses started by women also continues to increase.[68] Because of equal pay and equal opportunity legislation in many countries, relative pay for women is increasing. However, pay differentials between men and women still exist. Among Western European countries, the pay gap between men and women is greatest in the United Kingdom, where men earn 34 percent more than women do, and lowest in Sweden, where a 17-percent gap exists.[69]

The growing gender, ethnic, and cultural diversity in the workforce creates challenges and opportunities,[70] including those related to combining the best of both men's and women's traditional leadership styles for a firm's benefit and identifying ways to facilitate all employees' contributions to their firms. Some companies provide training to nurture the leadership potential of women and members of ethnic minorities. Changes in organizational structure and management practices often are required to eliminate subtle barriers that may exist. Learning to manage diversity in the domestic workforce can increase a firm's effectiveness in managing a globally diverse workforce, as the firm acquires more international operations.

Another manifestation of changing attitudes toward work is the continuing growth of contingency workers (part-time, temporary, and contract employees) throughout the global economy. This trend is significant in several parts of the world, including Canada, Japan, Latin America, Western Europe, and the United States. The fastest growing group of contingency workers is in the technical and professional area. Contributing to this growth are corporate restructurings and a breakdown of lifetime employment practices.

The continued growth of suburban communities in the United States and abroad is another sociocultural trend. The increasing number of people living in the suburbs has a number of effects. For example, because of the resulting often-longer commute times to urban businesses, there is pressure for better transportation and superhighway systems (e.g., outer beltways to serve the suburban communities). On the other hand, some businesses are locating in the suburbs closer to their employees. Suburban growth also affects the number of electronic telecommuters, which is increasing rapidly in the 21st century.[71] This work-style option is feasible because of changes in the technological segment. Also, beyond the suburbs, "micropolitan" areas are increasing in importance. These are classified by the U.S. Census Bureau as communities that are often 100 miles or more away from a large city and have 10,000 to 49,999 residents. These areas offer big-city amenities such as strip malls and major chain restaurants, but living costs are much lower.[72]

## The Technological Segment

Pervasive and diversified in scope, technological changes affect many parts of societies. These effects occur primarily through new products, processes, and materials. The **technological segment** includes the institutions and activities involved with creating new knowledge and translating that knowledge into new outputs, products, processes, and materials.

Given the rapid pace of technological change, it is vital for firms to thoroughly study the technological segment.[73] The importance of these efforts is suggested by the finding that firms that adopt new technology early often achieve higher market shares and earn higher returns. Thus, executives must verify that their firm is continuously scanning the external environment to identify potential substitutes for technologies that are in current use, as well as to spot newly emerging technologies from which their firm could derive competitive advantage.[74] Chapter 1 outlined three categories of technological trends that are altering the nature of competition: the increasing rate of technological change and diffusion, changes in information technology, and increasing knowledge intensity. The Internet is at the heart of all of these trends.

Among its other valuable uses, the Internet is an excellent source of data and information that can help a firm to understand its external environment. Access to experts on topics from chemical engineering to semiconductor manufacturing, to the Library of Congress, and even to satellite photographs is available through the Internet. Other information available through this technology includes Securities and Exchange Commission (SEC) filings, Commerce Department data, Bureau of the Census information, new patent filings, and stock market updates. Internet technology is also facilitating business transactions between companies, as well as between a company and its customers. Thus, a competitive advantage may accrue to the company that derives full value from the Internet in terms of both e-commerce activities and transactions taken to process the firm's work flow.

Wireless communication technologies, including handheld wireless devices, represent another important technological opportunity. The use of handheld computers with wireless network connectivity, Web-enabled mobile phone handsets, and other emerging platforms (i.e., consumer Internet access devices) are expected to increase substantially, soon becoming the dominant form of communication and commerce.[75] Wireless local area networks, known as Wi-Fi ("wireless fidelity"), are already available in many restaurants, hotels, office buildings, schools, and other venues.

Clearly, the Internet and wireless forms of communication are important technological developments for many reasons. One reason is that they facilitate the diffusion of other technology and knowledge critical for achieving and maintaining a competitive advantage.[76] Technological knowledge is particularly important. Certainly on a global scale, the technological opportunities and threats in the general environment affect whether firms obtain new technology from external sources (such as licensing and acquisition) or develop it internally.

## The Global Segment

The **global segment** includes relevant new global markets, existing markets that are changing, important international political events, and critical cultural and institutional characteristics of global markets.[77] Globalization was defined in Chapter 1 as the increasing economic interdependence among countries as reflected in the flow of goods and services, financial capital, and knowledge across country borders. Globalization of business markets creates opportunities for firms;[78] for example, they can identify and enter valuable global markets.[79] Economically maturing countries such as China and India may be particularly advantageous as a result of an increase in developing country funds, reduced trade barriers, and substantial macroeconomic reforms in those countries.[80] China's admission to the World Trade Organization in 2001 was a significant milestone in facilitating trade and investment in that country. India produces more people with technical degrees than any other country except the United States. As a result, many multinational companies are dramatically increasing their investments there. IBM, for instance, plans to triple its investment to $6 billion, which means that the company may eventually employ more workers in

India than in the United States.[81] Cisco Systems, Intel, and Microsoft have each committed more than $1 billion to their Indian operations for research and the hiring of thousands of workers.

Moving into international markets extends a firm's reach and potential. The larger total market increases the probability that a firm will earn a return on its innovations. Toyota receives about half of its total sales revenue from outside Japan, its home country. Well over half of the sales revenues of McDonald's and almost all of those of Nokia are from outside their home countries.[82] Certainly, firms entering new markets can diffuse new knowledge they have created and learn from the new markets as well.[83] Global markets also offer firms more opportunities to obtain the resources needed for success. For example, the Kuwait Investment Authority is the second largest shareholder of DaimlerChrysler.[84]

Nevertheless, globalization of business markets creates challenges as well as opportunities for firms.[85] The low cost of Chinese products threatens many global firms in industries such as textiles, where average wage rates make Chinese garments so inexpensive that companies in other countries find it hard to compete.[86] Also, the large number of technically trained workers in India does not mean that non-Indian multinationals have a monopoly on hiring them. In fact, rapidly developing Indian firms are hiring more of them and even expanding their operations outside India into regions that have traditionally been dominated by Western firms. Tata Consultancy Services Ltd. and Infosys Technologies Ltd. have begun to make acquisitions in Europe and the United States to expand their presence in those markets.[87]

Of course, investment risks abound in less economically mature countries. For instance, a few years ago Argentina's market was full of promise, but in 2001 Argentina experienced a financial crisis that placed it on the brink of bankruptcy.[88] By 2005 Argentina was still struggling to complete its debt restructuring. Also, although economic growth has increased since its recession in 2002, it will still have difficulties raising needed investment capital because of its tarnished reputation from failing to pay its debts.[89]

As firms expand into global markets, they need to recognize their differing sociocultural and institutional attributes. Companies competing in South Korea, for example, must understand the value placed in that country on hierarchical order, formality, and self-control, as well as on duty rather than rights. Furthermore, Korean ideology emphasizes communitarianism, a characteristic of many Asian countries. Korea's approach differs from those of Japan and China, however, in that it focuses on *inhwa*, or harmony. Inhwa is based on a respect of hierarchical relationships and obedience to authority. Alternatively, the approach in China stresses *guanxi*—personal relationships or good connections— while in Japan, the focus is on *wa*, or group harmony and social cohesion.[90] From an institutional perspective, China can be characterized by a major emphasis on centralized government planning,[91] in contrast to the United States and many other Western countries. These types of differences create the necessity to have a top management team with the experience, knowledge, and sensitivity that are necessary to effectively analyze this segment of the environment.[92]

## Industry Environment Analysis

A key objective of analyzing the general environment is identifying anticipated changes and trends among external elements. With a focus on the future, the analysis of the general environment allows firms to identify opportunities and threats. Also critical to a firm's future operations is an understanding of its industry environment and its competitors.

An **industry** is a group of firms producing products that are close substitutes. In the course of competition, these firms influence one another. Typically, industries include a rich mix of competitive strategies that companies use in pursuing value creation and above-average returns. In part, these strategies are chosen because of the influence of an industry's characteristics.[93] Compared with the general environment, the industry environment more directly affects the firm's value creation and above-average returns.[94] The intensity of industry competition and an industry's profit potential (as measured by the long-run return on invested capital) are functions of five forces of competition: the threats posed by new entrants, the power of suppliers, the power of buyers, product substitutes, and the intensity of rivalry among competitors (see Figure 3.2).

The five forces model of competition expands the arena for competitive analysis. Historically, when studying the competitive environment, firms concentrated on companies with which they competed directly. However, firms must search more broadly to identify current and potential competitors by identifying potential customers as well as the firms serving them. Competing for the same customers and thus being influenced by how customers value location and firm capabilities in their decisions is referred to as the *market microstructure*.[95] Understanding this area is particularly important because in recent years industry boundaries have become blurred. For example, in the electrical utilities industry, cogenerators (firms that also produce power) are competing with regional utility companies. Moreover, telecommunications companies now compete with broadcasters, software manufacturers provide personal financial services, airlines sell mutual funds, and automakers sell insurance and provide financing.[96] In addition to focusing on customers rather than specific industry boundaries to define markets, geographic boundaries are also relevant. Research suggests that different geographic markets for the same product can have considerably different competitive conditions.[97]

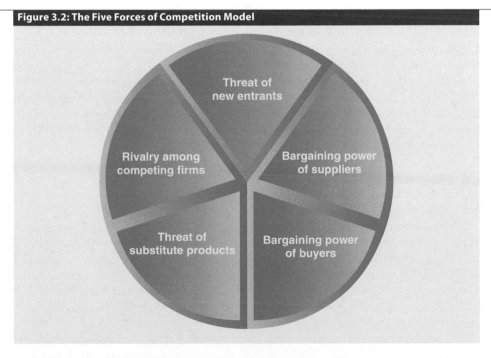

**Figure 3.2: The Five Forces of Competition Model**

Threat of new entrants

Rivalry among competing firms

Bargaining power of suppliers

Threat of substitute products

Bargaining power of buyers

The five forces model recognizes that suppliers can become a firm's competitors (by integrating forward), as can buyers (by integrating backward). Several firms have integrated forward in the pharmaceutical industry by acquiring distributors or wholesalers. In addition, firms choosing to enter a new market and those producing products that are adequate substitutes for existing products can become competitors of a company.

## Threat of New Entrants

Identifying new entrants is important because they can threaten the market share of existing competitors. One reason new entrants pose such a threat is that they bring additional production capacity. Unless the demand for a good or service is increasing, additional capacity holds consumers' costs down, resulting in less revenue and lower returns for competing firms. Often, new entrants have a keen interest in gaining a large market share. As a result, new competitors may force existing firms to be more effective and efficient and to learn how to compete in new dimensions (for example, using an Internet-based distribution channel).

The likelihood that firms will enter an industry is a function of several factors, two of which are *barriers to entry* and the *retaliation* expected from current industry participants. Entry barriers make it difficult for new firms to enter an industry and often place them at a competitive disadvantage even when they are able to enter. As such, high entry barriers increase the returns for existing firms in the industry and may allow some firms to dominate the industry.[98]

**Barriers to Entry.** Existing competitors try to develop barriers to entry. In contrast, potential entrants seek markets in which the entry barriers are relatively insignificant. The absence of entry barriers increases the probability that a new entrant can operate profitably. There are several kinds of potentially significant entry barriers, including economies of scale, product differentiation, capital requirements, switching costs, access to distribution channels, cost advantages independent of scale, and government policy.

**Economies of Scale.** *Economies of scale* are "the marginal improvements in efficiency that a firm experiences as it incrementally increases its size."[99] Therefore, as the quantity of a product produced during a given period increases, the cost of manufacturing each unit declines. Economies of scale can be developed in most business functions, such as marketing, manufacturing, R&D, and purchasing. Increasing economies of scale enhances a firm's flexibility. For example, a firm may choose to reduce its price and capture a greater share of the market. Alternatively, it may keep its price constant to increase profits.

New entrants face a dilemma when confronting current competitors' scale economies. Small-scale entry places them at a cost disadvantage. Alternatively, large-scale entry, in which the new entrant manufactures large volumes of a product to gain economies of scale, risks strong competitive retaliation.

Also important for the firm to understand are instances of current competitive realities that reduce the ability of economies of scale to create an entry barrier. Many companies now customize their products for large numbers of small customer groups. Customized products are not manufactured in the volumes necessary to achieve economies of scale. Customization is made possible by new flexible manufacturing systems. In fact, the new manufacturing technology facilitated by advanced computerization has allowed the development of mass customization in some industries. Mass customized products can be individualized to the customer in a very short time, often within a day. Mass customization is becoming increasingly common in manufacturing products.[100] Companies manufacturing customized products learn how to respond quickly to customers' desires rather than developing scale economies.

**Product Differentiation.** Over time, customers may come to believe that a firm's product is unique. This belief can result from the firm's service to the customer, effective advertising campaigns, or being the first to market a good or service. Companies such as Coca-Cola, PepsiCo, and the world's automobile manufacturers spend a great deal of money on advertising to convince potential customers of their products' distinctiveness. Customers valuing a product's uniqueness tend to become loyal to both the product and the company producing it. Typically, new entrants must allocate many resources to overcome existing customer loyalties. To combat the perception of uniqueness, new entrants frequently offer products at lower prices. This decision, however, may result in lower profits or even losses.

**Capital Requirements.** Competing in a new industry requires the firm to meet certain *capital requirements*. In addition to physical facilities, capital is needed for inventories, marketing activities, and other critical business functions. Even when competing in a new industry is attractive, the capital required for successful market entry may not be available for a firm to pursue an apparent market opportunity. For example, entering the steel and defense industries would be very difficult because of the substantial resource investments required to be competitive. One way a firm could enter the steel industry, however, is with a highly efficient mini-mill. A firm might enter the defense industry through the acquisition of an existing firm because of the knowledge requirements.

**Switching Costs.** *Switching costs* are the one-time costs customers incur when they buy from a different supplier. The costs of buying new ancillary equipment and of retraining employees, and even the psychic costs of ending a relationship, may be incurred in switching to a new supplier. In some cases, switching costs are low, such as when a consumer switches to a different soft drink. Switching costs can vary as a function of time. For example, in terms of hours toward graduation, the cost to a student to transfer from one university to another as a freshman is much lower than it is when that student transfers as a senior. Occasionally, a decision a manufacturer makes to produce a new, innovative product creates high switching costs for the final consumer. Customer loyalty programs, such as airlines awarding frequent flier miles, are intended to increase the customer's switching costs.

If switching costs are high, a new entrant must offer either a substantially lower price or a much better product to attract buyers. Usually, the more established the relationship between parties, the greater is the cost incurred to switch to an alternative offering.

**Access to Distribution Channels.** Over time, industry participants typically develop effective means of distributing products. Once a relationship with its distributors has been developed, a firm will nurture it to create switching costs for the distributors. *Access to distribution channels* can be a strong barrier to entry, particularly in consumer nondurable goods industries (for example, in grocery stores where shelf space is limited) and in international markets. Thus, new entrants have to persuade distributors to carry their products, either in addition to or in place of those currently distributed. Price breaks and cooperative advertising allowances may be used for this purpose; however, such practices reduce the new entrant's profit potential.

**Cost Advantages Independent of Scale.** Sometimes, established competitors have cost advantages—such as proprietary product technology, favorable access to raw materials, desirable locations, and government subsidies—that new entrants cannot duplicate. Successful competition requires new entrants to reduce the strategic relevance of these factors. Delivering purchases directly to the buyer can counter the advantage of a desirable location; new food establishments in an undesirable location often follow this practice. Similarly, automobile dealerships located in unattractive areas can provide superior service (such as picking up a car to be serviced and then delivering it to the customer) to overcome a competitor's location advantage.

**Government Policy.** Through licensing and permit requirements, *government policy* can also control entry into an industry. Liquor retailing, banking, and trucking are examples of industries in which government decisions and actions affect entry possibilities. Also, governments often restrict entry into some industries because of the need to provide quality service or to protect jobs. Alternatively, deregulation of industries, such as airlines or utilities in the United States, can increase competition as more firms are permitted to enter.[101] Some of the most widely publicized government actions are those involving antitrust cases. For instance, both the U.S. and European governments pursued an antitrust case against Microsoft. The final settlement in the United States involved a relatively small penalty for the company; however, the EU judgments were more severe.[102]

**Expected Retaliation.** Firms seeking to enter an industry also anticipate the reactions of firms in the industry. An expectation of swift and vigorous competitive responses reduces the likelihood of entry. Vigorous retaliation can be expected when the existing firm has a major stake in the industry (for example, it has fixed assets with few, if any, alternative uses), when it has substantial resources, and when industry growth is slow or constrained. For example, any firms that attempt to enter the steel or information technology industries at the current time can expect significant retaliation from existing competitors.

Locating market niches not served by incumbents allows the new entrant to avoid entry barriers. Small entrepreneurial firms are generally best suited for identifying and serving neglected market segments. When Honda first entered the U.S. market, it concentrated on small-engine motorcycles, a market that firms such as Harley-Davidson ignored. By targeting this neglected niche, Honda avoided competition. After consolidating its position, Honda used its strength to attack rivals by introducing larger motorcycles and competing in the broader market. (Competitive actions and competitive responses between firms such as Honda and Harley-Davidson are discussed briefly at the end of this chapter and fully in Chapter 6.)

## Bargaining Power of Suppliers

Supplier firms can use tactics such as increasing their prices and reducing the quality or availability of their products to exert power over firms competing within an industry. If a particular firm is unable to recover cost increases by its suppliers through its pricing structure, its profitability is reduced by its suppliers' actions. A supplier group is powerful when

- ■ It is dominated by a few large companies and is more concentrated than the industry to which it sells.
- ■ Satisfactory substitute products are not available to industry firms.
- ■ Industry firms are not a significant customer for the supplier group.
- ■ Suppliers' goods are critical to buyers' marketplace success.

- The effectiveness of suppliers' products has created high switching costs for industry firms.
- It poses a credible threat to integrate forward into the buyers' industry. Credibility is enhanced when suppliers have substantial resources and provide a highly differentiated product.

The automobile manufacturing industry is an example of an industry in which suppliers' bargaining power is relatively low. For example, Nissan and Toyota place significant pressure on their suppliers to provide parts at reduced prices.[103] Because they sell their products to a small number of large firms and because they aren't credible threats to integrate forward, auto parts suppliers have little power relative to automobile manufacturers such as Toyota and Nissan.

## Bargaining Power of Buyers

Firms seek to maximize their return on invested capital. Alternatively, buyers (customers of an industry or firm) want to buy products at the lowest possible price—the point at which the industry earns the lowest acceptable rate of return on its invested capital. To reduce their costs, buyers bargain for higher quality, greater levels of service, and lower prices. These outcomes are achieved by encouraging competitive battles among the industry's firms. Customers (buyer groups) are powerful when

- They purchase a large portion of an industry's total output.
- The sales of the product being purchased account for a significant portion of the seller's annual revenues.
- They could switch to another product at little, if any, cost.
- The industry's products are undifferentiated or standardized, and the buyers would pose a credible threat if they were to integrate backward into the sellers' industry.

Armed with greater amounts of information about the manufacturer's costs and the power of the Internet as a shopping and distribution alternative, consumers appear to be increasing their bargaining power in the automobile industry and auto dealers in particular. One reason is that individual buyers incur virtually zero switching costs when they decide to purchase from one manufacturer rather than another or from one dealer as opposed to another. These realities are forcing companies in the automobile industry to become more focused on the needs and desires of the people actually buying cars, trucks, minivans, and sport utility vehicles. In so doing, they can better serve and satisfy their customers, who have considerable power.

## Threat of Substitute Products

*Substitute products* are goods or services from outside an industry that perform similar or the same functions as a product that the industry produces. For example, NutraSweet and sugar perform the same function, but with different characteristics; as a sugar substitute, NutraSweet places an upper limit on sugar manufacturers' prices. Other product substitutes include people using e-mail instead of fax machines, filling plastic containers rather than glass jars, drinking tea instead of coffee, and buying satellite services in the place of digital cable services. Newspaper circulation has declined in recent years because of many substitute news outlets, including cable television, the Internet, e-mail, and cell phones.[104]

In general, product substitutes present a strong threat to a firm when customers have few, if any, switching costs and when the substitute product's price is lower or its quality and performance capabilities are equal to or greater than those of the competing product. Differentiating a product along dimensions that customers value (such as price, quality, service after the sale, and location) reduces a substitute's attractiveness.

## Intensity of Rivalry among Competitors

Because an industry's firms are mutually dependent, actions taken by one company usually invite competitive responses. *Competitive rivalry* intensifies when a firm is challenged by a competitor's actions or when an opportunity to improve its market position is recognized.

Firms within industries are rarely homogeneous; they differ in resources and capabilities and seek to differentiate themselves from competitors.[105] Typically, firms seek to differentiate their products from competitors' offerings in ways that customers value and in which the firms have a competitive advantage. Visible dimensions on which rivalry is based include price, quality, and innovation. Various factors influence the intensity of rivalry between or among competitors.

**Numerous or Equally Balanced Competitors.** Intense rivalries are common in industries with many companies. With multiple competitors, it is common for a few firms to believe that they can act without eliciting a response. However, evidence suggests that other firms generally are aware of competitors' actions, often choosing to respond to them. At the other extreme, industries with only a few firms of equivalent size and power also tend to have strong rivalries. The large and often similar-sized resource bases of these firms permit vigorous actions and responses. The competitive battles between Fuji and Kodak in the photo industry and Airbus and Boeing in aircraft manufacturing exemplify intense rivalries between pairs of relatively equivalent competitors.

**Slow Industry Growth.** When a market is growing, firms try to effectively use resources to serve an expanding customer base. Growing markets reduce the pressure to take customers from competitors. However, rivalry in no-growth or slow-growth markets becomes more intense as firms battle to increase their market shares by attracting competitors' customers.

Typically, battles to protect market shares are fierce. Certainly, this has been the case with Fuji and Kodak. The instability in the market that results from these competitive engagements reduces profitability for firms throughout the industry, as is demonstrated by the commercial aircraft industry. The market for large aircraft is expected to decline or grow only slightly over the next few years. To expand market share, Boeing and Airbus compete aggressively by introducing new products and differentiating products and services. Both firms are likely to win some battles and lose others.

**High Fixed Costs or High Storage Costs.** When fixed costs account for a large part of total costs, companies try to maximize the use of their productive capacity. Doing so allows the firm to spread costs across a larger volume of output. However, when many firms attempt to maximize their productive capacity, excess capacity is created throughout the industry. To then reduce inventories, individual companies typically cut the price of their product and offer rebates and other special discounts to customers. These practices often intensify competition. The pattern of excess capacity at the industry level followed by intense rivalry at the firm level is observed frequently in industries with high storage costs. Perishable products, for example, lose their value rapidly. As their inventories grow, producers of perishable goods often use pricing strategies to sell products quickly.

**Lack of Differentiation or Low Switching Costs.** When buyers find a differentiated product that satisfies their needs, they frequently purchase the product loyally over time. Industries with many companies that have successfully differentiated their products have less rivalry, resulting in lower competition for individual firms.[106] However, when buyers view products as commodities (as products with few differentiated features or capabilities), rivalry intensifies. In these instances, buyers' purchasing decisions are based primarily on price and, to a lesser degree, service. Film for cameras is an example of a commodity. Thus, the competition between Fuji and Kodak is expected to be strong.

The effect of switching costs is identical to that described for differentiated products. The lower the buyers' switching costs, the easier it is for competitors to attract buyers through pricing and service offerings. High switching costs, however, at least partially insulate the firm from rivals' efforts to attract customers. Interestingly, the switching costs—such as pilot and mechanic training—are high in aircraft purchases, yet the rivalry between Boeing and Airbus remains intense because the stakes for both are extremely high.

**High Strategic Stakes.** Competitive rivalry is likely to be high when it is important for several of the competitors to perform well in the market. For example, although Samsung is diversified and is a market leader in other businesses, it has targeted market leadership in the consumer electronics market. This market is quite important to Sony and other major competitors such as Hitachi, Matsushita, NEC, and Mitsubishi. Thus, we can expect substantial rivalry in this market over the next several years.

High strategic stakes can also exist in terms of geographic location. For example, Japanese automobile manufacturers are committed to a significant presence in the U.S. marketplace. A key reason for this is that the United States is the world's single largest market for auto manufacturers' products. Because of the stakes involved in this country for Japanese and U.S. manufacturers, rivalry among firms in the United States and the global automobile industry is intense. It should be noted that while close proximity tends to promote greater rivalry, physically proximate competition has potentially positive benefits as well. For example, when competitors are located near each other, it is easier for suppliers to serve them and they can develop economies of scale that lead to lower production costs. Additionally, communications with key industry stakeholders such as suppliers are facilitated and more efficient when they are located close to the firm.[107]

**High Exit Barriers.** Sometimes companies continue competing in an industry even though the returns on their invested capital are low or negative. Firms making this choice likely face high exit barriers, which include economic, strategic, and emotional factors causing companies to remain in an industry when the profitability of doing so is questionable. Common exit barriers are

- Specialized assets (assets with values linked to a particular business or location)
- Fixed costs of exit (such as labor agreements)

- Strategic interrelationships (relationships of mutual dependence, such as those between one business and other parts of a company's operations, including shared facilities and access to financial markets)

- Emotional barriers (aversion to economically justified business decisions because of fear for one's own career, loyalty to employees, and so forth)

- Government and social restrictions (more common outside the United States, these restrictions often are based on government concerns for job losses and regional economic effects)

## Complementors

A five forces analysis is a powerful way to examine competitive forces in an industry. However, complementors, sometimes labeled a sixth force, can also have a powerful influence on competition.[108] **Complementors** are the companies that sell complementary goods or services that are compatible with the focal firm's own products or services. They could also include suppliers and buyers who have a strong "network" relationship with the focal firm. A strong network of complementors can solidify a competitive advantage. For instance, Google's position as an Internet search engine is solidified because of the number of Internet access products with which it functions smoothly. If a complementor's good or service adds value to the sale of a firm's good or service, it is likely to create value for the firm. For instance, airlines are complementors to the hotel industry and engineering schools are complementors to high-tech industries.

Complementors can also have the effect of hurting firm competitiveness. For instance, poor airline performance can reduce the economic performance of hotels, theme parks, and other tourist destinations. Similarly, a reduction in the number of new homes built can negatively affect the furniture and home appliance industries. For instance, in late 2006 Masco Corporation, maker of ready-to-assemble furniture, cut its earnings forecast, stating that a decline in housing starts was hurting demand for its products.[109]

## Interpreting Industry Analyses

Effective industry analyses are products of careful study and interpretation of data and information from multiple sources. A wealth of industry-specific data is available. Because of globalization, international markets and rivalries must be included in the firm's analyses. In fact, research shows that in some industries, international variables are more important than domestic ones as determinants of value creation. Furthermore, because of the development of global markets, a country's borders no longer restrict industry structures. Movement into international markets enhances the chances of success for new ventures as well as for more established firms.[110]

Following study of the five forces of competition, the firm can develop the insights required to determine an industry's attractiveness regarding the potential to earn adequate or superior returns on its invested capital. In general, the stronger competitive forces are, the lower the profit potential for an industry's firms. An unattractive industry has low entry barriers, suppliers and buyers with strong bargaining positions, strong competitive threats from product substitutes, and intense rivalry among competitors. These industry characteristics make it very difficult for firms to achieve value creation and earn above-average returns. Alternatively, an attractive industry has high entry barriers, suppliers and buyers with little bargaining power, few competitive threats from product substitutes, and relatively moderate rivalry.[111]

# Analysis of Direct Competitors

Evaluating the five forces helps firms understand the nature and level of competition in its industry, and thus its profit potential. Firms can then use this information to help them develop strategies for dealing with each of the forces. For instance, a firm may be able to reduce the power of strong suppliers through joint ventures with a supplier company or through outright purchase. Also, a firm may be able to help erect higher entry barriers by building a very large plant to produce economies of scale. Firms can also use a five forces analysis to gain information that is useful in understanding the positions, intentions, and performance of direct competitors. Some of the closest of these competitors fall into what is sometimes called a *strategic group*.

## Strategic Groups

A set of firms emphasizing similar strategic dimensions to use a similar strategy is called a **strategic group**.[112] The competition between firms within a strategic group is greater than the competition between a member of a strategic group and companies outside that group. Thus, intra–strategic group competition is more intense than is inter–strategic group competition.

*Strategic dimensions*—such as the extent of technological leadership, product quality, pricing policies, distribution channels, and customer service—are areas that firms in a strategic group treat similarly. Describing patterns of competition within strategic groups suggests that "organizations in a strategic group occupy similar positions in the market, offer similar goods to a similar set of customers, and may also use similar production technology and other organizational processes."[113] Thus, membership in a particular strategic group partially defines the essential characteristics of the firm's strategy.[114]

The notion of strategic groups can be useful for analyzing an industry's competitive structure. Such analyses can be helpful in diagnosing competition, positioning, and the profitability of firms within an industry.[115] Research has found that strategic groups differ in performance, suggesting their importance.[116] Interestingly, research also suggests that strategic group membership remains relatively stable over time, making analysis easier and more useful.[117]

Using strategic groups to understand an industry's competitive structure requires the firm to plot companies' competitive actions and competitive responses along strategic dimensions such as pricing decisions, product quality, distribution channels, and so forth. Doing this shows the firm how certain companies are competing using similar strategic dimensions. For example, there are unique radio markets because consumers prefer different music formats and programming (news radio, talk radio, and so forth). Typically, a radio format is created through choices made regarding music or nonmusic style, scheduling, and announcer style.[118] It is estimated that approximately 30 different radio formats exist, suggesting that there are 30 strategic groups in this industry. The strategies within each of the 30 groups are similar, whereas the strategies across the total set of strategic groups are dissimilar. Thus, firms could increase their understanding of competition in the commercial radio industry by plotting companies' actions and responses in terms of important strategic dimensions.

Strategic groups have several implications. First, because firms within a group offer similar products to the same customers, the competitive rivalry among them can be intense. The more intense the rivalry, the greater the threat to each firm's profitability. Second, the strengths of the five industry forces (the threats posed by new entrants, the power of suppliers, the power of buyers, product substitutes, and the intensity of rivalry among competitors) differ across strategic groups. Third, the more similar the strategies across the strategic groups, the greater the likelihood of rivalry among the groups.

## Understanding Competitors and Their Intentions

Competitor analysis focuses on each company with which a firm directly competes. The five forces analysis examines forces that influence the strength of rivalry among competitors, but it does not address their intentions. Fuji and Kodak, Airbus and Boeing, and Sun Microsystems and Microsoft should be keenly interested in understanding each other's objectives, strategies, assumptions, and capabilities. Furthermore, the more intense the rivalry is in an industry, the greater the need to understand competitors. In a competitor analysis, the firm seeks to understand the following:

- What drives the competitor, as shown by its *future objectives*
- What the competitor is doing and can do, as revealed by its *current strategy and resources*
- What the competitor believes about the industry, as shown by its *assumptions*
- What the competitor's strengths and weaknesses are, as shown by its *capabilities*[119]

Information about these four components helps the firm prepare an anticipated *response profile* for each competitor (see Figure 3.3). Thus, the results of an effective competitor analysis help a firm understand, interpret, and predict its competitors' actions and responses.

Critical to an effective competitor analysis is gathering data and information that can help the firm understand its competitors' intentions and the strategic implications resulting from them.[120] **Competitor intelligence** is the set of data and information the firm gathers to better understand and better anticipate competitors' objectives, strategies, assumptions, and capabilities. In competitor analysis, the firm should gather intelligence not only about its competitors, but also regarding public policies in countries across the world. Intelligence about public policies "provides an early warning of threats and opportunities emerging from the global public policy environment, and analyzes how they will affect the achievement of the company's strategy."[121]

Through effective competitive and public policy intelligence, the firm gains the insights it needs to create a competitive advantage and to increase the quality of the strategic decisions it makes when determining how to compete against its rivals. Clare Hart, CEO of Factiva, a news and information service, believes that competitor intelligence helped her firm to move from the number three to the number two position in her industry. Additionally, she states that competitor intelligence will play an important role in her firm's efforts to reach its objective of becoming the top firm in the industry.[122]

Firms should follow generally accepted ethical practices in gathering competitor intelligence. Industry associations often develop such lists. Practices considered both legal and ethical include (1) obtaining publicly available information (such as court records, competitors' help-wanted advertisements, annual reports, financial reports of publicly held corporations, and Uniform Commercial Code filings), and (2) attending trade fairs and shows to obtain competitors' brochures, view their exhibits, and listen to discussions about their products.

In contrast, certain practices (including blackmail; trespassing; eavesdropping; and stealing drawings, samples, or documents) are widely viewed as unethical and often are

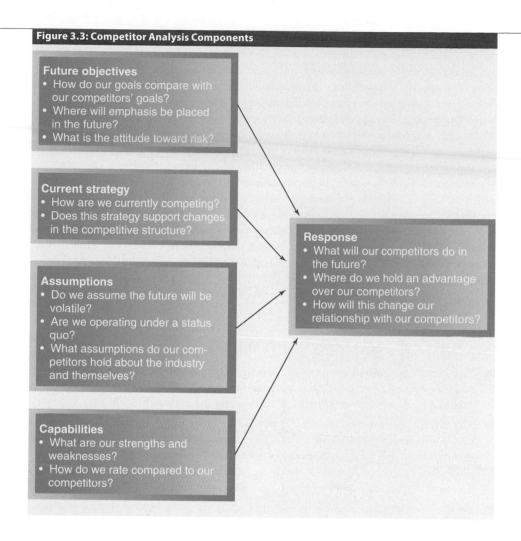

**Figure 3.3: Competitor Analysis Components**

**Future objectives**
- How do our goals compare with our competitors' goals?
- Where will emphasis be placed in the future?
- What is the attitude toward risk?

**Current strategy**
- How are we currently competing?
- Does this strategy support changes in the competitive structure?

**Assumptions**
- Do we assume the future will be volatile?
- Are we operating under a status quo?
- What assumptions do our competitors hold about the industry and themselves?

**Capabilities**
- What are our strengths and weaknesses?
- How do we rate compared to our competitors?

**Response**
- What will our competitors do in the future?
- Where do we hold an advantage over our competitors?
- How will this change our relationship with our competitors?

illegal.[123] For instance, an employee of Coca-Cola, working with two others, stole information about a new Coke product, complete with a sample, and offered to sell it to Pepsi. Pepsi immediately informed Coke of the breach, and the perpetrators were apprehended. According to Pepsi spokesman Dave DeCecco: "We were just doing whatever any responsible company would do. Despite the fierce competition in this industry, it should also be fair."[124]

To protect themselves from digital fraud or theft that occurs through competitors' breaking into their employees' PCs, some companies buy insurance to protect against PC hacking. Chubb's ForeFront plan, for example, offers up to $10 million coverage against digital fraud, theft, and extortion. Cigna's information asset protection division sells anti-hacker policies that cover up to 10 percent of a firm's revenues. The number of clients making claims seems to suggest the value of having one of these policies.[125]

Some competitor intelligence practices may be legal, but a firm must decide whether they are also ethical, given the image it desires as a corporate citizen. Especially with electronic transmissions, the line between legal and ethical practices can be difficult to determine. For example, a firm may develop Website addresses that are very similar to those of its competitors and thus occasionally receive e-mail transmissions that were intended for its competitors. According to legal experts, the legality of this "e-mail snagging" remains unclear.[126] Nonetheless, the practice is an example of the challenges companies face when deciding how to gather intelligence about competitors while simultaneously determining what to do to prevent competitors from learning too much about them. Open discussions of intelligence-gathering techniques can help a firm to ensure that people understand its convictions to follow ethical practices for gathering competitor intelligence. An appropriate guideline for competitor intelligence practices is to respect the principles of common morality and the right of competitors not to reveal certain information about their products, operations, and strategic intentions.[127]

Despite the importance of studying competitors, evidence suggests that only some firms use formal processes to collect and disseminate competitive intelligence. Other firms forget to analyze competitors' future objectives as they try to understand their current strategies, assumptions, and capabilities, which will yield incomplete insights about those competitors.[128]

# Summary

- The firm's external environment is challenging and complex. Because of the external environment's potential effect on performance, the firm must develop the skills required to identify opportunities and threats existing in that environment.

- The external environment has three major parts: (1) the general environment (elements in the broader society that affect industries and their firms), (2) the industry environment (factors that influence a firm, its competitive actions and responses, and the industry's profit potential), and (3) the competitor environment (each major competitor's future objectives, current strategies, assumptions, and capabilities).

- Analysis of the external environment has four steps: scanning, monitoring, forecasting, and assessing. Through environmental analysis, the firm identifies opportunities and threats.

- The general environment has six segments: demographic, economic, political/legal, sociocultural, technological, and global. For each segment, the firm wants to determine the strategic relevance of environmental changes and trends.

- Compared with the general environment, the industry environment has a more direct effect on the firm's strategic actions. The five forces model of competition includes the threat of entry, the power of suppliers, the power of buyers, product substitutes, and the intensity of rivalry among competitors. Complementors (sometimes labeled a sixth force) can also influence industry competition. Complementors are companies that sell complementary goods or services compatible with the focal firm's own product or service. By studying these forces, the firm finds a position in an industry where it can influence the forces to its benefit or where it can buffer itself from the power of the forces in order to increase its ability to earn above-average returns.

- Industries are populated with different strategic groups. A strategic group is a collection of firms that follow similar strategies and serve similar customers. Competitive rivalry is greater within a strategic group than it is among strategic groups.

- Competitor analysis informs the firm about the future objectives, current strategies, assumptions, and capabilities of the companies with which it competes directly.

- Different techniques are used to create competitor intelligence, defined as data, information, and knowledge that allow the firm to better understand its competitors and thereby predict their likely strategic and tactical actions. Firms should use only legal and ethical practices to gather intelligence. The Internet enhances firms' capabilities to gather insights about competitors and their strategic intentions.

# Ethics Questions

1. How can a firm use its "code of ethics" as it analyzes the external environment?
2. What ethical issues, if any, may be relevant to a firm's monitoring of its external environment? Does use of the Internet to monitor the environment lead to additional ethical issues? If so, what are they?
3. What is an ethical issue associated with each segment of a firm's general environment? Are firms across the globe doing enough to deal with this issue?
4. Why are ethical practices critical in the relationships between a firm and its suppliers?
5. In an intense rivalry, especially one that involves competition in the global marketplace, how can the firm gather competitor intelligence ethically while maintaining its competitiveness?
6. What do you believe determines whether an intelligence-gathering practice is or is not ethical? Do you see this changing as the world's economies become more interdependent? If so, why? Do you see this changing because of the Internet? If so, how?

# Notes

[1] D. G. Sirmon, M. A. Hitt, & R. D. Ireland, 2007, Managing firm resources in dynamic environments to create value: Looking inside the black box, *Academy of Management Review*, 32: 273–292; C. Williams & W. Mitchell, 2004, Focusing firm evolution: The impact of information infrastructure on market entry by U.S. telecommunications companies, 1984–1998, *Management Science*, 5: 1561–1575; J. Song, 2002, Firm capabilities and technology ladders: Sequential foreign direct investments of Japanese electronics firms in East Asia, *Strategic Management Journal*, 23: 191–210.

[2] J. A. Zuniga-Vicente & J. D. Vicente-Lorente, 2006, Strategic moves and organizational survival in turbulent environments: The case of Spanish banks (1983–97); J. Tan, 2005, Venturing in turbulent water: A historical perspective of economic reform and entrepreneurial transformation, *Journal of Business Venturing*, 20: 689–704; J. Chattopadhyay, W. H. Glick, & G. P. Huber, 2001, Organizational actions in response to threats and opportunities, *Academy of Management Journal*, 44: 937–955.

[3] J. Gimeno, R. E. Hoskisson, B. D. Beal, & W. P. Wan, 2005, Explaining the clustering of international expansion moves: A critical test in the U.S telecommunications industry, *Academy of Management Journal*, 48: 297–319; C. M. Grimm, H. Lee, & K. G.

Smith, 2005, *Strategy as Action: Competitive Dynamics and Competitive Advantages*, New York: Oxford University Press.

[4] S. Rangan & A. Drummond, 2004, Explaining outcomes in competition among foreign multinationals in a focal host market, *Strategic Management Journal*, 25: 285–293; J. M. Mezias, 2002, Identifying liabilities of foreignness and strategies to minimize their effects: The case of labor lawsuit judgments in the United States, *Strategic Management Journal*, 23: 229–244.

[5] K. G Smith, C. J. Collins, & K. D. Clark, 2005, Existing knowledge, knowledge creation capability, and the rate of new product introduction in high technology firms, *Academy of Management Journal*, 48: 346–357; R. M. Kanter, 2002, Strategy as improvisational theater, *MIT Sloan Management Review*, 43(2): 76–78.

[6] M. A. Hitt, J. E. Ricart, I. Costa, & R. D. Nixon, 1998, The new frontier, in M. A. Hitt, J. E. Ricart, I. Costa, & R. D. Nixon (eds.), *Managing Strategically in an Interconnected World*, Chichester, UK: Wiley, 1–12.

[7] M. Song, C. Droge, S. Hanvanich, & R. Calantone, 2005, Marketing and technology resource complementarity: An analysis of their interaction effect in two environmental contexts, *Strategic Management Journal*, 26: 259–276; D. M. De Carolis, 2003, Competencies and imitability in the pharmaceutical

industry: An analysis of their relationship with firm performance, *Journal of Management*, 29: 27–50.

8   L. Fahey, 1999, *Competitors*, New York: Wiley; B. A. Walters & R. L. Priem, 1999, Business strategy and CEO intelligence acquisition, *Competitive Intelligence Review*, 10(2): 15–22.

9   M. Song, R. J. Calantone, & C. Anthony, 2002, Competitive forces and strategic choice decisions: An experimental investigation in the United States and Japan, *Strategic Management Journal*, 23: 969–978; R. D. Ireland & M. A. Hitt, 1999, Achieving and maintaining value creation in the 21st century: The role of strategic leadership, *Academy of Management Executive*, 13(1): 43–57; M. A. Hitt, B. W. Keats, & S. M. DeMarie, 1998, Navigating in the new competitive landscape: Building strategic flexibility and competitive advantage in the 21st century, *Academy of Management Executive*, 12(4): 22–42.

10  L. Valikangas & M. Gibbert, 2005, Boundary-setting strategies for escaping innovation traps, *MIT Sloan Management Review*, 46(3): 58–65; Q. Nguyen & H. Mintzberg, 2003, The rhythm of change, *MIT Sloan Management Review*, 44(4): 79–84.

11  G. Smith, 2006, In Mexico, banco Wal-Mart, *Business Week*, November 20, 80.

12  P. Wonacott, 2006, IBM seeks bigger footprint in India, *Wall Street Journal*, June 7, B2.

13  R. Karlgaard, 1999, Digital rules: Technology and the new economy, *Forbes*, May 17, 43.

14  V. Prior, 1999, The language of competitive intelligence: Part four, *Competitive Intelligence Review*, 10(1): 84–87.

15  D. Machalba, 2003, Diesel prices force small truckers off the road, *Wall Street Journal*, March 11, B6.

16  G. Young, 1999, "Strategic value analysis" for competitive advantage, *Competitive Intelligence Review*, 10(2): 52–64.

17  M. A. Hitt, R. D. Ireland, S. M. Camp, & D. L. Sexton, 2001, Strategic entrepreneurship: Entrepreneurial strategies for wealth creation, *Strategic Management Journal*, 22(summer special issue): 479–491.

18  L. Rosenkopf & A. Nerkar, 2001, Beyond local search: Boundary-spanning exploration, and impact in the optical disk industry, *Strategic Management Journal*, 22: 287–306.

19  K. M. Patton & T. M. McKenna, 2005, Scanning for competitive intelligence, *Competitive Intelligence Magazine*, 8(2): 24–26; D. F. Kuratko, R. D. Ireland, & J. S. Hornsby, 2001, Improving firm performance through entrepreneurial actions: Acordia's corporate entrepreneurship strategy, *Academy of Management Executive*, 15(4): 60–71.

20  K. M. Eisenhardt, 2002, Has strategy changed? *MIT Sloan Management Review*, 43(2): 88–91; I. Goll & A. M. A. Rasheed, 1997, Rational decision-making and firm performance: The moderating role of environment, *Strategic Management Journal*, 18: 583–591.

21  J. R. Hough & M. A. White, 2004, Scanning actions and environmental dynamism: Gathering information for strategic decision making, *Management Decision*, 42: 781–793; V. K. Garg, B. A. Walters, & R. L. Priem, 2003, Chief executive scanning emphases, environmental dynamism, and manufacturing firm performance, *Strategic Management Journal*, 24: 725–744.

22  R. Donkin, 1999, Too young to retire, *Financial Times*, July 2, 9.

23  C. Wei & Y. Lee, 2004, Event detection from online news documents for supporting environmental scanning, *Decision Support Systems*, 36: 385–401.

24  R. Goldsborough, 2005, The benefits and fears of cookie technology, *Tech Directions*, May, 9.

25  Fahey, *Competitors*, 71–73.

26  P. Yip, 1999, The road to wealth, *Dallas Morning News*, August 2, D1, D3.

27  F. Dahlsten, 2003, Avoiding the customer satisfaction rut, *MIT Sloan Management Review*, 44(4): 73–77; Y. Luo & S. H. Park, 2001, Strategic alignment and performance of market-seeking MNCs in China, *Strategic Management Journal*, 22: 141–155.

28  K. Buysse & A. Verbeke, 2003, Proactive strategies: A stakeholder management perspective, *Strategic Management Journal*, 24: 453–470; I. M. Jawahar & G. L. McLaughlin, 2001, Toward a prescriptive stakeholder theory: An organizational life cycle approach, *Academy of Management Review*, 26: 397–414.

29  M. L. Perry, S. Sengupta, & R. Krapfel, 2004, Effectiveness of horizontal strategic alliances in technologically uncertain environments: Are trust and commitment enough? *Journal of Business Research*, 9: 951–956; M. Song & M. M. Montoya-Weiss, 2001, The effect of perceived technological uncertainty on Japanese new product development, *Academy of Management Journal*, 44: 61–80.

30  M. H. Zack, 2003, Rethinking the knowledge-based organization, *MIT Sloan Management Review*, 44(4): 67–71; H. Yli-Renko, E. Autio, & H. J. Sapienza, 2001, Social capital, knowledge acquisition, and knowledge exploitation in young technologically-based firms, *Strategic Management Journal*, 22(summer special issue): 587–613.

31  Fahey, *Competitors*.

32  2006, Texas Instruments Inc.: Earnings forecast is increased as sales forecast is narrowed, *Wall Street Journal*, March 7, D7.

33  2006, TI cuts forecast on lower-than-expected chip revenue, Reuters, http://news.com.com, December 11.

34  K. M. Sutcliffe & K. Weber, 2003, The high cost of accurate knowledge, *Harvard Business Review*, 81(5): 74–82.

35  E. Brown, 2005, Coming soon to a tiny screen near you, *Forbes*, May 23, 64–78.

36  L. Fahey & V. K. Narayanan, 1986, *Macroenvironmental Analysis for Strategic Management*, St. Paul, MN: West Publishing Co., 58.

37  2004, World population prospects: 2004 revision, www.un.org/esa/population/unpop.htm; D. Fishburn, 1999, The world in 1999, *The Economist Publications*, 9; 1999, Six billion . . . and counting, *Time*, October 4, 16.

38  J. F. Coates, J. B. Mahaffie, & A. Hines, 1997, *2025: Scenarios of US and Global Society Reshaped by Science and Technology*, Greensboro, NC: Oakhill.

39  2006, U.S. and world population clocks, U.S. Census Bureau, http://www.census.gov/main/www/popclock.html, December 28.

40  2001, Fewer seniors in the 1990s, *Business Week*, May 28, 30.

41  P. F. Drucker, 2002, They're not employees, they're people, *Harvard Business Review*, 80(2): 70–77.

42  B. Ritholz, 2006, Wal-Mart's prescription drug plan could impact entire U.S. health care system, Seeking Alpha, http://retail.seekingalpha.com/article/17334, December 28.

43  D. Stipp, 1999, Hell no, we won't go! *Fortune*, July 19, 102–108; G. Colvin, 1997, How to beat the boomer rush, *Fortune*, August 18, 59–63.

[44] S. Moffett, 2005, Fast-aging Japan keeps its elders on the job longer, *Wall Street Journal*, June 15, A1, A8.

[45] C. Bryan, 2005, The south owes its growth to 20th-century invention, *Richmond Times-Dispatch*, July 24, E6.

[46] J. Ordonez, 2005, Speak English. Live Latin, *Newsweek*, May 30, 30.

[47] 1999, U.S. Department of Labor, Demographic change and the future workforce, *Futurework*, November 8, http://www.dol.gov.

[48] G. Dessler, 1999, How to earn your employees' commitment, *Academy of Management Executive*, 13(2): 58–67; S. Finkelstein & D. C. Hambrick, 1996, *Strategic Leadership: Top Executives and Their Effect on Organizations*, Minneapolis, MN: West Publishing Co.

[49] L. H. Pelled, K. M. Eisenhardt, & K. R. Xin, 1999, Exploring the black box: An analysis of work group diversity, conflict, and performance, *Administrative Science Quarterly*, 44: 1–28.

[50] E. S. Rubenstein, 1999, Inequality, *Forbes*, November 1, 158–160.

[51] D. Roberts, 2006, China's online ad boom, *Business Week*, May 15, 46.

[52] Fahey & Narayanan, *Macroenvironmental Analysis*, 105.

[53] H. Berument, N. B. Ceylan, & H. Olgun, 2007, Inflation uncertainty and interest rates: Is the Fisher relation universal? *Applied Economics*, 39: 53–73.

[54] R. McKinnon, 2006, The worth of the dollar, *Wall Street Journal*, December 13, A18.

[55] G. Chon, 2006, Kia's new U.S. plant advances sales push in North America, *Wall Street Journal*, October 23, B2; A. Chozick, 2006, Toyota lifts profit outlook, *Wall Street Journal*, November 8, A3.

[56] S. Panchal, 2006, India Inc eyes the world, *India Abroad*, November 10, A28.

[57] P. Garnham, 2006, Dollar's rise loses momentum, *Financial Times*, December 22, 34.

[58] 2006, Japan to toughen regulations on foreign acquisitions, *Jiji Press English News Service*, December 19, 1.

[59] J.-P. Bonardi, A. J. Hillman, & G. D. Keim, 2005, The attractiveness of political markets: Implications for firm strategy, *Academy of Management Review*, 30: 397–413; G. Keim, 2001, Business and public policy: Competing in the political marketplace, in M. A. Hitt, R. E. Freeman, & J. S. Harrison (eds.), *Handbook of Strategic Management*, Oxford, UK: Blackwell Publishers, 583–601.

[60] M. Jacoby, 2006, EU hits Microsoft with $358.3 million penalty, *Wall Street Journal*, July 13, A3.

[61] M. D. Lord, 2003, Constituency building as the foundation for corporate political strategy, *Academy of Management Executive*, 17(1): 112–124; D. A. Schuler, K. Rehbein, & R. D. Cramer, 2003, Pursuing strategic advantage through political means: A multivariate approach, *Academy of Management Journal*, 45: 659–672; A. J. Hillman & M. A. Hitt, 1999, Corporate political strategy formulation: A model of approach, participation, and strategy decisions, *Academy of Management Review*, 24: 825–842.

[62] N. Zamiska, 2006, Beijing court backs patent protection for Viagra, *Wall Street Journal*, June 3, A3.

[63] M. Carson, 1998, *Global Competitiveness Quarterly*, March 9, 1.

[64] 2006, NAFTA trade soaring, *Traffic World*, November 27, 1.

[65] 2003, U.S. spends the most on healthcare but dollars do not equal health, Medica Portal, http://www.medica.de; J. Macintyre, 1999, Figuratively speaking, *Across the Board*, May 11, 1.

[66] C. Debaise, 2005, U.S. workers start early on retirement savings, *Wall Street Journal*, January 20, D2.

[67] B. Beck, 1999, The world in 1999: Executive, thy name is woman, *Economist*, November 6, 89; P. Thomas, 1995, Success at a huge personal cost: Comparing women around the world, *Wall Street Journal*, July 26, B1.

[68] 2005, U.S Department of Labor, Bureau of Labor Statistics data, http://www.bls.gov, April; 2004, Center for Women's Business Research, http://www.womensbusinessresearch.org, May.

[69] R. Taylor, 1999, Pay gap between the sexes widest in W. Europe, *Financial Times*, June 29, 9.

[70] C. A. Bartlett & S. Ghoshal, 2002, Building competitive advantage through people, *MIT Sloan Management Review*, 43(2): 33–41.

[71] T. Fleming, 2003, Benefits of taking the superhighway to work, *Canadian HR Reporter*, 16(11): G7.

[72] M. J. McCarthy, 2004, New outposts: Granbury, Texas, isn't a rural town: it's a "micropolis"; Census bureau adopts term for main street America, and marketers take note; beans, ribs and Starbucks, *Wall Street Journal*, June 3, A1.

[73] A. L. Porter & S. W. Cunningham, 2004, *Tech Mining: Exploiting New Technologies for Competitive Advantage*, Hoboken, NJ: Wiley.

[74] C. W. L. Hill & F. T. Rothaermel, 2003, The performance of incumbent firms in the face of radical technological innovation, *Academy of Management Review*, 28: 257–274; A. Afuah, 2002, Mapping technological capabilities into product markets and competitive advantage: The case of cholesterol drugs, *Strategic Management Journal*, 23: 171–179.

[75] N. Wingfield, 2003, Anytime, anywhere: The number of Wi-Fi spots is set to explode, bringing the wireless technology to the rest of us, *Wall Street Journal*, March 31, R6, R12.

[76] A. Andal-Ancion, P. A. Cartwright, & G. S. Yip, 2003, The digital transformation of traditional businesses, *MIT Sloan Management Review*, 44(4): 34–41; M. A. Hitt, R. D. Ireland, & H. Lee, 2000, Technological learning, knowledge management, firm growth and performance, *Journal of Technology and Engineering Management*, 17: 231–246.

[77] M. A. Hitt, R. M. Holmes, T. Miller, & M. P. Salmador, 2006, Modeling country institutional profiles: The dimensions and dynamics of institutional environments, paper presented at Strategic Management Society, Vienna, Austria (October); W. P. Wan, 2005, Country resource environments, firm capabilities, and corporate diversification strategies, *Journal of Management Studies*, 42: 161–182; M. Wright, I. Filatotchev, R. E. Hoskisson, & M. W. Peng, 2005, Strategy research in emerging economies: Challenging the conventional wisdom, *Journal of Management Studies*, 42: 1–30; W. P. Wan & R. E. Hoskisson, 2003, Home country environments, corporate diversification strategies and firm performance, *Academy of Management Journal*, 46: 27–45.

[78] F. Vermeulen & H. Barkema, 2002, Pace, rhythm, and scope: Process dependence in building a multinational corporation, *Strategic Management Journal*, 23: 637–653.

[79] J. Lu & P. Beamish, 2004, International diversification and firm performance: The S-curve hypothesis, *Academy*

of *Management Journal*, 47: 598–609; L. Tihanyi, R. A. Johnson, R. E. Hoskisson, & M. A. Hitt, 2003, Institutional ownership differences, and international diversification: The effects of boards of directors and technological opportunity, *Academy of Management Journal*, 46: 195–211.

80 F. Balfour, 2006, Dipping a toe in the risk pool, *Business Week*, December 25, 83.

81 K. Kranhold, 2006, GE chief sets an $8 billion goal for sales in India in four years, *Wall Street Journal*, May 30, A2; P. Wonacott & P. R. Venkat, India's economic growth ratchets up to 9.3%, *Wall Street Journal*, June 1, A6; P. Wonacott, IBM seeks bigger footprint in India, *Wall Street Journal*, June 7, B2.

82 R. D. Ireland, M. A. Hitt, S. M. Camp, & D. L. Sexton, 2001, Integrating entrepreneurship and strategic management actions to create firm wealth, *Academy of Management Executive*, 15(1): 49–63.

83 M. Subramaniam & N. Venkatraman, 2001, Determinants of transnational new product development capability: Testing the influence of transferring and deploying tacit overseas knowledge, *Strategic Management Journal*, 22: 359–378; P. J. Lane, J. E. Salk, & M. A. Lyles, 2001, Absorptive capacity, learning and performance in international joint ventures, *Strategic Management Journal*, 22: 1139–1161.

84 T. Burt, 2001, DaimlerChrysler in talks with Kuwaiti investors, *Financial Times*, http://www.ft.com, February 11.

85 Vermeulen & Barkema, Pace, rhythm, and scope.

86 M. Fong, 2005, Unphased by barriers, retailers flock to China for clothes, *Wall Street Journal*, May 27, B1, B2.

87 Wonacott & Venkat, India's economic growth.

88 J. Fuerbringer & R. W. Stevenson, 2001, No bailout is planned for Argentina, *New York Times*, http://www.nytimes.com, July 14; K. L. Newman, 2000, Organizational transformation during institutional upheaval, *Academy of Management Review*, 25: 602–619.

89 M. A. O'Grady, 2005, Americas: After the haircut, Argentina readies the shave, *Wall Street Journal*, May 27, A13.

90 S. H. Park & Y. Luo, 2001, Guanxi and organizational dynamics: Organizational networking in Chinese firms, *Strategic Management Journal*, 22: 455–477; M. A. Hitt, M. T. Dacin, B. B. Tyler, & D. Park, 1997, Understanding the differences in Korean and U.S. executives' strategic orientations, *Strategic Management Journal*, 18: 159–167.

91 M. A. Hitt, D. Ahlstrom, M. T. Dacin, E. Levitas, & L. Svobodina, 2004, The institutional effects on strategic alliance partner selection: China versus Russia, *Organization Science*, 15: 173–185.

92 M. A. Carpenter & J. W. Fredrickson, 2001, Top management teams, global strategic posture and the moderating role of uncertainty, *Academy of Management Journal*, 44: 533–545.

93 V. K. Narayanan & L. Fahey, 2005, The relevance of the institutional underpinnings of Porter's five forces framework to emerging economies: An epistemological analysis, *Journal of Management Studies*, 42: 207–223; N. Argyres & A. M. McGahan, 2002, An interview with Michael Porter, *Academy of Management Executive*, 16(2): 43–52; Y. E. Spanos & S. Lioukas, 2001, An examination into the causal logic of rent generation: Contrasting Porter's competitive strategy framework and

the resource-based perspective, *Strategic Management Journal*, 22: 907–934.

94 J. C. Short, D. J. Ketchen Jr., T. B. Palmer, & G. T. M. Hult, 2007, Firm, strategic group and industry influences on performance, *Strategic Management Journal*, 28: 147–167.

95 S. Zaheer & A. Zaheer, 2001, Market microstructure in a global b2b network, *Strategic Management Journal*, 22: 859–873.

96 Hitt, Ricart, Costa, & Nixon, The new frontier.

97 Y. Pan & P. S. K. Chi, 1999, Financial performance and survival of multinational corporations in China, *Strategic Management Journal*, 20: 359–374; G. R. Brooks, 1995, Defining market boundaries, *Strategic Management Journal*, 16: 535–549.

98 J. Shamsie, 2003, The context of dominance: An industry-driven framework for exploiting reputation, *Strategic Management Journal*, 24: 199–215; K. C. Robinson & P. P. McDougall, 2001, Entry barriers and new venture performance: A comparison of universal and contingency approaches, *Strategic Management Journal*, 22(summer special issue): 659–685.

99 R. Makadok, 1999, Interfirm differences in scale economies and the evolution of market shares, *Strategic Management Journal*, 20: 935–952.

100 B. J. Pine II, 2004, Mass customization: The new imperative, *Strategic Direction*, January, 2–3; R. Wise & P. Baumgartner, 1999, Go downstream: The new profit imperative in manufacturing, *Harvard Business Review*, 77(5): 133–141.

101 G. Walker, T. L. Madsen, & G. Carini, 2002, How does institutional change affect heterogeneity among firms? *Strategic Management Journal*, 23: 89–104.

102 A. Reinhardt, 2005, The man who said no to Microsoft, *Business Week*, May 31, 49; 2002, The long shadow of big blue, *Economist*, November 9, 63–64.

103 C. Dawson, 2001, Machete time: In a cost-cutting war with Nissan, Toyota leans on suppliers, *Business Week*, April 9, 42–43.

104 J. Angwin & J. T. Haliinan, 2005, Newspaper circulation continues to decline, forcing tough decisions, *Wall Street Journal*, May 2, A1, A6.

105 S. Dutta, O. Narasimhan, & S. Rajiv, 2005, Conceptualizing and measuring capabilities: Methodology and empirical application, *Strategic Management Journal*, 26: 277–285; T. Noda & D. J. Collies, 2001, The evolution of intraindustry firm heterogeneity: Insights from a process study, *Academy of Management Journal*, 44: 897–925.

106 De Carolis, Competencies and imitability; D. L. Deephouse, 1999, To be different, or to be the same? It's a question (and theory) of strategic balance, *Strategic Management Journal*, 20: 147–166.

107 L. Canina, C. A. Enz, & J. S. Harrison, 2005. Agglomeration effects and strategic orientations: Evidence from the U.S. lodging industry. *Academy of Management Journal*, 48: 565–581; W. Chung & A. Kalnins, 2001, Agglomeration effects and performance: Test of the Texas lodging industry, *Strategic Management Journal*, 22: 969–988.

108 A. Afuah, 2000, How much do your competitors' capabilities matter in the face of technological change? *Strategic Management Journal*, 21: 387–404; A. Brandenburger & B. Nalebuff, 1996, *Co-opetition*, New York: Currency Doubleday.

[109] 2006, Masco cuts earnings forecasts, citing decline in housing starts, *Furniture Today*, http://furnituretoday .com/article/CA6373894.html, September 20.

[110] K. D. Brouthers, L. E. Brouthers, & S. Werner, 2003, Transaction cost enhanced entry mode choices and firm performance, *Strategic Management Journal*, 24: 1239–1248; W. Kuemmerle, 2001, Home base and knowledge management in international ventures, *Journal of Business Venturing*, 17: 99–122.

[111] M. E. Porter, 1980, *Competitive Strategy*, New York: The Free Press.

[112] M. S. Hunt, 1972, Competition in the major home appliance industry, 1960–1970, doctoral dissertation, Harvard University, Cambridge, MA; Porter, *Competitive Strategy*, 129.

[113] H. R. Greve, 1999, Managerial cognition and the mimetic adoption of market positions: What you see is what you do, *Strategic Management Journal*, 19: 967–988.

[114] M. W. Peng, J. Tan, & T. W. Tong, 2004, Ownership types and strategic groups in an emerging economy, *Journal of Management Studies*, 41: 1105–1129; R. K. Reger & A. S. Huff, 1993, Strategic groups: A cognitive perspective, *Strategic Management Journal*, 14: 103–123.

[115] M. Peteraf & M. Shanely, 1997, Getting to know you: A theory of strategic group identity, *Strategic Management Journal*, 18(special issue): 165–186.

[116] A. Nair & S. Kotha, 2001, Does group membership matter? Evidence from the Japanese steel industry, *Strategic Management Journal*, 22: 221–235.

[117] J. A. Zuniga-Vicente, J. M. de la Fuente Sabate, & I. S. Gonzalez, 2004, Dynamics of the strategic group membership-performance linkage in rapidly changing environments, *Journal of Business Research*, 57: 1378–1390; J. D. Osborne, C. I. Stubbart, & A. Ramaprasad, 2001, Strategic groups and competitive enactment: A study of dynamic relationships between mental models and performance, *Strategic Management Journal*, 22: 435–454.

[118] Greve, Managerial cognition.

[119] Porter, *Competitive Strategy*, 49.

[120] P. M. Norman, R. D. Ireland, K. W. Artz, & M. A. Hitt, 2000, Acquiring and using competitive intelligence in entrepreneurial teams, paper presented at the Academy of Management, Toronto, Canada.

[121] C. S. Fleisher, 1999, Public policy competitive intelligence, *Competitive Intelligence Review*, 10(2): 24.

[122] 2001, Fuld & Co., CEO interview: Clare Hart, President and CEO, Factiva from Dow Jones, http://www .dowjones.com, April 4.

[123] A. Crane, 2005, In the company of spies: When competitive intelligence gathering becomes industrial espionage, *Business Horizons*, 48(3): 233–240.

[124] C. Harlan, 2006, Trade secret plot pulls Coke, Pepsi together, *Pittsburgh Post-Gazette*, http://www.post-gazette.com/pg/06188/704045-28.stm, July 7.

[125] V. Drucker, 1999, Is your computer a sitting duck during a deal? *Mergers & Acquisitions*, July/August, 25–28; J. Hodges, 1999, Insuring your PC against hackers, *Fortune*, May 24, 280.

[126] M. Moss, 1999, Inside the game of e-mail hijacking, *Wall Street Journal*, November 9, B1, B4.

[127] J. H. Hallaq & K. Steinhorst, 1994, Business intelligence methods: How ethical? *Journal of Business Ethics*, 13: 787–794.

[128] L. Fahey, 1999, Competitor scenarios: Projecting a rival's marketplace strategy, *Competitive Intelligence Review*, 10(2): 65–85.

# CHAPTER 4

# The Internal Organization: Resources, Capabilities, and Core Competencies

## KNOWLEDGE OBJECTIVES

*Studying this chapter should provide you with the strategic management knowledge needed to:*

1. Explain the need for firms to study and understand their internal organization.
2. Define value creation and discuss its importance.
3. Describe the differences between tangible and intangible resources.
4. Define capabilities and discuss how they are developed.
5. Describe four criteria used to determine whether resources and capabilities are core competencies.
6. Explain how value chain analysis is used to identify and evaluate resources and capabilities.
7. Define outsourcing and discuss the reasons for its use.
8. Discuss the importance of preventing core competencies from becoming core rigidities.
9. Explain several methods to measure firm performance and how firms can use multiple measures to balance stakeholder interests and enhance value creation.

---

As discussed in Chapter 1, rapidly developing technology and increasing globalization make it increasingly difficult for firms to develop a competitive advantage that can be sustained for a long time.[1] For instance, an organization may develop a new process that cuts production costs 10 percent, only to find out that a competitor has developed a new technology that is superior to the newly developed process. Or a firm may create a new product with some very attractive new features, but its novelty is quickly eclipsed by a new product that comes from a firm in a country halfway around the world. These are not unusual circumstances, but rather a reflection of the reality that strategic decision makers face today.[2] As a result, competitive advantage tends to be more closely associated with intangible resources that are hard to imitate rather than any one product or technology. For instance, although any particular product or service may be easy to imitate or surpass, the ability to constantly produce cutting-edge products or services is more difficult for competitors to address. Nokia attributes much of its success to "the Nokia Way," which involves an emphasis on continuous learning and a flat, networked organization that allows rapid decision making. New ideas are encouraged and embraced. About one-third of Nokia's workforce is devoted to research and development.[3]

Firm resources provide a foundation for creating strategies. Possession of a unique and valuable bundle of resources puts a firm in a strong position to develop competitive advantage, leading to the creation of wealth for shareholders and other stakeholders.[4] The strategic management process helps a firm successfully identify and use sources of competitive advantage over time.[5] This chapter will show how firms create value and earn high returns when they effectively leverage their unique core competencies to take advantage of opportunities in the external environment.

Over time, the benefits of any firm's value-creating strategy can be duplicated by its competitors. In other words, all competitive advantages have a limited life.[6] The question of duplication is not *if* it will happen, but *when*. In general, the sustainability of a competitive advantage is a function of three factors: (1) the rate of core competence obsolescence caused by environmental changes, (2) the availability of substitutes for the core competence, and (3) the imitability of the core competence.[7] The challenge in all firms is to effectively manage current core competencies while simultaneously developing new ones.[8] Michael Dell, CEO and chairman of Dell Inc., once said: "No [competitive] advantage and no success is ever permanent. The winners are those who keep moving. The only constant in our business is that everything is changing. We have to be ahead of the game."[9] His words have proved prophetic, as Dell is now struggling to retake the top spot in PC sales from rival Hewlett-Packard.[10]

In Chapter 3, we examined general, industry, and competitor environments. Armed with knowledge about the realities and conditions of these environments, firms have a better understanding of marketplace opportunities and the goods or services through which they can be pursued. In this chapter, we focus on the firm. Through an analysis of its internal organization, a firm determines what it *can do*—that is, the actions permitted by its unique resources, capabilities, and core competencies. As discussed in Chapter 1, core competencies are a firm's source of competitive advantage. The magnitude of that competitive advantage is a function primarily of the uniqueness of the firm's core competencies compared with those of its competitors.[11] Matching what a firm *can do* with what it *might do* (a function of opportunities and threats in the external environment) allows the firm to develop strategic intent, pursue its strategic mission, and select and implement its strategies. Figure 4.1 shows outcomes resulting from internal and external environmental analyses.

We examine several topics in this chapter, beginning with the importance and challenge of studying the firm's internal organization. We then discuss the roles of resources, capabilities, and core competencies in developing sustainable competitive advantage. Included in this discussion are the techniques firms can use to identify and evaluate resources and capabilities and the criteria for selecting core competencies from among them. Resources, capabilities, and core competencies are not inherently valuable, but they create value when the firm can use them to perform certain activities that result in a competitive advantage. Accordingly, we also discuss the value chain concept and examine four criteria for evaluating core competences that establish competitive advantage.[12] The primary objective of both internal resource analysis and evaluation of the value chain is to create competitive advantage leading to higher firm performance. The final section of this chapter examines the dimensions of firm performance from financial and stakeholder perspectives. Measuring firm performance is an essential part of internal analysis.

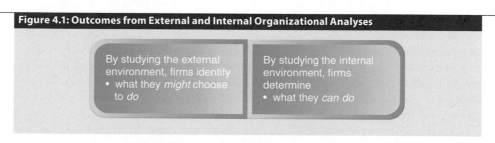

**Figure 4.1: Outcomes from External and Internal Organizational Analyses**

By studying the external environment, firms identify
- what they *might* choose to do

By studying the internal environment, firms determine
- what they *can do*

# Internal Analysis and Value Creation

The decisions managers make in terms of the firm's resources, capabilities, and core competencies significantly influence its performance.[13] Making these decisions—identifying, developing, deploying, and protecting resources, capabilities, and core competencies—may appear to be relatively easy. In fact, however, this task is as challenging and difficult as any other with which managers are involved; moreover, it is increasingly internationalized and linked with the firm's success.[14] The pressure managers face to pursue only those strategies that help the firm meet the quarterly earning numbers expected by market analysts can reduce their abilities to make objective, accurate assessments of the long-term potential of firm resources.[15] Recognizing its core competencies is essential before the firm can make important strategic decisions, including those to enter or exit markets, invest in new technologies, build new or additional manufacturing capacity, or form strategic partnerships.[16]

The challenge and difficulty of making effective decisions are implied by preliminary evidence suggesting that one-half of organizational decisions fail.[17] Sometimes, mistakes are made as the firm analyzes its internal organization. Managers might, for example, choose to emphasize resources and capabilities that do not create a competitive advantage. When a mistake occurs, decision makers must have the confidence to admit it and take corrective actions.[18] A firm can still grow through well-intended errors—the learning generated by making and correcting mistakes can be important to the creation of new competitive advantages.[19] Moreover, firms can learn from the failure resulting from a mistake; that is, they can learn what *not* to do when seeking competitive advantage.[20]

## Conditions Influencing Internal Analysis

In the global economy, traditional factors—such as labor costs, access to financial resources and raw materials, and protected or regulated markets—continue to be sources of competitive advantage for firms in some countries, but to a lesser degree than was previously the case.[21] An important reason for this decline is that the advantages created by these sources can be duplicated through an international strategy (see Chapter 10). For instance, Japanese auto manufacturers have overcome the relative advantages that U.S. auto manufacturers used to enjoy, such as reduced transportation and importing costs, by building automobile assembly operations in the United States. The relatively free flow of resources throughout the global economy has facilitated this trend. Consequently, those analyzing the firm's internal environment should adopt a **global mind-set,** defined as the ability to study an internal environment in ways that do not depend on the assumptions of a single country, culture, or context.[22]

Significant changes in the value-creating potential of a firm's resources and capabilities can occur in a rapidly changing global economy.[23] Because these changes affect a company's power and social structure, inertia or resistance to change may surface. Even though these reactions may happen, decision makers should not deny the changes needed to assure the firm's value creation. Denial is an unconscious coping mechanism used to block out and prevent initiation of painful changes.[24] Because some people have a strong tendency to resist the changes needed to cope with intensely competitive environments, involving a range of individuals and groups in the decision-making process is important when making changes in a firm's value-creating abilities.[25] (See Chapter 2 for the importance of heterogeneous top management teams.)

Few firms can consistently make the most effective strategic decisions unless they can change rapidly. A key challenge to developing the ability to change rapidly is fostering an organizational setting in which experimentation and learning are expected and pro-moted.[26] The demands of 21st-century competition require top-level managers to rethink earlier concepts of the firm and competition. For example, Polaroid Corporation sought to accommodate a significant technological shift by changing from analog to digital imaging. Polaroid's managers needed to gain a different understanding of their competitive world and the firm's existing capabilities as well as the new capabilities that were needed. The firm had to overcome the trajectory of its analog imaging capabilities so it could focus on developing and using capabilities required by digital imaging.[27] The Polaroid story clearly illustrates the importance of managers seeking to direct the firm through a completely new competitive environment. However, as mentioned previously, Polaroid's management was not successful in that endeavor.[28]

To facilitate the development and use of core competencies, managers must have cour-age, self-confidence, integrity, the capacity to deal with uncertainty and complexity, and a willingness to hold people accountable for their work and to be held accountable them-selves. Thus, difficult managerial decisions concerning resources, capabilities, and core competencies are characterized by three conditions: uncertainty, complexity, and intraor-ganizational conflicts (see Figure 4.2).[29]

Managers face *uncertainty* from a number of sources, including those of new proprietary technologies, rapid changes in economic and political trends, transformations in societal values, and shifts in customer demands.[30] *Complexity* results from the dependence firms have on one another and on the sheer number of factors that influence firm performance. Furthermore, environmental uncertainty increases the complexity and range of issues the firm needs to examine when studying its internal organization. Biases about how to cope with uncertainty affect decisions about the resources and capabilities that will become the foundation of the firm's competitive advantage. Chapter 2 examined several biases that tend to influence strategic decisions. Finally, *intraorganizational conflicts* often surface when deci-sions are made about which core competencies to nurture as well as how to nurture them.

A critical characteristic of effective resource analysis is the perspective that firms are bundles of heterogeneous resources, capabilities, and core competencies that can be used to

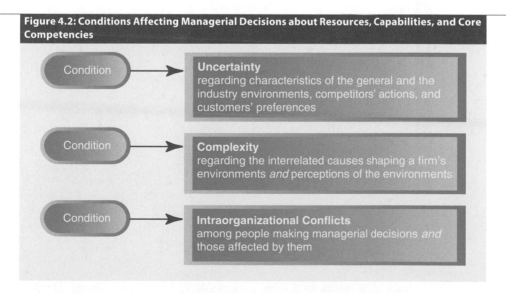

**Figure 4.2: Conditions Affecting Managerial Decisions about Resources, Capabilities, and Core Competencies**

Condition → **Uncertainty** regarding characteristics of the general and the industry environments, competitors' actions, and customers' preferences

Condition → **Complexity** regarding the interrelated causes shaping a firm's environments *and* perceptions of the environments

Condition → **Intraorganizational Conflicts** among people making managerial decisions *and* those affected by them

**Figure 4.3: Components of Internal Analysis Leading to Competitive Advantage and Value Creation**

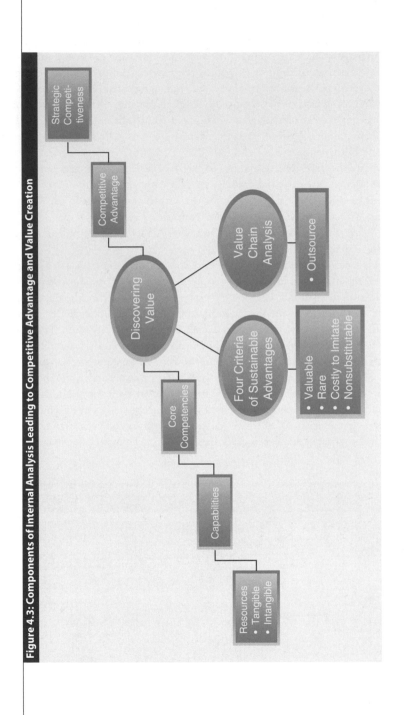

create an exclusive market position.[31] This perspective suggests that individual firms possess at least some resources and capabilities that other companies do not—at least not in the same combination. Resources are the source of capabilities, some of which lead to the development of a firm's core competencies.[32] Figure 4.3 illustrates the relationships among resources, capabilities, and core competencies and shows how firms use the four criteria of sustainable competitive advantage and value chain analysis to identify sources of value and ultimately competitive advantage and strategic competitiveness. Figure 4.3 provides an outline of topics for much of the rest of this chapter.

The mind-set needed in the global economy requires decision makers to define their firm's strategy in terms of a *unique competitive position*, rather than strictly in terms of operational effectiveness. For instance, Michael Porter argues that quests for productivity, quality, and speed from using a number of management techniques—total quality management (TQM), benchmarking, time-based competition, and reengineering—have resulted in operational efficiency, but have not resulted in strong sustainable strategies.[33] As discussed in Chapter 1, value creation results when the firm satisfies the operational efficiency demands of its external environment while simultaneously using its own unique capabilities to establish a viable strategic position.

## Creating Value

By exploiting core competencies and meeting the demanding standards of global competition, firms create value for customers.[34] **Value** is measured by a product's performance characteristics and by its attributes for which customers are willing to pay.[35] Firms must provide value to customers that is superior to the value competitors provide in order to create a competitive advantage. For instance, sales are soaring for Eclipse Aviation's new five-seater very light jet (VLJ), a product targeted at a segment of the market that typically cannot afford more expensive jets.[36] Nucor Steel provides basic steel products at lower cost than its competitors. A typical Lamborghini sports car, at well over $100,000, may not seem like it offers a value proposition to its customers, but the benefits of owning such a car outweigh the costs for some consumers, and sales have been steadily increasing.

Ultimately, creating customer value is the source of a firm's potential to earn above-average returns. What the firm intends regarding value creation affects its choice of business-level strategy and its organizational structure.[37] Value is created by a product's low cost, by its highly differentiated features, or by a combination of low cost and high differentiation compared with competitors' offerings (see Chapter 5). A business-level strategy is effective only when its use is grounded in exploiting the firm's current core competencies while actions are being taken to develop the core competencies that will be needed to effectively use "tomorrow's" business-level strategy. Thus, successful firms continuously examine the effectiveness of current and future core competencies.[38]

At one time the strategic management process was concerned largely with understanding the characteristics of the industry in which a firm competed and, in light of those characteristics, determining how the firm should position itself relative to competitors. This emphasis on industry characteristics and competitive strategy likely understated the role of the firm's resources and capabilities in developing competitive advantage. In the current competitive landscape, core competencies, in combination with product-market positions, are the firm's most important sources of competitive advantage.[39] The core competencies of a firm, in addition to its analysis of its general, industry, and competitor environments, should drive its selection of strategies. Clayton Christensen speaks to this matter: "Successful strategists need to cultivate a deep understanding of the processes of competition and progress and of the factors that undergird each advantage. Only thus will they be able to see when old advantages are poised to disappear and how new advantages can be built in their stead."[40] By emphasizing core competencies when formulating strategies, companies learn to compete primarily on the basis of firm-specific resources that differ from their competitors' resources.

## Resources, Capabilities, and Core Competencies

Resources, capabilities, and core competencies are the characteristics that provide the foundation for competitive advantage. Resources are the source of a firm's capabilities. Capabilities in turn are the source of a firm's core competencies, which are the basis of competitive advantages. As shown in Figure 4.3, combinations of resources and capabilities are managed to create core competencies. We now define and provide examples of these building blocks of competitive advantage.

### Resources

Broad in scope, resources cover a spectrum of individual, social, and organizational phenomena.[41] Typically, any one resource, on its own, does not yield a competitive advantage; a competitive advantage normally is created through the unique bundling of several resources.[42] For example, Amazon.com has combined service and distribution resources to create its competitive advantages. The firm started as an online bookseller, directly shipping orders to customers. It quickly grew large and established a distribution network through which it could ship many different products to millions of customers. Compared with Amazon's use of combined resources, traditional bricks-and-mortar companies, such as Toys "R" Us and Borders, found it difficult to establish an effective online presence. These difficulties led them to develop partnerships with Amazon. Amazon now handles the online presence and shipping of goods for several firms, including Toys "R" Us and Borders—companies that now focus on sales in their stores. Arrangements such as these are useful to the bricks-and-mortar companies because they are not accustomed to shipping so much diverse merchandise directly to individuals.[43]

Some of a firm's resources are tangible while others are intangible. **Tangible resources** are assets that can be observed and quantified, such as production equipment, manufacturing plants, and formal reporting structures. **Intangible resources** include assets that typically are rooted deeply in the firm's history and have accumulated over time. Because they are embedded in unique patterns of routines, intangible resources are relatively difficult for competitors to analyze and imitate. Knowledge, trust between managers and employees, ideas, the capacity for innovation, managerial capabilities, organizational routines (the unique ways people work together), scientific capabilities, and the firm's reputation for its goods or services and how it interacts with people (such as employees, customers, and suppliers) are all examples of intangible resources.[44]

**Tangible Resources.** The four types of tangible resources are financial, organizational, physical, and technological (see Table 4.1). As tangible resources, a firm's financial assets and the status of its plant and equipment are visible. The value of many tangible resources can be established through financial statements, but these statements do not account for the value of all of a firm's assets because they disregard some intangible resources.[45] As such, each of the firm's sources of competitive advantage typically are not reflected fully on corporate financial statements. The value of tangible resources is also constrained because

| Table 4.1: Tangible Resources | |
|---|---|
| Financial Resources | • The firm's borrowing capacity |
| | • The firm's ability to generate internal funds |
| Organizational Resources | • The firm's formal reporting structure and its formal planning, controlling, and coordinating systems |
| Physical Resources | • Sophistication and location of a firm's plant and equipment |
| | • Access to raw materials |
| Technological Resources | • Stock of technology, such as patents, trademarks, copyrights, and trade secrets |

SOURCES: Adapted from J. B. Barney, 1991, Firm resources and sustained competitive advantage, *Journal of Management*, 17: 101; R. M. Grant, 1991, *Contemporary Strategy Analysis,* Cambridge, U.K.: Blackwell Business, 100–102.

they are difficult to leverage—a firm generally cannot derive additional business or value from a tangible resource. For example, an airplane is a tangible resource or asset, but "You can't use the same airplane on five different routes at the same time. You can't put the same crew on five different routes at the same time. And the same goes for the financial investment you've made in the airplane."[46]

Although manufacturing assets are tangible, many of the processes for using these assets are intangible. Thus, the learning and potential proprietary processes associated with a tangible resource, such as manufacturing equipment, can have unique intangible attributes such as quality, just-in-time management practices, and unique manufacturing processes that develop over time and create competitive advantage.[47]

**Intangible Resources.** The three types of intangible resources are human, innovation, and reputational (see Table 4.2). As suggested above, compared with tangible resources, intangible resources are a superior and more potent source of core competencies.[48] In fact, in the global economy, "the success of a corporation lies more in its intellectual and systems capabilities than in its physical assets. [Moreover], the capacity to manage human intellect—and to convert it into useful products and services—is fast becoming the critical executive skill of the age."[49]

There is some evidence that the value of intangible assets is growing relative to that of tangible assets. John Kendrick, a well-known economist studying the main drivers of economic growth, found a general increase in the contribution of intangible assets to U.S. economic growth since the early 1900s: "In 1929, the ratio of intangible business capital to tangible business capital was 30 percent to 70 percent. In 1990, that ratio was 63 percent to 37 percent."[50]

Because intangible resources are less visible and more difficult for competitors to understand, purchase, imitate, or substitute for, firms prefer to rely on them rather than tangible resources as the foundation for their capabilities and core competencies. In fact, the more unobservable (that is, intangible) a resource is, the more sustainable will be the competitive advantage that is based on it. Another benefit of intangible resources is that, unlike most tangible resources, their use can be leveraged. With intangible resources, the larger the network of users, the greater is the benefit to each party.[51] For instance, sharing knowledge among employees does not diminish its value for any one person. On the contrary, two people sharing their individualized knowledge sets often can be leveraged to create additional knowledge that, although new to each of them, contributes to performance improvements for the firm.[52]

**Table 4.2: Intangible Resources**

| Human Resources | • Knowledge |
|---|---|
| | • Trust |
| | • Managerial capabilities |
| | • Organizational routines |
| Innovation Resources | • Ideas |
| | • Scientific capabilities |
| | • Capacity to innovate |
| Reputational Resources | • Reputation with customers |
| | • Brand name |
| | • Perceptions of product quality, durability, and reliability |
| | • Reputation with suppliers |
| |   • For efficient, effective, supportive, and mutually beneficial interactions and relationships |

SOURCES: Adapted from R. Hall, 1992, The strategic analysis of intangible resources, *Strategic Management Journal*, 13: 136–139; R. M. Grant, 1991, *Contemporary Strategy Analysis*, Cambridge, U.K.: Blackwell Business, 101–104.

The intangible resource of *reputation* is an important source of competitive advantage for companies such as Coca-Cola, General Electric, and Southwest Airlines. Earned primarily through the firm's actions, goods and services, and communications with its stakeholders, a value-creating reputation is a product of years of superior marketplace competence as perceived by stakeholders.[53] A reputation indicates the level of awareness a firm has been able to develop among stakeholders and the degree to which they hold the firm in high esteem.[54] A well-known and highly valued brand name is an application of reputation as a source of competitive advantage. The Harley-Davidson brand name, for example, has such cachet that it adorns a limited-edition Barbie doll, a popular restaurant in New York City, and a line of L'Oréal cologne. Moreover, Harley-Davidson Motor Clothes annually generates more than $100 million in revenue for the firm and offers a broad range of clothing items, from black leather jackets to fashions for tots.[55]

A firm's reputation is reciprocally interrelated with its *social capital*. A firm's social capital is its relationships with other organizations (e.g., suppliers, government units) that contribute to the creation of value.[56] Effective relationships allow firms to gain access to resources of partners that complement or supplement their resource base. Access to such resources helps them create higher value. A positive reputation helps firms establish alliances with good partners. And good relationships with other organizations contribute to a positive reputation.

Decision makers are challenged to understand fully the strategic value of their firm's tangible and intangible resources. The *strategic value of resources* is indicated by the degree to which they can contribute to the development of capabilities, core competencies, and, ultimately, competitive advantage. For example, as a tangible resource, a distribution facility is assigned a monetary value on the firm's balance sheet. The real value of the facility, however, is grounded in a variety of factors, such as its proximity to raw materials and customers, but also in intangible factors such as the manner in which workers integrate their actions internally and with other stakeholders, including suppliers and customers.[57]

## Capabilities

As a source of capabilities, tangible and intangible resources are a critical part of the pathway to the development of competitive advantage (as shown earlier in Figure 4.3). **Capabilities** are the firm's capacity to deploy resources that have been purposely integrated to achieve a desired end state.[58] As the glue binding an organization together, capabilities emerge over time through complex interactions among tangible and intangible resources. Critical to the forming of competitive advantages, capabilities are often based on developing, carrying, and exchanging information and knowledge through the firm's human capital.[59] Because a knowledge base is grounded in organizational actions that may not be explicitly understood by all employees, repetition and practice increase the value of a firm's capabilities.

The foundation of many capabilities lies in the skills and knowledge of a firm's employees and, often, their functional expertise.[60] Hence, the value of human capital in developing and using capabilities and, ultimately, core competencies cannot be overstated. Firms committed to continuously developing their people's capabilities are the most likely to sustain a competitive advantage longer than those firms that do not make such commitments. Educational benefits and employee training can have immediate positive effects on the skill levels of employees and managers, as well as new ideas leading to technological innovation. Also, applicants are drawn to firms that have a reputation for excellent employee treatment, which can increase the quality of human resources in the firm.[61] *Fortune* publishes a list each year of the best U.S. companies to work for. Recently Genentech, Wegmans Food Markets, and Valero Energy topped that list.[62] Recognition such as this can increase the effectiveness of a recruiting program. BP, one of the largest petrochemical groups in the world, is very deliberate about the way it treats its employees. The company has specified six values that guide decisions: nurturing human capability, treating employees fairly and with respect, providing clear expectations, enabling diverse employees to feel included, using merit in decisions associated with selection and advancement of its people, and rewarding employees on the basis of their roles in the group and their contributions.[63]

Global business leaders increasingly support the view that the knowledge possessed by human capital is among the most significant of an organization's capabilities and may ultimately be at the root of all competitive advantages.[64] But firms must also be able to utilize the knowledge that they have and transfer it among their operating businesses.[65] For example, it has been suggested that "in the information age, things are ancillary, knowledge is central. A company's value derives not from things, but from knowledge, know-how, intellectual assets, competencies—all of it embedded in people."[66] Given this reality, the firm's challenge is to create an environment that allows people to fit their individual pieces of knowledge together so that, collectively, employees possess as much organizational knowledge as possible.[67]

To help them develop an environment in which important knowledge is widely shared with as many employees as possible, some organizations have created a new upper-level managerial position often referred to as chief learning officer (CLO). Establishing a CLO highlights a firm's belief that "future success will depend on competencies that traditionally have not been actively managed or measured—including creativity and the speed with which new ideas are learned and shared."[68] In general, the firm should manage knowledge in ways that will support its efforts to create value for customers.[69]

As illustrated in Table 4.3, capabilities are often developed in specific functional areas (such as manufacturing, R&D, and marketing) or in a part of a functional area (for example, advertising). Research suggests that a relationship exists between capabilities developed in particular functional areas and the firm's financial performance at both the corporate and business-unit levels,[70] suggesting the need to develop capabilities at all levels.

**Table 4.3: Examples of Firms' Capabilities**

| Functional Areas | Capabilities | Examples of Firms |
|---|---|---|
| Distribution | Effective use of logistics management techniques | Wal-Mart |
| Human resources | Motivating, empowering, and retaining employees | AEROJET<br>Starbucks |
| Management information systems | Effective and efficient control of inventories through point-of-purchase data collection methods | Wal-Mart |
| Marketing | Effective promotion of brand-name products | Gillette<br>Ralph Lauren Clothing<br>McKinsey & Co. |
| | Effective customer service | Nordstrom<br>Norwest<br>Solectron Corporation<br>Norrell Corporation |
| | Innovative merchandising | Crate & Barrel |
| Management | Ability to envision the future of clothing | Chanel |
| | Effective organizational structure | PepsiCo |
| Manufacturing | Design and production skills yielding reliable products | Komatsu |
| | Product and design quality | Toyota |
| | Production of technologically sophisticated automobile engines | Mazda |
| | Miniaturization of components and products | Sony |
| Research & development | Exceptional technological capability | Corning |
| | Development of sophisticated elevator control solutions | Motion Control Engineering Inc. |
| | Rapid transformation of technology into new products and processes | Chaparral Steel |
| | Digital technology | Thomson Consumer Electronics |

## Core Competencies

Defined in Chapter 1, **core competencies** are resources and capabilities that serve as a source of a firm's competitive advantage over rivals. They distinguish a company competitively and reflect its personality. They emerge over time through an organizational process of accumulating and learning how to deploy different resources and capabilities.[71] As the capacity to take action, core competencies are "crown jewels of a company," the activities the company performs especially well compared with competitors and through which the firm adds unique value to its goods or services over a long time.[72]

Not all of a firm's resources and capabilities are *strategic assets*—that is, assets that have competitive value and the potential to serve as a source of competitive advantage.[73] Some resources and capabilities may result in competitive disadvantages, because they represent areas in which the firm is weak compared with competitors. Thus, some resources or capabilities cannot be developed into a core competence. Firms with substantial tangible resources such as financial capital (e.g., Microsoft and Exxon Mobil) may be able to purchase facilities or hire the skilled workers required to manufacture products that produce value for customers. However, firms without financial capital have a weakness in their ability to buy or build new capabilities. To be successful, firms must locate external environmental opportunities that can be exploited through their capabilities, while avoiding competition in areas of weakness.[74]

An important question is "How many core competencies are required for the firm to have a sustained competitive advantage?" Responses to this question vary. McKinsey & Co. recommends that its clients identify three or four competencies around which their strategic actions can be framed.[75] Supporting and nurturing more than four core competencies may prevent a firm from developing the focus it needs to fully exploit its competencies in the marketplace.

Not all capabilities are core competencies. For instance, safety is a necessary capability in the airline industry; however, because most of the airlines in the world are arguably safe, this capability cannot be a source of competitive advantage. Similarly, it would be hard to use food safety as a distinguishing feature in the restaurant industry or room cleanliness in the luxury hotel industry. These are necessary but not sufficient capabilities for firm success. The next section explains how firms can understand which competencies now constitute or will likely lead to competitive advantage.

## Building Core Competencies

Two tools help a firm identify and build its core competencies.[76] The first tool is application of the four criteria of sustainable advantage to determine whether resources are or have the potential to be core competencies: whether they are valuable, rare, costly to imitate, and nonsubstitutable. Because the capabilities shown in Table 4.3 have satisfied these four criteria, they are core competencies. The second tool is value chain analysis. Firms use this tool to select the value-creating competencies that should be maintained, upgraded, or developed and those that should be outsourced.

### Four Criteria of Sustainable Competitive Advantage

As shown in Table 4.4, capabilities that satisfy the four criteria of sustainable competitive advantage are core competencies; alternatively, those that do not satisfy the criteria are not core competencies. Thus, as shown in Figure 4.4, every core competence is a capability, but not every capability is a core competence. Operationally, for a capability to be a core competence, it must be "valuable and nonsubstitutable, from a customer's point of view, and unique and inimitable, from a competitor's point of view."[77]

A sustained competitive advantage is achieved only when competitors have failed in efforts to duplicate the benefits of a firm's strategy. For some period of time, the firm may earn a competitive advantage by using capabilities that are, for example, valuable and rare but can be imitated.[78] In this instance, the length of time a firm can expect to retain its competitive advantage is a function of how quickly competitors can successfully imitate a good, service, or process. Sustainable competitive advantage results only when all four criteria are satisfied.

**Valuable.** **Valuable capabilities** allow the firm to exploit opportunities or neutralize threats in its external environment. By effectively using capabilities to exploit opportunities, a firm creates value for its customers. Under the leadership of former CEO Jack Welch, General Electric built a valuable competence in financial services. It built this powerful competence largely through acquisitions and its core competence in integrating newly

**Table 4.4: Four Criteria for Determining Core Competencies**

| | |
|---|---|
| Valuable Capabilities | • Help a firm neutralize threats or exploit opportunities |
| Rare Capabilities | • Are not possessed by many others |
| Costly-to-Imitate Capabilities | • Historical: A unique and a valuable organizational culture or brand name |
| | • Ambiguous cause: The causes and uses of a competence are unclear |
| | • Social complexity: Interpersonal relationships, trust, and friendship among managers, suppliers, and customers |
| Nonsubstitutable Capabilities | • No strategic equivalent |

**Figure 4.4: Core Competence as a Strategic Capability**

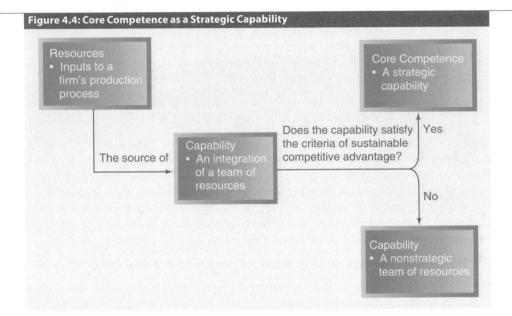

acquired businesses. In addition, to make such competencies as financial services highly successful, Welch placed the right people in the right jobs. He recognized that human capital is important to creating value for customers.[79]

**Rare.** **Rare capabilities** are possessed by few, if any, current or potential competitors. A key question managers answer when evaluating this criterion is, "Do rival firms possess these valuable capabilities, and if so, how many possess them?" Capabilities possessed by many rivals are unlikely to be a source of competitive advantage for any of them. Instead, valuable but common (i.e., not rare) resources and capabilities are sources of competitive parity.[80] Competitive advantage results only when firms develop and exploit capabilities that differ from those shared with competitors.

**Costly to Imitate.** **Costly-to-imitate capabilities** cannot easily be developed by other firms. Capabilities that are costly to imitate are created because of one or a combination of three reasons (see Table 4.4). First, a firm sometimes is able to develop capabilities because of *unique historical conditions*. "As firms evolve, they pick up skills, abilities and re-sources that are unique to them, reflecting their particular path through history."[81] That is, firms sometimes are able to develop capabilities because they were in the right place at the right time.[82]

A firm with a unique and valuable organizational culture that emerged in the early stages of the company's history "may have an imperfectly imitable advantage over firms founded in another historical period"[83]—one in which less valuable or less competitively useful values and beliefs strongly influenced the development of the firm's culture. This may be the case for the consulting firm McKinsey & Co. "It is that culture, unique to McKinsey and eccentric, which sets the firm apart from virtually any other business or-ganization and which often mystifies even those who engage [its] services."[84] An organi-zational culture can be a source of advantage when employees are held together tightly by their belief in it.[85]

UPS has been the prototype in many areas of the parcel delivery business because of its excellence in products, systems, marketing, and other operational business capabilities. "Its fundamental competitive strength, however, derives from the organization's unique culture, which has spanned almost a century, growing deeper all along. This culture pro-vides solid, consistent roots for everything the company does, from skills training to tech-nological innovation."[86]

A second condition of being costly to imitate occurs when the link between the firm's capabilities and its competitive advantage is *causally ambiguous*.[87] In these instances, com-petitors can't clearly understand how a firm uses its capabilities as the foundation for com-petitive advantage. As a result, firms are uncertain what capabilities they should develop or how the capabilities they identify in a competitor create a competitive advantage. Thus, they cannot duplicate the benefits of a competitor's value-creating strategy. For years, firms have tried to duplicate the success of companies such as Southwest Airlines and Lincoln Electric (the world leader in arc welders). In both cases, most companies have failed be-cause they do not understand how these firms' culture, technology, and human capital work together as a basis for competitive advantage.

*Social complexity* is the third reason that capabilities can be costly to imitate. Social complexity means that at least some, and frequently many, of the firm's capabilities are the product of complex social phenomena. Interpersonal relationships, trust, and friendships among managers and between managers and employees and a firm's reputation with suppli-ers and customers are examples of socially complex capabilities. Nucor Steel has been able to create "a hunger for new knowledge through a high-powered incentive system for every employee." This socially complex process has allowed the company "to push the boundaries of manufacturing process know-how."[88]

**Nonsubstitutable.** **Nonsubstitutable capabilities** do not have strategic equivalents. This final criterion for a capability to be a source of competitive advantage "is that there must be no strategically equivalent valuable resources that are themselves either not rare or imitable. Two valuable firm resources (or two bundles of firm resources) are strategically equivalent when they each can be separately exploited to implement the same strategies."[89] In general, the strategic value of capabilities increases as they become more difficult to sub-stitute.[90] The more invisible capabilities are, the more difficult it is for firms to find substi-tutes and the greater the challenge is to competitors trying to imitate a firm's value-creating strategy. Firm-specific knowledge and trust-based working relationships between manag-ers and nonmanagerial personnel are examples of capabilities that are difficult to identify

**Table 4.5: Outcomes from Combinations of the Criteria for Sustainable Competitive Advantage**

| Is the Resource or Capability Valuable? | Is the Resource or Capability Rare? | Is the Resource of Capability Costly to Imitate? | Is the Resource of Capability Nonsub-stitutable? | Competitive Consequences | Performance Implications |
|---|---|---|---|---|---|
| No | No | No | No | Competitive disadvantage | Below-average returns |
| Yes | No | No | Yes/No | Competitive parity | Average returns |
| Yes | Yes | No | Yes/no | Temporary competitive advantage | Above-average returns to average returns |
| Yes | Yes | Yes | Yes | Sustainable competitive advantage | Above-average returns |

and for which finding a substitute is challenging. However, causal ambiguity may make it difficult for the firm to learn and thus may stifle progress because the firm may not know how to improve processes that are not easily codified and thus ambiguous.[91]

In summary, sustainable competitive advantage is created only by using valuable, rare, costly-to-imitate, and nonsubstitutable capabilities. Table 4.5 shows the competitive consequences and performance implications resulting from combinations of the four criteria of sustainability. The analysis suggested by the table helps managers determine the strategic value of a firm's capabilities. Resources and capabilities exemplified in the first row in the table (that is, resources and capabilities that are neither valuable nor rare and that are imitable and for which strategic substitutes exist) should not be emphasized by the firm to formulate and implement strategies. Capabilities yielding competitive parity and either temporary or sustainable competitive advantage, however, can and likely should be supported. Large competitors such as Coca-Cola and PepsiCo may have capabilities that can yield only competitive parity. In such cases, the firms will nurture these capabilities while simultaneously trying to develop capabilities that can yield either a temporary or sustainable competitive advantage.

## Value Chain Analysis

Value chain analysis allows the firm to understand the parts of its operations that create value and those that do not. Understanding these issues is important because the firm earns high returns for its stakeholders only when the value it creates is greater than the costs incurred to create that value.[92]

The value chain is a template that firms use to understand their cost position and to identify the multiple means they might use to facilitate implementation of a chosen business-level strategy.[93] As shown in Figure 4.5, a firm's value chain is segmented into primary and support activities. **Primary activities** are involved with a product's physical creation, its sale and distribution to buyers, and its service after the sale. **Support activities** provide the support needed by the primary activities to be implemented.

**Figure 4.5: The Basic Value Chain**

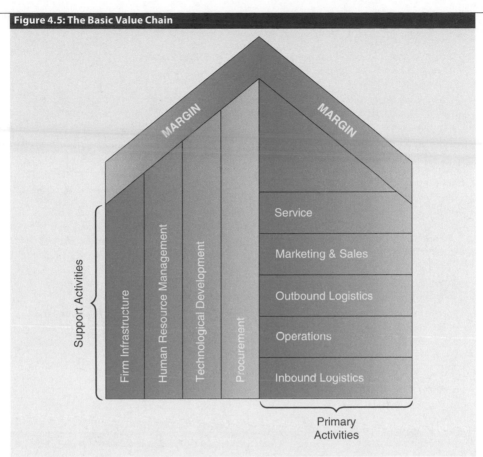

MARGIN

MARGIN

Support Activities

- Firm Infrastructure
- Human Resource Management
- Technological Development
- Procurement

Service

Marketing & Sales

Outbound Logistics

Operations

Inbound Logistics

Primary Activities

The value chain shows how a product moves from the raw-material stage to the final customer. For individual firms, the essential idea of the value chain "is to add as much value as possible as cheaply as possible, and, most important, to capture that value."[94] In a globally competitive economy, the most valuable links on the chain tend to belong to people who have knowledge about customers.[95] This locus of value-creating possibilities applies similarly to retail and service firms and to manufacturers alike. Moreover, for organizations in all sectors, it has become increasingly necessary for companies to develop value-adding knowledge processes to compensate for the value and margin that the Internet (e-commerce) strips from physical processes.[96]

Tables 4.6 and 4.7 list the items to consider when assessing the value-creating potential of primary activities and support activities, respectively. The intent in examining both primary and support activities is to determine areas where the firm has the potential to create and capture value. All activities in both tables should be evaluated relative to competitors' capabilities. To be a source of competitive advantage, a resource or capability must allow the firm (1) to perform an activity in a manner superior to the way competitors perform it, or (2) to perform a value-creating activity that competitors cannot perform. Only under

## Table 4.6: Examining the Value-Creating Potential of Primary Activities

**Inbound Logistics**
Activities, such as materials handling, warehousing, and inventory control, used to receive, store, and disseminate inputs to a product.

**Operations**
Activities necessary to convert the inputs provided by inbound logistics into final product form. Machining, packaging, assembly, and equipment maintenance are examples of operations activities.

**Outbound Logistics**
Activities involved with collecting, storing, and physically distributing the final product to customers. Examples of these activities include finished-goods warehousing, materials handling, and order processing.

**Marketing and Sales**
Activities completed to provide means through which customers can purchase products and to induce them to do so. To effectively market and sell products, firms develop advertising and promotional campaigns, select appropriate distribution channels, and select, develop, and support their sales force.

**Service**
Activities designed to enhance or maintain a product's value. Firms engage in a range of service-related activities, including installation, repair, training, and adjustment.

Each activity should be examined relative to competitors' abilities. Accordingly, firms rate each activity as *superior, equivalent,* or *inferior.*

SOURCE: Adapted with the permission of The Free Press, A Division of Simon & Schuster Adult Publishing Group, from *Competitive Advantage: Creating and Sustaining Superior Performance,* by Michael E. Porter, pp. 39–40, Copyright © 1985, 1988 by Michael E. Porter.

## Table 4.7: Examining the Value-Creating Potential of Support Activities

**Procurement**
Activities completed to purchase the inputs needed to produce a firm's products. Purchased inputs include items fully consumed during the manufacture of products (e.g., raw materials and supplies, as well as fixed assets—machinery, laboratory equipment, office equipment, and buildings).

**Technological Development**
Activities completed to improve a firm's product and the processes used to manufacture it. Technological development takes many forms, such as process equipment, basic research and product design, and servicing procedures.

**Human Resource Management**
Activities involved with recruiting, hiring, training, developing, and compensating all personnel.

**Firm Infrastructure**
Firm infrastructure includes activities such as general management, planning, finance, accounting, legal support, and governmental relations that are required to support the work of the entire value chain. Through its infrastructure, the firm strives to effectively and consistently identify external opportunities and threats, identify resources and capabilities, and support core competencies.

Each activity should be examined relative to competitors' abilities. Accordingly, firms rate each activity as *superior, equivalent,* or *inferior.*

SOURCE: Adapted with the permission of The Free Press, A Division of Simon & Schuster Adult Publishing Group, from *Competitive Advantage: Creating and Sustaining Superior Performance,* by Michael E. Porter, pp. 40–43, Copyright © 1985, 1988 by Michael E. Porter.

these conditions does a firm create value for customers and have opportunities to capture that value.

Sometimes start-up firms create value by uniquely reconfiguring or recombining parts of the value chain. Federal Express (FedEx) changed the nature of the delivery business by reconfiguring outbound logistics (a primary activity) and human resource management (a support activity) to originate the overnight delivery business, creating value in the process. The Internet has changed several aspects of the value chain for a broad range of firms. For instance, Amazon.com has affected actions firms take to sell, distribute, and service an array of consumer products, including books and various household items.

Rating a firm's capability to execute its primary and support activities is challenging. As already noted, identifying and assessing the value of a firm's resources and capabilities requires judgment. Judgment is equally necessary for value chain analysis because no known accurate model or rule is available to help in the process. Nevertheless, firms that involve a heterogeneous group of managers in such activities can get good results.[97]

## Outsourcing

Managers sometimes determine that their firms do not have capabilities in areas that are necessary to success. Similarly, they may realize that the firm lacks a resource or possesses an inadequate resource or skill that is essential to a strategy it intends to pursue. In some instances, outsourcing becomes a viable option for a firm to try to develop a competency inside the organization.

Concerned with how components, finished goods, or services will be obtained, **outsourcing** is the purchase of a value-creating activity from an external supplier.[98] Firms engaging in effective outsourcing can increase their flexibility, mitigate risks, and reduce their capital investments. In multiple global industries, the trend toward outsourcing continues at a rapid pace.[99] Moreover, in some industries, such as the automobile manufacturing and electronics industries, virtually all firms seek the value that can be captured through effective outsourcing.[100]

Outsourcing can be effective when few, if any, organizations possess the resources and capabilities required to achieve competitive superiority in all primary and support activities. With respect to technologies, for example, research suggests that few companies can afford to develop internally all the technologies that might lead to competitive advantage.[101] By nurturing a smaller number of capabilities, a firm increases the probability of developing a competitive advantage because it does not become overextended. In addition, by outsourcing activities in which it lacks a distinctive competence, the firm can fully concentrate on those areas in which it can create value.[102] Intermediaries such as the Outsourcing Institute facilitate outsourcing by concentrating on joining purchasers of outsourced goods and services with the firms that provide them.[103] With more than 70,000 members, the Outsourcing Institute publishes annual buyers guides, provides consulting and training on best practices, and facilitates networking among peers.

Other research suggests that outsourcing does not work effectively without extensive internal capabilities to effectively coordinate external sourcing as well as internal coordination of core competencies.[104] Furthermore, critics of outsourcing argue that too much outsourcing can lead to a loss of innovative activity within the firm and that it certainly leads to fewer positions.[105] Also, firms should be careful not to take advantage of suppliers once they have created a mutually dependent relationship with them, such as giving them lead times that are too short or making other unrealistic demands on them in the interest of cutting costs. Such behaviors can lead suppliers to integrate forward and become direct competitors to the firm they previously supplied.[106] Companies should be aware of all these risks and be both willing and able to address them when various stakeholders raise them.

To verify that the appropriate primary and support activities are outsourced, four skills are essential for managers: strategic thinking, deal making, partnership governance, and managing change.[107] Managers should understand whether and how outsourcing creates competitive advantage within their company—they need to be able to think strategically.[108] To complete effective outsourcing transactions, these managers must also be deal makers, to be able to secure rights from external providers that internal managers can fully use. They must be able to oversee and govern appropriately the relationship with the company to which the services were outsourced. Because outsourcing can significantly change how an organization operates, managers administering these programs must also be able to manage that change, including resolving employee resistance that accompanies any significant change effort.[109]

## When Core Competencies Lose Their Value

Tools such as outsourcing can help a firm focus on its core competencies. However, evidence shows that the value-creating ability of core competencies should never be taken for granted,[110] nor should the ability of a core competence to be a permanent competitive advantage be assumed. One reason for these cautions is that core competencies have the potential to become *core rigidities*. As Leslie Wexner, CEO of Limited Brands Inc., once said: "Success doesn't beget success. Success begets failure because the more that you know a thing works, the less likely you are to think that it won't work. When you've had a long string of victories, it's harder to foresee your own vulnerabilities."[111] Thus, each competence is a strength and a weakness—a strength because it is the source of competitive advantage and, hence, value creation, and a weakness because, if emphasized when it is no longer competitively relevant, it can be a seed of resistance to change.[112]

Events occurring in the firm's external environment create conditions through which core competencies can become core rigidities, generate resistance to change, and stifle innovation. "Often the flip side, the dark side, of core capabilities is revealed due to external events when new competitors figure out a better way to serve the firm's customers, when new technologies emerge, or when political or social events shift the ground underneath."[113] In the final analysis, however, changes in the external environment do not cause core capabilities or core competencies to become core rigidities; rather, inflexibility on the part of managers stemming from the strength of their shared beliefs (strategic myopia) is the cause.[114]

This concludes our discussion of tools firms use to determine how their resources and value chain activities can lead to core competencies and sustainable competitive advantage. High firm performance is the primary objective of these activities. Furthermore, evaluating firm performance is an important part of internal analysis. We close this chapter with a discussion of firm performance.

---

## Firm Performance

Firms seek to develop core competencies and enhance value-creating activities in an effort to achieve competitive advantage for the purpose of creating value for their shareholders and other stakeholders.[115] Firm performance is inherently multidimensional. Each stakeholder group expects those making strategic decisions in a firm to provide the leadership through which its valued objectives will be accomplished.[116] Stakeholders continue to support an organization when its performance meets or exceeds their expectations. When performance is lower than these expectations, they may withdraw their support. For instance, shareholders may sell their stock, and although a single stock sale rarely influences firm outcomes significantly, a trend of many shareholders or a very large shareholder selling stock can dramatically reduce the value of the stock in the market. Also, large shareholders such as investment funds may have political power to persuade others to withdraw or withhold resources from the firm. In addition, stakeholders' rights are grounded in laws governing private property and private enterprise. Consequently, top managers tend to give shareholder needs high priority when they make decisions.

Although organizations have dependency relationships with all of their primary stakeholders, they are not equally dependent on all stakeholders at all times; as a consequence, not every stakeholder has the same level of influence.[117] The more critical and valued a stakeholder's participation, the greater a firm's dependence on it. Greater dependence, in turn, gives the stakeholder more potential influence over a firm's commitments, decisions, and actions. Effective managers must find ways to either accommodate or insulate the organization from the demands of stakeholders controlling critical resources.[118]

## Stakeholder Objectives and Power

The objectives of the various stakeholder groups often differ from one another, sometimes placing managers in situations in which they must make trade-offs. Shareholders want the return on their investment (and, hence, their wealth) to be maximized. Maximization of short-term returns sometimes is accomplished at the expense of investing in a firm's future. For instance, research has demonstrated that newly appointed CEOs of large companies tend to curtail R&D investments immediately after their appointment, resulting in short-term increases in profitability.[119] However, this short-term enhancement of shareholders' wealth can negatively affect the firm's future competitive ability, and sophisticated shareholders with diversified portfolios may sell their interests if a firm fails to invest in its future. Those making strategic decisions are responsible for a firm's survival in both the short and the long term.[120] Accordingly, it is not in the interests of any stakeholders for investments in the company to be unduly minimized.

In contrast to shareholders, another group of stakeholders—the firm's customers—could have their interests maximized when the quality and reliability of a firm's products are improved, but without a price increase. Employees, on the other hand, prefer that companies provide better working conditions and higher compensation and benefits. At the extreme, serving the needs and desires of customers and employees may come at the expense of lower returns for capital market shareholders. Because of potential conflicts, each firm is challenged to manage its stakeholders. A firm must carefully prioritize the needs and desires of important stakeholders in case it cannot satisfy all of them.

Power is the most critical criterion in prioritizing stakeholders. The level of stakeholder influence can come from economic power, political power, or formal power. **Economic power** comes from the ability to withhold economic support from the firm. **Political power** results from the ability to influence others to withhold economic support or to change the rules of the game, as in the example of a special interest group that lobbies a government body for legal changes.[121] **Formal power** means that laws or regulations specify the legal relationship that exists between a firm and a particular stakeholder group.[122] For instance, firms have legal obligations to shareholders and they are legally obligated to follow government regulations. Stakeholders can enjoy multiple sources of power.[123] Firms may also give a particular stakeholder group priority because of its strategic importance to future plans. For instance, a company may begin to build excellent community relations in a nearby community where it hopes to build a new plant. Or top executives may simply choose to give a stakeholder priority, as in the case of a firm that makes large donations to universities because top managers value education, even if the direct benefits to the firm are negligible.

When the firm earns high economic returns, the challenge of balancing stakeholder interests is lessened substantially. With the capability and flexibility provided by high returns, a firm can more easily satisfy multiple stakeholders simultaneously. When the firm is earning only average returns, however, the management of its stakeholders may be more difficult. With average returns, the firm is unable to maximize the interests of all stakeholders. The objective then becomes one of at least minimally satisfying each stakeholder. Trade-off decisions are made in light of how dependent the firm is on the support of its stakeholder groups. A firm earning below-average returns does not have the capacity to minimally satisfy all stakeholders. The managerial challenge in this case is to make trade-offs that minimize the amount of support lost from stakeholders.

## Measures of Firm Performance

Because various types of firm performance influence stakeholders differently, measures of firm performance can be divided into categories based on the three primary stakeholder groups defined in Chapter 1: capital market, product market, and organizational stakeholders. Table 4.8 shows examples of measures that are highly relevant to capital market stakeholders. Capital market stakeholders, shareholders and lenders, expect a firm to preserve and enhance the wealth they have entrusted to the firm. Shareholders are particularly interested in receiving high returns for the investment they have made in a stock. Those returns may also be compared with the average return of all stocks in the market as a whole or in a designated industry for a particular period.

In addition, both shareholders and lenders expect returns that are commensurate with the degree of risk accepted with those investments (that is, lower returns are expected with low-risk investments, and higher returns are expected with high-risk investments). In this context, **risk** is an investor's uncertainty about the economic gains or losses that will result from a particular investment.[124] Strategic leaders must assess the risks involved in pursuing various courses of action.[125] Decisions that lead to lower variance in returns can enhance the value of an organization from the perspective of capital market stakeholders. Consequently, Table 4.8 contains a few common examples of measures that can be used to assess risk. These measures also can be used to adjust shareholder returns. Shareholders can deduct the average or market return for a particular period from the return that was actually received and then divide the result by the standard deviation of returns or beta.[126] Comparing this risk-adjusted return to the risk-adjusted return of other firms could provide a better sense of how well the stock is performing relative to the amount of risk the shareholder is assuming. Note also that lenders are interested in risk measures such as standard deviation or beta because they are one indication of the financial stability of the firm.

In addition, capital market stakeholders are concerned about the growth of the firm because growth is so closely associated with other measures of performance. They also become concerned when liquidity becomes too low or debt levels too high because these factors can influence the ability of a company to remain solvent. Furthermore, capital market stakeholders are interested in firm efficiency because of its influence on future profitability. Consequently, measures like asset or inventory turnover and days receivable are also relevant.

## Table 4.8: Firm Performance from a Capital Market Perspective

| Stakeholder | Needs/Desires | Examples | Measurement |
|---|---|---|---|
| **Capital Market** | | | |
| Shareholders | High returns | Total shareholder return | $\dfrac{(\text{Share Price at Period End} - \text{Price at Start of Period}) + \text{Dividends}}{\text{Share Price at Start of Period}}$ |
| | | Adjusted for: | |
| | High relative returns | Market return | Average return for other firms in market for same period |
| | High relative returns | Industry return | Average return for other firms in industry for same period |
| Lenders and shareholders | Low risk (variance) | Standard deviation | Standard deviation of shareholder return for the period |
| | Low risk (systematic) | Beta | Degree to which stock returns for the firm are correlated with stock returns for the whole market (systematic risk) |
| | High profitability | Return on assets | $\dfrac{\text{Net Profit after Taxes}}{\text{Total Assets}}$ |
| | | Return on equity | $\dfrac{\text{Net Profit after Taxes}}{\text{Shareholders' Equity}}$ |
| | Growth | Growth in revenues | $\dfrac{\text{This Year Total Revenues} - \text{Last Year Total Revenues}}{\text{Last Year Total Revenues}}$ |
| | Low financial risk | Debt-to-equity | $\dfrac{\text{Total Debt}}{\text{Shareholders' Equity}}$ |
| | | Debt-to-assets | $\dfrac{\text{Total Debt}}{\text{Total Assets}}$ |
| | Internal efficiency | Current ratio | $\dfrac{\text{Current Assets}}{\text{Current Liabilities}}$ |
| | | Worker productivity | $\dfrac{\text{Sales}}{\text{Number of Employees}}$ |
| | | Asset turnover | $\dfrac{\text{Sales}}{\text{Total Assets}}$ |
| | | Inventory turnover | $\dfrac{\text{Sales}}{\text{Total Inventories}}$ |
| | | Collections period | $\dfrac{\text{Receivables} \times 365\ \text{Days}}{\text{Annual Credit Sales}}$ |

The needs and desires of other key stakeholders are also important to the success of the firm, so managers should also establish measures that reflect how well the firm is responding to them. Table 4.9 contains a few examples of the types of measures firms might use. Product market stakeholders include primary customers, suppliers, communities, and, where applicable, unions. Customers demand reliable products at the lowest possible prices. Firms can measure customer satisfaction with products and services as well as their perceptions of the value they are receiving relative to prices paid. Suppliers seek reliable customers who are willing to pay high prices for the goods and services they receive. Firms can measure success in supplier relationships in terms of the way suppliers serve them and their eagerness to engage in business, based on the assumption that suppliers are best motivated to serve a customer who is satisfying their needs. Also, although suppliers may desire the highest prices possible, they tend to be satisfied with fair prices and good treatment

**Table 4.9: Other Measures of Firm Performance**

| Stakeholder | Needs/Desires | Examples | Measurement |
|---|---|---|---|
| *Product Market* | | | |
| Primary customers | High-quality, reliable products at low prices | Satisfaction | Customer satisfaction survey |
| | | Dissatisfaction | Product returns or customer complaints (for service firms) |
| Suppliers | High prices for goods and trustworthy, reliable behavior | Motivation to deliver | Delivery speed |
| | | Availability of goods | Number of stockouts |
| | | Fair contracts | Percentage of contract renewals; prices paid relative to competitors |
| Communities | Jobs, tax revenues, contributions to community, low negative influences | Job growth | Number of new jobs created in local community per year |
| | | Philanthropy | Donations of time and money to community |
| | | Dissatisfaction | Number of community complaints or legal suits |
| Unions | Job growth and security, high compensation, good working conditions | Compensation | Wages and other benefits relative to competitors |
| | | Worker safety | Reports of injuries |
| *Organizational* | | | |
| Managers and other employees | High compensation, opportunities for advancement, job security, professional development, job satisfaction | Desire to stay | Manager or other employee turnover |
| | | Education | Percentage of workforce receiving company-sponsored training per year |
| | | Satisfaction with job | Employee or manager satisfaction survey |
| | | Advancement opportunities | Percentage of upper-level positions filled internally |

(reliable orders and payments). Consequently, from the buying firm's perspective, lower prices paid to suppliers might actually be an indication that the supplier perceives the firm in a favorable light, if the other indicators of supplier satisfaction support such a perspective.

Host communities want companies that are long-term employers and providers of tax revenues without placing excessive demands on public support services. They also turn to businesses, in part, to provide contributions of money and time to help build the community. Union officials are interested in secure jobs, under highly desirable working conditions, for the employees they represent. Their demands typically are consistent with employees' needs. For instance, at the organizational level, managers and other employees want high levels of compensation and job security. They also desire professional development, job satisfaction, and advancement opportunities.[127]

## Balancing Stakeholder Performance

As already noted, the needs and desires of both product market and organizational stakeholders at least partly conflict with each other and with those of capital market stakeholders. Resources a firm expends to satisfy one stakeholder group can reduce resources available for others. Optimal value creation means that managers must balance the interests of stakeholders to ensure that each of them is highly motivated to continue to contribute resources and energy to the organization and its goals. Trade-off decisions are made on the basis of how important the support of each stakeholder group is to the firm, which is also a function of the power each group possesses.[128]

Fortunately, the goals of stakeholders do not conflict entirely. It is in the interest of all of an organization's stakeholders that a firm provides a steady and high return to shareholders because doing so reduces the cost of capital to the firm, thus increasing its ability to grow and prosper. Prosperity also means that more resources are available for all stakeholders. For instance, a prosperous firm can provide job security and higher compensation; the firm has more resources available to build innovative and reliable products that serve its customers well; and it has more resources to use to help foster excellent community relations. Even the most ardent supporters of a focus on shareholder wealth admit that other stakeholders are important for achieving high shareholder returns.[129]

## Sustainable Development

We have focused on a firm's primary stakeholders rather than taking the broader perspective of social responsibility. A firm that provides safe and high-quality products, treats its suppliers fairly, adds positively to its community, treats employees and managers well, pays its financial obligations, and provides a higher-than-average and stable return to shareholders is well on its way to being what most people would call a socially responsible firm.[130] Also, obedience to laws and regulations is assumed, since violations interfere with the firm's ability to create value. Nevertheless, there is one aspect of social performance that deserves separate attention because of its strategic importance. It is a firm's environmental performance.[131]

The concept of sustainability has gained strategic importance in recent years. **Sustainable development** is defined as business growth that does not deplete the natural environment or damage society. Most organizations define their sustainability programs in terms of what they are doing to advance technology while at the same time protect the environment and serve and protect the communities and societies in which they operate. According to John Chambers, CEO of the networking giant Cisco Systems, "At Cisco we believe that corporations have a responsibility to consider the broader effects of operations on the communities in which they do business and on the world in general."[132] Chiquita Brands International, Inc., a leading international marketer and distributor of high-quality fresh produce, has adopted sustainability as a core value.[133]

One of the keys to sustainability is to transform value-creating activities so that they benefit society while advancing the other goals of the firm.[134] CEMEX, the giant international cement company based in Mexico, serves a broad group of external constituencies through what the firm calls its Sustainable Management System. The system contains sustainability requirements and instructions covering environmental, health, safety, well-being, and community issues. CEMEX has integrated this system into business operations by focusing on key business areas. It sees sustainability as a strategic dimension of the business and as a key to the company's long-term viability. The progress of its sustainability initiatives is reported annually in a sustainable development report.[135]

One reason for measuring firm performance is to make sure that none of the firm's primary stakeholders are being neglected to such a point that they might withdraw their support from the organization. Of course, a more positive approach suggests that serving the needs of stakeholders above their minimum requirements brings substantial benefits to the firm, such as superior knowledge creation, attraction of resources, reduced transaction costs, and higher stakeholder motivation levels. Another reason for using multiple measures of firm performance is that traditional financial measures may not reflect the actual value created by a firm. If nonshareholder stakeholders are very powerful, they may be taking a disproportionate share of the value the firm is creating.[136] For instance, powerful unions for years absorbed a large share of the value being created by companies competing in the automobile and airline industries. Powerful suppliers can also extract a large share of the profits of an organization, as the oil companies are now demonstrating. This reasoning is consistent with the I/O model. Also, in firms that are predominantly owned by one family or by a business group, much of the value may not be reflected by shareholder returns.[137] Instead, value is redistributed to other business ventures under control of the group or family or directly to family members in the form of wages, benefits, and perquisites.

# Summary

- In a new landscape of rapid technological change and globalization, a firm's internal resources, capabilities, and core competencies have a strong influence on its competitiveness. The most effective firms recognize that creating value and generating high returns for shareholders and other stakeholders result only when core competencies (critical strengths identified through the analysis of the firm's internal organization) are matched with opportunities (determined by studying the firm's external environment).

- No competitive advantage lasts forever. Over time, rivals use their own unique resources, capabilities, and core competencies to form different value-creating propositions that duplicate the value-creating ability of the firm's competitive advantages. In general, the Internet's capabilities (e.g., diffusion of information and knowledge) are reducing the sustainability of many competitive advantages. Thus, firms must exploit their current advantages while simultaneously using their resources and capabilities to form new advantages that can lead to future competitive success.

- Effective management of core competencies requires careful internal analysis of the firm's resources (inputs to the production process) and capabilities (capacities for integrated bundles of resources to perform a task or activity).

- Single sets of resources are usually not a source of competitive advantage. Capabilities, which are groupings of tangible and intangible resources, are a more likely source of competitive advantages, especially relatively sustainable ones. A key reason for this is that the firm's nurturing and support of core competencies that are based on capabilities are less visible to rivals and, as such, more complex and difficult to imitate.

- Only when a capability is valuable, rare, costly to imitate, and nonsubstitutable is it a core competence and a source of competitive advantage. Over time, core competencies must be supported, but they cannot be allowed to become core rigidities. Core competencies are a source of competitive advantage only when they allow the firm to create value by exploiting opportunities in the external environment. When this is no longer the case, attention shifts to selecting or forming other capabilities that meet the four criteria of sustainable competitive advantage.

- Value chain analysis can be used to identify and evaluate the competitive potential of resources and capabilities. By studying their skills to perform primary and support activities, firms can understand their cost structure and identify the activities through which they can create value.

- When the firm cannot create value in either a primary or support activity, outsourcing, or the purchase of a value-creating activity from an external supplier, is an option. The firm must outsource only to companies possessing a competitive advantage in the particular primary or support activity under consideration. In addition, the firm must continuously verify that it is not outsourcing activities from which it could create value.

- Firm performance is inherently multidimensional. Each stakeholder group expects those making strategic decisions in a firm to provide the leadership through which its valued objectives will be accomplished. The priority given to each stakeholder group when making strategic decisions depends on its power and on its importance to the firm's strategies. When the firm earns high economic returns, the challenge of balancing stakeholder interests is lessened substantially.

# Ethics Questions

1. Can efforts to develop sustainable competitive advantages result in employees using unethical practices? If so, what unethical practices might be used to compare a firm's core competencies with those held by rivals?
2. Do ethical practices affect a firm's ability to develop a brand name as a source of competitive advantage? If so, how does this happen? Identify some brands that are a source of competitive advantage in part because of the firm's ethical practices.
3. What is the difference between exploiting a firm's human capital and using that capital as a source of competitive advantage? Are there situations in which the exploitation of human capital can be a source of advantage? If so, can you name such a situation? If the exploitation of human capital can be a source of competitive advantage, is this a sustainable advantage? Why or why not?
4. Are there any ethical dilemmas associated with outsourcing? If so, what are they? How would you deal with such ethical dilemmas?
5. What ethical responsibilities do managers have if they determine that a set of employees has skills that are valuable only to a core competence that is becoming a core rigidity?
6. Through the Internet, firms sometimes make a vast array of data, information, and knowledge available to competitors as well as to customers and suppliers. What ethical issues, if any, are involved when the firm finds competitively relevant information on a competitor's Website?
7. To what extent does a firm have a moral obligation to distribute value back to stakeholders based on their relative contributions to its creation? Does a firm have any legal obligations to do so?

# Notes

1  D. Lei & J. W. Slocum Jr., 2005, Strategic and organizational requirements for competitive advantage, *Academy of Management Executive*, 19(1): 31–45; A. Andal-Ancion, P. A. Cartwright, & G. S. Yip, 2003, The digital transformation of traditional businesses, *MIT Sloan Management Review*, 44(4): 34–41; R. R. Wiggins & T. W. Ruefli, 2002, Sustained competitive advantage: Temporal dynamics and the incidence of persistence of superior economic performance, *Organization Science*, 13: 82–105.

2  S. K. McEvily, K. M. Eisenhardt, & J. E. Prescott, 2004, The global acquisition, leverage, and protection of technological competencies, *Strategic Management Journal*, 25: 713–722.

3  2007, The Nokia way and values, http://www.nokia.com, January 23.

4  A. M. Knott, 2003, Persistent heterogeneity and sustainable innovation, *Strategic Management Journal*, 24: 687–705; C. G. Brush, P. G. Greene, & M. M. Hart, 2001, From initial idea to unique advantage: The entrepreneurial challenge of constructing a resource base, *Academy of Management Executive*, 15(1): 64–78.

5  R. Makadok, 2001, Toward a synthesis of the resource-based and dynamic-capability views of rent creation, *Strategic Management Journal*, 22: 387–401; K. M. Eisenhardt & J. A. Martin, 2000, Dynamic capabilities: What are they? *Strategic Management Journal*, 21: 1105–1121.

6  J. Shamsie, 2003, The context of dominance: An industry-driven framework for exploiting reputation, *Strategic Management Journal*, 24: 199–215; E. Autio, H. J. Sapienza, & J. G. Almeida, 2000, Effects of age at entry, knowledge intensity, and imitability on international growth, *Academy of Management Journal*, 43: 909–924.

7  M. Makhija, 2003, Comparing the resource-based and market-based view of the firm: Empirical evidence from Czech privatization, *Strategic Management Journal*, 24: 433–451; P. L. Yeoh & K. Roth, 1999, An empirical analysis of sustained advantage in the U.S. pharmaceutical industry: Impact of firm resources and capabilities, *Strategic Management Journal*, 20: 637–653.

8  D. F. Abell, 1999, Competing today while preparing for tomorrow, *Sloan Management Review*, 40(3): 73–81; D. Leonard-Barton, 1995, *Wellsprings of Knowledge: Building and Sustaining the Sources of Innovation* (Boston: Harvard Business School Press); R. A. McGrath, I. C. MacMillan, & S. Venkataraman, 1995, Defining and developing competence: A strategic process paradigm, *Strategic Management Journal*, 16: 251–275.

9  K. M. Eisenhardt, 1999, Strategy as strategic decision making, *Sloan Management Review*, 40(3): 65–72.

10  2007, Hewlett-Packard extends lead over Dell, msnbc, http://www.msnbc.msn.com/id/16687613/, January 23.

11  H. K. Steensma & K. G. Corley, 2000, On the performance of technology-sourcing partnerships: The interaction between partner interdependence and technology attributes, *Academy of Management Journal*, 43: 1045–1067.

12  J. B. Barney, 2001, Is the resource-based "view" a useful perspective for strategic management research? Yes, *Academy of Management Review*, 26: 41–56.

13  C. M. Christensen & M. E. Raynor, 2003, Why hard-nosed executives should care about management theory, *Harvard Business Review*, 81(9): 66–74; T. H. Davenport, 2001, Data to knowledge to results: Building an analytic capability, *California Management Review*, 43(2): 117–138; J. B. Barney, 1999, How a firm's capabilities affect boundary decisions, *Sloan Management Review*, 40(3): 137–145.

14  N. Checa, J. Maguire, & J. Barney, 2003, The new world disorder, *Harvard Business Review*, 81(8): 70–79; P. Westhead, M. Wright, & D. Ucbasaran, 2001, The internationalization of new and small firms: A resource-based view, *Journal of Business Venturing*, 16(4): 333–358; A. McWilliams, D. D. Van Fleet, & P. M. Wright, 2001, Strategic management of human resources for global competitive advantage, *Journal of Business Strategies*, 18(1): 1–24; N. Athanassiou & D. Nigh, 1999, The impact of U.S. company internationalization on top management team advice networks: A tacit knowledge perspective, *Strategic Management Journal*, 20: 83–92.

15  H. J. Smith, 2003, The shareholders vs. stakeholders debate, *MIT Sloan Management Review*, 44(4): 85–90; H. Collingwood, 2001, The earnings game: Everyone plays, nobody wins, *Harvard Business Review*, 79(6): 65–74.

16  Eisenhardt, Strategy as strategic decision making.

17  P. C. Nutt, 2002, *Why Decisions Fail*, San Francisco: Berrett-Koehler; P. C. Nutt, 1999, Surprising but true: Half the decisions in organizations fail, *Academy of Management Executive*, 13(4): 75–90.

18  J. M. Mezias & W. H. Starbuck, 2003, What do managers know, anyway? *Harvard Business Review*, 81(5): 16–17; M. Keil, 2000, Cutting your losses: Extricating your organization when a big project goes awry, *Sloan Management Review*, 41(3): 55–68.

19  P. G. Audia, E. Locke, & K. G. Smith, 2000, The paradox of success: An archival and a laboratory study of strategic persistence following radical environmental change, *Academy of Management Journal*, 43: 837–853; D. A. Aaker & E. Joachimsthaler, 1999, The lure of global branding, *Harvard Business Review*, 77(6): 137–144; R. G. McGrath, 1999, Falling forward: Real options reasoning and entrepreneurial failure, *Academy of Management Review*, 24: 13–30.

20  G. P. West III & J. DeCastro, 2001, The Achilles heel of firm strategy: Resource weaknesses and distinctive inadequacies, *Journal of Management Studies*, 38: 417–442; G. Gavetti & D. Levinthal, 2000, Looking forward and looking backward: Cognitive and experimental search, *Administrative Science Quarterly*, 45: 113–137.

21  M. Subramani & N. Venkatraman, 2003, Safeguarding investments in asymmetric interorganizational relationships: Theory and evidence, *Academy of Management Journal*, 46: 46–62; J. K. Sebenius, 2002, The hidden challenge of cross-border negotiations, *Harvard Business Review*, 80(3): 76–85; P. W. Liu & X. Yang, 2000, The theory of irrelevance of the size of the firm, *Journal of Economic Behavior & Organization*, 42: 145–165.

22  T. M. Begley & D. P. Boyd, 2003, The need for a corporate global mind-set, *MIT Sloan Management Review*, 44(2): 25–32.

23  H. Thomas, T. Pollock, & P. Gorman, 1999, Global strategic analyses: Frameworks and approaches, *Academy of Management Executive*, 13(1): 70–82.

24 J. M. Mezias, P. Grinyer, & W. D. Guth, 2001, Changing collective cognition: A process model for strategic change, *Long Range Planning*, 34(1): 71–95.

25 N. Tichy, 1999, The teachable point of view, *Harvard Business Review*, 77(2): 82–83.

26 P. F. Drucker, 2002, They're not employees, they're people, *Harvard Business Review*, 80(2): 70–77; G. Verona, 1999, A resource-based view of product development, *Academy of Management Review*, 24: 132–142.

27 M. Tripsas & G. Gavetti, 2000, Capabilities, cognition, and inertia: Evidence from digital imaging, *Strategic Management Journal*, 21: 1147–1161.

28 D. Whitford, 2001, Polaroid, R.I.P., *Fortune*, November 12, 44.

29 R. Amit & P. J. H. Schoemaker, 1993, Strategic assets and organizational rent, *Strategic Management Journal*, 14: 33–46.

30 R. E. Hoskisson & L. W. Busenitz, 2001, Market uncertainty and learning distance in corporate entrepreneurship entry mode choice, in M. A. Hitt, R. D. Ireland, S. M. Camp, & D. L. Sexton (eds.), *Strategic Entrepreneurship: Creating a New Integrated Mindset*, Oxford, UK: Blackwell Publishers, 151–172.

31 Barney, Is the resource-based "view" a useful perspective?; V. P. Rindova & C. J. Fombrun, 1999, Constructing competitive advantage: The role of firm-constituent interactions, *Strategic Management Journal*, 20: 691–710; M. A. Peteraf, 1993, The cornerstones of competitive strategy: A resource-based view, *Strategic Management Journal*, 14: 179–191.

32 Barney, Is the resource-based "view" a useful perspective?; T. H. Brush & K. W. Artz, 1999, Toward a contingent resource-based theory: The impact of information asymmetry on the value of capabilities in veterinary medicine, *Strategic Management Journal*, 20: 223–250.

33 M. E. Porter, 1996, What is strategy? *Harvard Business Review*, 74(6): 61–78.

34 S. K. McEvily & B. Chakravarthy, 2002, The persistence of knowledge-based advantage: An empirical test for product performance and technological knowledge, *Strategic Management Journal*, 23: 285–305; P. J. Buckley & M. J. Carter, 2000, Knowledge management in global technology markets: Applying theory to practice, *Long Range Planning*, 33(1): 55–71.

35 1998, Pocket Strategy, Value, *Economist Books*, 165.

36 B. Hindo, 2006, The best of 2006, *Business Week*, December 18, 82–92.

37 J. Wolf & W. G. Egelhoff, 2002, A reexamination and extension of international strategy-structure theory, *Strategic Management Journal*, 23: 181–189; R. Ramirez, 1999, Value co-production: Intellectual origins and implications for practice and research, *Strategic Management Journal*, 20: 49–65.

38 V. Shankar & B. L. Bayus, 2003, Network effects and competition: An empirical analysis of the home video game industry, *Strategic Management Journal*, 24: 375–384; S. W. Floyd & B. Wooldridge, 1999, Knowledge creation and social networks in corporate entrepreneurship: The renewal of organizational capability, *Entrepreneurship: Theory and Practice*, 23(3): 123–143; A. Campbell & M. Alexander, 1997, What's wrong with strategy? *Harvard Business Review*, 75(6): 42–51.

39 G. Hawawini, V. Subramanian, & P. Verdin, 2003, Is performance driven by industry- or firm-specific factors?

A new look at the evidence, *Strategic Management Journal*, 24: 1–16; M. A. Hitt, R. D. Nixon, P. G. Clifford, & K. P. Coyne, 1999, The development and use of strategic resources, in M. A. Hitt, P. G. Clifford, R. D. Nixon, & K. P. Coyne (eds.), *Dynamic Strategic Resources*, Chichester, UK: Wiley, 1–14.

40 C. M. Christensen, 2001, The past and future of competitive advantage, *Sloan Management Review*, 42(2): 105–109.

41 G. Ahuja & R. Katila, 2004, Where do resources come from? The role of idiosyncratic situations, *Strategic Management Journal*, 25: 887–907; M. D. Michalisin, D. M. Kline, & R. D. Smith, 2000, Intangible strategic assets and firm performance: A multi-industry study of the resource-based view, *Journal of Business Strategies*, 17(2): 91–117.

42 S. Berman, J. Down, & C. Hill, 2002, Tacit knowledge as a source of competitive advantage in the National Basketball Association, *Academy of Management Journal*, 45: 13–31; D. L. Deeds, D. DeCarolis, & J. Coombs, 2000, Dynamic capabilities and new product development in high technology ventures: An empirical analysis of new biotechnology firms, *Journal of Business Venturing*, 15: 211–229.

43 S. Shepard, 2001, Interview: "The company is not in the stock," *Business Week*, April 30, 94–96.

44 M. S. Feldman, 2000, Organizational routines as a source of continuous change, *Organization Science*, 11: 611–629; A. M. Knott & B. McKelvey, 1999, Nirvana efficiency: A comparative test of residual claims and routines, *Journal of Economic Behavior & Organization*, 38: 365–383.

45 R. Lubit, 2001, Tacit knowledge and knowledge management: The keys to sustainable competitive advantage, *Organizational Dynamics*, 29(3): 164–178; S. A. Zahra, A. P. Nielsen, & W. C. Bogner, 1999, Corporate entrepreneurship, knowledge, and competence development, *Entrepreneurship: Theory and Practice*, 23(3): 169–189.

46 A. M. Webber, 2000, New math for a new economy, *Fast Company*, January–February, 214–224.

47 R. G. Schroeder, K. A. Bates, & M. A. Junttila, 2002, A resource-based view of manufacturing strategy and the relationship to manufacturing performance, *Strategic Management Journal*, 23: 105–117.

48 Brush & Artz, Toward a contingent resource-based theory.

49 J. B. Quinn, P. Anderson, & S. Finkelstein, 1996, Making the most of the best, *Harvard Business Review*, 74(2): 71–80.

50 Webber, New math, 217.

51 Ibid., 218.

52 R. D. Ireland, M. A. Hitt, & D. Vaidyanath, 2002, Managing strategic alliances to achieve a competitive advantage, *Journal of Management*, 28: 413–434.

53 D. L. Deephouse, 2000, Media reputation as a strategic resource: An integration of mass communication and resource-based theories, *Journal of Management*, 26: 1091–1112.

54 J. Shamsie, 2003, The context of dominance: An industry-driven framework for exploiting reputation, *Strategic Management Journal*, 24: 199–215; P. W. Roberts & G. R. Dowling, 2002, Corporate reputation and sustained superior financial performance, *Strategic Management Journal*, 23: 1077–1093.

55. 2007, Harley-Davidson MotorClothes merchandise, http://www.harleydavidson.com, January 25; M. Kleinman, 2001, Harley pushes brand prestige, *Marketing*, May 17, 16; G. Rifkin, 1998, How Harley-Davidson revs its brand, *Strategy & Business*, 9: 31–40.

56. M. A. Hitt, H. Lee, & E. Yucel, 2002, The importance of social capital to the management of multinational enterprises: Relational networks among Asian and western firms, *Asia Pacific Journal of Management*, 19: 353–372.

57. Gavetti & Levinthal, Looking forward and looking backward; R. W. Coff, 1999, How buyers cope with uncertainty when acquiring firms in knowledge-intensive industries: Caveat emptor, *Organization Science*, 10: 144–161; S. J. Marsh & A. L. Ranft, 1999, Why resources matter: An empirical study of knowledge-based resources on new market entry, in M. A. Hitt, P. G. Clifford, R. D. Nixon, & K. P. Coyne (eds.), *Dynamic Strategic Resources*, Chichester, UK: Wiley, 43–66.

58. C. E. Helfat & R. S. Raubitschek, 2000, Product sequencing: Co-evolution of knowledge, capabilities and products, *Strategic Management Journal*, 21: 961–979.

59. M. A. Hitt, L. Bierman, K. Shimizu, & R. Kochhar, 2001, Direct and moderating effects of human capital on strategy and performance in professional service firms: A resource-based perspective, *Academy of Management Journal*, 44: 13–28; M. A. Hitt, R. D. Ireland, & H. Lee, 2000, Technological learning, knowledge management, firm growth and performance: An introductory essay, *Journal of Engineering and Technology Management*, 17: 231–246; D. G. Hoopes & S. Postrel, 1999, Shared knowledge: "Glitches," and product development performance, *Strategic Management Journal*, 20: 837–865; J. B. Quinn, 1994, *The Intelligent Enterprise*, New York: The Free Press.

60. N. W. Hatch & J. H. Dyer, 2004, Human capital and learning as a source of sustainable competitive advantage, *Strategic Management Journal*, 25: 1155–1178; R. W. Griffith, P. W. Hom, & S. Gaertner, 2000, A meta-analysis of correlates of employee turnover: Update, moderator tests and research implications for the new millennium, *Journal of Management*, 26: 463–488.

61. D. B. Turban & D. W. Greening, 1996, Corporate social performance and organizational attractiveness to prospective employees, *Academy of Management Journal*, 40: 658–672.

62. 2006, 100 best companies to work for, CNNMoney.com, *Fortune*, http://www.cnnmoney.com/magazines/fortune, August 8.

63. 2006, People and capability, BP, http://www.bp.com/, August 8.

64. D. L. Deeds, 2003, Alternative strategies for acquiring knowledge, in S. E. Jackson, M. A. Hitt, & A. S. DeNisi (eds.), *Managing Knowledge for Sustained Competitive Advantage*, San Francisco: Jossey-Bass, 37–63.

65. G. Fink & N. Holden, 2005, The global transfer of management knowledge, *Academy of Management Executive*, 19(2): 5–8; R. A. Noe, J. A. Colquitt, M. J. Simmering, & S. A. Alvarez, 2003, Knowledge management: Developing intellectual and social capital, in S. E. Jackson, M. A. Hitt, & A. S. DeNisi (eds.), *Managing Knowledge for Sustained Competitive Advantage*, San Francisco: Jossey-Bass: 209–242; L. Argote & P. Ingram, 2000, Knowledge transfer: A basis for competitive advantage in firms, *Organizational Behavior and Human Decision Processes*, 82: 150–169.

66. G. G. Dess & J. C. Picken, 1999, *Beyond Productivity*, New York: AMACOM.

67. M. J. Tippins & R. S. Sohi, 2003, IT competency and firm performance: Is organizational learning a missing link? *Strategic Management Journal*, 24: 745–761; P. Coy, 2002, High turnover, high risk, *Business Week* (special issue), spring, 24.

68. T. T. Baldwin & C. C. Danielson, 2000, Building a learning strategy at the top: Interviews with ten of America's CLOs, *Business Horizons*, 43(6): 5–14.

69. D. F. Kuratko, R. D. Ireland, & J. S. Hornsby, 2001, Improving firm performance through entrepreneurial actions: Acordia's corporate entrepreneurship strategy, *Academy of Management Executive*, 15(4): 60–71; M. T. Hansen, N. Nhoria, & T. Tierney, 1999, What's your strategy for managing knowledge? *Harvard Business Review*, 77(2): 106–116.

70. M. A. Hitt & R. D. Ireland, 1986, Relationships among corporate level distinctive competencies, diversification strategy, corporate structure, and performance, *Journal of Management Studies*, 23: 401–416; M. A. Hitt & R. D. Ireland, 1985, Corporate distinctive competence, strategy, industry, and performance, *Strategic Management Journal*, 6: 273–293; M. A. Hitt, R. D. Ireland, & K. A. Palia, 1982, Industrial firms' grand strategy and functional importance, *Academy of Management Journal*, 25: 265–298; M. A. Hitt, R. D. Ireland, & G. Stadter, 1982, Functional importance and company performance: Moderating effects of grand strategy and industry type, *Strategic Management Journal*, 3: 315–330; C. C. Snow & L. G. Hrebiniak, 1980, Strategy, distinctive competence, and organizational performance, *Administrative Science Quarterly*, 25: 317–336.

71. C. Zott, 2003, Dynamic capabilities and the emergence of intraindustry differential firm performance: Insights from a simulation study, *Strategic Management Journal*, 24: 97–125.

72. K. Hafeez, Y. B. Zhang, & N. Malak, 2002, Core competence for sustainable competitive advantage: A structured methodology for identifying core competence, *IEEE Transactions on Engineering Management*, 49(1): 28–35; C. K. Prahalad & G. Hamel, 1990, The core competence of the corporation, *Harvard Business Review*, 68(3): 79–93.

73. C. Bowman & V. Ambrosini, 2000, Value creation versus value capture: Towards a coherent definition of value in strategy, *British Journal of Management*, 11: 1–15; T. Chi, 1994, Trading in strategic resources: Necessary conditions, transaction cost problems, and choice of exchange structure, *Strategic Management Journal*, 15: 271–290.

74. C. Bowman, 2001, "Value" in the resource-based view of the firm: A contribution to the debate, *Academy of Management Review*, 26: 501–502.

75. C. Ames, 1995, Sales soft? Profits flat? It's time to rethink your business, *Fortune*, June 25, 142–146.

76. Barney, How a firm's capabilities affect boundary decisions; J. B. Barney, 1995, Looking inside for competitive advantage, *Academy of Management Executive*, 9(4): 59–60; J. B. Barney, 1991, Firm resources and sustained competitive advantage, *Journal of Management*, 17: 99–120.

77. C. H. St. John & J. S. Harrison, 1999, Manufacturing-based relatedness, synergy, and coordination, *Strategic Management Journal*, 20: 129–145.

78. Barney, Looking inside for competitive advantage.

79. 2005, Jack Welch: It's all in the sauce, CNNMoney.com, *Fortune*, http://money.cnn.com/magazines/fortune/, April 4.

80  Barney, Looking inside for competitive advantage, 52.

81  Ibid., 53.

82  Barney, How a firm's capabilities affect boundary decisions, 141.

83  Barney, Firm resources and sustained competitive advantage, 108.

84  J. Huey, 1993, How McKinsey does it, *Fortune*, November 1, 56–81.

85  L. E. Tetrick & N. Da Silva, 2003, Assessing the culture and climate for organizational learning, in S. E. Jackson, M. A. Hitt, & A. S. DeNisi (eds.), *Managing Knowledge for Sustained Competitive Advantage*, San Francisco: Jossey-Bass, 333–359; R. Burt, 1999, When is corporate culture a competitive asset? Mastering strategy (part six), *Financial Times*, November 1, 14–15.

86  L. Soupata, 2001, Managing culture for competitive advantage at United Parcel Service, *Journal of Organizational Excellence*, 20(3): 19–26.

87  A. W. King & C. P. Zeithaml, 2001, Competencies and firm performance: Examining the causal ambiguity paradox, *Strategic Management Journal*, 22: 75–99; R. Reed & R. DeFillippi, 1990, Causal ambiguity, barriers to imitation, and sustainable competitive advantage, *Academy of Management Review*, 15: 88–102.

88  A. K. Gupta & V. Govindarajan, 2000, Knowledge management's social dimension: Lessons from Nucor steel, *Sloan Management Review*, 42(1): 71–80.

89  Barney, Firm resources and sustained competitive advantage, 111.

90  Amit & Schoemaker, Strategic assets and organizational rent, 39.

91  M. J. Benner & M. L. Tushman, 2003, Exploitation, exploration, and process management: The productivity dilemma revisited, *Academy of Management Review*, 28: 238–256; S. K. McEvily, S. Das, & K. McCabe, 2000, Avoiding competence substitution through knowledge sharing, *Academy of Management Review*, 25: 294–311.

92  M. E. Porter, 1985, *Competitive Advantage*, New York: The Free Press, 33–61.

93  G. G. Dess, A. Gupta, J. F. Hennart, & C. W. L. Hill, 1995, Conducting and integrating strategy research at the international corporate and business levels: Issues and directions, *Journal of Management*, 21: 376; Porter, What is strategy?

94  J. Webb & C. Gile, 2001, Reversing the value chain, *Journal of Business Strategy*, 22(2): 13–17.

95  T. A. Stewart, 1999, Customer learning is a two-way street, *Fortune*, May 10, 158–160.

96  R. Amit & C. Zott, 2001, Value creation in E-business, *Strategic Management Journal*, 22(special issue): 493–520; M. E. Porter, 2001, Strategy and the Internet, *Harvard Business Review*, 79(3): 62–78.

97  M. A. Cusumano & A. Gawer, 2002, The elements of platform leadership, *MIT Sloan Management Review*, 43(3): 51–58; C. Pegels, Y. Song, & B. Yang, 2000, Management heterogeneity, competitive interaction groups, and firm performance, *Strategic Management Journal*, 21: 911–923; N. Athanassiou & D. Nigh, 1999, The impact of U.S. company internationalization on top management team advice networks: A tacit knowledge perspective, *Strategic Management Journal*, 20: 83–92.

98  T. W. Gainey & B. S. Klaas, 2003, The outsourcing of training and development: Factors impacting client satisfaction, *Journal of Management*, 29: 207–229; J. Y. Murray & M. Kotabe, 1999, Sourcing strategies of U.S.

service companies: A modified transaction-cost analysis, *Strategic Management Journal*, 20: 791–809.

99  K. Madigan & M. J. Mandel, 2003, Commentary: Outsourcing jobs: Is it bad? *Business Week* online, http://www.businessweek.com, August 25; S. Jones, 1999, Growth process in global market, *Financial Times*, June 22, 17.

100  A. Takeishi, 2001, Bridging inter- and intra-firm boundaries: Management of supplier involvement in automobile product development, *Strategic Management Journal*, 22: 403–433; H. Y. Park, C. S. Reddy, & S. Sarkar, 2000, Make or buy strategy of firms in the U.S., *Multinational Business Review*, 8(2): 89–97.

101  J. C. Linder, S. Jarvenpaa, & T. H. Davenport, 2003, Toward an innovation sourcing strategy, *MIT Sloan Management Review*, 44(4): 43–49.

102  K. Hafeez, Y. B. Zhang, & N. Malak, 2002, Core competence for sustainable competitive advantage: A structured methodology for identifying core competence, *IEEE Transactions on Engineering Management*, 49(1): 28–35; B. H. Jevnaker & M. Bruce, 1999, Design as a strategic alliance: Expanding the creative capability of the firm, in M. A. Hitt, P. G. Clifford, R. D. Nixon, & K. P. Coyne (eds.), *Dynamic Strategic Resources*, Chichester, UK: Wiley, 266–298; C. K. Prahalad & G. Hamel, 1990, The core competence of the corporation, *Harvard Business Review*, 68(3): 79–93.

103  2007, The Outsourcing Institute: Gateway to the outsourcing marketplace, http://www.outsourcing.com, February 5.

104  M. J. Leiblein, J. J. Reuer, & F. Dalsace, 2002, Do make or buy decisions matter? The influence of organizational governance on technological performance, *Strategic Management Journal*, 23: 817–833; Takeishi, Bridging inter- and intra-firm boundaries.

105  M. J. Mol, P. Pauwels, P. Matthyssens, & L. Quintens, 2004, A technological contingency perspective on the depth and scope of international outsourcing, *Journal of International Management*, 10: 287–305.

106  C. Rossetti & T. Y. Choi, 2005, On the dark side of strategic sourcing: Experiences from the aerospace industry, *Academy of Management Executive*, 19(1): 46–60.

107  M. Useem & J. Harder, 2000, Leading laterally in company outsourcing, *Sloan Management Review*, 41(2): 25–36.

108  R. C. Insinga & M. J. Werle, 2000, Linking outsourcing to business strategy, *Academy of Management Executive*, 14(4): 58–70.

109  M. Katz, 2001, Planning ahead for manufacturing facility changes: A case study in outsourcing, *Pharmaceutical Technology*, March, 160–164.

110  T. C. Powell, 2002, The philosophy of strategy, *Strategic Management Journal*, 23: 873–880.

111  G. G. Dess & J. C. Picken, 1999, Creating competitive (dis)advantage: Learning from Food Lion's freefall, *Academy of Management Executive*, 13(3): 97–111.

112  M. Hannan & J. Freeman, 1977, The population ecology of organizations, *American Journal of Sociology*, 82: 929–964.

113  Leonard-Barton, *Wellsprings of Knowledge*, 30–31.

114  West & DeCastro, The Achilles heel of firm strategy; Keil, Cutting your losses.

115  E. T. Prince, 2005, The fiscal behavior of CEOs, *MIT Sloan Management Review*, 46(3): 23–26; C. A.

de Kluyver, 2000, *Strategic Thinking: An Executive Perspective*, Upper Saddle River, NJ: Prentice Hall, 3.

[116] C. Caldwell & R. Karri, 2005, Organizational governance and ethical systems: A covenantal approach to building trust, *Journal of Business Ethics*, 58: 249–267; A. McWilliams & D. Siegel, 2001, Corporate social responsibility: A theory of the firm perspective, *Academy of Management Review*, 26: 117–127.

[117] J. M. Stevens, H. K. Steensma, D. A. Harrison, & P. L. Cochran, 2005, Symbolic or substantive document? The influence of ethics codes on financial executives' decisions, *Strategic Management Journal*, 26: 181–195.

[118] R. E. Freeman & J. McVea, 2001, A stakeholder approach to strategic management, in M. A. Hitt, R. E. Freeman, & J. S. Harrison (eds.), *Handbook of Strategic Management*, Oxford, UK: Blackwell Publishers, 189–207.

[119] J. S. Harrison & J. O. Fiet, 1999, New CEOs pursue their own self-interests by sacrificing stakeholder value, *Journal of Business Ethics*, 19: 301–308.

[120] J. Magretta, 2002, Why business models matter, *Harvard Business Review*, 80(5): 86–92.

[121] J. Frooman, 1999, Stakeholder influence strategies, *Academy of Management Review*, 24: 191-205.

[122] R. E. Freeman, 1984, *Strategic Management: A Stakeholder Approach*, Boston: Pitman.

[123] Freeman & McVea, A stakeholder approach; R. K. Mitchell, B. R. Agle, & D. J. Wood, 1997, Toward a theory of stakeholder identification and salience: Defining the principle of who and what really count, *Academy of Management Review*, 22: 853–886.

[124] P. Shrivastava, 1995, Ecocentric management for a risk society, *Academy of Management Review*, 20: 119.

[125] P. Bromiley, K. D. Miller, & D. Rau, 2001, Risk in strategic management research, in M. A. Hitt, R. E. Freeman, & J. S. Harrison (eds.), *Handbook of Strategic Management*, Oxford, UK: Blackwell Publishers, 259–288.

[126] W. F. Sharpe, 1966, Mutual fund performance, *Journal of Business*, January, 119–138; J. L. Treynor, 1965, How to rate mutual fund performance, *Harvard Business Review*, January–February: 63–75.

[127] D. Ancona, H. Bresman, & K. Kaeufer, 2002, The comparative advantage of X-teams, *MIT Sloan Management Review*, 43(3): 33–39.

[128] S. Maitlis, 2005, The social process of organizational sensemaking, *Academy of Management Journal*, 48: 21–49.

[129] M. C. Jensen, 2001, Value maximization, stakeholder theory, and the corporate objective function, *European Financial Management*, 7(3): 297–317.

[130] M. E. Porter & M. R. Kramer, 2006, Strategy and society: The link between competitive advantage and corporate social responsibility, *Harvard Business Review*, 84(12): 78–92.

[131] G. Kassinis & N. Vafeas, 2006, Stakeholder pressures and environmental performance, *Academy of Management Journal*, 49: 145–159.

[132] J. Chambers, 2005, From the president and CEO, *Corporate Citizenship Report*, Cisco Systems company document, San Jose, CA: 1.

[133] Chiquita Brands International, Inc., 2005, Annual Report, 21.

[134] Porter & Kramer, Strategy and society.

[135] CEMEX, 2005 Annual Report, *CEMEX 2005 Sustainable Development Interim Report*, 7, http://www.cemex.com/, August 1, 2006.

[136] M. Blyler & R. W. Coff, 2003, Dynamic capabilities, social capital, and rent appropriation: Ties that split pies, *Strategic Management Journal*, 24: 677–686; R. Coff, 1999, When competitive advantage doesn't lead to performance: The resource-based view and stakeholder bargaining power, *Organization Science*, 10: 119–133.

[137] S. J. Chang, 2003, Ownership structure, expropriation, and performance of group-affiliated companies in Korea, *Academy of Management Journal*, 46: 238–253.

# CHAPTER 5

# Business-Level Strategy

## KNOWLEDGE OBJECTIVES

*Studying this chapter should provide you with the strategic management knowledge needed to:*

1. Define business-level strategies.
2. Discuss the relationship between customers and business-level strategies in terms of who, what, and how.
3. Explain the differences among business-level strategies.
4. Describe the relationships between strategy and structure.
5. Discuss the simple and functional structures used to implement business-level strategies.
6. Use the five forces model of competition to explain how value can be created through each business-level strategy.
7. Describe the risks of using each of the business-lev el strategies.

Strategy is concerned with making choices among two or more alternatives.[1] When choosing a strategy, the firm decides to pursue one course of action instead of others. Indeed, the main point of strategy is to help decision makers choose among the competing priorities and alternatives facing their firm.[2] The choices are important, as an established link exists between a firm's strategies and its long-term performance.[3] The fundamental objective of all strategies is to create value for stakeholders. Each strategy used should specify desired outcomes and how they are to be achieved.[4] Strategies are purposeful, precede the taking of actions to which they apply, and demonstrate a shared understanding of the firm's strategic intent and strategic mission.[5]

The chapters in this part of this book explore several types of strategies. **Business-level strategy,** the focus of this chapter, is an integrated and coordinated set of commitments and actions the firm uses to gain a competitive advantage by exploiting core competencies in specific product markets.[6] Consequently, every firm needs a business-level strategy for each of the markets in which it competes.[7] Business-level strategy is described by five basic approaches that combine the scope of an organization's activities in the market (broad or narrow) with the primary source of its competitive advantage (low cost or uniqueness).[8] Business-level strategies provide a basic approach to the market; however, there is also a dynamic aspect of competitive strategy that is defined by the particular actions and reactions of firms in a market. Chapter 6 covers *competitive rivalry and competitive dynamics*. *Cooperative strategies* fall within the topic area of competitive dynamics, but they are so important in today's business environment that Chapter 7 is devoted to them.

While business-level strategies and competitive dynamics relate to competition in particular product markets, determining the markets in which a firm will compete is the domain of *corporate-level strategy*, the topic of Chapter 8. *Acquisitions and restructuring*, discussed in Chapter 9, are among the vehicles firms use to carry out a corporate-level strategy. For instance, if a firm decides to enter a new market, it might pursue an acquisition in that market. On the other hand, a restructuring often involves moving out of certain products or markets. Finally, Chapter 10 deals with *international strategies*, which apply at both the business and corporate levels of a firm.

The strategies in these chapters can also be understood in terms of the five major elements of strategy described in Chapter 2.[9] (1) *Arenas* deal with the question, "Where will we be active (and with how much emphasis)?" This question is answered through a firm's corporate-level and international strategies. (2) *Vehicles* ask, "How will we get there?" Acquisition and restructuring strategies facilitate execution of the corporate-level strategy, whereas cooperative strategies are vehicles for business-level strategy. (3) *Differentiators*, described in depth in this chapter, address the issue of "How will we win?" (4) *Staging* deals with the question, "What will be our speed and sequence of moves?" Competitive rivalry and competitive dynamics address this important aspect of strategy. (5) Finally, *economic logic* asks, "How will we achieve above-average returns?" To some extent each of the strategies deals with this question because they share a common theme: how to create competitive advantage—a topic explored thoroughly in this chapter. Business-level strategy is primarily about the economic logic behind a firm's strategy in a particular product market. In this sense, business-level strategy can be thought of as the firm's core strategy in each market or industry.[10]

This chapter begins with a discussion of the economic logic behind the selection of a business-level strategy. Because of the strategic importance of customers in the strategy selection process, we then focus on these stakeholders. Specifically, a business-level strategy determines (1) *who* will be served, (2) *what* customer needs the strategy will satisfy, and (3) *how* those needs will be satisfied. We then introduce how organizational structures are related to business-level strategy and discuss the five basic business-level strategies in detail. Our analysis of these strategies describes how the effective use of each strategy allows the firm to favorably position itself relative to the five competitive forces in the industry (see Chapter 3). We introduce and explain organizational structures that are linked with successful use of each business-level strategy, and then we use the value chain (see Chapter 4) to show examples of the primary and support activities that are needed to implement each one. We also describe the different risks firms may encounter when using one of these strategies.

## Economic Logic and Business-Level Strategy

A business-level strategy reflects where and how the firm has an advantage over its rivals.[11] An effectively formulated strategy marshals, integrates, and allocates the firm's resources, capabilities, and competencies so that it will be properly aligned with its external environment.[12] In the end, sound strategic choices that reduce the uncertainty a firm faces and facilitate its success are the foundations upon which successful strategies are built.[13] Only firms that continuously upgrade their competitive advantages over time are able to achieve long-term success with their business-level strategies.[14] Accordingly, information about a host of variables, including markets, customers, technology, worldwide finance, and the changing world economy, must be collected and analyzed to properly form, use, and revise business-level strategies.[15]

Key issues the firm must address when choosing a business-level strategy are which good or service to offer customers, how to manufacture or create it, and how to distribute it to the marketplace.[16] The essence of a firm's business-level strategy is "choosing to perform activities differently or to perform different activities than rivals."[17] Thus, the firm's business-level strategy is a deliberate choice about how it will perform the value chain's primary and support activities in ways that create unique value.[18] Value is delivered to customers when the firm is able to use competitive advantages resulting from the integration of activities. Superior fit among primary and support activities forms an *activity system*. In turn, an effective activity system helps the firm establish and exploit its strategic position.

## Types of Business-Level Strategy

Firms choose from among five business-level strategies to establish and defend their desired strategic position against rivals: *cost leadership, differentiation, focused cost leadership, focused differentiation, and integrated cost leadership/differentiation* (see Figure 5.1). These five strategies are sometimes called generic because they can be used in any business and in any industry.[19] Each business-level strategy helps the firm to establish and exploit a competitive advantage within a particular competitive scope.

When selecting a business-level strategy, a firm evaluates two types of potential competitive advantage: "lower cost than rivals, or the ability to differentiate and command a premium price that exceeds the extra cost of doing so."[20] Having lower cost derives from the firm's ability to perform activities differently from rivals; being able to differentiate indicates the firm's capacity to perform different (and valuable) activities from those of rivals.[21] Competitive advantage is thus achieved within a particular scope of activities.

Scope has several dimensions, including the group of product and customer segments served and the array of geographic markets in which the firm competes. Competitive ad-

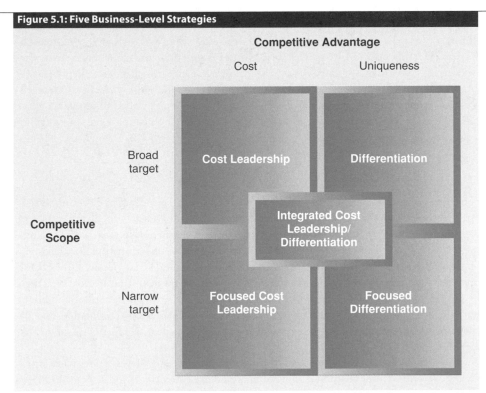

**Figure 5.1: Five Business-Level Strategies**

**Competitive Advantage**

Cost — Uniqueness

**Competitive Scope**

Broad target — Cost Leadership | Differentiation

Integrated Cost Leadership/ Differentiation

Narrow target — Focused Cost Leadership | Focused Differentiation

SOURCE: Adapted with the permission of The Free Press, A Division of Simon & Schuster Adult Publishing Group, from *Competitive Advantage: Creating and Sustaining Superior Performance*, by Michael E. Porter, p. 12. Copyright © 1985, 1988 by Michael E. Porter.

vantage is sought by competing in many customer segments when implementing either the cost leadership or the differentiation strategy. In contrast, when using focus strategies, the firm seeks a cost competitive advantage or a differentiation competitive advantage in a narrow competitive scope, segment, or niche. With focus strategies, the firm "selects a segment or group of segments in the industry and tailors its strategy to serving them to the exclusion of others."[22]

None of the five business-level strategies is inherently or universally superior to the others.[23] The effectiveness of each strategy is contingent both on the opportunities and threats in a firm's external environment and on the possibilities provided by the firm's unique resources, capabilities, and core competencies.[24] It is critical, therefore, for the firm to select an appropriate strategy in light of its opportunities, threats, and competencies.

## Serving Customers

Orientation toward customers is the foundation of all successful business-level strategies. The "source of competitive advantage" dimension deals with the question of whether firms will try to satisfy their customers through focusing on low costs (and presumably lower prices) or creating features that are highly attractive. Scope examines the nature and size of the customer group the firm seeks.

Strategic competitiveness results only when the firm is able to satisfy a group of customers by using its competitive advantages to compete in individual product markets. Firms must satisfy customers through their business-level strategies because the returns earned from relationships with customers are the lifeblood of all organizations.[25] The most successful companies constantly seek to chart new competitive space in order to serve new customers as they simultaneously try to find ways to better serve existing customers. Executives at the Motley Fool, an Internet venture, capture this reality crisply by noting that "the customer is the person who pays us."[26]

The firm's relationships with its customers are strengthened when it is committed to offering them superior value. In business-to-business transactions, superior value is often created when the firm's product helps its customers to develop a new competitive advantage or to enhance the value of its existing competitive advantages.[27] Receiving superior value enhances customers' loyalty to the firm that provides it. Evidence suggests that loyalty has a positive relationship with profitability. For example, Ford Motor Company estimates that each percentage-point increase in customer loyalty—defined as how many Ford owners purchase a Ford product the next time—creates at least $100 million in additional profits annually. As Ford struggles to turn around, it sorely needs the loyalty of its customer base. Norm Brodsky, a veteran entrepreneur who has had three businesses listed in *Inc.* magazine's list of the 500 fastest-growing companies, puts it this way: "There is a basic rule of business that's easy to forget, especially when you're competing for customers. Winning is not just about closing the sale. You win when you close the sale and also lay the foundation for a good relationship that will allow you to keep your customer for a long, long time."[28]

A number of companies have become skilled at the art of managing all aspects of their relationship with their customers.[29] In the fast-paced, technologically sophisticated global economy, firms that participate in e-commerce can understand their customers and manage their relationships with them more effectively than can companies without an Internet presence. The probability of successful competition increases when the firm carefully integrates Internet technology with its strategy, rather than using Internet technology on a "stand-alone basis."[30] CEMEX SA, a major global cement company based in Mexico, uses the Internet to link its customers, cement plants, and main control room, allowing the firm to automate orders and optimize truck deliveries in highly congested Mexico City. Analysts believe that CEMEX's integration of Web technology with its cost leadership strategy is helping to differentiate it from competitors.[31] Land's End is using the Internet to manage its relationships with women. Its Swim Finder online feature allows a shopper "to see a version of the suit on a three-dimensional likeness of her body."[32] Effective management of customer relationships, especially in this era of e-commerce, helps the firm answer questions related to the issues of who, what, and how to serve.

From a business-level strategy perspective, customer relationships involve answering questions related to *who, what,* and *how.*

### Who: Determining the Customers to Serve.
A crucial decision related to a business-level strategy is the one a company makes about *who,* or which customers, to target for the firm's goods or services.[33] To make this decision, companies divide customers into groups based on differences in the customers' needs (discussed below). This process, called **market segmentation,** clusters people with similar needs into individual and identifiable groups.[34] As part of its business-level strategy, the firm develops a marketing program to effectively sell products to a target customer group.[35]

Almost any identifiable human or organizational characteristic can be used to subdivide a market into segments that differ from one another on a given characteristic. Table 5.1 lists common characteristics on which customers' needs vary. On the basis of their core competencies and opportunities in the external environment, companies choose a business-level strategy to deliver value to target customers and satisfy their specific needs. For example, companies in the automobile industry segment markets using demographic factors, such as income and age; socioeconomic factors, such as stage in family life cycle; and psychological factors, such as lifestyle. Rolls-Royce and Porsche both appeal to wealthy individuals; however, Rolls-Royce focuses on older people and Porsche appeals to the young at heart.[36] Most of the major automobile companies have created separate product lines, with associated business infrastructures, to appeal to different segments of the market. General Motors has Cadillac, Buick, Chevrolet, Pontiac, Saturn, GMC, Hummer, Opel, and SAAB lines, with

---

**Table 5.1: Basis for Customer Segmentation**

**Consumer Markets**
1. Demographic factors (age, income, sex, etc.)
2. Socioeconomic factors (social class, stage in the family life cycle)
3. Geographic factors (cultural, regional, and national differences)
4. Psychological factors (lifestyle, personality traits)
5. Consumption patterns (heavy, moderate, and light users)
6. Perceptual factors (benefit segmentation, perceptual mapping)

**Industrial Markets**
1. End-use segments (identified by SIC code)
2. Product segments (based on technological differences or production economics)
3. Geographic segments (defined by boundaries between countries or by regional differences within them)
4. Common buying factor segments (cut across product market and geographic segments)
5. Customer size segments

SOURCE: Adapted from S. C. Jain, 2000, *Marketing Planning and Strategy,* Cincinnati: South-Western College Publishing, 120.

PART 3 / CREATING COMPETITIVE ADVANTAGE

each brand appealing to a different type of customer.[37] Toyota created its Lexus line and Honda its Acura line specifically to compete with Cadillac for people with higher incomes.

**What: Determining Which Customer Needs to Satisfy.** As a firm decides who it will serve, it must simultaneously identify *what* the targeted customer group needs that its goods or services can satisfy.[38] The two generalized forms of value that products provide are low cost with acceptable features or highly differentiated features with acceptable cost. For instance, in the department store retail market, Wal-Mart appeals to value-conscious consumers, whereas Saks Fifth Avenue seeks to appeal to consumers who expect the latest fashions and the highest quality merchandise.[39] Similarly, Apple Computer's strategy is to develop computers and other products that are highly differentiated. Its major competitors, such as Hewlett-Packard and Dell, focus on keeping costs low and selling a high volume of products.

**How: Determining Core Competencies Necessary to Satisfy Customer Needs.** *How* is addressed through core competencies, or the resources and capabilities that serve as a source of competitive advantage for the firm over its rivals (see Chapters 1 and 4). Firms use core competencies to implement value-creating strategies and thereby satisfy customers' needs. Only those firms with the capacity to continuously improve, innovate, and upgrade their competencies can expect to meet and, it is hoped, exceed customers' expectations across time.[40]

SAS Institute is the world's largest privately owned software company. Its programs are used for data warehousing, data mining, and decision support. Allocating more than 30 percent of revenues to R&D, the firm relies on its core competence in this area to satisfy the data-related needs of such customers as the U.S. Census Bureau and a host of consumer goods firms (e.g., hotels, banks, and catalog companies).[41] Vans Inc. relies on its core competencies in innovation and marketing to design and sell skateboards. The firm also pioneered thick-soled, slip-on sneakers that can absorb the shock of five-foot leaps on wheels. Vans uses what is recognized as an offbeat marketing mix to capitalize on its pioneering products. In lieu of mass media ads, the firm sponsors skateboarding events, has supported the making of a documentary film that celebrates the "outlaw nature" of the skateboarding culture, and is building skateboard parks around the country.[42]

All organizations, including SAS and Vans, must be able to use their core competencies (the *how*) to satisfy the needs (the *what*) of the target group of customers (the *who*) that the firm has chosen to serve by using its business-level strategy. Much of the success of any strategy, business-level or corporate-level (Chapter 8), depends on its implementation. But before we discuss each of the business-level strategies in detail, we introduce some of the structures that will be used to examine how each strategy can be implemented.

## Strategy and Structure

Research shows that organizational structure and the controls that are a part of it affect firm performance.[43] In particular, when the firm's strategy isn't matched with the most appropriate structure and controls, performance declines.[44] **Organizational structure** specifies the firm's formal reporting relationships, procedures, controls, and authority and decision-making processes.[45] Developing an organizational structure that will effectively support the firm's strategy is difficult, especially because of the uncertainty about cause-effect relationships in the global economy's rapidly changing and dynamic competitive environments.[46] When a structure's elements (e.g., reporting relationships, procedures, and so forth) are properly aligned with one another, that structure facilitates effective implementation of the firm's strategies.[47]

Strategy and structure have a reciprocal relationship, with structure flowing from the selection of the firm's strategy.[48] Once in place, structure can influence current strategic actions as well as choices about future strategies. The general nature of the strategy–structure relationship means that changes to the firm's strategy create the need to change how the organization completes its work. In the "structure influences strategy" direction, firms must be vigilant in their efforts to verify that how their structure calls for work to be completed remains consistent with the implementation requirements of chosen strategies. Research shows, however, that strategy has a more important influence on structure than structure does on strategy.[49]

Three major types of organizational structures are used to implement strategies: simple structure, functional structure, and multidivisional structure. The **simple structure** is a structure in which the owner-manager makes all major decisions and monitors all activities while the staff serves as an extension of the manager's supervisory authority.[50] Typically, the owner-manager actively works in the business on a daily basis. Informal relationships, few rules, limited task specialization, and unsophisticated information systems describe the simple structure. Frequent and informal communications between the owner-manager and employees make it relatively easy to coordinate the work that is to be done.

As the small firm grows and becomes more complex, managerial and structural challenges emerge, and firms tend to move from the simple structure to a functional organizational structure.[51] The **functional structure** is a structure consisting of a chief executive officer and a limited corporate staff, with functional line managers in dominant organizational areas such as production, accounting, marketing, R&D, engineering, and human resources.[52] This structure allows for functional specialization, thereby facilitating active sharing of knowledge within each functional area.[53] Knowledge sharing facilitates career paths as well as the professional development of functional specialists. However, a functional orientation can have a negative effect on communication and coordination among those representing different organizational functions. Because of this, the CEO must work hard to verify that the decisions and actions of individual business functions promote the entire firm rather than a single function.[54] The functional structure supports implementation of the business-level strategies described in this chapter and some corporate-level strategies (e.g., single or dominant business, described in Chapter 8) with low levels of product diversification.

With continuing growth and success, firms often consider greater levels of diversification. Successful diversification requires analysis of substantially greater amounts of data and information when the firm offers the same products in different markets (market or geographic diversification) or offers different products in several markets (product diversification). In addition, trying to manage high levels of diversification through functional structures creates serious coordination and control problems.[55] Thus, greater diversification leads to a new structural form.[56] The **multidivisional structure** (M-form) consists of operating divisions, each representing a separate business or profit center in which the top corporate officer delegates responsibilities for day-to-day operations and business-unit strategy to division managers. Each division represents a distinct, self-contained business with its own functional hierarchy.[57] This structure and its variants in relationship to corporate-level strategy will be described in Chapter 8.

We now discuss each business-level strategy and the structures they require.

# Cost Leadership Strategy

The **cost leadership strategy** is an integrated set of actions designed to produce or deliver goods or services with features that are acceptable to customers at the lowest cost, relative to that of competitors.[58] In terms of the two characteristics that define business-level strategies, competitive advantage and competitive scope, low-cost leaders seek cost advantages while serving a broad customer segment. Southwest Airlines, JetBlue Airways, and AirTran Airways all began with cost leadership strategies; however, they are now adding features and services that make them more similar to the large carriers. On the other hand, Europe's Ryanair Holdings may actually be *the* low-cost leader. Ryanair makes its flight crew members buy their own uniforms and charges customers to check luggage. A bottle of water on a Ryanair flight costs customers $3.40. Flight attendants use flight time to increase revenues by selling products such as digital cameras and iPocket MP3 players. Says CEO Michael O'Leary, "You want luxury? Go somewhere else."[59] Even in the face of large increases in fuel prices in 2006, Ryanair was enjoying huge increases in profits.

## Successful Execution of the Cost Leadership Strategy

Firms using the cost leadership strategy sell no-frills, standardized goods or services to the industry's most typical customers. Although cost leadership implies keeping costs as low as possible, products and services provided by a firm pursuing cost leadership must still have qualities and features that customers find acceptable.[60] For instance, even the lowest cost automobiles must meet minimum standards for safety and include features that customers have come to expect from all automobiles, such as a reliable radio, a spare tire, and some level of comfort. Indeed, emphasizing cost reductions while ignoring competitive features is ineffective. At the extreme, concentrating only on reducing costs could find the firm very efficiently producing products that no customer wants to purchase. When the firm designs, produces, and markets a comparable product more efficiently than its rivals, there is evidence that it is successfully using the cost leadership strategy.[61]

As described in Chapter 4, firms use value chain analysis to determine the parts of the company's operations that create value and those that do not. Cost leaders concentrate on finding ways to lower their costs relative to those of their competitors by constantly rethinking how to complete their primary and support activities to reduce costs further while still maintaining important features.[62] Figure 5.2 demonstrates the primary and support activities that allow a firm to create value through the cost leadership strategy. Companies unable to link the activities shown in this figure typically lack the resources, capabilities, and core competencies needed to successfully use the cost leadership strategy.

As primary activities, inbound logistics (e.g., materials handling, warehousing, and inventory control) and outbound logistics (e.g., collecting, storing, and distributing products to customers) often account for significant portions of the total cost to produce some goods and services. Research suggests that having a competitive advantage in terms of logistics creates more value when using the cost leadership strategy than when using the differentiation strategy (discussed below).[63] Thus, cost leaders seeking competitively valuable ways to reduce costs may want to concentrate on the primary activities of inbound logistics and outbound logistics.

Cost leaders also carefully examine all support activities to find additional sources of potential cost reductions. Developing new systems for finding the optimal combination of low cost and acceptable quality in the raw materials required to produce the firm's goods or

| | Inbound Logistics | Operations | Outbound Logistics | Marketing and Sales | Service |
|---|---|---|---|---|---|
| **Firm Infrastructure** | Cost-effective management information systems | Relatively few managerial layers in order to reduce overhead costs | | Simplified planning practices to reduce planning costs | |
| **Human Resource Management** | Consistent policies to reduce turnover costs | | Intense and effective training programs to improve worker efficiency and effectiveness | | |
| **Technology Development** | Easy-to-use manufacturing technologies | | Investments in technologies in order to reduce costs associated with a firm's manufacturing processes | | |
| **Procurement** | Systems and procedures to find the lowest cost (with acceptable quality) products to purchase as raw materials | | Frequent evaluation processes to monitor suppliers' performances | | |
| | Highly efficient systems to link suppliers' products with the firm's production processes | Use of economies of scale to reduce production costs | A delivery schedule that reduces costs | A small, highly trained sales force | Efficient and proper product installations in order to reduce the frequency and severity of recalls |
| | | Construction of efficient-scale production facilities | Selection of low-cost transportation carriers | Products priced so as to generate significant sales volume | |

MARGIN

MARGIN

SOURCE: Adapted with the permission of The Free Press, A Division of Simon & Schuster Adult Publishing Group, from *Competitive Advantage: Creating and Sustaining Superior Performance,* by Michael E. Porter, p. 47. Copyright © 1985, 1988 by Michael E. Porter.

services is an example of how the procurement support activity can facilitate successful use of the cost leadership strategy.

Big Lots Inc. uses the cost leadership strategy. With its vision of being "The World's Best Bargain Place," Big Lots is the largest broad-line closeout discount chain in the United States. Operating under the format names of Big Lots, Big Lots Furniture, Wisconsin Toy, Consolidated International, Big Lots Capital, and Big Lots Wholesale, the firm strives constantly to drive its costs lower by relying on what some analysts see as a highly disciplined merchandise cost and inventory management system.[64] The firm's stores sell name-brand products at prices that are 15 to 35 percent lower than those of discount retailers and roughly 70 percent lower than those of traditional retailers.[65] Big Lots's buyers travel the country looking through manufacturer overruns and discontinued styles, finding goods priced well below wholesale prices. In addition, the firm buys from overseas suppliers. Big Lots thinks of itself as the undertaker of the retailing business, purchasing merchandise that others can't sell or don't want. The company has a goal of "Helping People Connect with Their Inner Bargain Hunter."[66]

Effective use of the cost leadership strategy allows a firm to create value despite the presence of strong competitive forces described in the five forces model of competition (see Chapter 3). We now turn to how firms are able to do this, examining each of the five forces.

**Rivalry with Existing Competitors.** Having the low-cost position is a valuable defense against rivals. Because of the cost leader's advantageous position, rivals hesitate to compete on the basis of price. Wal-Mart is known for its ability to both control and reduce costs, making it difficult for firms to compete against it on the basis of price. The discount retailer achieves strict cost control in several ways. As one reporter described the company's Arkansas headquarters: "Wal-Mart's 660,000-square foot main headquarters, with its drab gray interiors and frayed carpets, looks more like a government building than the home of one of the world's largest corporations. Business often is done in the no-frills cafeteria, and suppliers meet with managers in stark, cramped rooms. Employees have to throw out their own garbage at the end of the day and double up in hotel rooms on business trips."[67] Kmart's inability to compete against Wal-Mart on the basis of cost led to its bankruptcy and eventually its merger with Sears.[68] However, the new company will still have difficulty competing with Wal-Mart in terms of cost because of Wal-Mart's comparative advantage in logistics. As noted earlier, research suggests that having a competitive advantage in terms of logistics significantly contributes to the cost leader's ability to create value.[69]

**Bargaining Power of Buyers (Customers).** Powerful customers can force a cost leader to reduce its prices, but not below the level at which the cost leader's next-most-efficient industry competitor can earn average returns. Although powerful customers might be able to force the cost leader to reduce prices even below this level, they probably would not choose to do so. Prices that are low enough to prevent the next-most-efficient competitor from earning average returns would force that firm to exit the market, leaving the cost leader with less competition and in an even stronger position. Customers would thus lose their power and pay higher prices when they are forced to purchase from a single firm operating in an industry without competitive rivals.

**Bargaining Power of Suppliers.** The cost leader operates with margins greater than those of competitors. Among other benefits, higher margins relative to those of competitors make it possible for the cost leader to absorb its suppliers' price increases. When an industry faces substantial increases in the cost of its supplies, only the cost leader may be able to pay the higher prices and continue to earn either average or above-average returns. Alternatively, a powerful cost leader may be able to force its suppliers to hold down their prices, which would reduce the suppliers' margins in the process.

**Potential Entrants.** Through continuous efforts to reduce costs to levels that are lower than those of its competitors, a cost leader becomes highly efficient. Because ever-improving levels of efficiency enhance profit margins, they serve as a significant entry barrier to potential competitors. New entrants must be willing and able to accept average to below-average returns until they gain the experience required to approach the cost leader's efficiency. To earn even average returns, new entrants must have the competencies required to match the cost levels of competitors other than the cost leader. The low profit margins (relative to margins earned by firms implementing the differentiation strategy) make it necessary for the cost leader to sell large volumes of its product to create value. However, firms striving to be the cost leader must avoid pricing their products so low that their ability to operate profitably is reduced, even though volume increases.

**Product Substitutes.** Compared with its industry rivals, the cost leader also holds an attractive position in terms of product substitutes. A product substitute becomes an issue for the cost leader when its features and characteristics, in terms of cost and differentiated features, are potentially attractive to the firm's customers. When faced with possible substitutes, the cost leader has more flexibility than its competitors. To retain customers, it can reduce the price of its good or service. With still lower prices and competitive levels of differentiation, the cost leader increases the probability that customers will prefer its product rather than a substitute.

## Using the Functional Structure to Implement the Cost Leadership Strategy

Different forms of the functional organizational structure are used to support implementation of the cost leadership, differentiation, and integrated cost leadership/differentiation strategies. The differences in these forms are accounted for primarily by different uses of three important structural characteristics or dimensions: *specialization* (concerned with the type and number of jobs required to complete work[70]), *centralization* (the degree to which decision-making authority is retained at higher managerial levels), and *formalization* (the degree to which formal rules and procedures govern work[71]).

Firms using the cost leadership strategy want to sell large quantities of standardized products to an industry's or a segment's typical customer. Simple reporting relationships, few layers in the decision-making and authority structure, a centralized corporate staff, and a strong focus on process improvements through the manufacturing function rather than the development of new products through an emphasis on product R&D characterize the cost leadership form of the functional structure (see Figure 5.3).[72] This structure contributes to the emergence of a low-cost culture—a culture in which all employees constantly try to find ways to reduce the costs incurred to complete their work.

In terms of centralization, decision-making authority is centralized in a staff function to maintain a cost-reducing emphasis within each organizational function (for example, engineering, marketing, etc.). While encouraging continuous cost reductions, the centralized staff also verifies that further cuts in costs in one function won't adversely affect the productivity levels in other functions.

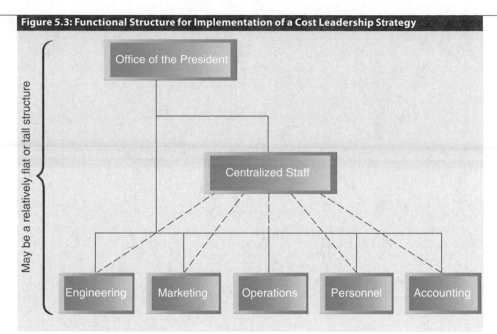

**Figure 5.3: Functional Structure for Implementation of a Cost Leadership Strategy**

Office of the President

Centralized Staff

Engineering | Marketing | Operations | Personnel | Accounting

*May be a relatively flat or tall structure*

Notes: • Operations is the main function
  • Process engineering is emphasized rather than new product R&D
  • Relatively large centralized staff coordinates functions
  • Formalized procedures allow for emergence of a low-cost culture
  • Overall structure is mechanical; job roles are highly structured

Jobs are highly specialized in the cost leadership functional structure. Job specialization is accomplished by dividing work into homogeneous subgroups. Organizational functions are the most common subgroup, although work is sometimes batched on the basis of products produced or clients served. Specializing in their work allows employees to increase their efficiency, reducing the firm's costs as a result. Highly formalized rules and procedures, often emanating from the centralized staff, guide the work completed in the cost leadership form of the functional structure. Predictably following formal rules and procedures creates cost-reducing efficiencies. Known for its commitment to EDLP ("everyday low price"), Wal-Mart's functional organizational structures in both its retail (e.g., Wal-Mart Stores, Supercenters, Sam's Club) and specialty (e.g., Wal-Mart Vacations, Used Fixture Auctions) divisions are formed to continuously drive costs lower.[73] Competitors' efforts to duplicate the success of Wal-Mart's cost leadership strategies have failed, partly because of Wal-Mart's effective strategy–structure configurations in its business units.

## Competitive Risks of the Cost Leadership Strategy

The cost leadership strategy is not risk free. One risk is that the processes the cost leader uses to produce and distribute its good or service could become obsolete because of innovations by its competitors. These innovations may allow rivals to produce at costs lower than those of the original cost leader, or to provide additional differentiated features without increasing the product's price to customers.

A second risk is that the cost leader may focus on cost reductions at the expense of trying to understand customers' perceptions of "competitive levels of differentiation." As noted earlier, Wal-Mart is known for constantly and aggressively reducing its costs. However, the firm must simultaneously remain focused on understanding when a cost-reducing decision to eliminate differentiated features that can create value in a low-cost environment (e.g., extended shopping hours, increases in the number of checkout counters to reduce customer waiting time) in order to reduce costs to still lower levels would create an unattractive value proposition for customers.

A final risk of the cost leadership strategy concerns imitation. Using their own core competencies (see Chapter 3), competitors sometimes learn how to successfully imitate the cost leader's strategy. When this occurs, the cost leader must increase the value that its good or service provides to customers. Commonly, value is increased by selling the current product at an even lower price or by adding differentiated features that customers value while maintaining price.

Even cost leaders must be careful when reducing prices to a still lower level. If the firm prices its good or service at an unrealistically low level (a level at which it will be difficult to retain satisfactory margins), customers' expectations about a reasonable price become difficult to reverse.

## Differentiation Strategy

The **differentiation strategy** is an integrated set of actions designed by a firm to produce or deliver goods or services (at an acceptable cost) that customers perceive as being different in ways that are important to them.[74] Competitive scope is still fairly broad, in that firms that pursue this strategy seek to sell their products to a broad group of customers. Mary Frances Accessories follows a differentiation strategy. The company sells elaborately designed, constructed, and decorated women's handbags and other accessories at thousands of boutiques and department stores throughout the United States, such as Macy's and Dillard's. As part of its differentiation strategy, Mary Frances has had its handbags on the arms of some very influential people, including Oprah Winfrey. It also provides an assortment of more than 100 handbags at any given time. The company, which employs women only, grew 515 percent in a three-year period, putting it on *Inc.* magazine's list of the fastest growing private companies in 2006.[75]

### Successful Execution of the Differentiation Strategy

While cost leaders serve an industry's typical customer, differentiators target customers who perceive that value is added by the manner in which the firm's products are differentiated. Firms must be able to produce differentiated products at competitive costs, however, to reduce upward pressure on the price customers pay for them. When a product's differentiated features are produced through noncompetitive costs, the price for the product can exceed what the firm's target customers are willing to pay. When the firm has a thorough understanding of what its target customers value, the relative importance they attach to the satisfaction of different needs, and for what they are willing to pay a premium, the differentiation strategy can be successfully used.[76] The key to success in a differentiation strategy is that customers must perceive that the additional cost of a product or service is more than offset by its differentiating features. Commonly recognized differentiated goods include Bose stereo equipment, Ralph Lauren clothing, and Caterpillar heavy-duty earth-moving equipment. McKinsey & Co., thought by some to be the world's most expensive and prestigious consulting firm, is a well-known example of a firm that offers differentiated services.

Through the differentiation strategy, the firm produces nonstandardized products for customers who value differentiated features more than they value lowest possible cost. For example, superior product reliability and durability and high-performance sound systems are among the differentiated features of Toyota's Lexus products. The often-used Lexus promotional statement—"The Relentless Pursuit of Perfection"—suggests a strong commitment to overall product quality as a source of differentiation.[77] However, Lexus offers its vehicles to customers at a competitive purchase price. As with Lexus products, a good or service's unique attributes, rather than its purchase price, provide the value for which customers are willing to pay. Similarly, clothing manufacturer Robert Talbott follows stringent standards of crafts and pays meticulous attention to every detail of production. The firm imports exclusive fabrics from the world's finest mills to make men's dress shirts. Single-needle tailoring is used, and precise collar cuts are made. According to the company, customers purchasing one of its shirts can be assured that they are being provided with the finest quality available.[78] Thus, Robert Talbott's success in shirt making rests on the firm's ability to produce and sell its differentiated shirts at a price significantly higher than the costs of imported fabrics and its unique manufacturing processes.

A firm using the differentiation strategy seeks to be different from its competitors on as many dimensions as possible. The less similarity between a firm's goods or services and those of competitors, the more buffered it is from rivals' actions. A product can be differentiated in many ways. Unusual features, responsive customer service, rapid product innovations, technological leadership, perceived prestige and status, different tastes, and engineering design and performance are examples of approaches to differentiation. For customers to be willing to pay a premium price, a "firm must truly be unique at something or be perceived as unique."[79] The ability to sell a good or service at a price that substantially exceeds the cost of creating its differentiated features allows the firm to outperform rivals and create value.

A firm's value chain can be analyzed to determine whether the firm is able to link the activities required to create value by using the differentiation strategy. Figure 5.4 shows examples of primary and support activities that are commonly used to differentiate a good or service. Companies without the core competencies needed to link these activities cannot expect to successfully use the differentiation strategy. Next, we explain how firms using the differentiation strategy can successfully position themselves in terms of the five forces of competition (see Chapter 3) to create value.

**Rivalry with Existing Competitors.** Customers tend to be loyal purchasers of products that are differentiated in ways that are meaningful to them. As their loyalty to a brand increases, their sensitivity to price increases is reduced. This is especially true of those purchasing high-end, big-ticket items (e.g., luxury automobiles and custom interior design services for the home and office). The relationship between brand loyalty and price sensitivity insulates a firm from competitive rivalry. Thus, McKinsey & Co. is insulated from its competitors, even on the basis of price, as long as it continues to satisfy the differentiated needs of its customer group. Bose is insulated from intense rivalry as long as customers continue to perceive that its stereo equipment offers superior sound quality at a competitive price.

**Bargaining Power of Buyers (Customers).** The uniqueness of differentiated goods or services reduces customers' sensitivity to price increases. Customers are willing to accept a price increase when a product still satisfies their perceived unique needs better than a competitor's offering can. Thus, the golfer whose needs are uniquely satisfied by Callaway golf clubs will likely continue buying those products even if their cost increases. Similarly, the

| | Inbound Logistics | Operations | Outbound Logistics | Marketing and Sales | Service |
|---|---|---|---|---|---|
| **Firm Infrastructure** | Highly developed information systems to better understand customers' purchasing preferences | | | | |
| **Human Resource Management** | Compensation programs intended to encourage worker creativity and productivity | | Somewhat extensive use of subjective rather than objective performance measures | | Superior personnel training |
| **Technology Development** | Strong capability in basic research | | Investments in technologies that will allow the firm to produce highly differentiated products | | |
| **Procurement** | Systems and procedures used to find the highest quality raw materials | | Purchase of highest quality replacement parts | | |
| | Superior handling of incoming raw materials so as to minimize damage and to improve the quality of the final product | Consistent manufacturing of attractive products. Rapid responses to customers' unique manufacturing specifications | Accurate and responsive order-processing procedures. Rapid and timely product deliveries to customers | Extensive granting of credit buying arrangements for customers. Extensive personal relationships with buyers and suppliers | Extensive buyer training to assure high-quality product installations. Complete field stocking of replacement parts |

SOURCE: Adapted with the permission of The Free Press, A Division of Simon & Schuster Adult Publishing Group, from *Competitive Advantage: Creating and Sustaining Superior Performance*, by Michael E. Porter, p. 47. Copyright © 1985, 1988 by Michael E. Porter.

person who has been highly satisfied with a 10-year-old Louis Vuitton wallet will proba-bly replace that wallet with another wallet from the same company even though the price is higher than the original one. Purchasers of brand-name items (e.g., Heinz ketchup and Kleenex tissues) will continue to purchase them even at higher prices than comparable prod-ucts as long as they perceive that the extra value they are receiving from those products sur-passes the additional costs.

**Bargaining Power of Suppliers.** Because the firm using the differentiation strategy charges a premium price for its products, suppliers must provide high-quality components, driving up the firm's costs. However, the high margins the firm earns in these cases par-tially insulate it from the influence of suppliers in that higher supplier costs can be paid through these margins. Alternatively, because of buyers' relative insensitivity to price in-creases, the differentiated firm might choose to pass the additional cost of supplies on to the customer by increasing the price of its unique product.

**Potential Entrants.** Customer loyalty and the need to overcome the uniqueness of a dif-ferentiated product present substantial entry barriers to potential entrants. Entering an in-dustry under these conditions typically demands significant investments of resources and patience while seeking customers' loyalty.

**Product Substitutes.** Firms selling brand-name goods and services to loyal custom-ers are positioned effectively against product substitutes. In contrast, companies without brand loyalty face a higher probability of their customers switching either to products that offer differentiated features that serve the same function (particularly if the substitute has a lower price) or to products that offer more features and perform more attractive functions.

## Using the Functional Structure to Implement the Differentiation Strategy

Firms using the differentiation strategy produce products that customers perceive as be-ing different in ways that create value for them. With this strategy, the firm wants to sell nonstandardized products to customers with unique needs. Relatively complex and flex-ible reporting relationships, frequent use of cross-functional product development teams, and a strong focus on marketing and product R&D rather than manufacturing and process R&D (as with the cost leadership form of the functional structure) characterize the dif-ferentiation form of the functional structure (see Figure 5.5). This structure contributes to the emergence of a development-oriented culture—a culture in which employees try to find ways to further differentiate current products and to develop new, highly differenti-ated products.

Continuous product innovation demands that people throughout the firm be able to interpret and take action based on information that is often ambiguous, incomplete, and uncertain. With a strong focus on the external environment to identify new opportuni-ties, employees often gather this information from people outside the firm, such as cus-tomers and suppliers. Commonly, rapid responses to the possibilities indicated by the col-lected information are necessary, suggesting the need for decision-making responsibility and authority to be decentralized. To support creativity and the continuous pursuit of new sources of differentiation and new products, jobs in this structure are not highly special-ized. This lack of specialization means that workers have a relatively large number of tasks in their job descriptions. Few formal rules and procedures are also characteristic of this

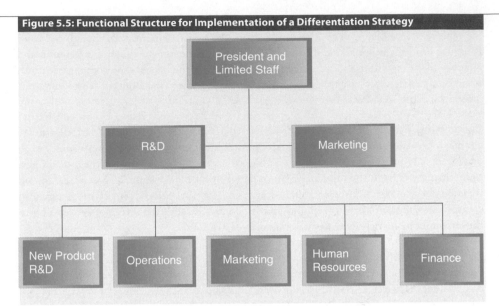

**Figure 5.5: Functional Structure for Implementation of a Differentiation Strategy**

President and Limited Staff

R&D

Marketing

New Product R&D

Operations

Marketing

Human Resources

Finance

Notes:
- Marketing is the main function for keeping track of new product ideas
- New product R&D is emphasized
- Most functions are decentralized, but R&D and marketing may have centralized staffs that work closely with each other
- Formalization is limited so that new product ideas can emerge easily and change is more readily accomplished
- Overall structure is organic; job roles are less structured

structure. Low formalization, decentralization of decision-making authority and responsibility, and low specialization of work tasks combine to create a structure in which people interact frequently to exchange ideas about how to further differentiate current products while developing ideas for new products that can be differentiated to create value for customers.

## Competitive Risks of the Differentiation Strategy

As with the other business-level strategies, the differentiation strategy is not risk free. One risk is that customers might decide that the price differential between the differentiator's product and the cost leader's product is too large. In this instance, a firm may be offering differentiated features that exceed target customers' needs. The firm then becomes vulnerable to competitors that are able to offer customers a combination of features and price that is more consistent with their needs.

Another risk of the differentiation strategy is that a firm's means of differentiation may cease to provide value for which customers are willing to pay. A differentiated product becomes less valuable if imitation by rivals causes customers to perceive that competitors offer essentially the same good or service, but at a lower price. For example, Walt Disney Company operates different theme parks, including the Magic Kingdom, Epcot, Animal Kingdom, and Disneyland. Each park offers entertainment and educational opportunities. However, Disney's competitors, such as Six Flags Corporation and NBC Universal (Universal Studios and Islands of Adventure), also offer entertainment and educational experiences similar to those available at Disney's locations. To ensure that its facilities create value for which customers will be willing to pay, Disney continuously reinvests in its operations to more crisply differentiate them from those of its rivals.[80]

A third risk of the differentiation strategy is that experience can narrow customers' perceptions of the value of a product's differentiated features. For example, the value of the IBM name provided a differentiated feature for the firm's personal computers for which some users were willing to pay a premium price in the early life cycle of the product. However, as customers familiarized themselves with the product's standard features, and as a host of other firms' personal computers entered the market, IBM brand loyalty ceased to create value for which some customers were willing to pay. Competitors offered features similar to those found in the IBM product at a substantially lower price, reducing the attractiveness of IBM's product. Ultimately, IBM sold its PC business to China's Lenovo Group, although IBM kept a stake in the business.[81]

Counterfeiting is the differentiation strategy's fourth risk. Makers of counterfeit goods—products that attempt to convey differentiated features to customers at significantly reduced prices—are a concern for many firms using the differentiation strategy. For example, Callaway Golf Company's success at producing differentiated products that create value, coupled with golf's increasing global popularity, has created great demand for counterfeited Callaway equipment. Through the U.S. Customs Service's "Project Teed Off" program, agents seized more than 110 shipments with a total of more than 100,000 counterfeit Callaway golf club components over three years.[82] Companies such as Callaway also work with government officials in other nations to influence the formation of tighter import regulations to curb the flow of counterfeit products.

---

## Focus Strategies

Firms choose a **focus strategy** when they want their core competencies to serve the needs of a particular industry segment or niche at the exclusion of others. Examples of specific market segments that can be targeted by a focus strategy include (1) a particular buyer group (e.g., youths or senior citizens), (2) a different segment of a product line (e.g., products for professional painters or those for "do-it-yourselfers"), or (3) a different geographic market (e.g., the East or the West in the United States).[83] Thus, the focus strategy is an integrated set of actions designed to produce or deliver goods or services that serve the needs of a particular competitive segment.

Although the breadth of a target is clearly a matter of degree, the essence of the focus strategy "is the exploitation of a narrow target's differences from the balance of the industry."[84] Firms using the focus strategy intend to serve a particular segment of an industry more effectively than can industry-wide competitors. They succeed when they effectively serve a segment whose unique needs are so specialized that broad-based competitors choose not to serve that segment or when they satisfy the needs of a segment being served poorly by industry-wide competitors.[85]

Through successful use of the focus strategy, firms gain a competitive advantage in specific market niches or segments, even though they do not possess an industry-wide competitive advantage.[86] Firms can create value for customers in specific and unique market segments by using the *focused cost leadership strategy* or the *focused differentiation strategy*.

### Focused Cost Leadership Strategy

Based in Sweden, Ikea, an international furniture retailer, follows the focused cost leadership strategy.[87] Young buyers desiring style at a low cost are Ikea's market segment. For these customers, the firm offers home furnishings that combine good design, function, and acceptable quality with low prices. According to the firm, low cost applies to every phase of their activities. For example, instead of relying on third-party manufacturers, the firm's engineers design low-cost, modular furniture ready for assembly by customers. Ikea also displays its products in roomlike settings, which reduces the need for sales associates or decorators to help the customer imagine how a batch of furniture will look when placed in the customer's home. This approach requires fewer sales personnel, allowing Ikea to keep its costs low. A third practice that keeps Ikea's costs low is expecting customers to transport their own purchases rather than providing delivery service. Ikea makes sure that its services and products "are uniquely aligned with the needs of (its) customers, who are young, are not wealthy, are likely to have children (but no nanny), and, because they work for a living, have a need to shop at odd hours."[88]

Firms that provide services can also pursue a focused cost leadership strategy. Morgan Lynch created Logoworks because he was dismayed when hiring a firm to create a company logo for one of his other ventures. Logoworks is an online company with a team of 225 designers who have created logos for firms in more than 100 countries. At least two designers create logo concepts for each project. According to Lynch, "The most popular deal is three designers for $399. Every designer gets paid for concepting, and the one who gets chosen gets a bonus."[89] The budget-conscious Internet logo company had sales of $7.3 million in 2005.

## Focused Differentiation Strategy

Other firms implement the focused differentiation strategy in the pursuit of competitive advantage. As noted earlier, firms can differentiate their products in many ways. Harley-Davidson focuses on older consumers with an adventurous spirit. In fact, only 15 percent of its sales are to buyers younger than age 35. Harley differentiates its motorcycles on quality and image rather than speed. It makes frequent improvements to existing models and introduced 10 new models (out of 38 total) in a period of only two years. Despite all these improvements, Harley's motorcycles still have the look and feel of a Harley. As Jay Leno, owner of 80 motorcycles, said, "When you look at a 1936 Harley, the family resemblance to the modern Harley holds up."[90] According to Cook Neilson, former top motorcycle racer, "The company has a death grip on who it is they are, and they know that for them to stray off in some direction would be stupid and suicidal, and they're not going to do it."[91] Despite their high price tags, Harley motorcycles are still growing in popularity. In 2006 sales grew in double digits, and even in Japan, home of rivals Honda and Suzuki, Harley owns the top spot in the big bike segment.

Like the focused cost leadership strategy, the focused differentiation strategy also applies to service and to manufacturing firms. The share price of Live Nation Inc., which was spun off from Clear Channel Communications at the end of 2005, more than doubled in just 13 months. The company focuses specifically on rock and roll fans who are willing to spend $100 or more to see aging artists such as the Rolling Stones, Eagles, and Madonna.[92]

Firms must be able to complete various primary and support activities in a competitively superior manner to achieve and sustain a competitive advantage and create value with a focus strategy. The activities required to use the focused cost leadership strategy are virtually identical to those shown in Figure 5.2, and the activities required to use the focused differentiation strategy are virtually identical to those shown in Figure 5.4. Similarly, each of the two focus strategies allows a firm to deal successfully with the five competitive forces in a manner parallel to that described with respect to the cost leadership strategy and the differentiation strategy. The only difference is that the competitive scope changes from an industry-wide market to a narrow industry segment. Thus, a review of Figures 5.2 and 5.4

and the text regarding the five competitive forces yields a description of the relationship between each of the two focus strategies and competitive advantage.

## Using the Simple or Functional Structures to Implement Focus Strategies

The simple structure is matched with focus strategies as firms compete by offering a single product line in a single geographic market. Local restaurants, repair businesses, and other specialized enterprises are examples of firms relying on the simple structure to implement their strategy. However, as firms grow larger, a functional structure will be required. If they pursue a focused cost leadership or focused differentiation strategy, they will implement the functional structures illustrated in Figure 5.3 or Figure 5.5, respectively.

## Competitive Risks of Focus Strategies

With either focus strategy, the firm faces the same general risks as does the company using the cost leadership or the differentiation strategy on an industry-wide basis. However, focus strategies have three additional risks.

First, a competitor may be able to focus on a more narrowly defined competitive segment and "outfocus" the focuser. For example, Big Dog Motorcycles is trying to outfocus Harley-Davidson, which is pursuing a broader-focus differentiation strategy. While Harley focuses solely on producing heavyweight motorcycles, Big Dog builds motorcycles that target only the very high end of the heavyweight market—the high-end premium cruiser market—with names such as Pitbull, Wolf, Mastiff, and Bulldog. Big Dog is careful to differentiate its products from those of Harley-Davidson, citing its larger motors, fat rear tires, unique state-of-the-art electronics, and four-piston caliber brakes as examples of value-creating features. With additional value-creating differentiated features (e.g., performance capabilities made possible by larger engines), Big Dog may be able to better serve the unique needs of a narrow customer group.[93]

Second, a company competing on an industry-wide basis may decide that the market segment served by the focus strategy firm is attractive and worthy of competitive pursuit. For instance, Anne Fontaine specializes in designing, producing, and selling "uniquely feminine" white shirts for women through 70 of its own stores.[94] Gap, Inc.'s new Forth & Towne retail concept, targeted at upscale women older than age 35, may pose a direct threat to Anne Fontaine.[95]

The third risk involved with a focus strategy is that the needs of customers within a narrow competitive segment may become more similar to those of industry-wide customers as a whole. As a result, the advantages of a focus strategy are either reduced or eliminated. At some point, for example, Harley's customers may begin to focus more on speed and handling, areas where the other big motorcycle manufacturers have an advantage.

## Integrated Cost Leadership/Differentiation Strategy

Particularly in global markets, the firm's ability to integrate the means of competition necessary to implement the cost leadership and differentiation strategies may be critical to developing competitive advantages. In fact, with globalization and technological advancements, many markets demand that firms not only "run harder" than competitors, they must also run differently and smarter.[96] Doing so requires the use of the **integrated cost leadership/differentiation strategy.** Compared with firms implementing one dominant business-level strategy, the company that successfully uses an integrated cost leadership/ differentiation strategy should be in a better position to (1) adapt quickly to environmental changes, (2) learn new skills and technologies more quickly, and (3) effectively leverage its core competencies while competing against its rivals.

Concentrating on the needs of its core customer group (higher-income, fashion-conscious discount shoppers), Target Corporation uses an integrated strategy. It relies on its relationships with Michael Graves in home, garden, and electronics products; Sonia Kashuk in cosmetics; Mossimo in apparel; and Eddie Bauer in camping and outdoor gear, among others, to offer differentiated products at discounted prices. Committed to presenting a consistent upscale image to its core customer group, the firm carefully studies trends to find new branded items that it believes can satisfy its customers' needs.[97]

## Successful Execution of the Integrated Cost Leadership/Differentiation Strategy

Evidence suggests a relationship between successful use of the integrated strategy and above-average returns.[98] Thus, firms able to produce relatively differentiated products at relatively low costs can expect to perform well.[99] Indeed, a researcher found that the most successful firms competing in low-profit-potential industries were integrating the attributes of the cost leadership and differentiation strategies.[100] Other researchers have discovered that "businesses which combined multiple forms of competitive advantage outperformed businesses that only were identified with a single form."[101] The results of another study showed that the highest-performing companies in the Korean electronics industry combined the value-creating aspects of the cost leadership and differentiation strategies.[102] This finding suggests the usefulness of integrated strategy in settings outside the United States.

Unlike Target, which uses the integrated cost leadership/differentiation strategy on an industry-wide basis, air-conditioning and heating-systems maker Aaon concentrates on a particular competitive scope. Thus, Aaon is implementing a focused integrated strategy. Aaon manufactures semicustomized rooftop air-conditioning systems for large retailers, including Wal-Mart, Target, and Home Depot. The company positions its rooftop systems between low-priced commodity equipment and high-end customized systems. Aaon's objective is to make and offer "performance oriented products that perform beyond expectations and provide life-cycle dependability at a reasonable first cost."[103] The firm's innovative manufacturing capabilities allow it to tailor a production line for units with special heat-recovery options unavailable on low-end systems. Combining custom features with assembly-line production methods results in significant cost savings. Aaon's prices are approximately 5 percent higher than low-end products but are only one-third the price of comparable customized systems.[104] Thus, the firm's narrowly defined target customers receive some differentiated features (e.g., special heat-recovery options) at a low, but not the lowest, cost.

The integrated cost leadership/differentiation strategy is a common strategy, although it is difficult to successfully implement. This difficulty largely is due to the fact that cost leadership and differentiation strategies emphasize different primary and support activities. To achieve the low-cost position, emphasis is placed on production and process engineering, with infrequent product changes. To achieve a differentiated position, marketing and new-product R&D are emphasized, whereas production and process engineering are not. Thus, successful implementation of the integrated strategy requires a careful combination of activities intended to reduce costs with activities intended to create additional differentiation features. This balancing act requires a flexible organizational structure.

## Using a Flexible Structure to Implement the Integrated Cost Leadership/Differentiation Strategy

As a result of the need to balance the various objectives associated with both cost leadership and differentiation, the type of functional structure needed for the integrated strategy must have flexible decision-making patterns that are partially centralized and partially decentralized. Additionally, jobs are less specialized than in a traditional functional structure so that workers are more sensitive to the need for a balance between low cost and differentiation. Some firms use modular products to create differentiation (easier customization) and simultaneously to hold down costs. Firms that use modular products often also use modular organizational structures to implement the strategy of modular products. Modular structures are more flexible and less hierarchical.[105]

A commitment to *strategic flexibility* (see Chapter 1) is necessary for firms such as Target and Aaon to effectively use the integrated cost leadership/differentiation strategy. Strategic flexibility results from developing systems, procedures, and methods that enable a firm to quickly and effectively respond to opportunities that reduce costs or increase differentiation. Because of the need for additional strategic flexibility, other system processes help to facilitate implementation of the integrated strategy. *Flexible manufacturing systems, information networks*, and *total quality management systems* are three sources of strategic flexibility that facilitate use of the integrated strategy. Valuable to the successful use of each business-level strategy, the strategic flexibility provided by these three tools is especially important to firms trying to balance the objectives of continuous cost reductions and continuous enhancements to sources of differentiation.

**Flexible Manufacturing Systems.** Modern information technologies have helped make flexible manufacturing systems (FMS) possible. These systems increase the "flexibilities of human, physical, and information resources" that the firm integrates to create differentiated products at low costs.[106] A flexible manufacturing system (FMS) is a computer-controlled process used to produce a variety of products in moderate, flexible quantities with a minimum of manual intervention.[107] Particularly in situations where parts are too heavy for people to handle or when other methods are less effective in creating manufacturing and assembly flexibility, robots are integral to use of an FMS.[108] Despite their promise, only one in five Fortune 1000 companies is using the productive capabilities of an FMS.[109]

The goal of an FMS is to eliminate the "low-cost-versus-product-variety" trade-off that is inherent in traditional manufacturing technologies. Firms use an FMS to change quickly and easily from making one product to making another.[110] Used properly, an FMS allows the firm to respond more effectively to changes in its customers' needs, while retaining low-cost advantages and consistent product quality.[111] Because an FMS also enables the firm to reduce the lot size needed to manufacture a product efficiently, the firm increases its capacity to serve the unique needs of a narrow competitive scope. Thus, FMS technology is a significant technological advance that allows firms to produce a large variety of products at a relatively low cost. Levi Strauss, for example, uses an FMS to make jeans for women that fit their exact measurements. Customers of Andersen Windows can design their own windows using proprietary software the firm has developed. Tire manufacturers Pirelli and Goodyear are turning to robots and other advanced technologies as part of their quest to transform the traditional time-consuming, complex, and costly method of making tires into a more flexible and responsive system.[112]

The effective use of an FMS is linked with a firm's ability to understand the constraints these systems may create (in terms of materials handling and the flow of supporting resources in scheduling, for example) and to design an effective mix of machines, computer systems, and people.[113] In service industries, the processes used must be flexible enough to increase delivery speed and to satisfy changing customer needs. In industries of all types, effective mixes of the firm's tangible assets (e.g., machines) and intangible assets (e.g., people's skills) facilitate implementation of complex competitive strategies, especially the integrated cost leadership/differentiation strategy.[114]

**Information Networks.** By linking companies with their suppliers, distributors, and customers, information networks provide another source of strategic flexibility. Used correctly, these networks facilitate the firm's efforts to satisfy customer expectations in terms of product quality and delivery speed.[115] For instance, customer relationship management (CRM) is one form of an information-based network process that firms use to better understand customers and their needs. The effective CRM system provides a 360-degree view of the company's relationship with customers, encompassing all contact points, involving all business processes, and incorporating all communication media and sales channels.[116] The firm can then use this information to determine the trade-offs its customers are willing to make between differentiated features and low cost, which is vital for companies using the integrated cost leadership/differentiation strategy.

Information networks are also critical to the establishment and successful use of an enterprise resource planning (ERP) system. ERP is an information system used to identify and plan the resources required across the firm to receive, record, produce, and ship customer orders.[117] For example, salespeople for aircraft parts distributor Aviall use handheld equipment to scan bar-code labels on bins in customers' facilities to determine when parts need to be restocked. Data gathered through this procedure are uploaded via the Web to the Aviall back-end replenishment and ERP system, allowing the order fulfillment process to begin within minutes of scanning.[118] Growth in ERP applications such as the one used at Aviall has been significant.[119] Full installations of an ERP system are expensive, running into the tens of millions of dollars for large-scale applications.

Improving efficiency on a company-wide basis is a primary objective of using an ERP system. Efficiency improvements result from the use of systems through which financial and operational data are moved rapidly from one department to another. The transfer of sales data from Aviall salespeople to the order entry point at the firm's manufacturing facility demonstrates the rapid movement of information from one function to another. Integrating data across parties that are involved with detailing product specifications and then manufacturing those products and distributing them in ways that are consistent with customers' unique needs enable the firm to respond with flexibility to customer preferences relative to cost and differentiation.

**Total Quality Management Systems.** In the 1970s and 1980s, executives in Western nations, including the United States, recognized that their firms' success and even survival in some industries (e.g., automobile manufacturing) depended on developing an ability to dramatically improve the quality of their goods and services while simultaneously reducing their cost structures. The relatively low costs of relatively high-quality products from a host of Japanese companies emphasized this message with resounding clarity.[120]

Focused on doing things right through increases in efficiency, total quality management (TQM) systems are used in firms across multiple nations and economic regions to increase their competitiveness.[121] TQM systems incorporate customer definitions of quality instead of those derived by the firm, and demand that the firm focus on the root causes of a problem rather than on its symptoms.[122] A key assumption underlying the use of a TQM system is that "the costs of poor quality (such as inspection, rework, lost customers, and so on) are far greater than the costs of developing processes that produce high-quality products and services."[123]

Firms use TQM systems to achieve several specific objectives, including (1) increasing customer satisfaction, (2) cutting costs, and (3) reducing the amount of time required to introduce innovative products to the marketplace.[124] Achieving these objectives improves a firm's flexibility and facilitates use of all business-level strategies. However, the outcomes suggested by these objectives are particularly important to firms implementing the integrated cost leadership/differentiation strategy. At least meeting (and perhaps exceeding) customers' expectations regarding quality is a differentiating feature, and eliminating process inefficiencies allows the firm to offer that quality at a relatively low cost. Thus, an effective TQM system helps the firm develop the flexibility needed to spot opportunities to simultaneously increase differentiation and/or reduce costs.

## Competitive Risks of the Integrated Cost Leadership/Differentiation Strategy

The potential to create value by successfully using the integrated cost leadership/differentiation strategy is appealing. However, experience shows that substantial risk accompanies this potential. Selecting a business-level strategy requires the firm to make choices about how it intends to compete.[125] Achieving the low-cost position in an industry or a segment of an industry by using a focus strategy demands that the firm reduce its costs consistently relative to the costs of its competitors. The use of the differentiation strategy, with either an industry-wide (broad target) or a focused (narrow target) competitive scope (see Figure 5.1), requires the firm to provide its customers with differentiated goods or services they value and for which they are willing to pay a premium price.

The firm that uses the integrated strategy yet fails to establish a leadership position risks becoming "stuck in the middle."[126] Being in this position prevents the firm from dealing successfully with the competitive forces in its industry and from having a distinguishable competitive advantage. The firm will not be able to create value, and it will be able to earn only average returns only when the structure of the industry in which it competes is highly favorable or if its competitors are also in the same position.[127] Without these conditions, the firm will earn below-average returns. Thus, companies implementing the integrated cost leadership/differentiation strategy, such as Target and Aaon, must be certain that their competitive actions allow them both to offer some differentiated features that their customers value and to provide them with products at a relatively low cost.

Little if any research evidence shows that the attributes of the cost leadership and differentiation strategies cannot be effectively integrated.[128] The integrated strategy therefore is an appropriate strategic choice for firms with the core competencies required to produce somewhat differentiated products at relatively low costs. It is also important that the appropriate structure with additional processes be used to facilitate proper implementation of the strategy.

# Summary

- A business-level strategy is an integrated and coordinated set of commitments and actions the firm uses to gain a competitive advantage by exploiting core competencies in specific product markets. This chapter examines five business-level strategies: cost leadership, differentiation, focused cost leadership, focused differentiation, and integrated cost leadership/differentiation. A firm's strategic competitiveness is enhanced when it is able to develop and exploit new core competencies faster than competitors can mimic the competitive advantages yielded by the firm's current competencies.

- Customers are the foundation of successful business-level strategies. When considering customers, a firm simultaneously examines *who* to serve (which customer groups), *what* they want (the needs the firm seeks to satisfy), and *how* to serve them (the core competencies that will meet those needs). Increasing market segmentation throughout the global economy creates opportunities for firms to identify unique customer needs.

- Strategy and structure influence each other, although strategy has an overall stronger influence on structure. Research indicates that firms tend to change structure when declining performance forces them to do so. Effective managers anticipate the need for structural change, quickly modifying structure to better accommodate the firm's strategy implementation needs when evidence calls for that action.

- Business-level strategies are implemented through the functional structure. The cost leadership strategy requires a centralized functional structure in which manufacturing efficiency and process engineering are emphasized. The differentiation strategy's functional structure decentralizes implementation-related decisions, especially those concerned with marketing, and emphasizes those involved with individual organizational functions. Focus strategies, often used in small firms, require a simple structure until such time that the firm diversifies in terms of products and/or markets. The integrated low cost/differentiation strategy requires a functional structure with well-developed processes to manage partial centralization and jobs that are semispecialized.

- Firms seeking competitive advantage through the cost leadership strategy produce no-frills, standardized products for an industry's typical customer. These low-cost products must be offered with competitive levels of differentiation. Above-average returns are earned when firms continuously drive their costs lower than those of their competitors, while providing customers with products that have low prices and acceptable levels of differentiated features.

- Competitive risks associated with the cost leadership strategy include (1) a loss of competitive advantage to newer technologies, (2) a failure to detect changes in customers' needs, and (3) the ability of competitors to imitate the cost leader's competitive advantage through their own unique strategic actions.

- The differentiation strategy enables firms to provide customers with products that have different (and valued) features. Differentiated products must be sold at a cost that customers believe is competitive given the product's features as compared with the cost–feature combination available through competitors' offerings. Because of their uniqueness, differentiated goods or services are sold at a premium price. Products can be differentiated along any dimension that some customer group values. Firms using this strategy seek to differentiate their products from competitors' goods or services along as many dimensions as possible. The less similarity with competitors' products, the more buffered a firm is from competition with its rivals.

- Risks associated with the differentiation strategy include (1) a customer group's decision that the differences between the differentiated product and the cost leader's good or service are no longer worth a premium price, (2) the inability of a differentiated product to create the type of value for which customers are willing to pay a premium price, (3) the ability of competitors to provide customers with products that have features similar to those associated with the differentiated product, but at a lower cost, and (4) the threat of counterfeiting, whereby firms produce a cheap imitation of a differentiated good or service.

- Through the cost leadership and the differentiated focus strategies, firms serve the needs of a narrow competitive segment (e.g., a buyer group, product segment, or geographic area). This strategy is successful when firms have the core competencies required to provide value to a narrow competitive segment that exceeds the value available from firms serving customers on an industry-wide basis.

- The competitive risks of focus strategies include (1) a competitor's ability to use its core competencies to "outfocus" the focuser by serving an even more narrowly defined competitive segment, (2) decisions by industry-wide competitors to serve a customer group's specialized needs that the focuser has been serving, and (3) a reduction in differences of the needs between customers in a narrow competitive segment and the industry-wide market.

- Firms using the integrated cost leadership/differentiation strategy strive to provide customers with relatively low-cost products that have some valued differentiated features. The primary risk of this strategy is that a firm might produce products that do not offer sufficient value in terms of either low cost or differentiation. When this occurs, the company is "stuck in the middle," competing at a disadvantage and unable to earn more than average returns.

# Ethics Questions

1. Can a commitment to ethical conduct on issues such as the environment, product quality, and fulfilling contractual agreements affect a firm's competitive advantage? If so, how?
2. Is there more incentive for differentiators or cost leaders to pursue stronger ethical conduct?
3. Can an overemphasis on cost leadership or differentiation lead to ethical challenges?
4. A brand image is one way a firm can differentiate its good or service. However, many questions are now being raised about the effect brand images have on consumer behavior. For example, considerable concern has arisen about brand images that are managed by tobacco firms and their effect on the smoking habits of teenagers. Should firms be concerned about how they form and use brand images? Why or why not?
5. To what extent should an individual manager be concerned about the accuracy of the claims the company makes about its products in its advertisements?

# Notes

1  G. Gavetti, D. A. Levinthal, & J. W. Rivkin, 2005, Strategy making in novel and complex worlds: The power of analogy, *Strategic Management Journal*, 26: 691–712.

2  J. Stopford, 2001, Should strategy makers become dream weavers? *Harvard Business Review*, 79(1): 165–169.

3  C. A. De Kluyver, 2000, *Strategic Thinking*, Upper Saddle River, NJ: Prentice Hall, 3.

4  R. S. Kaplan & D. P. Norton, 2001, *The Strategy-Focused Organization*, Boston: Harvard Business School Press, 90.

5  D. J. Ketchen Jr., C. C. Snow, & V. L. Street, 2004, Improving firm performance by matching strategic decision-making processes to competitive dynamics, *Academy of Management Executive*, 18(4): 29–43; R. D. Ireland, M. A. Hitt, S. M. Camp, & D. L. Sexton, 2001, Integrating entrepreneurship and strategic management actions to create firm wealth, *Academy of Management Executive*, 15(1): 49–63.

6  N. Park, J. M. Mezias, & J. Song, 2004, Increasing returns, strategic alliances, and the values of E-commerce firms, *Journal of Management*, 30: 7–27; V. P. Rindova & C. J. Fombrun, 1999, Constructing competitive advantage: The role of firm-constituent interactions, *Strategic Management Journal*, 20: 691–710; G. G. Dess, A. Gupta, J. F. Hennart, & C. W. L. Hill, 1995, Conducting and integrating strategy research at the international, corporate, and business levels: Issues and directions, *Journal of Management*, 21: 357–393.

7  J. B. Barney & T. B. Mackey, 2005, Testing resource-based theory, in D. J. Ketchen Jr. & D. D. Bergh (eds.), *Research Methodology in Strategy and Management*, 2nd ed., London: Elsevier, 1–13; E. H. Bowman & C. E. Helfat, 2001, Does corporate strategy matter? *Strategic Management Journal*, 22: 1–23.

8  M. E. Porter, 1980, *Competitive Strategy*, New York: The Free Press.

9  D. C. Hambrick & J. W. Fredrickson, 2001, Are you sure you have a strategy? *Academy of Management Executive*, 15(4): 48–59.

10  C. B. Dobni & G. Luffman, 2003, Determining the scope and impact of market orientation profiles on strategy implementation and performance, *Strategic Management Journal*, 24: 577–585; G. Hamel, 2000, *Leading the Revolution*, Boston: Harvard Business School Press, 71.

11  S. F. Slater & E. M. Olsen, 2000, Strategy type and performance: The influence of sales force management, *Strategic Management Journal*, 21: 813–829; M. E. Porter, 1998, *On Competition*, Boston: Harvard Business School Press.

12  K. Shimizu & M. A. Hitt, 2004, Strategic flexibility: Organizational preparedness to reverse ineffective strategic decisions, *Academy of Management Executive*, 18(4): 44–59; M. A. Geletkanycz & S. S. Black, 2001, Bound by the past? Experience-based effects on commitment to the strategic status quo, *Journal of Management*, 27: 3–21; C. E. Helfat, 1997, Know-how and asset complementarity and dynamic capability accumulation: The case of R&D, *Strategic Management Journal*, 18: 339–360.

13  R. D. Ireland & C. C. Miller, 2005, Decision-making and firm success, *Academy of Management Executive*, 18(4): 8–12; J. J. Janney & G. G. Dess, 2004, Can real-options analysis improve decision making? Promises and pitfalls, *Academy of Management Executive*, 18(4): 60–75.

14  Hamel, *Leading the Revolution*.

15  L. Tihanyi, A. E. Ellstrand, C. M. Daily, & D. R. Dalton, 2000, Composition of top management team and firm international diversification, *Journal of Management*, 26: 1157–1177; P. F. Drucker, 1999, *Management in the 21st Century*, New York: Harper Business.

16  De Kluyver, *Strategic Thinking*, 7.

17  M. E. Porter, 1996, What is strategy? *Harvard Business Review*, 74(6): 61–78.

18  M. E. Porter, 1985, *Competitive Advantage*, New York: The Free Press, 26.

19  Porter, *Competitive Strategy*.

20  M. E. Porter, 1994, Toward a dynamic theory of strategy, in R. P. Rumelt, D. E. Schendel, & D. J. Teece (eds.), *Fundamental Issues in Strategy*, Boston: Harvard Business School Press, 423–461.

21  Porter, What is strategy? 62.

22  Porter, *Competitive Advantage*, 15.

23  G. G. Dess, G. T. Lumpkin, & J. E. McGee, 1999, Linking corporate entrepreneurship to strategy, structure, and process: Suggested research directions, *Entrepreneurship: Theory & Practice*, 23(3): 85–102; P. M. Wright, D. L. Smart, & G. C. McMahan, 1995, Matches between human resources and strategy among NCAA basketball teams, *Academy of Management Journal*, 38: 1052–1074.

24  L. E. Brouthers, E. O'Donnell & J. Hadjimarcou, 2005, Generic product strategies for emerging market exports into triad nation markets: A mimetic isomorphism approach, *Journal of Management Studies*, 42: 225–245.

25  F. E. Webster Jr., A. J. Malter, & S. Ganesan, 2005, The decline and dispersion of marketing competence, *MIT Sloan Management Review*, 6(4): 35–43; L. L. Berry, 2001, The old pillars of new retailing, *Harvard Business Review*, 79(4): 131–137.

26  N. Irwin, 2001, Motley Fool branches out, *Washington Post*, May 22, B5.

27  M. Schrage, 2001, Don't scorn your salespeople—you will soon be one, *Fortune*, May 14, 256; D. Peppers, M. Rogers, & B. Dorf, 1999, Is your company ready for one-to-one marketing? *Harvard Business Review*, 77(5): 59–72.

28  N. Brodsky, 2006, It's hard to make Inc. 500 if you're always churning clients, *Inc.* magazine, September, 57.

29  P. B. Seybold, 2001, Get inside the lives of your customers, *Harvard Business Review*, 79(5): 81–89.

30  M. E. Porter, 2001, Strategy and the Internet, *Harvard Business Review*, 79(3): 62–78.

31  L. Walker, 2001, Plugged in for maximum efficiency, *Washington Post*, June 20, G1, G4.

32  B. Tedeschi, 2005, Women are keen to shop online; merchants are eager to oblige, *New York Times*, http://www.nytimes.com, June 6.

33  A. Reed II & L. E. Bolton, 2005, The complexity of identity, *MIT Sloan Management Review*, 46(3): 18–22.

34  C. W. Lamb Jr., J. F. Hair Jr., & C. McDaniel, 2006, *Marketing*, 8th ed., Mason, OH: Thomson/South-Western, 224; A. Dutra, J. Frary, & R. Wise, 2004, Higher-order needs drive new growth in mature consumer markets, *Journal of Business Strategy*, 25(5): 26–34; W. D. Neal & J. Wurst, 2001, Advances in

market segmentation, *Marketing Research*, 13(1): 14–18; S. C. Jain, 2000, *Marketing Planning and Strategy*, Cincinnati: South-Western, 104–125.

35. S. S. Hassan & S. H. Craft, 2005, Linking global market segmentation decisions with strategic positioning options, *Journal of Consumer Marketing*, 22(2/3): 81–88.

36. 2007, Porsche, http://www.porsche.com/usa, January 30; 2007, Rolls-Royce, Trusted to deliver excellence, http://www.rolls-royce.com, January 30.

37. 2007, GM, Vehicle showroom, http://www.gm.com, January 30.

38. 2003, Unions and Gen-X: What does the future hold? *HR Focus*, March, 3; F. Marshall, 2003, Storehouse wakes up to Gen-X employees, *Furniture Today*, February 10, 2–3; J. Pereira, 2003, Best on the street, *Wall Street Journal*, May 12, R7; D. A. Aaker, 1998, *Strategic Marketing Management*, 5th ed., New York: Wiley, 20.

39. 2007, Saks Fifth Avenue, http://www.saksfifthavenue .com, January 30.

40. C. W. L. Hill & F. T. Rothaermel, 2003, The performance of incumbent firms in the face of radical technological innovation, *Academy of Management Review*, 28: 257–274; A. W. King, S. W. Fowler, & C. P. Zeithaml, 2001, Managing organizational competencies for competitive advantage: The middle-management edge, *Academy of Management Executive*, 15(2): 95–106; Porter, Strategy and the Internet, 72.

41. 2007, SAS Institute, The power to know, http://www .sas.com, January 30; C. A. O'Reilly III & J. Pfeffer, 2000, *Hidden Value: How Great Companies Achieve Extraordinary Results with Ordinary People*, Boston: Harvard Business School Press, 102.

42. 2007, Vans Inc., http://www.vans.com, January 30; A. Weintraub & G. Khermouch, 2001, Chairman of the board, *Business Week*, May 28, 94.

43. T. Burns & G. M. Stalker, 1961, *The Management of Innovation*, London: Tavistok; P. R. Lawrence & J. W. Lorsch, 1967, *Organization and Environment*, Homewood, IL.: Richard D. Irwin; J. Woodward, 1965, *Industrial Organization: Theory and Practice*, London: Oxford University Press.

44. W. D. Sine, H. Mitsuhashi, & D. A. Kirsch, 2006, Revisiting Burns and Stalker: Formal structure and new venture performance in emerging economy sectors, *Academy of Management Journal*, 49: 121–132; H. Kim, R. E. Hoskisson, L. Tihanyi, & J. Hong, 2004, Evolution and restructuring of diversified business groups in emerging markets: The lessons from chaebols in Korea, *Asia Pacific Journal of Management*, 21: 25–48; P. Jenster & D. Hussey, 2001, *Company Analysis: Determining Strategic Capability*, Chichester, UK: Wiley, 135–171; D. J. Teece, G. Pisano, & A. Shuen, 1997, Dynamic capabilities and strategic management, *Strategic Management Journal*, 18: 509–533.

45. B. Keats & H. O'Neill, 2001, Organizational structure: Looking through a strategy lens, in M. A. Hitt, R. E. Freeman, & J. S. Harrison (eds.), *Handbook of Strategic Management*, Oxford, UK: Blackwell Publishers, 520–542; J. R. Galbraith, 1995, *Designing Organizations*, San Francisco: Jossey-Bass, 6.

46. H. J. Leavitt, 2003, Why hierarchies thrive, *Harvard Business Review*, 81(3): 96–102; V. P. Rindova & S. Kotha, 2001, Continuous "morphing": Competing through dynamic capabilities, form, and function, *Academy of Management Journal*, 44: 1263–1280.

47. H. Barth, 2003, Fit among competitive strategy, administrative mechanisms, and performance:

A comparative study of small firms in mature and new industries, *Journal of Small Business Management*, 41(2): 133–147; J. G. Covin, D. P. Slevin, & M. B. Heeley, 2001, Strategic decision making in an intuitive vs. technocratic mode: Structural and environmental consideration, *Journal of Business Research*, 52: 51–67.

48. M. Sengul, 2001, Divisionalization: Strategic effects of organizational structure, paper presented during the 21st Annual Strategic Management Society Conference, San Francisco, October.

49. Keats & O'Neill, Organizational structure, 531.

50. C. Levicki, 1999, *The Interactive Strategy Workout*, 2nd ed., London: Prentice Hall.

51. J. J. Chrisman, A. Bauerschmidt, & C. W. Hofer, 1998, The determinants of new venture performance: An extended model, *Entrepreneurship: Theory & Practice*, 23(3): 5–29; H. M. O'Neill, R. W. Pouder, & A. K. Buchholtz, 1998, Patterns in the diffusion of strategies across organizations: Insights from the innovation diffusion literature, *Academy of Management Review*, 23: 98–114.

52. Galbraith, *Designing Organizations*, 25.

53. Keats & O'Neill, Organizational structure, 539.

54. Lawrence & Lorsch, *Organization and Environment*.

55. O. E. Williamson, 1975, *Markets and Hierarchies: Analysis and Anti-trust Implications*, New York: The Free Press.

56. A. Chandler, 1962, *Strategy and Structure*, Cambridge, MA: MIT Press.

57. J. Greco, 1999, Alfred P. Sloan, Jr. (1875–1966): The original organizational man, *Journal of Business Strategy*, 20(5): 30–31.

58. Porter, *Competitive Strategy*, 35–40.

59. K. Capell, 2006, "Wal-Mart" with wings, *Business Week*, November 27, 44.

60. D. F. Spulber, 2004, *Management Strategy*, New York: McGraw-Hill/Irwin, 175.

61. J. A. Parnell, 2000, Reframing the combination strategy debate: Defining forms of combination, *Journal of Management Studies*, 9(1): 33–54.

62. C. Malburg, 2000, Competing on costs, *Industry Week*, October 16, 31.

63. D. F. Lynch, S. B. Keller, & J. Ozment, 2000, The effects of logistics capabilities and strategy on firm performance, *Journal of Business Logistics*, 21(2): 47–68.

64. 2005, Big Lots, Standard & Poor's, http://www .standardandpoors.com, July 16.

65. 2005, Big Lots Inc. names Steve Fishman chairman, chief executive officer, and president, Reuters, http://www .reuters.com, June 10.

66. 2007, Big Lots, About our company, http://www .biglotscorporate.com, January 30.

67. A. D'Innocenzio, 2001, We are paranoid, *Richmond Times-Dispatch*, June 10, E1, E2.

68. L. Grant, 2001, Kmart, Wal-Mart face off in price-cutting fight, *USA Today*, June 8, B1; A. R. Moses, 2001, Kmart's long road back, *Richmond Times-Dispatch*, November 24, C1, C10.

69. Lynch, Keller, & Ozment, The effects of logistics capabilities.

70. R. H. Hall, 1996, *Organizations: Structures, Processes, and Outcomes*, 6th ed., Englewood Cliffs, NJ: Prentice Hall, 13; S. Baiman, D. F. Larcker, & M. V. Rajan,

1995, Organizational design for business units, *Journal of Accounting Research*, 33: 205–229.

71 Hall, *Organizations*, 64–75.

72 J. B. Barney, 2002, *Gaining and Sustaining Competitive Advantage*, 2nd ed., Upper Saddle River, NJ: Prentice Hall, 257.

73 2002, Wal-Mart stores pricing policy, http://www .walmart.com, February 2.

74 Porter, *Competitive Strategy*, 35–40.

75 2006, Mary Frances Accessories, *Inc.* September 2006, 106.

76 Porter, *Competitive Strategy*, 35–40.

77 2007, Lexus, http://www.lexus.com, January 31.

78 2007, Robert Talbott, Robert Talbott history, http:// www.roberttalbott.com/history.html, January 31.

79 Porter, *Competitive Advantage*, 14.

80 Barney, *Gaining and Sustaining Competitive Advantage*, 268.

81 M. Williams & P. Kallendar, 2004, China's Lenovo to buy IBM's PC business, *IDG News*, December 7.

82 H. R. Goldstein, A. E. Roth, T. Young, & J. D. Lawrence, 2001, US manufacturers take a swing at counterfeit golf clubs, *Intellectual Property & Technology Law Journal*, May, 23.

83 Porter, *Competitive Strategy*, 98.

84 Porter, *Competitive Advantage*, 15.

85 Ibid., 15–16.

86 Ibid., 15.

87 2007, Ikea, The Ikea concept and Ikea franchising, http://www.ikea.com, January 31.

88 Porter, What is strategy? 65.

89 M. Lynch, 2006, It was, get sales up to fund the growth or stop operations, *Inc.* September, 92.

90 J. Weber, 2006, Harley just keeps on cruisin', *Business Week*, November 6, 71.

91 Ibid.

92 T. Lowry, 2007, Music to the Street's ears, *Business Week*, January 8, 38.

93 2007, Big Dog Motorcycles, http://www.bdm.com, January 31.

94 2007, Anne Fontaine, http://www.annefontaine.com, January 31.

95 2007, Forth & Towne, http://www.forthandtowne.com, January 31.

96 S. Voelpel, M. Leibold, E. Tekie, & G. Von Krogh, 2005, Escaping the red queen effect in competitive strategy: Sense-testing business models, *European Management Journal*, 23: 37–49.

97 2001, The engine that drives differentiation, *DSN Retailing Today*, April 2, 52.

98 G. G. Dess, G. T. Lumpkin, & J. E. McGee, 1999, Linking corporate entrepreneurship to strategy, structure, and process: Suggested research directions, *Entrepreneurship: Theory & Practice*, 23(3): 89.

99 P. Ghemawat, 2001, *Strategy and the Business Landscape*, Upper Saddle River, NJ: Prentice Hall, 56.

100 W. K. Hall, 1980, Survival strategies in a hostile environment, *Harvard Business Review* 58, 5: 75–87.

101 Dess, Gupta, Hennart, & Hill, Conducting and integrating strategy research, 377.

102 L. Kim & Y. Lim, 1988, Environment, generic strategies, and performance in a rapidly developing country: A taxonomic approach, *Academy of Management Journal*, 31: 802–827.

103 2007, Aaon Inc. heating and cooling products, http:// www.aaonnet.com, January 31.

104 S. A. Forest, 2001, When cool heads prevail, *Business Week*, June 11, 114.

105 G. Hoetker, 2006, Do modular products lead to modular organizations? *Strategic Management Journal*, 27: 501–518.

106 R. Sanchez, 1995, Strategic flexibility in product competition, *Strategic Management Journal*, 16(summer special issue): 140.

107 A. Faria, P. Fenn, & A. Bruce, 2005, Production technologies and technical efficiency: Evidence from Portuguese manufacturing industry, *Applied Economics*, 37: 1037–1046.

108 R. Olexa, 2001, Flexible parts feeding boosts productivity, *Manufacturing Engineering*, 126(4): 106–114.

109 I. Mount & B. Caulfield, 2001, The missing link, *Ecompany Now*, May, 82–88.

110 J. Baljko, 2003, Built for speed—When putting the reams of supply chain data they've amassed to use, companies are discovering that agility counts, *EBN*, 1352: 25–28.

111 E. K. Bish, A. Muriel, & S. Biller, 2005, Managing flexible capacity in a make-to-order environment, *Management Science*, 51: 167–180.

112 M. Maynard, 2001, Tiremaking technology is on a roll, *Fortune*, May 28, 148B–148L; J. Martin, 1997, Give 'em exactly what they want, *Fortune*, November 10, 283–285.

113 M. Savsar, 2005, Performance analysis of an FMS operating under different failure rates and maintenance policies, *International Journal of Flexible Manufacturing Systems*, 16: 229–249.

114 S. M. Iravani, M. P. van Oyen, & K. T. Sims, 2005, Structural flexibility: A new perspective on the design of manufacturing and service operations, *Management Science*, 51: 151–166.

115 A. McAfee, 2003, When too much IT knowledge is a dangerous thing, *McKinsey Quarterly*, 44(2): 83–89; F. Mattern, S. Schonwalder, & W. Stein, 2003, Fighting complexity in IT, *McKinsey Quarterly*, No. 1: 57–65.

116 S. Isaac & R. N. Tooker, 2001, The many faces of CRM, *LIMRA's MarketFacts Quarterly*, 20(1): 84–89.

117 P. J. Rondeau & L. A. Litteral, 2001, The evolution of manufacturing planning and control systems: From reorder point to enterprise resource planning, *Production and Inventory Management*, 42(2): 1–7.

118 M. L. Songini, 2001, Companies test their wireless supply chain wings, *Computerworld*, May 21, 35.

119 N. Checker, 2001, An integrated approach, *Chemical Market Reporter*, June 4, S8–S10.

120 D. Chatterji & J. M. Davidson, 2001, Examining TQM's legacies for R&D, *Research Technology Management*, 44(1): 10–12.

121 Kaplan & Norton, *The Strategy-Focused Organization*, 361; M. A. Mische, 2001, *Strategic Renewal: Becoming a High-Performance Organization*, Upper Saddle River, NJ: Prentice Hall, 15.

122 J. Pfeffer, 1998, *The Human Equation: Building Profits by Putting People First*, Boston: Harvard Business School Press, 156.

[123] J. R. Hackman & R. Wageman, 1995, Total quality management: Empirical, conceptual, and practical issues, *Administrative Science Quarterly*, 40: 310.

[124] V. W. S. Yeung & R. W. Armstrong, 2003, A key to TQM benefits: Manager involvement in customer processes, *International Journal of Services Technology and Management*, 4(1): 14–29.

[125] De Kluyver, *Strategic Thinking*, 3; C. H. St. John & J. S. Harrison, 1999, Manufacturing-based relatedness, synergy, and coordination, *Strategic Management Journal*, 20: 129–145.

[126] Porter, *Competitive Advantage*, 16.

[127] Ibid., 17.

[128] Parnell, Reframing the combination strategy debate, 33.

**CHAPTER 6**

# Competitive Rivalry and Competitive Dynamics

## KNOWLEDGE OBJECTIVES

*Studying this chapter should provide you with the strategic management knowledge needed to:*

1. Define competitors, competitive rivalry, competitive behavior, and competitive dynamics.
2. Describe market commonality and resource similarity as the building blocks of a competitor analysis.
3. Explain awareness, motivation, and ability as drivers of competitive behavior.
4. Discuss factors affecting the likelihood a competitor will take competitive actions.
5. Discuss factors affecting the likelihood a competitor will respond to actions taken against it.
6. Explain competitive dynamics in slow-cycle, fast-cycle, and standard-cycle markets.

As previous chapters have demonstrated, continuous increases in globalization and technological change have altered the fundamental nature of competition in many of the world's industries.[1] These changes both expand and complicate the competitive environment a firm faces.[2] In fact, they have created an environment that might be called *hypercompetitive* (see Chapter 1).[3] A team of experts on competitive rivalry put it this way:

> The new age of competition is distinct because of the dramatic increase in competitive actions and reactions between firms. As a consequence of the accelerating rate of actions and reactions, the time firms have to make decisions has decreased, and the speed with which new ideas are created and brought to market has increased. Above all, the speed at which data, information, and knowledge pulse between competitors has skyrocketed. In this new age of competition, fast companies generate advantages and market power while faster ones generate more advantages and greater market power, and no one's advantages are guaranteed to last long.[4]

The speed and strength of competitive reactions are easy to see in technologically advanced, global industries such as handheld communications devices, where new products and features are introduced at an astounding rate. However, the general climate change influences virtually all industries, even those where one might expect a measure of stability. For instance, Quaker Oats bought Gaines Pet Food, making Quaker the number-two player in the dry dog food segment. Ralston, the market leader, quickly announced that it would double the number of new products it introduces. One of its introductions was a semimoist dog food to compete directly with Gainesburgers, a Quaker product. Also, Ralston acquired Benco Pet Foods, manufacturer of Moist & Meaty. Quaker responded by introducing an imitation called Moist & Beefy. Ralston then introduced a new dry dog food called Graavy to compete with Quaker's Gravy Train, at a price that was nearly 40 percent cheaper. Ralston apparently ended up winning this battle. Quaker lost significant market share in the pet foods segment and recently sold its pet food business.[5]

This chapter focuses on competitive rivalry and competitive dynamics. **Competitors** are firms operating in the same market, offering similar products and targeting similar customers.[6] For instance, FedEx and UPS compete against each other in several product markets, including package delivery by both land and air and emerging e-commerce and logistics markets. **Competitive rivalry** is the ongoing set of competitive actions and competitive responses occurring between competitors as they contend with each other for an advantageous market position. Competitive rivalry influences a firm's ability to gain and sustain competitive advantages.[7] It also affects the scope and nature of its operations.[8] Rivalry results from firms both initiating their own competitive actions and responding to actions their competitors take.[9]

**Competitive behavior** is the set of competitive actions and competitive responses the firm takes to build or defend its competitive advantages and to improve its market position.[10] Through competitive behavior, the firm tries to successfully position itself relative to the five forces of competition (see Chapter 3) and to defend and use current competitive advantages while building advantages for the future (see Chapter 4). **Competitive dynamics** describe the total set of actions and responses all firms competing within a market take. Figure 6.1 shows the relationships among competitors, competitive rivalry, competitive behavior, and competitive dynamics.

Another way of highlighting competitive rivalry's effect on the firm's strategies is to say that a strategy's success is determined not only by the firm's initial competitive actions but also by how well it anticipates competitors' responses to them and by how well the firm anticipates and responds to its competitors' initial actions (also called *attacks*).[11] Although competitive rivalry affects all types of strategies, its most dominant influence is on the firm's business-level strategy or strategies. Business-level strategy is concerned with what the firm does to successfully use its competitive advantages in specific product markets

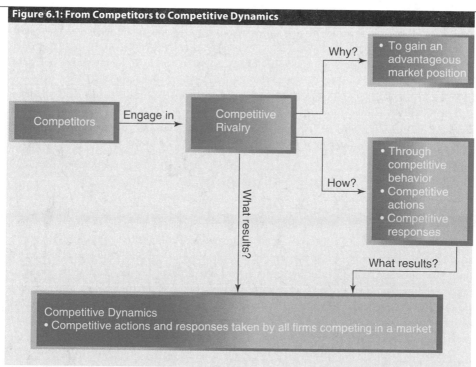

**Figure 6.1: From Competitors to Competitive Dynamics**

Competitors — Engage in → Competitive Rivalry

Why? → • To gain an advantageous market position

How? → • Through competitive behavior • Competitive actions • Competitive responses

What results?

What results? → Competitive Dynamics • Competitive actions and responses taken by all firms competing in a market

SOURCE: Adapted from M.-J. Chen, 1996, Competitor analysis and interfirm rivalry: Toward a theoretical integration, *Academy of Management Review*, 21: 100–134.

(see Chapter 5). Firms with business-level strategies allowing them to be different from competitors in ways that customers value are effectively positioned to successfully engage in competitive rivalry.[12]

The essence of these important topics is that a firm's strategies are dynamic in nature. Actions one firm takes elicit responses from competitors that, in turn, typically result in responses from the firm that took the initial action.[13] Increasingly, competitors engage in competitive actions and responses in more than one market.[14] Firms competing against each other in several product or geographic markets are engaged in **multimarket competition**.[15] For instance, Hilton and Marriott both compete in the upscale and midscale hotel segments throughout the world, as well as the vacation time-share industry. Often, their various brands are located side-by-side in geographic markets.[16] The implication is that actions in one market can influence a competitive response in another market.

The trend toward firms expanding their geographic scope contributes to the increasing intensity in the competitive rivalry between firms. Some believe, for example, that an aptitude for cross-border management practices and a facility with cultural diversity find EU firms emerging as formidable global competitors.[17] Similarly, former General Electric CEO Jack Welch believes that GE's most significant future competitive threats may be from companies not currently in prominent positions on the firm's radar screen, such as those in emerging countries.[18] Thus, the firm trying to predict competitive rivalry should anticipate that in the future it will encounter a larger number of increasingly diverse competitors. This trend also suggests that firms should expect competitive rivalry to have a stronger effect on their strategies' success than historically has been the case.[19] Furthermore, research shows that intensified rivalry within an industry can result in decreased financial performance.[20]

We begin this chapter by presenting an integrative model of competitive rivalry at the firm level. We then describe market commonality and resource similarity as the building blocks of a competitor analysis. Next, we discuss the effects of three organizational characteristics—awareness, motivation, and ability—on the firm's competitive behavior. We then examine competitive rivalry in detail by describing the factors that affect the likelihood a firm will take a competitive action and the factors that affect the likelihood a firm will respond to a competitor's action. In the chapter's final section, we turn our attention to competitive dynamics to describe how market characteristics affect competitive rivalry in slow-cycle, fast-cycle, and standard-cycle markets.

## A Model of Competitive Rivalry

Figure 6.2 shows a straightforward model of competitive rivalry at the firm level. Of course, firm rivalry tends to be more dynamic and complex than the model indicates;[21] nevertheless, it provides a useful way to discuss the various aspects of competitive dynamics. Rivalry is studied at the firm level because the competitive actions and responses the firm takes are the foundation for successfully building and using its competitive advantages to gain an advantageous market position.[22] Thus, we use the model in Figure 6.2 to help us explain competition between a particular firm and each of its competitors as they compete for the most advantageous market position. The sum of all the individual rivalries shown in Figure 6.2 that are occurring in a particular market reflects the competitive dynamics in that market.

Over time, the firm is involved with many competitive actions and competitive responses.[23] Competitive rivalry evolves from this pattern of action and response as one

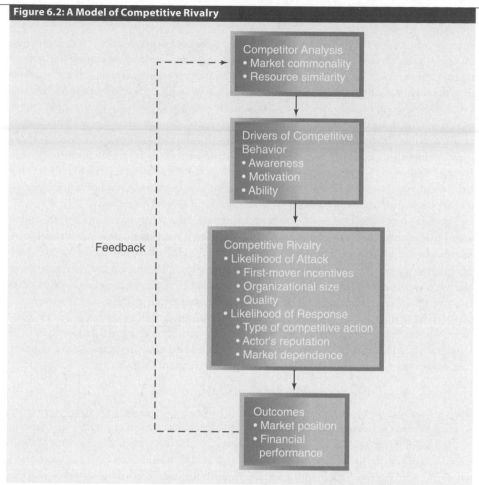

SOURCE: Adapted from M.-J. Chen, 1996, Competitor analysis and interfirm rivalry: Toward a theoretical integration, *Academy of Management Review*, 21: 100–134.

firm's competitive actions noticeably affect a competitor's, eliciting competitive responses from that firm.[24] This pattern shows that firms are mutually interdependent, that they feel each other's actions and responses, and that marketplace success is a function of both individual strategies and the consequences of their use.[25]

The intensity of rivalry within a market, such as that in the pet food market, is affected by many factors, including the total number of competitors, market characteristics, and the quality of individual firms' strategies. Firms that develop and use effective business-level strategies tend to outperform competitors in particular product markets, even when experiencing intense competitive rivalry.[26] For instance, for years Microsoft has dominated the personal computer software market through its integrated cost leadership/differentiation strategy, despite continual attacks from competitors, as well as government regulators in the United States and abroad. We now turn directly to Figure 6.2 as our foundation for further discussion of competitive rivalry.

# Competitor Analysis

A *competitor analysis* is the first step the firm takes to be able to predict the extent and nature of its rivalry with each competitor. Recall that a competitor is a firm operating in the same market, offering similar products, and targeting similar customers. The number of markets in which firms compete against each other and the similarity in their resources (called *market commonality* and *resource similarity*, respectively, defined below) determine the extent to which the firms are competitors. Firms with high market commonality and highly similar resources are "clearly direct and mutually acknowledged competitors."[27] However, being direct competitors does not necessarily mean that the rivalry between the firms will be intense. The *drivers of competitive behavior*—as well as factors influencing the likelihood that a competitor will initiate competitive actions and will respond to its competitor's competitive actions—influence the intensity of rivalry, even for direct competitors.[28]

In Chapter 3, we discussed competitor analysis as a technique firms use to understand their competitive environment, which, along with the general and industry environments, is part of the firm's external environment. We described how firms use competitor analysis to help them understand their competitors. This understanding results from studying competitors' future objectives, current strategies, assumptions, and capabilities (see Figure 3.3). In this chapter, the discussion of competitor analysis is extended to describe what firms study as the first step to being able to predict competitors' behavior in the form of their competitive actions and responses. The discussions of competitor analysis in Chapter 3 and this chapter are complementary in that firms must first understand competitors before their competitive actions and competitive responses can be predicted.

## Market Commonality

Each industry is composed of various markets. The financial services industry, for instance, has markets for insurance, brokerage services, banks, and so forth. By concentrating on the needs of different, unique customer groups, one can further subdivide markets. The insurance market can be broken into market segments (such as commercial and consumer), product segments (such as health insurance and life insurance), and geographic markets (such as Western Europe and Southeast Asia).

In general, competitors agree about the different characteristics of individual markets that form an industry.[29] For example, in the transportation industry, there is an understanding that the commercial air travel market differs from the ground transportation market that is served by firms such as Yellow Freight System. Although differences exist, most industries' markets are somewhat related in terms of technologies used or core competencies needed to develop a competitive advantage.[30] For example, different types of transportation companies need to provide reliable and timely service. Commercial airline carriers such as Southwest Airlines and Singapore Airlines must therefore develop service competencies to satisfy their passengers, while Yellow Freight System must develop such competencies to serve the needs of those using its fleet to ship their goods.

Firms competing in several or even many markets, some of which may be in different industries, are likely to come into contact with a particular competitor several times,[31] a situation bringing forth the issue of market commonality. **Market commonality** is concerned with the number of markets with which the firm and a competitor are jointly involved and the degree of importance of the individual markets to each.[32] Firms competing against one another in several or many markets engage in multimarket competition.[33] For example, McDonald's and Burger King compete against each other in multiple geographic markets around the world,[34] and Prudential and CIGNA compete against each other in several market segments (institutional and retail) as well as product markets (such as life insurance and health insurance).[35] Airlines, chemicals, pharmaceuticals, and consumer foods are other industries in which firms often simultaneously engage each other in multiple market competitions.

Firms competing in several markets have the potential to respond to a competitor's actions not only within the market in which the actions are taken, but also in other markets in which they compete with the rival. This potential complicates the rivalry between competitors. In fact, recent research suggests that "a firm with greater multimarket contact is less likely to initiate an attack, but more likely to move (respond) aggressively when attacked."[36] Thus, in general, multimarket competition reduces competitive rivalry.[37]

## Resource Similarity

**Resource similarity** is the extent to which the firm's tangible and intangible resources are comparable to a competitor's in terms of both type and amount.[38] Firms with similar types and amounts of resources are likely to have similar strengths and weaknesses and use similar strategies.[39] Such is the case with the big hotel chains. Marriott, Accor, Hilton, and Intercontinental, the top hospitality companies, all have high brand recognition, advanced information and reservations systems, and strong marketing programs.[40] Furthermore, they all have a strong international presence and draw their managers from many of the same hospitality schools, mostly in the United States and Europe. It is not uncommon for a manager to work for several different hotel companies during a typical career, which adds to the similarity of human resources across the major companies. Also, all of the major hospitality companies are highly vulnerable to global economic conditions, changes in information technology, and sociocultural shifts, such as changing demographics.[41]

When performing a competitor analysis, a firm analyzes each of its competitors in terms of resource similarity and market commonality. Assessing market commonality is easier than assessing resource similarity, particularly when critical resources are intangible (such as brand name, knowledge, trust, and the capacity to innovate) rather than tangible (for example, access to raw materials and a competitor's ability to borrow capital). A competitor's intangible resources are difficult to identify and understand, making an assessment of their value challenging. Marriott and Hilton can easily determine the market segments and geographic locations in which they are competing, but it is more difficult for them to determine whether any intangible resources (such as knowledge and trust among employees) are a source of competitive advantage.

The results of a firm's competitor analyses can be mapped for visual comparisons. In Figure 6.3, we show different hypothetical intersections between the firm and individual competitors in terms of market commonality and resource similarity. These intersections indicate the extent to which the firm and those to which it has compared itself are competitors.[42] For example, the firm and its competitor displayed in quadrant I of Figure 6.3 have similar types and amounts of resources and use them to compete against each other in many markets that are important to each. These conditions lead to the conclusion that the firms modeled in quadrant I are direct and mutually acknowledged competitors. FedEx and UPS would fall into quadrant I, as would Marriott and Hilton. In contrast, the firm and its competitor shown in quadrant III share few markets and have little similarity in their resources, indicating that they aren't direct and mutually acknowledged competitors. The firm's mapping of its competitive relationship with rivals is fluid as firms enter and

**Figure 6.3: A Framework of Competitor Analysis**

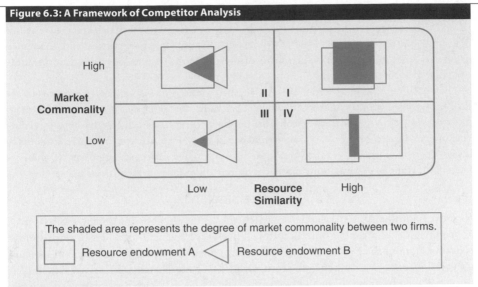

The shaded area represents the degree of market commonality between two firms.

☐ Resource endowment A ◁ Resource endowment B

SOURCE: Adapted from M.-J. Chen, 1996, Competitor analysis and interfirm rivalry: Toward a theoretical integration, *Academy of Management Review*, 21: 100–134.

exit markets and as companies' resources change in type and amount. Thus, the companies with which the firm is a direct competitor change over time.

## Drivers of Competitive Actions and Responses

As shown in Figure 6.2, market commonality and resource similarity influence the drivers of competitive behavior (awareness, motivation, and ability). In turn, the drivers influence the firm's competitive behavior, as shown by the actions and responses it takes while engaging in competitive rivalry.[43]

*Awareness*, which is a prerequisite to any competitive action or response being taken by the firm or its competitor, refers to the extent to which competitors recognize the degree of their mutual interdependence that results from market commonality and resource similarity.[44] A lack of awareness can lead to excessive competition, resulting in a negative effect on all competitors' performance.[45] Awareness tends to be greatest when firms have highly similar resources (in terms of types and amounts) to use while competing against each other in multiple markets. Dell and Hewlett-Packard are fully aware of each other, as are Wal-Mart and France's Carrefour. The last two firms' joint awareness has increased as they use similar resources to compete against each other for dominant positions in multiple European and South American markets.[46] Awareness affects the extent to which the firm understands the consequences of its competitive actions and responses.

*Motivation*, which concerns the firm's incentive to take action or to respond to a competitor's attack, relates to perceived gains and losses. Thus, a firm may be aware of competitors but may not be motivated to engage in rivalry with them if it perceives that its position will not improve as a result of doing so or that its market position won't be damaged if it doesn't respond.[47]

Market commonality affects the firm's perceptions and resulting motivation. For example, all else being equal, the firm is more likely to attack the rival with which it has low market commonality than the one with which it competes in multiple markets. The primary reason is that high stakes are involved in trying to gain a more advantageous position over a rival with whom the firm shares many markets. As mentioned earlier, multimarket competition can find a competitor responding to the firm's action in a market different from the one in which the initial action was taken. Actions and responses of this type can cause both firms to lose focus on core markets and to battle each other with resources that had been allocated for other purposes. Because of the high stakes of competition under the condition of market commonality, the probability is high that the attacked firm will respond to its competitor's action in an effort to protect its position in one or more markets.[48]

In some instances, the firm may be aware of the large number of markets it shares with a competitor and may be motivated to respond to an attack by that competitor, but it lacks the ability to do so. *Ability* relates to each firm's resources and the flexibility they provide. Without available resources (such as financial capital and people), the firm lacks the ability to attack a competitor or respond to its actions. However, similar resources suggest similar abilities to attack and respond. When a firm faces a competitor with similar resources, it must carefully study a possible attack before initiating it because the similarly resourced competitor is likely to respond to that action.[49]

*Resource dissimilarity* also influences competitive actions and responses between firms. The greater the "resource imbalance" between a firm and its competitors, the longer it will take the firm with a resource disadvantage to respond.[50] For example, Wal-Mart initially used its cost leadership strategy to compete only in small communities (those with a population of 25,000 or less). Using sophisticated logistics systems and extremely efficient purchasing practices as competitive advantages, among others, Wal-Mart created what was at that time a new type of value (primarily in the form of wide selections of products at the lowest competitive prices) for customers in small retail markets. Local stores, facing resource deficiencies relative to Wal-Mart, lacked the ability to marshal resources at the pace required to respond quickly and effectively. However, even when facing competitors with greater resources (greater ability) or more attractive market positions, firms should eventually respond, no matter how daunting doing so seems.[51] Choosing not to respond can ultimately result in failure, as happened with at least some local retailers who didn't respond to Wal-Mart's competitive actions.

## Competitive Rivalry

As already defined, *competitive rivalry* is the ongoing set of competitive actions and competitive responses occurring between competing firms for an advantageous market position. Because the ongoing competitive action-response sequence between a firm and a competitor affects the performance of both firms,[52] it is important for companies to carefully study competitive rivalry to successfully use their strategies. Understanding a competitor's awareness, motivation, and ability helps the firm to predict the likelihood of an attack by that competitor and how likely it is that a competitor will respond to the actions taken against it.

As described above, the predictions drawn from the study of competitors in terms of awareness, motivation, and ability are grounded in market commonality and resource similarity. These predictions are fairly general. The value of the final set of predictions the firm develops about each of its competitor's competitive actions and competitive responses is enhanced by studying the "Likelihood of Attack" factors (such as first-mover incentives and organizational size) and the "Likelihood of Response" factors (such as the actor's reputation) that are shown in Figure 6.2. Studying these factors allows the firm to develop a deeper understanding of its competitor in order to refine the predictions it makes about that competitor's actions and responses.

## Strategic and Tactical Actions

Firms use both strategic and tactical actions when forming their competitive actions and competitive responses in the course of engaging in competitive rivalry.[53] A **competitive action** is a strategic or tactical action the firm takes to build or defend its competitive advantages or improve its market position. A **competitive response** is a strategic or tactical action the firm takes to counter the effects of a competitor's competitive action. A strategic action or a strategic response is a market-based move that involves a significant commitment of organizational resources and is difficult to implement and reverse. A **tactical action** or a **tactical response** is a market-based move that is taken to fine-tune a strategy; it involves fewer resources and is relatively easy to implement and reverse. Hyundai Motor Co.'s R&D expenditures and plant expansions are strategic actions that support the firm's desire to be one of the world's largest carmakers by 2010, selling at least a million units annually in the United States.[54] Fine-tuning of pricing and sales strategies are considered tactical actions. Adding rebates in response to rebates offered by competitors would be a tactical response. Tactical actions like these, which have negative effects on industry profitability, are common in the automobile and airline industries.

---

# Likelihood of Attack

In addition to market commonality, resource similarity, and the drivers of awareness, motivation, and ability, other factors also affect the likelihood a competitor will use strategic actions and tactical actions to attack its competitors. Three of these factors are first-mover incentives, organizational size, and quality.

## First-Mover Incentives

A **first mover** is a firm that takes an initial competitive action to build or to defend its competitive advantages or to improve its market position. Superior R&D skills are often the foundation of the first mover's competitive success.[55] The first-mover concept has been influenced by the work of the famous economist Joseph Schumpeter, who argued that firms achieve competitive advantage by taking innovative actions[56] (we define and fully describe innovation in Chapter 12). In general, first movers "allocate funds for product innovation and development, aggressive advertising, and advanced research and development."[57]

The benefits of being a successful first mover can be substantial. Especially in fast-cycle markets (discussed later in this chapter) where changes occur rapidly and where it is virtually impossible to sustain a competitive advantage for any period of time, "a first mover may experience five to ten times the valuation and revenue of a second mover."[58] This evidence suggests that although first-mover benefits are never absolute, they are often critical to firm success in industries experiencing rapid technological developments and relatively short product life cycles.[59]

In addition to earning above-average returns until its competitors respond to its successful competitive action, the first mover can gain (1) the loyalty of customers who may become committed to the goods or services of the firm that first made them available and (2) market share that can be difficult for competitors to take during future competitive rivalry. For example, Yahoo! Japan moved first to establish an online auction market service in Japan. Rival eBay entered the market five months later. eBay's delayed response in an industry rife with rapid technological change was a critical mistake. Yahoo! Japan quickly controlled 95 percent of the online auction market in Japan while rival eBay's share was only 3 percent. eBay eventually withdrew from Japan because of Yahoo!'s sizeable advantage.[60] A company official commented about why Yahoo! Japan moved first to establish an online auction market in Japan: "We knew catching up with a front-runner is hard, because in auctions, more buyers bring more sellers."[61] Never able to completely recover, eBay continues to have competitive problems in other parts of Asia, most recently in China.[62]

First movers tend to be aggressive and willing to experiment with innovation and take higher, yet reasonable, levels of risk.[63] To be a first mover, the firm must have readily available the amount of resources required to significantly invest in R&D as well as to rapidly and successfully produce and market a stream of innovative products. Organizational slack makes it possible for firms to have the ability (as measured by available resources) to be first movers. *Slack* is the buffer or cushion provided by actual or obtainable resources that aren't currently in use and are in excess of the minimum resources needed to produce a given level of organizational output.[64] Thus, slack is liquid resources that the firm can quickly allocate to support the actions such as R&D investments and aggressive marketing campaigns that lead to first-mover benefits. Slack allows a competitor to take aggressive competitive actions to continuously introduce innovative products. Furthermore, a first mover will try to rapidly gain market share and customer loyalty in order to earn above-average returns until its competitors are able to effectively respond to its first move.

Being a first mover also carries risk. For example, it is difficult to accurately estimate the returns that will be earned from introducing product innovations.[65] Additionally, the first mover's cost to develop a product innovation can be substantial, reducing the slack available to support further innovation. Also, research has shown that in some cases, a first mover is less likely to make the conversion to the product design that eventually becomes the dominant design in the industry.[66] In such cases, a first mover enjoys most of the benefits from its new product in the period before adoption of a dominant design. These risks mean that a firm should carefully study the results a competitor achieves as a first mover. Continuous success by the competitor suggests additional product innovations, while lack of product acceptance over the course of the competitor's innovations may indicate less willingness in the future to accept the risks of being a first mover.

A **second mover** is a firm that responds to the first mover's competitive action, typically through imitation. More cautious than the first mover, the second mover studies customers' reactions to product innovations. In the course of doing so, the second mover also tries to find any mistakes the first mover made so that it can avoid the problems resulting from them. Often, successful imitation of the first mover's innovations allows the second mover "to avoid both the mistakes and the huge spending of the pioneers (first movers)."[67] Second movers also have the time to develop processes and technologies that are more efficient than those the first mover used.[68] Greater efficiencies could result in lower costs for the second mover. Overall, the outcomes of the first mover's competitive actions may provide an effective blueprint for second and even late movers (as described below) as they determine the nature and timing of their competitive responses.[69] Texas Instruments (TI) tends to be a second mover in chip manufacturing to its cutting-edge rival Intel. Consequently, Intel's chips typically are the most advanced and sought after in the PC industry. However, keeping that first-mover position also means that Intel spends more than any of its competitors on R&D. TI, on the other hand, has made use of its less costly position as a second mover to make impressive inroads into markets such as cell phones, consumer electronics, and medical devices.[70]

Determining that a competitor thinks of itself as an effective second mover allows the firm to predict that that competitor will tend to respond quickly to first movers' successful, innovation-based market entries. If the firm itself is a first mover, then it can expect a successful second-mover competitor to study its market entries and to respond to them quickly. As a second mover, the competitor will try to respond with a product that creates customer value exceeding the value provided by the product that the firm introduced initially as a first mover. The most successful second movers are able to rapidly and meaningfully interpret market feedback to respond quickly, yet productively, to the first mover's innovations.[71]

A **late mover** is a firm that responds to a competitive action, but only after considerable time has elapsed after the first mover's action and the second mover's response. Typically, a late response is better than no response at all, although any success achieved from the late competitive response tends to be slow in coming and considerably less than that achieved by first and second movers. Thus, the firm competing against a late mover can predict that that competitor will likely enter a particular market only after both the first and second movers have achieved success. Moreover, on a relative basis, the firm can predict that the late mover's competitive action will allow it to earn even average returns only when enough time has elapsed for it to understand how to create value that is more attractive to customers than is the value offered by the first and second movers' products. Although exceptions do exist, the firm can predict that the late mover's competitive actions will be relatively ineffective, certainly as compared with those initiated by first movers and second movers.

## Organizational Size

An organization's size affects the likelihood that it will take competitive actions as well as the types of actions it will take and their timing.[72] In general, compared with large companies, small firms are nimble and flexible competitors who rely on speed and surprise to defend their competitive advantages or develop new ones while engaged in competitive rivalry, especially with large companies, to gain an advantageous market position.[73] Small firms' flexibility and nimbleness allow them to develop greater *variety* in their competitive actions relative to larger firms.[74] Nevertheless, because they tend to have more slack resources, large firms are likely to initiate *more* competitive and strategic actions during a given time.[75] Thus, the competitive actions a firm likely will encounter from competitors larger than itself are different from the competitive actions it will encounter from competitors who are smaller.

Relying on a limited variety of competitive actions (which is the large firm's tendency) can lead to reduced competitive success across time, partly because competitors learn how to effectively respond to a predictable set of competitive actions taken by a firm. In contrast, remaining flexible and nimble (which is the small firm's tendency) in order to develop and use a wide variety of competitive actions contributes to success against rivals.

The Website MySpace.com, with more than 100 million users, dominates the U.S. social networking market. However, a smaller, more limber rival is moving in on its "space." Backed by South Korea's SK Telecom, Cyworld hired Look-Look, a youth research firm, to help it understand American teenagers. It also hired Native Instinct, a digital design firm, to scrutinize the site's look and feel. The result is a relaxed hangout that stresses friendships and hosts nearly 3,000 clubs. It also includes "avatars," which are cartoon characters that can be programmed to dance, play, or sulk in a custom online miniroom. Cyworld hopes to lure users through its wholesomeness, as opposed to the "everything goes" culture at MySpace. So far, the approach has led to steady growth.[76]

## Quality

Quality has many definitions, including well-established ones relating it to the production of goods or services with zero defects[77] and seeing it as a never-ending cycle of continuous improvement.[78] **Quality** exists when the firm's goods or services meet or exceed customers' expectations. Thus, in the eyes of customers, quality is about doing the right things relative to performance measures that are important to them.[79] From a strategic perspective, quality is an outcome of how the firm completes primary and support activities (see Chapter 4). Some evidence suggests that quality is one of the most critical components of being able to satisfy a firm's customers.[80]

Customers may be interested in measuring the quality of a firm's products against a broad range of dimensions. Table 6.1 shows sample quality dimensions for goods and services in which customers commonly express an interest. Quality is possible only when top-level managers support it and when its importance is part of the organizational culture.[81] When employees and managers value quality, they become vigilant about continuously finding ways to improve it.[82]

Quality is a universal theme in the global economy and is a necessary but not sufficient condition for competitive success.[83] Without quality, a firm's products lack credibility, meaning that customers don't think of them as viable options. Indeed, customers won't consider buying a product until they believe that it can satisfy at least their base-level expectations in terms of quality dimensions that are important to them. For years, quality was an issue for Jaguar automobiles as the carmaker endured frequent complaints from drivers about poor quality. As a result of recent actions addressing this issue, quality has improved to the point at which customers now view the cars as credible products.[84]

Quality affects competitive rivalry. The firm studying a competitor whose products suffer from poor quality can predict that the competitor's costs are high and that its sales

### Table 6.1: Quality Dimensions of Goods and Services

**Product Quality Dimensions**
1. *Performance*—Operating characteristics
2. *Features*—Important special characteristics
3. *Flexibility*—Meeting operating specifications over some period of time
4. *Durability*—Amount of use before performance deteriorates
5. *Conformance*—Match with preestablished standards
6. *Serviceability*—Ease and speed of repair
7. *Aesthetics*—How a product looks and feels
8. *Perceived quality*—Subjective assessment of characteristics (product image)

**Service Quality Dimensions**
1. *Timeliness*—Performed in the promised period of time
2. *Courtesy*—Performed cheerfully
3. *Consistency*—Giving all customers similar experiences each time
4. *Convenience*—Accessibility to customers
5. *Completeness*—Fully serviced, as required
6. *Accuracy*—Performed correctly each time

SOURCE: Adapted from J. W. Dean, Jr., & J. R. Evans, 1994, *Total Quality: Management, Organization and Society*, St. Paul, MN: West Publishing Company; H. V. Roberts & B. F. Sergesketter, 1993, *Quality Is Personal*, New York: The Free Press; D. Garvin, 1988, *Managed Quality: The Strategic and Competitive Edge*, New York: The Free Press.

revenue likely will decline until the quality issues are resolved. In addition, the firm can predict that the competitor likely won't be aggressive in terms of taking competitive actions, given that its quality problems must be corrected in order to gain credibility with customers. Once the problems are corrected, however, that competitor is likely to take competitive actions emphasizing significant product quality improvements.

Hyundai's experiences illustrate these expectations. Immediately upon becoming CEO of the company in March 1999, Chung Mong Koo started touring the firm's manufacturing facilities. Appalled at what he saw, he told both workers and managers, "The only way we can survive is to raise our quality to Toyota's level."[85] To dramatically improve quality, a quality-control unit was established, and significant resources (more than $1 billion annually) were allocated to R&D in order to build cars that could compete on price and deliver on quality. Outcomes from Hyundai's focus on quality improvements are impressive. In 2006 Hyundai ranked third in the J. D. Power's survey for initial quality (which measures design problems and defects in the first 90 days of ownership), behind only Porsche and Toyota's luxury brand Lexus. According to Jack Nerad, a market analyst at Kelley Blue Book, this recognition indicates that Hyundai has become a force to be reckoned with in both North American and international automobile markets.[86]

## Likelihood of Response

So far in this chapter we have examined how market commonality, resource similarity, awareness of mutual interdependence, motivation to act based on perceived gains and losses, and the ability of a firm to take action can influence competitive behavior. We have also described how first-mover incentives, organizational size, and a firm's emphasis on quality can help a firm predict whether a competitor will pursue a competitive action. These same factors should also be evaluated to help a firm predict whether a competitor will respond to an action it is considering. In addition, this section describes other factors that a firm should consider when predicting competitive responses from one or more competitors.

The success of a firm's competitive action is affected both by the likelihood that a competitor will respond to it and by the type (strategic or tactical) and effectiveness of that response. As noted earlier, a competitive response is a strategic or tactical action the firm takes to counter the effects of a competitor's competitive action. In general, a firm is likely to respond to a competitor's action if the action either significantly strengthens the position of the competitor or significantly weakens the competitive position of the firm.[87] For instance, the actions of a competitor may lead to better use of its capabilities to create competitive advantages or an improved market position. Alternatively, the actions of a competitor could damage the firm's own ability to use its capabilities to create or maintain an advantage or could make its market position less defensible.

The introduction of wireless Internet access (Wi-Fi) into hotel rooms provides an excellent example of why firms may feel compelled to respond to a competitor's actions. Omni Hotels launched a marketing campaign in February 2003 announcing that it was the first luxury hotel chain to have Wi-Fi in its rooms. This action would both improve the ability of Omni to create a competitive advantage and weaken the ability of larger competitors such as Marriott to claim that their luxury hotels were superior to other hotels. Shortly thereafter, Starwood and Intel announced a joint marketing campaign to promote Wi-Fi in several of Starwood's brands, including Westin, Sheraton, and W Hotels. Marriott followed with a similar announcement. According to Lou Paladeau, Marriott's vice president of technology development, "Customers are making decisions about where they stay based on where this technology is available."[88] Although only an estimated 10 percent of Marriott's guests had Wi-Fi enabled laptops at the time, the technology was symbolic of the elite image the luxury hotel competitors were trying to convey. Now, only a few years later, Wi-Fi is standard even in midscale hotels.

Three factors can help a firm predict how a competitor is likely to respond to competitive actions: the type of competitive action, reputation, and market dependence.

## Type of Competitive Action

Competitive responses to strategic actions differ from responses to tactical actions. These differences allow the firm to predict a competitor's likely response to a competitive action that has been launched against it. Of course, a general prediction is that strategic actions receive strategic responses while tactical responses are taken to counter the effects of tactical actions.

In general, strategic actions elicit fewer total competitive responses.[89] The reason this is the case is that as with strategic actions, strategic responses, such as market-based moves, involve a significant commitment of resources and are difficult to implement and reverse. Moreover, the time needed for a strategic action to be implemented and its effectiveness assessed delays the competitor's response to that action.[90] In contrast to the time often required to respond to a strategic action, a competitor likely will respond quickly to a tactical action, such as when an airline company almost immediately matches a competitor's tactical action of reducing prices in certain markets. Either strategic actions or tactical actions that target a large number of a rival's customers are likely to be targeted with strong responses.[91] In fact, if the effects of a competitor's action on the focal firm are significant (e.g., loss of market share, loss of major resources such as critical employees), a response is likely to be swift and strong.[92]

## Actor's Reputation

In the context of competitive rivalry, an *actor* is the firm taking an action or response; *reputation* is "the positive or negative attribute ascribed by one rival to another based on past competitive behavior."[93] A positive reputation may be a source of competitive advantage and high returns, especially for producers of consumer goods.[94] To predict the likelihood of a competitor's response to a current or planned action, the firm studies the responses that the competitor has taken previously when attacked—past behavior is assumed to be a reasonable predictor of future behavior.

Competitors are more likely to respond to either strategic or tactical actions that are taken by a market leader.[95] In particular, successful actions will be quickly imitated. For example, Apple Computer was the dominant manufacturer of personal computers when IBM, the market leader in the computer industry, devoted significant resources to enter the market. When IBM was immediately successful in this endeavor, competitors such as Dell, Compaq, and Gateway responded with strategic actions to enter the market. IBM's reputation as well as its successful strategic action strongly influenced entry by these competitors. Once the market became saturated and the product became more standardized, IBM's reputation was no longer a large source of competitive advantage relative to the cost advantages of competitors. As mentioned in the last chapter, IBM eventually sold its PC business to China's Lenovo Group, although IBM kept a stake in it.[96]

In contrast to a firm with a strong reputation, such as IBM, competitors are less likely to respond to companies with reputations for competitive behavior that is risky, complex, and unpredictable. For instance, a firm with a reputation as a price predator (an actor that frequently reduces prices to gain or maintain market share) generates few responses to its tactical actions. This is because price predators, which typically increase prices once their market share objective is reached, lack credibility with their competitors.[97] On the other hand, a firm with a reputation for pricing integrity, such as Wal-Mart, is much more likely to get a competitive response to its pricing policies.[98]

## Dependence on the Market

*Market dependence* denotes the extent to which a firm's revenues or profits are derived from a particular market.[99] In general, firms can predict that competitors with high market dependence are likely to respond strongly to attacks threatening their market position.[100] For example, firms that depend almost exclusively on one market, such as the Wrigley Company (chewing gum), Lincoln Electric (arc welders), or American Airlines (airline transportation), are much more likely to exhibit strong reactions to the strategic and tactical actions of competitors. Interestingly, the threatened firm in these instances may not respond quickly, but rather take more of a calculated approach so that its response is more effective.

Several software companies took aim at Microsoft's operating system by developing software to handle media applications and security issues. Microsoft, the largest seller of operating systems for PCs, did not respond immediately with a new operating system. Instead, the company introduced a series of minor changes to existing software to address pressing issues. When the company did finally launch its new Vista operating system, it was a strong response to the previous actions of competitors, especially in the areas of media management and security.[101] Microsoft exhibited the same type of strong but delayed response when it introduced its new version of Internet Explorer.[102]

---

# Competitive Dynamics

Whereas competitive rivalry concerns the ongoing actions and responses between a firm and its competitors for an advantageous market position, *competitive dynamics* concerns the ongoing actions and responses taking place among *all* firms competing within a market for advantageous positions.

To explain competitive rivalry, we described (1) factors that determine the degree to which firms are competitors (market commonality and resource similarity), (2) the drivers of competitive behavior for individual firms (awareness, motivation, and ability), and (3) factors affecting the likelihood a competitor will act or attack (first-mover incentives, organizational size, and quality) and respond (type of competitive action, reputation, and market dependence). Building and sustaining competitive advantages are at the core of competitive rivalry, in that advantages are the link to an advantageous market position.

To explain competitive dynamics, we discuss the effects of varying rates of competitive speed in different markets (called slow-cycle, fast-cycle, and standard-cycle markets) on the behavior (actions and responses) of all competitors within a given market. Competitive behaviors as well as the reasons or logic for taking them are similar within each market type, but differ across market types.[103] Thus, competitive dynamics differs in slow-cycle, fast-cycle, and standard-cycle markets. The sustainability of the firm's competitive advantages is an important difference among the three market types.

As noted in Chapter 1, firms want to sustain their advantages for as long as possible, although no advantage is permanently sustainable. The degree of sustainability is affected by how quickly competitive advantages can be imitated and how costly it is to do so.

## Slow-Cycle Markets

**Slow-cycle markets** are markets in which the firm's competitive advantages are shielded from imitation for what are commonly long periods of time and where imitation is costly.[104] Competitive advantages are sustainable in slow-cycle markets.

Building a one-of-a-kind competitive advantage that is proprietary leads to competitive success in a slow-cycle market. This type of advantage is difficult for competitors to understand. As discussed in Chapter 4, a difficult-to-understand and costly-to-imitate advantage results from unique historical conditions, causal ambiguity, and/or social complexity. Copyrights, geography, patents, and ownership of an information resource are examples of what leads to one-of-a-kind advantages.[105] Once a proprietary advantage is developed, the firm's competitive behavior in a slow-cycle market is oriented to protecting, maintaining, and extending that advantage. Thus, the competitive dynamics in slow-cycle markets involve all firms concentrating on competitive actions and responses that enable them to protect, maintain, and extend their proprietary competitive advantage.

Walt Disney Co. continues to extend its proprietary characters, such as Mickey Mouse, Minnie Mouse, and Goofy. These characters have a unique historical development as a result of Walt and Roy Disney's creativity and vision for entertaining people. Products based on the characters seen in Disney's animated cartoons and films are sold through Disney's theme park shops as well as self-standing retail outlets called Disney Stores. The list of character-based products is extensive, including everything from the characters to clothing decorated with the characters' images. Patents shield the use of these characters, so the proprietary nature of Disney's advantage in terms of animated characters protects the firm from imitation by competitors.

Consistent with another attribute of competition in a slow-cycle market, Disney remains committed to protecting its exclusive rights to its characters and their use as shown by the fact that "the company once sued a day-care center, forcing it to remove the likeness of Mickey Mouse from a wall of the facility."[106] As with all firms competing in slow-cycle markets, Disney's competitive actions (such as building theme parks in France, Japan, and Hong Kong) and responses (such as lawsuits to protect its right to fully control use of its animated characters) maintain and extend its proprietary competitive advantage while protecting it. Disney has been able to establish through actions and defend through responses an advantageous market position as a result of its competitive behavior.

In the pharmaceutical industry, patent laws and regulatory requirements, such as those in the United States requiring approval by the Federal Food and Drug Administration (FDA) to launch new products, shield pharmaceutical companies' positions. Once a patent expires, the firm is no longer shielded from competition, a situation that has severe financial implications. Consequently, competitors in this market try to extend patents on their drugs to maintain advantageous positions that the patents provide. The generic version of the allergy drug Flonase didn't hit the market until two years after GlaxoSmithKline's patent expired. The delay resulted from several aggressive administrative and legal maneuvers that finally ended in a courtroom in Baltimore when a judge turned down GlaxoSmithKline's final appeal. According to the consulting firm Bain & Co., patents will expire on 252 drugs by 2014, which could save consumers millions of dollars. Commenting on the situation, Sid Wolfe, director of the Health Research Group, a watchdog organization, said: "Big, big fights are ahead. The brand-name companies will do everything possible to prolong the day when the generic drugs become available. Buying an extra six months, two years or three

**Figure 6.4: Gradual Erosion of a Sustained Competitive Advantage**

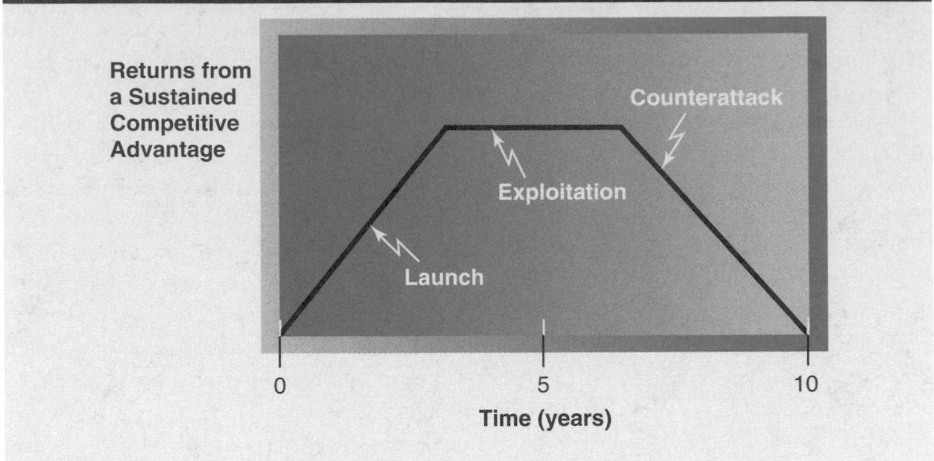

SOURCE: Adapted from I. C. MacMillan, 1988, Controlling competitive dynamics by taking strategic initiative, *Academy of Management Executive*, 11(2): 111–118.

years for a big-selling drug is going to mean a difference of tens or hundreds of millions of dollars."[107]

Figure 6.4 shows the competitive dynamics generated by firms competing in slow-cycle markets. In slow-cycle markets, firms launch a product (e.g., a new drug) that has been developed through a proprietary advantage (e.g., R&D) and then exploit it for as long as possible while the product is shielded from competition. Eventually, competitors respond to the action with a counterattack. In markets for drugs, this counterattack commonly occurs as patents expire, creating the need for another product launch by the firm seeking a shielded market position.

## Fast-Cycle Markets

**Fast-cycle markets** are markets in which the firm's capabilities that contribute to competitive advantages aren't shielded from imitation and where imitation is often rapid and inexpensive. Thus, competitive advantages aren't sustainable in fast-cycle markets. Firms competing in fast-cycle markets recognize the importance of speed; these companies appreciate that "time is as precious a business resource as money or head count—and that the costs of hesitation and delay are just as steep as going over budget or missing a financial forecast."[108] Such high-velocity environments place considerable pressures on top managers to make strategic decisions quickly, but they must also be effective.[109] The often substantial competition and technology-based strategic focus make the strategic decisions complex, increasing the need for a comprehensive approach integrated with decision speed, two often-conflicting characteristics of the strategic decision process.[110]

Reverse engineering and the rate of technology diffusion in fast-cycle markets facilitate rapid imitation. A competitor uses reverse engineering to quickly gain the knowledge required to imitate or improve the firm's products, usually in only a few months. Technology is diffused rapidly in fast-cycle markets, making it available to competitors in a short period of time. The technology often used by fast-cycle competitors isn't proprietary, nor is it protected by patents, as in slow-cycle markets. For example, only a few hundred parts, which are readily available on the open market, are required to build a personal computer. Patents protect only a few of these parts, such as microprocessor chips.[111]

Fast-cycle markets are more volatile than slow-cycle markets and standard-cycle markets. Indeed, the pace of competition in fast-cycle markets is almost frenzied, as companies rely on ideas and the innovations resulting from them as the engines of their growth. Because prices fall quickly in these markets, companies need to profit quickly from their product innovations. For example, rapid declines in the prices of microprocessor chips produced by Intel and Advanced Micro Devices, among others, make it possible for PC manufacturers to continuously reduce their prices to end users. Imitation of many fast-cycle products is relatively easy, as demonstrated by Dell and Hewlett-Packard, along with a host of other vendors. All of these firms have partly or largely imitated IBM's initial PC design to create their products. Continuous declines in the costs of parts, as well as the fact that the information and knowledge required to assemble a PC isn't especially complicated and is readily available, make it possible for additional competitors to enter this market without significant difficulty.[112]

Fast-cycle market characteristics make it virtually impossible for companies in this type of market to develop sustainable competitive advantages. Recognizing this, firms avoid "loyalty" to any of their products, preferring to cannibalize their current product by launching a new product before competitors learn how to do so through successful imitation. This emphasis creates competitive dynamics that differ substantially from those in slow-cycle markets. Instead of concentrating on protecting, maintaining, and extending competitive advantages, as is the case for firms in slow-cycle markets, companies competing in fast-cycle markets focus on learning how to rapidly and continuously develop new competitive advantages that are superior to those they replace. In fast-cycle markets, firms don't concentrate on trying to protect a given competitive advantage because they understand that the advantage won't exist long enough to extend it.

Figure 6.5 shows the competitive behavior of firms competing in fast-cycle markets. Competitive dynamics in this market type finds firms taking actions and responses in the course of competitive rivalry that are oriented to rapid and continuous product introductions and the use of a stream of ever-changing competitive advantages. The firm launches

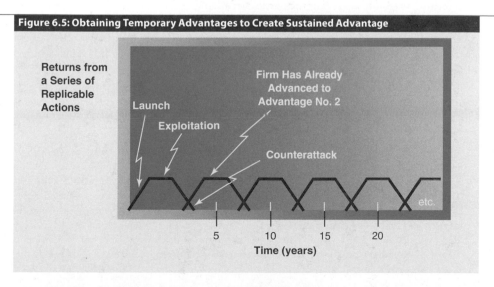

**Figure 6.5: Obtaining Temporary Advantages to Create Sustained Advantage**

Returns from a Series of Replicable Actions

Launch

Exploitation

Firm Has Already Advanced to Advantage No. 2

Counterattack

etc.

5    10    15    20

Time (years)

a product as a competitive action and then exploits the advantage associated with it for as long as possible. However, the firm also tries to move to another temporary competitive action before competitors can respond to the first one. Thus, competitive dynamics in fast-cycle markets, in which all firms seek to achieve new competitive advantages before competitors learn how to effectively respond to current ones, often result in rapid product upgrades as well as quick product innovations.[113]

As our discussion suggests, innovation has a dominant effect on competitive dynamics in fast-cycle markets. For individual firms, this means that innovation is a key source of competitive advantage. Through innovation, the firm can cannibalize its own products before competitors successfully imitate them.[114]

## Standard-Cycle Markets

**Standard-cycle markets** are those in which the firm's competitive advantages are moderately shielded from imitation and where imitation is moderately costly. Competitive advantages are partially sustainable in standard-cycle markets, but only when the firm is able to continuously upgrade the quality of its competitive advantages. The competitive actions and responses that form a standard-cycle market's competitive dynamics find firms seeking large market shares, trying to gain customer loyalty through brand names, and carefully controlling their operations to consistently provide the same positive experience for customers.[115]

Companies competing in standard-cycle markets serve many customers. Because the capabilities on which their competitive advantages are based are less specialized, imitation is faster and less costly for standard-cycle firms than for those competing in slow-cycle markets. However, imitation is less quick and more expensive in these markets than in fast-cycle markets. Thus, the competitive dynamics in standard-cycle markets rest midway between the characteristics of dynamics in slow-cycle and fast-cycle markets. The quickness of imitation is reduced and becomes more expensive for standard-cycle competitors when a firm is able to develop economies of scale by combining coordinated and integrated design and manufacturing processes with a large sales volume.

Because of large volumes, the size of mass markets, and the need to develop scale economies, the competition for market share is intense in standard-cycle markets. This form of competition is readily evident in the battles between Coca-Cola and PepsiCo. These companies compete all over the world. In recent years, PepsiCo has been winning battles in domestic and international markets. These outcomes are partially a result of effective strategic actions by PepsiCo as well as ineffective actions by Coca-Cola, including rapid turnover of individuals serving as the firm's CEO and its ineffective product innovation.[116]

This example illustrates that innovation can also drive competitive actions and responses in standard-cycle markets such as beverages, especially when rivalry is intense. A stock analyst recently commented on the nonalcoholic beverages market:

> The need for innovation has been especially strong in this space, where Coke and Pepsi fight for market share. Carbonated soft drinks, though still the dominant category, are not growing. Consumers seem to have reached a saturation point with iconic offerings, especially colas, and are instead gravitating toward noncarbonated beverages such as sports drinks, bottled water, and bottled iced teas and coffees. This shifting playing field has clearly benefited PepsiCo at the expense of Coke—Coke has been slow where PepsiCo has been nimble, and Coke has continued to push doors when it should have been watching what doors consumers were pulling open. PepsiCo, in contrast, concentrated on finding out what consumers wanted and making sure that a PepsiCo product met that need.[117]

In the final analysis, innovation substantially influences competitive dynamics as it affects the actions and responses of all companies competing in a slow-cycle, fast-cycle, or standard-cycle market. We have emphasized the importance of innovation to the firm's value creation in earlier chapters and will do so again in Chapter 12. Our discussion of innovation in terms of competitive dynamics extends the earlier discussions by showing its importance in all types of markets in which firms compete.

## Summary

- Competitors are firms competing in the same market, offering similar products and targeting similar customers. Competitive rivalry is the ongoing set of competitive actions and competitive responses occurring between competitors as they compete against each other for an advantageous market position. The outcomes of competitive rivalry influence the firm's ability to sustain its competitive advantages as well as the level (below-average, average, or above-average) of its financial returns.

- The set of competitive actions and responses the firm takes while engaged in competitive rivalry is called competitive behavior. Competitive dynamics is the set of actions all firms competing within a particular market take.

- A firm studies competitive rivalry to be able to predict the competitive actions and responses that each of its competitors likely will take. Competitive actions are either strategic or tactical in nature. The firm takes competitive actions to defend or build its competitive advantages or improve its market position. Competitive responses are taken to counter the effects of a competitor's competitive action. A strategic action or a strategic response requires a significant commitment of organizational resources, is difficult to successfully implement, and is hard to reverse. A tactical action or a tactical response requires fewer organizational resources and is easier to implement and reverse.

- A competitor analysis is the first step the firm takes to be able to predict its competitors' actions and responses. In their analysis, firms study market commonality (the number of markets with which competitors are jointly involved and their importance to each) and resource similarity (how comparable competitors' resources are in terms of type and amount). In general, the greater the market commonality and resource similarity, the more firms acknowledge that they are direct competitors.

- Market commonality and resource similarity shape the firm's awareness (the degree to which it and its competitor understand their mutual interdependence), motivation (the firm's incentive to attack or respond), and ability (the quality of the resources available to the firm to attack and respond). Having knowledge of a competitor in terms of these characteristics increases the quality of the firm's predictions about a competitor's actions and responses.

- First-mover incentive is another factor that affects the likelihood of a competitor taking competitive actions. First movers, those firms taking an initial competitive action, often earn above-average returns until competitors can successfully respond to their action and gain loyal customers. Not all firms can be first movers in that they may lack the awareness, motivation, or ability required to engage in this type of competitive behavior. Moreover, some firms prefer to be a second mover (the firm responding to the first mover's action). One reason for this is that second movers, especially those acting quickly, can successfully compete against the first mover. By studying the first mover's good or service, customers' reactions to it, and the responses of other competitors to the first mover, the second mover can often avoid the early entrant's mistakes and find ways to improve upon the value created for customers by the first mover's good or service. Late movers (those that respond a long time after the original action was taken) commonly are lower performers and much less competitive.

■ A large organizational size tends to reduce the number of different types of competitive actions that large firms launch; smaller competitors use a wide variety of actions. Ideally, the firm would like to initiate a large number of diverse actions when engaged in competitive rivalry.

■ Poor product quality dampens a firm's ability to take competitive actions, in that it is a base denominator to successful competition in the global economy.

■ The type of action (strategic or tactical) the firm takes, the competitor's reputation for the nature of its competitor behavior, and its dependence on the market in which the action is taken are studied to predict a competitor's response. In general, the number of tactical responses exceeds the number of strategic responses. Competitors respond more frequently to the actions taken by the firm with a reputation for predictable and understandable competitive behavior, especially if that firm is a market leader. In general, the firm can predict that when its competitor is highly dependent for its revenue and profitability in the market in which the firm takes a competitive action, that competitor is likely to launch a strong response. However, firms that are more diversified across markets are less likely to respond to a particular action that affects only one of the markets in which they compete.

■ Competitive dynamics concerns the ongoing competitive behavior occurring among all firms competing in a market for advantageous positions. Market characteristics affect the set of actions and responses firms take while competing in a market as well as the sustainability of firms' competitive advantages. In slow-cycle markets, where competitive advantages can be maintained, competitive dynamics finds firms taking actions and responses that are intended to protect, maintain, and extend their proprietary advantages. In fast-cycle markets, competition is almost frenzied as firms concentrate on developing a series of temporary competitive advantages. This emphasis is necessary because firms' advantages in fast-cycle markets aren't proprietary and, as such, are subject to rapid and relatively inexpensive imitation. In standard-cycle markets, firms are moderately shielded from competition as they use competitive advantages that are moderately sustainable. Competitors in standard-cycle markets serve mass markets and try to develop economies of scale to enhance their profitability. Innovation is vital to competitive success in each of these market types.

## Ethics Questions

1. When competing against one another, firms jockey for a market position that is advantageous, relative to competitors. In this jockeying, what are the ethical implications associated with the way competitor intelligence is gathered?
2. Second movers often respond to a first mover's competitive actions through imitation. Is there anything unethical about a company imitating a competitor's good or service as a means of engaging in competition?

3. The standards for competitive rivalry differ in countries throughout the world. What should firms do to cope with these differences? What guidance should a firm give to employees as they deal with competitive actions and competitive responses that are ethical in one country but unethical in others?

4. In slow-cycle markets, effective competitors are able to shield their competitive advantages from imitation by competitors for relatively long periods of time. However, this isn't the case in fast-cycle markets. Do these conditions have implications in terms of ethical business practices? Is what is ethical in slow-cycle markets different from what is ethical in fast-cycle markets?

5. Is it ethical for the firm competing against a competitor in several markets to launch a competitive response in a market that differs from the one in which that competitor took a competitive action against the local firm? Why or why not?

# Notes

1. R. Belderbos & L. Sleuwaegen, 2005, Competitive drivers and international plant configuration strategies: A product-level test, *Strategic Management Journal*, 26; 577–593; G. J. Castrogiovanni, 2002, Organization task environments: Have they changed fundamentally over time? *Journal of Management*, 28: 129–150; D. Tapscott, 2001, Rethinking strategy in a networked world, *Strategy & Business*, 24(third quarter), 34–41.

2. S. J. Chang & S. Park, 2005, Types of firms generating network externalities and MNCs' co-location decisions, *Strategic Management Journal*, 26: 595–615; S. C. Voelpel, M. Dous, & T. H. Davenport, 2005, Five steps to creating global knowledge-sharing systems: Siemens' ShareNet, *Academy of Management Executive*, 19(2): 9–23; A. Seth, K. P. Song, & R. R. Pettit, 2002, Value creation and destruction in cross-border acquisitions: An empirical analysis of foreign acquisitions of U.S. firms, *Strategic Management Journal*, 23: 921–940; D. G. McKendrick, 2001, Global strategy and population level learning: The case of hard disk drives, *Strategic Management Journal*, 22: 307–334.

3. G. Hamel, 2000, *Leading the Revolution*, Boston: Harvard Business School Press.

4. C. M. Grimm, H. Lee, & K. G. Smith, 2006, *Strategy as Action: Competitive Dynamics and Competitive Advantage*, Oxford, UK: Oxford University Press.

5. Ibid.

6. M.-J. Chen, 1996, Competitor analysis and interfirm rivalry: Toward a theoretical integration, *Academy of Management Review*, 21: 100–134.

7. S. Jayachandran, J. Gimeno, & P. R. Varadarajan, 1999, Theory of multimarket competition: A synthesis and implications for marketing strategy, *Journal of Marketing*, 63(3): 49–66.

8. D. Barton, R. Newell, & G. Wilson, 2002, How to win in a financial crisis, *McKinsey Quarterly*, 4: 21–33.

9. R. E. Caves, 1984, Economic analysis and the quest for competitive advantage, in *Papers and Proceedings of the 96th Annual Meeting of the American Economic Association*, 127–132.

10. Grimm, Lee, & Smith, *Strategy as Action*; G. Young, K. G. Smith, C. M. Grimm, & D. Simon, 2000, Multimarket contact and resource dissimilarity: A competitive dynamics perspective, *Journal of Management*, 26: 1217–1236; C. M. Grimm & K. G. Smith, 1997, *Strategy as Action: Industry Rivalry and Coordination*, Cincinnati: South-Western, 53–74.

11. H. D. Hopkins, 2003, The response strategies of dominant U.S. firms to Japanese challengers, *Journal of Management*, 29: 5–25; G. S. Day & D. J. Reibstein, 1997, The dynamic challenges for theory and practice, in G. S. Day & D. J. Reibstein (eds.), *Wharton on Competitive Strategy*, New York: Wiley, 2.

12. J. Magretta, 2002, Why business models matter, *Harvard Business Review*, 80(5): 86–92.

13. G. Young, K. G. Smith, & C. M. Grimm, 1996, "Austrian" and industrial organization perspectives on firm-level competitive activity and performance, *Organization Science*, 73: 243–254.

14. H. A. Haveman & L. Nonnemaker, 2000, Competition in multiple geographic markets: The impact on growth and market entry, *Administrative Science Quarterly*, 45: 232–267.

15. L. Fuentelsaz & J. Gomez, 2006, Multipoint competition, strategic similarity and entry into geographic markets, *Strategic Management Journal*, 27: 477–499; K. G. Smith, W. J. Ferrier, & H. Ndofor, 2001, Competitive dynamics research: Critique and future directions, in M. A. Hitt, R. E. Freeman, & J. S. Harrison (eds.), *Handbook of Strategic Management*, Oxford, UK: Blackwell Publishers, 326.

16. L. Canina, C. A. Enz, & J. S. Harrison, 2005, Agglomeration effects and strategic orientations: Evidence from the U.S. lodging industry, *Academy of Management Journal*, 48: 565–581.

17. S. Crainer, 2001, And the new economy winner is . . . Europe, *Strategy & Business*, second quarter, 40–47.

18. J. E. Garten, 2001, The wrong time for companies to beat a global retreat, *Business Week*, December 17, 22.

19. Young, Smith, Grimm, & Simon, Multimarket contact and resource dissimilarity, 1230–1233.

20. K. Ramaswamy, 2001, Organizational ownership, competitive intensity, and firm performance: An empirical study of the Indian manufacturing sector, *Strategic Management Journal*, 22: 989–998; K. Cool, L. H. Roller, & B. Leleux, 1999, The relative impact of

actual and potential rivalry on firm profitability in the pharmaceutical industry, *Strategic Management Journal*, 20: 1–14.

21  D. R. Gnyawali & R. Madhavan, 2001, Cooperative networks and competitive dynamics: A structural embeddedness perspective, *Academy of Management Review*, 26: 431–445.

22  Young, Smith, Grimm, & Simon, Multimarket contact and resource dissimilarity, 1217; M. E. Porter, 1991, Towards a dynamic theory of strategy, *Strategic Management Journal*, 12: 95–117.

23  S. J. Marsh, 1998, Creating barriers for foreign competitors: A study of the impact of anti-dumping actions on the performance of U.S. firms, *Strategic Management Journal*, 19: 25–37; K. G. Smith, C. M. Grimm, G. Young, & S. Wally, 1997, Strategic groups and rivalrous firm behavior: Toward a reconciliation, *Strategic Management Journal*, 18: 149–157.

24  D. Simon, 2005, Incumbent pricing responses to entry, *Strategic Management Journal*, 26: 1229–1248; W. J. Ferrier, 2001, Navigating the competitive landscape: The drivers and consequences of competitive aggressiveness, *Academy of Management Journal*, 44: 858–877; M. E. Porter, 1980, *Competitive Strategy*, New York: The Free Press.

25  Smith, Ferrier, & Ndofor, Competitive dynamics research, 319.

26  W. P. Putsis Jr., 1999, Empirical analysis of competitive interaction in food product categories, *Agribusiness*, 15(3): 295–311.

27  Chen, Competitor analysis and interfirm rivalry, 108.

28  Ibid., 109.

29  G. K. Deans, F. Kroeger, & S. Zeisel, 2002, The consolidation curve, *Harvard Business Review*, 80(12): 20–21; E. Abrahamson & C. J. Fombrun, 1994, Macrocultures: Determinants and consequences, *Academy of Management Review*, 19: 728–755.

30  C. Salter, 2002, On the road again, *Fast Company*, January, 50–58.

31  Young, Smith, Grimm, & Simon, Multimarket contact and resource dissimilarity, 1219.

32  Chen, Competitor analysis and interfirm rivalry, 106.

33  L. Fuentelsaz & J. Gomez, 2006, Multipoint competition, strategic similarity and entry into geographic markets, *Strategic Management Journal*, 27: 477–499; J. Gimeno & C. Y. Woo, 1999, Multimarket contact, economies of scope, and firm performance, *Academy of Management Journal*, 42: 239–259.

34  S. Stevenson, 2007, Return of the King, *Slate*, http://www.slate.com/id/2107697, February 2.

35  2007, Prudential Financial, Inc., Hoover's online, http://www.hoovers.com/prudential, February 2.

36  Young, Smith, Grimm, & Simon, Multimarket contact and resource dissimilarity, 1230.

37  J. Gimeno, 1999, Reciprocal threats in multimarket rivalry: Staking out "spheres of influence" in the U.S. airline industry, *Strategic Management Journal*, 20: 101–128; N. Fernandez & P. L. Marin, 1998, Market power and multimarket contact: Some evidence from the Spanish hotel industry, *Journal of Industrial Economics*, 46: 301–315.

38  Jayachandran, Gimeno, & Varadarajan, Theory of multimarket competition, 59; Chen, Competitor analysis and interfirm rivalry, 107.

39  J. Gimeno & C. Y. Woo, 1996, Hypercompetition in a multimarket environment: The role of strategic similarity and multimarket contact on competitive de-escalation, *Organization Science*, 7: 322–341.

40  Canina, Enz, & Harrison, Agglomeration effects and strategic orientations.

41  J. W. O'Neill & A. S. Mattila, 2006, Strategic hotel development and positioning: The effects of revenue drivers on profitability, *Cornell Hotel and Restaurant Administration Quarterly*, 47(2): 146–155.

42  Chen, Competitor analysis and interfirm rivalry, 107–108.

43  Ibid., 110.

44  Ibid.; W. Ocasio, 1997, Towards an attention-based view of the firm, *Strategic Management Journal*, 18(summer special issue): 187–206; Smith, Ferrier, & Ndofor, Competitive dynamics research, 320.

45  S. Tallman, M. Jenkins, N. Henry, & S. Pinch, 2004, Knowledge, clusters and competitive advantage, *Academy of Management Review*, 29: 258–271; G. P. Hodgkinson & G. Johnson, 1994, Exploring the mental models of competitive strategists: The case for a processual approach, *Journal of Management Studies*, 31: 525–551; J. F. Porac & H. Thomas, 1994, Cognitive categorization and subjective rivalry among retailers in a small city, *Journal of Applied Psychology*, 79: 54–66.

46  M. Selva, 2003, Wal-Mart, France's Carrefour set sights on Ahold businesses, *Sunday Business*, April 6, 83; 2001, Wal around the world, *Economist*, December 8, 55–56.

47  S. H. Park & D. Zhou, 2005, Firm heterogeneity and competitive dynamics in alliance formation, *Academy of Management Review*, 30: 531–554; Smith, Ferrier, & Ndofor, Competitive dynamics research, 320.

48  Chen, Competitor analysis and interfirm rivalry, 113.

49  R. Belderbos & L. Sleuwaegen, 2005, Competitive drivers and international plant configuration strategies: A product-level test, *Strategic Management Journal*, 26: 577–593.

50  Grimm & Smith, Strategy as Action, 125.

51  2002, Blue light blues, *Economist*, January 29, 54; D. B. Yoffie & M. Kwak, 2001, Mastering strategic movement at Palm, *MIT Sloan Management Review*, 43(1): 55–63.

52  K. G. Smith, W. J. Ferrier, & C. M. Grimm, 2001, King of the hill: Dethroning the industry leader, *Academy of Management Executive*, 15(2): 59–70.

53  W. J. Ferrier & H. Lee, 2003, Strategic aggressiveness, variation, and surprise: How the sequential pattern of competitive rivalry influences stock market returns, *Journal of Managerial Issues*, 14: 162–180; G. S. Day, 1997, Assessing competitive arenas: Who are your competitors? in G. S. Day & D. J. Reibstein (eds.), *Wharton on Competitive Strategy*, New York: Wiley, 25–26.

54  R. Truett, 2003, A chance to shape design destiny, *Automotive News*, April 7, D2; M. Ihlwan, L. Armstrong, & K. Kerwin, 2001, Hyundai gets hot, *Business Week*, December 17, 84–86.

55  W. T. Robinson & J. Chiang, 2002, Product development strategies for established market pioneers, early followers, and late entrants, *Strategic Management Journal*, 23: 855–866.

56  J. Schumpeter, 1934, *The Theory of Economic Development*, Cambridge, MA: Harvard University Press.

57. J. L. C. Cheng & I. F. Kesner, 1997, Organizational slack and response to environmental shifts: The impact of resource allocation patterns, *Journal of Management*, 23: 1–18.

58. F. Wang, 2000, Too appealing to overlook, *America's Network*, December, 10–12.

59. D. P. Forbes, 2005, Managerial determinants of decision speed in new ventures, *Strategic Management Journal*, 26: 355–366; G. Hamel, 2000, *Leading the Revolution*, Boston: Harvard Business School Press, 103.

60. K. Hafner & B. Stone, 2006, eBay is expected to close its auction site in China, *New York Times*, http://www .nytimes.com/2006/12/19/technology, December 19.

61. K. Belson, R. Hof, & B. Elgin, 2001, How Yahoo! Japan beat eBay at its own game, *Business Week*, June 4, 58.

62. Hafner & Stone, eBay is expected to close its auction site.

63. A. Srivastava & H. Lee, 2005, Predicting order and timing of new product moves: The role of top management in corporate entrepreneurship, *Journal of Business Venturing*, 20: 459–481; A. Nerer & P. W. Roberts, 2004, Technological and product-market experience and the success of new product introductions in the pharmaceutical industry, *Strategic Management Journal*, 25: 779–799.

64. S. W. Geiger & L. H. Cashen, 2002, A multidimensional examination of slack and its impact on innovation, *Journal of Managerial Issues*, 14: 68–84; L. J. Bourgeois III, 1981, On the measurement of organizational slack, *Academy of Management Review*, 6: 29–39.

65. M. B. Lieberman & D. B. Montgomery, 1988, First-mover advantages, *Strategic Management Journal*, 9: 41–58.

66. G. Dowell & A. Swaminathan, 2006, Entry timing, exploration, and firm survival in the early U.S. bicycle industry, *Strategic Management Journal*, 27: 1159–1182.

67. 2001, Older, wiser, webbier, *Economist*, June 30, 10.

68. M. Shank, 2002, Executive strategy report, IBM business strategy consulting, http://www.ibm.com, March 14; W. Boulding & M. Christen, 2001, First-mover disadvantage, *Harvard Business Review*, 79(9): 20–21.

69. J. Gimeno, R. E. Hoskisson, B. B. Beal, & W. P. Wan, 2005, Explaining the clustering of international expansion moves: A critical test in the U.S. telecommunications industry, *Academy of Management Journal*, 48: 297–319; K. G. Smith, C. M. Grimm, & M. J. Gannon, 1992, *Dynamics of Competitive Strategy*, Newbury Park, CA: Sage Publications.

70. C. Edwards, 2006, To see where tech is headed, watch TI, *Business Week*, November 6, 74.

71. H. R. Greve, 1998, Managerial cognition and the mimetic adoption of market positions: What you see is what you do, *Strategic Management Journal*, 19: 967–988.

72. S. D. Dobrev & G. R. Carroll, 2003, Size (and competition) among organizations: Modeling scale-based selection among automobile producers in four major countries, 1885–1981, *Strategic Management Journal*, 24: 541–558; Smith, Ferrier, & Ndofor, Competitive dynamics research, 327.

73. W. S. Desarbo, R. Grewal, & J. Wind, 2006, Who competes with whom? A demand-based perspective for identifying and representing asymmetric competition, *Strategic Management Journal*, 27: 101–129; F. K. Pil & M. Hoiweg, 2003, Exploring scale: The advantage of thinking small, *McKinsey Quarterly*, 44(2): 33–39; M.-J. Chen & D. C. Hambrick, 1995, Speed, stealth and selective attack: How small firms differ from large

firms in competitive behavior, *Academy of Management Journal*, 38: 453–482.

74. D. Miller & M.-J. Chen, 1996, The simplicity of competitive repertoires: An empirical analysis, *Strategic Management Journal*, 17: 419–440.

75. Young, Smith, & Grimm, "Austrian" and industrial organization perspectives.

76. E. Woyke, 2006, The Korean upstart in MySpace's face, *Business Week*, November 13, 72.

77. P. B. Crosby, 1980, *Quality Is Free*, New York: Penguin.

78. W. E. Deming, 1986, *Out of the Crisis*, Cambridge, MA: MIT Press.

79. R. S. Kaplan & D. P. Norton, 2001, *The Strategy-Focused Organization*, Boston: Harvard Business School Press.

80. L. B. Crosby, R. DeVito, & J. M. Pearson, 2003, Manage your customers' perception of quality, *Review of Business*, 24(1): 18–24.

81. R. Cullen, S. Nicholls, & A. Halligan, 2001, Measurement to demonstrate success, *British Journal of Clinical Governance*, 6(4): 273–278.

82. K. E. Weick & K. M. Sutcliffe, 2001, *Managing the Unexpected*, San Francisco: Jossey-Bass, 81–82.

83. G. Yeung & V. Mok, 2005, What are the impacts of implementing ISOs on the competitiveness of manufacturing industry in China, *Journal of World Business*, 40: 139–157.

84. J. Green & D. Welch, 2001, Jaguar may find it's a jungle out there, *Business Week*, March 26, 62.

85. Ihlwan, Armstrong, & Kerwin, Hyundai gets hot, 84.

86. R. Jones, 2006, Quality gains driving Hyundai's success, http://www.msnbc.msn.com/id/13207035, June 9.

87. J. Schumpeter, 1950, *Capitalism, Socialism and Democracy*, New York: Harper; Smith, Ferrier, & Ndofor, Competitive dynamics research, 323.

88. C. Binkley and D. Clark, 2003, Wi-Fi is now a must for big hotels, *Wall Street Journal*, February 27, D3.

89. M.-J. Chen & I. C. MacMillan, 1992, Nonresponse and delayed response to competitive moves, *Academy of Management Journal*, 35: 539–570; Smith, Ferrier, & Ndofor, Competitive dynamics research, 335.

90. M.-J. Chen, K. G. Smith, & C. M. Grimm, 1992, Action characteristics as predictors of competitive responses, *Management Science*, 38: 439–455.

91. M.-J. Chen & D. Miller, 1994, Competitive attack, retaliation and performance: An expectancy-valence framework, *Strategic Management Journal*, 15: 85–102.

92. T. Gardner, 2005, Interfirm competition for human resources: Evidence from the software industry, *Academy of Management Journal*, 48: 237–258; N. Huyghebaert & L. M. van de Gucht, 2004, Incumbent strategic behavior in financial markets and the exit of entrepreneurial startups, *Strategic Management Journal*, 25: 669–688.

93. Smith, Ferrier, & Ndofor, Competitive dynamics research, 333.

94. P. W. Roberts & G. R. Dowling, 2003, Corporate reputation and sustained superior financial performance, *Strategic Management Journal*, 24: 1077–1093; J. Shamsie, 2003, The context of dominance: An industry-driven framework for exploiting reputation, *Strategic Management Journal*, 24: 199–215.

95. W. J. Ferrier, K. G. Smith, & C. M. Grimm, 1999, The role of competitive actions in market share erosion and industry dethronement: A study of industry leaders

and challengers, *Academy of Management Journal*, 42: 372–388.

⁹⁶ M. Williams & P. Kallendar, 2004, China's Lenovo to buy IBM's PC business, *IDG News*, December 7.

⁹⁷ Smith, Grimm, & Gannon, *Dynamics of Competitive Strategy*.

⁹⁸ S. Vranica & G. McWilliams, 2006, Wal-Mart hits a crossroads on ad approach: Retailer could go back to low-prices pitch or pursue targeted tack, *Wall Street Journal*, December 12, B4.

⁹⁹ A. Karnani & B. Wernerfelt, 1985, Research note and communication: Multiple point competition, *Strategic Management Journal*, 6: 87–97.

¹⁰⁰ Smith, Ferrier, & Ndofor, Competitive dynamics research, 330.

¹⁰¹ J. Greene, 2007, The real value of Vista, *Business Week*, February 5, 48; S. Wildstrom, 2007, Burglar-proof windows? *Business Week*, January 22, 26.

¹⁰² S. Wildstrom, 2006, Explorer's long awaited update, *Business Week*, November 13, 24.

¹⁰³ A. Kalnins & W. Chung, 2004, Resource-seeking agglomeration: A study of market entry in the lodging industry, *Strategic Management Journal*, 25: 689–699; J. R. Williams, 1999, *Renewable Advantage: Crafting Strategy through Economic Time*, New York: The Free Press.

¹⁰⁴ J. R. Williams, 1992, How sustainable is your competitive advantage? *California Management Review* 34(3): 29–51.

¹⁰⁵ Williams, *Renewable Advantage*, 6.

¹⁰⁶ Ibid., 57.

¹⁰⁷ T. Pugh, 2006, Generic drug's path to retail market often long and contentious, *Knight Ridder Tribune Business News*, April 30, 1.

¹⁰⁸ 2003, How fast is your company? *Fast Company*, June, 18.

¹⁰⁹ T. Talaulicar, J. Grundei, & A. V. Werder, 2005, Strategic decision making in start-ups: The effect of top management team organization and processes on speed and comprehensiveness, *Journal of Business Venturing*, 20: 519–541.

¹¹⁰ M. Song, C. Droge, S. Hanvanich, & R. Calantone, 2005, Marketing and technology resource complementarity: An analysis of their interaction effect in two environmental contexts, *Strategic Management Journal*, 26: 259–276.

¹¹¹ Williams, *Renewable Advantage*, 8.

¹¹² Ibid.

¹¹³ R. Sanchez, 1995, Strategic flexibility in production competition, *Strategic Management Journal*, 16(summer special issue): 9–26.

¹¹⁴ Schumpeter, *The Theory of Economic Development*.

¹¹⁵ Williams, *Renewable Advantage*, 7.

¹¹⁶ B. Morris, 2004, Coca-Cola: The real story, *Fortune*, May 31, 84–91.

¹¹⁷ M. Reilly, 2007, Stock strategist: Which beverage stock makes the best investment? *Knight Ridder Tribune Business News*, January 19, 1.

# CHAPTER 7

# Cooperative Strategy

## KNOWLEDGE OBJECTIVES

*Studying this chapter should provide you with the strategic management knowledge needed to:*

1. Define cooperative strategies and explain why they are important in the current competitive environment.

2. Explain how the primary reasons for the use of cooperative strategy differ depending on market context (fast-cycle, slow-cycle, or standard-cycle).

3. Define and discuss equity and nonequity strategic alliances.

4. Discuss the types of cooperative strategies that are formed primarily to reduce costs or increase differentiation.

5. Identify and describe cooperative strategies that help a firm address forces in the external environment.

6. Explain the cooperative strategies that firms use primarily to foster growth.

7. Discuss the risks associated with cooperative strategies.

8. Describe how firms can effectively implement and manage their cooperative strategies.

Globalization and rapid technological changes have created a business environment in which interorganizational cooperation is required for success. To be competitive, for example, a firm that assembles and markets handheld electronic devices may have business relationships with 100 companies in 20 countries, simply because those companies produce the best products and provide the best services at the best prices. Although many relationships of this nature are contractual, some of them will be cooperative. A **cooperative strategy** is a strategy in which firms work together to achieve a shared objective.[1]

Boeing is an excellent example of how times have changed. The development process for its 787 model was very different from the process used for earlier models. Before the 787, Boeing did all of the engineering design work on its own. However, the company realized that to be competitive with its main rival Airbus it would have to work with the best suppliers in the world. Boeing selected fewer than 100 suppliers for the 787, compared with more than 500 for the 777, and gave them much more responsibility for the project. As noted in the *Economist*: "The difference is not just in the numbers, but in the relationship. Suppliers provide what they are asked for; partners share responsibility for a project."[2]

We examine several topics in this chapter. First, we discuss some of the reasons cooperative strategies are important in the current competitive environment. We examine these reasons in general and also by market type: slow-cycle, fast-cycle, or standard-cycle. Then we offer examples of various types of cooperative strategies on the basis of their primary strategic objectives: to increase differentiation or reduce costs, to deal with forces in the external environment, or to grow and diversify. Many of the examples fall into the category of strategic alliances because they are the most frequently used form of cooperative strategy. A **strategic alliance** is a cooperative strategy in which firms combine resources and capabilities to create a competitive advantage.[3] The chapter closes with discussions of the risks of using cooperative strategies as well as how effective management of them can reduce those risks and enhance performance.

## The Importance of Cooperative Strategy

Cooperative strategies have become an integral part of the competitive landscape and are now quite important to many companies.[4] Surveyed executives of technology companies stated that partnerships are central to their firms' success.[5] Speaking directly to the issue of technology acquisition and development for these firms, a manager noted: "You have to partner today or you will miss the next wave. You cannot possibly acquire the technology fast enough, so partnering is essential."[6] Similarly, Jack Welch, previous CEO of General Electric, has been widely quoted as saying, "If you think you can go it alone in today's global economy, you are highly mistaken."[7] Most (if not virtually all) firms lack the full set of resources and capabilities needed to reach their objectives, which indicates that partnering with others will increase the probability of reaching them.[8] Cooperative behavior allows partners to create value that they couldn't develop by acting independently.[9]

From a stakeholder perspective, organizations coordinate an entire network of cooperative relationships, both inside and outside the firm.[10] The underlying assumption is that organizations are inherently cooperative systems.[11] Because of their cooperative nature, organizations are inclined to form partnerships with stakeholders to achieve common objectives.[12] Cooperative relationships can be powerful mechanisms for aligning stakeholder interests and can also help a firm reduce environmental uncertainty.[13] For example, much of a firm's success in the automobile industry depends on the strength of its suppliers. But just as an automobile manufacturer depends on its suppliers, so also its suppliers depend on the manufacturer. Their fortunes are closely aligned, and thus a lot of the uncertainty they face depends on the strategic and tactical actions each takes. Mutual dependence suggests that manufacturers and their suppliers should form strong partnerships in order to reduce uncertainty and enhance joint value creation.[14] Toyota admits that a lot of its success comes from special relationships with suppliers. A senior executive of a firm that supplies Toyota described the relationship in simple terms: "Toyota helped us dramatically improve our production system."[15] The payoff to Toyota is a better, and more loyal, supplier.

Increasingly, cooperative strategies are formed by firms who also compete against one another, a situation sometimes called **co-opetition**.[16] For instance, fierce rivals Microsoft and Apple are using a shared set of tools and libraries for developing certain types of software.[17] Lockheed Martin and Boeing formed an alliance to promote advancement of the future U.S. air transportation industry.[18] At a speech in Japan, Antonio Perez, CEO of Eastman Kodak, provided the following insights about Kodak's partnering philosophy:

> Kodak today is involved with partnerships that would have been unthinkable a few short years ago. Throughout my time here today, you'll hear me refer to collaborative programs with companies like Hewlett-Packard, Sony, Canon, Xerox and Fuji and many others. We're partnering with competitors on many universal projects, and on others we're competing with them fiercely in the marketplace arena. For example, we compete with H-P in the commercial and home printing markets, but our Kodak-Creo unit supplies the workflow for H-P's Indigo printer. We compete with Xerox in commercial printing, but we sell controllers for their iGen3 digital presses.[19]

The effects of the greater use of cooperative strategies—particularly in the form of strategic alliances—are noticeable. In large firms, for example, alliances now account for more than 20 percent of revenue.[20] Many senior-level executives believe that alliances are a prime vehicle for firm growth.[21] Many firms, especially large global competitors, establish multiple strategic alliances. Eli Lilly and Company, the global pharmaceutical giant, has established an office of alliance management to establish and coordinate its many alliances in R&D, commercialization, and manufacturing. In manufacturing alone, Lilly has more than 100 alliances in 40 countries. According to Lilly, "Our strategy for 'manufacturing without walls' generates opportunities for a large number of partners. These alliances have supported the development of supplier capabilities and created significant value for both the partner and Lilly."[22]

In some industries, alliance versus alliance is becoming more prominent than firm against firm as a point of competition. In the global airline industry, for example, "competition increasingly is between . . . alliances rather than between airlines."[23] The SkyTeam alliance includes Continental Airlines, Northwest Airlines, and KLM Royal Dutch Airlines.[24] The Star Alliance involves seventeen airlines around the globe, including U.S. Airways, United Airlines, Air Canada, SAS, Austrian Airlines, Singapore Airlines, and South African Airways.[25]

The individually unique competitive conditions of slow-cycle, fast-cycle, and standard-cycle markets (discussed in Chapter 6) find firms using cooperative strategies for slightly different reasons (see Table 7.1).[26] Slow-cycle markets are markets where the firm's competitive advantages are shielded from imitation for relatively long periods and where imitation is costly. These markets have close to monopolistic conditions. Railroads and, historically, telecommunications, utilities, and financial services are examples of industries characterized as slow-cycle markets. In fast-cycle markets the firm's competitive advantages aren't shielded from imitation, preventing their long-term sustainability. Competitive advantages are moderately shielded from imitation in standard-cycle markets, typically allowing them to be sustained for a longer time compared with fast-cycle market situations, but for a shorter time than in slow-cycle markets. In this chapter, we focus specifically on the most common form of cooperative strategy, strategic alliances, to describe how purposes tend to vary across the three types of markets.

### Table 7.1: Reasons for Strategic Alliances by Market Type

| Market | Reason |
|---|---|
| Slow-Cycle | • Gain access to a restricted market |
| | • Establish a franchise in a new market |
| | • Maintain market stability (e.g., establishing standards) |
| Fast-Cycle | • Speed up development of new goods or services |
| | • Speed up new market entry |
| | • Maintain market leadership |
| | • Form an industry technology standard |
| | • Share risky R&D expenses |
| | • Overcome uncertainty |
| Standard-Cycle | • Gain market power (reduce industry overcapacity) |
| | • Gain access to complementary resources |
| | • Establish better economies of scale |
| | • Overcome trade barriers |
| | • Meet competitive challenges from other competitors |
| | • Pool resources for very large capital projects |
| | • Learn new business techniques |

## Strategic Alliances in Slow-Cycle Markets

Firms in slow-cycle markets often use strategic alliances to enter restricted markets or to establish franchises in new markets. Strategic alliances sometimes allow firms to enter new markets more easily and with more speed.[27] The alliance partner better understands conditions in the new market, including sociocultural, legal, regulatory, economic, and industry influences, and provides knowledge of and relationships with customers and suppliers. Restricted entry to India's insurance market prompted American International Group (AIG) to form a joint venture—Tata AIG—with Mumbai-based Tata Group, a reputable Indian company.[28] AIG executives believed that cooperative strategies were the only viable way for their firm to enter a market in which state-operated insurers had played a monopolistic role for decades.

Slow-cycle markets are becoming rare in the 21st-century competitive landscape for several reasons, including the privatization of industries and economies, the rapid expansion of the Internet's capabilities in terms of the quick dissemination of information, and the speed with which advancing technologies make quickly imitating even complex products possible.[29] Firms competing in slow-cycle markets should recognize the future likelihood that they'll encounter situations in which their competitive advantages become partially sustainable (in the case of a standard-cycle market) or unsustainable (in the case of a fast-cycle market). Cooperative strategies can be helpful to firms making the transition from relatively sheltered markets to more competitive ones.[30]

## Strategic Alliances in Fast-Cycle Markets

Fast-cycle markets tend to be unstable, unpredictable, and complex.[31] These three conditions virtually preclude the establishment of long-lasting competitive advantages, forcing firms to constantly seek sources of new competitive advantages while creating value by using current ones. Alliances between firms with current excess resources and capabilities and those with promising capabilities help companies competing in fast-cycle markets to make an effective transition from the present to the future and also to gain rapid entry to new markets.

The information technology (IT) industry is a fast-cycle market. The IT landscape continues to change rapidly as businesses are becoming more and more focused on selecting a handful of strategic partners to help drive down costs, integrate technologies that provide significant business advantages or productivity gains, and aggressively look for applications that can be shifted to more flexible and cost-effective platforms. For example, in 2007 Ricoh of Japan and IBM formed a joint venture company called InfoPrint Solutions Company. The joint venture, initially 51 percent owned by Ricoh, will involve IBM's Printing Systems Division. When the venture was announced, Samuel J. Palmisano, IBM's chairman and CEO, noted that the two companies had "benefited from a strong relationship for many years" and called the new venture "a natural extension of that relationship." He pointed out that Ricoh's investment would help the new company "innovate and grow, which will benefit current and future customers." Masamitsu Sakurai, president and CEO of Ricoh, said his company looked forward "to creating an infrastructure" with IBM "that can address complex solutions and mission critical environments."[32]

## Strategic Alliances in Standard-Cycle Markets

In standard-cycle markets, which are often large and oriented toward economies of scale (e.g., the commercial aerospace industry), alliances are more likely to be made by partners with complementary resources and capabilities. For example, the Star Alliance was formed with the goal to "combine the best routes worldwide and then offer seamless world travel through shared booking."[33] With airlines now in every major economic region of the world, the alliance has come a long way toward achieving that goal.

Companies also may cooperate in standard-cycle markets to gain market power. In 2006, Cantrex Group, a subsidiary of Sears Canada, formed a partnership with La Clef de Sol of Quebec. Cantrex is Canada's largest buying group representing independent merchants of furniture, appliances, electronics, photography equipment, and floor coverings. La Clef de Sol serves independent electronics retailers. The purpose of the partnership is to increase market share in the Canadian consumer electronics retail sector.[34]

Finally, cooperative strategies are important in standard-cycle markets because they allow firms to learn new business techniques and new technologies. For instance, the National Concrete Masonry Association (NCMA) combines the major firms in the industry in a cooperative association that sponsors research and communicates information about important trends and technical advances to all of its members.[35]

Firms can and should learn from each of their alliance partners.[36] Indeed, learning from alliances may be most critical in standard-cycle markets, but it can also help firms in slow-cycle and fast-cycle markets. Cooperative strategies are especially helpful in transferring *tacit knowledge*, which is complex and difficult to codify.[37]

## Types of Alliances and Other Cooperative Strategies

As already mentioned, strategic alliances allow firms to combine resources and capabilities to create a competitive advantage.[38] Thus, strategic alliances involve firms with some degree of exchange and sharing of resources and capabilities to co-develop or distribute goods or services.[39] Strategic alliances allow firms to leverage their existing resources and capabilities while working with partners to develop additional resources and capabilities as the foundation for new competitive advantages.[40]

Strategic alliances can be divided into two basic types on the basis of their legal form, depending on whether they involve equity. An **equity strategic alliance** is an alliance in which two or more firms own a portion of the equity in the venture they have created. Many direct foreign investments, such as those made by U.S. and Japanese companies in China, are completed through equity strategic alliances.[41] Sometimes they take the form of purchase of stock in an existing company, as when Citigroup purchased 5 percent of the equity in the Shanghai Pudong Development Bank, China's ninth largest bank. Later, Citigroup obtained permission to increase its investment to more than 20 percent. The equity alliance allowed Citigroup to enter the Chinese credit card business.[42]

A **joint venture** is a strategic alliance in which two or more firms create a legally independent company to share resources and capabilities to develop a competitive advantage. Joint ventures also involve equity. Typically, partners in a joint venture own equal percentages and contribute equally to its operations. For example, Boeing and Lockheed Martin are equal partners in the joint venture called United Space Alliance, which runs all of the space shuttle operations in central Florida.[43] Joint ventures are effective in establishing long-term relationships and in transferring tacit knowledge. Because it can't be codified, tacit knowledge is learned through experiences, such as those taking place when people from partner firms work together in a joint venture.[44] Tacit knowledge is an important source of competitive advantage for many firms.[45]

A **nonequity strategic alliance** is an alliance in which two or more firms develop a contractual relationship to share some of their unique resources and capabilities to create a competitive advantage. In this type of strategic alliance, firms do not establish a separate independent company and therefore don't take equity positions. Because of this, nonequity strategic alliances are less formal and demand fewer partner commitments than joint ventures and equity strategic alliances.[46] The relative informality and lower commitment levels characterizing nonequity strategic alliances make them unsuitable for complex projects in which success requires effective transfers of tacit knowledge between partners.[47]

Firms today increasingly use nonequity alliances in many different forms, such as licensing agreements, distribution agreements, and supply contracts.[48] For example, Foamix signed a licensing agreement with the German pharmaceutical giant Bayer Schering Pharma to produce and market its dermatological foam. The agreement is expected to lead to tens of millions of dollars in revenue for Foamix.[49] A key reason for the growth in types of cooperative strategies is the complexity and uncertainty that characterize most global industries and make it difficult for firms to be successful without some sort of partnerships.[50]

Typically, outsourcing commitments take the form of a nonequity strategic alliance.[51] Discussed in Chapter 4, outsourcing is the purchase of a value-creating primary or support activity from another firm. Magna International, a leading global supplier of technologically advanced automotive systems, components, and modules, has formed many nonequity strategic alliances with automotive manufacturers who have outsourced work to it. Magna's effectiveness with nonequity strategic alliances is suggested by the awards honoring work quality that Magna has received from many of its partners/customers, including General Motors, Ford Motor Company, Honda, DaimlerChrysler, and Toyota.[52] Magna's success has made it one of the top 500 largest global companies.

Many other forms of cooperative strategy exist. For instance, trade groups, associations, and research consortia combine firms in common purposes. Also, firms may cooperate in other ways, either formally (e.g., a cartel or *keiretsu*, a group of firms tied together by cross-shareholdings) or informally (e.g., collusion). Equity, nonequity, and other forms of alliances and cooperative strategies can be divided into categories based on their primary strategic objectives. Figure 7.1 lists the most common types of cooperative strategies based on whether they are primarily intended to enhance differentiation or reduce costs, help the firm deal more effectively with forces in its external environment, or increase the firm's growth and diversification. Obviously, any particular alliance can have two or more of these objectives; however, dividing them on the basis of their primary strategic objective will facilitate this discussion.

**Figure 7.1: Strategic Objectives of Cooperative Strategies**

| Primary Intention | Type of Strategy |
|---|---|
| Enhance Differentiation or Reduce Costs | Complementary strategic alliances |
| | Network cooperative strategies |
| Effectively Address Forces in the External Environment | Competitive response alliances |
| | Uncertainty-reducing alliances |
| | Competition-reducing cooperative strategies |
| | Associations and consortia |
| Promote Growth and/or Diversification | Diversifying strategic alliances |
| | Franchising |
| | International cooperative strategies |

# Cooperative Strategies That Enhance
# Differentiation or Reduce Costs

Cooperative strategies are used at the business level to help improve a firm's performance in individual product markets. As discussed in Chapter 5, business-level strategy details what the firm intends to do to gain a competitive advantage in specific product markets. Thus, the firm forms a business-level cooperative strategy when it believes that combining its resources and capabilities with those of one or more partners will create competitive advantages that it can't create by itself and that will lead to success in a specific product market. Chapter 5 described two primary means of creating above-normal value for customers in product markets: producing goods or services at lower costs or differentiating a good or service so that customers prefer it.[53] Cooperative strategies that are intended to achieve these objectives fall into two general categories: complementary strategic alliances and network cooperative strategies.

## Complementary Strategic Alliances

**Complementary strategic alliances** are business-level alliances in which firms share some of their resources and capabilities in complementary ways to develop competitive advantages.[54] There are two types of complementary strategic alliances—vertical and horizontal (see Figure 7.2).

**Vertical Complementary Strategic Alliances.** In a *vertical complementary strategic alliance*, firms share their resources and capabilities from different stages of the value chain to create a competitive advantage. McDonald's has formed vertical complementary alliances with major oil companies and independent store operators. With units located in these firms' storefronts, the customer can buy gas, food, and other items with one stop. The cooperative strategy has worked so well in the United States that McDonald's recently formed a similar alliance with China's largest gas station operator, China Petroleum and Chemical Corp. According to a market analyst, this strategy is simply more efficient for McDonald's at this time.[55]

Similarly, the global consulting firm Accenture formed an alliance with Confederated Tribes of the Umatilla Indian Reservation in the United States to provide call center, document preparation, and software programming services. The alliance, called Cayuse Technologies, will be owned by the Umatilla Indians but managed by Accenture. The alliance resulted from a year of research on Native American tribes by Accenture Managing Director Randall L. Willis. According to Willis, demand for domestic services like these is tremendous because government agencies are requiring that more outsourced work be done in the United States: "Whether it's cost concerns or security, a number of industries would like to keep it in the U.S."[56]

**Horizontal Complementary Alliances.** A *horizontal complementary strategic alliance* is an alliance in which firms share some of their resources and capabilities from the same stage of the value chain to create a competitive advantage.[57] Commonly, firms use this type of alliance to focus on long-term product development and distribution opportunities.[58] Shin Caterpillar Mitsubishi (SCM), for example, is a joint venture between Caterpillar and Mitsubishi Heavy Industries that is now more than forty years old. These partners continue to share resources and capabilities to produce innovative products that neither

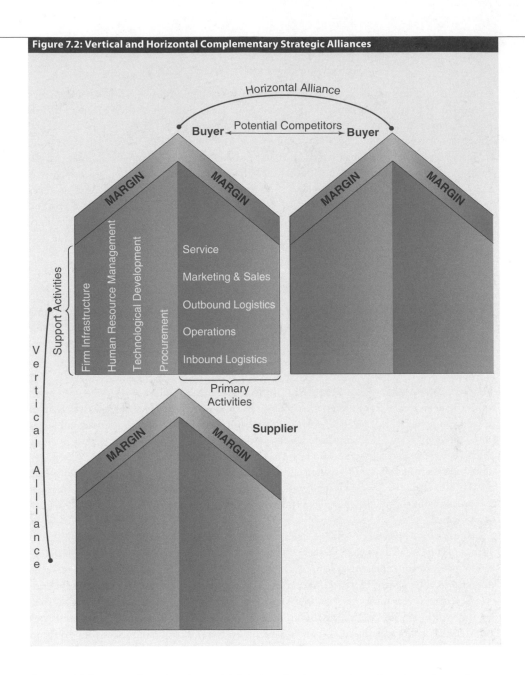

firm could design and produce by itself. SCM is a leading supplier of earthmoving and construction equipment in Japan and also sells the products it produces to other Caterpillar units globally.[59]

Another example is Raffles International, which signed a strategic marketing alliance with Taj Hotels Resorts and Palaces, an entity of Indian Hotels Company, India's largest group of hotels. The geographical distribution of the companies is complementary, with Raffles International hotels found throughout Asia, Australia, Europe, and North and South America. Taj Hotels Resorts and Palaces, on the other hand, primarily has a strong domestic network in India. The two companies will "undertake joint sales events at travel and trade fairs, implement sales information exchanges and cross-promote their hotels."[60]

Although complementary alliances may require similar levels of investment from the partners, the benefits tend to be different. There are several potential reasons for the imbalance of benefits.[61] Frequently, the partners have different opportunities as a result of the alliance. Partners may learn at different rates and have different capabilities to leverage the complementary resources provided by the alliance. Some firms are more effective at managing alliances and deriving the benefits from them. The partners may also have different reputations in the market, thus differentiating the types of actions they can legitimately take in the marketplace. Facing huge losses in global sales revenues because of management missteps and product defects, Mitsubishi created an alliance with Peugeot to manufacture new sport utility vehicles to be sold under the Peugeot brand name.[62] The alliance provides Mitsubishi with an opportunity to use its production capacity while borrowing Peugeot's reputation. Peugeot is able to introduce a new product without increasing its own production capacity. Consequently, both sides enjoy potential benefits from the alliance, but the benefits are very different.

## Network Cooperative Strategies

Increasingly, firms are engaging in several cooperative strategies simultaneously. In addition to forming their own alliances with individual companies, a growing number of firms are joining forces in multiple networks.[63] A **network cooperative strategy** is a cooperative strategy in which multiple firms agree to form partnerships to achieve shared objectives. A network cooperative strategy is particularly effective when it is formed by geographically clustered firms,[64] such as those in Silicon Valley in California or Singapore's Silicon Island.[65]

The set of strategic alliance partnerships resulting from the use of a network cooperative strategy is commonly called an *alliance network*. Firms involved in alliance networks gain information and knowledge from multiple sources.[66] They can use this heterogeneous knowledge to produce more and better innovation. As a result, firms involved in alliance networks tend to be more innovative.[67] Research evidence suggests that the positive financial effects of network cooperative strategies will continue to make these strategies important to the success of both suppliers and buyers.[68] However, one of the disadvantages to belonging to an alliance network is that a firm can be locked into its partners, precluding the development of alliances with others. In certain types of networks, such as a Japanese *keiretsu*, firms in the network are expected to help other firms in the network whenever they need aid. Such expectations can become a burden to the firm rendering assistance, thus reducing its performance.[69]

Effective social relationships and interactions among partners while sharing their resources and capabilities make it more likely that a network cooperative strategy will be successful.[70] Also important is having an effective *strategic center firm*, which is at the core or center of an alliance network and around which the network's cooperative relationships revolve (see Figure 7.3).

Because of its central position, the strategic center firm is the foundation for the alliance network's structure. Concerned with various aspects of organization, such as formal reporting relationships and procedures, the strategic center firm manages what are often complex, cooperative interactions among network partners. Its four primary tasks are:[71]

■ *Strategic Outsourcing.* The strategic center firm outsources and partners with more firms than do other network members. At the same time, the strategic center firm

**Figure 7.3: A Strategic Network**

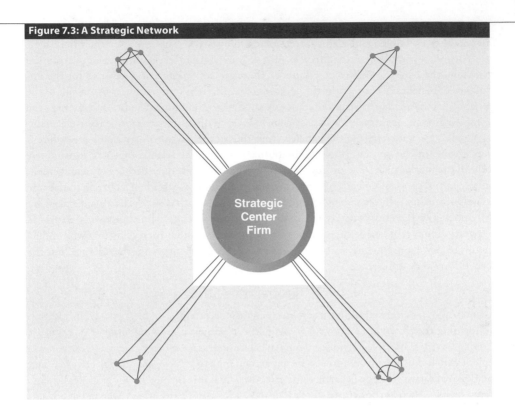

requires network partners to be more than contractors. Members are expected to find opportunities for the network to create value through its cooperative work.

■ *Competencies.* To increase network effectiveness, the strategic center firm seeks ways to support each member's efforts to develop core competencies that can benefit the network.

■ *Technology.* The strategic center firm is responsible for managing the development and sharing of technology-based ideas among network members. The structural requirement that members submit formal reports detailing the technology-oriented outcomes of their efforts to the strategic center firm facilitates this activity.

■ *Race to Learn.* The strategic center firm emphasizes that the principal dimensions of competition are between value chains and between networks of value chains. Because of this, the strategic network is only as strong as its weakest value-chain link. With its centralized decision-making authority and responsibility, the strategic center firm guides participants in efforts to form network-specific competitive advantages. The need for each participant to have capabilities that can be the foundation for the network's competitive advantages encourages friendly rivalry among participants seeking to develop the skills needed to quickly form new capabilities that create value for the network.[72]

An important advantage of a network cooperative strategy is that firms gain access "to their partners' partners."[73] As noted throughout this chapter, having access to multiple

PART 3 / CREATING COMPETITIVE ADVANTAGE

collaborations increases the likelihood that additional competitive advantages will be formed as the set of resources and capabilities being shared expands.[74] In turn, increases in competitive advantages further stimulate the development of product innovations that are critical to value creation in the global economy.[75]

Alliance networks vary by industry condition and goal orientation. A *stable alliance network* is formed in mature industries in which demand is relatively constant and predictable. Through a stable alliance network, firms try to extend their competitive advantages to other settings while continuing to profit from operations in their core, relatively mature industry. Thus, stable networks are built for exploitation of the economies (scale and/or scope) available between firms.[76] These economies can help reduce a firm's cost structure. Toyota's alliance network, described previously, is an example of a stable alliance network.

*Dynamic alliance networks* are used in industries characterized by frequent product innovations and short product life cycles.[77] For instance, the pace of innovation in the IT industry is too fast for any one company to maintain success over time. Therefore, the ability to develop and nurture strategic partnerships can make the difference between success and failure in the industry. IBM, Intel, and all of the other major players in the industry play significant roles in dynamic alliance networks.[78] Thus, dynamic alliance networks are primarily used to stimulate rapid, value-creating product innovations and subsequent successful market entries, demonstrating that their purpose is often the exploration of new ideas.[79]

---

## Cooperative Strategies That Address Forces in the External Environment

Participation in stable alliance networks tends to be directed primarily toward producing products at low cost, while that in dynamic alliance networks is more directed toward continuing to produce goods and services that are highly attractive to customers. However, membership in a dynamic alliance network can also help a firm deal with uncertainty in the external environment by keeping firm managers abreast of important technological and other changes.

As already mentioned repeatedly, the external environment of most firms is increasingly complex and ever changing.[80] One of the great challenges managers face is helping their firms to prosper in their respective environments. Several types of cooperative strategies can assist managers in this task. *Competitive response alliances* help firms deal with the actions of competitors. *Uncertainty-reducing alliances* help firms take some of the uncertainty out of the environments they are facing. *Competition-reducing cooperative strategies* give the partnering firms differential advantages in their markets. Finally, *associations and consortia* can strengthen member firms in dealing with external stakeholders such as legislators, suppliers, and customers.

### Competitive Response Alliances

As discussed in Chapter 6, competitors initiate competitive actions to attack rivals and launch competitive responses to their competitors' actions. Strategic alliances can be used to respond to competitors' attacks. Because they can be difficult to reverse and expensive to operate, strategic alliances are primarily formed to respond to strategic rather than tactical actions.

Steel companies, especially in Asia, are forming joint ventures, taking stakes in other companies, and signing technology-licensing agreements in response to some large mergers, including the €28 billion (more than $35 billion) combination of Mittal Steel and Arcelor SA. According to Ku Taek Lee, CEO of South Korea's Posco, the third-largest steel producer, all of the major steel companies are trying to find competitive solutions to the consolidation that is taking place in the industry. Many steel companies say they want to avoid mergers because of their costs and political risks. Instead, they are leaning toward cooperative strategies. For instance, Posco is considering buying small stakes in other Asian steelmakers, forming research alliances, or combining with other companies in purchasing raw materials. Japan's Nippon Steel likewise is considering boosting its equity positions in Japanese steelmakers Sumitomo Metal Industries and Kobe Steel. Nippon is also considering expanding its joint venture with North American Mittal Steel to make high-quality steel for the automobile industry. Top managers at Nucor, based in Charlotte, North Carolina, are considering acquisitions but favor growth through licensing new technologies it is developing.[81]

## Uncertainty-Reducing Alliances

Cooperative strategies can be a powerful mechanism for responding to the strategic actions of competitors, but they can also help a firm reduce environmental uncertainty.[82] Particularly in fast-cycle markets, business-level strategic alliances can be used to hedge against risk and uncertainty.[83] Also, they are used where uncertainty exists, such as in entering new product markets or emerging economies. For instance, Dutch bank ABN AMRO developed a venture called ShoreCap International involving a multisector partnership of organizations, including private businesses, financial institutions, development funds, and foundations. ShoreCap invests in and advises local financial institutions that do small and microbusiness lending in developing economies, targeting Asia, Africa, and Central and Eastern Europe. The venture's leading sponsor, ShoreBank Corporation, is a for-profit community development and environmental bank. It has a history of collaboration with financial institutions and other partners, including the World Bank. Through this cooperative strategy with other financial institutions, ShoreBank's goal is to reduce the risk of providing credit to smaller borrowers in disadvantaged regions. It also hopes to reduce poverty in the regions where it invests.[84]

In other instances, firms form strategic alliances to reduce the uncertainty associated with developing new products or establishing a technology standard.[85] NTT DoCoMo, a Japanese mobile communications company, bought a stake in Fuji Television Network to prepare for a new digital broadcasting service. At the same time, NTT DoCoMo was considering a variety of alliances with Nippon Television Network with the objective of unifying telecommunications and broadcasting services. The two companies already had an alliance that brings terrestrial digital broadcasting to mobile-phone users, referred to as "one-seg," as well as a limited partnership to provide television programs for mobile users.[86] As this example illustrates, the uncertainty and risk of the 21st-century landscape finds firms, such as those competing in the communications industry, forming multiple strategic alliances to create more value.

## Competition-Reducing Cooperative Strategies

Virtually all cooperative strategies between or among competitors have the effect of reducing competition in an industry. For instance, a Japanese *keiretsu* typically includes executives from a number of competing firms in an industry, among other stakeholders. As these companies work together, competition is reduced. Horizontal cooperative strategies reduce competition in a similar way, as do many alliance networks. Alliance networks, in particular, provide advantages to member firms that make it hard for nonmember firms to compete.[87]

Another common and more direct competition-reducing cooperative strategy is *collusion*. Collusive strategies often are illegal. There are two types of collusive strategies—explicit collusion and tacit collusion. *Explicit collusion* "exists when firms directly negotiate production output and pricing agreements in order to reduce competition."[88]

Explicit collusion strategies are illegal in the United States and most developed economies (except in regulated industries). Therefore, firms that use such strategies may face litigation and may be found guilty of noncompetitive actions. For instance, in 2006 Toyota paid $35 million to settle its part of a class action lawsuit alleging that it colluded with six other automakers to keep less-expensive Canadian vehicle models from being imported into the U.S. market. The suit charged the automakers with violating the Sherman Antitrust Act by preventing consumers from taking advantage of the lower prices. The other companies involved in the suit were General Motors, Ford, Daimler Chrysler, BMW, American Honda Motor Co., and Nissan North America.[89]

*Tacit collusion* exists when several firms in an industry indirectly coordinate their production and pricing decisions by observing each other's competitive actions and responses.[90] Firms that engage in tacit collusion recognize that they are interdependent and that their competitive actions and responses significantly affect competitors' behaviors toward them.

Tacit collusion results in less than fully competitive production levels and prices that are higher than they might otherwise be. Firms engaging in tacit collusion do not directly negotiate output and pricing decisions, as they do in explicit collusion. This type of competition-reducing strategy is more common in industries that are highly concentrated, such as breakfast cereals. Four firms (Kellogg, General Mills, Post, and Quaker) have accounted for as much as 80 percent of the sales volume in the ready-to-eat segment of the U.S. cereal market.[91] Some believe that this high degree of concentration results in prices that are much higher than the costs of production.[92] Prices above the competitive level in this industry suggest the possibility that the dominant firms are using a tacit collusion cooperative strategy.

*Mutual forbearance* is a form of tacit collusion "in which firms avoid competitive attacks against those rivals they meet in multiple markets."[93] Rivals learn a great deal about each other when engaging in multimarket competition, including how to deter the effects of their rivals' competitive attacks and responses. Given what they know about each other as competitors, firms choose not to engage in what could be destructive competition in multiple product markets.[94]

Governments in free market economies need to determine how rivals can collaborate to increase their competitiveness without violating established regulations.[95] It is challenging to reach this determination when evaluating collusive strategies, particularly tacit ones. For example, it is difficult to determine where to draw the line when evaluating global pharmaceutical and biotechnology firms that must collaborate in order to stay competitive. Some regulation is necessary to maintain an effective balance between collaboration and competition; however, sometimes regulation can interfere with efficient markets.[96]

## Associations and Consortia

Because they are inherently cooperative systems,[97] organizations are inclined to form coalitions with stakeholders to achieve common objectives.[98] These coalitions can take a variety of forms, including associations, trade groups, industry and labor panels, and research consortia. Firms join associations to gain access to information and to obtain legitimacy, acceptance, and influence.[99] Associations and consortia can also enhance creative efforts leading to innovation.[100]

Often one of the primary purposes of associations and consortia is to provide a common voice when dealing with an important external stakeholder, such as the government. For instance, many trade groups employ lobbyists at the federal, state, regional, or local level. These lobbyists work to ensure that government legislation is as favorable as possible to the member firms. Trade group representatives may also work directly with government leaders and representatives to enhance business relationships. For instance, the National Concrete Masonry Association (NCMA), mentioned previously, has a representative who works directly with the U.S. Army Corps of Engineers on construction projects where concrete masonry should be used.[101] The NCMA also promotes research that is relevant to members and communicates the results to them. In this sense, it is also a research consortium.

Associations and consortia can also be used to influence nongovernment stakeholders. For example, Cisco Systems, Intel, and Oracle provided leadership in the formation of a consortium of leading technology companies, medical groups, and independent practice associations. The consortium "will reward doctors that use technology to share information and improve patient care. The consortium is unique in that it is employer-led and bands together thousands of employees and healthcare providers working toward the goal of improving healthcare quality."[102]

## Cooperative Strategies That Promote Growth and/or Diversification

So far we have described cooperative strategies that help firms enhance differentiation, reduce costs, or effectively address trends and forces in their external environments. These cooperative strategies can also be used to promote growth or diversification (or both).

Growth is a primary goal in most organizations.[103] Firms can decide to pursue growth through a variety of internal strategies, such as new product development or market development. Other firms pursue growth externally through mergers and acquisitions, the topic of Chapter 9. However, cooperative strategies are sometimes an attractive alternative to mergers and acquisitions as a vehicle for growth.[104] Cooperative strategies can be more attractive than mergers and acquisitions because typically they require fewer resource commitments[105] and permit greater strategic flexibility because they are not as permanent.[106] In fact, an alliance can be used as a way to determine if the partners might benefit from a future merger or acquisition between them. This "testing process" often characterizes alliances formed to combine firms' unique technological resources and capabilities.[107] Cooperative strategies that are frequently used to stimulate growth include diversifying strategic alliances, franchising, and international cooperative strategies. These strategies may also promote market diversification (increased market scope) and sometimes product diversification.

### Diversifying Strategic Alliances

A **diversifying strategic alliance** is a corporate-level cooperative strategy in which firms share some of their resources and capabilities to diversify into new product or market areas. (Product diversification will be explored more comprehensively in Chapter 8.) For instance, Intelligent Energy, an international fuel-cell company, formed an alliance with Seymourpowell, a diversified engineering and technology company (both based in London) to create a clean, quiet motorcycle that runs on a hydrogen fuel cell. A prototype called the ENV bike (for "emissions neutral vehicle" and pronounced "envy") has received a lot of global attention because the fuel cell it uses is both compact and practical. The companies employed Andy Eggleston, a former vice president with Ford Europe, to create a production-ready vehicle. The ENV is described by some as "irresistible."[108]

## Franchising

**Franchising** is a cooperative strategy in which a firm (the *franchisor*) uses a franchise as a contractual relationship to describe and control the sharing of its resources and capabilities with partners (the *franchisees*).[109] A **franchise** is a "contractual agreement between two legally independent companies whereby the franchisor grants the right to the franchisee to sell the franchisor's product or do business under its trademarks in a given location for a specified period of time."[110] Franchising is a popular strategy; companies using it account for $1 trillion in annual U.S. retail sales and compete in more than 75 industries. McDonald's, Hilton International, and Krispy Kreme are well-known examples of firms that use the franchising corporate-level cooperative strategy.[111]

In the most successful franchising strategies, the partners (the franchiser and the franchisees) closely work together.[112] A primary responsibility of the franchisor is to develop programs to transfer to the franchisees the knowledge and skills that they need to successfully compete at the local level.[113] In return, franchisees should provide feedback to the franchisor regarding how their units could become more effective and efficient.[114] Working cooperatively, the franchisor and its franchisees find ways to strengthen the core company's brand name, which is often the most important competitive advantage for franchisees operating in their local markets.[115]

Aaron Kennedy founded Noodles & Company, a restaurant serving noodle dishes from around the world, in 1995. By 2003 the company had 79 company-owned locations in nine states. However, new competitors were appearing and Kennedy wanted to maintain the firm's position as the market leader in the noodle segment. He was concerned about losing control over his brand but nonetheless decided to franchise, signing up five franchisees in 2004. He developed an extensive training program for managers, which now includes three months of training. According to Kennedy, this helps them "understand the soul of Noodles & Co." He also developed uniform menus and pricing. As of 2007, the company had 142 locations, 22 of which were franchises, and sales had doubled compared with their 2004 levels. Kennedy is very careful about the rate of growth, working closely with managers at every location. "We are the franchisees' partners and parents," he says, "reinforcing good behavior while establishing guardrails."[116]

Franchising is a particularly attractive strategy in fragmented industries, such as retailing and commercial printing. In such industries, a large number of small and medium-sized firms compete as rivals; however, no firm or small set of firms has a dominant share, making it possible for a company to gain a large market share by consolidating independent companies through contractual relationships.[117] This is why franchising is such a common cooperative strategy in food chains.

## International Cooperative Strategies

A **cross-border strategic alliance** is an international cooperative strategy in which firms with headquarters in different nations combine some of their resources and capabilities to create a competitive advantage. In virtually all industries, the number of cross-border alliances being completed continues to increase,[118] in some cases at the expense of mergers and acquisitions.[119] For example, a $6 billion joint venture between British Petroleum (BP) and the Russian oil company Tyumen Oil in 2003 created the tenth largest oil company in the world.[120]

There are several reasons for the increasing use of cross-border strategic alliances. In general, multinational corporations outperform firms that operate only domestically.[121] Thus, a firm may form cross-border strategic alliances to leverage core competencies that are the foundation of its domestic success to expand into international markets.[122] For example, Sybase, a mobile messaging and data services provider based in Chantilly, Virginia, formed a joint venture with Oxford Bookstore, the leading online bookstore in India, to create a nationwide interactive short message service (SMS) featuring Oxford's books.[123] Sybase has considerable expertise in message delivery, having delivered 25 billion mobile messages in 2006, but Oxford Bookstore has the reputation, contacts, and market knowledge to make the venture a success.

Limited domestic growth opportunities and governmental economic policies are additional reasons firms use cross-border alliances. Local ownership is an important national policy objective in some nations. In India and China, for example, governmental policies reflect a strong preference to license local companies. Indeed, investment by foreign firms in these countries may be allowed only through a partnership with a local firm, such as in a cross-border alliance. A cross-border strategic alliance can also be helpful to foreign partners from an operational perspective, because the local partner has significantly more information about factors contributing to competitive success such as local markets, sources of capital, legal procedures, and cultural and institutional norms.[124] For example, Bharti Enterprises, an Indian telecommunications company, formed a joint venture "of equal partnership" with Wal-Mart to create a chain of retail stores in India. Wal-Mart's contributions will be made in the back-end supply part of the business, providing both logistics and technological support, while Bharti will act as a Wal-Mart franchisee, owning and operating the retail stores. "India is yet to fully open up the retail sector but allows 51 percent foreign investment in single-brand retail with prior government permission," explained Sunil Bharti Mittal, chairman of Bharti Enterprises. The agreement "allows the two companies to study and evaluate the retail market in India and identify business opportunities together within the existing guidelines."[125] Mittal expected the venture to open several hundred stores beginning in August 2007.

In general, cross-border alliances are more complex and risky than domestic strategic alliances.[126] However, the fact that firms competing internationally tend to outperform domestic-only competitors suggests the importance of learning how to diversify into international markets. Compared with mergers and acquisitions, cross-border alliances may be a better way to learn this process, especially in the early stages of the firms' efforts to diversify geographically. Careful and thorough study of a proposed cross-border alliance contributes to success,[127] as do precise specifications of each partner's alliance role.[128]

Because firms often have multiple alliances in different geographical regions, alliance networks are frequently formed to implement international cooperative strategies.[129] Differences among countries' regulatory environments increase the challenge of managing international networks and verifying that, at a minimum, the network's operations comply with all legal requirements.[130] *Distributed alliance networks* are often the organizational structure used to manage international cooperative strategies. As shown in Figure 7.4, several regional strategic center firms are included in the distributed network to manage partner firms' multiple cooperative arrangements.[131] Strategic centers for Ericsson (telecommunications exchange equipment) and Electrolux (white goods, washing machines) are

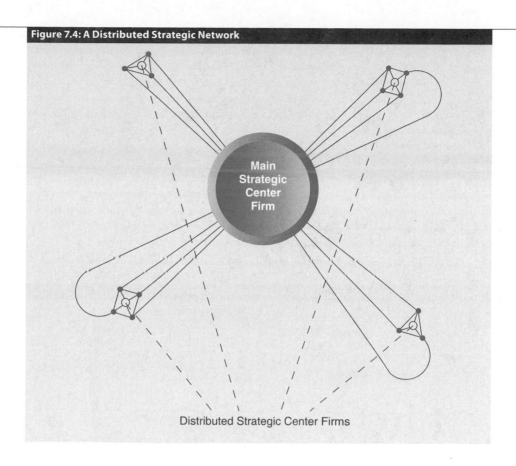

Distributed Strategic Center Firms

located in countries throughout the world, instead of only in Sweden where the firms are headquartered. Ericsson, for example, is active in more than 140 countries and employs more than 90,000 people. The company has five major alliance networks and has formed cooperative agreements with companies throughout the world through each network. As a founding member of an Ethernet alliance (Intel and Cisco are also members), Ericsson acts as the strategic center firm for this cooperative arrangement, which promotes open industry standards and provides interoperability testing for its members.[132]

## Competitive Risks of Cooperative Strategies

Although their use by firms has increased significantly, many cooperative strategies fail.[133] In fact, evidence shows that two-thirds of cooperative strategies have serious problems in their first two years and that as many as 70 percent of them fail.[134] This failure rate suggests that even when the partnership has potential complementarities and synergies, alliance success is elusive.

Finger-pointing and a legal suit resulted from a failed joint venture between Belgium's Flying Group and France's Euralair Airport Services (EAS) to develop business aviation operations at a base in Le Bourget, France. Flying Group alleges that EAS's founder, Alexandre Couvelaire, is in breach of certain aspects of the agreement: "Couvelaire is trying to defend himself with isolated arguments that are not related to the context of the deal. Those minor issues would have been clarified if he had not decided to withdraw and stop communication." Couvelaire claims that "in no way is EAS in breach of any of its obligations under the parties' preliminary protocol or any agreement whatsoever with Flying Group, which is fully liable for the parties' failure in reaching their final agreement." In addition to a legal suit, Flying Group planned to demolish EAS's infrastructure at Le Bourget and build a new terminal, hangar, and offices.[135]

Prominent risks of cooperative strategy are shown in the top box of Figure 7.5 (the rest of the figure is explained later in this chapter). One is that a partner may act opportunistically.[136] Opportunistic behaviors surface either when formal contracts fail to prevent them or when an alliance is based on a false perception of partner trustworthiness. Not infrequently, the opportunistic firm wants to acquire as much of its partner's tacit knowledge as it can.[137] Full awareness of what a partner wants in a cooperative strategy reduces the likelihood that a firm will suffer from another's opportunistic actions.[138]

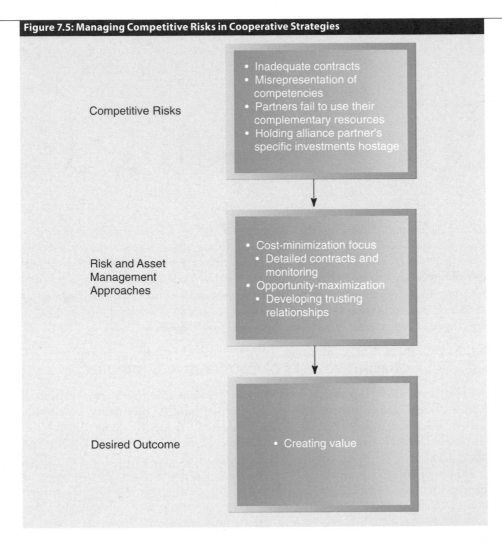

**Figure 7.5: Managing Competitive Risks in Cooperative Strategies**

Competitive Risks

- Inadequate contracts
- Misrepresentation of competencies
- Partners fail to use their complementary resources
- Holding alliance partner's specific investments hostage

Risk and Asset Management Approaches

- Cost-minimization focus
  - Detailed contracts and monitoring
- Opportunity-maximization
  - Developing trusting relationships

Desired Outcome

- Creating value

Some cooperative strategies fail when it is discovered that a firm has *misrepresented the competencies* it can bring to the partnership. This risk is more common when the partner's contribution is grounded in some of its intangible assets. Superior knowledge of local conditions is an example of an intangible asset that partners often fail to deliver. Asking the partner to provide evidence that it does possess the resources and capabilities it is to share in the cooperative strategy (even when they are largely intangible) may be an effective way to deal with this risk.

Another risk is that a firm fails to make available to its partners the complementary resources and capabilities (such as its most sophisticated technologies) that it committed to the cooperative strategy. This risk surfaces most commonly when firms form an international cooperative strategy.[139] In these instances, different cultures can result in different interpretations of contractual terms or trust-based expectations.

A final risk is that the firm may make investments that are specific to the alliance while its partner does not. For example, the firm might commit resources and capabilities to develop manufacturing equipment that can be used only to produce items coming from the alliance. If the partner isn't also making alliance-specific investments, the firm is at a relative disadvantage in terms of returns earned from the alliance compared with investments made to earn the returns.

---

## Implementing and Managing Cooperative Strategies

As our discussion shows, cooperative strategies are an important option for firms competing in the global economy.[140] However, our discussion also shows that they are complex and prone to failure.[141] Firms gain the most benefit from cooperative strategies when they are effectively managed.[142] Because the ability to effectively implement and manage cooperative strategies is unevenly distributed across organizations, firms that develop superior skills in these areas may develop a competitive advantage.[143] The key is to develop cooperative strategies and implement them in ways that are valuable, rare, imperfectly imitable, and non-substitutable (see Chapter 4).

Learning from the experiences associated with both successful and unsuccessful cooperative strategies is important to the success of future cooperative strategies.[144] Learning is more likely to happen when experiences are internalized. In other words, those involved with forming and using cooperative strategies should make a deliberate attempt to use these experiences to develop useful knowledge about how to succeed in the future.[145] To gain maximum value from this knowledge, firms should organize it and verify that it is always properly distributed to those involved with forming and using cooperative strategies. Thus, companies should invest significant efforts in learning from successes and failures and recording and disseminating this knowledge within the firm.

Also important to implementation and management of cooperative strategies is the establishment of appropriate controls. For example, McDonald's uses strategic controls and financial controls to verify that its franchisees' operations create the greatest value for its entire franchising network. One strategic control issue is the location of franchisee units. McDonald's now believes that its greatest expansion opportunities are outside the United States. Density percentages seem to support this conclusion. According to the company, although in the United States "there are 22,000 people per McDonald's, in the rest of the world there is only one McDonald's for every 605,000 people."[146] As a result, McDonald's is devoting its capital expenditures primarily to develop units in non-U.S. markets. Financial controls are framed around the requirements an interested party must satisfy to become a McDonald's franchisee as well as performance standards that party must meet when operating a unit.[147] In addition, the financial controls used to determine the bonuses for regional teams are being changed. The headquarters office also administers an evaluation system to improve customer service, especially in the U.S. units, as well as requiring its franchisees to participate in company training programs to increase efficiency and quality.[148]

In general, assigning managerial responsibility for a firm's cooperative strategies to a high-level executive or to a team improves the likelihood that the strategies will be well managed. IBM, Johnson Controls, Coca-Cola, Northwest Airlines, and Siebel Systems have all made such assignments.[149] Those responsible for managing the firm's set of cooperative strategies coordinate activities, categorize knowledge learned from previous experiences, and make certain that what the firm knows about how to effectively form and use cooperative strategies is in the hands of the right people at the right time. Firms generally use one of two primary approaches to manage cooperative strategies: cost minimization and opportunity maximization[150] (see Figure 7.5). This is the case whether or not the firm has formed a separate cooperative strategy management function.

In the *cost minimization* management approach, the firm develops formal contracts with its partners. These contracts specify how the cooperative strategy is to be monitored and how partner behavior is to be controlled. The goal of this approach is to minimize the cooperative strategy's cost and to prevent opportunistic behavior by a partner. The focus of the second managerial approach—*opportunity maximization*—is on maximizing a partnership's value-creation opportunities. In this case, partners are prepared to take advantage of unexpected opportunities to learn from each other and to explore additional marketplace possibilities.[151] Less formal contracts, with fewer constraints on partners' behaviors, make it possible for partners to explore how they can share their resources and capabilities in multiple value-creating ways.

Firms can successfully use either approach to manage cooperative strategies. However, the costs to monitor the cooperative strategy are greater with cost minimization, in that writing detailed contracts and using extensive monitoring mechanisms are expensive, even though the approach is intended to reduce alliance costs. Although monitoring systems may prevent partners from acting in their own best interests, they also preclude positive responses to those situations in which opportunities to use the alliance's competitive advantages surface unexpectedly.[152] Thus, formal contracts and extensive monitoring systems tend to stifle partners' efforts to gain maximum value from their participation in a cooperative strategy and require significant resources to be put into place and used.[153]

The relative lack of detail and formality that is a part of the contract developed by firms using opportunity maximization means that firms need to trust each other to act in the partnership's best interests. A psychological state, *trust* involves a willingness to be vulnerable because of the expectations of positive behavior from the firm's alliance partner.[154] When partners trust each other, there is less need to write detailed formal contracts to specify each firm's alliance behaviors,[155] and the cooperative relationship tends to be more stable.[156] On a relative basis, trust tends to be more difficult to establish in international cooperative strategies compared with domestic ones.[157] Differences in trade policies, cultures, laws, and politics that are part of cross-border alliances account for the increased difficulty. When trust exists, partners' monitoring costs are reduced and opportunities to create value are maximized.

Research showing that trust between partners increases the likelihood of alliance success seems to highlight the benefits of the opportunity maximization approach to managing cooperative strategies.[158] Trust may also be the most efficient way to influence and control alliance partners' behaviors.[159] Consistent with the stakeholder perspective that is one of the foundations of this book, research indicates that trust can be a capability that is valuable, rare, imperfectly imitable, and often nonsubstitutable.[160] Thus, firms known to be trustworthy can have a competitive advantage in terms of how they develop and use cooperative strategies. This is partly because it is impossible to specify all operational details of a cooperative strategy in a formal contract. When a firm has confidence that its partner can be trusted, its concern about the inability to contractually control all alliance details is reduced.

# Summary

■ A cooperative strategy is one in which firms work together to achieve a shared objective. Strategic alliances, which are cooperative strategies in which firms combine some of their resources and capabilities to create a competitive advantage, are the primary form of cooperative strategy.

■ Strategic alliances can be divided into two basic legal forms: equity strategic alliances (in which firms own different shares of a newly created venture) and nonequity strategic alliances (in which firms cooperate through a contractual relationship). Joint ventures are a type of equity alliance in which firms create and own equal shares of a new business venture that is intended to develop competitive advantages.

■ Co-opetition describes a situation in which cooperative strategies are formed by firms who also compete against one another.

■ Firms in slow-cycle markets often use strategic alliances to enter restricted markets or to establish franchises in new markets. In standard-cycle markets, alliances are more likely to be made by partners with complementary resources and capabilities. Companies also may cooperate in standard-cycle markets to gain market power or to learn new business techniques and new technologies. Alliances between firms with current excess resources and capabilities and those with promising capabilities help companies competing in fast-cycle markets to make an effective transition from the present to the future and also to gain rapid entry to new markets.

■ Some cooperative strategies are used at the business level to help improve a firm's performance in individual product markets, either through reducing costs or increasing differentiation. Cooperative strategies that are intended to achieve these objectives fall into two general categories: complementary strategic alliances (vertical or horizontal) and network cooperative strategies.

■ In a network cooperative strategy, several firms agree to form multiple partnerships to achieve shared objectives. One of the primary benefits of this strategy is the firm's opportunity to gain access to its partner's other partnerships. The probability of this happening improves when a strategic center firm facilitates partner relationships that provide unique ways to share resources and capabilities to form competitive advantages.

■ Firms can also use cooperative strategies to deal with an environment that is increasingly complex and ever changing. Competitive response alliances help firms deal with the actions of competitors. Competition-reducing cooperative strategies give the partnering firms differential advantages in their markets. Uncertainty-reducing alliances help firms take some of the uncertainty out of the environments they are facing. Finally, associations and consortia can strengthen member firms in dealing with external stakeholders such as legislators, suppliers, and customers.

■ Diversifying alliances, franchising, and international cooperative strategies tend to promote firm growth. These cooperative strategies are sometimes an attractive alternative to mergers and acquisitions because typically they require fewer resource commitments and permit greater strategic flexibility because they are not as permanent.

■ Cooperative strategies aren't risk free. If a contract is not developed appropriately, or if a partner misrepresents its competencies or fails to make them available, failure is likely. Furthermore, a firm may be held hostage through asset-specific investments made in conjunction with a partner, which may be exploited.

■ Cooperative strategies are more likely to be successful if they are effectively implemented and managed. Consequently, firms should devote resources to learning from their cooperative strategies, establish appropriate strategic and financial controls, assign responsibility for cooperative strategies to high-level executives, and decide on a cost minimization or opportunity maximization approach.

■ Trust is another important aspect of successful cooperative strategies. Firms recognize the value of partnering with companies known for their trustworthiness. When trust exists, a cooperative strategy is managed to maximize the pursuit of opportunities between partners. Without trust, formal contracts and extensive monitoring systems are used to manage cooperative strategies. In this case, the interest is to minimize costs rather than to maximize opportunities by participating in a cooperative strategy.

# Ethics Questions

1. From an ethical perspective, how much information is a firm obliged to provide to a potential complementary alliance partner about what it expects to learn from a cooperative arrangement?
2. "A contract is necessary because most firms cannot be trusted to act ethically in a cooperative venture such as a strategic alliance." In your opinion, is this statement true or false? Why? Does the answer vary by country? Why?
3. Ventures in foreign countries without strong contract law are more risky because managers may be subjected to bribery attempts once their firms' assets have been invested in the country. How can managers deal with these problems?
4. This chapter mentions international strategic alliances being formed by the world's airline companies. Do these companies face any ethical issues as they participate in multiple alliances? If so, what are the issues? Are they different for airline companies headquartered in the United States than for those with European home bases? If so, what are the differences, and what accounts for them?
5. Firms with a reputation for ethical behavior in strategic alliances are likely to have more opportunities to form cooperative strategies than companies that have not earned this reputation. What actions can firms take to earn a reputation for behaving ethically as a strategic alliance partner?

# Notes

1. T. A. Hemphill, 2003, Cooperative strategy, technology innovation and competition policy in the United States and the European Union, *Technology Analysis & Strategic Management*, 1: 93–101; J. B. Barney, 2002, *Gaining and Sustaining Competitive Advantage*, 2nd ed., Upper Saddle River, NJ: Prentice Hall, 339.

2. 2006, Survey: Partners in wealth, *Economist*, January 21, 18.

3. R. D. Ireland, M. A. Hitt, & D. Vaidyanath, 2002, Alliance management as a source of competitive advantage, *Journal of Management*, 28: 413–446; J. G. Combs & D. J. Ketchen, 1999, Explaining interfirm cooperation and performance: Toward a reconciliation of predictions from the resource-based view and organizational economics, *Strategic Management Journal*, 20: 867–888.

4. Y. Awazu, 2006, Managing technology alliances: The case for knowledge management, *International Journal of Information Management*, 26: 484–498; J. J. Reuer, M. Zollo, & H. Singh, 2002, Post-formation dynamics in strategic alliances, *Strategic Management Journal*, 23: 135–151; D. Campbell, 2001, High-end strategic alliances as fundraising opportunities, *Nonprofit World*, 19(5): 8–12; M. D. Hutt, E. R. Stafford, B. A. Walker, & P. H. Reingen, 2000, Case study: Defining the social network of a strategic alliance, *Sloan Management Review*, 41(2): 51–62.

5. M. J. Kelly, J.-L. Schaan, & H. Jonacas, 2002, Managing alliance relationships: Key challenges in the early stages of collaboration, *R&D Management*, 32(1): 11–22.

6. A. C. Inkpen & J. Ross, 2001, Why do some strategic alliances persist beyond their useful life? *California Management Review*, 44(1): 132–148.

7. J. R. Harbison & P. Pekar, 1998, *Smart Alliances*, San Francisco: Jossey-Bass, 11.

8. K. R. Harrigan, 2001, Strategic flexibility in the old and new economies, in M. A. Hitt, R. E. Freeman, & J. S. Harrison (eds.), *Handbook of Strategic Management*, Oxford, UK: Blackwell Publishers, 97–123.

9. A. C. Inkpen, 2001, Strategic alliances, in M. A. Hitt, R. E. Freeman, & J. S. Harrison (eds.), *Handbook of Strategic Management*, Oxford, UK: Blackwell Publishers, 409–432.

10. C. W. L. Hill & T. M. Jones, 1992, Stakeholder-agency theory, *Journal of Management Studies*, 29: 131–154; R. E. Freeman, 1984, *Strategic Management: A Stakeholder Approach*. Boston: Pitman.

11. A. A. Lado, N. G. Boyd, & S. C. Hanlon, 1997, Competition, cooperation and the search for economic rents: A syncretic model, *Academy of Management Review*, 22: 110–141; C. Barnard, 1938, *The Functions of the Executive*, Cambridge, MA: Harvard University Press.

12. R. Axelrod, W. Mitchell, R. E. Thomas, D. S. Bennett, & E. Bruderer, 1995, Coalition formation in standard-setting alliances, *Management Science*, 41: 1493–1513.

13. M. S. Kraatz, 1998, Learning by association? Interorganizational networks and adaptation to environmental change, *Academy of Management Journal*, 41: 621–643; J. S. Harrison & C. H. St. John, 1996, Managing and partnering with external stakeholders, *Academy of Management Executive*, 10(2): 46–59.

14. Harrison & St. John, Managing and partnering with external stakeholders.

15. J. K. Liker & T. Y. Choi, 2004, Building deep supplier relationships, *Harvard Business Review*, 82(12): 104.

16. M. A. Hitt, R. D. Ireland, S. M. Camp, & D. L. Sexton, 2002, Strategic entrepreneurship: Integrating entrepreneurial and strategic management perspectives, in M. A. Hitt, R. D. Ireland, S. M. Camp, & D. L. Sexton (eds.), *Strategic Entrepreneurship: Creating a New Mindset*, Oxford, UK: Blackwell Publishers, 8.

17. 2007, Microsoft, http://www.microsoft.com/globaldev, February 6.

18. 2007, Lockheed Martin and Boeing form strategic alliance to promote next-generation air transportation system, http://money.cnn.com/news, January 22.

19. A. Perez, 2007, The power of partnering, Kodak, http://www.kodak.com, February 6.

20. G. W. Dent Jr., 2001, Gap fillers and fiduciary duties in strategic alliances, *Business Lawyer*, 57(1): 55–104.

21. M. Gonzalez, 2001, Strategic alliances, *Ivey Business Journal*, 66(1): 47–51.

22. 2007, Lilly, Achieving value through partnership, http://www.lilly.com/about/partnering/alliances, February 12.

23. M. Johnson, 2001, Airlines rush for comfort alliances, *Global Finance*, 15(11): 119–120.

24. 2007, Continental Airlines, http://www.continental.com/web/en-US/content/company/alliance/northwest, February 6.

25. 2007, Star Alliance: The airline alliance for the earth, http://www.staralliance.com, February 6.

26. J. R. Williams, 1998, *Renewable Advantage: Crafting Strategy through Economic Time*, New York: The Free Press.

27. L. Fuentelsaz, J. Gomez, & Y. Polo, 2002, Followers' entry timing: Evidence from the Spanish banking sector after deregulation, *Strategic Management Journal*, 23: 245–264.

28. 2007, Tata AIG Life Insurance Company, http://www.tata-aig-life.com, February 6; V. Kumari, 2001, Joint ventures bolster credibility of new players in India, *National Underwriter*, 105(14): 46.

29. S. A. Zahra, R. D. Ireland, I. Gutierrez, & M. A. Hitt, 2000, Privatization and entrepreneurial transformation: Emerging issues and a future research agenda, *Academy of Management Review*, 25: 509–524.

30. I. Filatotchev, M. Wright, K. Uhlenbruck, L. Tihanyi, & R. E. Hoskisson, 2003, Governance, organizational capabilities, and restructuring in transition economies, *Journal of World Business*, 38(4): 331–347.

31. K. M. Eisenhardt, 2002, Has strategy changed? *MIT Sloan Management Review*, 43(2): 88–91.

32. 2007, IBM and Ricoh to create joint venture printing systems company, http://www-03.ibm.com/press/us/en/pressrelease/20965.wss, February 6.

33. B. Berentson, 2001, United Airlines, *Forbes Best of the Web*, May 21, 68.

34. M. J. Knell, 2006, Cantrex allies with Quebec-based electronics buying group, *Furniture/Today*, 30(35): 2–6.

35. 2007, National Concrete Masonry Association, http://www.ncma.org, February 17.

36 D. C. Mowery, J. E. Oxley, & B. S. Silverman, 1996, Strategic alliances and interfirm knowledge transfer, *Strategic Management Journal*, 17: 77–91.

37 B. McEvily & A. Marcus, 2005, Embedded ties and the acquisition of competitive capabilities, *Strategic Management Journal*, 26: 1033–1055.

38 Ireland, Hitt, & Vaidyanath, Alliance management; J. G. Combs & D. J. Ketchen, 1999, Explaining interfirm cooperation and performance: Toward a reconciliation of predictions from the resource-based view and organizational economics, *Strategic Management Journal*, 20: 867–888.

39 M. R. Subramani & N. Venkatraman, 2003, Safeguarding investments in asymmetric interorganizational relationships: Theory and evidence, *Academy of Management Journal*, 46(1): 46–62; P. Kale, H. Singh, & H. Perlmutter, 2000, Learning and protection of proprietary assets in strategic alliances: Building relational capital, *Strategic Management Journal*, 21: 217–237.

40 P. Kale, J. H. Dyer, & H. Singh, 2002, Alliance capability, stock market response, and long-term alliance success: The role of the alliance function, *Strategic Management Journal*, 23: 747–767; D. F. Kuratko, R. D. Ireland, & J. S. Hornsby, 2001, Improving firm performance through entrepreneurial actions: Acordia's corporate entrepreneurship strategy, *Academy of Management Executive*, 15(4): 60–71; D. Ernst & T. Halevy, 2000, When to think alliance, *McKinsey Quarterly*, No. 4: 46–55.

41 A.-W. Harzing, 2002, Acquisitions versus Greenfield investments: International strategy and management of entry modes, *Strategic Management Journal*, 23: 211–227; S. J. Chang & P. M. Rosenzweig, 2001, The choice of entry mode in sequential foreign direct investment, *Strategic Management Journal*, 22: 747–776.

42 2007, Shanghai Pudong Development Bank and Citibank launch credit cards in China, http://www.citigroup.com/ citigroup, February 8; 2003, Citibank can boost China stake, *Wall Street Journal*, April 28, C11.

43 2006, Lockheed: A bold choice, *Flight International*, September 5, 3.

44 S. L. Berman, J. Down, & C. W. L. Hill, 2002, Tacit knowledge as a source of competitive advantage in the National Basketball Association, *Academy of Management Journal*, 45: 13–31.

45 H. Hoang & F. T. Rothaermel. 2005, The effect of general and partner specific alliance experience on joint R&D project performance, *Academy of Management Journal*, 48: 332–345; P. E. Bierly III & E. H. Kessler, 1999, The timing of strategic alliances, in M. A. Hitt, P. G. Clifford, R. D. Nixon, & K. P. Coyne (eds.), *Dynamic Strategic Resources: Development, Diffusion and Integration*, Chichester, UK: Wiley, 299–345.

46 S. Das, P. K. Sen, & S. Sengupta, 1998, Impact of strategic alliances on firm valuation, *Academy of Management Journal*, 41: 27–41.

47 Bierly & Kessler, The timing of strategic alliances, 303.

48 Barney, *Gaining and Sustaining Competitive Advantage*, 339; T. B. Folta & K. D. Miller, 2002, Real options in equity partnerships, *Strategic Management Journal*, 23: 77–88.

49 G. Weinreb, 2007, Foamix licenses dermatological product to German Co., *Knight Ridder Tribune Business News*, January 14, 1.

50 Inkpen, Strategic alliances.

51 M. Delio, 1999, Strategic outsourcing, *Knowledge Management*, 2(7): 62–68.

52 2007, Magna International, http://www.magnaint.com/ magna/en, February 8.

53 M. E. Porter, 1994, Toward a dynamic theory of strategy, in R. P. Rumelt, D. E. Schendel, & D. J. Teece (eds.), *Fundamental Issues in Strategy*, Boston: Harvard Business School Press, 423–461.

54 D. R. King, J. G. Covin, & H. Hegarty, 2003, Complementary resources and the exploitation of technological innovations, *Journal of Management*, 29: 589–606; J. S. Harrison, M. A. Hitt, R. E. Hoskisson, & R. D. Ireland, 2001, Resource complementarity in business combinations: Extending the logic to organizational alliances, *Journal of Management*, 27: 679–699; S. H. Park & G. R. Ungson, 1997, The effect of national culture, organizational complementarity, and economic motivation on joint venture dissolution, *Academy of Management Journal*, 40: 297–307.

55 J. Ong, 2006, Gas station partnership drives McD's China plan, *Chicago Sun-Times*, June 22, 60.

56 J. McGregor, 2006, The other Indian oursourcer: Accenture and the Umatilla tribes' bold plan, *Business Week*, November 6: 40.

57 R. Cairo, 2006, Co-opetition and strategic business alliances in telecommunications, *Business Review*, 5: 147–154.

58 M. Kotabe & K. S. Swan, 1995, The role of strategic alliances in high technology new product development, *Strategic Management Journal*, 16: 621–636.

59 2007, Caterpillar history, http://www.cat.com/cda, February 8.

60 2007, Raffles International signs strategic marketing alliance with Taj Hotels, Resorts and Palaces, http:// www.asiatraveltips.com/travelnews04/198-Alliance. shtml, February 6.

61 P. Dussauge, B. Garrette, & W. Mitchell, 2004, Asymmetric performance: The market share impact of scale and link alliances in the global auto industry, *Strategic Management Journal*, 25: 701–711.

62 2005, Peugeot in pact with Mitsubishi for new SUVs, *Wall Street Journal* online, http://www.wsj.com, July 12.

63 Z. Zhao, J. Anand, & W. Mitchell, 2005, A dual networks perspective on inter-organizational transfer of R&D capabilities: International joint ventures in the Chinese automotive industry, *Journal of Management Studies*, 42: 127–160.

64 L. Canina, C. A. Enz, & J. S. Harrison, 2005, Agglomeration effects and strategic orientations: Evidence from the U.S. lodging industry, *Academy of Management Journal*, 48: 565–581; C. B. Copp & R. L. Ivy, 2001, Networking trends of small tourism businesses in post-Socialist Slovakia, *Journal of Small Business Management*, 39: 345–353.

65 M. Ferrary, 2003, Managing the disruptive technologies life cycle by externalising the research: Social network and corporate venturing in the Silicon Valley, *International Journal of Technology Management*, 25(1,2): 165–180; S. S. Cohen & G. Fields, 1999, Social capital and capital gains in Silicon Valley, *California Management Review*, 41(2): 108–130; J. A. Matthews, 1999, A silicon island of the east: Creating a semiconductor industry in Singapore, *California Management Review*, 41(2): 55–78; M. E. Porter, 1998, Clusters and the new economics of competition, *Harvard Business Review*, 78(6): 77–90; R. Pouder &

C. H. St. John, 1996, Hot spots and blind spots: Geographical clusters of firms and innovation, *Academy of Management Review*, 21: 1192–1225.

66 J. H. Dyer & N. W. Hatch, 2006, Relation-specific capabilities and barriers to knowledge transfers: Creating advantage through network relationships, *Strategic Management Journal*, 27: 701–719.

67 G. G. Bell, 2005, Clusters, networks, and firm innovativeness, *Strategic Management Journal*, 26: 287–295.

68 A. Echols & W. Tsai, 2005, Niche and performance: The moderating role of network embeddedness, *Strategic Management Journal*, 26: 219–238; S. Chung & G. M. Kim, 2003, Performance effects of partnership between manufacturers and suppliers for new product development: The supplier's standpoint, *Research Policy*, 32: 587–604.

69 H. Kim, R. E. Hoskisson, & W. P. Wan, 2004, Power, dependence, diversification strategy and performance in keiretsu member firms, *Strategic Management Journal*, 25: 613–636.

70 A. C. Cooper, 2001, Networks, alliances, and entrepreneurship, in M. A. Hitt, R. D. Ireland, S. M. Camp, & D. L. Sexton (eds.), *Strategic Entrepreneurship: Creating a New Mindset*, Oxford, UK: Blackwell Publishers, 203–222.

71 S. Harryson, 1998, *Japanese Technology and Innovation Management*, Northampton, MA: Edward Elgar.

72 P. Dussauge, B. Garrette, & W. Mitchell, 2000, Learning from competing partners: Outcomes and duration of scale and link alliances in Europe, North America and Asia, *Strategic Management Journal*, 21: 99–126; G. Lorenzoni & C. Baden-Fuller, 1995, Creating a strategic center to manage a web of partners, *California Management Review*, 37(3): 146–163.

73 R. S. Cline, 2001, Partnering for strategic alliances, *Lodging Hospitality*, 57(9): 42.

74 D. Lavie, 2006, The competitive advantage of interconnected firms: An extension of the resource-based view, *Academy of Management Review*, 31: 638–658; M. Rudberg & J. Olhager, 2003, Manufacturing networks and supply chains: An operations strategy perspective, *Omega*, 31(1): 29–39.

75 G. J. Young, M. P. Charns, & S. M. Shortell, 2001, Top manager and network effects on the adoption of innovative management practices: A study of TQM in a public hospital system, *Strategic Management Journal*, 22: 935–951.

76 F. T. Rothaermel, 2001, Complementary assets, strategic alliances, and the incumbent's advantage: An empirical study of industry and firm effects in the biopharmaceutical industry, *Research Policy*, 30: 1235–1251.

77 V. Shankar & B. L. Bayus, 2003, Network effects and competition: An empirical analysis of the home video game industry, *Strategic Management Journal*, 24: 375–384.

78 2007, Strategic alliance Intel and IBM, http://www.intel.com/cd/business/enterprise/emea/eng/casestudies, February 7.

79 Z. Simsek, M. H. Lubatkin, & D. Kandemir, 2003, Inter-firm networks and entrepreneurial behavior: A structural embeddedness perspective, *Journal of Management*, 29: 401–426; D. C. Hambrick, J. Li, K. Xin, & A. S. Tsui, 2001, Compositional gaps and downward spirals in international joint venture management groups, *Strategic Management Journal*, 22: 1033–1053; T. K. Das & B.-S. Teng, 2000, Instabilities of strategic alliances: An internal tensions perspective, *Organization Science*, 11: 77–101.

80 G. McNamara, P. M. Vaaler, & C. Devers, 2003, Same as it ever was: The search for evidence of increasing hypercompetition, *Strategic Management Journal*, 24: 261–278; R. A. D'Aveni, 1995, Coping with hypercompetition: Utilizing the new 7S's framework, *Academy of Management Executive*, 9(3): 46.

81 P. Glader, 2006, Politics and economics: Steelmakers seek new tie-ups that are short of true mergers, *Wall Street Journal*, October 13, A1.

82 M. S. Kraatz, 1998, Learning by association? Interorganizational networks and adaptation to environmental change. *Academy of Management Journal*, 41: 621–643; J. S. Harrison & C. H. St. John, 1996, Managing and partnering with external stakeholders, *Academy of Management Executive*, 10(2): 46–59.

83 J. J. Reuer & R. Ragozzino, 2006, Agency hazards and alliance portfolios, *Strategic Management Journal*, 27: 27–43; J. J. Reuer & T. W. Tong, 2005, Real options in international joint ventures, *Journal of Management*, 31: 403–423; S. Chatterjee, R. M. Wiseman, A. Fiegenbaum, & C. E. Devers, 2003, Integrating behavioural and economic concepts of risk into strategic management: The twain shall meet, *Long Range Planning*, 36(1): 61–80; Hitt, Ireland, Camp, & Sexton, Strategic entrepreneurship, 9; R. G. McGrath, 1999, Falling forward: Real options reasoning and entrepreneurial failure, *Academy of Management Journal*, 22: 13–30.

84 2007, ShoreCap International, http://www.shorecap.net/bins/site/templates/splash.asp, February 7; Dow Jones, 2003, ABN, ShoreBank set up co to invest in developing economies, *Wall Street Journal* online, http://www.wsj.com, July 10.

85 G. Hoetker, 2005, How much you know versus how well I know you: Selecting a supplier for a technically innovative component, *Strategic Management Journal*, 26: 75–96, M. Sakakibara, 2002, Formation of R&D consortia: Industry and company effects, *Strategic Management Journal*, 23: 1033–1050.

86 2006, NTT DoCoMo Inc., *Wall Street Journal*, July 20, B10.

87 B. R. Barringer & J. S. Harrison, 2000, Walking a tightrope: Creating value through interorganizational relationships, *Journal of Management*, 26: 367–404; K. R. Harrigan, 1986, *Managing for Joint Venture Success*. Lexington, MA: Lexington Books.

88 Barney, *Gaining and Sustaining Competitive Advantage*, 339.

89 M. Rectin, 2006, Toyota settles suit alleging collusion on imports, *Automotive News*, 80(6194, April 20): 6–9.

90 D. Leahy & S. Pavelin, 2003, Follow-my-leader and tacit collusion, *International Journal of Industrial Organization*, 21(3): 439–454.

91 G. K. Price & J. M. Connor, 2003, Modeling coupon values for ready-to-eat breakfast cereals, *Agribusiness*, 19(2): 223–244.

92 G. K. Price, 2000, Cereal sales soggy despite price cuts and reduced couponing, *Food Review*, 23(2): 21–28.

93 S. Jayachandran, J. Gimeno, & P. Rajan, 1999, Theory of multimarket competition: A synthesis and implications for marketing strategy, *Journal of Marketing*, 63(3): 49–66.

94  B. R. Golden & H. Ma, 2003, Mutual forbearance: The role of intrafirm integration and rewards, *Academy of Management Review*, 28: 479–493.

95  S. B. Garland & A. Reinhardt, 1999, Making antitrust fit high tech, *Business Week*, March 22, 34–36.

96  E. G. Rogoff & H. S. Guirguis, 2002, Legalized price-fixing, *Forbes*, December 9, 48.

97  A. A. Lado, N. G. Boyd, & S. C. Hanlon, Competition, cooperation and the search for economic rents: A syncretic model, *Academy of Management Review*, 22: 110–141; C. Barnard, 1938, *The Functions of the Executive*, Cambridge, MA: Harvard University Press.

98  R. Axelrod, W. Mitchell, R. E. Thomas, D. S. Bennett, & E. Bruderer, 1995, Coalition formation in standard-setting alliances. *Management Science*, 41: 1493–1513.

99  M. T. Dacin, C. Oliver, & J.-P. Roy, 2007, The legitimacy of strategic alliances: An institutional perspective, *Strategic Management Journal*, 28: 169–182; W. R. Scott, 1992, *Organizations: Rational, Natural, and Open Systems*, 3rd ed., Englewood Cliffs, NJ: Prentice Hall.

100  S. Rangan, R. Samhi, & L. N. Van Wassenhove, 2006, Constructive partnerships: When alliances between private firms and public actors can enable creative strategies, *Academy of Management Review*, 31: 738–751.

101  2007, National Concrete Masonry Association, http://www.ncma.org.

102  2006, Cisco, Intel and Oracle create consortium to accelerate sharing and exchange of medical information using health information technologies, http://newsroom.cisco.com, February 22.

103  T. R. Eisenmann, 2006, Internet companies' growth strategies: determinants of investment intensity and long-term performance, *Strategic Management Journal*, 27: 1183–1200; C. Lu, 2006, Growth strategies and merger patterns among small and medium-sized enterprises: An empirical study, *International Journal of Management*, 23: 529–547.

104  J. H. Dyer, P. Kale & H. Singh, 2004, When to ally and when to acquire, *Harvard Business Review*, (July–August): 109–115; S. Chaudhuri & B. Tabrizi, 1999, Capturing the real value in high-tech acquisitions, *Harvard Business Review*, 77(5): 123–130; J. F. Hennart & S. Reddy, 1997, The choice between mergers/acquisitions and joint ventures in the United States, *Strategic Management Journal*, 18: 1–12.

105  Inkpen, Strategic alliances, 413.

106  J. L. Johnson, R. P.-W. Lee, A. Saini, & B. Grohmann, 2003, Market-focused strategic flexibility: Conceptual advances and an integrative model, *Academy of Marketing Science Journal*, 31: 74–90; C. Young-Ybarra & M. Wiersema, 1999, Strategic flexibility in information technology alliances: The influence of transaction cost economics and social exchange theory, *Organization Science*, 10: 439–459.

107  T. B. Folta & K. D. Miller, 2002, Real options in equity partnerships, *Strategic Management Journal*, 23: 77–88.

108  M. Vella, 2006, A motorcycle that runs clean and quiet, *Business Week*, November 27, 38.

109  J. G. Combs & D. J. Ketchen Jr., 2003, Why do firms use franchising as an entrepreneurial strategy? A meta-analysis, *Journal of Management*, 29: 427–443; S. A. Shane, 1996, Hybrid organizational arrangements and their implications for firm growth and survival: A study of new franchisers, *Academy of Management Journal*, 39: 216–234.

110  F. Lafontaine, 1999, Myths and strengths of franchising, *Financial Times*, Mastering Strategy (Part 9), November 22, 8–10.

111  M. Sullivan, 2001, McDonald's, *Forbes Best of the Web*, May 21, 100.

112  S. C. Michael, 2002, Can a franchise chain coordinate? *Journal of Business Venturing*, 17: 325–342; R. P. Dant & P. J. Kaufmann, 1999, Franchising and the domain of entrepreneurship research, *Journal of Business Venturing*, 14: 5–16.

113  M. Gerstenhaber, 2000, Franchises can teach us about customer care, *Marketing*, March 16, 18.

114  P. J. Kaufmann & S. Eroglu, 1999, Standardization and adaptation in business format franchising, *Journal of Business Venturing*, 14: 69–85.

115  S. C. Michael, 2002, First mover advantage through franchising, *Journal of Business Venturing*, 18: 61–68; L. Wu, 1999, The pricing of a brand name product: Franchising in the motel services industry, *Journal of Business Venturing*, 14: 87–102.

116  2007, Serving up success, *Inc.*, January, 59.

117  Barney, *Gaining and Sustaining Competitive Advantage*, 110–111.

118  R. Narula & G. Duysters, 2004, Globalization and trends in international R&D alliances, *Journal of International Management*, 10: 199–218; M. A. Hitt, M. T. Dacin, E. Levitas, J. L. Arregle, & A. Borza, 2000, Partner selection in emerging and developed market contexts: Resource-based and organizational learning perspectives, *Academy of Management Journal*, 43: 449–467; M. D. Lord & A. L. Ranft, 2000, Organizational learning about new international markets: Exploring the internal transfer of local market knowledge, *Journal of International Business Studies*, 31: 573–589.

119  D. Kovaleski, 2003, More firms shaking hands on strategic partnership agreements, *Pensions & Investments*, February 3, 20; A. L. Velocci Jr., 2001, U.S.-Euro strategic alliances will outpace company mergers, *Aviation Week & Space Technology*, 155(23): 56.

120  H. Timmons, 2003, BP signs deal with Russian firm for venture in oil and gas, *New York Times*, June 27, WI.

121  I. M. Manev, 2003, The managerial network in a multinational enterprise and the resource profiles of subsidiaries, *Journal of International Management*, 9: 133–152; M. A. Hitt, R. E. Hoskisson, & H. Kim, 1997, International diversification: Effects on innovation and firm performance in product diversified firms, *Academy of Management Journal*, 40: 767–798.

122  H. K. Steensma, L. Tihanyi, M. A. Lyles, & C. Dhanaraj, 2005, The evolving value of foreign partnerships in transitioning economies, *Academy of Management Journal*, 48: 213–235; L. Nachum & D. Keeble, 2003, MNE linkages and localized clusters: Foreign and indigenous firms in the media cluster of Central London, *Journal of International Management*, 9: 171–192; J. Hagedoorn, 1995, A note on international market leaders and networks of strategic technology partnering, *Strategic Management Journal*, 16: 241–250.

123  2006, Mobile 365 partners with Indian bookstore, VA Newswire, http://www.vanewswire.com, August 30.

124  J. W. Lu & P. W. Beamish, 2006, Partnering strategies and performance of SMEs' international joint ventures, *Journal of Business Venturing*, 21: 461–480; S. R. Miller & A. Parkhe, 2002, Is there a liability of foreignness in global banking? An empirical test of banks' X-efficiency, *Strategic Management Journal*, 23: 55–75; Y. Luo, 2001,

Determinants of local responsiveness: Perspectives from foreign subsidiaries in an emerging market, *Journal of Management*, 27: 451–477.

125. 2006, Bharti plumps for Wal-Mart, *Businessline*, November 28, 1–4.

126. J. E. Oxley & R. C. Sampson, 2004, The scope and governance of international R&D alliances, *Strategic Management Journal*, 25: 723–749.

127. P. Ghemawat, 2001, Distance matters: The hard reality of global expansion, *Harvard Business Review*, 79(8): 137–147.

128. J. K. Sebenius, 2002, The hidden challenge of cross-border negotiations, *Harvard Business Review*, 80(3): 76–85.

129. C. Jones, W. S. Hesterly, & S. P. Borgatti, 1997, A general theory of network governance: Exchange conditions and social mechanisms, *Academy of Management Review*, 22: 911–945.

130. A. Goerzen, 2005, Managing alliance networks: Emerging practices of multinational corporations, *Academy of Management Executive*, 19(2): 94–107; J. M. Mezias, 2002, Identifying liabilities of foreignness and strategies to minimize their effects: The case of labor lawsuit judgments in the United States, *Strategic Management Journal*, 23: 229–244.

131. R. E. Miles, C. C. Snow, J. A. Mathews, G. Miles, & J. J. Coleman Jr., 1997, Organizing in the knowledge age: Anticipating the cellular form, *Academy of Management Executive*, 11(4): 7–20.

132. 2006, Ethernet alliance develops further, *Competitive Response Newsletter*, June 7, 1; 2002, Ericsson NewsCenter, http://www.ericsson.com, February 10.

133. D. C. Hambrick, J. Li, K. Xin, & A. S. Tsui, 2001, Compositional gaps and downward spirals in international joint venture management groups, *Strategic Management Journal*, 22: 1033–1053; T. K. Das & B.-S. Teng, 2000, Instabilities of strategic alliances: An internal tensions perspective, *Organization Science*, 11: 77–101.

134. Ireland, Hitt, & Vaidyanath, Alliance management; A Madhok & S. B. Tallman, 1998, Resources, transactions and rents: Managing value through interfirm collaborative relationships, *Organization Science*, 9: 326–339.

135. A. Turner, 2006, EAS and Flying Group row over failed venture, *Flight International*, March 14, 22.

136. T. K. Das, 2006, Strategic alliance temporalities and partner opportunism, *British Journal of Management*, 17(1): 1–20; C. Rossetti & T. Y. Choi, 2005, On the dark side of strategic sourcing: Experience from the aerospace industry, *Academy of Management Executive*, 19(1): 46–60.

137. P. M. Norman, 2002, Protecting knowledge in strategic alliances: Resource and relational characteristics, *Journal of High Technology Management Research*, 13(2): 177–202; P. M. Norman, 2001, Are your secrets safe? Knowledge protection in strategic alliances, *Business Horizons*, November–December, 51–60.

138. M. A. Hitt, M. T. Dacin, B. B. Tyler, & D. Park, 1997, Understanding the differences in Korean and U.S. executives' strategic orientations, *Strategic Management Journal*, 18: 159–168.

139. R. Abratt & P. Motlana, 2002, Managing co-branding strategies: Global brands into local markets, *Business Horizons*, 45(5): 43–50; P. Lane, J. E. Salk, & M. A. Lyles, 2001, Absorptive capacity, learning, and performance in international joint ventures, *Strategic Management Journal*, 22: 1139–1161.

140. R. Larsson, L. Bengtsson, K. Henriksson, & J. Sparks, 1998, The interorganizational learning dilemma: Collective knowledge development in strategic alliances, *Organization Science*, 9: 285–305.

141. Ireland, Hitt, & Vaidyanath, Alliance management.

142. Reuer, Zollo, & Singh, Post-formation dynamics, 148.

143. J. Sammer, 2006, Alliances: How to get desired outcomes, *Business Finance*, 12(4): 38–40; J. H. Dyer, P. Kale, & H. Singh, 2001, How to make strategic alliances work, *MIT Sloan Management Review*, 42(4): 37–43.

144. R. C. Sampson, 2005, Experience effects and collaborative returns in R&D alliances, *Strategic Management Journal*, 26: 1009–1030; J. H. Dyer & N. W. Hatch, 2004, Using supplier networks to learn faster, *MIT Sloan Management Review*, 45(1): 57–63; D. De Cremer & D. van Knippenberg, 2002, How do leaders promote cooperation? The effects of charisma and procedural fairness, *Journal of Applied Psychology*, 87: 858–867; B. L. Simonin, 1997, The importance of collaborative know-how: An empirical test of the learning organization, *Academy of Management Journal*, 40: 1150–1174.

145. Y. Awazu, 2006, Managing technology alliances: The case for knowledge management, *International Journal of Information Management*, 26: 484–498.

146. 2002, McDonald's USA franchising, http://www.mcdonalds.com, February 9.

147. 2007, Financial requirements, McDonald's, http://www.mcdonalds.com/corp/franchise, February 10.

148. 2007, World class training, McDonald's http://www.mcdonalds.com/corp/franchise, February 10; 2002, Argus Company Report, McDonald's Corp., http://argusresearch.com, February 10.

149. S. Lott, 2005, Northwest names new exec to lead alliance department, *Aviation Daily*, August 26, 4.

150. M. H. Hansen, R. E. Hoskisson, & J. B. Barney, 2007, Competitive advantage in alliance governance: Resolving the opportunism minimization–gain maximization paradox, *Managerial and Decision Economics*, forthcoming.

151. Ibid.

152. J. J. Reuer & A. Arino, 2002, Contractual renegotiations in strategic alliances, *Journal of Management*, 28: 47–68.

153. J. H. Dyer & C. Wujin, 2003, The role of trustworthiness in reducing transaction costs and improving performance: Empirical evidence from the United States, Japan, and Korea, *Organization Science*, 14: 57–69.

154. Hutt, Stafford, Walker, & Reingen, Case study: Defining the social network, 53.

155. D. L. Ferrin & K. T. Dirks, 2003, The use of rewards to increase and decrease trust: Mediating processes and differential effects, *Organization Science*, 14(1): 18–31; D. F. Jennings, K. Artz, L. M. Gillin, & C. Christodouloy, 2000, Determinants of trust in global strategic alliances: Amrad and the Australian biomedical industry, *Competitiveness Review*, 10(1): 25–44.

156. V. Perrone, A. Zaheer, & B. McEvily, 2003, Free to be trusted? Boundary constraints on trust in boundary spanners, *Organization Science*, 14: 422–439; H. K. Steensma, L. Marino, & K. M. Weaver, 2000, Attitudes toward cooperative strategies: A cross-cultural

analysis of entrepreneurs, *Journal of International Business Studies*, 31: 591–609.

157 Y. Luo, 2005, How important are shared perceptions of procedural justice in cooperative alliances? *Academy of Management Journal*, 48: 695–709.

158 R. Krishnan, X. Martin, & N. G. Noorderhaven, 2006, When does trust matter to alliance performance? *Academy of Management Journal*, 49: 894–917; A. Arino & J. de la Torre, 1998, Learning from failure: Towards an evolutionary model of collaborative ventures, *Organization Science*, 9: 306–325; J. B. Barney & M. H. Hansen, 1994, Trustworthiness: Can it be a source of competitive advantage? *Strategic Management Journal*, 15(special winter issue): 175–203.

159 Dyer & Wujin, The role of trustworthiness; R. Gulati & H. Singh, 1998, The architecture of cooperation: Managing coordination costs and appropriation concerns in strategic alliances, *Administrative Science Quarterly*, 43: 781–814; R. Gulati, 1996, Social structure and alliance formation patterns: A longitudinal analysis, *Administrative Science Quarterly*, 40: 619–652.

160 J. H. Davis, F. D. Schoorman, R. C. Mayer, & H. H. Tan, 2000, The trusted general manager and business unit performance: Empirical evidence of a competitive advantage, *Strategic Management Journal*, 21: 563–576; R. C. Mayer, J. H. Davis, & F. D. Schoorman, 1995, An integrative model of organizational trust, *Academy of Management Review*, 20: 709–734.

# CHAPTER 8

# Corporate-Level Strategy

## KNOWLEDGE OBJECTIVES

*Studying this chapter should provide you with the strategic management knowledge needed to:*

1. Define corporate-level strategy and discuss its importance to the diversified firm.

2. Describe the advantages and disadvantages of single and dominant business strategies.

3. Explain three primary reasons why firms move from single and dominant business strategies to more diversified strategies to enhance value creation.

4. Describe the multidivisional structure (M-form) and controls and discuss the difference between strategic controls and financial controls.

5. Describe how related diversified firms create value by sharing or transferring core competencies.

6. Explain the two ways value can be created with an unrelated diversification strategy.

7. Explain the use of the three versions of the multidivisional structure (M-form) to implement different diversification strategies.

8. Discuss the incentives and resources that encourage diversification.

9. Describe motives that can be incentives for managers to overdiversify a firm.

Our discussions of business-level strategies (Chapter 5) and the rivalry and competitive dynamics associated with them (Chapter 6) concentrated on firms competing in a single industry or product market.[1] However, some of the cooperative strategies described in Chapter 7 move firms beyond their traditional business-level focused markets and industries. **Corporate-level strategy** specifies actions a firm takes to gain a competitive advantage by selecting and managing a portfolio of businesses that compete in different product markets or industries. With regard to the five major elements of strategy described in Chapter 2, corporate-level strategy answers the question regarding arenas: where will we be active (and with how much emphasis)?[2]

A *diversification strategy* allows the firm to use its core competencies to pursue opportunities in the external environment.[3] As such, diversification strategies play a major role in the behavior of large firms.[4] Royal Philips Electronics of the Netherlands, for instance, has diversified into a wide variety of industries, including semiconductors, lighting, medical systems, domestic appliances, personal care, and consumer electronics. The firm has 161,500 employees in more than 60 countries.

Like a firm's business-level and cooperative strategies, corporate-level strategies are intended to help a firm create value leading to high performance.[5] Some suggest that few corporate-level strategies actually create value.[6] A corporate-level strategy's value is ultimately determined by the degree to which "the businesses in the portfolio are worth more under the management of the company than they would be under any other ownership."[7] Thus, one way to measure the success of a corporate-level strategy is to determine whether the aggregate returns across all of a firm's business units exceed what those returns would be without the overall corporate strategy, in terms of the firm's ability to create value and achieve high performance.[8] This is still an important, and not entirely resolved, research question.[9]

*Product diversification*, a primary form of corporate-level strategy, concerns the scope of the industries and markets in which the firm competes as well as "how managers buy, create and sell different businesses to match skills and strengths with opportunities presented to the firm."[10] Successful diversification is expected to reduce variability in the firm's profitability in that its earnings are generated from several different business units.[11] Because firms incur development and monitoring costs when diversifying, the ideal business portfolio balances diversification's costs and benefits.[12] CEOs and their top management team are ultimately responsible for determining the ideal portfolio of businesses for the firm.[13]

We begin the chapter by examining different levels (from low to high) of diversification. Value-creating reasons for firms to use a corporate-level strategy are explored next, along with vertical integration strategy as a means to gain power over competitors. Two types of diversification strategies denoting moderate to very high levels of diversification—related and unrelated—are then examined. The specific structural design that should be used to facilitate implementation of each corporate-level strategy is presented. Finally, the chapter explores value-neutral incentives to diversify as well as managerial motives for diversification, which can be destructive because of overdiversification.

## Levels of Diversification

Diversified firms vary according to their level of diversification and the connections between and among their businesses. Figure 8.1 defines five categories of diversification. In addition to the *single* and *dominant* business categories, which denote relatively low levels of diversification, more fully diversified firms are classified into *related* and *unrelated* categories. A firm is related through its diversification when there are several links between its business units; for example, units may share products or services, technologies, or distribution channels. The more links among businesses, the more constrained is the relatedness of diversification. Unrelatedness refers to the absence of direct links between businesses.

### Low Levels of Diversification

A firm pursing a low level of diversification uses either a single or a dominant corporate-level diversification strategy. A *single business strategy* is a corporate-level strategy in which the firm generates 95 percent or more of its sales revenue from its core business area.[14] With more than 100 aircraft, JetBlue Airways Corp. is involved in only one business area: domestic airline transportation.[15]

With the *dominant business diversification strategy*, the firm generates between 70 and 95 percent of its total revenue within a single business area. United Parcel Service (UPS) uses this strategy. Recently, UPS generated 74 percent of its revenue from its U.S. package delivery business and 17 percent from its international package business, with the remaining 9 percent coming from the firm's nonpackage business.[16] Although the U.S. package delivery business currently generates the largest percentage of the firm's sales revenue, UPS anticipates that in the future its international and nonpackage businesses will account for the majority of its growth in revenues. This expectation suggests that UPS may become more diversified, in terms of both the goods and services it offers and the number of countries in which those goods and services are offered. If this happens, UPS would likely become a moderately diversified firm.

## Figure 8.1: Levels and Types of Diversification

**Low Levels of Diversification**

| | | |
|---|---|---|
| Single business: | More than 95% of revenue comes from a single business. |  |

Dominant business:    Between 70% and 95% of revenue comes from a single business.

**Moderate to High Levels of Diversification**

Related constrained:    Less than 70% of revenue comes from the dominant business, and all businesses share product, technological, and distribution linkages.

Related linked (mixed related and unrelated):    Less than 70% of revenue comes from the dominant business, and there are only limited links between businesses.

**Very High Levels of Diversification**

Unrelated:    Less than 70% of revenue comes from the dominant business, and there are no common links between businesses.

SOURCE: Adapted from R. P. Rumelt, 1974, *Strategy, Structure and Economic Performance*, Boston: Harvard Business School.

## Moderate and High Levels of Diversification

A firm generating more than 30 percent of its sales revenue outside a dominant business and whose businesses are related to each other in some manner uses a *related diversification strategy*. When the links between the diversified firm's businesses are rather direct, a *related constrained diversification strategy* is being used. A related constrained firm shares a number of resources and activities among its businesses. The Campbell Soup Company, Procter & Gamble, Kodak, and Merck & Co. use a related constrained strategy, as do some large cable companies. With a related constrained strategy, resources and activities are shared among a firm's businesses. Cable firms such as Comcast and Time Warner, for example, share technology-based resources and billing service activities across their television programming, high-speed Internet connection, and phone service businesses.[17]

The diversified company with a portfolio of businesses with only a few links between them is called a mixed related and unrelated firm and is using the *related linked diversification strategy*. Compared with related constrained firms, related linked firms share fewer resources and assets among their businesses, concentrating on transferring knowledge and competencies among the businesses instead. Johnson & Johnson, General Electric, and Cendant follow this corporate-level diversification strategy. Johnson & Johnson, for example, has more than 200 operating companies "that manufacture and market thousands of branded health care products in hundreds of categories."[18] Despite the diversity of the company's products, the products are still "linked" by a focus on health care. As with firms using each type of diversification strategy, companies implementing the related linked strategy constantly adjust the mix in their portfolio of businesses as well as decisions about how to manage their businesses.

A highly diversified firm, which has no well-defined relationships between its businesses, follows an *unrelated diversification strategy*. These types of firms are also referred to as *conglomerates*. United Technologies, Textron, and Samsung are examples of firms using this type of corporate-level strategy. United Technologies' major operating companies, for instance, include air-conditioning systems, industrial and aerospace products, engines, elevators and escalators, helicopters, security systems, and fuel cells.[19]

Research evidence suggests that a curvilinear relationship may exist between level of diversification and firm performance.[20] As illustrated in Figure 8.2, the dominant business and unrelated business strategies are expected to have lower performance than the related constrained diversification strategy. The related linked strategy would fall somewhere between the related constrained and the unrelated diversification strategies; the single business strategy is not included in the figure because it does not involve a significant level of diversification. There are many reasons why a diversification strategy that involves a portfolio of closely related firms is likely to be higher performing than other types of diversification strategies. However, it is important to note two caveats to this pattern of diversification and performance: first, some firms are successful with each type of diversification strategy; second, some research suggests that *all* diversification leads to trade-offs and a certain level of suboptimization.[21]

As a result of low performance, many firms using the unrelated diversification strategy have refocused to become less diversified;[22] however, many others continue to have high levels of diversification. In Latin America and other emerging economies such as China, Korea, and Taiwan, conglomerates continue to dominate the private sector.[23] Typically family controlled, these corporations also account for the greatest percentage of private firms in India.[24] Similarly, the largest business groups in emerging markets such as Brazil, Mexico, Argentina, and Colombia are family-owned, diversified enterprises.[25] However, questions

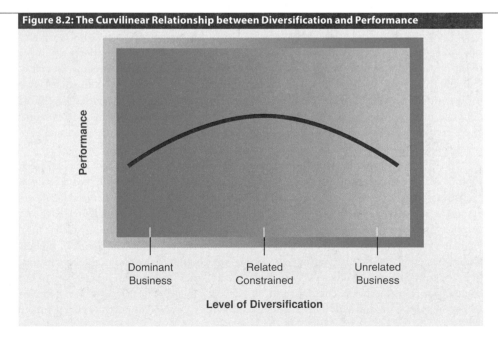

**Figure 8.2: The Curvilinear Relationship between Diversification and Performance**

Performance

Dominant
Business

Related
Constrained

Unrelated
Business

**Level of Diversification**

are being raised about the viability of these large diversified business groups, especially in developed economies such as Japan.[26]

## Reasons for Diversification

There are many reasons firms use a corporate-level diversification strategy (see Table 8.1). Typically, a diversification strategy is used to increase the firm's value by improving its overall performance (*value-creating diversification* in Table 8.1). Value is created through related diversification when the strategy allows a company's business units to increase revenues or reduce costs while implementing their business-level strategies. Another reason for diversification is to gain market power relative to competitors. Often, this is achieved through multimarket competition (introduced in Chapter 6) or vertical integration (defined later in the chapter). In addition, a firm may diversify in an effort to allocate capital more efficiently to those businesses that have the greatest potential for high performance or as a part of a business restructuring plan.

*Value-neutral diversification* does not necessarily guide the firm toward any particular type of value-creating diversification strategy. Value-neutral reasons for diversifying include government-induced stimuli such as antitrust regulation and tax laws, as well as particular concerns managers may have about a firm's low performance, uncertainty of future cash flows, or other types of risk. In addition, the firm may possess tangible or intangible resources that would facilitate diversification. The prevailing logic of diversification suggests that the firm should diversify into additional markets when it has excess resources, capabilities, and core competencies with multiple value-creating uses.[27] Although these factors might push a firm toward diversification, hopefully its managers will actually pursue a type of diversification that will add value to the firm.

**Table 8.1: Reasons for Diversification**

**Value-Creating Diversification**
- Economies of scope (related diversification)
  - —Sharing activities
  - —Transferring core competencies
- Market power (related diversification)
  - —Blocking competitors through multimarket competition
  - —Vertical integration
- Financial economies (unrelated diversification)
  - —Efficient internal capital allocation
  - —Business restructuring

**Value-Neutral Diversification**
- Antitrust regulation
- Tax laws
- Low performance
- Uncertain future cash flows
- Risk reduction for firm
- Tangible resources
- Intangible resources

**Value-Reducing Diversification**
- Diversifying managerial employment risk
- Increasing managerial compensation

Other reasons for using a diversification strategy may not increase the firm's value; in fact, diversification could have neutral effects, increase costs, or reduce a firm's revenue and its value (*value-reducing diversification* in Table 8.1). These reasons include diversification to match and thereby neutralize a competitor's market power (such as to neutralize another firm's advantage by acquiring a distribution outlet similar to its rival) and to expand a firm's portfolio of businesses to reduce managerial employment risk (if one of the businesses in a diversified firm fails, the top executive of the firm has an opportunity to remain employed). Because diversification can increase a firm's size and thus managerial compensation, managers have motives to diversify a firm to a level that reduces its value. Diversification rationales that may have a neutral or negative effect on the firm's value are discussed in a later section.

*Operational relatedness* and *corporate relatedness* are two ways diversification strategies can create value (see Figure 8.3). Study of these independent relatedness dimensions shows the importance of resources and key competencies.[28] The vertical dimension of Figure 8.3 indicates sharing activities (operational relatedness), and its horizontal dimension depicts corporate capabilities for transferring knowledge (corporate relatedness). The firm with a strong capability in managing operational synergy, especially in sharing assets between its businesses, falls in the upper left quadrant, which also represents vertical sharing of assets through vertical integration. The lower right quadrant represents a highly developed corporate capability for transferring a skill across businesses. This capability is located primarily in the corporate office. The use of either operational relatedness or corporate relatedness is

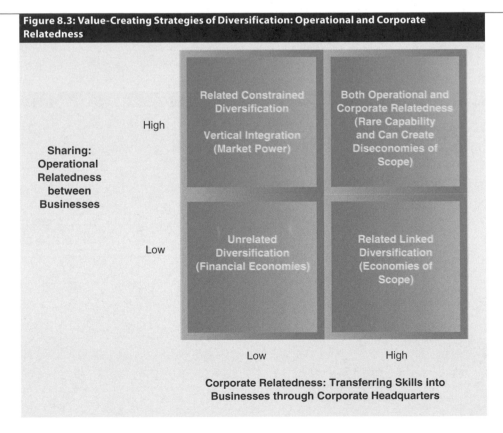

**Figure 8.3: Value-Creating Strategies of Diversification: Operational and Corporate Relatedness**

|  | Low Corporate Relatedness | High Corporate Relatedness |
|---|---|---|
| **Sharing: Operational Relatedness between Businesses — High** | Related Constrained Diversification / Vertical Integration (Market Power) | Both Operational and Corporate Relatedness (Rare Capability and Can Create Diseconomies of Scope) |
| **Low** | Unrelated Diversification (Financial Economies) | Related Linked Diversification (Economies of Scope) |

**Corporate Relatedness: Transferring Skills into Businesses through Corporate Headquarters**

based on a knowledge asset that the firm can either share or transfer.[29] Unrelated diversification is also shown in Figure 8.3 in the lower left quadrant. The unrelated diversification strategy creates value through financial economies rather than through either operational relatedness or corporate relatedness among business units.

## Diversification and the Multidivisional Structure

In Chapter 5 we introduced the idea that value can be created by effectively using an organizational structure—a simple structure, functional structure, or flexible structure—to facilitate implementation of one of the business-level strategies. By definition, corporate-level diversification strategies are multi-business and therefore a different type of structure is appropriate when implementing these strategies.[30] In Chapter 5, the *multidivisional structure* (M-form) was described as consisting of several operating divisions, each representing a separate business or profit center in which the top corporate officer delegates responsibilities for day-to-day operations and business unit strategy to division managers. Each division represents a distinct, self-contained business with its own business-level structure.[31] The M-form ties all those divisions together. Diversification is a dominant corporate-level strategy in the global economy, resulting in extensive use of the M-form.[32] Proper use of the M-form in a diversified firm can lead to value creation.[33]

Alfred Chandler viewed the M-form as an innovative response to coordination and control problems that surfaced during the 1920s in the functional structures then used by large firms such as DuPont and General Motors.[34] As initially designed, the M-form was thought to have three major benefits: "(1) it enabled corporate officers to more accurately monitor the performance of each business, which simplified the problem of control; (2) it facilitated comparisons between divisions, which improved the resource allocation process; and (3) it stimulated managers of poorly performing divisions to look for ways of improving performance."[35] Active monitoring of performance through the M-form increases the likelihood that decisions made by managers heading individual units will be in the shareholders' best interests. The M-form is used to support implementation of both related and unrelated diversification strategies. It helps firms successfully manage the many demands of diversification, including those related to processing vast amounts of information.[36] Partly because of its value to diversified corporations, some consider the M-form to be one of the 20th century's most significant organizational innovations.[37]

**Organizational controls** are an important aspect of the M-form. They guide the use of strategy, indicate how to compare actual results with expected results, and suggest corrective actions to take when the difference between actual and expected results is unacceptable. The fewer the differences between actual and expected outcomes, the more effective the organization's controls.[38] It is hard for a company to successfully exploit its competitive advantages without effective organizational controls.[39] Properly designed organizational controls provide clear insights regarding behaviors that enhance firm performance.[40] Firms rely on strategic controls and financial controls as part of their structures to support the use of their strategies.[41]

**Strategic controls** are largely subjective criteria intended to verify that the firm is using appropriate strategies for the conditions in the external environment and the company's competitive advantages. Thus, strategic controls are concerned with examining the fit between what the firm *might* do (as suggested by opportunities in its external environment) and what it *can* do (as indicated by its competitive advantages) (see Chapters 2 and 4). Effective strategic controls help the firm understand what it takes to be successful and set appropriate strategic goals, as well as monitor such goal achievement.[42] Strategic controls demand rich communications between top managers responsible for evaluating overall firm performance and those with primary responsibility for implementing the firm's strategies in its divisions. These frequent exchanges are both formal and informal in nature.[43] Because related diversification requires more information processing, strategic controls are more important to a firm that is pursuing this strategy.

Partly because strategic controls are difficult to use with extensive diversification,[44] **financial controls** are emphasized to evaluate the performance of the firm following the unrelated diversification strategy. Financial controls are largely objective criteria used to measure the firm's performance against previously established quantitative standards. Accounting-based measures, such as return on investment and return on assets, and market-based measures, such as economic value added, are examples of financial controls. As explained below, a corporate-wide emphasis on sharing among business units (as called for by the related constrained diversification strategy) results in an emphasis on strategic controls while financial controls are emphasized for strategies in which activities or capabilities aren't shared (e.g., unrelated diversification). As such, different variants of the M-form that have significantly different control system emphases are necessary for the successful use of each unique diversification strategy.

---

## Related Diversification

With the related diversification corporate-level strategy, the firm builds upon or extends its resources, capabilities, and core competencies to create value.[45] The company using the related diversification strategy wants to develop and exploit economies of scope between its business units. Available to companies operating in multiple industries or product markets,[46] **economies of scope** are cost savings that the firm creates by successfully transferring some of its capabilities and competencies that were developed in one of its businesses to another of its businesses. **Synergy** exists when the value created by business units working together exceeds the value those same units create working independently.

As illustrated in Figure 8.3, firms seek to create value from economies of scope through two basic kinds of operational economies: sharing activities (operational relatedness) and transferring skills or corporate core competencies (corporate relatedness). The difference between sharing activities and transferring competencies is based on how separate resources are jointly used to create economies of scope. To create economies of scope, tangible resources, such as plant and equipment or other business-unit physical assets, often must be shared. Less tangible resources, such as manufacturing know-how, also can be shared.[47] However, know-how transferred between separate activities with no physical or tangible resource involved is a transfer of a corporate-level core competence and not an operational sharing of activities.

### Operational Relatedness: Sharing Activities

Firms can create operational relatedness by sharing either a primary activity such as inventory delivery systems or a support activity such as purchasing practices (see discussion of the value chain in Chapter 4). Sharing activities is quite common, especially among related constrained firms. Procter & Gamble's (P&G) paper towel business and baby diaper business both use paper products as a primary input to the manufacturing process.[48] The firm's joint paper production plant that produces inputs for the two divisions is an example of a shared activity. In addition, these two businesses are likely to share distribution channels and sales networks because they both produce consumer products.

Firms expect activity sharing among units to result in increased value creation and improved financial returns.[49] When P&G acquired Gillette in 2005, top management promised shareholders more than $1 billion in annual cost synergies by 2008. Within nine months of the acquisition, P&G had integrated Gillette's operations into its systems in 31 countries, covering five geographic regions. The integration efforts mean that P&G is "taking orders, shipping products, and receiving payments as a single company in those countries," according to CEO A. G. Lafley. "I have no doubt that P&G and Gillette are stronger together than alone, and that our combined company can deliver our accelerated growth targets over the balance of the decade."[50]

Several issues affect the degree to which activity sharing creates positive outcomes. For example, activity sharing requires sharing strategic control over business units. Research has shown that firms that are successful in creating economies of scope in their related businesses often demonstrate a corporate passion for pursuing appropriate coordination mechanisms.[51] Also, activity sharing can be risky because business-unit ties create links between outcomes. For instance, if demand for one business's product is reduced, there may not be sufficient revenues to cover the fixed costs required to operate the facilities being shared. Moreover, one business unit manager may feel that another unit is receiving a disproportionate share of the gains being accrued through activity sharing. Such a perception could create conflicts between division managers. Organizational difficulties such as these can prevent activity sharing from being successful.[52]

Although activity sharing across business units isn't risk free, research shows that it can create value. For example, studies that examined acquisitions of firms in the same industry (called *horizontal acquisitions*), such as the banking industry, have found that sharing resources and activities and thereby creating economies of scope contributed to post-acquisition increases in performance and higher returns to shareholders.[53] Additionally, firms that sold related units in which resource sharing was a possible source of economies of scope have been found to produce lower returns than those that sold businesses unrelated to the firm's core business.[54] Still other research discovered that firms with more related units had lower risk.[55] These results suggest that gaining economies of scope by sharing activities across a firm's businesses may be important in reducing risk and creating value. Furthermore, more attractive results are obtained through activity sharing when a strong corporate office facilitates it.[56]

## Using the Cooperative Form of the Multidivisional Structure to Implement the Related Constrained Strategy

The **cooperative form** is a structure in which horizontal integration is used to bring about interdivisional cooperation. The divisions in the firm using the related constrained diversification strategy commonly are formed around products and markets, or both. The objective of P&G to "think globally, act locally," for example, is supported by a cooperative structure of five global business product units (baby, feminine and family care, fabric and home care, food and beverage, and health and beauty care) and seven market development organizations (MDOs), each formed around a region of the world, such as Northeast Asia. Using the five global product units to create strong brand equities through ongoing innovation is how P&G "thinks globally"; interfacing with customers to ensure that a division's marketing plans fully capitalize on local opportunities is how P&G "acts locally." Information is shared between the product-oriented and the marketing-oriented efforts to enhance the corporation's performance. Indeed, some corporate staff members are responsible for making certain that knowledge is meaningfully categorized and then rapidly transferred throughout P&G's businesses.[57]

In Figure 8.4, we use product divisions as part of the representation of the cooperative form of the M-form. As the P&G example suggests, market divisions could be used instead of or in addition to product divisions to develop the structure. Thus, as should be the case in all diversified companies, P&G has implemented a form of the M-form to satisfy its unique requirements for matching strategy and structure.

All of the divisions of the related constrained firm share one or more corporate strengths, such as production competencies, marketing competencies, or channel dominance.[58] Marketing expertise is one of the strengths shared across P&G's divisions. Interdivisional sharing of competencies depends on cooperation, suggesting the use of the cooperative form of the M-form.[59] Increasingly, it is important that the links resulting from effective use of integration mechanisms support the cooperative sharing of both intangible resources (such as knowledge) and tangible resources (such as facilities and equipment).[60]

Different characteristics of structure are used as integrating mechanisms by the cooperative structure to facilitate interdivisional cooperation. *Centralization* is one of these

**Figure 8.4: Cooperative Form of the Multidivisional Structure for Implementation of a Related Constrained Strategy**

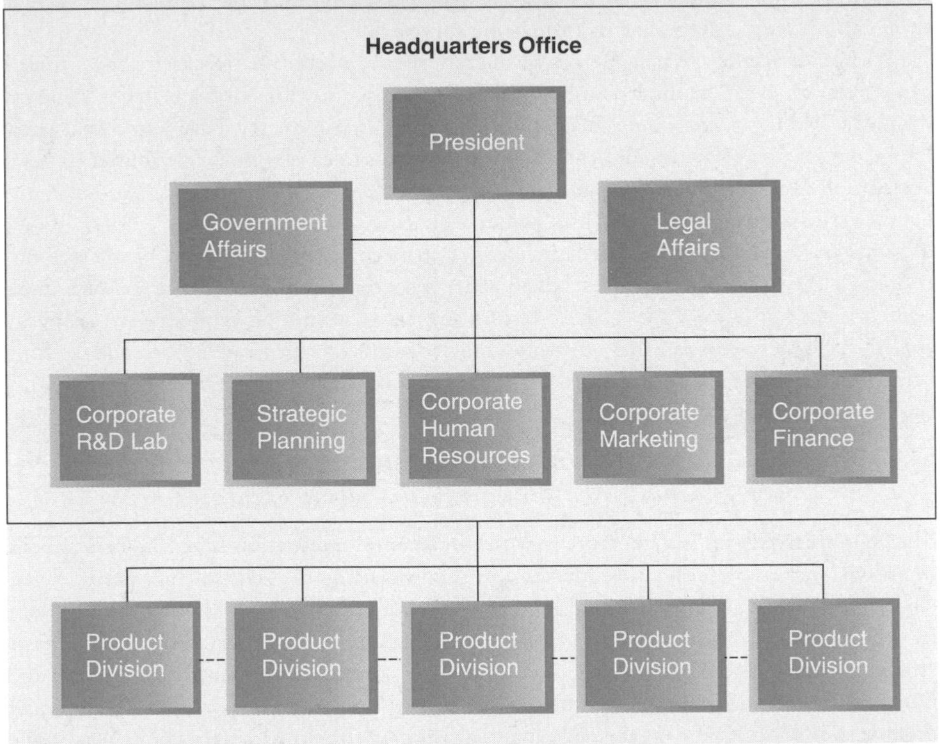

Notes: • Structural integration devices create tight links among all divisions
   • Corporate office emphasizes centralized strategic planning, human resources, and marketing to foster cooperation between divisions
   • R&D is likely to be centralized
   • Rewards are subjective and tend to emphasize overall corporate performance in addition to divisional performance
   • Culture emphasizes cooperative sharing

mechanisms (see Chapter 5). Centralizing some organizational functions (human resource management, R&D, marketing, or finance) at the corporate level allows the linking of activities among divisions. Work completed in these centralized functions is managed by the firm's central office with the purpose of exploiting common strengths among divisions by sharing competencies.

The success of the cooperative M-form is significantly affected by how well information is processed among divisions. But because cooperation among divisions implies a loss of managerial autonomy, division managers may not readily commit themselves to the type of integrative information-processing activities that this structure demands. Moreover, coordination among divisions sometimes results in an unequal flow of positive outcomes to divisional managers. In other words, when managerial rewards are based partly on the performance of individual divisions, the manager of the division that is able to benefit the most by the sharing of corporate competencies might be viewed as receiving gains at the expense of others. Strategic controls are important in these instances, as divisional managers' performance can be evaluated at least partly on the basis of how well they have facilitated interdivisional cooperative efforts. Furthermore, using reward systems that emphasize overall company performance, besides financial outcomes achieved by individual divisions, helps overcome problems associated with the cooperative form.

## Corporate Relatedness: Transferring of Core Competencies

Over time, the firm's intangible resources, such as its know-how, become the foundation of core competencies. **Corporate-level core competencies** are complex sets of resources and capabilities that link different businesses, primarily through managerial and technological knowledge, experience, and expertise.[61] Related linked firms (see Figure 8.3) often transfer competencies across businesses, thereby creating value in at least two ways.[62] First, because the expense of developing a competence has been incurred in one unit, transferring it to a second business unit eliminates the need for the second unit to allocate resources to develop the competence.[63] This is the case at Henkel, which intends to transfer its competence in nanotechnology from its commercial adhesives business to its industrial adhesives business.[64] Resource intangibility is a second source of value creation through corporate relatedness. Intangible resources are difficult for competitors to understand and imitate; therefore, the unit receiving a transferred competence often gains an immediate competitive advantage over its rivals.[65]

A number of firms have successfully transferred some of their resources and capabilities across businesses. Virgin Group transfers its marketing core competence across businesses involved in travel, cosmetics, music, drinks, mobile phones, health clubs, and other areas.[66] Cooper Industries, which manages a number of manufacturing-related businesses, transfers its expertise in electrical products and tools across all of its businesses.[67] Honda has developed and transferred its expertise in small and now larger engines for different types of vehicles, from motorcycles and lawnmowers to a range of automotive products.[68]

## Using the Strategic Business-Unit Form of the Multidivisional Structure to Implement the Related Linked Strategy

As noted above, when the firm has fewer links or less constrained links among its divisions, the related linked diversification strategy is used. The **strategic business-unit form** of the M-form supports implementation of this strategy and consists of three levels: corporate headquarters, strategic business units (SBUs), and SBU divisions (see Figure 8.5).

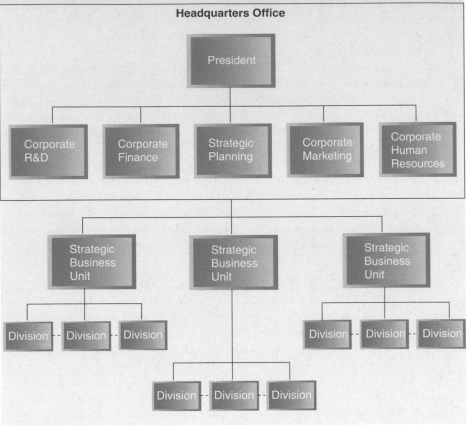

**Figure 8.5: SBU Form of the Multidivisional Structure for Implementation of a Related Linked Strategy**

Notes: • Structural integration among divisions within SBUs, but independence across SBUs
• Strategic planning may be the most prominent function in headquarters for managing the strategic planning approval process of SBUs for the president
• Each SBU may have its own budget for staff to foster integration
• Corporate headquarters staff serve as consultants to SBUs and divisions, rather than having direct input to product strategy as in the cooperative form

The divisions within each SBU are related in terms of shared products or markets or both, but the divisions of one SBU have little in common with the divisions of the other SBUs. Divisions within each SBU share product or market competencies to develop economies of scope and possibly economies of scale. The integration mechanisms used by the divisions in a cooperative structure can be equally well used by the divisions within the individual SBUs that are part of the SBU form of the M-form. In the SBU structure, each SBU is a profit center that is controlled and evaluated by the headquarters office. Although both financial and strategic controls are important, on a relative basis, financial controls are more vital to headquarters' evaluation of each SBU; strategic controls are critical when the heads of SBUs evaluate their divisions' performance. Strategic controls are also critical to the headquarters' efforts to determine whether the company has chosen an effective portfolio of businesses and whether those businesses are being effectively managed.

One way managers facilitate the transfer of competencies is to move key people into new management positions.[69] However, a business-unit manager of an older division may be reluctant to transfer key people who have accumulated knowledge and experience critical to the business unit's success. Thus, managers with the ability to facilitate the transfer of a core competence may come at a premium, or the key people involved may not want to transfer. Additionally, the top-level managers from the transferring division may not want the competencies transferred to a new division to fulfill the firm's diversification objectives.

The SBU structure can be complex, depending on the organization's size and product and market diversity. For example, General Electric (GE), a related linked firm, has six major SBUs, each with multiple divisions.[70] For instance, GE Industrial includes businesses involved in advanced materials, consumer and industrial products, equipment services, plastics, sensing, security and inspection technologies, and automation products and services. In many of GE's SBUs, efforts are undertaken to form competencies in services and technology as a source of competitive advantage. For instance, the company has developed skills in system integration and automation in its GE Health Care SBU that are expected to enhance the in vitro diagnostics business it recently acquired from Abbott Laboratories.[71]

## Market Power through Multimarket Competition and Vertical Integration

Related diversification can also be used to gain market power. **Market power** exists when a firm is able to sell its products above the existing competitive level or to reduce the costs of its primary and support activities below the competitive level, or both.[72] Two avenues firms might pursue to increase their market power through diversification are *multimarket competition* and *vertical integration*.

Introduced in Chapter 6 as a strategy that influences competitive rivalry, **multimarket** (also called **multipoint**) **competition** exists when two or more diversified firms simultaneously compete in the same product or geographic markets.[73] The actions taken by phone and cable companies in their primary U.S. markets illustrate multimarket competition. Dial-up phone connections were once the most common Internet connection for home users in the United States. However, the large cable companies, such as Comcast, began offering high-speed Internet connections and then digital phone services through their cable lines at attractive prices.[74] In response, phone companies such as Verizon began offering super high-speed Internet connections through newly installed fiber-optic lines.[75] Competitive attacks are less common in multipoint competition because the threat of a counterattack may prevent strategic actions from being taken, or more likely, firms may retract their strategic actions when faced with the threat of counterattack.[76] By virtue of the fact that the phone and cable companies are now competing in the same product markets and often in the same geographic markets, they are less likely to take aggressive competitive actions against each other (i.e., drastic price reductions). This is often called *mutual forbearance*.

Some firms choose to create value by using vertical integration to gain market power (see Figure 8.3). **Vertical integration** exists when a company produces its own inputs (*backward integration*) or owns its own source of distribution of outputs (*forward integration*). In some instances, firms partially integrate their operations, producing and selling their products by using both company business units and outside sources.[77] **Taper integration,** as this strategy is sometimes called, "arises when a firm sources inputs externally from independent suppliers as well as internally within the boundaries of the firm, or disposes of its outputs through independent outlets in addition to company-owned distribution channels."[78] Research has shown that carefully balancing vertical integration and strategic outsourcing provides competitive benefits leading to superior performance when a high level of innovation is required for success.[79]

Vertical integration is commonly used in the firm's core business to gain market power over rivals. Market power is gained as the firm develops the ability to save on its operations, avoid market costs, improve product quality, and, possibly, protect its technology from imitation by rivals.[80] Market power also is created when firms have strong ties between their assets for which no market prices exist. Establishing a market price would result in high search and transaction costs, so firms seek to vertically integrate rather than remain separate businesses.[81] When they do, a cooperative M-form similar to that described in association with the related constrained firm is implemented (see Figure 8.4).

Smithfield Foods is a vertically integrated company with hog processing as its core business. Smithfield has vertically integrated backward by raising the hogs that it later processes in its plants. Most packaging plants operate profitably when the price of meat is low and suffer when prices are high. In contrast, Smithfield can better control its costs because it owns the facilities that provide the raw materials required for its core processing operations. This control often results in Smithfield having market power over its competitors because it typically produces products at below the average industry production cost. The company has made more than 30 acquisitions since 1981, supporting the firm's use of vertical integration to yield competitively attractive options to consumers.[82]

There are also limits to vertical integration. For example, an outside supplier may produce the product at a lower cost. As a result, internal transactions from vertical integration may be expensive and reduce profitability relative to competitors. Also, bureaucratic costs may occur with vertical integration. And, because vertical integration can require substantial investments in specific technologies, it may reduce the firm's flexibility, especially when technology changes quickly. Finally, changes in demand create capacity balance and coordination problems. If one division is building a part for another internal division, but achieving economies of scale requires the first division to manufacture quantities that are beyond the capacity of the internal buyer to absorb, it would be necessary to sell the parts outside the firm as well as to the internal division. Thus, although vertical integration can create value, especially through market power, it is not without risks and costs.[83]

Many manufacturing firms no longer pursue vertical integration as a means of gaining market power.[84] In fact, reducing vertical integration is the focus of most manufacturing firms, such as Intel and Dell, and even among large automobile companies, such as Ford and General Motors, as they develop independent supplier networks.[85] Solectron, a contract manufacturer, represents a new breed of large contract manufacturers that is helping to foster this revolution in supply-chain management.[86] Such firms often manage their customers' entire product lines and offer services ranging from inventory management to delivery and after-sales service. Conducting business through e-commerce also allows vertical integration to be changed into "virtual integration."[87] Thus, closer relationships are possible with suppliers and customers through virtual integration or electronic means of integration, allowing firms to reduce the costs of processing transactions while improving their supply-chain management skills and tightening the control of their inventories. This evidence suggests that *virtual* integration rather than *vertical* integration may be a more common source of market power for today's firms.

## Simultaneous Operational Relatedness and Corporate Relatedness

As Figure 8.3 suggests, some firms simultaneously seek operational and corporate forms of economies of scope.[88] Firms have difficulty simultaneously creating economies of scope by sharing activities (operational relatedness) and transferring core competencies (corporate relatedness). There are two implications associated with this difficulty. First, because managing two sources of knowledge is very difficult, such efforts often fail, creating what might be called "diseconomies" of scope.[89] Second, firms that are successful may be able to achieve a sustainable competitive advantage because it will be difficult for competitors to imitate their success.

The Walt Disney Company uses a related diversification strategy to simultaneously create economies of scope through operational and corporate relatedness. Within the firm's Studio Entertainment business, for example, Disney can gain economies of scope by sharing activities among its different movie distribution companies, such as Touchstone Pictures, Hollywood Pictures, and Dimension Films, among others. Broad and deep knowledge about its customers is a capability on which Disney relies to develop corporate-level core competencies in terms of marketing and distribution. With these competencies, Disney is able to create economies of scope through corporate relatedness as it cross-sells products that are highlighted in its movies through the distribution channels that are part of its theme parks, media, resorts, and consumer products businesses. Thus, characters created in cartoons and movies become figures that are promoted on the Disney Channel and sold in Disney's stores and resorts. In addition, themes found in movies frequently become rides or shows at theme parks. Or, in the case of *Pirates of the Caribbean*, a theme park ride inspired a movie. Currently, the company "is sketching out a string of niche resorts and attractions around the world. That could include everything from stand-alone, Disney themed hotels in cities and beach resorts to Disney branded retail and dining districts, and smaller, more specialized theme parks."[90]

Either cooperative or SBU M-forms are likely to be implemented with this dual strategy, depending on the degree of diversification (i.e., more diversification would likely require the SBU form). However, with this strategy more process mechanisms to facilitate integration and coordination may be required. For example, more frequent, direct contact between division managers may be essential. This integrating mechanism encourages and supports cooperation and the sharing of either competencies or resources that have the possibility of being used to create new advantages. Sometimes, liaison roles could be established in each division to reduce the amount of time division managers spend integrating and coordinating their unit's work with the work taking place in other divisions. Temporary teams or task forces may be formed around projects for which success depends on sharing competencies that are embedded within several divisions. Formal integration departments might be established in firms that frequently use temporary teams or task forces. Ultimately, a matrix organization may evolve in firms implementing this dual strategy. A **matrix organization** is an organizational structure in which a dual structure combines both functional specialization and business product or project specialization. Although complicated, an effective matrix structure can lead to improved coordination among a firm's divisions that seek to simultaneously implement operational and corporate relatedness.[91]

## Unrelated Diversification

Firms do not seek either operational relatedness or corporate relatedness when using the unrelated diversification corporate-level strategy. An unrelated diversification strategy (see Figure 8.3) can create value through two types of financial economies. **Financial economies** are cost savings realized through improved allocations of financial resources based on investments inside or outside the firm.[92]

Efficient internal capital allocations lead to financial economies. One way they do this is by reducing total corporate risk through creation of a portfolio of businesses with different risk profiles. The second type of financial economy is concerned with purchasing other corporations and restructuring their assets. Here, the diversified firm buys another firm, restructures that company's assets in ways that allow it to operate more profitably, and then sells it for a profit in the external market.[93] These two types of financial economies will now be discussed in greater detail.

## Efficient Internal Capital Market Allocation

In a market economy, capital markets are thought to efficiently allocate capital. Efficiency results from investors purchasing firm equity shares (ownership) that have high future cash-flow values. Capital is also allocated through debt as shareholders and debtholders try to improve the value of their investments by taking stakes in businesses with high growth prospects.

In large diversified firms, the corporate office distributes capital to business divisions to create value for the overall company. The nature of these distributions may generate gains that exceed the gains that would accrue to shareholders as a result of capital being allocated by the external capital market.[94] This happens because while managing the firm's portfolio of businesses, the corporate office may gain access to detailed and accurate information regarding those businesses' actual and prospective performance.

Compared with corporate office personnel, investors have relatively limited access to internal information and can only estimate divisional performance and future business prospects. Although businesses seeking capital must provide information to potential suppliers (such as banks or insurance companies), firms with internal capital markets may have at least two informational advantages. First, information provided to capital markets through annual reports and other sources may not include negative information, instead emphasizing positive prospects and outcomes. External sources of capital have limited ability to understand the dynamics inside large organizations. Even external shareholders who have access to information have no guarantee of full and complete disclosure.[95] Second, although a firm must disseminate information, that information also becomes simultaneously available to the company's current and potential competitors. With insights gained by studying such information, competitors may find it easier to attempt to duplicate a firm's competitive advantage. Thus, an ability to efficiently allocate capital through an internal market may help the firm protect its competitive advantages.

If intervention from outside the firm is required to make corrections to capital allocations, only significant changes are possible, such as forcing the firm into bankruptcy or changing the top management team. Alternatively, in an internal capital market, the corporate office can fine-tune its corrections, such as choosing to adjust managerial incentives or suggesting strategic changes in a division. Thus, capital can be allocated according to more specific criteria than possible with external market allocations. Because it has less accurate information, the external capital market may fail to allocate resources adequately to high-potential investments compared with corporate office investments. The corporate office of a diversified company can more effectively perform tasks such as disciplining underperforming management teams through resource allocations.[96]

Research suggests, however, that in efficient capital markets, the unrelated diversification strategy may be discounted.[97] "For years, stock markets have applied a 'conglomerate discount': they value diversified manufacturing conglomerates at 20 percent less, on average, than the value of the sum of their parts. The discount still applies, in good economic times and bad. Extraordinary manufacturers (like GE) can defy it for a while, but more ordinary ones (like Philips and Siemens) cannot."[98] One reason for this discount could be that firms sometimes substitute acquisitions for innovation. In these instances, too many resources are allocated to analyzing and completing acquisitions to further diversify a firm instead of allocating an appropriate amount of resources to nurturing internal innovation. This happened for some Japanese drug firms between 1975 and 1995, a period during which "corporate diversification was a strategic substitute for significant innovation."[99]

Despite the challenges associated with unrelated diversification, some firms still use it.[100] These large diversified business groups are found in many European countries, where the number of firms using the conglomerate or unrelated diversification strategy has actually increased, and throughout emerging economies as well.[101] Although many conglomerates, such as ITT and Hansen Trust, have refocused, other unrelated diversified firms have replaced them.

The Achilles heel of the unrelated diversification strategy is that conglomerates in developed economies have a fairly short life cycle because financial economies are more easily duplicated than are the gains derived from operational relatedness and corporate relatedness. This is less of a problem in emerging economies, where the absence of a "soft infrastructure" (including effective financial intermediaries, sound regulations, and contract laws) supports and encourages use of the unrelated diversification strategy.[102] In fact, in emerging economies, such as those in India and Chile, diversification increases the performance of firms affiliated with large diversified business groups.[103] The increasing skill levels of people working in corporations located in emerging markets may support the successful use of the unrelated diversification strategy.[104]

## Restructuring

Financial economies can also be created when firms learn how to create value by buying and selling other companies' assets in the external market.[105] As in the real estate business, buying assets at low prices, restructuring them, and selling them at a price exceeding their cost generates a positive return on the firm's invested capital. Some conglomerates have pursued value creation through restructuring firms in this way. Today, this strategy is often pursued by private equity firms, which are like an unrelated diversified firm in that they have large portfolios of acquired businesses that they buy, restructure, and sell, either to another company or through a public offering.

The Blackstone Private Equity Group bought and then restructured the assets of the 143-hotel AmeriSuites chain before profitably selling the chain to Hyatt Corp.[106] The group pursues a strategy of active portfolio management: "The Private Equity Group takes an active role in monitoring and supporting enhancement of equity value for its portfolio company investments. In recognition of the importance of initiating and supporting post-acquisition programs to enhance portfolio company value, the Group has a full-time dedicated team responsible for monitoring the strategic, operational, and financial performance of [the Group's] portfolio investments. All Private Equity professionals participate in regular portfolio company reviews."[107]

Creating financial economies by acquiring and restructuring other companies' assets requires an understanding of significant trade-offs. Success usually calls for a focus on mature, low-technology businesses because of the uncertainty of demand for high-technology products. In high-technology businesses, decisions about resource allocation become too complex, creating information-processing overload on the small corporate staffs of unrelated diversified firms. Furthermore, high-technology businesses often depend on human resources; these people can leave or demand higher pay and thus appropriate or deplete the value of an acquired firm.[108]

Service businesses with a client orientation are also difficult to buy and sell in this way because of their client-based sales orientation and the mobility of sales people.[109] This is especially so in professional service businesses such as accounting, law, advertising, consulting, and investment banking.

## Using the Competitive Form of the Multidivisional Structure to Implement the Unrelated Diversification Strategy

As noted above, firms using the unrelated diversification strategy want to create value through efficient internal capital allocations or by buying, restructuring, and selling businesses.[110] The competitive form of the M-form supports implementation of this strategy.

The **competitive form** is a structure in which the firm's divisions are completely independent (see Figure 8.6). Unlike the divisions in the cooperative structure (see Figure 8.4), the divisions that are part of the competitive structure do not share common corporate strengths (e.g., marketing competencies or channel dominance). Because strengths aren't shared in the competitive structure, integrating devices aren't developed for the divisions to use.

The efficient internal capital market that is the foundation for use of the unrelated diversification strategy requires organizational arrangements that emphasize divisional competition rather than cooperation.[111] Three benefits are expected from the internal competition that the competitive form of the M-form facilitates. First, internal competition creates flexibility—corporate headquarters can have divisions working on different technologies

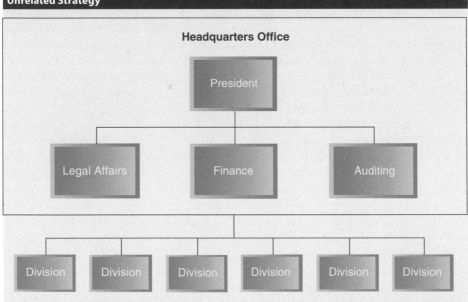

**Figure 8.6: Competitive Form of the Multidivisional Structure for Implementation of an Unrelated Strategy**

Notes:
- Corporate headquarters has a small staff
- Finance and auditing are the most prominent functions in the headquarters office to manage cash flow and assure the accuracy of performance data coming from divisions
- The legal affairs function becomes important when the firm acquires or divests assets
- Divisions are independent and separate for financial evaluation purposes
- Divisions retain strategic control, but cash is managed by the corporate office
- Divisions compete for corporate resources

to identify those with the greatest future potential. Resources can then be allocated to the division that is working with the most promising technology to fuel the entire firm's success. Second, internal competition challenges the status quo and inertia, because division heads know that future resource allocations are a product of excellent current performance as well as superior positioning of their division in terms of future performance. Last, internal competition motivates effort. The challenge of competing against internal peers can be as great as the challenge of competing against external marketplace competitors.[112]

Independence among divisions, as shown by a lack of sharing of corporate strengths and the absence of integrating devices, allows the firm using the unrelated diversification strategy to form specific profit performance expectations for each division to stimulate internal competition for future resources. The benefits of internal capital allocations or restructuring cannot be fully realized unless divisions are held accountable for their own independent performance. In the competitive structure, organizational controls (primarily financial controls) are used to emphasize and support internal competition among separate divisions and as the basis for allocating corporate capital based on divisions' performances. Textron, a highly diversified conglomerate with operations as varied as fasteners, golf carts, and helicopters, has a vision of being "the premier multi-industry company."[113] Top managers continuously seek to reshape the firm's portfolio by buying businesses in attractive industries and divesting businesses that are no longer attractive.[114] Managers of each of Textron's numerous independent businesses are completely responsible for their own operations.

Selling underperforming divisions and placing the rest under rigorous financial controls may increase business unit value. A firm creating financial economies at least partly through rigorous controls may have to use hostile takeovers or tender offers, because target firm managers often do not find this environment attractive and are less willing to be acquired. Hostile takeovers have the potential to increase the resistance of the target firm's top-level managers.[115] In these cases, corporate-level managers often are discharged, while division managers are retained, depending on how important each is to future operational success.

To emphasize competitiveness among divisions, the headquarters office maintains an arms-length relationship with them and does not intervene in divisional affairs, except to audit operations and discipline managers whose divisions perform poorly. In this situation, the headquarters office relies on strategic controls to set rate-of-return targets and financial controls to monitor divisional performance relative to those targets. The headquarters office then allocates cash flow on a competitive basis, rather than automatically returning cash to the division that produced it. Thus, the focus of the headquarters' work is on performance appraisal, resource allocation, and legal aspects related to acquisitions to verify that the firm's portfolio of businesses will lead to financial success.[116]

## Value-Neutral Diversification: Incentives and Resources

The objectives described in the last two sections on related and unrelated diversification are all focused on helping the firm create value through its corporate-level strategy. However, diversification is sometimes pursued with value-neutral rather than value-creating objectives in mind.

### Incentives to Diversify

Incentives to diversify come from both the external environment and a firm's internal organization. The term *incentive* implies that managers have choices. External incentives include antitrust regulations and tax laws. Internal incentives include low performance, uncertain future cash flows, and an overall reduction of risk for the firm. Diversification strategies taken in light of these various incentives sometimes increase the firm's ability to create value, but often the effect is neutral.

**Antitrust Regulation and Tax Laws.** Government antitrust policies and tax laws provided incentives for U.S. firms to diversify in the 1960s and 1970s.[117] Antitrust laws against mergers that created increased market power (via either vertical or horizontal integration) were stringently enforced during that period.[118] As a result, many of the mergers during that time were unrelated, involving companies pursuing different lines of business. Thus, the merger wave of the 1960s was "conglomerate" in character. Merger activity that produced conglomerate diversification was encouraged primarily by the Celler-Kefauver Act, which discouraged horizontal and vertical mergers. For example, in the 1973–1977 period, 79.1 percent of all mergers were conglomerate.[119]

During the 1980s, antitrust enforcement lessened, resulting in more and larger horizontal mergers (acquisitions of target firms in the same line of business, such as a merger between two oil companies).[120] In addition, investment bankers became more open to the kinds of mergers they tried to facilitate; as a consequence, hostile takeovers increased to unprecedented numbers.[121] The conglomerates or highly diversified firms of the 1960s and 1970s became more "focused" in the 1980s and early 1990s as merger constraints were relaxed and restructuring was implemented.[122]

In the late 1990s and early 2000s, however, antitrust concerns emerged again with the large volume of mergers and acquisitions (see Chapter 9).[123] Thus, mergers and acquisitions are receiving more scrutiny than they did in the 1980s and through the early 1990s. Partially as a result of the trend toward increased scrutiny, the U.S. government enacted the Antitrust Modernization Act of 2002. As a result of this act, the Antitrust Modernization Commission was created to examine whether antitrust laws need to be modernized, to solicit the views of all of the parties concerned with regard to operation of the antitrust laws, to evaluate relevant proposals for changes, and to prepare a report for the president and Congress. In early 2007 a bill to extend the existence of the commission passed both houses of Congress. The activities of this commission could alter the regulatory incentives to pursue diversifying acquisitions.[124]

The tax effects of diversification stem not only from individual tax rates, but also from corporate tax changes. Some companies (especially mature ones) generate more cash from their operations than they can reinvest profitably. Some argue that *free cash flows* (liquid financial assets for which investments in current businesses are no longer economically viable) should be redistributed to shareholders as dividends.[125] However, in the 1960s and 1970s, dividends were taxed more heavily than ordinary personal income. As a result, before 1980, shareholders preferred that firms use free cash flows to buy and build companies in high-performance industries. If the firm's stock value appreciated over the long term, shareholders might receive a better return on those funds than if they had been redistributed as dividends, because they would be taxed more lightly under capital-gains rules than dividends when they sold their stock.

Under the 1986 Tax Reform Act, however, the top individual ordinary income tax rate was reduced from 50 to 28 percent, and the special capital-gains tax was also changed, treating capital gains as ordinary income. These changes created an incentive for shareholders to stop encouraging firms to retain funds for purposes of diversification. These changes in the tax law also influenced an increase in divestitures of unrelated business units after 1984. Thus, while individual tax rates for capital gains and dividends created a shareholder incentive to increase diversification before 1986, they encouraged less diversification after 1986, unless it was funded by tax-deductible debt. The elimination of personal-interest deductions, as well as the lower attractiveness of retained earnings to shareholders, might prompt the use of more leverage by firms, for which interest expense is tax deductible.

Corporate tax laws also affect diversification. Acquisitions typically increase a firm's depreciable asset allowances. Increased depreciation (a non-cash-flow expense) produces lower taxable income, thereby providing an additional incentive for acquisitions. Before 1986, acquisitions may have been the most attractive means for securing tax benefits,[126] but the 1986 Tax Reform Act diminished some of the corporate tax advantages of diversification.[127] Changes recommended by the Financial Accounting Standards Board (FASB) regarding the elimination of the "pooling of interests" method for accounting for the acquired firm's assets and the elimination of the write-off for research and development in process reduce some of the incentives to make acquisitions, especially related acquisitions in high-technology industries (these changes are discussed further in Chapter 9).[128]

**Low Performance.** Some research shows that low returns are related to greater levels of diversification.[129] Even as "high performance eliminates the need for greater diversification,"[130] low performance may provide an incentive for diversification. Firms plagued by poor performance often take higher risks in an effort to turn things around.[131] Once a global powerhouse, Eastman Kodak Co. was recently described as an "ailing film giant." However, the company embarked on a high-risk diversification strategy to take on the market leader, Hewlett-Packard, in the inkjet printer market of the $50 billion printer industry. The effort is led by Antonio M. Perez, who left Hewlett-Packard after he was passed over for the top job in favor of Carly Fiorina. According to the company, the Kodak printers use ink that will "stay vibrant for 100 years rather than 15." Also, replacement ink cartridges "will cost half of what consumers are used to paying," which Perez says will "disrupt the industry's business model and address consumers' key dissatisfaction: the high cost of ink."[132]

**Uncertain Future Cash Flows.** As a firm's product line matures or is threatened, a firm may diversify as an important defensive strategy.[133] Small firms and companies in mature or maturing industries sometimes find it necessary to diversify for long-term survival.[134] For example, uncertainty was one of the dominant reasons for diversification among railroad firms during the 1960s and 1970s. Railroads diversified primarily because the trucking industry created uncertainty for railroad operators regarding the future level of demand for their services.

Diversifying into other product markets or into other businesses can reduce uncertainty about a firm's future cash flows. For example, Brinker International has reduced the uncertainty of its cash flows by competing in several segments of the casual dining industry. The company owns Chili's Grill & Bar, Romano's Macaroni Grill, On the Border Mexican Grill & Cantina, and Maggiano's Little Italy and has been called "the mutual fund of casual dining."[135] In this instance, while the demand for one of its restaurants might decline at any time, demand for one or more of its other restaurants might increase.

**Synergy and Firm Risk Reduction.** As mentioned previously, firms may pursue economies of scope between their diversified business units in an effort to realize synergy. Synergy is more likely to be produced if the firm's business units are highly related. But as a firm increases its relatedness between business units, it also increases its risk of corporate failure, because synergy produces interdependence among business units, which can reduce a firm's flexibility to respond to changes in its external environment.

Concerns about this flexibility can make a firm risk averse, resulting in its diversifying into industries in which more certainty exists. Risk aversion of this type may prevent firms from pursuing new product lines that have potential, but are not proved. Alternatively, the firm may constrain its level of activity sharing and forego synergy's benefits. The latter condition likely will result in additional, but unrelated, diversification.[136] For instance, Wal-Mart recently diversified into video-downloading services, competing directly with Apple's iTunes.[137] Research suggests that a firm using a related diversification strategy is more careful in bidding for new businesses, whereas a firm pursuing an unrelated diversification strategy may be more likely to overprice its bid because an unrelated bidder may not have full information about the acquired firm.[138]

## Resources and Diversification

As we have discussed, there are several value-neutral incentives for firms to diversify as well as value-creating incentives, such as the ability to create economies of scope. However, even when incentives to diversify exist, a firm must have the types and levels of resources and capabilities needed to successfully use a corporate-level diversification strategy.[139] Although tangible, intangible, and financial resources all facilitate diversification, they vary in their ability to create value. Indeed, the degree to which resources are valuable, rare, costly to imitate, and nonsubstitutable (see Chapter 4) influence their ability to create value through diversification. For instance, free cash flows are a financial resource that may be used to diversify the firm. However, compared with diversification that is grounded in intangible resources, diversification based on financial resources is more visible to competitors and thus more imitable and less likely to create value over the long term.[140]

Tangible resources usually include the plant and equipment necessary to produce a good or service and tend to be less flexible assets. Any excess capacity often can be used only for closely related products, especially those requiring highly similar manufacturing technologies. Excess capacity of other tangible resources, such as a sales force, can be used to diversify more easily. Again, excess capacity in a sales force is more effective with related diversification, because it may be utilized to sell similar products. The sales force would be more knowledgeable about the characteristics, customers, and distribution channels of related products.[141] Tangible resources may create resource interrelationships in production, marketing, procurement, and technology, defined earlier as activity sharing. Intangible resources are more flexible than tangible physical assets in facilitating diversification. Although the sharing of tangible resources may induce diversification, intangible resources such as tacit knowledge could encourage even more diversification.[142]

## Value-Reducing Diversification: Managerial Motives to Diversify

Managerial motives for diversification may exist independently of value-neutral reasons (i.e., incentives and resources) and value-creating reasons (e.g., economies of scope).[143] The desire for increased compensation is one motive for top executives to diversify their firm beyond value-creating and value-neutral levels.[144] Because diversification and firm size are highly correlated, as size increases, so does executive compensation.[145] Also, large firms are more complex and difficult to manage, so managers of larger firms usually receive more compensation.[146] Furthermore, top executives may diversify a firm in order to diversify their own employment risk;[147] that is, managers may have a perception that firms that are diversified are less likely to experience performance peaks and valleys that could lead to job loss.

Since the desire for increased compensation and reduced managerial risk may serve the interests of top executives at the expense of other stakeholders such as shareholders, internal governance mechanisms are intended to limit managers' tendencies to overdiversify. Such mechanisms, such as the board of directors, monitoring by owners, and executive compensation, are discussed in detail in Chapter 11. Even when these internal governance mechanisms are not strong, the external market for corporate control can act as a disciplining force for top managers. For instance, loss of adequate internal governance may result in poor performance, thereby triggering a threat of takeover.[148] A takeover may improve efficiency by replacing ineffective managerial teams; however, the at-risk managers may pursue defensive tactics or "poison pills" to fend off the acquisition and thus preserve their jobs. One example of a poison pill is the "golden parachute," which provides high compensation to managers of the acquired firm as they leave the firm after a takeover (other defensive tactics are discussed in Chapter 11).[149] Therefore, a threat of external governance, although restraining managers, does not flawlessly control managerial motives for diversification.[150]

Top executives may also be held in check by concerns for their reputation. If a positive reputation facilitates use of power, a poor reputation may reduce it. Likewise, a strong external market for managerial talent may deter managers from pursuing inappropriate diversification.[151] In addition, a diversified firm may police other diversified firms to acquire those poorly managed firms in order to restructure its own asset base. Knowing that their firms could be acquired if they are not managed successfully encourages managers to use value-creating strategies.

Even when governance mechanisms cause managers to correct a problem of poorly implemented diversification or overdiversification, these moves are not without trade-offs. For instance, firms that are spun off may not realize productivity gains, even though spinning them off is in the best interest of the divesting firm.[152] Accordingly, the assumption that managers need disciplining may not be entirely correct, and sometimes governance may create consequences that are worse than those resulting from overdiversification.

Excessive governance may cause a firm's managers to be overly cautious and risk averse.[153] Stephen Odland, the CEO of Office Depot, supports the Sarbanes–Oxley Act of 2002, which revised governance for publicly traded companies in the United States, but he has pointed out that "if we frighten managers to the point that they're not willing to risk anything we could damage our economy and our ability to compete in the world."[154] Most large publicly held firms are profitable because managers are positive stewards of firm resources, and many of their strategic actions, including those related to selecting a diversification strategy contribute to the firm's competitive success.[155] Thus, it is overly pessimistic to assume that managers usually act in their own self-interest as opposed to their firm's interest.[156] Governance devices should be designed to deal with exceptions to the norms of value creation and increasing shareholder wealth.

As shown in Figure 8.7, the level of diversification that can be expected to have the greatest positive effect on performance is based partly on how the interaction of value-creating influences, value-neutral influences, and value-reducing influences affects the adoption of particular diversification strategies. As indicated earlier, the greater the incentives and the more flexible the resources, the higher the level of expected diversification.

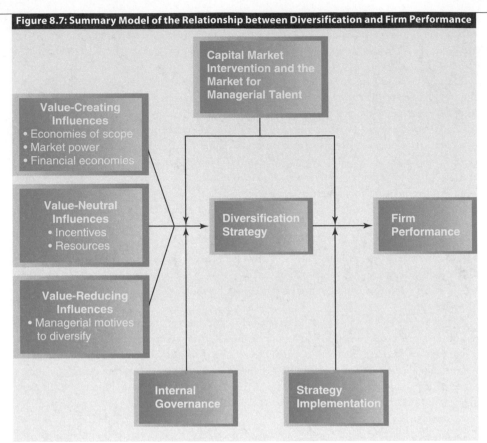

**Figure 8.7: Summary Model of the Relationship between Diversification and Firm Performance**

Capital Market Intervention and the Market for Managerial Talent

Value-Creating Influences
- Economies of scope
- Market power
- Financial economies

Value-Neutral Influences
- Incentives
- Resources

Value-Reducing Influences
- Managerial motives to diversify

Diversification Strategy

Firm Performance

Internal Governance

Strategy Implementation

SOURCE: R. E. Hoskisson & M. A. Hitt, 1990, Antecedents and performance outcomes of diversification: A review and critique of theoretical perspectives, *Journal of Management*, 16: 498.

Financial resources (the most flexible) should have a stronger relationship to the extent of diversification than either tangible or intangible resources. Tangible resources (the most inflexible) are useful primarily for related diversification.

As discussed in this chapter, firms can create more value by effectively using diversification strategies; however, diversification must be kept in check by internal corporate governance (see Chapter 11). Also, the governing effects of the capital market (i.e., threat of a takeover) and the external market for managerial talent help keep in check value-reducing motivations of top executives to diversify. Appropriate strategy implementation tools, such as the organizational structures discussed in this chapter, are also important.

## Summary

- A single or dominant business corporate-level strategy may be preferable to a more diversified strategy, unless a corporation can develop economies of scope or financial economies between businesses, or unless it can obtain market power through additional levels of diversification. These economies and market power are the main sources of value creation when the firm diversifies.

- Strategic controls (largely subjective criteria) and financial controls (largely objective criteria) are the two types of organizational controls used to successfully implement the firm's chosen corporate-level strategy within the M-form. Both types of controls are critical, although their degree of emphasis varies on the basis of individual matches between strategy and structure.

- Related diversification creates value through the sharing of activities or the transfer of core competencies. Sharing activities usually involves sharing tangible resources between businesses. Transferring core competencies involves transferring core competencies developed in one business to another one. It also may involve transferring competencies between the corporate office and a business unit.

- Sharing activities is usually associated with the corporate-level related constrained diversification strategy. Activity sharing is costly to implement and coordinate, may create unequal benefits for the divisions involved in the sharing, and may lead to fewer managerial risk-taking behaviors.

- Transferring core competencies is often associated with related linked (or mixed related) diversification, although firms pursuing both sharing activities and transferring core competencies can use it.

- Efficiently allocating resources or restructuring a target firm's assets and placing them under rigorous financial controls are two ways to accomplish successful unrelated diversification. These methods focus on obtaining financial economies.

- Unique combinations of different forms of the M-form are matched with different corporate-level diversification strategies to properly implement these strategies. The cooperative M-form, used to implement the related constrained corporate-level strategy, has a centralized corporate office and extensive integrating mechanisms. Divisional incentives are linked to overall corporate performance. The related linked SBU M-form establishes separate profit centers within the diversified firm. Each profit center may have divisions offering similar products, but the centers are unrelated to each other. The competitive M-form, used to implement the unrelated diversification strategy, is highly decentralized, lacks integrating mechanisms, and utilizes objective financial criteria to evaluate each unit's performance.

- The primary reason a firm diversifies is to create more value. However, diversification is sometimes pursued because of incentives from tax and governmental antitrust policies, performance disappointments, and uncertainties about future cash flow or to reduce risk.

- Managerial motives to diversify (including to increase compensation) can lead to over-diversification and a reduction in the firm's value-creating ability. On the other hand, managers can also be effective stewards of the firm's assets.

- Decision makers should pay attention to their firm's internal organization and external environment when making decisions about the optimal level of diversification for their company. Internal resources are important determinants of the direction that diversification should take. However, opportunities in the firm's external environment may facilitate additional levels of diversification, as might unexpected threats from competitors.

# Ethics Questions

1. Assume that you overheard the following statement: "Those managing an unrelated diversified firm face far more difficult ethical challenges than do those managing a dominant business firm." Based on your reading of this chapter, do you believe this statement true or false? Why?

2. Is it ethical for managers to diversify a firm rather than return excess earnings to shareholders? Provide reasoning to support your answer.

3. Are ethical issues associated with the use of strategic controls? With the use of financial controls? If so, what are they?

4. Are ethical issues involved in implementing the cooperative and competitive M-forms? If so, what are they? As a top-level manager, how would you deal with them?

5. What unethical practices might occur when a firm restructures? Explain.

6. Do you believe that ethical managers are unaffected by the managerial motives to diversify discussed in this chapter? If so, why? In addition, do you believe that ethical managers should help their peers learn how to avoid making diversification decisions on the basis of the managerial motives to diversify (e.g., increased compensation)? Why or why not?

# Notes

1. M. E. Porter, 1980, *Competitive Strategy*, New York: The Free Press, xvi.

2. D. C. Hambrick & J. W. Fredrickson, 2005, Are you sure you have a strategy? *Academy of Management Executive*, 19(4): 54.

3. R. E. Hoskisson, R. A. Johnson, D. Yiu, & W. P. Wan, 2001, Restructuring strategies of diversified business groups: Differences associated with country institutional environments, in M. A. Hitt, R. E. Freeman, & J. S. Harrison (eds.), *Handbook of Strategic Management*, Oxford, UK: Blackwell Publishers, 433–463; Y. Luo, 2001, Determinants of entry in an emerging economy: A multilevel approach, *Journal of Management Studies*, 38: 443–472; T. B. Palmer & R. M. Wiseman, 1999, Decoupling risk taking from income stream uncertainty: A holistic model of risk, *Strategic Management Journal*, 20: 1037–1062.

4. E. H. Bowman & C. E. Helfat, 2001, Does corporate strategy matter? *Strategic Management Journal*, 22: 1–23; M. A. Hitt, R. E. Hoskisson, & H. Kim, 1997, International diversification: Effects on innovation and firm performance in product-diversified firms, *Academy of Management Journal*, 40: 767–798.

5. P.-Y. Chu, M.-J. Teng, C.-H. Huang, & H.-S. Lin, 2005, Virtual integration and profitability: Some evidence from Taiwan's IC industry, *International Journal of Technology Management*, 29: 152–172; M. Kwak, 2002, Maximizing value through diversification, *MIT Sloan Management Review*, 43(2): 10; R. A. Burgelman & Y. L. Doz, 2001, The power of strategic integration, *MIT Sloan Management Review*, 42(3): 28–38; C. C. Markides, 1997, To diversify or not to diversify? *Harvard Business Review*, 75(6): 93–99.

6. P. Wright, M. Kroll, A. Lado, & B. Van Ness, 2002, The structure of ownership and corporate acquisition

strategies, *Strategic Management Journal*, 23: 41–53; C. C. Markides & P. J. Williamson, 1996, Corporate diversification and organizational structure: A resource-based view, *Academy of Management Journal*, 39: 340–367.

7. A. Campbell, M. Goold, & M. Alexander, 1995, Corporate strategy: The question for parenting advantage, *Harvard Business Review*, 73(2): 120–132.

8. J. B. Barney, 2002, *Gaining and Sustaining Competitive Advantage*, 2nd ed., Upper Saddle River, NJ: Prentice Hall.; T. H. Brush, P. Bromiley, & M. Hendrickx, 1999, The relative influence of industry and corporation on business segment performance: An alternative estimate, *Strategic Management Journal*, 20: 519–547; T. H. Brush & P. Bromiley, 1997, What does a small corporate effect mean? A variance components simulation of corporate and business effects, *Strategic Management Journal*, 18: 825–835.

9. C. E. Helfat & K. M. Eisenhardt, 2004, Inter-temporal economies of scope, organizational modularity, and the dynamics of diversification, *Strategic Management Journal*, 25: 1217–1232; D. D. Bergh, 2001, Diversification strategy research at a crossroads: Established, emerging and anticipated paths, in M. A. Hitt, R. E. Freeman, & J. S. Harrison (eds.), *Handbook of Strategic Management*, Oxford, UK: Blackwell Publishers, 363–383.

10. Bergh, Diversification strategy research at a crossroads, 363.

11. C. Kim, S. Kim, & C. Pantzalis, 2001, Firm diversification and earnings volatility: An empirical analysis of U.S.-based MNCs, *American Business Review*, 19(1): 26–38; W. Lewellen, 1971, A pure financial rationale for the conglomerate merger, *Journal of Finance*, 26: 521–537.

12 A.-W. Harzing, 2002, Acquisitions versus greenfield investments: International strategy and management of entry modes, *Strategic Management Journal*, 23: 211–227; J. D. Fisher & Y. Liang, 2000, Is sector diversification more important than regional diversification? *Real Estate Finance*, 17(3): 35–40.

13 Hambrick & Fredrickson, Are you sure you have a strategy?

14 R. P. Rumelt, 1974, *Strategy, Structure, and Economic Performance*, Boston: Harvard Business School Press; L. Wrigley, 1970, Divisional autonomy and diversification, doctoral dissertation, Harvard University, Cambridge, MA.

15 2007, JetBlue Airways Corporation, Hoovers, http://www.hoovers.com/jetblue, February 12.

16 R. D. Ireland, R. E. Hoskisson, & M. A. Hitt, 2006, *Understanding Business Strategy*, Mason, OH: Thomson/South-Western, 139.

17 2007, Time Warner, http://timewarner.broadbandnational.com, February 12; 2007, Comcast, http://www.comcast.com/Corporate, February 12.

18 2007, Johnson & Johnson, Brands from our operating companies, http://www.jnj.com/product/brands/index.htm, February 13.

19 2007, United Technologies, http://www.utc.com/units/power.htm, February 13.

20 L. E. Palich, L. B. Cardinal, & C. C. Miller, 2000, Curvilinearity in the diversification-performance linkage: An examination of over three decades of research, *Strategic Management Journal*, 21: 155–174.

21 E. Stickel, 2001, Uncertainty reduction in a competitive environment, *Journal of Business Research*, 51: 169–177; S. Chatterjee & J. Singh, 1999, Are tradeoffs inherent in diversification moves? A simultaneous model for type of diversification and mode of expansion decisions, *Management Science*, 45: 25–41.

22 R. E. Hoskisson, R. A. Johnson, L. Tihanyi, & R. E. White, 2005, Diversified business groups and corporate refocusing in emerging economies, *Journal of Management*, 31: 941–965; R. A. Johnson, 1996, Antecedents and outcomes of corporate refocusing, *Journal of Management*, 22: 437–481.

23 C. Chung, 2006, Beyond Guanxi: Network contingencies in Taiwanese business groups, *Organization Studies*, 27: 461–480; S. J. Chang & J. Hong, 2002, How much does the business group matter in Korea? *Strategic Management Journal*, 23: 265–274; C. Chung, 2001, Markets, culture and institutions: The emergence of large business groups in Taiwan, 1950s–1970s, *Journal of Management Studies*, 38: 719–745; L. A. Keister, 2000, *Chinese Business Groups: The Structure and Impact of Inter-Firm Relations during Economic Development*, New York: Oxford University Press; T. Khanna & K. Palepu, 1997, Why focused strategies may be wrong for emerging markets, *Harvard Business Review*, 75(4): 41–50.

24 N. Lakshman, 2007, Private equity invades India, *Business Week*, January 8, 40; S. Manikutty, 2000, Family business groups in India: A resource-based view of the emerging trends, *Family Business Review*, 13: 279–292.

25 A. Mishra & M. Akbar, 2007, Empirical examination of diversification strategies in business groups: Evidence from emerging markets, *International Journal of Emerging Markets*, 2: 22–38; 1997, Inside story, *Economist*, December 6, 7–9.

26 Hoskisson, Johnson, Tihanyi, & White, Diversified business groups; K. Dewenter, W. Novaes, & R. H. Pettway, 2001, Visibility versus complexity in business groups: Evidence from Japanese keiretsus, *Journal of Business*, 74: 79–100.

27 B. S. Silverman, 1999, Technological resources and the direction of corporate diversification: Toward an integration of the resource-based view and transaction cost economics, *Administrative Science Quarterly*, 45: 1109–1124; D. Collis & C. A. Montgomery, 1995, Competing on resources: Strategy in the 1990s, *Harvard Business Review*, 73(4): 118–128; M. A. Peteraf, 1993, The cornerstones of competitive advantage: A resource-based view, *Strategic Management Journal*, 14: 179–191.

28 W. S. DeSarbo, C. A. Di Benedetto, M. Song, & I. Sinha, 2005, Revisiting the Miles and Snow strategic framework: Uncovering interrelationships between strategic types, capabilities, environmental uncertainty, and firm performance, *Strategic Management Journal*, 26: 47–74; J. Song, 2002, Firm capabilities and technology ladders, *Strategic Management Journal*, 23: 191–210; M. Farjoun, 1998, The independent and joint effects of the skill and physical bases of relatedness in diversification, *Strategic Management Journal*, 19: 611–630.

29 R. E. Hoskisson & L. W. Busenitz, 2002, Market uncertainty and learning distance in corporate entrepreneurship entry mode choice, in M. A. Hitt, R. D. Ireland, S. M. Camp, & D. L. Sexton (eds.), *Strategic Entrepreneurship: Creating a New Mindset*, Oxford, UK: Blackwell Publishers, 150–172; S. K. McEvily & B. Chakravarthy, 2002, The persistence of knowledge-based advantage: An empirical test for product performance and technological knowledge, *Strategic Management Journal*, 23: 285–305.

30 A. Chandler, 1962, *Strategy and Structure*, Cambridge, MA: MIT Press.

31 J. Greco, 1999, Alfred P. Sloan, Jr. (1875–1966): The original organizational man, *Journal of Business Strategy*, 20(5): 30–31.

32 H. Zhou, 2005, Market structure and organizational form, *Southern Economic Journal*, 71: 705–719; H. Itoh, 2003, Corporate restructuring in Japan, Part I: Can M-form organization manage diverse businesses? *Japanese Economic Review*, 54: 49 73.

33 S. Karim, 2006, Modularity in organizational structure: The reconfiguration of internally developed and acquired business units, *Strategic Management Journal*, 27: 799–823.

34 O. E. Williamson, 1994, Strategizing, economizing, and economic organization, in R. P. Rumelt, D. E. Schendel, & D. J. Teece (eds.), *Fundamental Issues in Strategy*, Cambridge, MA: Harvard Business School Press, 361–401; Chandler, *Strategy and Structure*.

35 R. E. Hoskisson, C. W. L. Hill, & H. Kim, 1993, The multidivisional structure: Organizational fossil or source of value? *Journal of Management*, 19: 269–298.

36 A. D. Chandler, 1994, The functions of the HQ unit in the multibusiness firm, in R. P. Rumelt, D. E. Schendel, & D. J. Teece (eds.), *Fundamental Issues in Strategy*, Cambridge, MA: Harvard Business School Press, 327.

37 O. E. Williamson, 1985, *The Economic Institutions of Capitalism: Firms, Markets, and Relational Contracting*, New York: Macmillan.

38 S. Venkataraman & S. D. Sarasvathy, 2001, Strategy and entrepreneurship: Outlines of an untold story, in M. A. Hitt, R. E. Freeman, & J. S. Harrison (eds.), *Handbook of Strategic Management*, Oxford, UK: Blackwell Publishers, 650–668.

39 Y. Luo, 2002, Contract, cooperation, and performance in international joint ventures, *Strategic Management*

*Journal*, 23: 903–919; D. E. W. Marginson, 2002, Management control systems and their effects on strategy formation at middle-management levels: Evidence from a U.K. organization, *Strategic Management Journal*, 23: 1019–1031.

40. D. F. Kuratko, R. D. Ireland, & J. S. Hornsby, 2001, Improving firm performance through entrepreneurial actions: Acordia's corporate entrepreneurship strategy, *Academy of Management Executive*, 15(4): 60–71.

41. J. S. Harrison & C. H. St. John, 2008, *Foundations in Strategic Management*, 4th ed., Cincinnati: South-Western.

42. D. Incandela, K. L. McLaughlin, & C. S. Shi, 1999, Retailers to the world, *McKinsey Quarterly*, 3: 84–97.

43. R. E. Hoskisson, M. A. Hitt, & R. D. Ireland, 1994, The effects of acquisitions and restructuring strategies (strategic refocusing) on innovation, in G. von Krogh, A. Sinatra, & H. Singh (eds.), *Managing Corporate Acquisition*, London: Macmillan, 144–169.

44. R. E. Hoskisson & M. A. Hitt, 1988, Strategic control and relative R&D investment in multiproduct firms, *Strategic Management Journal*, 9: 605–621.

45. M. S. Gary, 2005, Implementation strategy and performance outcomes in related diversification, *Strategic Management Journal*, 26: 643–664; H. Tanriverdi & N. Venkatraman, 2005, Knowledge relatedness and the performance of multibusiness firms, *Strategic Management Journal*, 26: 97–119.

46. M. W. Peng, S. H. Lee, & D. Y. L. Wang, 2005, What determines the scope of the firm over time? A focus on institutional relatedness, *Academy of Management Review*, 30: 622–633; M. E. Porter, 1985, *Competitive Advantage*, New York: The Free Press, 328.

47. J. W. Lu & P. W. Beamish, 2004, International diversification and firm performance: The S-curve hypothesis, *Academy of Management Journal*, 47: 598–609; R. G. Schroeder, K. A. Bates, & M. A. Junttila, 2002, A resource-based view of manufacturing strategy and the relationship to manufacturing performance, *Strategic Management Journal*, 23: 105–117.

48. 2007, Procter & Gamble, All P&G Products, http://www.pg.com/en_US/products/all_products/index.jhtml, February 13.

49. A. Pehrsson, 2006, Business relatedness and performance: A study of managerial perceptions, *Strategic Management Journal*, 27: 265–282; D. Gupta & Y. Gerchak, 2002, Quantifying operational synergies in a merger/acquisition, *Management Science*, 48: 517–533.

50. A. G. Lafley, 2006, Letter to shareholders, P&G 2006 Annual Report, 3–4.

51. C. H. St. John & J. S. Harrison, 1999, Manufacturing-based relatedness, synergy, and coordination, *Strategic Management Journal*, 20: 129–145.

52. M. L. Marks & P. H. Mirvis, 2000, Managing mergers, acquisitions, and alliances: Creating an effective transition structure, *Organizational Dynamics*, 28(3): 35–47.

53. C. Park, 2003, Prior performance characteristics of related and unrelated acquirers, *Strategic Management Journal*, 24: 471–480; G. Delong, 2001, Stockholder gains from focusing versus diversifying bank mergers, *Journal of Financial Economics*, 2: 221–252; T. H. Brush, 1996, Predicted change in operational synergy and post-acquisition performance of acquired businesses, *Strategic Management Journal*, 17: 1–24; H. Zhang, 1995, Wealth effects of U.S. bank takeovers, *Applied Financial Economics*, 5: 329–336.

54. D. D. Bergh, 1995, Size and relatedness of units sold: An agency theory and resource-based perspective, *Strategic Management Journal*, 16: 221–239.

55. M. Lubatkin & S. Chatterjee, 1994, Extending modern portfolio theory into the domain of corporate diversification: Does it apply? *Academy of Management Journal*, 37: 109–136.

56. A. Van Oijen, 2001, Product diversification, corporate management instruments, resource sharing, and performance, *Academy of Management Best Paper Proceedings* (on CD-ROM, Business Policy and Strategy Division); T. Kono, 1999, A strong head office makes a strong company, *Long Range Planning*, 32(2): 225.

57. Lafley, Letter to shareholders, 6; R. Brooker, 2002, The Un-CEO, *Fortune*, September 12, 88–96.

58. Rumelt, *Strategy, Structure and Economic Performance*.

59. C. C. Markides & P. J. Williamson, 1996, Corporate diversification and organizational structure: A resource-based view, *Academy of Management Journal*, 39: 340–367; C. W. L. Hill, M. A. Hitt, & R. E. Hoskisson, 1992, Cooperative versus competitive structures in related and unrelated diversified firms, *Organization Science*, 3: 501–521.

60. P. F. Drucker, 2002, They're not employees, they're people, *Harvard Business Review*, 80(2): 70–77; J. Robins & M. F. Wiersema, 1995, A resource-based approach to the multibusiness firm: Empirical analysis of portfolio interrelationships and corporate financial performance, *Strategic Management Journal*, 16: 277–299.

61. M. Kotabe, X. Martin, & H. Domoto, 2003, Gaining from vertical partnerships: Knowledge transfer, relationship duration, and supplier performance improvement in the U.S. and Japanese automotive industries, *Strategic Management Journal*, 24: 293–316; M. Y. Brannen, J. K. Liker, & W. M. Fruin, 1999, Recontextualization and factory-to-factory knowledge transfer from Japan to the US: The case of NSK, in J. K. Liker, W. M. Fruin, & P. Adler (eds.), *Remade in America: Transplanting and Transforming Japanese Systems*, New York: Oxford University Press, 117–153; L. Capron, P. Dussauge, & W. Mitchell, 1998, Resource redeployment following horizontal acquisitions in Europe and the United States, 1988–1992, *Strategic Management Journal*, 19: 631–661.

62. L. Capron & N. Pistre, 2002, When do acquirers earn abnormal returns? *Strategic Management Journal*, 23: 781–794.

63. D. J. Miller, 2006, Technological diversity, related diversification and firm performance, *Strategic Management Journal*, 27: 601–619.

64. 2005, Henkel's Lehner to expand adhesives unit through acquisitions, http://www.Bloomberg.com, August 17.

65. J. W. Spencer, 2003, Firms' knowledge-sharing strategies in the global innovation system: Empirical evidence from the flat panel display industry, *Strategic Management Journal*, 24: 217–233.

66. 2007, Virgin Group Ltd., Hoovers, http://www.hoovers.com, February 13.

67. 2007, History of Cooper Industries, http://www.cooperindustries.com/common/aboutCooper/index.cfm, February 13.

68. 2007, Honda Investor Relations, http://world.honda.com/investors, February 15.

69. G. Stalk Jr., 2005, Rotate the core, *Harvard Business Review*, 83(3): 18–19; C. Zellner & D. Fornahl, 2002,

Scientific knowledge and implications for its diffusion, *Journal of Knowledge Management*, 6(2): 190–198.

70. 2007, General Electric, http://www.ge.com/en/company/businesses/index.htm, February 13.

71. 2007, GE to acquire Abbott's *in vitro* and point-of-care diagnostics businesses for $8.13 billion, broadening capabilities in growing global industry, http://home.businesswire.com, February 13.

72. W. G. Shepherd, 1986, On the core concepts of industrial economics, in H. W. deJong & W. G. Shepherd (eds.), *Mainstreams in Industrial Organization*, Boston: Kluwer Publications.

73. D. Genesove & W. P. Mullin, 2001, Rules, communication, and collusion: Narrative evidence from the Sugar Institute Case, *American Economic Review*, 91: 379–398; J. Gimeno & C. Y. Woo, 1999, Multimarket contact, economies of scope, and firm performance, *Academy of Management Journal*, 42: 239–259.

74. 2007, Comcast Digital Voice, http://www.comcast.com/comcastdigitalvoice/default.html, February 13.

75. D. Bricklin, 2007, Installing Verizon FIOS fiber-optic Internet service to my house, http://www.bricklin.com/fiosinstall.htm, February 13.

76. H. A. Haveman & L. Nonnemaker, 2000, Competition in multiple geographic markets: The impact on growth and market entry, *Administrative Science Quarterly*, 45: 232–267.

77. I. Geyskens, J.-B. E. M. Steenkamp, & N. Kumar, 2006, Make, buy, or ally: A transaction cost theory meta-analysis, *Strategic Management Journal*, 49: 519–543; R. Gulati, P. R. Lawrence, & P. Puranam, 2005, Adaptation in vertical relationships: Beyond incentive conflict, *Strategic Management Journal*, 26: 415–440.

78. F. T. Rothaermel, M. A. Hitt, & L. A. Jobe, 2006, Balancing vertical integration and strategic outsourcing: Effects on product portfolio, product success, and firm performance, *Strategic Management Journal*, 27: 1033.

79. Ibid.

80. D. A. Griffin, A. Chandra, & T. Fealey, 2005, Strategically employing natural channels in an emerging market, *Thunderbird International Business Review*, 47(3): 287–311; A. Darr & I. Talmud, 2003, The structure of knowledge and seller-buyer networks in markets for emergent technologies, *Organization Studies*, 24: 443–461.

81. O. E. Williamson, 1996, Economics and organization: A primer, *California Management Review*, 38(2): 131–146.

82. 2007, Smithfield, Acquisitions at a glance, http://www.smithfieldfoods.com/Investor/Acquisitions, February 17; S. Killman, 2001, Smithfield Foods CEO welcomes backlash over its hog farms, *Wall Street Journal*, August 21, B4.

83. M. G. Jacobides, 2005, Industry change through vertical disintegration: How and why markets emerged in mortgage banking, *Academy of Management Journal*, 48: 465–498.

84. L. R. Kopczak & M. E. Johnson, 2003, The supply-chain management effect, *MIT Sloan Management Review*, 3: 27–34; K. R. Harrigan, 2001, Strategic flexibility in the old and new economies, in M. A. Hitt, R. E. Freeman, & J. S. Harrison (eds.), *Handbook of Strategic Management*, Oxford, UK: Blackwell Publishers, 97–123.

85. M. R. Subramani & N. Venkatraman, 2003, Safeguarding investments in asymmetric interorganizational relationships: Theory and evidence, *Academy of Management Journal*, 46: 46–62; R. E. Kranton & D. F. Minehart, 2001, Networks versus vertical integration, *Rand Journal of Economics*, 3: 570–601.

86. 2007, Solectron Corporation, http://www.solectron.com/main/index.html, February 13.

87. P. Kothandaraman & D. T. Wilson, 2001, The future of competition: Value-creating networks, *Industrial Marketing Management*, 30: 379–389.

88. K. M. Eisenhardt & D. C. Galunic, 2000, Coevolving: At last, a way to make synergies work, *Harvard Business Review*, 78(1): 91–111.

89. R. Schoenberg, 2001, Knowledge transfer and resource sharing as value creation mechanisms in inbound continental European acquisitions, *Journal of Euro-Marketing*, 10: 99–114.

90. M. Marr, 2007, The Magic Kingdom looks to hit the road, *Wall Street Journal*, February 8, B1.

91. J. G. March, 1994, *A Primer on Decision Making: How Decisions Happen*, New York: The Free Press, 117–118; J. G. Galbraith & R. K. Kazanjian, *Strategy Implementation: Structure, Systems, and Processes*, St. Paul, MN: West Publishing Co.

92. D. D. Bergh, 1997, Predicting divestitures of unrelated acquisitions: An integrative model of ex ante conditions, *Strategic Management Journal*, 18: 715–732; C. W. L. Hill, 1994, Diversification and economic performance: Bringing structure and corporate management back into the picture, in R. P. Rumelt, D. E. Schendel, & D. J. Teece (eds.), *Fundamental Issues in Strategy*, Boston: Harvard Business School Press, 297–321.

93. M. E. Porter, 1985, *Competitive Advantage*, New York: The Free Press.

94. O. E. Williamson, 1975, *Markets and Hierarchies: Analysis and Antitrust Implications*, New York: Macmillan Free Press.

95. J. McTague, 2002, Security in numbers, *Barron's*, December 30, 26; C. Botosan & M. Harris, 2000, Motivations for changes in disclosure frequency and its consequences: An examination of voluntary quarterly segment disclosure, *Journal of Accounting Research*, 38: 329–353; R. Kochhar & M. A. Hitt, 1998, Linking corporate strategy to capital structure: Diversification strategy, type, and source of financing, *Strategic Management Journal*, 19: 601–610.

96. D. Miller, R. Eisenstat, & N. Foote, 2002, Strategy from the inside out: Building capability-creating organizations, *California Management Review*, 44(3): 37–54; P. Taylor & J. Lowe, 1995, A note on corporate strategy and capital structure, *Strategic Management Journal*, 16: 411–414.

97. J. M. Campa & S. Kedia, 2002, Explaining the diversification discount, *Journal of Finance*, 57: 1731–1762; M. Kwak, 2001, Spinoffs lead to better financing decisions, *MIT Sloan Management Review*, 42(4): 10; O. A. Lamont & C. Polk, 2001, The diversification discount: Cash flows versus returns, *Journal of Finance*, 56: 1693–1721; R. Rajan, H. Servaes, & L. Zingales, 2001, The cost of diversity: The diversification discount and inefficient investment, *Journal of Finance*, 55: 35–79.

98. 2001, Spoilt for choice, *Economist* online, http://www.economist.com, July 5.

99. L. G. Thomas III, 2004, Are we all global now? Local vs. foreign sources of corporate competence: The case of the Japanese pharmaceutical industry, *Strategic Management Journal*, 25(special issue): 865–886.

100 T. R. Eisenmann, 2002, The effects of CEO equity ownership and firm diversification on risk taking, *Strategic Management Journal*, 23: 513–534; D. J. Denis, D. K. Denis, & A. Sarin, 1999, Agency theory and the reference of equity ownership structure on corporate diversification strategies, *Strategic Management Journal*, 20: 1071–1076; R. Amit & J. Livnat, 1988, A concept of conglomerate diversification, *Journal of Management*, 14: 593–604.

101 R. Whittington, 1999, In praise of the evergreen conglomerate, Mastering Strategy (Part 6), *Financial Times*, November 1, 4.

102 T. Khanna, K. G. Palepu, & J. Sinha, 2005, Strategies that fit emerging markets, *Harvard Business Review*, 83(6): 63–76; T. Khanna & J. W. Rivkin, 2001, Estimating the performance effects of business groups in emerging markets, *Strategic Management Journal*, 22: 45–74.

103 T. Khanna & K. Palepu, 2000, Is group affiliation profitable in emerging markets? An analysis of diversified Indian business groups, *Journal of Finance*, 55: 867–892; T. Khanna & K. Palepu, 2000, The future of business groups in emerging markets: Long-run evidence from Chile, *Academy of Management Journal*, 43: 268–285.

104 S. Sams, 2005, Emerging expertise, *Harvard Business Review*, 83(5): 24–26.

105 R. E. Hoskisson, R. A. Johnson, D. Yiu, & W. P. Wan, 2001, Restructuring strategies and diversified business groups: Differences associated with country institutional environments, in M. A. Hitt, R. E. Freeman, & J. S. Harrison (eds.), *Handbook of Strategic Management*, Oxford, UK: Blackwell Publishers, 433–463; S. J. Chang & H. Singh, 1999, The impact of entry and resource fit on modes of exit by multibusiness firms, *Strategic Management Journal*, 20: 1019–1035.

106 J. Robertson, 2005, Hotel chain to be sold, *Dallas Morning News*, http://www.dallasnews.com, June 14.

107 2007, The Blackstone Group, Private equity group, http://www.blackstone.com/private_equity/investment.html, February 13.

108 R. Coff, 2003, Bidding wars over R&D-intensive firms: Knowledge, opportunism, and the market for corporate control, *Academy of Management Journal*, 46: 74–85.

109 S. Nambisan, 2001, Why service businesses are not product businesses, *MIT Sloan Management Review*, 42(4): 72–80; T. A. Doucet & R. M. Barefield, 1999, Client base valuation: The case of a professional service firm, *Journal of Business Research*, 44: 127–133.

110 Hoskisson, Hill, & Kim, The multidivisional structure; R. E. Hoskisson & M. A. Hitt, 1990, Antecedents and performance outcomes of diversification: A review and critique of theoretical perspectives, *Journal of Management*, 16: 461–509.

111 Hill, Hitt, & Hoskisson, Cooperative versus competitive structures, 512.

112 J. Birkinshaw, 2001, Strategies for managing internal competition, *California Management Review*, 44(1): 21–38.

113 2007, Textron, Our company, http://www.textron.com/about/company/index.jsp, February 13.

114 2005, Textron profile, http://www.textron.com, August 27.

115 J. S. Harrison, H. M. O'Neill, & R. E. Hoskisson, 2000, Acquisition strategy and target resistance: A theory of countervailing effects of pre-merger bidding and post-merger integration, in C. Cooper & A. Gregory (eds.), *Advances in Mergers and Acquisitions*, Vol. 1, Greenwich, CT: JAI/Elsevier, 157–182.

116 M. Maremont, 2004, Leadership (a special report); more can be more: Is the conglomerate a dinosaur from a bygone era? The answer is no with a caveat, *Wall Street Journal*, October 24, R4; T. R. Eisenmann & J. L. Bower, 2000, The entrepreneurial M-form: Strategic integration in global media firms, *Organization Science*, 11: 348–355.

117 M. Lubatkin, H. Merchant, & M. Srinivasan, 1997, Merger strategies and shareholder value during times of relaxed antitrust enforcement: The case of large mergers during the 1980s, *Journal of Management*, 23: 61–81.

118 D. P. Champlin & J. T. Knoedler, 1999, Restructuring by design? Government's complicity in corporate restructuring, *Journal of Economic Issues*, 33(1): 41–57.

119 R. M. Scherer & D. Ross, 1990, *Industrial Market Structure and Economic Performance*, Boston: Houghton Mifflin.

120 A. Shleifer & R. W. Vishny, 1994, Takeovers in the 1960s and 1980s: Evidence and implications, in R. P. Rumelt, D. E. Schendel, & D. J. Teece (eds.), *Fundamental Issues in Strategy*, Boston: Harvard Business School Press, 403–422.

121 S. Chatterjee, J. S. Harrison, & D. D. Bergh, 2003, Failed takeover attempts, corporate governance and refocusing, *Strategic Management Journal*, 24: 87–96; Lubatkin, Merchant, & Srinivasan, Merger strategies and shareholder value; D. J. Ravenscraft & R. M. Scherer, 1987, *Mergers, Sell-Offs and Economic Efficiency*, Washington, DC: Brookings Institution, 22.

122 D. A. Zalewski, 2001, Corporate takeovers, fairness, and public policy, *Journal of Economic Issues*, 35: 431–437; P. L. Zweig, J. P. Kline, S. A. Forest, & K. Gudridge, 1995, The case against mergers, *Business Week*, October 30, 122–130; J. R. Williams, B. L. Paez, & L. Sanders, 1988, Conglomerates revisited, *Strategic Management Journal*, 9: 403–414.

123 E. J. Lopez, 2001, New anti-merger theories: A critique, *Cato Journal*, 20: 359–378; 1998, The trustbusters' new tools, *Economist*, May 2, 62–64.

124 2007, American Bar Association, http://www.abanet.org/litigation/committees/antitrust/news.html, February 13.

125 M. C. Jensen, 1986, Agency costs of free cash flow, corporate finance, and takeovers, *American Economic Review*, 76: 323–329.

126 R. Gilson, M. Scholes, & M. Wolfson, 1988, Taxation and the dynamics of corporate control: The uncertain case for tax motivated acquisitions, in J. C. Coffee, L. Lowenstein, & S. Rose-Ackerman (eds.), *Knights, Raiders, and Targets: The Impact of the Hostile Takeover*, New York: Oxford University Press, 271–299.

127 C. Steindel, 1986, Tax reform and the merger and acquisition market: The repeal of the general utilities, *Federal Reserve Bank of New York Quarterly Review*, 11(3): 31–35.

128 M. A. Hitt, J. S. Harrison, & R. D. Ireland, 2001, *Mergers and Acquisitions: A Guide to Creating Value for Stakeholders*, New York: Oxford University Press.

129 C. Park, 2002, The effects of prior performance on the choice between related and unrelated acquisitions: Implications for the performance consequences of diversification strategy, *Journal of Management Studies*, 39: 1003–1019; Y. Chang & H. Thomas, 1989, The impact of diversification strategy on risk-return performance, *Strategic Management Journal*, 10: 271–

284; R. M. Grant, A. P. Jammine, & H. Thomas, 1988, Diversity, diversification, and profitability among British manufacturing companies, 1972–1984, *Academy of Management Journal*, 31: 771–801.

130 Rumelt, *Strategy, Structure and Economic Performance*, 125.

131 M. N. Nickel & M. C. Rodriguez, 2002, A review of research on the negative accounting relationship between risk and return: Bowman's paradox, *Omega*, 30(1): 1–18; R. M. Wiseman & L. R. Gomez-Mejia, 1998, A behavioral agency model of managerial risk taking, *Academy of Management Review*, 23: 133–153; E. H. Bowman, 1982, Risk seeking by troubled firms, *Sloan Management Review*, 23: 33–42.

132 S. Hamm, 2007, Kodak's moment of truth, *Business Week*, February 19, 42.

133 A. E. Bernardo & B. Chowdhry, 2002, Resources, real options, and corporate strategy, *Journal of Financial Economics*, 63: 211–234.

134 N. W. C. Harper & S. P. Viguerie, 2002, Are you too focused? *McKinsey Quarterly* (mid-summer): 29–38; J. C. Sandvig & L. Coakley, 1998, Best practices in small firm diversification, *Business Horizons*, 41(3): 33–40; C. G. Smith & A. C. Cooper, 1988, Established companies diversifying into young industries: A comparison of firms with different levels of performance, *Strategic Management Journal*, 9: 111–121.

135 2007, Brinker International, http://www.brinker.com, February 14.

136 N. M. Kay & A. Diamantopoulos, 1987, Uncertainty and synergy: Towards a formal model of corporate strategy, *Managerial and Decision Economics*, 8: 121–130.

137 2007, Wal-Mart watch, *Business Week*, February 19, 31.

138 R. W. Coff, 1999, How buyers cope with uncertainty when acquiring firms in knowledge-intensive industries: Caveat emptor, *Organization Science*, 10: 144–161.

139 J. G. Matsusaka, 2001, Corporate diversification, value maximization, and organizational capabilities, *Journal of Business*, 74: 409–432; S. J. Chatterjee & B. Wernerfelt, 1991, The link between resources and type of diversification: Theory and evidence, *Strategic Management Journal*, 12: 33–48.

140 W. Keuslein, 2003, The Ebitda folly, *Forbes*, March 17, 165–167; Kochhar & Hitt, Linking corporate strategy to capital structure.

141 L. Capron & J. Hulland, 1999, Redeployment of brands, sales forces, and general marketing management expertise following horizontal acquisitions: A resource-based view, *Journal of Marketing*, 63(2): 41–54.

142 A. M. Knolt, D. J. Bryce, & H. E. Pose, 2003, On the strategic accumulation of intangible assets, *Organization Science*, 14: 192–207; R. D. Smith, 2000, Intangible strategic assets and firm performance: A multi-industry study of the resource-based view, *Journal of Business Strategies*, 17(2): 91–117.

143 A. Rappaport, 2006, 10 ways to create shareholder value, *Harvard Business Review*, 84(9): 66–80.

144 J. G. Combs & M. S. Skill, 2003, Managerialist and human capital explanation for key executive pay premiums: A contingency perspective, *Academy of Management Journal*, 46: 63–73; M. A. Geletkanycz, B. K. Boyd, & S. Finklestein, 2001, The strategic value of CEO external directorate networks: Implications for CEO compensation, *Strategic Management Journal*, 9: 889–898; W. Grossman & R. E. Hoskisson, 1998, CEO pay at the crossroads of Wall Street and Main: Toward the strategic design of executive compensation, *Academy of Management Executive*, 12(1): 43–57; S. Finkelstein & D. C. Hambrick, 1996, *Strategic Leadership: Top Executives and Their Effects on Organizations*, St. Paul, MN: West Publishing Co.

145 J. J. Cordeiro & R. Veliyath, 2003, Beyond pay for performance: A panel study of the determinants of CEO compensation, *American Business Review*, 21(1): 56–66; S. R. Gray & A. A. Cannella Jr., 1997, The role of risk in executive compensation, *Journal of Management*, 23: 517–540; H. Tosi & L. Gomez-Mejia, 1989, The decoupling of CEO pay and performance: An agency theory perspective, *Administrative Science Quarterly*, 34: 169–109.

146 R. Bliss & R. Rosen, 2001, CEO compensation and bank mergers, *Journal of Financial Economics*, 1: 107–138; S. Finkelstein & R. A. D'Aveni, 1994, CEO duality as a double-edged sword: How boards of directors balance entrenchment avoidance and unity of command, *Academy of Management Journal*, 37: 1070–1108.

147 M. Goranova, T. M. Alessandri, P. Brandes, & R. Dharwadkar, 2007, Managerial ownership and corporate diversification: A longitudinal view, *Strategic Management Journal*, 28: 211–225; W. Shen & A. A. Cannella Jr., 2002, Power dynamics within top management and their impacts on CEO dismissal followed by inside succession, *Academy of Management Journal*, 45: 1195–1206; W. Shen & A. A. Cannella Jr., 2002, Revisiting the performance consequences of CEO succession: The impacts of successor type, postsuccession senior executive turnover, and departing CEO tenure, *Academy of Management Journal*, 45: 717–733; Y. Amihud and B. Lev, 1981, Risk reduction as a managerial motive for conglomerate mergers, *Bell Journal of Economics*, 12: 605–617.

148 J. J. Janney, 2002, Eat or get eaten? How equity ownership and diversification shape CEO risk-taking, *Academy of Management Executive*, 14(4): 157–158; J. W. Lorsch, A. S. Zelleke, & K. Pick, 2001, Unbalanced boards, *Harvard Business Review*, 79(2): 28–30; R. E. Hoskisson & T. Turk, 1990, Corporate restructuring: Governance and control limits of the internal market, *Academy of Management Review*, 15: 459–477.

149 M. Kahan & E. B. Rock, 2002, How I learned to stop worrying and love the pill: Adaptive responses to takeover law, *University of Chicago Law Review*, 69(3): 871–915.

150 R. C. Anderson, T. W. Bates, J. M. Bizjak, & M. L. Lemmon, 2000, Corporate governance and firm diversification, *Financial Management*, 29(1): 5–22; J. D. Westphal, 1998, Board games: How CEOs adapt to increases in structural board independence from management, *Administrative Science Quarterly*, 43: 511–537; J. K. Seward & J. P. Walsh, 1996, The governance and control of voluntary corporate spin offs, *Strategic Management Journal*, 17: 25–39; J. P. Walsh & J. K. Seward, 1990, On the efficiency of internal and external corporate control mechanisms, *Academy of Management Review*, 15: 421–458.

151 E. F. Fama, 1980, Agency problems and the theory of the firm, *Journal of Political Economy*, 88: 288–307.

152 R. A. Johnson, 1996, Antecedents and outcomes of corporate refocusing, *Journal of Management*, 22: 439–483; C. Y. Woo, G. E. Willard, & U. S. Dallenbach, 1992, Spin-off performance: A case of overstated expectations, *Strategic Management Journal*, 13: 433–448.

153 M. Wright, R. E. Hoskisson, & L. W. Busenitz, 2001, Firm rebirth: Buyouts as facilitators of strategic growth

and entrepreneurship, *Academy of Management Executive*, 15(1): 111–125; H. Kim & R. E. Hoskisson, 1996, Japanese governance systems: A critical review, in S. B. Prasad (ed.), *Advances in International Comparative Management*, Greenwich, CT: JAI Press, 165–189.

154 J. McTague, 2005, Corporate tangle, *Barron's*, April 4, 19.

155 M. Wiersema, 2002, Holes at the top: Why CEO firings backfire, *Harvard Business Review*, 80(12): 70–77.

156 V. Kisfalvi & P. Pitcher, 2003, Doing what feels right: The influence of CEO character and emotions on top management team dynamics, *Journal of Management Inquiry*, 12(10): 42–66; R. Larsson, K. R. Brousseau, M. J. Driver, & M. Homqvist, 2003, International growth through cooperation: Brand-driven strategies, leadership, and career development in Sweden, *Academy of Management Executive*, 17(1): 7–21; W. G. Bennis & R. J. Thomas, 2002, Crucibles of leadership, *Harvard Business Review*, 80(9): 39–45; W. G. Rowe, 2001, Creating wealth in organizations: The role of strategic leadership, *Academy of Management Executive*, 15(1): 81–94; Finkelstein & D'Aveni, CEO duality as a double-edged sword.

# Acquisition and Restructuring Strategies

**KNOWLEDGE OBJECTIVES**

*Studying this chapter should provide you with the strategic management knowledge needed to:*

1. Explain the popularity of acquisition strategies.
2. Discuss reasons firms use an acquisition strategy to create value.
3. Describe seven problems that work against developing a competitive advantage using an acquisition strategy.
4. Name and describe attributes of effective acquisitions.
5. Define the restructuring strategy and distinguish among its common forms.
6. Explain the short- and long-term outcomes of the different types of restructuring strategies.

In Chapter 8, we studied corporate-level strategies, focusing on types and levels of product diversification strategies that can build core competencies and create competitive advantage. As noted in the previous chapter, diversification allows a firm to create value by productively using excess resources.[1] However, as is the case for each strategy examined in Part 3 of this book, a diversification strategy can be expected to enhance performance only when the firm has the competitive advantages required to successfully use the strategy. In the case of diversification strategies, the firm should possess the competitive advantages needed to form and manage an effective portfolio of businesses and to restructure that portfolio as necessary.[2]

In this chapter, we explore mergers and acquisitions, often combined with a diversification strategy, as a major strategy that firms use throughout the world. Merger and acquisition strategies are developed as a part of the decisions top-level managers make during the strategic management process.[3] In the latter half of the 20th century, mergers and acquisitions became a popular strategy used by major corporations. Even smaller and more focused firms began employing merger and acquisition strategies to grow and enter new markets.[4] However, these strategies are not without problems, and many acquisitions fail. Thus, the focus of this chapter is on how mergers and acquisitions can be used to produce value for the firm's stakeholders while avoiding the pitfalls of the acquisition process.[5]

Before describing attributes associated with effective mergers and acquisitions, we examine the most significant problems companies experience when pursuing these strategies. For example, when a merger or acquisition contributes to poor performance, a firm may deem it necessary to restructure its operations. Closing the chapter are descriptions of three restructuring strategies, as well as the short- and long-term outcomes resulting from their use. Setting the stage for these topics is an examination of the popularity of mergers and acquisitions and a discussion of the differences among mergers, acquisitions, and takeovers.

# The Popularity of Merger and Acquisition Strategies

The acquisition strategy has been popular among U.S. firms for many years. Some believe that this strategy has played a central role in an effective restructuring of U.S. businesses over the past few decades.[6] Increasingly, acquisition strategies are becoming more popular with firms in other nations and economic regions, including Europe.[7] In fact, a large percentage of acquisitions in recent years have been made across country borders (i.e., a firm headquartered in one country acquiring a firm headquartered in another country).[8] For example, in 2006 Mittal Steel, based in the Netherlands, acquired Arcelor of Luxembourg, creating Arcelor Mittal, the largest steel company in the world.[9]

Five waves of mergers and acquisitions occurred in the 20th century, with the last two in the 1980s and 1990s.[10] There were 55,000 acquisitions valued at $1.3 trillion in the 1980s, but acquisitions in the 1990s exceeded $11 trillion in value.[11] World economies, particularly the U.S. economy, slowed in the new millennium, reducing the number of completed mergers and acquisitions.[12] The annual value of mergers and acquisitions peaked in 2000 at about $3.41 trillion and fell to about $1.75 trillion in 2001.[13] However, as the worldwide economy improved, acquisition activity increased again, and the 2006 level was at a new record of approximately $3.44 trillion.[14] Furthermore, lots of corporate cash and increased involvement by private equity firms was expected to make 2007 even stronger, especially in the mining and energy, manufacturing, health care, media, finance, and transportation industries.[15]

Strategic decisions regarding the use of a merger or acquisition strategy are complex because of a highly uncertain global economy.[16] However, these strategies are sometimes used precisely because of this uncertainty. A firm may make an acquisition to increase its market power because of a competitive threat, to enter a new market because of the opportunity available in that market, or to spread the risk due to the uncertain environment.[17] In addition, as volatility brings undesirable changes to its primary markets, a firm may acquire other companies as options that allow the firm to shift its core business into different markets.[18]

A merger or acquisition strategy should be used only when the acquiring firm will be able to increase its economic value through ownership and the use of an acquired firm's assets.[19] Evidence suggests, however, that, at least for acquiring firms, acquisition strategies may not result in these desirable outcomes.[20] Researchers have found that shareholders of acquired firms often earn above-average returns from an acquisition, while shareholders of acquiring firms are less likely to do so, typically earning returns from the transaction that are close to zero.[21] In approximately two-thirds of all acquisitions, the acquiring firm's stock price falls immediately after the intended transaction is announced.[22] During one three-year period, acquiring firm shareholders lost $0.12 per share on average when a deal was announced.[23] When pharmaceutical company Gilead Sciences announced it would acquire Myogen, its share price dropped 10 percent compared with an increase of 50 percent in Myogen stock (this acquisition will be examined in more depth later in this chapter).[24] A negative response such as this is an indication of investor skepticism about the likelihood that the acquirer will be able to achieve the synergies required to justify the premium paid.[25]

## Mergers, Acquisitions, and Takeovers: What Are the Differences?

Before examining the reasons firms engage in mergers and acquisitions, the problems they encounter, and the keys to success, we should define a few terms that will make the discussion easier to follow. A **merger** is a strategy through which two firms agree to integrate their operations on a relatively co-equal basis. A merger of equals took place when, in 2006, Regions Financial Corp. merged with AmSouth Bancorp to form the tenth largest U.S. bank.[26] There are not many true mergers, however, because one party is usually dominant. For example, the DaimlerChrysler merger was originally envisioned as a combination of equals, but Daimler executives quickly became dominant.[27]

We define an **acquisition** as a strategy through which one firm buys a controlling, 100 percent interest in another firm with the intent of making the acquired firm a subsidiary business within its portfolio. *Partial acquisitions* occur when the acquiring firm obtains less than 100 percent of the target firm. To avoid confusion, the word *acquisition* will always refer to a complete acquisition in the remainder of this book. In the case of an acquisition, the management of the acquired firm reports to the management of the acquiring firm.

While most mergers are friendly transactions, acquisitions include unfriendly take-overs. A **takeover** is a special type of acquisition strategy wherein the target firm did not solicit the acquiring firm's bid. Oftentimes, takeover bids spawn bidding wars. For exam-ple, in October 2006 India's Tata Steel made a bid of $8 billion for the British steelmaker Corus Group. In November Companhia Siderurgica Nacional (CSN) of Brazil announced that it intended to make a competing bid. In December, in anticipation of the CSN bid, Tata sweetened its offer to $9.38 billion. CSN's actual bid came in at $9.8 billion, but Tata eventually won the contest at a price of $12 billion.[28] As this example points out, the bid-ding process is one reason why it is difficult for the acquiring firm to create value in an acquisition.

**Hostile takeovers** are not only unexpected, but undesired by the target firm's man-agers. When Gold Kist, an Atlanta-based poultry producer, turned down an unsolicited takeover bid from Pilgrim's Pride, another poultry company based in Texas, Pilgrim's Pride initiated a proxy battle "to appeal directly to shareholders." After four months, Gold Kist's board of directors finally agreed to sell the company for $1.1 billion. The deal makes Pilgrim's Pride the largest chicken producer in the United States. According to chief finan-cial officer Richard Cogdill, the hostile bid "might not have been friendly to members of the board or management, [but] our proposal was very friendly to shareholders."[29]

Acquisitions are much more common than mergers and takeovers; as a result, this chapter focuses on acquisitions.

## Reasons for Acquisitions

There are several reasons that support the use of an acquisition strategy. Although each reason can provide a legitimate rationale for an acquisition, the acquisition may not neces-sarily lead to a competitive advantage.

### Increase Market Power

A primary reason for acquisitions is to achieve greater market power.[30] *Market power* (de-fined in Chapter 8) exists when a firm is able to sell its goods or services above competitive levels or when the costs of its primary or support activities are below those of its competi-tors. Market power usually is derived from the size of the firm and its resources and capa-bilities to compete in the marketplace.[31] It is also affected by the firm's share of the mar-ket. Therefore, most acquisitions designed to achieve greater market power entail buying a competitor, a supplier, a distributor, or a business in a highly related industry to allow exer-cise of a core competence and to gain competitive advantage in the acquiring firm's primary market. One goal in achieving market power is to become a market leader.[32] For example, the acquisition of Compaq by Hewlett-Packard (along with some missteps by Dell) ulti-mately led the combined company to become the market leader in the PC market.[33]

Firms use horizontal, vertical, and related acquisitions to increase their market power.

**Horizontal Acquisitions.** The acquisition of a company competing in the same industry in which the acquiring firm competes is referred to as a *horizontal acquisition*. GateHouse Media is pursuing a horizontal acquisition strategy by buying small-town papers across the United States to add to its already large portfolio of small-town papers. It currently controls more than 400 publications in places like Heber Springs, Arkansas, and Canandaigua, New York. Although papers in large U.S. cities are struggling as more people turn to the Internet for news, GateHouse has discovered that small towns still represent solid markets. In 2007 the company is expected to generate $23 million in profit on $400 million in revenues.[34]

Horizontal acquisitions increase a firm's market power by exploiting cost-based and rev-enue-based synergies.[35] Research suggests that horizontal acquisitions of firms with simi-lar characteristics result in higher performance than when firms with dissimilar charac-teristics combine their operations.[36] Examples of important similar characteristics include strategy, managerial styles, and resource allocation patterns. Similarities in these charac-teristics make the integration of the two firms proceed more smoothly.[37] Horizontal acqui-sitions are often most effective when the acquiring firm integrates the acquired firm's assets with its assets, but only after evaluating and divesting excess capacity and assets that do not complement the newly combined firm's core competencies.[38]

**Vertical Acquisitions.** A *vertical acquisition* refers to a firm acquiring a supplier or distrib-utor of one or more of its goods or services. A firm becomes vertically integrated through this type of acquisition, in that it controls additional parts of the value chain (see Chapter 4). For example, railroad company Burlington Northern Santa Fe Corp. acquired Pro-Am Trans-portation Services, a company specializing in third-party logistics, which strengthens Burl-ington Northern's integration of transportation services and warehousing.[39]

**Related Acquisitions.** The acquisition of a firm in a highly related industry is called a *re-lated acquisition*. Cooper Industries, a diversified manufacturer of electrical products, tools, and hardware, acquired WPI Interconnect Products, a privately owned manufacturer of cus-tom connectors and cable assemblies. Cooper Industries' CEO Kirk S. Hachigian pointed out that "WPI's capabilities add substantial depth to our portfolio of highly customized specification-grade connector technologies for use in harsh, heavy-duty and hazardous lo-cations." He noted that this acquisition, along with previous acquisitions, expands the com-panies offerings of "highly engineered interconnect products" and continues "the theme we laid out for investors in the 2006 Outlook meeting, specifically that we will build on existing platforms in the Cooper portfolio, expanding into highly customized and technical adjacen-cies that leverage our core strengths and represent solid profitable growth opportunities."[40]

Acquisitions intended to increase market power are subject to regulatory review and to analysis by financial markets. In September 2006 U.S. specialty pharmaceutical and medication delivery company Hospira announced it would acquire the Australian generic-pharmaceutical maker Mayne Pharma for $2 billion. The deal was subjected to antitrust review by the U.S. Department of Justice and was approved in January 2007.[41] Thus, firms seeking growth and market power through acquisitions must understand the political/legal segment of the general environment (see Chapter 3) in order to successfully use an acquisi-tion strategy.

## Overcome Entry Barriers

*Barriers to entry* (introduced in Chapter 3) are factors associated with the market or with the firms currently operating in it that increase the expense and difficulty new ventures face as they try to enter that particular market. For example, well-established competitors may have substantial economies when manufacturing their products. In addition, enduring relationships with customers often create product loyalties that are difficult for new entrants to overcome. When facing differentiated products, new entrants typically must spend considerable resources to advertise their goods or services and may find it necessary to sell at a price below competitors' to entice customers.

Facing the entry barriers created by economies of scale and differentiated products, a new entrant may find the acquisition of an established company to be more effective than entering the market as a competitor offering a new good or service that is unfamiliar to current buyers. In fact, the higher the barriers to market entry, the greater the probability that a firm will acquire an existing firm to overcome them. Although an acquisition can be expensive, it does provide the new entrant with immediate market access.

Firms trying to enter international markets often face quite steep entry barriers.[42] In response, acquisitions are commonly used to overcome those barriers.[43] At least for large multinational corporations, another indicator of the importance of entering and then competing successfully in international markets is the fact that five emerging markets (China, India, Brazil, Mexico, and Indonesia) are among the 12 largest economies in the world, with a combined purchasing power that is already one-half that of the Group of Seven industrial nations (United States, Japan, Britain, France, Germany, Canada, and Italy).[44]

Acquisitions made between companies with headquarters in different countries are called *cross-border acquisitions*. These acquisitions are often made to overcome entry barriers. Compared with a cross-border alliance (discussed in Chapter 10), a cross-border acquisition gives a firm more control over its international operations.[45] Acquisitions often represent the fastest means to enter international markets and help firms overcome the liabilities associated with such strategic moves.[46] The results of cross-border acquisitions are somewhat encouraging, in that research evidence indicates that "the average cross-border acquisition reflects an increase of about 7.5 percent in the value of the combined firms relative to their pre-acquisition value."[47]

Historically, U.S. firms have been the most active acquirers of companies outside their domestic markets.[48] However, in the global economy, companies throughout the world are increasingly choosing this strategic option. In recent years, cross-border acquisitions have represented as much as 45 percent of the total number of acquisitions made annually. Because of relaxed regulations, the amount of cross-border activity among nations within the European community also continues to increase. Some analysts believe that the growth of cross-border acquisitions in Europe stems from the fact that many large European corporations have approached the limits of growth within their domestic markets and thus seek growth in other markets. Additionally, they are trying to achieve market power to compete effectively throughout the European Union and thus have made acquisitions in other European countries.

European and Asian firms are also acquiring North American firms with increasing frequency. In one recent example, Evraz Group, one of Russia's largest vertically integrated steelmakers, announced it would acquire Oregon Steel Mills for $2.3 billion. According to Evraz chairman Alexander Frolov, the acquisition will make the combined company "the leading rail producer globally" and will "secure an important place on the attractive plate market and in the expanding pipe business in North America."[49] The U.S. Committee on Foreign Investment approved the acquisition in January 2007.

## Reduce Costs and Risks Associated with New Product Development

Developing new products internally and successfully introducing them into the marketplace often require significant investments of a firm's resources, including time, making it difficult to quickly earn a profitable return.[50] Also of concern to firms' managers is achieving adequate returns from the capital invested to develop and commercialize new products—an estimated 88 percent of innovations fail to achieve adequate returns. Perhaps contributing to these less-than-desirable rates of return is the successful imitation of approximately 60 percent of innovations within four years after the patents are obtained. Because of outcomes such as these, managers often perceive internal product development as a costly, high-risk activity.[51]

Acquisitions are another means a firm can use to gain access to new products and to current products that are new to the firm. Compared to internal product development processes, acquisitions provide more predictable returns. Because of this, managers may view acquisitions as lowering risk.[52] Possibly for this reason, acquisitions that involve extensive bidding wars are common in high-technology industries.[53]

Acquisition activity is also extensive throughout the pharmaceutical industry, in which firms frequently use acquisitions to overcome the high costs of developing products internally and to increase the predictability of returns on their investments. High acquisition prices are also common. For instance, Gilead Sciences paid approximately $2.5 billion to acquire Myogen, a company with sales of only $7 million. At the time, 80 percent of Gilead's revenues and virtually all of its robust growth was coming from an HIV drug called Atripla. Although Gilead arguably paid too much for the company, Myogen had a promising drug for treating hypertension that offered instant diversification value.[54]

While acquisitions have become a common means of avoiding risky internal ventures (and therefore risky R&D investments), they may also become a substitute for innovation.[55] This can be a problem because innovation is so vital to the future competitiveness of firms.[56] For instance, at the time of the Myogen acquisition, Gilead was spending only about 13 percent of its revenues on R&D, a very small amount for the pharmaceutical industry.[57] Furthermore, as mentioned previously, acquisitions can depress firm performance. Thus, acquisitions are not a risk-free alternative to entering new markets.

## Increase Speed to Market

Compared with internal product development, acquisitions result in more rapid market entries.[58] Entry speed is important, in that quick market entries are critical to successful competition in the highly uncertain, complex global environment.[59] Acquisitions provide rapid access both to new markets and to new capabilities. For instance, Google's acquisition of YouTube for $1.65 billion in 2006 gave the company immediate entry into the online video market segment.[60]

## Increase Diversification and Reshape the Firm's Competitive Scope

Firms also use acquisitions to diversify. Based on experience and the insights resulting from it, firms typically find it easier to develop and introduce new products in markets they currently serve. In contrast, it is difficult for companies to develop products that differ from their current lines for markets in which they lack experience. Thus, it is uncommon for a firm to develop new products internally to diversify its product lines.[61] Using acquisitions to diversify a firm is the quickest and, typically, the easiest way to change a firm's portfolio of businesses.[62]

Both related and unrelated diversification strategies can be implemented through acquisitions.[63] However, research has shown that the more related the acquired firm is to the acquiring firm, the greater the probability that the acquisition will be successful.[64] Thus, horizontal acquisitions (through which a firm acquires a competitor) and other types of related acquisitions tend to contribute more to the firm's ability to create value than acquiring a company that operates in quite different product markets from those in which the firm competes.[65] For example, firms in the financial services industry have become more diversified over time, often through acquisitions. One study suggests that these firms are diversifying not only to provide a more complete line of products for their customers but also to create strategic flexibility. In other words, they diversify into some product lines to provide options for future services they may wish to emphasize. As noted earlier, such acquisitions are a means of dealing with an uncertain competitive environment.[66]

Firms may use diversifying acquisitions to alter the scope of their activities. Scope falls within the major strategy element of arenas, defined in Chapter 2 as the breadth of a firm's activities across products, markets, geographic regions, core technologies, and value-creation stages.[67] A firm may desire to alter its scope if the intensity of competitive rivalry in an industry is affecting profitability.[68] To reduce the negative effect of an intense rivalry on their financial performance, firms may use acquisitions to reduce their dependence on one or more products or markets. Many years ago General Electric reduced its emphasis on electronics markets by making acquisitions in the financial services industry. Today, GE gets about half of its revenues and profits from service businesses.[69]

## Learn and Develop New Capabilities

Some acquisitions are made to gain capabilities that the firm does not possess. For example, acquisitions may be used to acquire a special technological capability.[70] Research has shown that firms can broaden their knowledge base and reduce inertia through acquisitions.[71] Therefore, acquiring other firms with skills and capabilities that differ from its own helps the acquiring firm learn new knowledge and remain agile.[72] Using new capabilities to pioneer new products and to enter markets quickly can create advantageous market positions.[73]

Of course, firms are better able to learn these capabilities if they share some similar properties with the firm's current capabilities. Thus, firms should seek to acquire companies with different but related and complementary capabilities in order to build their own knowledge base.[74] In 2006 the software giant Oracle bought Stellant for $440 million. They are both software companies, but Stellant gives Oracle needed expertise in non-database information management. Oracle provides Stellant with a powerful brand name, distribution network, and the capital needed for growth. Consequently, their strengths are complementary.[75]

---

## Problems in Achieving Acquisition Success

Acquisition strategies based on legitimate reasons described in this chapter can increase value and help firms to earn above-average returns. However, acquisition strategies are not risk free. Figure 9.1 shows reasons for the use of acquisition strategies and potential problems with such strategies.

Research suggests that perhaps 20 percent of all mergers and acquisitions are successful, approximately 60 percent produce disappointing results, and the remaining 20 percent are clear failures.[76] Successful acquisitions generally involve a well-conceived strategy in selecting the target, avoiding too high of a premium, and an effective integration process.[77] As shown in Figure 9.1, several problems may prevent successful acquisitions.

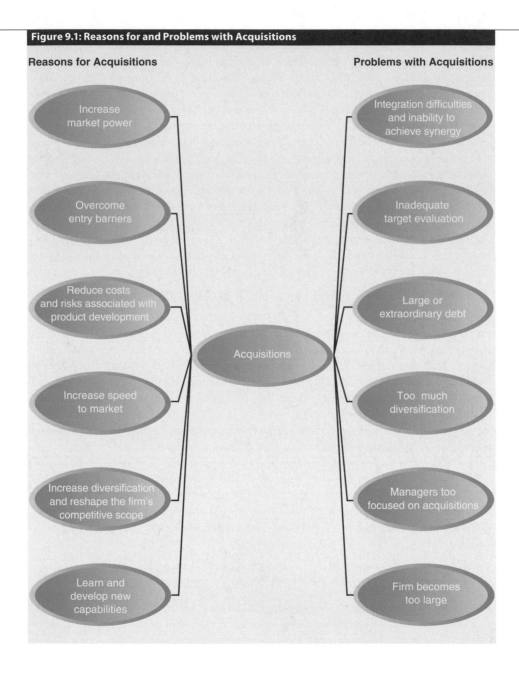

**Figure 9.1: Reasons for and Problems with Acquisitions**

Reasons for Acquisitions

- Increase market power
- Overcome entry barriers
- Reduce costs and risks associated with product development
- Increase speed to market
- Increase diversification and reshape the firm's competitive scope
- Learn and develop new capabilities

Acquisitions

Problems with Acquisitions

- Integration difficulties and inability to achieve synergy
- Inadequate target evaluation
- Large or extraordinary debt
- Too much diversification
- Managers too focused on acquisitions
- Firm becomes too large

## Integration Difficulties and an Inability to Achieve Synergy

The importance of a successful integration should not be underestimated.[78] Without it, an acquisition is unlikely to produce positive returns. As suggested by a researcher studying the process, "managerial practice and academic writings show that the post-acquisition integration phase is probably the single most important determinant of shareholder value creation (and equally of value destruction) in mergers and acquisitions."[79]

Integration is complex and involves a large number of activities. Integration challenges include melding two disparate corporate cultures, linking different financial and control systems, building effective working relationships (particularly when management styles differ), and resolving problems regarding the status of the newly acquired firm's executives.[80] As this list suggests, many of the important integration activities revolve around people. It is especially important to focus on effective management of human capital in the target firm after an acquisition because that is where much of an organization's knowledge is contained.[81] Turnover of key personnel from the acquired firm can have a negative effect on the performance of the merged firm.[82] The loss of key personnel, such as critical managers, weakens the acquired firm's capabilities and reduces its value. If implemented effectively, the integration process can have a positive effect on target firm managers and reduce the probability that key human resources will leave.[83]

If the potential for synergy exists between an acquired and a target firm, the potential is released primarily during the integration stage.[84] Defined in Chapter 8, *synergy* refers to the value created by business units working together that would not have been created in those same units working independently. That is, synergy exists when assets are worth more when used in conjunction than when used separately.[85] Synergy is created by the efficiencies derived from economies of scale and economies of scope and by sharing resources (e.g., human capital and knowledge) across the businesses of the combined firm.[86] Externally acquired capabilities do not always integrate well with the acquiring firm's internal processes and procedures—a reality necessitating committed effort during the integration stage.[87]

A firm develops a competitive advantage through an acquisition strategy only when a transaction generates private synergy.[88] *Private synergy* is created when the combination and integration of the acquiring and acquired firms' assets yield capabilities and core competencies that could not be developed by combining and integrating either firm's assets with another company. Private synergy is possible when firms' assets are complementary in unique ways; that is, the unique type of asset complementarity is not possible by combining either company's assets with another firm's assets.[89] Because of its uniqueness, private synergy is difficult for competitors to understand and imitate. However, private synergy is difficult to create.

Even if the potential for private synergy exists and managers work diligently to realize it during the integration process, it is still possible that the net effect of an acquisition on firm value will be negative because the costs exceed the benefits. Beyond the purchase price, a firm's ability to account for costs that are necessary to create anticipated revenue- and cost-based synergies affects the acquisition's success.[90] Firms experience several types of expenses when trying to create private synergy through acquisitions. Called *transaction costs*, these expenses are incurred when firms use acquisition strategies to create synergy.[91] Transaction costs may be direct or indirect. Direct costs include legal fees and charges from investment bankers who complete due diligence for the acquiring firm. Indirect costs include managerial time to evaluate target firms and then to complete negotiations, as well as the loss of key managers and employees after an acquisition.[92] Another type of costs in-volves the actual time and resources used for integration processes, such as the time man-agers spend in meetings and the cost of integrating information systems, manufacturing systems, R&D processes, and retirement systems. Firms tend to underestimate these costs when determining the value of the synergy that may be created by combining and integrat-ing the acquired firm's assets with the acquiring firm's assets. This may help explain why so many acquisitions fail to live up to expectations.

## Inadequate Evaluation of Target

*Due diligence* is a process through which a potential acquirer evaluates a target firm for ac-quisition. In an effective due-diligence process hundreds of items are examined in areas as diverse as the financing for the intended transaction, differences in cultures between the acquiring and target firm, tax consequences of the transaction, and actions that would be necessary to successfully meld the two workforces. Due diligence is commonly performed by investment bankers, accountants, lawyers, and management consultants specializing in that activity, although firms actively pursuing acquisitions may form their own internal due-diligence team.[93]

The failure to complete an effective due-diligence process may easily result in the ac-quiring firm paying an excessive premium for the target company. In fact, research shows that without due diligence, "the purchase price is driven by the pricing of other 'comparable' acquisitions rather than by a rigorous assessment of where, when, and how management can drive real performance gains. [In these cases], the price paid may have little to do with achievable value."[94]

Many firms once used investment banks to perform their due diligence, but in the post-Enron era the process is increasingly performed in-house. While investment bankers such as Credit Suisse First Boston and Citibank still play a large role in due diligence for large mergers and acquisitions, their role in smaller mergers and acquisitions seems to be de-creasing. A growing number of companies are building their own internal operations to offer advice about mergers and how to finance them. However, although investment banks are playing a lesser role, there will always be the need for an outside opinion for a company's board of directors—to reassure them about a planned merger and reduce their liability.[95]

## Large or Extraordinary Debt

To finance a number of acquisitions completed during the 1980s and 1990s, some compa-nies significantly increased their levels of debt. A financial innovation called junk bonds helped make this possible. *Junk bonds* are a financing option through which risky acquisi-tions are financed with money (debt) that provides a large potential return to lenders (bond-holders). Because junk bonds are unsecured obligations that are not tied to specific assets for collateral, interest rates for these high-risk debt instruments sometimes reached be-tween 18 and 20 percent during the 1980s.[96] Some prominent financial economists viewed debt as a means to discipline managers, causing them to act in shareholders' best interests.[97] Junk bonds are now used less frequently to finance acquisitions, and the conviction that debt disciplines managers is less strong.

The $12 billion acquisition of Corus Group by Tata Steel, mentioned earlier in this chapter, came with an enormous debt burden. Analysts who were following the deal de-scribed the implications of the debt for Tata: "Even Tata's initial bid of $8 billion drew the attention of credit rating agencies such as Standard & Poor's, which placed Tata on its Cred-itWatch list with 'negative implications' back in October. Investors, meanwhile, dumped

Tata Steel shares with unrelenting fury in trading on the Bombay Stock Exchange, where the benchmark stock index fell about one percent. Tata Steel shares were pounded down 11 percent."[98]

High debt can have several negative effects on the firm. For example, because high debt increases the likelihood of bankruptcy, it can lead agencies such as Moody's and Standard & Poor's to downgrade the firm's credit rating.[99] In addition, high debt may preclude needed investment in activities that contribute to the firm's long-term success, such as R&D, human resource training, and marketing.[100] Still, use of leverage can be a positive force in a firm's development, allowing it to take advantage of attractive expansion opportunities. Too much leverage (such as extraordinary debt), however, can lead to negative outcomes, including postponing or eliminating investments, such as critical R&D expenditures, that are necessary to create value over the long term.

## Too Much Diversification

As explained in Chapter 7, diversification strategies can lead to improved firm performance. In general, firms using related diversification strategies outperform those using unrelated diversification strategies. However, conglomerates, formed by using an unrelated diversification strategy, can be successful. United Technologies and General Electric are examples of conglomerates that have been highly successful with their unrelated acquisition strategies.[101]

At some point, however, firms become overdiversified. The level at which overdiversification occurs varies across companies because each firm has different capabilities to manage diversification. Recall from Chapter 8 that related diversification requires more information processing than does unrelated diversification. The need for related diversified firms to process more information of greater diversity is such that they become overdiversified with a smaller number of business units, compared with firms using an unrelated diversification strategy.[102] Regardless of the type of diversification strategy implemented, however, declines in performance result from overdiversification, after which business units are often divested.[103] The pattern of excessive diversification followed by divestments of underperforming business units was frequently observed among U.S. firms from the 1960s through the 1980s.[104]

Even when a firm is not overdiversified, a high level of diversification can have a negative effect on the firm's long-term performance. For example, the scope created by additional amounts of diversification often causes managers to rely on financial rather than strategic controls to evaluate business units' performances. Top-level executives often rely on financial controls to assess the performance of business units when they do not have a rich understanding of business units' objectives and strategies. Use of financial controls, such as return on investment (ROI), causes individual business-unit managers to focus on short-term outcomes at the expense of long-term investments. When long-term investments are reduced to increase short-term profits, a firm's overall ability to create value may be harmed.[105]

Another problem resulting from too much diversification is the tendency for acquisitions to become substitutes for innovation. Earlier in this chapter, we mentioned that sometimes firms make acquisitions in order to avoid the costs and risks associated with new product development. In other words, they buy innovation instead of producing it internally. This problem is magnified in firms that overdiversify because a reinforcing cycle evolves.[106] Costs associated with acquisitions may result in fewer allocations to activities, such as R&D, that are linked to innovation. Without adequate support, a firm's innovation skills begin to atrophy. Without internal innovation skills, the only option available to a firm is to make still additional acquisitions to gain access to innovation. Evidence suggests that firms that use acquisitions as a substitute for internal innovation eventually encounter performance problems.[107]

## Managers Too Focused on Acquisitions

Typically, a fairly substantial amount of managerial time and energy is required for acquisition strategies to enhance the firm's value. Activities with which managers become involved include (1) searching for viable acquisition candidates, (2) completing effective due-diligence processes, (3) preparing for negotiations, and (4) managing the integration process after the acquisition is completed.

Top-level managers do not personally gather all data and information required to make acquisitions. However, these executives do make critical decisions about the firms to be targeted, the nature of the negotiations, and so forth. Company experiences show that participating in and overseeing the activities required for making acquisitions can divert managerial attention from other matters that are necessary for long-term competitive success, such as identifying and taking advantage of other opportunities and interacting with important external stakeholders.[108] Evidence suggests that the acquisition process can create a short-term perspective and a greater aversion to risk among top-level executives in a target firm.[109]

Both theory and research suggest that managers can become overly involved in the process of making acquisitions.[110] One observer suggested: "The urge to merge is still like an addiction in many companies: doing deals is much more fun and interesting that fixing fundamental problems. So, as in dealing with any other addiction or temptation, maybe it is best to just say no."[111] When acquisitions do fail, leaders are tempted to blame failure on others or on unforeseen circumstances rather than on their excessive involvement in the acquisition process.[112] An active board that questions decisions regarding acquisitions can help counteract the tendency for managers to become too involved in acquisitions.[113]

## Firm Becomes Too Large

Most acquisitions create a larger firm that should help increase its economies of scale. These economies can then lead to more efficient operations; for example, the two sales organizations can be integrated using fewer sales representatives because a sales representative can sell the products of both firms (particularly if the products of the acquiring and target firms are highly related).

There is a managerial incentive to grow larger through acquisitions because size serves as a defense against takeovers.[114] Also, many firms seek increases in size because of the potential economies of scale and enhanced market power (discussed earlier). At some level, however, the additional costs required to manage the larger firm will exceed the benefits of the economies of scale and additional market power. In addition, the complexities generated by the larger size often lead managers to implement more bureaucratic controls to manage the combined firm's operations. *Bureaucratic controls* are formalized supervisory and behavioral rules and policies designed to ensure that decisions and actions across different units of a firm are consistent. However, through time, formalized controls often lead to relatively rigid and standardized managerial behavior. Certainly, in the long run, the diminished flexibility that accompanies rigid and standardized managerial behavior may produce less innovation as well as fewer searches for entrepreneurial opportunities (see Chapter 12). Because of innovation's importance to competitive success, the bureaucratic controls resulting from a large organization (that is, built by acquisitions) can have a detrimental effect on performance.[115]

## Effective Acquisitions

Earlier in the chapter, we noted that acquisition strategies do not consistently produce above-average returns for the acquiring firm's shareholders.[116] Nonetheless, some companies are able to create value when using an acquisition strategy.[117] Results from a research study shed light on the differences between unsuccessful and successful acquisition strategies and suggest that there is a pattern of actions and attributes that can improve the probability of acquisition success.[118] Table 9.1 summarizes the attributes and actions and the results of successful acquisitions.

First, the study shows that when the target firm's assets *complement* the acquired firm's assets, an acquisition is more successful. With complementary assets, integrating two firms' operations has a higher probability of creating synergy. In fact, integrating two firms with complementary assets frequently produces unique capabilities and core competencies.[119] With complementary assets, the acquiring firm can maintain its focus on core businesses and leverage the complementary assets and capabilities from the acquired firm. Oftentimes, targets were selected and "groomed" by establishing a working relationship sometime before the acquisition.[120] As discussed in Chapter 7, strategic alliances are sometimes used to test the feasibility of a future merger or acquisition.[121]

The study's results also show that *friendly acquisitions*—in which firms work together to find ways to integrate their operations to create synergy—facilitate integration of the firms involved in an acquisition.[122] In hostile takeovers, animosity often results between the two top management teams, a condition that in turn affects working relationships in the newly created firm. As a result, more key personnel in the acquired firm may be lost, and those who remain may resist the changes necessary to integrate the two firms.[123] With effort,

### Table 9.1: Attributes and Results of Successful Acquisitions

| Attributes | Results |
|---|---|
| 1. Acquired firm has assets or resources that are complementary to the acquiring firm's core business | 1. High probability of synergy and competitive advantage by maintaining strengths |
| 2. Acquisition is friendly | 2. Faster and more effective integration and possibly lower premiums |
| 3. Acquiring firm conducts effective due diligence to select target firms and evaluate the target firm's health (financial, cultural, and human resources) | 3. Firms with strongest complementarities are acquired and overpayment is avoided |
| 4. Acquiring firm has financial slack (cash or a favorable debt position) | 4. Financing (debt or equity) is easier and less costly to obtain |
| 5. Merged firm maintains a low to moderate debt position | 5. Lower financing cost, lower risk (e.g., of bankruptcy), and avoidance of trade-offs that are associated with high debt |
| 6. Sustained and consistent emphasis on R&D and innovation | 6. Maintain long-term competitive advantage in markets |
| 7. Has experience with change and is flexible and adaptable | 7. Faster and more effective integration facilitates achievement of synergy |

cultural clashes can be overcome, and fewer key managers and employees will become discouraged and leave.[124] Efficient and effective integration helps produce the desired synergy in the newly created firm.

Additionally, *effective due-diligence processes* involving the deliberate and careful selection of target firms and an evaluation of the relative health of those firms (financial health, cultural fit, and the value of human resources) contribute to successful acquisitions. *Financial slack* in the form of debt equity or cash in both the acquiring and acquired firms also has frequently contributed to success in acquisitions. While financial slack provides access to financing for the acquisition, it is still important to maintain a *low or moderate level of debt* after the acquisition to keep debt costs low. When substantial debt was used to finance the acquisition, companies with successful acquisitions reduced the debt quickly, partly by selling off assets from the acquired firm, especially noncomplementary or poorly performing assets. For these firms, debt costs do not prevent long-term investments such as R&D, and managerial discretion in the use of cash flow is relatively flexible.

Another attribute of successful acquisition strategies is an *emphasis on innovation,* as demonstrated by continuing investments in R&D activities. Significant R&D investments show a strong managerial commitment to innovation and can help offset the tendency to substitute acquisitions for innovation. Innovation is increasingly important to overall competitiveness, as well as acquisition success.

*Flexibility and adaptability* are the final two attributes of successful acquisitions. When executives of both the acquiring and target firms have experience in managing change and learning from acquisitions, they will be more skilled at adapting their capabilities to new environments.[125] As a result, they will be more adept at integrating the two organizations, which is particularly important when firms have different organizational cultures.

---

## Restructuring

As we have learned, some acquisitions enhance strategic competitiveness. However, the majority of acquisitions that took place from the 1970s through the 1990s did not enhance firms' value. In fact, history has shown that between one-third and more than one-half of acquisitions are ultimately divested or spun off.[126] Thus, firms often use restructuring strategies to correct for the failure of a merger or an acquisition. Defined formally, **restructuring** is a strategy through which a firm changes its set of businesses or financial structure.[127] For more than 30 years, divesting of businesses from company portfolios and downsizing has accounted for a large percentage of firms' restructuring strategies. Restructuring is a global phenomenon.[128]

The failure of an acquisition strategy sometimes precedes a restructuring strategy. Among the famous restructurings undertaken to correct for an acquisition failure are (1) AT&T's $7.4 billion purchase of NCR and subsequent spin-off of the company to shareholders in a deal valued at $3.4 billion, (2) Novell's purchase of WordPerfect for stock valued at $1.4 billion and its sale of the company to Corel for $124 million in stock and cash, and (3) Quaker Oats' acquisition of Snapple Beverage Company for $1.7 billion, only to sell it three years later for $300 million.[129]

In other instances, however, firms purposefully pursue a restructuring strategy because their external or internal environments change.[130] For example, opportunities sometimes surface in the external environment that are particularly attractive to the diversified firm in light of its core competencies. Similarly, the firm may find ways to use its competitive advantages to create new products or to enter new markets. In such cases, restructuring may be appropriate to position the firm to create more value for stakeholders, given the environmental changes.[131]

Firms use three restructuring strategies: downsizing, downscoping, and leveraged buyouts.

## Downsizing

Once thought to be an indicator of organizational decline, downsizing is now recognized as a legitimate restructuring strategy.[132] *Downsizing* is a reduction in the number of a firm's employees and, sometimes, in the number of its operating units, but it may or may not change the composition of businesses in the company's portfolio. To increase the probability that downsizing will result in increased performance, it should be an intentional, proactive management strategy, rather than being forced on the firm as a result of involuntary decline.[133]

For example, the pharmaceutical giant Pfizer dramatically reduced its sales force both in the United States and Europe in response to criticism from doctors, consumer groups, and government regulators who were disturbed by the "hard-sell" tactics pharmaceutical sales people frequently use. In addition, in a survey by PricewaterhouseCoopers, 94 percent of doctors, hospital executives, and other healthcare providers believed that pharmaceutical companies spend too much promoting their products. The big pharmaceutical companies also began to question the effectiveness of their sales tactics. Reducing the workforce was seen as an opportunity to develop new, more effective sales techniques. According to Pfizer CEO Jeffrey B. Kindler, "What we really want is a culture of productivity and continuous improvement."[134]

Firms use downsizing as a restructuring strategy for different reasons. The most frequently cited reason is that the firm expects improved profitability from cost reductions and more efficient operations. For instance, Time Warner's AOL unit announced it would cut about one-quarter of its workforce over six months as part of a plan to reduce costs by $1 billion.[135] Downsizing is more likely to produce desired performance outcomes if a firm has a high level of slack, as indicated by insufficiently used resources.[136] If there is not much slack, then downsizing can cut into the core of a firm's operations and competencies, thus reducing overall long-term performance.

## Downscoping

*Downscoping*—which refers to a divestiture, spin-off, or some other means of eliminating businesses that are unrelated to a firm's core businesses—has a more positive effect on firm performance than downsizing.[137] Commonly, downscoping is described as a set of actions that causes a firm to strategically refocus on its core businesses.[138] In 2002, General Electric embarked on an ambitious restructuring plan. By the end of 2005, the company had announced or completed $30 billion in divestitures, including its insurance operations. According to CEO Jeffrey Immelt, the divestitures were part of an effort to strengthen GE's core business areas.[139]

A firm that downscopes often also downsizes simultaneously. However, it does not eliminate key employees from its primary businesses in the process, because such action could lead to a loss of one or more core competencies. Instead, a firm that is simultaneously downscoping and downsizing becomes smaller by reducing the diversity of businesses in its portfolio.[140] By refocusing on its core businesses, the firm can be managed more effectively by the top management team. Managerial effectiveness increases because the firm has become less diversified, allowing the management team to better understand and manage the remaining businesses.[141]

In general, U.S. firms use downscoping as a restructuring strategy more frequently than do companies in other regions of the world. The trend in Europe, Latin America, and Asia has been to build conglomerates. In Latin America, these conglomerates are called *grupos*. Many Asian and Latin American conglomerates have begun to adopt Western corporate strategies in recent years and have been refocusing on their core businesses. This downscoping has occurred simultaneously with increasing globalization and with more open markets, which have greatly enhanced the competition. By downscoping, these firms have been able to focus on their core businesses and improve their competitiveness.[142]

## Leveraged Buyouts

Leveraged buyouts are commonly used as a restructuring strategy to correct for managerial mistakes or because the firm's managers are making decisions that primarily serve their own interests rather than those of shareholders.[143] A *leveraged buyout* (LBO) is a restructuring strategy whereby a party buys all of a firm's assets in order to take the firm private (that is, the firm's stock will no longer be traded publicly). For example, in late 2006 Jerry Moyes, founder of Swift Transportation Co., initiated a takeover bid to take the company private for $29 per share (shares were trading at around $23 at the time).[144] Firms that facilitate or engage in taking public firms private are called *private equity firms*. Private equity firms may also be involved in taking business units of a public company private.

Usually, significant amounts of debt are incurred to finance the buyout, hence the buyout is "leveraged." LBOs typically fall into one of three general categories: management buyouts, employee buyouts, and whole-firm buyouts, in which a company or partnership purchases an entire company instead of a part of it. To support debt payments and to downscope the company to concentrate on the firm's core businesses, the new owners may immediately sell a number of assets.[145] It is not uncommon for those buying a firm through an LBO to restructure the firm to the point that it can be sold at a profit within five to eight years.

Very high debt brings with it significant risks, which can dramatically influence the performance of an LBO. For example, in 2004 Oak Hill Capital Partners bought Duane Reade, a 249-store pharmacy chain based in New York, for $750 million. However, as *Business Week* pointed out, Duane Reade "hemorrhaged cash from virtually the day the transaction closed" in July 2004, and the chain's credit rating was downgraded four times by Standard & Poor's. The "once-thriving retailer" slumped "in nearly every way." This kind of experience "shows how quickly companies can find themselves in trouble after taking on lots of debt."[146]

In part because of managerial incentives, management buyouts, more so than employee buyouts and whole-firm buyouts, have been found to lead to downscoping, an increased strategic focus, and improved performance.[147] In fact, research has shown that management buyouts can also lead to greater entrepreneurial activity and growth.[148] There may be different reasons for a buyout; one is to protect against a capricious financial market, allowing the owners to focus on developing innovations and bringing them to the market.[149] As such, buyouts can represent a form of firm rebirth to facilitate entrepreneurial efforts and stimulate effective growth.[150]

## Outcomes from Restructuring

Figure 9.2 shows the short-term and long-term outcomes resulting from the three restructuring strategies. Although downsizing may reduce labor costs in the short term, it does not commonly lead to higher firm performance. In fact, research has shown that downsizing

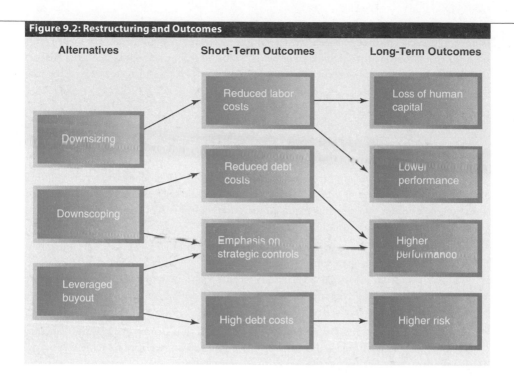

**Figure 9.2: Restructuring and Outcomes**

| Alternatives | Short-Term Outcomes | Long-Term Outcomes |

- Downsizing
- Downscoping
- Leveraged buyout

Short-Term Outcomes:
- Reduced labor costs
- Reduced debt costs
- Emphasis on strategic controls
- High debt costs

Long-Term Outcomes:
- Loss of human capital
- Lower performance
- Higher performance
- Higher risk

contributes to lower returns for both U.S. and Japanese firms.[151] Stock market participants in both nations tend to evaluate downsizing negatively, an indication that investors believe that downsizing will have a negative effect on companies' ability to create value in the long term. One reason for their pessimism could be that downsizing results in a loss of valuable human capital.[152] Losing employees with many years of experience with the firm represents a major loss of knowledge. As noted in Chapter 4, knowledge is vital to competitive success in the global economy.[153] Investors may also assume that downsizing occurs as a consequence of other problems in a company. Thus, in general, research evidence and corporate experience suggest that downsizing may be of more tactical (or short-term) value than strategic (or long-term) value.[154]

As Figure 9.2 indicates, downscoping generally leads to more positive outcomes in both the short and the long term than do downsizing and engaging in a leveraged buyout. Downscoping's desirable long-term outcome of higher performance is a product of reduced debt costs and the emphasis on strategic controls derived from concentrating on the firm's core businesses. In so doing, the refocused firm should be able to increase its ability to compete.[155]

Although whole-firm LBOs have been hailed as a significant innovation in the financial restructuring of firms, there can be negative trade-offs.[156] First, the resulting large debt increases the financial risk of the firm, as evidenced by the number of companies that filed for bankruptcy in the 1990s after executing a whole-firm LBO. Sometimes, the intent of the owners to increase the efficiency of the bought-out firm and then sell it within five to eight years creates a short-term and risk-averse managerial focus.[157] As a result, these firms may fail to invest adequately in R&D or take other major actions designed to maintain or improve the company's core competence.[158] Research also suggests that in firms with an entrepreneurial mind-set, buyouts can lead to greater innovation, especially if the debt load is not too great.[159] However, because they more often result in significant debt, most LBOs have taken place in mature industries in which stable cash flows are possible. This enables the buying firm to meet the recurring debt payments, which can mitigate some of the risk associated with a buyout.

# Summary

- Acquisition strategies are increasingly popular. Because of globalization, deregulation of multiple industries in many different economies, and favorable legislation, domestic and cross-border mergers and acquisitions remain a viable strategy for global competitors pursuing value creation.

- Firms use acquisition strategies to: (1) increase market power; (2) overcome entry barriers to new markets or regions; (3) reduce the costs and risks associated with developing new products; (4) increase the speed of entering a new market; (5) become more diversified and reshape the firm's competitive scope; and (6) enhance learning, thereby adding to the firm's knowledge base.

- Among the problems associated with use of an acquisition strategy are: (1) the difficulty of effectively integrating the firms involved, leading to an inability to achieve synergy; (2) inadequately evaluating the target firm's value relative to the costs of acquisition; (3) creating debt loads that preclude adequate long-term investments (e.g., in R&D); (4) creating a firm that is too diversified; (5) creating an internal environment in which managers devote increasing amounts of their time and energy to analyzing and completing acquisitions; and (6) developing a combined firm that is too large, necessitating extensive use of bureaucratic, rather than strategic, controls.

- Effective acquisitions have the following attributes: (1) the acquiring and target firms have complementary resources that can be the basis of core competencies in the newly created firm; (2) the acquisition is friendly, thereby facilitating integration of the two firms' resources; (3) the target firm is selected and purchased based on a thorough due diligence process; (4) the acquiring and target firms have considerable slack in the form of cash or debt capacity; (5) the merged firm maintains a low or moderate level of debt by selling off portions of the acquired firm or some of the acquiring firm's poorly performing units; (6) R&D and innovation are emphasized in the new firm; and (7) the acquiring and acquired firms have experience in terms of adapting to change.

- Restructuring is used to improve a firm's performance by correcting for problems created by ineffective management. Restructuring by downsizing involves reducing the number of employees and hierarchical levels in the firm. Although it can lead to short-term cost reductions, they may be realized at the expense of long-term success because of the loss of valuable human resources (and knowledge).

- The goal of restructuring through downscoping is to reduce the firm's level of diversification. Often, the firm divests unrelated businesses to achieve this goal. Eliminating unrelated businesses makes it easier for the firm and its top-level managers to refocus on the core businesses.

- Another restructuring strategy is the leveraged buyout (LBO), through which a firm is purchased so that it can become a private entity firm. LBOs usually are financed largely through debt, which creates substantial risks. Management buyouts, employee buyouts, and whole-firm buyouts are the three types of LBOs. Because they provide clear managerial incentives, management buyouts have been the most successful of the three. Often, the intent of a buyout is to improve efficiency and performance to the point at which the firm can be sold successfully within five to eight years.

■ Commonly, restructuring's primary goal is gaining or reestablishing effective strategic control of the firm. Of the three restructuring strategies, downscoping is aligned the most closely with establishing and using strategic controls.

# Ethics Questions

1. What are the ethical issues associated with takeovers, if any? Are mergers more or less ethical than takeovers? Why or why not?
2. One of the outcomes associated with market power is that the firm is able to sell its good or service above competitive levels. Is it ethical for firms to pursue market power? Does your answer to this question differ by the industry in which the firm competes? For example, are the ethics of pursuing market power different for firms producing and selling medical equipment compared with those producing and selling sports clothing?
3. What ethical considerations are associated with downsizing decisions? If you were part of a corporate downsizing, would you feel that your firm had acted unethically? If you believe that downsizing has an unethical component to it, what should firms do to avoid using this technique?
4. What ethical issues are involved with conducting a robust due-diligence process?
5. Some evidence suggests that there is a direct relationship between a firm's size and the level of compensation its top executives receive. If this is so, what inducement does this relationship provide to top-level managers? What can be done to influence this relationship so that it serves shareholders' best interests?

# Notes

1. J. Anand, 2004, Redeployment of corporate resources: A study of acquisition strategies in the US defense industries, 1978–1996, *Managerial and Decision Economics*, 2S: 383–400; D. D. Bergh, 2001, Diversification strategy research at a crossroads: Established, emerging and anticipated paths, in M. A. Hitt, R. E. Freeman, & J. S. Harrison, *Handbook of Strategic Management*, Oxford, UK: Blackwell Publishers, 362–383; P. Moran & S. Ghoshal, 1999, Markets, firms, and the process of economic development, *Academy of Management Review*, 24: 390–412; M. A. Hitt, R. E. Hoskisson, R. D. Ireland, & J. S. Harrison, 1991, Effects of acquisitions on R&D inputs and outputs, *Academy of Management Journal*, 34: 693–706.

2. M. Kwan, 2002, Maximizing value through diversification, *MIT Sloan Management Review*, 43(2): 10.

3. M. Farjoun, 2002, Towards an organic perspective on strategy, *Strategic Management Journal*, 23: 561–594.

4. R. A. Krishnan, S. Joshi, & H. Krishnan, 2004, The influence of mergers on firms' product-mix strategies, *Strategic Management Journal*, 2S: 587–611.

5. H. Shahrur, 2005, Industry structure and horizontal takeovers: Analysis of wealth effects on rivals, suppliers, and corporate customers, *Journal of Financial Economics*, 76: 61–98; K. Fuller, J. Netter, & M. Stegemoller, 2002, What do returns to acquiring firms tell us? Evidence from firms that make many acquisitions, *Journal of Finance*, 57: 1763–1793; M. A. Hitt, J. S. Harrison, & R. D. Ireland, 2001, *Mergers and Acquisitions: A Guide to Creating Value for Stakeholders*, New York: Oxford University Press.

6. B. E. Chappuis, K. A. Frick, & P. J. Roche, 2004, High-tech mergers take shape, *McKinsey Quarterly*, (1): 60–69; G. K. Deans, F. Kroeger, & S. Zeisel, 2002, The consolidation curve, *Harvard Business Review*, 80(12): 20–21; 2000, How M&As will navigate the turn into a new century, *Mergers & Acquisitions*, January, 29–35.

7. P. Quah & S. Young, 2005, Post-acquisition management: A phases approach for cross-border M&As, *European Management Journal*, 23(1): 65–80.

8. J. A. Schmidt, 2002, Business perspective on mergers and acquisitions, in J. A. Schmidt (ed.), *Making Mergers*

*Work*, Alexandria, VA: Society for Human Resource Management, 23–46.

9   J. Singer & P. Glader, 2006, Arcelor agrees to acquisition by rival Mittal, *Wall Street Journal*, June 26, A3.

10  E. R. Auster & M. L. Sirower, 2002, The dynamics of merger and acquisition waves: A three-stage conceptual framework with implications for practice, *Journal of Applied Behavioral Science*, 38: 216–244.

11  M. A. Hitt, R. D. Ireland, & J. S. Harrison, 2001, Mergers and acquisitions: A value creating or a value destroying strategy? In M. A. Hitt, R. E. Freeman, & J. S. Harrison, *Handbook of Strategic Management*, Oxford, UK: Blackwell Publishers, 385–408.

12  L. Saigol, 2002, Thin pickings in dismal year for dealmaking, *Financial Times* online, http://www.ft.com, January 2; 2001, Waiting for growth, *Economist* online, http://www.economist.com, April 27.

13  2002, Mergers snapshot: 2001 deal volume, *Wall Street Journal*, January 4, C12; 2001, The great merger wave breaks, *Economist*, January 27, 59–60.

14  J. Weber, 2007, An irresistible urge to merge, *Business Week*, January 1, 72–73.

15  E. Thornton, 2006, What's behind the buyout binge? *Business Week*, December 4, 38.

16  M. Song, R. J. Calantone, & C. Anthony, 2002, Competitive forces and strategic choice decisions: An experimental investigation in the United States and Japan, *Strategic Management Journal*, 23: 969–978.

17  R. Coff, 2003, Bidding wars over R&D-intensive firms: Knowledge, opportunism, and the market for corporate control, *Academy of Management Journal*, 46: 74–85; P. Chattopadhyay, W. H. Glick, & G. P. Huber, 2001, Organizational actions in response to threats and opportunities, *Academy of Management Journal*, 44: 937–955.

18  J. J. Reuer & T. W. Tong, 2005, Real options in international joint ventures, *Journal of Management*, 31: 403–423; A. E. M. A. Schilling & H. K. Steensma, 2002, Disentangling the theories of firm boundaries: A path model and empirical test, *Organization Science*, 13: 387–401; H. T. J. Smit, 2001, Acquisition strategies as option games, *Journal of Applied Corporate Finance*, 14(2): 79–89.

19  G. Cullinan, J.-M. Le Roux, & R.-M. Weddigen, 2004, When to walk away from a deal, *Harvard Business Review*, 82(4): 96–104; L. Selden & G. Colvin, 2003, M&A needn't be a loser's game, *Harvard Business Review*, 81(6): 70–73; L. Capron & N. Pistre, 2002, When do acquirers earn abnormal returns? *Strategic Management Journal*, 23: 781–794; J. Anand, 1999, How many matches are made in heaven? Mastering strategy (part five), *Financial Times*, October 25, 6–7.

20  J. J. Reuer, 2005, Avoiding lemons in M&A deals, *MIT Sloan Management Review*, 46(3): 15–17.

21  M. C. Jensen, 1988, Takeovers: Their causes and consequences, *Journal of Economic Perspectives*, 1(2): 21–48.

22  A. Rappaport & M. L. Sirower, 1999, Stock or cash? *Harvard Business Review*, 77(6): 147–158.

23  S. B. Moeller, F. P. Schlingemann, & R. M. Stulz, 2005, Wealth destruction on a massive scale? A study of acquiring-firm returns in the recent merger wave, *Journal of Finance*, 60: 757–782.

24  A. Weintraub, 2007, How Gilead primed the pipeline, *Business Week*, February 19, 66.

25  D. K. Berman, 2005, Mergers horror II: The rhetoric, *Wall Street Journal*, May 24, C1; T. Wright, M. Kroll, A. Lado, & B. Van Ness, 2002, The structure of ownership and corporate acquisition strategies, *Strategic Management Journal*, 23: 41–53; Rappaport & Sirower, Stock or cash?

26  D. Berman & V. Bauerlein, 2006, Regions to merge with AmSouth in $10 billion deal, *Wall Street Journal*, May 25, A1.

27  M. Karnitschnig, 2000, Eaton runs out of gas at DaimlerChrysler, *Business Week* online, http://www.businessweek.com, January 27.

28  E. Bellman, J. Singer, & P. Wonacott, 2006, Tata Steel offers $8 billion for Corus, *Wall Street Journal*, October 18, A6.

29  E. Thornton, 2007, Unsolicited aggression, *Business Week*, January 1, 34.

30  P. Haspeslagh, 1999, Managing the mating dance in equal mergers, Mastering strategy (part five), *Financial Times*, October 25, 14–15.

31  P. Wright, M. Kroll, & D. Elenkov, 2002, Acquisition returns, increase in firm size and chief executive officer compensation: The moderating role of monitoring, *Academy of Management Journal*, 45: 599–608.

32  G. Anders, 2002, Lessons from WaMU's M&A playbook, *Fast Company*, January, 100–107.

33  L. Lee, 2007, Is Dell too big for Michael Dell? *Business Week*, February 12, 33.

34  T. Lowry, 2007, Hot news in nowheresville, *Business Week*, February 19, 74.

35  L. Capron & N. Pistre, 2002, When do acquirers earn abnormal returns? *Strategic Management Journal*, 23: 781–794; L. Capron, 1999, Horizontal acquisitions: The benefits and risks to long-term performance, *Strategic Management Journal*, 20: 987–1018.

36  C. E. Fee & S. Thomas, 2004, Sources of gains in horizontal mergers: Evidence from customer, supplier, and rival firms, *Journal of Financial Economics*, 74: 423–460.

37  M. Lubatkin, W. S. Schulze, A. Mainkar, & R. W. Cotterill, 2001, Ecological investigation of firm effects in horizontal mergers, *Strategic Management Journal*, 22: 335–357; K. Ramaswamy, 1997, The performance impact of strategic similarity in horizontal mergers: Evidence from the U.S. banking industry, *Academy of Management Journal*, 40: 697–715.

38  L. Capron, W. Mitchell, & A. Swaminathan, 2001, Asset divestiture following horizontal acquisitions: A dynamic view, *Strategic Management Journal*, 22: 817–844.

39  A. Kuczynski, 2007, BNSF Logistics expands through acquisition of Pro-Am Transportation Services, Inc., Dow Jones Newswires, http://www.djnewswires.com, January 2.

40  2007, Cooper industries acquires WPI Interconnect Products, *Connector Specifier*, January 5, 1.

41  2007, Hospira acquisition of Mayne Pharma clears U.S. antitrust review, Dow Jones Newswires, http://www.djnewswires.com, January 18; D. K. Berman & T. M. Burton, 2006, Hospira to buy Mayne Pharma for $2 billion, *Wall Street Journal*, September, B4.

42  M. Lerner, 2001, Israeli Antitrust Authority's general director David Tadmor on corporate mergers, *Academy of Management Executive*, 15(1): 8–11.

43  S. F. S. Chen & M. Zeng, 2004, Japanese investors' choice of acquisitions vs. startups in the US: The role of

reputation barriers and advertising outlays, *International Journal of Research in Marketing*, 21(2): 123–136; S. J. Chang & P. M. Rosenzweig, 2001, The choice of entry mode in sequential foreign direct investment, *Strategic Management Journal*, 22: 747–776.

44 2004, Leaders: Grow up; emerging economies, *Economist*, October 16, 12; N. Dawar & A. Chattopadhyay, 2002, Rethinking marketing programs for emerging markets, *Long Range Planning*, 35(5): 457–474; J. A. Gingrich, 1999, Five rules for winning emerging market consumers, *Strategy & Business*, 15: 19–33.

45 K. Shimizu, M. A. Hitt, D. Vaidyanath, & V. Pisano, 2004, Theoretical foundations of cross-border mergers and acquisitions: A review of current research and recommendations for the future, *Journal of International Management*, 10: 307–353; J. A. Doukas & L. H. P. Lang, 2003, Foreign direct investment, diversification and firm performance, *Journal of International Business Studies*, 34: 153–172; Hitt, Harrison, & Ireland, *Mergers and Acquisitions*, Chapter 10; D. Angwin & B. Savill, 1997, Strategic perspectives on European cross-border acquisitions: A view from the top European executives, *European Management Review*, 15: 423–435.

46 J. W. Lu & P. W. Beamish, 2001, The internationalization and performance of SMEs, *Strategic Management Journal*, 22(special issue): 565–586.

47 A. Seth, K. P. Song, & R. R. Pettit, 2002, Value creation and destruction in cross-border acquisitions: An empirical analysis of foreign acquisitions of U.S. firms, *Strategic Management Journal*, 23: 921–940.

48 Ibid.

49 2007, Rail giant takes shape, *Railway Gazette International*, 163(1): 1.

50 V. Bannert & H. Tschirky, 2004, Integration planning for technology intensive acquisitions, *R&D Management*, 34(5): 481–494; R. E. Hoskisson, M. A. Hitt, R. A. Johnson, & W. Grossman, 2002, Conflicting voices: The effects of institutional ownership heterogeneity and internal governance on corporate innovation strategies, *Academy of Management Journal*, 45: 697–716.

51 H. Gatignon, M. L. Tushman, W. Smith, & P. Anderson, 2002, A structural approach to assessing innovation: Construct development of innovation locus, type, and characteristics, *Management Science*, 48: 1103–1122; Hitt, Harrison, & Ireland, *Mergers and Acquisitions*.

52 L.-F. Hsieh, Y.-T. Tsai, 2005, Technology investment mode of innovative technological corporations: M&A strategy intended to facilitate innovation, *Journal of American Academy of Business*, 6(1): 185–194; G. Ahuja & R. Katila, 2001, Technological acquisitions and the innovation performance of acquiring firms: A longitudinal study, *Strategic Management Journal*, 22: 197–220; M. A. Hitt, R. E. Hoskisson, & R. D. Ireland, 1990, Mergers and acquisitions and managerial commitment to innovation in M-form firms, *Strategic Management Journal*, 11(summer special issue): 29–47; M. A. Hitt, R. E. Hoskisson, R. A. Johnson, & D. D. Moesel, 1996, The market for corporate control and firm innovation, *Academy of Management Journal*, 39: 1084–1119.

53 R. Coff, 2003, Bidding wars over R&D intensive firms: Knowledge, opportunism and the market for corporate control, *Academy of Management Journal*, 46: 74–85.

54 Weintraub, How Gilead primed the pipeline, 66.

55 Hitt, Hoskisson, Johnson, & Moesel, The market for corporate control.

56 M. A. Hitt, R. E. Hoskisson, R. D. Ireland, & J. S. Harrison, 1991, Effects of acquisitions on R&D inputs and outputs, *Academy of Management Journal*, 34: 693–706.

57 Weintraub, How Gilead primed the pipeline, 66.

58 P. Kale & P. Puranam, 2004, Choosing equity stakes in technology sourcing relationships: An integrative framework, *California Management Review*, 46(3): 77–99; T. Yoshikawa, 2003, Technology development and acquisition strategy, *International Journal of Technology Management*, 25: 666–674; K. F. McCardle & S. Viswanathan, 1994, The direct entry versus takeover decision and stock price performance around takeovers, *Journal of Business*, 67: 1–43.

59 K. M. Eisenhardt, 2002, Has strategy changed? *MIT Sloan Management Review*, 43(2): 88–91.

60 A. Dolbeck, 2006, In print and online, acquisitions in the media sector, *Corporate Growth Report*, November, 1–2.

61 Hitt, Hoskisson, Ireland, & Harrison, Effects of acquisitions on R&D inputs and outputs.

62 Capron, Mitchell, & Swaminathan, Asset divestiture following horizontal acquisitions; D. D. Bergh, 1997, Predicting divestiture of unrelated acquisitions: An integrative model of ex ante conditions, *Strategic Management Journal*, 18: 715–731.

63 C. E. Helfat & K. M. Eisenhardt, 2004, Inter-temporal economies of scope, organizational modularity, and the dynamics of diversification, *Strategic Management Journal*, 25: 1217–1232; C. Park, 2003, Prior performance characteristics of related and unrelated acquirers, *Strategic Management Journal*, 24: 471–480.

64 Hitt, Harrison, & Ireland, *Mergers and Acquisitions*.

65 J. Anand & H. Singh, 1997, Asset redeployment, acquisitions and corporate strategy in declining industries, *Strategic Management Journal*, 18(summer special issue): 99–118.

66 M. Raynor, 2001, *Strategic Flexibility in the Financial Services Industry*, report published by Deloitte Consulting and Deloitte & Touche, Toronto, Canada.

67 D. C. Hambrick & J. W. Fredrickson, 2005, Are you sure you have a strategy? *Academy of Management Executive*, 19(4): 51–62, reprinted from 15(4).

68 W. J. Ferrier, 2001, Navigating the competitive landscape: The drivers and consequences of competitive aggressiveness, *Academy of Management Journal*, 44: 858–877.

69 2007, Operations: Segment operations, General Electric 2005 Annual Report, http://www.ge.com/ar2005, February 15; R. E. Hoskisson & M. A. Hitt, 1994, *Downscoping: How to Tame the Diversified Firm*, New York: Oxford University Press.

70 P. Puranam, H. Singh, & M. Zollo, 2006, Organizing for innovation: Managing the coordination-autonomy dilemma in technology acquisitions, *Academy of Management Journal*, 49: 263–280.

71 F. Vermeulen & H. Barkema, 2001, Learning through acquisitions, *Academy of Management Journal*, 44: 457–476.

72 K. Uhlenbruck, M. A. Hitt, & M. Semadeni, 2006, Market value effects of acquisitions involving Internet firms: A resource-based analysis, *Strategic Management Journal*, 27: 899–913; F. Vermeulen, 2005, How acquisitions can revitalize firms, *MIT Sloan Management Review*, 46(4): 45–51; J. Gammelgaard, 2004, Access to competence: An emerging acquisition motive, *European*

Business Forum, spring, 44–48; M. L. A. Hayward, 2002, When do firms learn from their acquisition experience? Evidence from 1990–1995, *Strategic Management Journal*, 23: 21–39.

73  G. Ahuja & C. Lampert, 2001, Entrepreneurship in the large corporation: A longitudinal study of how established firms create breakthrough inventions, *Strategic Management Journal*, 22(special issue): 521–543.

74  J. S. Harrison, M. A. Hitt, R. E. Hoskisson, & R. D. Ireland, 2001, Resource complementarities in business combinations: Extending the logic to organizational alliances, *Journal of Management*, 27: 679–690.

75  L. B. Suzukamo, 2006, Oracle buying Stellant for $440 million, *Knight Ridder Tribune Business News*, November 3, 1.

76  Schmidt, Business perspective on mergers and acquisitions.

77  M. Zollo & H. Singh, 2004, Deliberate learning in corporate acquisitions: Post-acquisition strategies and integration capability in U.S. bank mergers, *Strategic Management Journal*, 25: 1233–1256; P. Mallette, C. L. Fowler, & C. Hayes, 2003, The acquisition process map: Blueprint for a successful deal, *Southern Business Review*, 28(2): 1–13; Hitt, Harrison, & Ireland, *Mergers and Acquisitions*.

78  C. Homberg & M. Bucerius, 2006, Is speed of integration really a success factor of mergers and acquisitions? An analysis of the roles of internal and external relatedness, *Strategic Management Journal*, 27: 347–367; L. Schweizer, 2005, Organizational integration of acquired biotechnology companies into pharmaceutical companies: The need for a hybrid approach, *Academy of Management Journal*, 48: 1051–1074; J. R. Carleton & C. S. Lineberry, 2004, *Achieving Post-Merger Success*, New York: Wiley; Y. Weber & E. Menipaz, 2003, Measuring cultural fit in mergers and acquisitions, *International Journal of Business Performance Management*, 5(1): 54–72.

79  M. Zollo, 1999, M&A—The challenge of learning to integrate, Mastering strategy (part eleven), *Financial Times*, December 6, 14–15.

80  R. A. Weber & C. F. Camerer, 2003, Cultural conflict and merger failure: An experimental approach, *Management Science*, 49: 400–415; A. J. Viscio, J. R. Harbison, A. Asin, & R. P. Vitaro, 1999, Post-merger integration: What makes mergers work? *Strategy & Business*, 17: 26–33; D. K. Datta, 1991, Organizational fit and acquisition performance: Effects of post-acquisition integration, *Strategic Management Journal*, 12: 281–297.

81  A. Krug, 2003, Why do they keep leaving? *Harvard Business Review*, 81(2): 14–15; M. A. Hitt, L. Bierman, K. Shimizu, & R. Kochhar, 2001, Direct and moderating effects of human capital on strategy and performance in professional service firms, *Academy of Management Journal*, 44: 13–28.

82  G. G. Dess & J. D. Shaw, 2001, Voluntary turnover, social capital and organizational performance, *Academy of Management Review*, 26: 446–456; I. T. Kay & M. Shelton, 2000, The people problem in mergers, *McKinsey Quarterly*, http://www.mckinseyquarterly.com, October 8.

83  T. McIntyre, 2004, A model of levels of involvement and strategic roles of human resource development (HRD) professionals as facilitators of due diligence and the integration process, *Human Resource Development*

Review, 3(2): 173–182; J. A. Krug & H. Hegarty, 2001, Predicting who stays and leaves after an acquisition: A study of top managers in multinational firms, *Strategic Management Journal*, 22: 185–196.

84  J. M. Shaver, 2006, A paradox of synergy: Contagion and capacity effects in mergers and acquisitions, *Academy of Management Review*, 31: 962–976.

85  T. N. Hubbard, 1999, Integration strategies and the scope of the company, Mastering strategy (part eleven), *Financial Times*, December 6, 8–10.

86  T. Saxton & M. Dollinger, 2004, Target reputation and appropriability: Picking and deploying resources in acquisitions, *Journal of Management*, 30: 123–147.

87  S. A. Zahra & A. P. Nielsen, 2002, Sources of capabilities, integration and technology commercialization, *Strategic Management Journal*, 23: 377–398.

88  J. B. Barney, 1988, Returns to bidding firms in mergers and acquisitions: Reconsidering the relatedness hypothesis, *Strategic Management Journal*, 9(summer special issue): 71–78.

89  Harrison, Hitt, Hoskisson, & Ireland, Resource complementarities.

90  A. Rappaport, 2006, 10 ways to create shareholder value, *Harvard Business Review*, 84(9): 66–80.

91  O. E. Williamson, 1999, Strategy research: Governance and competence perspectives, *Strategic Management Journal*, 20: 1087–1108.

92  Hitt, Hoskisson, Johnson, & Moesel, The market for corporate control.

93  Cullinan, Le Roux, & Weddigen, When to walk away from a deal.

94  Rappaport & Sirower, Stock or cash? 149.

95  E. Thornton, 2003, Bypassing the street, *Business Week*, June 2, 79.

96  G. Yago, 1991, *Junk Bonds: How High Yield Securities Restructured Corporate America*, New York: Oxford University Press, 146–148.

97  M. C. Jensen, 1986, Agency costs of free cash flow, corporate finance, and takeovers, *American Economic Review*, 76: 323–329.

98  B. Bremner & N. Lakshman, 2007, Tata Steel bags Corus—but at what price? *Business Week* online, http://www.businessweek.com, February 1.

99  M. A. Hitt & D. L. Smart, 1994, Debt: A disciplining force for managers or a debilitating force for organizations? *Journal of Management Inquiry*, 3: 144–152.

100  Hitt, Harrison, & Ireland, *Mergers and Acquisitions*.

101  2007, United Technologies, http://www.utc.com, February 13; 2007, General Electric, http://www.ge.com, February 15.

102  C. W. L. Hill & R. E. Hoskisson, 1987, Strategy and structure in the multiproduct firm, *Academy of Management Review*, 12: 331–341.

103  R. A. Johnson, R. E. Hoskisson, & M. A. Hitt, 1993, Board of director involvement in restructuring: The effects of board versus managerial controls and characteristics, *Strategic Management Journal*, 14(special issue): 33–50; C. C. Markides, 1992, Consequences of corporate refocusing: Ex ante evidence, *Academy of Management Journal*, 35: 398–412.

104  D. Palmer & B. N. Barber, 2001, Challengers, elites and families: A social class theory of corporate acquisitions, *Administrative Science Quarterly*, 46: 87–120.

[105] Hitt, Harrison, & Ireland, *Mergers and Acquisitions*; R. E. Hoskisson & R. A. Johnson, 1992, Corporate restructuring and strategic change: The effect on diversification strategy and R&D intensity, *Strategic Management Journal*, 13: 625–634.

[106] J. Haleblian, J.-J. Kim, & N. Rajagopalan, 2006, The influence of acquisition experience and performance on acquisition behavior: Evidence from the U.S. commercial banking industry, *Academy of Management Journal*, 49: 357–370.

[107] Ibid.

[108] J. P. Hughes, W. W. Lang, L. J. Mester, C.-G. Moon, & M. S. Pagano, 2003, Do bankers sacrifice value to build empires? Managerial incentives, industry consolidation, and financial performance, *Journal of Banking and Finance*, 27: 417–477; Hitt, Hoskisson, Johnson, & Moesel, The market for corporate control.

[109] R. E. Hoskisson, M. A. Hitt, & R. D. Ireland, 1994, The effects of acquisitions and restructuring (strategic refocusing) strategies on innovation, in G. von Krogh, A. Sinatra, & H. Singh (eds.), *Managing Corporate Acquisitions*, London: Macmillan, 144–169.

[110] M. L. A. Hayward & D. C. Hambrick, 1997. Explaining the premiums paid for large acquisitions: Evidence of CEO hubris, *Administrative Science Quarterly*, 42: 103–127; R. Roll, 1986, The hubris hypothesis of corporate takeovers, *Journal of Business*, 59: 197–216.

[111] J. Pfeffer, 2003, The human factor: Curbing the urge to merge, *Business 2.0*, July, 58.

[112] Weber & Camerer, Cultural conflict and merger failure.

[113] Hayward, When do firms learn from their acquisition experience?

[114] R. M. Cyert, S.-H. Kang, & P. Kumar, 2002, Corporate governance, takeovers, and top-management compensation: Theory and evidence, *Management Science*, 48: 453–469.

[115] Hitt, Harrison, & Ireland, *Mergers and Acquisitions*.

[116] A. P. Dickerson, H. D. Gibson, & E. Tsakalotos, 2002, Takeover risk and the market for corporate control: The experience of British firms in the 1970s and 1980s, *International Journal of Industrial Organization*, 20: 1167–1195.

[117] Uhlenbruck, Hitt, & Semadeni, Market value effects of acquisitions involving Internet firms; Hitt, Harrison, & Ireland, *Mergers and Acquisitions*.

[118] M. A. Hitt, R. D. Ireland, J. S. Harrison, & A. Best, 1998, Attributes of successful and unsuccessful acquisitions of U.S. firms, *British Journal of Management*, 9: 91–114.

[119] Harrison, Hitt, Hoskisson, & Ireland, Resource complementarities.

[120] J. Hagedoorn & G. Dysters, 2002, External sources of innovative capabilities: The preference for strategic alliances or mergers and acquisitions, *Journal of Management Studies*, 39: 167–188.

[121] B. Villalonga & A. M. McGahan, 2005, The choice among acquisitions, alliances, and divestitures, *Strategic Management Journal*, 26: 1183–1208; P. Porrini, 2004, Can a previous alliance between an acquirer and a target affect acquisition performance? *Journal of Management*, 30: 545–562; J. Reuer, 2001, From hybrids to hierarchies: Shareholder wealth effects of joint venture partner buyouts, *Strategic Management Journal*, 22: 27–44.

[122] R. J. Aiello & M. D. Watkins, 2000, The fine art of friendly acquisition, *Harvard Business Review*, 78(6): 100–107.

[123] P. Gwynne, 2002, Keeping the right people, *MIT Sloan Management Review*, 43(2): 19; D. D. Bergh, 2001, Executive retention and acquisition outcomes: A test of opposing views on the influence of organizational tenure, *Journal of Management*, 27: 603–622; J. P. Walsh, 1989, Doing a deal: Merger and acquisition negotiations and their impact upon target company top management turnover, *Strategic Management Journal*, 10: 307–322.

[124] R. W. Coff, 2002, Human capital, shared expertise, and the likelihood of impasse in corporate acquisitions, *Journal of Management*, 28: 107–128; M. L. Marks & P. H. Mirvis, 2001, Making mergers and acquisitions work: Strategic and psychological preparation, *Academy of Management Executive*, 15(2): 80–92.

[125] J. Haleblian, J.-J. Kim, & N. Rajagopalan, The influence of acquisition experience and performance on acquisition behavior; Hitt, Harrison, & Ireland, *Mergers and Acquisitions*; Q. N. Huy, 2001, Time, temporal capability and planned change, *Academy of Management Review*, 26: 601–623; L. Markoczy, 2001, Consensus formation during strategic change, *Strategic Management Journal*, 22: 1013–1031.

[126] Anand, How many matches are made in heaven? 6.

[127] R. A. Johnson, 1996, Antecedents and outcomes of corporate refocusing, *Journal of Management*, 22: 437–481; J. E. Bethel & J. Liebeskind, 1993, The effects of ownership structure on corporate restructuring, *Strategic Management Journal*, 14(summer special issue): 15–31.

[128] R. E. Hoskisson, A. A. Cannella, L. Tihanyi, & R. Faraci, 2004, Asset restructuring and business group affiliation in French civil law countries, *Strategic Management Journal*, 25: 525–539; R. E. Hoskisson, R. A. Johnson, D. Yiu, & W. P. Wan, 2001, Restructuring strategies of diversified groups: Differences associated with country institutional environments, in M. A. Hitt, R. E. Freeman, & J. S. Harrison (eds.), *Handbook of Strategic Management*, Oxford, UK: Blackwell Publishers, 433–463; S. R. Fisher & M. A. White, 2000, Downsizing in a learning organization: Are there hidden costs? *Academy of Management Review*, 25: 244–251; A. Campbell & D. Sadtler, 1998, Corporate breakups, *Strategy & Business*, 12: 64–73; E. Bowman & H. Singh, 1990, Overview of corporate restructuring: Trends and consequences, in L. Rock & R. H. Rock (eds.), *Corporate Restructuring*, New York: McGraw-Hill.

[129] Hitt, Harrison, & Ireland, *Mergers and Acquisitions*.

[130] M. Brauer, 2006, What we have acquired and what should we acquire in diversification research? A review and research agenda, *Journal of Management*, 32: 751–785.

[131] J. L. Morrow Jr., R. A. Johnson, & L. W. Busenitz, 2004, The effects of cost and asset retrenchment on firm performance: The overlooked role of a firm's competitive environment, *Journal of Management*, 30: 199–208; T. A. Kruse, 2002, Asset liquidity and the determinants of asset sales by poorly performing firms, *Financial Management*, 31(4): 107–129.

[132] R. D. Nixon, M. A. Hitt, H.-U. Lee, & E. Jeong, 2004, Market reactions to announcements of corporate downsizing actions and implementation strategies, *Strategic Management Journal*, 25: 1121–1129.

[133] E. G. Love & N. Nohria, 2005, Reducing slack: The performance consequences of downsizing by large industrial firms, 1977–1993, *Strategic Management Journal*, 26: 1087–1108; W. McKinley, J. Zhao, & K. G. Rust, 2000, A sociocognitive interpretation of

organizational downsizing, *Academy of Management Review*, 25: 227–243.

[134] A. Weintraub, 2007, The doctor won't see you now, *Business Week*, February 5, 30.

[135] M. Karnitschnig, 2006, AOL to lay off as many as 5,000 in strategy shift, *Wall Street Journal*, August 4, A12.

[136] Love & Nohria, Reducing slack.

[137] Hoskisson & Hitt, *Downscoping*.

[138] L. Dranikoff, T. Koller, & A. Schneider, 2002, Divestiture: Strategy's missing link, *Harvard Business Review*, 80(5): 74–83.

[139] J. Immelt, 2007, Letter to stakeholders, General Electric, http://www.ge.com/ar2005/letter_strong.htm, February 15.

[140] M. Raj and & M. Forsyth, 2002, Hostile bidders, long-term performance, and restructuring methods: Evidence from the UK, *American Business Review*, 20(1): 71–81.

[141] Johnson, Hoskisson, & Hitt, Board of director involvement in restructuring; R. E. Hoskisson & M. A. Hitt, 1990, Antecedents and performance outcomes of diversification: A review and critique of theoretical perspectives, *Journal of Management*, 16: 461–509.

[142] R. E. Hoskisson, R. A. Johnson, L. Tihanyi, & R. E. White, 2005, Diversified business groups and corporate refocusing in emerging economies, *Journal of Management*, 31: 941–965; Hoskisson, Johnson, Yiu, & Wan, Restructuring strategies.

[143] D. D. Bergh & G. F. Holbein, 1997, Assessment and redirection of longitudinal analysis: Demonstration with a study of the diversification and divestiture relationship, *Strategic Management Journal*, 18: 557–571; C. C. Markides & H. Singh, 1997, Corporate restructuring: A symptom of poor governance or a solution to past managerial mistakes? *European Management Journal*, 15: 213–219.

[144] E. Thornton, 2007, Unsolicited aggression, *Business Week*, January 1, 34.

[145] M. F. Wiersema & J. P. Liebeskind, 1995, The effects of leveraged buyouts on corporate growth and diversification in large firms, *Strategic Management Journal*, 16: 447–460.

[146] D. Henry, 2006, Duane Reade: An LBO on the critical list, *Business Week*, December 4.

[147] R. Harris, D. S. Siegel, & M. Wright, 2005, Assessing the impact of management buyouts on economic efficiency: Plant-level evidence from the United Kingdom, *Review of Economics and Statistics*, 87: 148–153; A. Seth & J. Easterwood, 1995, Strategic redirection in large management buyouts: The evidence from post-buyout restructuring activity, *Strategic Management Journal*, 14: 251–274; P. H. Phan &

C. W. L. Hill, 1995, Organizational restructuring and economic performance in leveraged buyouts: An ex-post study, *Academy of Management Journal*, 38: 704–739.

[148] C. M. Daily, P. P. McDougall, J. G. Covin, & D. R. Dalton, 2002, Governance and strategic leadership in entrepreneurial firms, *Journal of Management*, 3: 387–412.

[149] M. Wright, R. E. Hoskisson, L. W. Busenitz, & J. Dial, 2000, Entrepreneurial growth through privatization: The upside of management buyouts, *Academy of Management Review*, 25: 591–601.

[150] M. Wright, R. E. Hoskisson, & L. W. Busenitz, 2001, Firm rebirth: Buyouts as facilitators of strategic growth and entrepreneurship, *Academy of Management Executive*, 15(1): 111–125.

[151] H. A. Krishnan & D. Park, 2002, The impact of work force reduction on subsequent performance in major mergers and acquisitions: An exploratory study, *Journal of Business Research*, 55(4): 285–292; P. M. Lee, 1997, A comparative analysis of layoff announcements and stock price reactions in the United States and Japan, *Strategic Management Journal*, 18: 879–894.

[152] W. F. Casio, 2005, Strategies for responsible restructuring, *Academy of Management Executive*, 19(4): 39–50.

[153] E. W. K. Tsang, 2002, Acquiring knowledge by foreign partners from international joint ventures in a transition economy: Learning-by-doing and learning myopia, *Strategic Management Journal*, 23: 835–854.

[154] N. Mirabal & R. DeYoung, 2005, Downsizing as a strategic intervention, *Journal of American Academy of Business*, 6(1): 39–45.

[155] K. Shimizu & M. A. Hitt, 2005, What constrains or facilitates divestitures of formerly acquired firms? The effects of organizational inertia, *Journal of Management*, 31: 50–72.

[156] S. Toms & M. Wright, 2005, Divergence and convergence within AngloAmerican corporate governance systems: Evidence from the US and UK, 1950–2000, *Business History*, 47(2): 267–295.

[157] P. Desbrieres & A. Schatt, 2002, The impacts of LBOs on the performance of acquired firms: The French case, *Journal of Business Finance & Accounting*, 29: 695–729.

[158] G. D. Bruton, J. K. Keels, & E. L. Scifres, 2002, Corporate restructuring and performance: An agency perspective on the complete buyout cycle, *Journal of Business Research*, 55: 709–724; W. F. Long & D. J. Ravenscraft, 1993, LBOs, debt, and R&D intensity, *Strategic Management Journal*, 14(summer special issue): 119–135.

[159] Wright, Hoskisson, Busenitz, & Dial, Entrepreneurial growth through privatization.

# CHAPTER 10

# International Strategy

## KNOWLEDGE OBJECTIVES

*Studying this chapter should provide you with the strategic management knowledge needed to:*

1. Explain the primary reasons firms pursue international diversification.

2. Explain the factors that influence decisions regarding the international scope of a firm's activities.

3. Define the three international corporate-level strategies along with the structures associated with each strategy.

4. Explain the relationship between international corporate-level strategy and the selection of business-level corporate strategies within business units, countries, or global regions.

5. Identify the factors that contribute to the advantage of firms in a dominant global industry and associated with a specific country or regional environment.

6. Name and describe the five modes for entering international markets.

7. Explain the effects of international diversification on firm returns and innovation.

8. Name and describe two major risks of international diversification.

9. Explain why the positive outcomes from international expansion are limited.

---

The dramatic success of Japanese firms (i.e., Toyota and Sony) in the United States and other international markets in the 1980s was a powerful jolt to U.S. managers and awakened them to the importance of international competition in what were rapidly becoming global markets. In the 21st century, China, Brazil, India, and Eastern Europe represent potential major international market opportunities for firms from many countries, including the United States, Japan, Korea, and European nations.[1] This chapter covers various aspects of **international diversification,** a strategy through which a firm expands the sales of its goods or services across the borders of global regions and countries into different geographic locations or markets. We examine opportunities that firms identify as they seek to develop and exploit core competencies by diversifying geographically into global markets.[2] In addition, we discuss different problems, complexities, and threats that might accompany use of the firm's international strategies. Although national boundaries, cultural differences, and geographical distances all pose barriers to entry into many markets, significant opportunities draw businesses into the international arena.[3]

A firm that plans to operate globally must formulate a successful strategy to take advantage of these global opportunities.[4] Furthermore, to mold their firms into truly global companies, managers must develop a global mind-set, which was defined in Chapter 4 as the ability to study an internal environment in ways that do not depend on the assumptions of a single country, culture, or context.[5] As firms move into international markets, they develop relationships with suppliers, customers, and partners and then learn from these relationships.[6] Especially with regard to managing human resources, traditional means of operating, with little cultural diversity and without global sourcing, are no longer effective.[7]

**Figure 10.1: Reasons for, Selection of, and Outcomes from International Strategies**

| Reasons for International Strategy | Selection of International Strategies | Selection of Mode of Entry | | Desired Strategic Competitiveness Outcomes |
|---|---|---|---|---|
| Increase market size | *Corporate-level strategy* | Exporting | | |
| Increase return on investment | • Multidomestic<br>• Global<br>• Transnational | Licensing<br><br>Strategic alliances | Management difficulties | Higher performance |
| Seek economies of scale, scope, and learning | | Acquisitions | Risks | Innovation |
| Obtain resources and achieve other location advantages | *Business-level strategy*<br><br>(overall or by market) | New wholly owned subsidiary | | |

Figure 10.1, which serves as an outline for this chapter, provides an overview of the various incentives, choices, and outcomes associated with international strategy. This chapter first focuses on the reasons firms internationalize. Once a firm decides to compete internationally, it must select its strategy and an associated structure. The chapter outlines both international business and corporate-level strategies and structures and then provides rationales for choosing a mode of entry into international markets. Entry may be accomplished by exporting from domestic-based operations, licensing products or services, forming strategic alliances with international partners, acquiring a foreign-based firm, or establishing a new subsidiary. International diversification can lead to increased strategic competitiveness by extending product life cycles, providing incentives for more innovation, and ultimately producing higher organizational performance. These benefits are tempered by political and economic risks and the problems of managing a complex international firm with operations in multiple countries.

## Incentives for Using an International Strategy

An **international strategy** is a strategy through which the firm sells its goods or services outside its domestic market.[8] An international strategy results in international diversification. Firms pursue an international strategy (as opposed to a purely domestic strategy) to seek new opportunities to create value in international markets.[9] When successful, firms can derive four basic benefits from using international strategies: (1) increased market size; (2) greater returns on major capital investments or on investments in new products and processes; (3) greater economies of scale, scope, or learning; and (4) a competitive advantage through location (for example, access to low-cost labor or critical resources).

### Increased Market Size

Firms can expand the size of their potential market—sometimes dramatically—by moving into international markets. New large-scale, emerging markets, such as China and India, provide a strong internationalization incentive because of the potential demand for consumer products and services.[10] Because of currency fluctuations, firms may also choose to distribute their operations across many countries, including emerging ones, in order to reduce the risk of devaluation in one country.[11] However, the uniqueness of emerging markets presents both opportunities and challenges.[12] India, for example, offers a huge potential market and its government is becoming more supportive of foreign direct investment.[13] Nevertheless, India differs from Western countries in many respects, including culture, politics, and the precepts of its economic system. The differences between India and Western countries pose serious challenges to Western competitive paradigms; these challenges emphasize the skills needed to manage financial, economic, and political risks.

A large majority of U.S.-based companies' international business is in European markets.[14] More foreign direct investment is targeted at Great Britain than any other country in Europe.[15] In 2006, the United States and India dramatically increased the number of their foreign investments in Great Britain. However, according to a survey of U.S. investors conducted by AmCham of Germany and the Boston Consulting Group, Germany is now becoming more attractive for investment than Great Britain because of differences in cost of living and wages, as well as superior resources in the areas of product development and marketing.[16] U.S. companies alone have invested €120 billion in Germany, accounting for 850,000 jobs. Spain is also an increasingly attractive market for investment. For much of the period from 1997 to 2006 Spain's economy grew at twice the European Union average.[17]

Companies seeking to internationalize their operations in Asia, Europe, or elsewhere need to understand the pressure on them to respond to local, national, or regional customs, especially where goods or services require customization because of cultural differences or effective marketing to entice customers to try a different product.[18] Although changing consumer tastes and practices linked to cultural values or traditions is not simple, following an international strategy is a particularly attractive option to firms competing in domestic markets that have limited growth opportunities.

The size of an international market also affects a firm's willingness to invest in R&D to build competitive advantages in that market.[19] Larger markets usually offer higher potential returns and thus pose less risk for a firm's investments. The strength of the science base in the country in question also can affect a firm's foreign R&D investments. Most firms prefer to invest more heavily in those countries with the scientific knowledge and talent to produce value-creating products and processes from their R&D activities.[20] The United States and Germany have strong reputations in R&D,[21] and China is also making very large investments in that area. In 2006 China invested an estimated $136 billion on R&D, making it second only to the United States, at an estimated $330 billion.[22]

International diversification can help extend a product's life cycle.[23] Typically, a firm discovers an innovation in its home-country market. Some demand for the product may then develop in other countries, and exports are provided by domestic operations. Increased demand in foreign countries justifies direct foreign investment in production capacity abroad, especially because foreign competitors also organize to meet increasing demand. As the product becomes standardized, the firm may rationalize its operations by moving production to a region with low manufacturing costs.[24]

## Return on Investment

Large markets may be crucial for earning a return on significant investments, such as plant and capital equipment or R&D. Therefore, most R&D-intensive industries, such as electronics, are international. In addition to the need for a large market to recoup heavy investment in R&D, the development pace for new technology is increasing. As a result, new products become obsolete more rapidly, and therefore investments need to be recouped more quickly. Moreover, firms' abilities to develop new technologies are expanding; and, because of different patent laws across country borders, imitation by competitors is more likely. Through reverse engineering, competitors are able to take apart a product, learn the new technology, and develop a similar product that imitates the new technology. Because their competitors can imitate the new technology relatively quickly, firms need to recoup new product development costs even more rapidly. Consequently, the larger markets provided by international expansion are particularly attractive in many industries, such as computer hardware, because they expand the opportunity for the firm to recoup a large capital investment and large-scale R&D expenditures.[25]

However, the primary reason for making investments in international markets is to generate higher returns than firms would achieve on investments made in their domestic markets.[26] For example, Gruma, Mexico's leading corn flour producer, has had difficulty earning high returns in its home market because of government price controls on both flour and tortillas. However, Gruma has used this dominant position in Mexico to buy new brands and build plants in other countries. It has a new factory in Shanghai that is producing millions of tortillas for Kentucky Fried Chicken and other customers. The company now produces tortillas and corn chips in 89 factories from Australia to Britain,[27] and its margins are significantly better in its international operations than they are in Mexico.

## Economies of Scale, Scope, and Learning

By expanding their markets, firms may be able to enjoy economies of scale, particularly in their manufacturing operations. To the extent that a firm can standardize its products across country borders and use the same or similar production facilities, thereby coordinating critical resource functions, it is more likely to achieve optimal economies of scale.[28]

In some industries, technology drives globalization because the economies of scale necessary to reduce costs to the lowest level often require an investment greater than that needed to meet domestic market demand. There is also pressure for cost reductions, achieved by purchasing from the lowest-cost global suppliers. For example, economies of scale are critical in the global auto industry. China's decision to join the World Trade Organization is allowing carmakers from other countries to enter China and causing China to lower tariffs (in the past Chinese carmakers have had an advantage over foreign carmakers because of tariffs). Ford, Honda, General Motors (GM), and Volkswagen are each producing an economy car to compete with the existing cars in China. Because of global economies of scale, all of these companies are likely to obtain market share in China. The Chinese government–owned Shanghai Automotive Industry Corp. (SAIC) has helped these foreign car companies achieve significant success in manufacturing cars in China. SAIC has joint ventures, for example, with both GM and Volkswagen. Furthermore, SAIC is seeking to develop opportunities for exporting vehicles as well. It aspires to be one of the six largest automakers in the world by 2020.[29]

Economies of scope are also an incentive for international expansion. Firms may be able to exploit core competencies in international markets through sharing resources and knowledge between units across country borders.[30] This sharing generates synergy, which helps the firm produce higher-quality goods or services at lower cost.

In addition, working across international markets provides the firm with new learning opportunities.[31] Multinational firms have substantial occasions to learn from the different practices they encounter in international markets. Moreover, R&D expertise for emerging products and businesses may not exist in the domestic market.[32] In this case, the firm will need to go to where it can obtain the necessary knowledge. Novartis, the world's fourth-largest pharmaceutical company, recently announced a $100 million investment in R&D in Shanghai not to reduce costs, but because "the city is packed with universities and hospitals bubbling with ideas."[33] To take advantage of international R&D investments, firms need to already have a strong R&D system in place to absorb the knowledge.[34]

## Obtain Resources and Achieve Other Location Advantages

Another traditional motive for firms to become multinational is to secure needed resources, whether in the form of scarce factors of production or lower costs.[35] Key supplies of raw material, especially minerals and energy, are important in some industries. For instance, aluminum producers need a supply of bauxite, tire firms need rubber, and oil companies scour the world to find new petroleum reserves. Other industries, such as the garment, electronics, and watch-making industries, seek low-cost factors of production and have moved portions of their operations to foreign locations in pursuit of lower costs.[36]

Some countries provide access to lower-cost labor, energy, or other natural resources. In North America, Mexico has well-developed infrastructures and a skilled, though inexpensive, labor force, and it has received significant amounts of foreign direct investment. The costs of locating in Mexico are significantly lower than in other countries regionally. Flextronics found the country's reasonably low labor rate and proximity to its customers in North America ideal. It therefore moved to a 124-acre industrial park in Guadalajara, Mexico, where it manufactures multiple products ranging from handheld computers to routers. The venture was so successful that the company later built two additional plants in different parts of Mexico.[37]

Location advantages can be influenced by the needs of intended customers as well as by costs.[38] For example, dozens of Chinese and Taiwanese companies have made significant investments in production facilities in Central Europe to get closer to wealthy European customers. Chinese consumer electronics maker Hisense opened a plant that makes televisions in Hungary, and Shanghai-based SVA Group is building a plant in Bulgaria. Taiwanese PC manufacturer Foxconn Technology and TV manufacturer Tatung both have major operations in the Czech Republic.[39] In fact, the Czech Republic is becoming a major distribution center for international companies because of its central location. Japanese tire manufacturer Bridgestone and DHL Worldwide Express are among the most recent firms to establish distribution centers near Prague.[40]

Cultural influences may also affect location advantages and disadvantages. If there is a strong match between the cultures in which international transactions are carried out, the liabilities associated with being a foreigner are lower than if the cultures are very different.[41] Research also suggests that regulatory differences influence the level of ownership multinational firms are willing to undertake in a foreign business venture as well as their strategies for managing expatriate human resources.[42]

Assuming that the reasons for expanding international strategic presence are sufficient, firms must make several decisions regarding how to proceed. As discussed in Chapters 5 and 8, firms expect to create value through the implementation of a business-level strategy and a corporate-level strategy.[43] Consequently, they must decide whether they will follow an international corporate-level strategy that emphasizes a different approach to each international market, a standardized approach, or something in between. They must also determine how to use their distinctive competencies to create advantages in international markets through a business-level strategy. In addition, they have to choose a mode for entering new markets.

# International Corporate-Level Strategy

**International corporate-level strategy** focuses on the scope of a firm's operations through both product and geographic diversification.[44] The firm must select which products or services will be provided to various regions around the world. Consequently, international corporate-level strategy is like corporate-level strategy described in Chapter 8 in the sense that it is largely about the decision of where a firm should compete. International corporate-level strategy adds an international dimension to the diversification decisions firms make. Although large firms have tended to reduce the scope of their product diversification over the past two decades, the trend toward refocusing on core activities has been accompanied by an increase in the scope of international operations.[45]

The essence of international corporate-level strategy is to allow firms to use their core competencies to pursue opportunities in the external environment.[46] To create competitive advantage, each strategy must realize a core competence based on difficult-to-duplicate resources and capabilities.[47]

## International Scope: Worldwide Presence or Regionalization

Because a firm's location can affect its value creation,[48] it must decide whether to compete in all or many global markets, or to focus on a particular region.[49] Competing in all markets provides the potential for economies because of the combined market size. Also, firms may be influenced to expand their global reach because competing in risky emerging markets can lead to higher performance.[50] However, a firm that competes in industries in which the international markets differ greatly may wish to narrow its focus to a particular region of the world.

**Regionalization.** In support of the trend toward strategies that focus on particular regions, many countries have developed trade agreements to increase the economic power of their regions. The European Union (EU) and the Organization of American States (OAS) in South America are associations that developed trade agreements to promote the flow of trade across country boundaries within their respective regions.[51] Many European firms acquire and integrate their businesses in Europe to better coordinate pan-European brands as the EU creates more unity in European markets.[52] Similarly, the North American Free Trade Agreement (NAFTA), signed by the United States, Canada, and Mexico, facilitates free trade across country borders in North America. NAFTA loosens restrictions on international strategies within a region and provides greater opportunity for international strategies. A treaty called the Central American Free Trade Agreement (CAFTA) was signed by President George W. Bush in 2005 and was ratified by many Central American countries in 2006. It is now frequently called CAFTA-DR because of the addition of the Dominican Republic. Like the rest of these agreements, the intention is to reduce trade barriers across borders and encourage trade in the region.[53]

The Canada–Mexico partnership, which includes a large group of Canadian and Mexican businesses as well as various local and regional government agencies, provides an example of the effects of regionalization on business. One of the goals of the partnership is to "increase prosperity for both countries through the promotion of further trade and investment through a network of high-level business representatives."[54] The partnership currently has working groups in areas such as housing, agribusiness, and sustainability. The housing group consists of more than a dozen organizations, including business firms such as Habitat Design and Consulting and Canada Mortgage and Housing Corporation in

Canada, and Brasca Homes in Mexico, as well as the Engineering Institute of the National Autonomous University of Mexico. One of the early successes of the group is that Mexican developers agreed to use Canadian technologies in future construction projects that will help conserve energy.

Firms that pursue regionalization can better understand the cultures, legal and social norms, and other factors that are important for effective competition in those markets. For example, a firm may focus only on Far East markets rather than compete simultaneously in the Middle East, Europe, and the Far East. Or, the firm may choose a region of the world where the markets are more similar and some coordination and sharing of resources would be possible. In this way, the firm may be able not only to better understand the markets in which it competes, but also to achieve some economies.

Most firms enter regional markets sequentially, beginning in markets with which they are more familiar. They also introduce their largest and strongest lines of business into these markets first, followed by their other lines of business once the first lines are successful. They also usually invest in the same area as their original investment location.[55]

**Liability of Foreignness.** In addition to the trend toward regionalization, another influential factor for the scope of a firm's international operations is the liability of foreignness. Liabilities associated with being a foreign business in a highly different business environment can make competing on a worldwide scale risky and expensive.[56] Research shows that worldwide strategies are not as prevalent as once thought and are very difficult to implement, even when using Internet-based strategies.[57]

A variety of factors make operating a business in a foreign country difficult. Employment contracts and labor forces differ significantly in international markets.[58] For example, it is more difficult to lay off employees in Europe than in the United States because of differences in employment contracts. Also, in many cases, host governments demand joint ownership, which allows the foreign firm to avoid tariffs. Furthermore, host governments frequently require a high percentage of procurements, manufacturing, and R&D to use local sources.[59] These issues increase the need for local investment and responsiveness compared with seeking global economies of scale.[60]

Some of the biggest difficulties associated with liability of foreignness have to do with an inability to understand customers in international markets. Wal-Mart discovered this when it tried to enter the German market. The company assumed that Germans would want to be treated as Americans are in Wal-Mart stores; when Wal-Mart staff greeted customers brightly and helped pack their purchases, Germans fled. The company did not know that many Germans regard shop assistants who try to help them with suspicion.[61] In 2006 Wal-Mart sold its German stores to Metro, a local rival.

In the 21st century, regionalization and the liability of foreignness may lead some firms to focus more on regional adaptation rather than global markets.[62] Although developments in the Internet and mobile telecommunication facilitate communications across the globe, the implementation of Web-based strategies also requires local adaptation.[63]

After a firm has decided where it will compete, whether in a particular global region or across multiple regions, one of the most important decisions corporate-level managers must make is the degree to which headquarters will guide the strategy of businesses outside the home country. Some firms pursue corporate strategies that give individual country units the authority to develop their own business-level strategies, while other firms dictate what their business-level strategies will be in order to standardize the firm's products and sharing of resources across countries.[64] The three basic approaches to international corporate-level

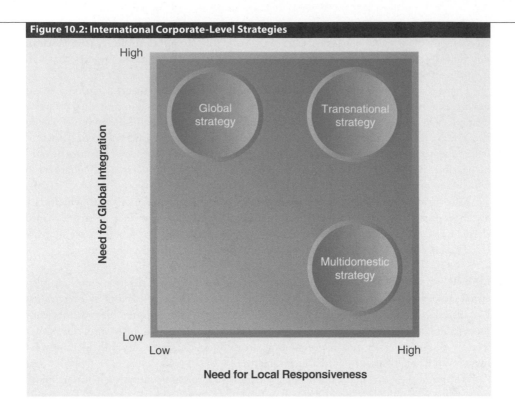

**Figure 10.2: International Corporate-Level Strategies**

High

**Need for Global Integration**

Global strategy

Transnational strategy

Multidomestic strategy

Low

Low          High

**Need for Local Responsiveness**

strategy are multidomestic (products adapted to each market), global (one product for the whole world), and transnational (a combination of multidomestic and global). As illustrated in Figure 10.2, two factors that influence the decision regarding type of corporate-level strategy are the need for global integration and the need for local responsiveness.

## Multidomestic Strategy

A **multidomestic strategy** is an international strategy in which strategic and operating decisions are decentralized to the strategic business unit in each country to allow that unit to tailor products to the local market.[65] A multidomestic strategy focuses on competition within each country. It assumes that the markets differ and therefore are segmented by country boundaries. In other words, consumer needs and desires, industry conditions (e.g., the number and type of competitors), political and legal structures, and social norms vary by country. With multidomestic strategies, the firm can customize its products to meet the specific needs and preferences of local customers. Therefore, these strategies should maximize a firm's competitive response to the idiosyncratic requirements of each market.[66] The use of multidomestic strategies usually expands the firm's local market share because the firm can pay attention to the needs of the local clientele.[67]

The multidomestic strategy decentralizes the firm's strategic and operating decisions to business units in each country so that product characteristics can be tailored to local preferences.[68] Firms using this strategy try to isolate themselves from global competitive forces by establishing protected market positions or by competing in industry segments that are most affected by differences among local countries. Also, the need for local repair and service capabilities can influence a firm to be responsive to local country conditions through its internationalization strategy.[69] This localization may even affect industries that are seen as needing more global economies of scale, such as home appliances.

The **worldwide geographic area structure,** which emphasizes national interests and facilitates the firm's efforts to satisfy local or cultural differences, is used to implement the multidomestic strategy (see Figure 10.3). Because using the multidomestic strategy requires little coordination between different country markets, integrating mechanisms among divisions in the worldwide geographic area structure aren't needed. Hence, formalization is low, and coordination among units in the structure is often informal.

The worldwide geographic area structure evolved as a natural outgrowth of the multicultural European marketplace. Friends and family members of the main business, who were sent as expatriates into foreign countries to develop the independent country subsidiary, often implemented this type of structure for the main business. The relationship to corporate headquarters by divisions took place through informal communication among "family members."[70]

One disadvantage of the multidomestic strategy with a worldwide geographic area structure is the inability to create global efficiency. For instance, multidomestic strategies make it more difficult to achieve economies of scale. Also, the use of these strategies results in more uncertainty for the corporation as a whole because of the differences across markets and thus the different strategies used by local country units.[71]

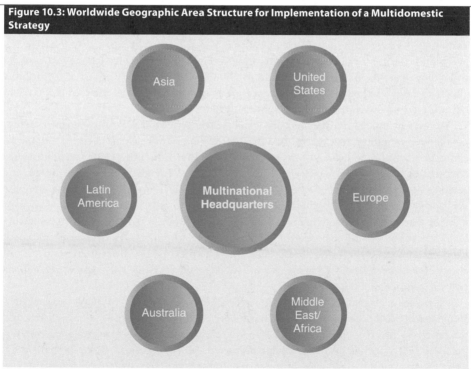

**Figure 10.3: Worldwide Geographic Area Structure for Implementation of a Multidomestic Strategy**

Notes:
- The perimeter circles indicate decentralization of operations
- Emphasis is on differentiation by local demand to fit an area or country culture
- Corporate headquarters coordinates financial resources among independent subsidies
- The organization is like a decentralized federation

## Global Strategy

In contrast to a multidomestic strategy, a **global strategy** is an international strategy through which the firm offers standardized products across country markets, with the competitive strategy being dictated by the home office.[72] The strategic business units operating in each country are assumed to be interdependent, and the home office attempts to achieve integration across these businesses.[73] A global strategy emphasizes economies of scale and offers greater opportunities to utilize innovations developed at the corporate level or in one country in other markets. Improvements in global accounting and financial reporting standards are facilitating this strategy.[74] Many Japanese firms have successfully used the global strategy.[75]

Pressure has increased for global integration of operations, mostly driven by more universal product demand. As nations industrialize, the demand for some products and commodities appears to become more similar. This "nationless," or borderless, demand for globally branded products may be due to similarities in lifestyle in developed nations. For instance, the Swedish firm IKEA International has become a global brand by selling company-designed furniture through about 250 stores in 34 countries.[76] To cut transportation costs, IKEA uses flat packaging; customers assemble the products at home. About 1,300 suppliers in more than 50 countries make the furniture. IKEA sells by mail order and online, and its stores also feature Swedish cuisine restaurants and playrooms for children.

While a global strategy produces lower risk, the firm may forgo growth opportunities in local markets, either because those markets are less likely to identify opportunities or because opportunities require that products be adapted to the local market.[77] The global strategy is not as responsive to local markets and is difficult to manage because of the need to coordinate strategies and operating decisions across country borders. For example, Vodafone, in implementing a global strategy, has had difficulty in Japan. "By focusing too much on building a globally oriented brand, Vodafone failed to give Japanese customers what they wanted, chiefly a wide lineup of phones with fancy features."[78] In addition, a global strategy can reduce the effectiveness of learning processes in a multinational firm because of the pressure to conform to a standard way of doing things.[79]

Achieving efficient operations with a global strategy requires the sharing of resources and coordination and cooperation across country boundaries, which in turn require centralization and headquarters control. The **worldwide product divisional structure** supports use of the global strategy (see Figure 10.4). In this kind of structure, decision-making authority is centralized in the worldwide division headquarters to coordinate and integrate decisions and actions among divisional business units. This structure is often used in rapidly growing firms seeking to manage their diversified product lines effectively, as in Japan's Kyowa Hakko.[80] With businesses in pharmaceuticals, chemicals, biochemicals, and food, this company uses the worldwide product divisional structure to facilitate its decisions about how to successfully compete in what it believes are rapidly shifting global competitive environments.

Integrating mechanisms are important for effective use of the worldwide product divisional structure. Direct contact between managers, liaison roles between departments, and "extensive and formal use of task forces and operating committees to supplement communication and coordination of worldwide operations" are examples of these mechanisms.[81] The evolution of a shared vision of the firm's strategy, and how structure supports its implementation, is one of the important outcomes resulting from the effective use of these mechanisms. The disadvantages of the combination of the global strategy and worldwide

**Figure 10.4: Worldwide Product Divisional Structure for Implementation of a Global Strategy**

Worldwide Products Division

Worldwide Products Division

Worldwide Products Division

**Global Corporate Headquarters**

Worldwide Products Division

Worldwide Products Division

Worldwide Products Division

Notes: • The headquarters' circle indicates centralization to coordinate information flow among worldwide products
• Corporate headquarters uses many intercoordination devices to facilitate global economies of scale and scope
• Corporate headquarters also allocates financial resources in a cooperative way
• The organization is like a centralized federation

structure are the difficulty involved with coordinating decisions and actions across country borders and the inability to quickly respond to local needs and preferences.

## Transnational Strategy

A **transnational strategy** is an international strategy through which the firm seeks to achieve both global efficiency and local responsiveness.[82] Realizing these goals is difficult: the first requires close global coordination and the second requires local flexibility. "Flexible coordination"—building a shared vision and individual commitment through an integrated network—is needed to implement the transnational strategy.[83] Such integrated networks allow a firm to manage its connections with customers, suppliers, partners, and other parties more efficiently rather than using arms-length transactions.[84] In reality, it is difficult to successfully use the transnational strategy because of its conflicting goals. On the positive side, effective implementation of a transnational strategy often produces higher performance than does implementation of either the multidomestic or global international corporate-level strategies.[85]

The worldwide combination structure is used to implement the transnational strategy. The **worldwide combination structure** draws characteristics and mechanisms from both the worldwide geographic area structure and the worldwide product divisional structure. The fit between the multidomestic strategy and the worldwide geographic area structure, and between the global strategy and the worldwide product divisional structure, are apparent. However, when a firm wants to implement both the multidomestic and the global strategies simultaneously through a combination structure, the appropriate integrating mechanisms for the two structures are less obvious.

Some assets and operations of the worldwide combination structure are centralized and others are decentralized. In addition, some functions are integrated and others are nonintegrated. These seemingly opposite characteristics must be managed by an overall structure that is capable of encouraging all employees to understand the effects of cultural diversity on a firm's operations. Consequently, a blend of formal and informal relationships and various mechanisms—including meetings, conference calls, subsidiary visits, cross-national teams, rotations and transfer of employees, and task forces that use inputs from across the firm—are developed throughout the organization to leverage both efficiency and flexibility.[86] Within a worldwide combination structure, some subsidiaries may be given a *global mandate*, which means that they are responsible for supplying a particular good or service to all parts of the organization throughout the world. Others may make a *specialized contribution* to an interdependent network of subsidiaries.[87] For instance, a subsidiary may be assigned the responsibility for one part of a production process. Still other subsidiaries within the structure may be responsible only for *local implementation*, which means that they play a well-defined role in the value chain, such as marketing and service in a single country.[88]

The requirements of a combination structure highlight the need for a strong educational component to change the whole culture of the organization. If the cultural change is effective, the combination structure should allow the firm to learn how to gain competitive benefits in local economies by adapting its core competencies, which often have been developed and nurtured in less culturally diverse competitive environments. As firms globalize and move toward the transnational strategy, the idea of a corporate headquarters has become increasingly important in fostering leadership and a shared vision to create a stronger company identity.[89] But fostering multiple and dispersed capabilities is also a challenge. Firms have been effectively managing "centers of excellence" as they emerge in foreign subsidiaries to help with this challenge.[90]

An example would be firms in the global automobile industry, which are choosing the transnational strategy to deal with global trends. Many of these companies produce automobiles with a basic design that is standard throughout the world but also a variety of models that reflect local markets. Standard designs help create efficiencies in engineering and production, while customized models appeal to individual markets. Also, automobile companies are increasing their production of models in the countries where they are sold. For example, in 1999 Ford spent $150 million on a plant near St. Petersburg, Russia. Cars started rolling off the production line in 2002. In 2006, New York Motors in southwest Moscow sold more cars than any other Ford dealership in the world.[91] Ford's prosperity in Russia, however, is in stark contrast to its lackluster performance in its domestic market.

Although the transnational strategy is difficult to implement, emphasis on global efficiency is increasing as more industries begin to experience global competition.[92] To add to the problem, emphasis on local requirements is also increasing: global goods and services often require some customization to meet government regulations within particular countries or to fit customer tastes and preferences. In addition, most multinational firms desire coordination and sharing of resources across country markets to hold down costs. Furthermore, some products and industries may be more suited than others for standardization across country borders.

As a result, most large multinational firms with diverse products employ a multidomestic strategy with certain product lines and a global strategy with others. Many multinational firms may require this type of flexibility if they are to be strategically competitive, partly because of trends such as regionalization and the liability of foreignness.

## International Business-Level Strategy

In addition to a corporate-level international strategy, firms must also determine the business-level strategies that will be pursued in each business and international location. The generic business-level strategies discussed in Chapter 5 include cost leadership, differentiation, focused cost leadership, focused differentiation, and integrated cost leadership/ differentiation. A firm must also respond to competitive rivalry and competitive dynamics within international markets, as discussed in Chapter 6.

International business-level strategies depend in part on the type of international corporate-level strategy the firm selects. If the firm adopts a global corporate-level strategy, then subsidiaries within particular countries may have very little liberty to choose their own business-level strategies because the essential characteristics of the product are already established. In these cases, the subsidiary would play the role of local implementer. The local implementer simply fine-tunes a strategy that is determined by international headquarters.

The cost leadership strategy is most closely associated with a global corporate-level strategy because global corporate-level strategies tend to produce standard products for the whole world, thus facilitating economies of scale. For example, the chemical giant BASF has created a sprawling complex of 250 individual chemical factories in its headquarters town of Ludwigshafen, Germany. The complex, called the *Verbund*, employs 36,000 people and turns out 8,000 different products, all in one place. The level of efficiency of the operation is "legendary" despite the high costs of doing business in the Mannheim region of Germany.[93]

If the firm's international corporate-level strategy is multidomestic or to some extent transnational, then each international subsidiary will have more control over its own approach to its domestic market. For example, Bausch & Lomb has different approaches to its various international markets in sunglasses as well as other eye care products.[94] Production and marketing policies are determined in individual markets, although the company does have some international plants to enhance production efficiency. Thus, its transnational corporate-level strategy allows some freedom to determine business-level strategies in individual markets.

In an international business-level strategy, the home country of operation is often the most important source of competitive advantage.[95] The resources and capabilities established in the home country frequently allow the firm to pursue the strategy into markets in other countries. Michael Porter's model, illustrated in Figure 10.5, describes the factors contributing to the advantage of firms in a dominant global industry and associated with a specific country or regional environment.[96]

The first dimension in Porter's model, *factors of production*, refers to the inputs necessary to compete in any industry—labor, land, natural resources, capital, and infrastructure (such as transportation, postal, and communication systems). Factors are basic (e.g., natural and labor resources) or advanced (e.g., digital communication systems and a highly educated workforce). Other production factors are generalized (highway systems and the supply of debt capital) and specialized (skilled personnel in a specific industry, such as the workers in a port who specialize in handling bulk chemicals). If a country has both advanced and specialized production factors, it is likely to serve an industry well by spawning strong home-country competitors that also can be successful global competitors.

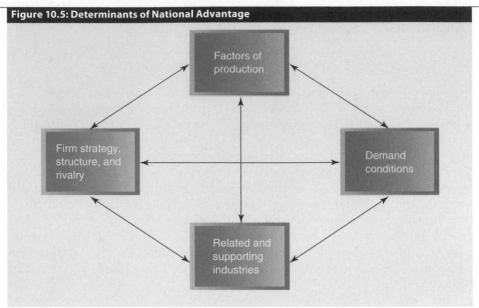

**Figure 10.5: Determinants of National Advantage**

SOURCE: Adapted with the permission of The Free Press, A Division of Simon & Schuster Adult Publishing Group, from *Competitive Advantage of Nations*, by Michael E. Porter, p. 72. Copyright © 1988, 1990 by Michael E. Porter.

Ironically, countries often develop advanced and specialized factors because they lack critical basic resources. For example, some Asian countries, such as South Korea, lack abundant natural resources but offer a strong work ethic, a large number of engineers, and systems of large firms to create an expertise in manufacturing. Similarly, Germany developed a strong chemical industry, partially because Hoechst and BASF spent years creating a synthetic indigo dye to reduce their dependence on imports, unlike Britain, whose colonies provided large supplies of natural indigo.[97]

The second dimension in Porter's model, *demand conditions*, is characterized by the nature and size of buyers' needs in the home market for the industry's goods or services. The sheer size of a market segment can produce the demand necessary to create scale-efficient facilities. This efficiency can also lead to domination of the industry in other countries. Specialized demand may create opportunities beyond national boundaries. For example, Swiss firms have long led the world in tunneling equipment because of the need to tunnel through mountains for rail and highway passage in Switzerland. Japanese firms have created a niche market for compact, quiet air conditioners, which are important in Japan because homes are often small and located closely together.[98]

*Related and supporting industries* is the third dimension in Porter's model. Italy has become the leader in the shoe industry because of related and supporting industries; a well-established leather-processing industry provides the leather needed to construct shoes and related products. Also, many people travel to Italy to purchase leather goods, providing support in distribution. Supporting industries in leather-working machinery and design services also contribute to the success of the shoe industry. In fact, the design services industry supports its own related industries, such as ski boots, fashion apparel, and furniture. In Japan, cameras and copiers are related industries. Similarly, it is argued that in Japan the "creative resources nurtured by [the] popular cartoons and animation sector, combined with technological knowledge accumulated in the consumer electronics industry, facilitated the emergence of a successful video game industry."[99]

*Firm strategy, structure, and rivalry* make up the final dimension of Porter's model and also foster the growth of certain industries. This dimension varies greatly from nation to nation. For instance, because of the excellent technical training system in Germany, firms strongly emphasize methodical product and process improvements. In Japan, unusual cooperative and competitive systems have facilitated the cross-functional management of complex assembly operations. In Italy, the national pride of the country's designers has spawned strong industries in sports cars, fashion apparel, and furniture. In the United States, competition among computer software producers has favored the development of this industry.

The four dimensions of the "diamond" model in Figure 10.5 emphasize the environmental and structural attributes of a national economy that contribute to national advantage. Government policies and regulations can also strongly influence the ability of firms in a country to compete successfully on a global scale. Airbus was originally formed as a multinational European consortium to challenge the dominant position of U.S. aircraft manufacturers. Now one of the two largest aircraft makers, Airbus has received much support from multiple European governments over its history.[100]

Although each firm must create its own success, not all firms will survive to become global competitors—not even those operating with the same country factors that spawned the successful firms. Furthermore, research indicates that as a firm continues its growth into multiple international locations, the country of origin is less important for competitive advantage.[101] The actual strategic choices managers make may be the most compelling reason for success or failure. Accordingly, the dimensions illustrated in Figure 10.5 are likely to produce competitive advantages only when the firm develops and implements an appropriate strategy that takes advantage of distinct country factors. Thus, these distinct country factors are necessary to consider when analyzing business-level strategies (i.e., cost leadership, differentiation, focused cost leadership, focused differentiation, and integrated cost leadership/differentiation) in an international context.

---

## Choice of International Entry Mode

After the firm selects its international strategies and decides whether to employ them in regional or world markets, it must choose a market entry mode.[102] International expansion is accomplished by exporting products, licensing arrangements, strategic alliances, acquisitions, and establishing new wholly owned subsidiaries (see Table 10.1). Each means of market entry has its advantages and disadvantages. Furthermore, the timing of international entry can influence its success.[103] Thus, choosing the appropriate mode or path to enter international markets affects the firm's performance in those markets.[104]

### Exporting

Many industrial firms begin their international expansion by exporting goods or services to other countries.[105] Exporting does not require the expense of establishing operations in host countries, but exporters must establish some means of marketing and distributing their products. Usually, exporting firms develop contractual arrangements with host-country firms.

The disadvantages of exporting include the often high costs of transportation and possible tariffs placed on incoming goods. Furthermore, the exporter has less control over the

**Table 10.1: Global Market Entry: Choice of Entry Mode**

| Type of Entry | Characteristics |
| --- | --- |
| Exporting | High cost, low control |
| Licensing | Low cost, low risk, little control, low returns |
| Strategic alliances | Shared costs, shared resources, shared risks, problems of integration (e.g., two corporate cultures) |
| Acquisition | Quick access to new market, high cost, complex negotiations, problems of merging with domestic operations |
| New wholly owned subsidiary | Complex, often costly, time consuming, high risk, maximum control, potential above-average returns |

marketing and distribution of its products in the host country and must either pay the distributor or allow the distributor to mark up the price to recoup its costs and earn a profit.[106] As a result, it may be difficult to market a competitive product through exporting or to provide a product that is customized to each international market.[107] However, evidence suggests that cost leadership strategies enhance the performance of exports in developed countries, whereas differentiation strategies are more successful in emerging economies.[108]

Firms export mostly to countries that are closest to their facilities because of the lower transportation costs and the usually greater similarity between geographic neighbors. For example, U.S. NAFTA partners Mexico and Canada account for more than half of the goods exported from Texas. The Internet has also made exporting easier.[109] Even small firms can access critical information about foreign markets, examine a target market, research the competition, and find lists of potential customers.[110] Governments also use the Internet to facilitate applications for export and import licenses. Although fears of terrorism may slow its progress, high-speed technology is still the wave of the future.[111]

Small businesses are most likely to use the exporting mode of international entry.[112] However, currency exchange rates are a significant problem for small businesses. Larger firms have specialists that manage the exchange rates, but small businesses rarely have this expertise. Changes in exchange rates can dramatically alter a firm's success in international markets. For example, in early 2007, Japanese exporters were enjoying a windfall in profits because the yen grew weak relative to the dollar.[113] Of course, the situation was opposite for U.S. companies exporting to Japan.

## Licensing

Licensing is one form of organizational network that is becoming common, particularly among smaller firms.[114] A licensing arrangement allows a foreign firm to purchase the right to manufacture and sell the firm's products within a host country or set of countries.[115] The licenser is normally paid a royalty on each unit produced and sold. The licensee takes the risks and makes the monetary investments in facilities for manufacturing, marketing, and distributing the goods or services. As a result, licensing is possibly the least costly form of international expansion.

Philip Morris International, Altria Group's international cigarette business, has seven of the top international cigarette brands in its portfolio, including the best-selling Marlboro. Its international sales have been increasing, primarily because of increased demand in Egypt, France, Mexico, the Philippines, Russia, Thailand, Turkey, and Ukraine. Nevertheless, U.S.-owned cigarette companies have had trouble entering the highly attractive

Chinese market because state-owned tobacco companies have lobbied against such entry. To overcome this problem, Philip Morris formed a licensing agreement with the China National Tobacco Corporation (CNTC). Under the terms of the agreement, CNTC has the right to sell cigarettes under the Marlboro brand name.[116]

Licensing is also a way to expand returns based on older innovations.[117] Even if product life cycles are short, licensing may be a useful tool. For instance, because the toy industry faces relentless change and unpredictable buying patterns, licensing is used and contracts are often completed in foreign markets where labor may be less expensive.[118]

Licensing also has disadvantages. For example, with a licensing agreement, the firm has very little control over the manufacture and marketing of its products in other countries, so structuring a licensing agreement properly is very important.[119] In addition, licensing provides the fewest potential returns, because returns must be shared between the licenser and the licensee. Worse, the international firm may learn the technology and produce and sell a similar competitive product after the license expires. Komatsu, for example, first licensed much of its technology from International Harvester, Bucyrus International, and Cummins to compete against Caterpillar in the earth-moving equipment business. Komatsu then dropped these licenses and developed its own products using the technology it had gained from the U.S. companies.[120]

In addition, if a firm wants to move to a different ownership arrangement, licensing may create some inflexibility. Thus, it is important that a firm thinks ahead and considers sequential forms of entry into international markets.[121] The key is to create needed flexibility in a licensing agreement so that a firm can pursue other means of approaching the market as conditions change.

## Strategic Alliances

In recent years, strategic alliances have become a popular means of international expansion.[122] Strategic alliances allow firms to share the risks and resources required to enter international markets.[123] Moreover, strategic alliances can facilitate the development of new core competencies that contribute to the firm's future strategic competitiveness.[124] Consequently, because their resources are so limited, alliances are an especially attractive way for small and medium-sized firms to enter international markets.[125]

Most strategic alliances are formed with a host-country firm that knows and understands the competitive conditions, legal and social norms, and cultural idiosyncrasies of the country. This helps the expanding firm produce and market a competitive product. For example, McDonald's formed a venture with China's largest gas retailer, the state-owned Sinopec, to create a chain of "Drive-Thru" restaurants at Sinopec gas stations. The agreement gives McDonald's the ability "to expand rapidly along highways and in fast-growing suburbs on the edges of China's sprawling cities, where cars are becoming ever more popular." The new "Drive-Thru" restaurants are being promoted as "fashionable and time saving"—"a brand new way of dining."[126]

Often, firms in emerging economies want to form international alliances and ventures to gain access to sophisticated technologies that are new to them. This type of arrangement can benefit the firm from the nonemerging economy as well, in that it gains access to a new market and doesn't have to pay tariffs to do so (because it is partnering with a local company).[127] In return, the host-country firm may find its new access to the expanding firm's technology and innovative products attractive. Each partner in an alliance brings knowledge or resources to the partnership.[128] Indeed, partners often enter an alliance with the purpose of learning new capabilities, such as technological skills.[129]

Not all alliances are successful, however; in fact, many fail.[130] Chinese electronics manufacturer TCL and Thomson Electronics of France formed a venture in 2004 to manufacture television sets, making it the largest manufacturer of TVs in the world. However, increasing global competition led to big losses, and by the end of 2006 most operations had been closed, "including a factory in Poland and an expensive distribution network."[131]

The primary reasons for failure—even more common than market changes—include incompatible partners and conflict between partners.[132] International strategic alliances are especially difficult to manage.[133] Several factors may cause a relationship to sour. Trust between the partners is critical and is affected by at least four fundamental issues: the initial condition of the relationship, the negotiation process used to arrive at an agreement, partner interactions, and external events.[134] Trust is also influenced by the cultures of the countries involved in the alliance or joint venture.[135]

The legal form of an international alliance depends on the nature of the alliance. Research has shown that equity-based alliances, over which a firm has more control, tend to produce more positive returns than non-equity–based alliances.[136] However, if trust is required for developing new capabilities, as is the case in a research collaboration, equity can serve as a barrier to the necessary relationship building.[137]

Research suggests that alliances are more favorable than acquisitions in the face of high uncertainty, where cooperation is needed to bring out the knowledge dispersed between partners, and where strategic flexibility is important, such as with small and medium-sized firms.[138] Acquisitions are better in situations that need less strategic flexibility and when the transaction is used to maintain economies of scale or scope.[139] Also, if conflict in a strategic alliance or joint venture will not be manageable, an acquisition may be a better option.[140]

## Acquisitions

As free trade has continued to expand in global markets, cross-border acquisitions have also been increasing significantly. In recent years, such acquisitions have comprised more than 45 percent of all acquisitions completed worldwide.[141] As explained in Chapter 9, acquisitions can provide quick access to a new market. In fact, acquisitions may provide the fastest, and often the largest, initial international expansion of any of the alternatives.[142] For example, the U.S. energy services company Superior Energy Services bought Duffy & McGovern Accommodations Services, based in Aberdeen, Scotland, to expand its offshore accommodations. Before the acquisition, Superior's offshore accommodations were primarily in the United States. According to Terence Hall, Superior's CEO, "This acquisition gives us immediate exposure to new rental markets around the world, and further broadens our international footprint."[143]

Although acquisitions have become a popular mode of entering international markets, they are not without costs. International acquisitions carry some of the disadvantages of domestic acquisitions, such as integration difficulties leading to an inability to achieve synergy (see Chapter 9). Like domestic acquisitions, they can be expensive and often require debt financing, which increases costs associated with the deal. In addition, negotiations for international acquisitions are generally more complicated than those for domestic acquisitions. For example, it is estimated that about half as many cross-border bids lead to a completed acquisition compared with domestic acquisitions.[144] Dealing with the legal and regulatory requirements in the target firm's country and obtaining appropriate information to negotiate an agreement frequently present significant problems.

Finally, the problems of merging the new firm into the acquiring firm often are more complex than in domestic acquisitions. The acquiring firm must deal not only with different corporate cultures, but also with potentially different social cultures and practices.[145] Therefore, while international acquisitions have been popular because of the rapid access to new markets that they provide, they also carry with them large costs and high risks.

## New Wholly Owned Subsidiary

The establishment of a new wholly owned subsidiary is called a *greenfield venture*. The process of establishing a greenfield venture is often complex and potentially costly, but it gives the firm maximum control and has the most potential to provide above-average returns. This potential is especially true of firms with strong intangible capabilities that might be leveraged through a greenfield venture.[146] For instance, Wal-Mart intends to draw on the strength of its brand name to enter the banking industry in Mexico. The Mexican market is especially attractive because 80 percent of Mexicans have never had a bank account and the existing big banks charge significantly higher interest rates and fees than banks in the United States.[147]

A firm maintains full control of its operations with a greenfield venture, which is especially advantageous if the firm has proprietary technology. Research also suggests that "wholly-owned subsidiaries and expatriate staff are preferred" in service industries where "close contact with end customers" and "high levels of professional skills, specialized know-how, and customization" are required.[148] Other research suggests that greenfield investments are more prominent where physical capital–intensive plants are planned and that acquisitions are more likely preferred when a firm is human capital–intensive—that is, where a strong local degree of unionization and large cultural differences would cause difficulty in transferring knowledge to a host nation through a greenfield approach.[149]

The risks are also high for a greenfield venture because of the costs of establishing a new business operation in a foreign country. The firm may have to acquire the knowledge and expertise of the existing market by hiring either host-country nationals, possibly from competitors, or consultants, which can be costly. Still, the firm maintains control over the technology, marketing, and distribution of its products.[150] Alternatively, the company would have to build new manufacturing facilities, establish distribution networks, and learn and implement appropriate marketing strategies to compete in the new market.[151]

Research shows that changes in government policies can influence whether a firm decides on a joint venture or a wholly owned approach. For instance, after the Asian financial crisis of the late 1990s many countries had to change their institutional policies to allow for more foreign ownership. As the institutional policy changed, many firms chose to go with a wholly owned approach rather than a joint venture.[152]

## Dynamics of Mode of Entry

A number of factors affect a firm's choice of mode of entry into international markets.[153] Initially, market entry will often be achieved through export, which requires no foreign manufacturing expertise and investment only in distribution. Licensing similarly requires relatively few resources, as in the case of Philip Morris International's entry into China. Both exporting and licensing are effective early entrance strategies.

Strategic alliances are popular because they allow a firm to connect with an experienced partner already in the targeted market. Strategic alliances also reduce risk through the sharing of costs. Consequently, a strategic alliance is often used in more uncertain situations, such as an emerging economy.[154] However, if intellectual property rights in the emerging economy are not well-protected, if the number of firms in the industry is growing quickly, and if the need for global integration is high, the greenfield entry mode is preferred.[155]

To secure a stronger presence in international markets, acquisitions or greenfield ventures may be required. Many Japanese automobile manufacturers, such as Honda, Nissan, and Toyota, have gained a presence in the United States through both greenfield ventures and joint ventures.[156] Toyota has particularly strong intangible production capabilities that it has been able to transfer through greenfield ventures.[157]

Both acquisitions and greenfield ventures are likely to come at later stages in the development of an international strategy. In addition, both of these strategies tend to be more successful when the firm making the investment possesses valuable core competencies.[158] Large diversified business groups, often found in emerging economies, not only gain resources through diversification, but also have specialized abilities in managing differences in inward and outward flows of foreign direct investment. In particular, Korean *chaebols*, a form of business conglomerate, have been adept at making acquisitions in emerging economies.[159]

Thus, to enter a global market, a firm selects the entry mode that is best suited to the situation at hand. In some instances, the various options will be followed sequentially, beginning with exporting and ending with greenfield ventures.[160] In other cases, the firm may use several, but not all, of the different entry modes, each in different markets. The decision regarding which entry mode to use is primarily a result of the industry's competitive conditions, the country's situation and government policies, and the firm's unique set of resources, capabilities, and core competencies.

## Strategic Competitiveness Outcomes

After a firm has chosen its international strategy and mode of entry, it turns its attention to implementation. Implementation is very important because, as explained next, international expansion is risky and may not result in a competitive advantage. The probability the firm will achieve success with an international strategy increases when that strategy is effectively implemented.

### International Diversification and Returns

As noted earlier, firms have many reasons for diversifying internationally. Because of its potential advantages, international diversification should be related positively to firms' returns. In fact, researchers have found that international diversification can lead to greater operational efficiency, which ultimately leads to higher financial performance.[161] A firm's returns may decrease at first as international diversification increases, but then returns increase as the firm learns to manage its international expansion.[162]

The stock market is particularly sensitive to investments in international markets. Firms that are broadly diversified into multiple international markets usually achieve the most positive returns, especially when they diversify geographically into core business areas.[163] There are many reasons for the positive effects of international diversification, such as potential economies of scale and experience, location advantages, increased market size, and the opportunity to stabilize returns, which helps reduce a firm's overall risk.[164] All of these outcomes can be achieved by both smaller and newer ventures and larger and established firms. New ventures can also enjoy higher returns when they learn new technologies through their international diversification.[165]

Firms in the Japanese automobile industry have found that international diversification may allow them to better exploit their core competencies because sharing knowledge resources between operations can produce synergy. Also, a firm's returns may affect its decision to diversify internationally. For example, poor returns in a domestic market may encourage a firm to expand internationally in order to enhance its profit potential. In addition, internationally diversified firms may have access to more flexible labor markets, as the Japanese do in the United States, and may thereby benefit from global scanning for competition and market opportunities. Also, through global networks with assets in many countries, firms can develop more flexible structures to adjust to changes that might occur.[166] "Offshore outsourcing," or *offshoring*, has allowed for significant value-creating opportunities for firms engaged in it, especially as firms move into regions with more flexible labor markets.[167] Furthermore, offshoring increases exports for the firms that receive the contract.[168]

Multinational firms with efficient and competitive operations are more likely to produce above-average returns for their investors and better products for their customers than are solely domestic firms. However, as explained later, international diversification can be carried too far.

## International Diversification and Innovation

In Chapter 1, we noted that the development of new technology is at the heart of value creation. A nation's competitiveness partly depends on the capacity of its industry to innovate. Eventually and inevitably, competitors outperform firms that fail to innovate and improve their operations and products. Therefore, the only way to sustain a competitive advantage is to upgrade it continually.[169]

International diversification provides the potential for firms to achieve greater returns on their innovations (through larger or more numerous markets) and lowers the often substantial risks of R&D investments. In addition, firms moving into international markets are exposed to new products and processes. If they learn about those products and processes and integrate this knowledge into their operations, they can develop further innovation.[170] Therefore, international diversification provides incentives for firms to innovate.[171] However, for firms to take advantage of R&D investment, they must have a well-developed capacity for knowledge absorption.[172]

International diversification may also be necessary to generate the resources required to sustain a large-scale R&D operation. An environment of rapid technological obsolescence makes it difficult for a firm to invest in new technologies and the capital-intensive operations required to take advantage of such investments. Firms operating solely in domestic markets may find such high-level investments problematic because of the length of time required to recoup the original costs. If that time is extended, it may not even be possible to recover the investment before the technology becomes obsolete.[173] As a result, international diversification improves a firm's ability to appropriate additional and necessary returns from innovation before competitors can overcome the initial competitive advantage created by the innovation. For instance, research suggests that Japanese foreign direct investment in developing countries is focused more on market-seeking and labor cost-saving purposes, whereas investment in developed economies is more focused on strategy development as well as market-seeking purposes. In these firms, a relatively strong ownership advantage is evident compared with firms in developing economies.[174]

The relationship among international diversification, innovation, and returns is complex. Researchers generally agree that technological and organizational learning through international diversification ultimately leads to higher financial performance.[175] However, some level of performance is necessary to provide the resources to generate international diversification, which in turn provides incentives and resources to invest in R&D. The latter, if done appropriately, should enhance the returns of the firm, which then provides more resources for continued international diversification and investment in R&D.[176] But as with many types of investments, higher returns mean higher risks.

## Risks in an International Environment

International strategy carries risks that are not associated with a purely domestic strategy.[177] Because of these risks, international expansion is difficult to implement, and it is difficult to manage after implementation. The chief risks are political and economic. Taking these risks into account, highly internationally diversified firms are accustomed to market conditions yielding competitive situations that differ from what was predicted. Sometimes, these situations contribute to the firm's value creation; on other occasions, they negatively affect the firm's efforts.[178]

**Political Risks.** Political risks are related to instability in national governments and to war, both civil and international. Instability in a national government creates numerous problems, including economic risks and uncertainty created by government regulations; the existence of many, possibly conflicting, legal authorities; and the potential nationalization of private assets.

Government corruption can have a very negative effect on business. Firms don't like to invest where corruption is prevalent because corruption leads to instability, sometimes in the form of protests, revolts, or revolutions. Often these actions are associated with changes in national leadership, which could also mean changes in economic policies. According to Transparency International's annual corruption index, the least corrupt governments in the world in 2006 were in Finland, Iceland, and New Zealand. The United States government was also among the least corrupt. In the middle of the list were the governments of Brazil and India. Iraq and Haiti were among the most corrupt governments in the ranking.[179]

Changes in government policies can dramatically influence the attractiveness of direct foreign investment. For example, "China's government has been creating some new hurdles for foreign investors in recent months, with increased scrutiny of foreign-backed mergers and proposed restrictions in areas from banking to retailing to manufacturing." The changes were a result of "the government's preoccupation with helping the ever-increasing universe of new Chinese companies and tackling pressing domestic issues such as poverty and wealth disparities."[180] Such changes can limit the attractiveness of foreign investment. On the other hand, some firms are able to achieve a favored position with the government in a particular country. In this case, they face less investment risk, which can put them at a competitive advantage relative to other firms.[181]

**Economic Risks.** Foremost among the economic risks of international diversification are the differences and fluctuations in the value of different currencies.[182] The value of the dollar relative to other currencies determines the value of the international assets and earnings of U.S. firms. For example, an increase in the value of the U.S. dollar can reduce the value of U.S. multinational firms' international assets and earnings in other countries. Furthermore, the value of different currencies can also, at times, dramatically affect a firm's competitiveness in global markets because of its effect on the prices of goods manufactured in different countries.[183] An increase in the value of the dollar can harm U.S. firms' exports to international markets because of the price differential of the products. It can also affect economies of other countries.

Economic and political risks are interdependent. Besides the fact that political instability in the Middle East has caused a great deal of political turmoil elsewhere,[184] Middle Eastern problems influence oil prices. Since the global economy is so dependent on oil, these fluctuations can have serious economic consequences. The terrorism that has grown out of militant political groups in the region also poses a huge risk for businesses around the globe.[185] The predictable economic effect of terrorism is an increase in insurance and risk-management costs, which results in increased production prices, forcing companies to reanalyze the risks of doing business in countries where security risks are higher.[186] Other costs and risks—such as the risk associated with damage to a country or region's infrastructure or financial system in the aftermath of a major disaster—are not easy to predict or measure.

## Complexity of Managing Multinational Firms

Although firms can realize many benefits by implementing an international strategy, doing so is complex and can produce greater risks.[187] Risk levels increase even more when a firm operates in several different countries. Because of this increased complexity and risk, firms can grow only so large and diverse before becoming unmanageable or before the costs of managing them exceed their benefits.[188]

Returns on international diversification tend to level off and become negative as the diversification increases past some point.[189] There are several reasons for the limits to the positive effects of international diversification. First, greater geographic dispersion across country borders increases the costs of coordination between units and the distribution of products. Second, trade barriers, logistical costs, cultural diversity, and other differences by country (e.g., access to raw materials and different employee skill levels) greatly complicate the implementation of an international diversification strategy.[190]

Institutional and cultural factors can present strong barriers to the transfer of a firm's competitive advantages from one country to another.[191] Marketing programs often have to be redesigned and new distribution networks established when firms expand into new countries. In addition, firms may encounter different labor costs and capital charges. In general, it is difficult to effectively implement, manage, and control a firm's international operations.[192]

The amount of international diversification that can be managed will vary from firm to firm and according to the abilities of each firm's managers. The problems of central coordination and integration are mitigated if the firm diversifies into more friendly countries that are geographically close and have cultures similar to its own country's culture. In that case, there are likely to be fewer trade barriers, the laws and customs are better understood, and the product is easier to adapt to local markets.[193] For example, U.S. firms may find it less difficult to expand their operations into Mexico, Canada, and Western European countries than into Asian countries.

Management must also be concerned with the relationship between the host government and the multinational corporation.[194] Although government policy and regulations are often barriers, many firms, such as Toyota and General Motors, have turned to strategic alliances to overcome those barriers.[195] By forming interorganizational networks, such as strategic alliances, firms can share resources and risks but also build flexibility.[196] However, large networks can be difficult to manage.[197]

Evidence suggests that more culturally diverse top management teams often have a greater knowledge of international markets and their idiosyncrasies[198] (see Chapter 2 for a discussion of top management teams). Moreover, an in-depth understanding of diverse markets among top-level managers facilitates intrafirm coordination and the use of long-term, strategically relevant criteria for evaluating the performance of managers and their units.[199] In turn, this approach facilitates improved innovation and performance.[200]

# Summary

■ The use of international strategies is increasing. Firms are pursuing international diversification to (1) increase market size; (2) increase return on investment; (3) seek economies of scale, scope, and learning; and (4) obtain resources and achieve other location advantages.

■ Firms that pursue an international strategy must decide whether to compete in all or many global markets, or to focus on a particular region. Competing in all markets provides the potential for economies because of the combined market size. Also, firms may be influenced to expand their global reach because competing in emerging markets can lead to higher performance. However, a firm that competes in industries in which the international markets differ greatly may wish to narrow its scope because of the liability of foreignness. Factors such as differences in labor forces or an inability to understand customers in a particular market can lead to disadvantages for firms competing outside their primary domestic markets. Also, the trend toward regionalization is supported by governments that have developed trade agreements to increase the economic power of their regions.

■ There are three types of international corporate-level strategies. A *multidomestic strategy* focuses on competition within each country in which the firm competes. Firms using a multidomestic strategy, implemented through the worldwide geographic area structure, decentralize strategic and operating decisions to the business units operating in each country so that each unit can tailor its goods and services to the local market.

■ A *global strategy* assumes more standardization of products across country boundaries. The worldwide product divisional structure is used to implement the global strategy. This structure is centralized in order to coordinate and integrate different functional activities so as to gain global economies of scope and scale. Decision-making authority is centralized in the firm's worldwide division headquarters.

■ A *transnational strategy* seeks to combine aspects of both multidomestic and global strategies in order to emphasize both local responsiveness and global integration and coordination. It is implemented through the combination structure. Because it must be simultaneously centralized and decentralized, integrated and nonintegrated, and formalized and nonformalized, the combination structure is difficult to organize and manage successfully. It requires an integrated network and a culture of individual commitment where training is continually emphasized.

■ Although the transnational strategy's implementation is a challenge, environmental trends are causing many multinational firms to consider the need for both global efficiency and local responsiveness. Many large multinational firms, particularly those with many diverse products, use a multidomestic strategy with some product lines and a global strategy with others.

■ International business-level strategies partly depend on the type of international corporate-level strategy the firm has selected. The cost leadership strategy is most closely associated with a global corporate-level strategy because global corporate-level strategies tend to produce standard products for the whole world, thus facilitating economies of scale. If the firm's international corporate-level strategy is multidomestic or transnational, then each international subsidiary will have more control over its own approach to its domestic market. An international business unit, whether in a particular country or a region, adopts an approach based on one of the generic business-level strategies, which are cost leadership, differentiation, focused cost leadership, focused differentiation, and integrated cost leadership/differentiation.

■ International business-level strategies are usually grounded in one or more home-country advantages, as Porter's "diamond" model suggests. The diamond model emphasizes four dimensions: factors of production; demand conditions; related and supporting industries; and patterns of firm strategy, structure, and rivalry.

■ Firms may enter international markets in one of several ways, including undertaking exporting or licensing, forming strategic alliances, making acquisitions, and establishing new wholly owned subsidiaries, often called greenfield ventures. Most firms begin with exporting or licensing, because of their lower costs and risks, but later may expand to strategic alliances and acquisitions. Establishing a new wholly owned subsidiary is the most expensive and risky means of entering a new international market However, such subsidiaries provide the advantages of maximum control by the firm and, if they are successful, the greatest returns.

■ In general, international diversification is related to above-average returns, but this assumes that the diversification is effectively implemented and the firm's international operations are well-managed. International diversification provides greater economies of scope and learning, which, along with greater innovation, help produce above-average returns.

■ International diversification facilitates innovation in a firm because it provides a larger market and faster returns from investments in innovation. In addition, international diversification may generate the resources necessary to sustain a large-scale R&D program.

■ Among the risks involved with managing multinational operations are political risks (e.g., instability of national governments) and economic risks (e.g., fluctuations in the value of a country's currency).

■ There are limits to the ability of a firm to effectively manage international expansion. International diversification increases coordination and distribution costs, and management problems are exacerbated by trade barriers, logistical costs, and cultural diversity, among other factors.

## Ethics Questions

1. As firms internationalize, they may be tempted to locate facilities where product liability laws are lax in testing new products. Is this an acceptable practice? Why or why not?

2. Regulation and laws regarding the sale and distribution of tobacco products are stringent in the U.S. market. What are the ethical implications of U.S. firms pursuing marketing strategies for tobacco products in other countries that would be illegal in the United States?

3. Some companies outsource production to firms in foreign countries to save money. To what extent is a company morally responsible for the way workers are treated by the firms in those countries?

4. Global and multidomestic strategies call for different competitive approaches. What ethical concerns might surface when firms try to market standardized products globally? When should firms develop different products or approaches for each local market?

5. Are companies morally responsible to support the U.S. government as it imposes trade sanctions on other countries, such as China, because of human rights violations? What if a significant amount of its international business is in one of those countries?

6. Latin America has been experiencing significant changes in both political orientation and economic development. What strategies should foreign international businesses implement, if any, to influence government policy in these countries? Can businesses realistically expect to influence political changes?

# Notes

1. N. Lakshman, 2007, Private equity invades India, *Business Week*, January 8, 40–41; P. Wonacott & P. R. Venkat, 2006, India's economic growth ratchets up to 9.3%: Pace rivals China's gains. *Wall Street Journal*, June 1, A6; T. Isobe, S. Makino, & D. B. Montgomery, 2000, Resource commitment, entry timing and market performance of foreign direct investments in emerging economies: The case of Japanese international joint ventures in China, *Academy of Management Journal*, 43: 468–484.

2. W. P. Wan, 2005, Country resource environments, firm capabilities, and corporate diversification strategies, *Journal of Management Studies*, 42: 161–182.

3. M. A. Hitt, L. Tihanyi, T. Miller, & B. Connelly, 2006, International diversification: Antecedents, outcomes and moderators, *Journal of Management*, 32: 831–867; M. Wright, I. Filatotchev, R. E. Hoskisson, & M. W. Peng, 2005, Strategy research in emerging economies: Challenging the conventional wisdom, *Journal of Management Studies*, 42: 1–30.

4. R. E. Hoskisson, H. Kim, R. E. White, & L. Tihanyi, 2004, A framework for understanding international diversification by business groups from emerging economies, in M. A. Hitt & J. L. C. Cheng (eds.), *Advances in International Management*, Oxford, UK: JAI/Elsevier, 137–163; A. K. Gupta & V. Govindarajan, 2001, Converting global presence into global competitive advantage, *Academy of Management Executive*, 15(2): 45–57.

5. M. Javidan, R. M. Steers, & M. A. Hitt (eds.), 2007, *The Global Mindset: Advances in International Management*, Vol. 19, Amsterdam: Elsevier Science; T. M. Begley & D. P. Boyd, 2003, The need for a corporate global mindset, *MIT Sloan Management Review*, 44(2): 25–32; A. K. Gupta & V. Govindarajan, 2002, Cultivating a global mindset, *Academy of Management Executive*, 16(1): 116–126.

6. S. A. Zahra, R. D. Ireland, & M. A. Hitt, 2000, International expansion by new venture firms: International diversity, mode of market entry, technological learning, and performance, *Academy of Management Journal*, 43: 925–950.

7. V. Mok & G. Yeung, 2005, Employee motivation, external orientation and the technical efficiency of foreign-financed firms in China: A stochastic frontier analysis, *Managerial and Decision Economics*, 26(3): 175–190; R. L. Mecham III, 2003, Success for the new global manager: What you need to know to work across distances, countries, and cultures, *Leadership Quarterly*, 14: 347–352; A. McWilliams, D. D. Van Fleet, & P. M. Wright, 2001, Strategic management of human resources for global competitive advantage, *Journal of Business Strategies*, 18(1): 1–24; B. L. Kedia & A. Mukherji, 1999, Global managers: Developing a mindset for global competitiveness, *Journal of World Business*, 34(3): 230–251.

8. L. Tongli, E. J. Ping, & W. K. C. Chiu, 2005, International diversification and performance: Evidence from Singapore, *Asia Pacific Journal of Management*, 22: 65–88; S. Tallman, 2001, Global strategic management, in M. A. Hitt, R. E. Freeman, & J. S. Harrison (eds.), *Handbook of Strategic Management*, Oxford, UK: Blackwell Publishers, 462–490; C. W. L. Hill, 2000, *International Business: Competing in the Global Marketplace*, 3rd ed., Boston: McGraw-Hill/Irwin, 378–380.

9. J. E. Ricart, M. J. Enright, P. Ghemawat, S. L. Hart, & T. Khanna, 2004, New frontiers in international strategy, *Journal of International Business Studies*, 35: 175–200; W. Hejazi & P. Pauly, 2003, Motivations for FDI and domestic capital formation, *Journal of International Business Studies*, 34: 282–289.

10. N. Lakshman, 2007, Private equity invades India, *Business Week*, January 8, 40; Wonacott & Venkat, India's economic growth ratchets up to 9.3%.

11. C. C. Y. Kwok & D. M. Reeb, 2000, Internationalization and firm risk: An upstream-downstream hypothesis, *Journal of International Business Studies*, 31: 611–629; J. J. Choi & M. Rajan, 1997, A joint test of market segmentation and exchange risk factor in international capital markets, *Journal of International Business Studies*, 28: 29–49.

12. Wright, Filatotchev, Hoskisson, & Peng, Strategy research in emerging economies; T. London & S. Hart,

2004, Reinventing strategies for emerging markets: Beyond the transnational model, *Journal of International Business Studies*, 35: 350–370; R. E. Hoskisson, L. Eden, C. M. Lau, & M. Wright, 2000, Strategy in emerging economies, *Academy of Management Journal*, 43: 249–267; D. J. Arnold & J. A. Quelch, 1998, New strategies in emerging markets, *Sloan Management Review*, 40: 7–20.

13   2006, Setting up shop in India, *Economist*, November 4, 73–74.

14   2005, EU economy: Building transatlantic bridges, *EIU Views Wire*, May 27; T. Aeppel, 2003, Manufacturers spent much less abroad last year—U.S. firms cut investing overseas by estimated 37 percent; the "high-wage paradox," *Wall Street Journal*, May 9, A8; J. P. Quinlan, 1998, Europe, not Asia, is corporate America's key market, *Wall Street Journal*, January 12, A20.

15   S. Daneshkhu, 2006, Foreign direct investment surges 34%, *Financial Times*, October 5, 4.

16   2006, Higher revenues, new jobs: Germany has become more attractive to U.S. investors, *PR Newswire*, http://www.prnewswire.com, March 16.

17   2006, Spain, long one of Europe's also-rans, is about to join the big league; Italy is going the other direction, *Economist*, November 4, 64.

18   T. Stein, 2005, Globe trotters: Venture firms are increasingly looking beyond U.S. shores, encouraged by the explosive growth, low development costs and surging entrepreneurship in emerging markets. But can U.S.-style venture capital be exported successfully? *Venture Capital Journal*, May 2, 1; W. Kuemmerle, 2001, Go global—or not? *Harvard Business Review*, 79(6): 37–49; Y. Luo & M. W. Peng, 1999, Learning to compete in a transition economy: Experience, environment and performance, *Journal of International Business Studies*, 30: 269–295.

19   K. Asakawa & M. Lehrer, 2003, Managing local knowledge assets globally: The role of regional innovation relays, *Journal of World Business*, 38: 31–42.

20   W. Chung & J. Alcacer, 2002, Knowledge seeking and location choice of foreign direct investment in the United States, *Management Science*, 48(12): 1534–1554.

21   2006, China's R&D prowess, *Business Week*, December 18, 37; Higher revenues, new jobs.

22   Higher revenues, new jobs.

23   R. Vernon, 1996, International investment and international trade in the product cycle, *Quarterly Journal of Economics*, 80: 190–207.

24   J. M.-S. Cheng, C. Blankson, P. C. S. Wu, & S. S. M. Chen, 2005, A stage model of an international brand development: The perspectives of manufacturers from two newly industrialized economies—South Korea and Taiwan, *Industrial Marketing Management*, 34: 504–514; S. Andersson, 2004, Internationalization in different industrial contexts, *Journal of Business Venturing*, 19: 851–875; H. F. Lau, C. C. Y. Kwok, & C. F. Chan, 2000, Filling the gap: Extending international product life cycle to emerging economies, *Journal of Global Marketing*, 13(4): 29–51.

25   F. Jiang, 2005, Driving forces of international pharmaceutical firms' FDI into China, *Journal of Business Research*, 22(1): 21–39; W. Shan & J. Song, 1997, Foreign direct investment and the sourcing of technological advantage: Evidence from the biotechnology industry, *Journal of International Business Studies*, 28: 267–284.

26   W. Chung, 2001, Identifying technology transfer in foreign direct investment: Influence of industry conditions and investing firm motives, *Journal of International Business Studies*, 32: 211–229.

27   G. Smith, 2007, Wrapping the globe in tortillas, *Business Week*, February 26, 54.

28   K. J. Petersen, R. B. Handfield, & G. L. Ragatz, 2005, Supplier integration into new product development: Coordinating product, process and supply chain design, *Journal of Operations Management*, 23: 371–388; S. Prasad, J. Tata, & M. Madan, 2005, Build to order supply chains in developed and developing countries, *Journal of Operations Management*, 23: 551–568; A. J. Mauri & A. V. Phatak, 2001, Global integration as inter-area product flows: The internalization of ownership and location factors influencing product flows across MNC units, *Management International Review*, 41(3): 233–249.

29   2007, Shanghai Automotive Industry Corp., http://www.hoovers.com, February 17; A. Taylor, 2004, Shanghai Auto wants to be the world's next great car company, *Fortune*, October 4, 103–109.

30   A. Inkpen & K. Ramaswamy, 2006, *Global Strategy: Creating and Sustaining Advantage across Borders*, New York: Oxford University Press; W. Kuemmerle, 2002, Home base and knowledge management in international ventures, *Journal of Business Venturing*, 2: 99–122; H. Bresman, J. Birkinshaw, & R. Nobel, 1999, Knowledge transfer in international acquisitions, *Journal of International Business Studies*, 30: 439–462; J. Birkinshaw, 1997, Entrepreneurship in multinational corporations: The characteristics of subsidiary initiatives, *Strategic Management Journal*, 18: 207–229.

31   Hitt, Tihanyi, Miller, & Connelly, International diversification; J. Cantwell, J. Dunning, & O. Janne, 2004, Towards a technology-seeking explanation of U.S. direct investment in the United Kingdom, *Journal of International Management*, 10: 5–20; S. Makino, C. M. Lau, & R. S. Yeh, 2002, Asset-exploitation versus asset-seeking: Implications for location choice of foreign direct investment from newly industrialized economies, *Journal of International Business Studies*, 33(3): 403–421.

32   D. Rigby & C. Zook, 2003, Open-market innovation, *Harvard Business Review*, 89(10): 80–89; J.-R. Lee & J. S. Chen, 2003, Internationalization, local adaptation and subsidiary's entrepreneurship: An exploratory study on Taiwanese manufacturing firms in Indonesia and Malaysia, *Asia Pacific Journal of Management*, 20: 51–72; K. Macharzina, 2001, The end of pure global strategies? *Management International Review*, 41(2): 105; W. Kuemmerle, 1999, Foreign direct investment in industrial research in the pharmaceutical and electronics industries: Results from a survey of multinational firms, *Research Policy*, 28(2/3): 179–193.

33   2006, A novel prescription, *Economist*, November 11, 73.

34   J. Penner-Hahn & J. M. Shaver, 2005, Does international research increase patent output? An analysis of Japanese pharmaceutical firms, *Strategic Management Journal*, 26: 121–140.

35   K. Ito & E. L. Rose, 2002, Foreign direct investment location strategies in the tire industry, *Journal of International Business Studies*, 33(3): 593–602; J. Bernstein & D. Weinstein, 2002, Do endowments predict the location of production? Evidence from national and international data, *Journal of International Economics*, 56(1): 55–76.

36   Mauri & Phatak, Global integration as inter-area product flows.

37   M. Bluetow, 2006, Report: Flextronics adding 3rd Mexico plant, *Circuits Assembly*, http://circuitsassembly

.com, October 27; R. Robertson & D. H. Dutkowsky, 2002, Labor adjustment costs in a destination country: The case of Mexico, *Journal of Development Economics*, 67: 29–54.

[38] R. Tahir & J. Larimo, 2004, Understanding the location strategies of the European firms in Asian countries, *Journal of American Academy of Business*, 5: 102–110.

[39] D. Rocks, 2007, Made in China—Er, Veliko Turnovo, *Business Week*, January 8, 43.

[40] S. Carney, 2006, Czech Republic's location leads to distribution-center boom, *Wall Street Journal*, May 24, A13.

[41] D. A. Waldman, A. S. de Luque, N. Washburn, R. J. House, et al., 2006, Cultural and leadership predictors of corporate social responsibility values of top management: A GLOBE study of 15 countries, *Journal of International Business Studies*, 37: 823–837; D. Xu & O. Shenkar, 2004, Institutional distance and the multinational enterprise, *Academy of Management Review*, 27: 608–618.

[42] D. Xu, Y. Pan, & P. W. Beamish, 2004, The effect of regulative and normative distances on MNE ownership and expatriate strategies, *Management International Review*, 44(3): 285–307.

[43] D. Tan & J. T. Mahoney, 2005, Examining the Penrose effect in an international business context: The dynamics of Japanese firm growth in U.S. industries, *Managerial and Decision Economics*, 26(2): 113–127; K. Uhlenbruck, 2004, Developing acquired foreign subsidiaries: The experience of MNEs for multinationals in transition economies, *Journal of International Business Studies*, 35: 109–123; Y. Luo, 2000, Dynamic capabilities in international expansion, *Journal of World Business*, 35(4): 355–378.

[44] W. P. Wan & R. E. Hoskisson, 2003, Home country environments, corporate diversification strategies and firm performance, *Academy of Management Journal*, 46: 27–45; J. M. Geringer, S. Tallman, & D. M. Olsen, 2000, Product and international diversification among Japanese multinational firms, *Strategic Management Journal*, 21: 51–80.

[45] H. P. Bowen & M. F. Wiersema, 2005, Foreign-based competition and corporate diversification strategy, *Strategic Management Journal*, 26: 1153–1171.

[46] R. E. Hoskisson, R. A. Johnson, D. Yiu, & W. P. Wan, 2001, Restructuring strategies of diversified business groups: Differences associated with country institutional environments, in M. A. Hitt, R. E. Freeman, & J. S. Harrison (eds.), *Handbook of Strategic Management*, Oxford, UK: Blackwell Publishers, 433–463; Y. Luo, 2001, Determinants of entry in an emerging economy: A multilevel approach, *Journal of Management Studies*, 38: 443–472; T. B. Palmer & R. M. Wiseman, 1999, Decoupling risk taking from income stream uncertainty: A holistic model of risk, *Strategic Management Journal*, 20: 1037–1062.

[47] S. Tallman & K. Fladmoe-Lindquist, 2002, Internationalization, globalization, and capability-based strategy, *California Management Review*, 45(1): 116–135; D. A. Griffith & M. G. Harvey, 2001, A resource perspective of global dynamic capabilities, *Journal of International Business Studies*, 32: 597–606; D. J. Teece, G. Pisano, & A. Shuen, 1997, Dynamic capabilities and strategic management, *Strategic Management Journal*, 18: 509–533.

[48] F. X. Molina-Morales, 2001, European industrial districts: Influence of geographic concentration on performance of the firm, *Journal of International Management*, 7: 277–294; M. E. Porter & S. Stern, 2001, Innovation: Location matters, *Sloan Management Review*, 42(4): 28–36.

[49] A. Rugman & A. Verbeke, 2004, A perspective on regional and global strategies of multinational enterprises, *Journal of International Business Studies*, 35: 3–18; B. Elango, 2004, Geographic scope of operations by multinational companies: An exploratory study of regional and global strategies, *European Management Journal*, 22(4): 431–441.

[50] C. Pantzalis, 2001, Does location matter? An empirical analysis of geographic scope and MNC market valuation, *Journal of International Business Studies*, 32: 133–155.

[51] R. D. Ludema, 2002, Increasing returns, multinationals and geography of preferential trade agreements, *Journal of International Economics*, 56: 329–358; L. Allen & C. Pantzalis, 1996, Valuation of the operating flexibility of multinational corporations, *Journal of International Business Studies*, 27: 633–653.

[52] 2006, Other EU candidates: A very long engagement, *Economist*, November 11: 56–57.

[53] 2007, Office of the United States Trade Representative, Central America-Dominican Republic Free Trade agreement, http://www.ustr.gov/Trade_Agreements, February 20.

[54] 2007, Foreign Affairs and International Trade Canada, Canada-Mexico Partnership: Report to leaders, http://www.itcan-cican.gc.ca/cmp-en.asp, February 20.

[55] W. Chung & J. Song, 2004, Sequential investment, firm motives, and agglomeration of Japanese electronics firms in the United States, *Journal of Economics and Management Strategy*, 13: 539–560; D. Xu & O. Shenkar, 2002, Institutional distance and the multinational enterprise, *Academy of Management Review*, 27(4): 608–618; J. Chang & P. M. Rosenzweig, 1998, Industry and regional patterns in sequential foreign market entry, *Journal of Management Studies*, 35: 797–822.

[56] L. Eden & S. Miller, 2004, Distance matters: Liability of foreignness, institutional distance and ownership strategy, in M. Hitt & J. L. Cheng (eds.), *Advances in International Management*. Oxford, UK: JAI/Elsevier, 187–221; S. R. Miller & A. Parkhe, 2002, Is there a liability of foreignness in global banking? An empirical test of banks' x-efficiency, *Strategic Management Journal*, 23: 55–75; T. Kostova & S. Zaheer, 1999, Organizational legitimacy under conditions of complexity: The case of the multinational enterprise, *Academy of Management Review*, 24: 64–81; S. Zaheer & E. Mosakowski, 1997, The dynamics of the liability of foreignness: A global study of survival in financial services, *Strategic Management Journal*, 18: 439–464.

[57] S. Zaheer & A. Zaheer, 2001, Market microstructure in a global B2B network, *Strategic Management Journal*, 22: 859–873.

[58] 2006, VW seeks return to longer work week; union balks, *Wall Street Journal*, June 13, A11.

[59] J. W. Spencer, T. P. Murtha, & S. A. Lenway, 2005, How governments matter to new industry creation, *Academy of Management Review*, 30: 321–337; I. P. Mahmood & C. Rufin, 2005, Government's dilemma: The role of government in imitation and innovation, *Academy of Management Review*, 30: 338–360.

[60] P. Ghemawat, 2001, Distance still matters: The hard reality of global expansion, *Harvard Business Review*, 79(8): 137–147.

[61] 2006, Global retailing: Trouble at till, *Economist*, November 4, 18.

62. A. Rugman & R. Hodgetts, 2001, The end of global strategy, *European Management Journal*, 19(4): 333–343.

63. F. T. Rothaermel, S. Kotha, & H. K. Steensma, 2006, International market entry by U.S. Internet firms: An empirical analysis of country risk, national culture and market size, *Journal of Management*, 32: 56–82.

64. J. Birkinshaw, 2001, Strategies for managing internal competition, *California Management Review*, 44(1): 21–38.

65. L. Li, 2005, Is regional strategy more effective than global strategy in the U.S. service industries? *Management International Review*, 45: 37–57; B. B. Alred & K. S. Swan, 2004, Global versus multidomestic: Culture's consequences on innovation, *Management International Review*, 44: 81–105; A.-W. Harzing, 2000, An empirical analysis and extension of the Bartlett and Ghoshal typology of multinational companies, *Journal of International Business Studies*, 32: 101–120; S. Ghoshal, 1987, Global strategy: An organizing framework, *Strategic Management Journal*, 8: 425–440.

66. L. Nachum, 2003, Does nationality of ownership make any difference and if so, under what circumstances? Professional service MNEs in global competition, *Journal of International Management*, 9: 1–32; J. Sheth, 2000, From international to integrated marketing, *Journal of Business Research*, 51(1): 5–9; J. Taggart & N. Hood, 1999, Determinants of autonomy in multinational corporation subsidiaries, *European Management Journal*, 17: 226–236.

67. Y. Luo, 2001, Determinants of local responsiveness: Perspectives from foreign subsidiaries in an emerging market, *Journal of Management*, 27: 451–477.

68. Inkpen & Ramaswamy, *Global Strategy*.

69. O. Gadiesh, 2004, Risk-proofing your brand, *European Business Forum*, summer, 82; Lee & Chen, Internationalization, local adaptation and subsidiary's entrepreneurship.

70. C. A. Bartlett & S. Ghoshal, 1989, *Managing across Borders: The Transnational Solution*, Boston: Harvard Business School Press.

71. M. Geppert, K. Williams, & D. Matten, 2003, The social construction of contextual rationalities in MNCs: An Anglo-German comparison of subsidiary choice, *Journal of Management Studies*, 40: 617–641; M. Carpenter & J. Fredrickson, 2001, Top management teams, global strategic posture, and the moderating role of uncertainty, *Academy of Management Journal*, 44: 533–545; T. T. Herbert, 1999, Multinational strategic planning: Matching central expectations to local realities, *Long Range Planning*, 32: 81–87.

72. L. Li, 2005, Is regional strategy more effective than global strategy in the U.S. service industries? *Management International Review*, 45: 37–57; Harzing, An empirical analysis and extension.

73. I. C. MacMillan, A. B. van Putten, & R. G. McGrath, 2003, Global gamesmanship, *Harvard Business Review*, 81(5): 62–71.

74. R. G. Barker, 2003, Trend: Global accounting is coming, *Harvard Business Review*, 81(4): 24–25.

75. H. D. Hopkins, 2003, The response strategies of dominant US firms to Japanese challengers, *Journal of Management*, 29: 5–25; S. Massini, A. Y. Lewin, T. Numagami, & A. Pettigrew, 2002, The evolution of organizational routines among large Western and Japanese firms, *Research Policy*, 31(8,9): 1333–1348; M. W. Peng, S. H. Lee, & J. J. Tan, 2001, The keiretsu in Asia: Implications for multilevel theories of competitive

advantage, *Journal of International Management*, 7: 253–276; A. Bhappu, 2000, The Japanese family: An institutional logic for Japanese corporate networks and Japanese management, *Academy of Management Review*, 25: 409–415; J. K. Johaansson & G. S. Yip, 1994, Exploiting globalization potential: U.S. and Japanese strategies, *Strategic Management Journal*, 15: 579–601.

76. 2007, Yahoo! Finance, IKEA International A/S company profile, http://biz.yahoo.com/ic/42/42925.html, February 17.

77. A. Yaprak, 2002, Globalization: Strategies to build a great global firm in the new economy, *Thunderbird International Business Review*, 44(2): 297–302; D. G. McKendrick, 2001, Global strategy and population level learning: The case of hard disk drives, *Strategic Management Journal*, 22: 307–334.

78. G. Parker, 2005, Going global can hit snags, Vodafone finds, *Wall Street Journal*, June 16, B1.

79. M. Zellmer-Bruhn & C. Gibson, 2006, Multinational organization context: Implications for team learning and performance, *Academy of Management Journal*, 49: 501–518.

80. 2007, Kyowa, http://www.kyowa.co.jp/eng/, February 20.

81. T. W. Malnight, 2002, Emerging structural patterns within multinational corporations: Toward process-based structures, *Academy of Management Journal*, 44: 1187–1210.

82. Inkpen & Ramaswamy, *Global Strategy*.

83. Bartlett & Ghoshal, *Managing across Borders*.

84. T. B. Lawrence, E. A. Morse, & S. W. Fowler, 2005, Managing your portfolio of connections, *MIT Sloan Management Review*, 46(2): 59–65; Y. Doz, J. Santos, & P. Williamson, 2001, *From Global to Metanational: How Companies Win in the Knowledge Economy*, Boston: Harvard Business School Press.

85. A. Abbott & K. Banerji, 2003, Strategic flexibility and firm performance: The case of US based transnational corporations, *Global Journal of Flexible Systems Management*, 4(1/2): 1–7; J. Child & Y. Van, 2001, National and transnational effects in international business: Indications from Sino-foreign joint ventures, *Management International Review*, 41(1): 53–75.

86. Inkpen & Ramaswamy, *Global Strategy*, 69.

87. J. Cantwell & R. Mudambi, 2005, MNE competence-creating subsidiary mandates, *Strategic Management Journal*, 26: 1109–1128.

88. Inkpen & Ramaswamy, *Global Strategy*; J. M. Birkinshaw & A. J. Morrison, 1995, Configurations of strategy and structure in subsidiaries of multinational corporations, *Journal of International Business Studies*, 26: 729–754.

89. R. J. Kramer, 1999, Organizing for global competitiveness: The corporate headquarters design, *Chief Executive Digest*, 3(2): 23–28.

90. T. S. Frost, J. M. Birkinshaw, & P. C. Ensign, 2002, Centers of excellence in multinational corporations, *Strategic Management Journal*, 23: 997–1018.

91. J. Bush, 2007, They've driven a Ford lately, *Business Week*, February 26, 52.

92. Inkpen & Ramaswamy, *Global Strategy*.

93. 2006, Molecular weight, *Economist*, November 4, 80–81.

94. 2007, Bausch & Lomb, Sunglasses: The bright side, http://www.bausch.com/en_US/consumer/age/sunglasses_senior.aspx; R. Jacob, 1992, Trust the locals, win worldwide, *Fortune*, May 4, 76.

95  J. Gimeno, R. E. Hoskisson, B. D. Beal, & W. P. Wan, 2005, Explaining the clustering of international expansion moves: A critical test in the U.S. telecommunications industry, *Academy of Management Journal*, 48: 297–319.

96  M. E. Porter, 1990, *The Competitive Advantage of Nations*, New York: The Free Press.

97  Ibid., 84.

98  Ibid., 89.

99  Y. Aoyama & H. Izushi, 2003, Hardware gimmick or cultural innovation? Technological, cultural, and social foundations of the Japanese video game industry, *Research Policy*, 32: 423–443.

100  2007, Airbus, Company evolution, http://www.airbus.com/en/corporate/people/Airbus_short_history.html, February 22.

101  L. Nachum, 2001, The impact of home countries on the competitiveness of advertising TNCs, *Management International Review*, 41(1): 77–98.

102  S. Zahra, J. Hayton, J. Marcel, & H. O'Neill, 2001, Fostering entrepreneurship during international expansion: Managing key challenges, *European Management Journal*, 19: 359–369.

103  H. J. Sapienza, E. Autio, G. George, & S. A. Zahra, 2006, A capabilities perspective on the effects of early internationalization on firm survival and growth, *Academy of Management Review*, 31: 914–933.

104  H. Zhao, Y. Luo, & T. Suh, 2004, Transaction costs determinants and ownership-based entry mode choice: A meta-analytical review, *Journal of International Business Studies*, 35: 524–544; K. D. Brouthers, 2003, Institutional, cultural and transaction cost influences on entry mode choice and performance, *Journal of International Business Studies*, 33: 203–221; R. Konopaske, S. Werner, & K. E. Neupert, 2002, Entry mode strategy and performance: The role of FDI staffing, *Journal of Business Research*, 55: 759–770.

105  C. Lages, C. R. Lages, & L. F. Lages, 2005, The RELQUAL scale: A measure of relationship quality in export market ventures, *Journal of Business Research*, 58: 1040–1048; R. Isaak, 2002, Using trading firms to export: What can the French experience teach us? *Academy of Management Executive*, 16(4): 155–156; M. W. Peng, C. W. L. Hill, & D. Y. L. Wang, 2000, Schumpeterian dynamics versus Williamsonian considerations: A test of export intermediary performance, *Journal of Management Studies*, 37: 167–184.

106  Y. Chui, 2002, The structure of the multinational firm: The role of ownership characteristics and technology transfer, *International Journal of Management*, 19(3): 472–477.

107  Luo, Determinants of local responsiveness.

108  M. A. Raymond, J. Kim, & A. T. Shao, 2001, Export strategy and performance: A comparison of exporters in a developed market and an emerging market, *Journal of Global Marketing*, 15(2): 5–29; P. S. Aulakh, M. Kotabe, & H. Teegen, 2000, Export strategies and performance of firms from emerging economies: Evidence from Brazil, Chile and Mexico, *Academy of Management Journal*, 43: 342–361.

109  W. Dou, U. Nielsen, & C. M. Tan, 2003, Using corporate Websites for export marketing, *Journal of Advertising Research*, 42(5): 105–115.

110  A. Haahti, V. Madupu, U. Yavas, & E. Babakus, 2005, Cooperative strategy, knowledge intensity and export performance of small and medium sized enterprises, *Journal of World Business*, 40(2): 124–138.

111  K. A. Houghton & H. Winklhofer, 2004, The effect of Web site and ecommerce adoption on the relationship between SMEs and their export intermediaries, *International Small Business Journal*, 22: 369–385; B. Walker & D. Luft, 2001, Exporting tech from Texas, *Texas Business Review*, August, 1–5.

112  P. Westhead, M. Wright, & D. Ucbasaran, 2001, The internationalization of new and small firms: A resource-based view, *Journal of Business Venturing*, 16: 333–358.

113  I. Rowley, 2007, Who's cashing in on the weak yen? *Business Week*, February 12, 42.

114  D. Kline, 2003, Sharing the corporate crown jewels, *MIT Sloan Management Review*, 44(3): 83–88; M. A. Hitt & R. D. Ireland, 2000, The intersection of entrepreneurship and strategic management research, in D. L. Sexton & H. Landstrom (eds.), *Handbook of Entrepreneurship*, Oxford, UK: Blackwell Publishers, 45–63.

115  A. Arora & A. Fosfuri, 2000, Wholly owned subsidiary versus technology licensing in the worldwide chemical industry, *Journal of International Business Studies*, 31: 555–572.

116  2007, The China National Tobacco Corporation and Philip Morris International announce the establishment of a long-term strategic cooperative partnership, http://www.altria.com/media, February 22; N. Zamiska & V. O'Connell, 2005, Philip Morris is in talks to make Marlboros in China, *Wall Street Journal*, April 21, B1, B2.

117  Y. J. Kim, 2005, The impact of firm and industry characteristics on technology licensing, *S.A.M. Advanced Management Journal*, 70(1): 42–49.

118  M. Johnson, 2001, Learning from toys: Lessons in managing supply chain risk from the toy industry, *California Management Review*, 43(3): 106–124.

119  D. Rigby & C. Zook, 2003, Open-market innovation, *Harvard Business Review*, 89(10): 80–89.

120  2007, Komatsu, Product outline, http://www.komatsu.com, February 22; C. A. Bartlett & S. Rangan, 1992, Komatsu limited, in C. A. Bartlett & S. Ghoshal (eds.), *Transnational Management: Text, Cases and Readings in Cross-Border Management*, Homewood, IL: Irwin, 311–326.

121  J. J. Reuer & T. W. Tong, 2005, Real options in international joint ventures, *Journal of Management*, 31: 403–423; B. Petersen, D. E. Welch, & L. S. Welch, 2000, Creating meaningful switching options in international operations, *Long Range Planning*, 33(5): 688–705.

122  R. Larsson, K. R. Brousseau, M. J. Driver, & M. Homqvist, 2003, International growth through cooperation: Brand-driven strategies, leadership, and career development in Sweden, *Academy of Management Executive*, 17(1): 7–21; J. W. Lu & P. W. Beamish, 2001, The internationalization and performance of SMEs, *Strategic Management Journal*, 22(special issue): 565–586; M. Koza & A. Lewin, 2000, Managing partnerships and strategic alliances: Raising the odds of success, *European Management Journal*, 18(2): 146–151.

123  J. S. Harrison, M. A. Hitt, R. E. Hoskisson, & R. D. Ireland, 2001, Resource complementarity in business combinations: Extending the logic to organization alliances, *Journal of Management*, 27: 679–690; T. Das & B. Teng, 2000, A resource-based theory of strategic alliances, *Journal of Management*, 26: 31–61.

124  M. A. Hitt, D. Ahlstrom, M. T. Dacin, E. Levitas, & L. Svobodina, 2004, The institutional effects on strategic

alliance partner selection in transition economies: China versus Russia, *Organization Science*, 15: 173–185; M. Peng, 2001, The resource-based view and international business, *Journal of Management*, 27: 803–829.

125 J. W. Lu & P. W. Beamish, 2006, Partnering strategies and performance of SMEs' international joint ventures, *Journal of Business Venturing*, 21: 461–480.

126 G. Fairclough & G. A. Fowler, 2006, Drive-through tips for China, *Wall Street Journal*, June 20, B1.

127 J. Bamford, D. Ernst, & D. G. Fubini, 2004, Launching a world-class joint venture, *Harvard Business Review*, 82(2): 91–100.

128 P. J. Lane, J. E. Salk, & M. A. Lyles, 2001, Absorptive capacity, learning, and performance in international joint ventures, *Strategic Management Journal*, 22: 1139–1161; B. L. Simonin, 1999, Transfer of marketing know-how in international strategic alliances: An empirical investigation of the role and antecedents of knowledge ambiguity, *Journal of International Business Studies*, 30: 463–490; M. A. Lyles & J. E. Salk, 1996, Knowledge acquisition from foreign parents in international joint ventures: An empirical examination in the Hungarian context, *Journal of International Business Studies*, 27(special issue): 877–903.

129 A. T. Mohr & J. F. Puck, 2005, Managing functional diversity to improve the performance of international joint ventures, *Long Range Planning*, 38(2): 163–182; R. C. Shrader, 2001, Collaboration and performance in foreign markets: The case of young high-technology manufacturing firms, *Academy of Management Journal*, 44: 45–60; M. A. Hitt, M. T. Dacin, E. Levitas, J. L. Arregle, & A. Borza, 2000, Partner selection in emerging and developed market contexts: Resource based and organizational learning perspectives, *Academy of Management Journal*, 43: 449–467.

130 M. W. Peng & O. Shenkar, 2002, Joint venture dissolution as corporate divorce, *Academy of Management Executive*, 16(2): 92–105; O. Shenkar & A. Van, 2002, Failure as a consequence of partner politics: Learning from the life and death of an international cooperative venture, *Human Relations*, 55: 565–601.

131 2006, A grim picture, *Economist*, November 4, 78.

132 J. A. Robins, S. Tallman, & K. Fladmoe-Lindquist, 2002, Autonomy and dependence of international cooperative ventures: An exploration of the strategic performance of U.S. ventures in Mexico, *Strategic Management Journal*, 23(10): 881–901; Y. Gong, O. Shenkar, Y. Luo, & M.-K. Nyaw, 2001, Role conflict and ambiguity of CEOs in international joint ventures: A transaction cost perspective, *Journal of Applied Psychology*, 86: 764–773.

133 P. K. Jagersma, 2005, Cross-border alliances: Advice from the executive suite, *Journal of Business Strategy*, 26(1): 41–50; D. C. Hambrick, J. Li, K. Xin, & A. S. Tsui, 2001, Compositional gaps and downward spirals in international joint venture management groups, *Strategic Management Journal*, 22: 1033–1053; M. T. Dacin, M. A. Hitt, & E. Levitas, 1997, Selecting partners for successful international alliances: Examination of U.S. and Korean firms, *Journal of World Business*, 32: 3–16.

134 J. Child & Y. Van, 2003, Predicting the performance of international joint ventures: An investigation in China, *Journal of Management Studies*, 40(2): 283–320; A. Arino, J. de la Torre, & P. S. Ring, 2001, Relational quality: Managing trust in corporate alliances, *California Management Review*, 44(1): 109–131.

135 L. Huff & L. Kelley, 2003, Levels of organizational trust in individualist versus collectivist societies: A seven-nation study, *Organization Science*, 14(1): 81–90.

136 Y. Pan & D. K. Tse, 2000, The hierarchical model of market entry modes, *Journal of International Business Studies*, 31: 535–554; Y. Pan, S. Li, & D. K. Tse, 1999, The impact of order and mode of market entry on profitability and market share, *Journal of International Business Studies*, 30: 81–104.

137 J. J. Reuer & M. Zollo, 2005, Termination outcomes of research alliances, *Research Policy*, 34(1): 101–115.

138 J. J. Reuer, 2005, Avoiding lemons in M&A deals, *MIT Sloan Management Review*, 46(3): 15–17; G. A. Knight & P. W. Liesch, 2002, Information internalisation in internationalising the firm, *Journal of Business Research*, 55(12): 981–995.

139 J. H. Dyer, P. Kale, & H. Singh, 2004, When to ally and when to acquire, *Harvard Business Review*, 82(7): 108–117; W. H. Hoffmann & W. Schaper-Rinkel, 2001, Acquire or ally? A strategy framework for deciding between acquisition and cooperation, *Management International Review*, 41(2): 131–159.

140 P. Porrini, 2004, Can a previous alliance between an acquirer and a target affect acquisition performance? *Journal of Management*, 30: 545–562; J. J. Reuer, 2002, Incremental corporate reconfiguration through international joint venture buyouts and selloffs, *Management International Review*, 42: 237–260.

141 K. Shimizu, M. A. Hitt, D. Vaidyanath, & V. Pisano, 2004, Theoretical foundations of cross-border mergers and acquisitions: A review of current research and recommendations for the future, *Journal of International Management*, 10: 307–353; M. A. Hitt, J. S. Harrison, & R. D. Ireland, 2001, *Creating Value through Mergers and Acquisitions*, New York: Oxford University Press.

142 M. A. Hitt & V. Pisano, 2003, The cross-border merger and acquisition strategy, *Management Research*, 1: 133–144.

143 2007, OilVoice, Superior Energy Services continues international expansion with acquisition of Duffy & McGovern Accommodations Services, http://www .oilvoice.com, January 23.

144 1999, French dressing, *Economist*, July 10, 53–54.

145 P. Quah & S. Young, 2005, Post-acquisition management: A phases approach for cross-border M&As, *European Management Journal*, 23(1): 65–80.

146 A.-W. Harzing, 2002, Acquisitions versus greenfield investments: International strategy and management of entry modes, *Strategic Management Journal*, 23: 211–227; K. D. Brouthers & L. E. Brouthers, 2000, Acquisition or greenfield start-up? Institutional, cultural and transaction cost influences, *Strategic Management Journal*, 21: 89–97.

147 G. Smith, 2006, In Mexico, Banco Wal-Mart, *Business Week*, November 20, 66–67.

148 C. Bouquet, L. Hebert, & A. Delios, 2004, Foreign expansion in service industries: Separability and human capital intensity, *Journal of Business Research*, 57: 35–46.

149 D. Elango, 2005, The influence of plant characteristics on the entry mode choice of overseas firms, *Journal of Operations Management*, 23(1): 65–79.

150 P. Deng, 2003, Determinants of full-control mode in China: An integrative approach, *American Business Review*, 21(1): 113–123.

151 R. Belderbos, 2003, Entry mode, organizational learning, and R&D in foreign affiliates: Evidence from Japanese firms, *Strategic Management Journal*, 34: 235–259.

152 K. E. Meyer & H. V. Nguyen, 2005, Foreign investment strategies in subnational institutions in emerging

markets: Evidence from Vietnam, *Journal of Management Studies*, 42: 63–93; J. Reuer, O. Shenkar, & R. Ragozzino, 2004, Mitigating risks in international mergers and acquisitions: The role of contingent payouts, *Journal of International Business Studies*, 35: 19–32.

153 S. J. Chang & P. Rosenzweig, 2001, The choice of entry mode in sequential foreign direct investment, *Strategic Management Journal*, 22: 747–776.

154 K. E. Myer, 2001, Institutions, transaction costs, and entry mode choice in Eastern Europe, *Journal of International Business Studies*, 32: 357–367.

155 S. Li, 2004, Why are property rights protections lacking in China? An institutional explanation, *California Management Review*, 46(3): 100–115; Y. Luo, 2001, Determinants of entry in an emerging economy: A multilevel approach, *Journal of Management Studies*, 38: 443–472.

156 A. Takeishi, 2001, Bridging inter- and intra-firm boundaries: Management of supplier involvement in automobile product development, *Strategic Management Journal*, 22: 403–433.

157 T. Keith, 2007, Will Texans now take to Toyota? *Business Week*, February 5, 10; I. Rowley, 2007, Even Toyota isn't perfect, *Business Week*, January 22, 54; D. K Sobek II, A. C. Ward, & J. K. Liker, 1999, Toyota's principles of set-based concurrent engineering, *Sloan Management Review*, 40(2): 53–83.

158 J. Hagedoorn & G. Dysters, 2002, External sources of innovative capabilities: The preference for strategic alliances or mergers and acquisitions, *Journal of Management Studies*, 39: 167–188; H. Chen, 1999, International performance of multinationals: A hybrid model, *Journal of World Business*, 34: 157–170.

159 J. E. Garten, 2005, A new threat to America, Inc., *Business Week*, July 25, 114; Hoskisson, Kim, Tihanyi, & White, A framework; S. J. Chang & J. Hong, 2002, How much does the business group matter in Korea? *Strategic Management Journal*, 23: 265–274.

160 J. Song, 2002, Firm capabilities and technology ladders: Sequential foreign direct investments of Japanese electronics firms in East Asia, *Strategic Management Journal*, 23: 191–210.

161 Hitt, Tihanyi, Miller, & Connelly, International diversification.

162 J. W. Lu & P. W. Beamish, 2004, International diversification and firm performance: The S-curve hypothesis, *Academy of Management Journal*, 47: 598–609; M. Ramirez-Aleson & M. A. Espitia-Escuer, 2001, The effect of international diversification strategy on the performance of Spanish-based firms during the period 1991–1995, *Management International Review*, 41(3): 291–315; A. Delios & P. W. Beamish, 1999, Geographic scope, product diversification, and the corporate performance of Japanese firms, *Strategic Management Journal*, 20: 711–727.

163 S.-C. Chang & C.-F. Wang, 2007, The effect of product diversification strategies on the relationship between international diversification and firm performance, *Journal of World Business*, 42: 61–77; S. E. Christophe & H. Lee, 2005, What matters about internationalization: A market-based assessment, *Journal of Business Research*, 58: 536–543; J. A. Doukas & L. H. P. Lang, 2003, Foreign direct investment, diversification and firm performance, *Journal of International Business Studies*, 34: 153–172.

164 J. M. Geringer, P. W. Beamish, & R. C. daCosta, 1989, Diversification strategy and internationalization: Implications for MNE performance, *Strategic*

*Management Journal*, 10: 109–119; R. E. Caves, 1982, *Multinational Enterprise and Economic Analysis*, Cambridge, UK: Cambridge University Press.

165 Zahra, Ireland, & Hitt, International expansion by new venture firms.

166 T. R. Holcomb & M. A. Hitt, 2007, Toward a model of strategic outsourcing, *Journal of Operations Management*, 25: 464–481; U. Andersson, M. Forsgren, & U. Holm, 2002, The strategic impact of external networks: Subsidiary performance and competence development in the multinational corporation, *Strategic Management Journal*, 23: 979–996; Malnight, Emerging structural patterns.

167 A. E. Harrison & M. S. McMillan, 2006, Dispelling some myths about offshoring, *Academy of Management Perspectives*, 20(4): 6–22.

168 D. Farrell, 2005, Offshoring: Value creation through economic change, *Journal of Management Studies*, 42: 675–683; J. P. Doh, 2005, Offshore outsourcing: Implications for international business and strategic management theory and practice, *Journal of Management Studies*, 42: 695–704.

169 J. Penner-Hahn & J. M. Shaver, 2005, Does international research and development increase patent output? An analysis of Japanese pharmaceutical firms, *Strategic Management Journal*, 26: 121–140; G. Hamel, 2000, *Leading the Revolution*, Boston: Harvard Business School Press.

170 Asakawa & Lehrer, Managing local knowledge assets globally; I. Zander & O. Solvell, 2000, Cross border innovation in the multinational corporation: A research agenda, *International Studies of Management and Organization*, 30(2): 44–67; Y. Luo, 1999, Time-based experience and international expansion: The case of an emerging economy, *Journal of Management Studies*, 36: 505–533.

171 L. Tihanyi, R. A. Johnson, R. E. Hoskisson, & M. A. Hitt, 2003, Institutional ownership differences and international diversification: The effects of board of directors and technological opportunity, *Academy of Management Journal*, 46: 195–211.

172 Penner-Hahn & Shaver, Does international research increase patent output?

173 B. Ambos, 2005, Foreign direct investment in industrial research and development: A study of German MNCs, *Research Policy*, 34: 395–410; F. Bradley & M. Gannon, 2000, Does the firm's technology and marketing profile affect foreign market entry? *Journal of International Marketing*, 8(4): 12–36; M. Kotabe, 1990, The relationship between off-shore sourcing and innovativeness of U.S. multinational firms: An empirical investigation, *Journal of International Business Studies*, 21: 623–638.

174 S. Makino, P. W. Beamish, & N. B. Zhao, 2004, The characteristics and performance of Japanese FDI in less developed and developed countries, *Journal of World Business*, 39(4): 377–392.

175 Hitt, Tihanyi, Miller, & Connelly, International diversification, 854.

176 O. E. M. Janne, 2002, The emergence of corporate integrated innovation systems across regions: The case of the chemical and pharmaceutical industry in Germany, the UK and Belgium, *Journal of International Management*, 8: 97–119; N. J. Foss & T. Pedersen, 2002, Transferring knowledge in MNCs: The role of sources of subsidiary knowledge and organizational context, *Journal of International Management*, 8: 49–67; Z. Liao, 2001,

International R&D project evaluation by multinational corporations in the electronics and IT industry of Singapore, *R&D Management*, 31: 299–307; M. Subramaniam & N. Venkatraman, 2001, Determinants of transnational new product development capability: Testing the influence of transferring and deploying tacit overseas knowledge, *Strategic Management Journal*, 22: 359–378.

177 Y. Paik, 2005, Risk management of strategic alliances and acquisitions between western MNCs and companies in central Europe, *Thunderbird International Business Review*, 47(4): 489–511; A. Delios & W. J. Henisz, 2003, Policy uncertainty and the sequence of entry by Japanese firms, 1980–1998, *Journal of International Business Studies*, 34: 227–241; D. M. Reeb, C. C. Y. Kwok, & H. Y. Baek, 1998, Systematic risk of the multinational corporation, *Journal of International Business Studies*, 29: 263–279.

178 C. Pompitakpan, 1999, The effects of cultural adaptation on business relationships: Americans selling to Japanese and Thais, *Journal of International Business Studies*, 30: 317–338.

179 2006, Corruption: Strains of sleaze, *Economist*, November 11, 69.

180 A. Batson, 2006, In strategic shift, China hits foreign investors with new hurdles, *Wall Street Journal*, August 30, A1.

181 J. G. Frynas, K. Mellahi & G. A. Pigman, 2006, First mover advantages in international business and firm-specific political resources, *Strategic Management Journal*, 27: 321–345.

182 T. Vestring, T. Rouse, & U. Reinert, 2005, Hedging your offshoring bets, *MIT Sloan Management Review*, 46(3): 26–29; L. L. Jacque & P. M. Vaaler, 2001, The international control conundrum with exchange risk: An EVA framework, *Journal of International Business Studies*, 32: 813–832.

183 T. G. Andrews & N. Chompusri, 2005, Temporal dynamics of crossvergence: Institutionalizing MNC integration strategies in post-crisis ASEAN, *Asia Pacific Journal of Management*, 22(1): 5–22; S. Mudd, R. Grosse, & J. Mathis, 2002, Dealing with financial crises in emerging markets, *Thunderbird International Business Review*, 44(3): 399–430.

184 2006, How much worse can it get? *Economist*, November 11, 52; 2006, Military solutions in the air, *Economist*, November 4, 53.

185 Inkpen & Ramaswamy, *Global Strategy*.

186 P. Engardio, R. Miller, G. Smith, D. Brady, M. Kripalani, A. Borrus, & D. Foust, 2001, What's at stake: How terrorism threatens the global economy, *Business Week*, October 22, 34–37.

187 Y. Li, L. Li, Y. Liu, & L. Wang, 2005, Linking management control systems with product development and process decisions to cope with environment complexity, *International Journal of Production Research*, 43: 2577–2591; J. Child, L. Chung, & H. Davies, 2003, The performance of cross-border units in China: A test of natural selection, strategic choice and contingency theories, *Journal of International Business Studies*, 34: 242–254; D. Rondinelli, B. Rosen, & I. Drori, 2001, The struggle for strategic alignment in multinational corporations: Managing readjustment during global expansion, *European Management Journal*, 19: 404–405; Carpenter & Fredrickson, Top management teams.

188 Y.-H. Chiu, 2003, The impact of conglomerate firm diversification on corporate performance: An empirical

study in Taiwan, *International Journal of Management*, 19: 231–237; Y. Luo, 2003, Market-seeking MNEs in an emerging market How parent-subsidiary links shape overseas success, *Journal of International Business Studies*, 34: 290–309.

189 Wan & Hoskisson, Home country environments; M. A. Hitt, R. E. Hoskisson, & H. Kim, 1997, International diversification: Effects on innovation and firm performance in product-diversified firms, *Academy of Management Journal*, 40: 767–798; S. Tallman & J. Li, 1996, Effects of international diversity and product diversity on the performance of multinational firms, *Academy of Management Journal*, 39: 179–196; M. A. Hitt, R. E. Hoskisson, & R. D. Ireland, 1994, A midrange theory of the interactive effects of international and product diversification on innovation and performance, *Journal of Management*, 20: 297–326; Geringer, Beamish, & daCosta, Diversification strategy.

190 B. Shimoni & H. Bergmann, 2006, Managing in a changing world: From multiculturalism to hybridization—the production of hybrid management cultures in Israel, Thailand, and Mexico, *Academy of Management Perspectives*, 20(3): 76–89; F. J. Contractor, S. K. Kundu, & C. C. Hsu, 2003, A three-stage theory of international expansion: The link between multinationality and performance in the service sector, *Journal of International Business Studies*, 34(1): 5–19; A. K. Rose & E. van Wincoop, 2001, National money as a barrier to international trade: The real case for currency union, *American Economic Review*, 91: 386–390.

191 M. A. Hitt, R. M. Holmes, T. Miller, & M. P. Salmador, 2006, Modeling country institutional profiles: The dynamics of institutional environments, paper presented at the Strategic Management Society Conference, November, Vienna, Austria; I. Bjorkman, W. Barner-Rasmussen, & L. Li, 2004, Managing knowledge transfer in MNCs: The impact of headquarters control mechanisms, *Journal of International Business Studies*, 35: 443–455.

192 I. M. Manev & W. B. Stevenson, 2001, Nationality, cultural distance, and expatriate status: Effects on the managerial network in a multinational enterprise, *Journal of International Business Studies*, 32: 285–303.

193 P. S. Barr & M. A. Glynn, 2004, Cultural variations in strategic issue interpretation: Relating cultural uncertainty avoidance to controllability in discriminating threat and opportunity, *Strategic Management Journal*, 25: 59–67; D. E. Thomas & R. Grosse, 2001, Country-of-origin determinants of foreign direct investment in an emerging market: The case of Mexico, *Journal of International Management*, 7: 59–79.

194 W. J. Henisz & B. A. Zelner, 2005, Legitimacy, interest group pressures and change in emergent institutions, the case of foreign investors and host country governments, *Academy of Management Review*, 30: 361–382; J. Feeney & A. Hillman, 2001, Privatization and the political economy of strategic trade policy, *International Economic Review*, 42: 535–556; R. Vernon, 2001, Big business and national governments: Reshaping the compact in a globalizing economy, *Journal of International Business Studies*, 32: 509–518; B. Shaffer & A. J. Hillman, 2000, The development of business-government strategies by diversified firms, *Strategic Management Journal*, 21: 175–190.

195 N. Shirouzu, 2005, Mean but lean, Toyota seeks outside help, *Wall Street Journal*, July 14, B4.

196 J. W. Lu & P. W. Beamish, 2004, Network development and firm performance: A field study of internationalizing Japanese firms, *Multinational Business Review*, 12(3):

41–61; B. Barringer & J. Harrison, 2000, Walking the tightrope: Creating value through interorganizational relationships, *Journal of Management*, 26: 367–404.

[197] S. J. Chang & S. Park, 2005, Types of firms generating network externalities and MNCs' co-location decisions, *Strategic Management Journal*, 26: 595–616.

[198] D. S. Elenkov, W. Judge, & P. Wright, 2005, Strategic leadership and executive innovation influence: An international multi-cluster comparative study, *Strategic Management Journal*, 26: 665–682; M. Carpenter & J. Fredrickson, 2001, Top management teams,

global strategic posture, and the moderating role of uncertainty, *Academy of Management Journal*, 44: 533–545; S. Finkelstein & D. C. Hambrick, 1996, *Strategic Leadership: Top Executives and Their Effects on Organizations*, St. Paul, MN: West Publishing Co.

[199] H. A. Krishnan & D. Park, 2003, Power in acquired top management teams and post-acquisition performance: A conceptual framework, *International Journal of Management*, 20: 75–80.

[200] Hitt, Hoskisson, & Kim, International diversification.

# CHAPTER 11

# Corporate Governance

**KNOWLEDGE OBJECTIVES**

*Studying this chapter should provide you with the strategic management knowledge needed to:*

1.  Define corporate governance and explain why it is used to monitor and control managers' strategic decisions.

2.  Explain how ownership came to be separated from managerial control in the modern corporation.

3.  Define an agency relationship and managerial opportunism and describe their strategic implications.

4.  Explain how three internal governance mechanisms—ownership concentration, the board of directors, and executive compensation—are used to monitor and control managerial decisions.

5.  Discuss trends among the three types of compensation executives receive and their effects on strategic decisions.

6.  Describe how the external corporate governance mechanism—the market for corporate control—acts as a restraint on top-level managers' strategic decisions.

7.  Discuss the use of corporate governance in international settings, in particular in Germany and Japan.

8.  Describe how corporate governance fosters ethical strategic decisions and the importance of such behaviors on the part of top-level executives.

Corporate governance is an increasingly important part of the strategic management process.[1] If the board of directors makes the wrong decision in compensating the firm's key strategic leader, the CEO, the whole firm suffers, as do its shareholders. Compensation is used to motivate CEOs to act in the best interests of the firm—in particular, the shareholders. When they do, the firm's value should increase.

What are a CEO's actions worth? The amount of compensation paid to CEOs suggests that they are worth a significant amount in the United States. While some critics argue that U.S. CEOs are paid too much,[2] the hefty increases in their compensation in recent years ostensibly have come from linking their pay to their firms' performance, and until recently, U.S. firms performed better than many firms in other countries. Research suggests that CEOs receive excessive compensation when corporate governance is the weakest.[3] Events in the early part of the 21st century suggest that the use of stock options, in particular, may have been abused by some boards because of the excessive amount of options awarded to CEOs and a tendency to reprice them at a lower level whenever the stock price falls.[4] In addition to repricing, some top executive teams engaged in an illegal practice called *options backdating*, which involves falsification of the date on which an options grant is awarded to ensure that executives are able to exercise their options at attractive prices.[5]

**Corporate governance** is the set of mechanisms used to manage the relationships among stakeholders and to determine and control the strategic direction and performance of organizations.[6] At its core, corporate governance is concerned with ensuring that strategic decisions are made effectively.[7] Governance can also be thought of as a means corporations use to establish effective relationships between parties (such as the firm's owners and its top-level managers) whose interests may be in conflict. Thus, corporate governance reflects and enforces the company's values.[8] In modern corporations—especially those in the United States and the United Kingdom—a primary objective of corporate governance is to ensure that the interests of top-level managers are aligned with the interests of the shareholders. Corporate governance involves oversight in areas in which owners, managers, and members of boards of directors may have conflicts of interest. These areas include the election of directors, the general supervision of CEO pay and more focused supervision of director pay, and the corporation's overall structure and strategic direction.[9] The primary goal is to ensure that the firm performs well and creates value for the shareholders.

Corporate governance has been emphasized in recent years because corporate governance mechanisms occasionally fail to adequately monitor and control top-level managers' decisions, as evidenced in scandals such as those at Enron and WorldCom. This situation has resulted in changes in governance mechanisms in corporations throughout the world, especially with respect to efforts intended to improve the performance of boards of directors.[10] These changes often cause confusion about the proper role of the board. According to one observer, "Depending on the company, you get very different perspectives: Some boards are settling for checking the boxes on compliance regulations, while others are thinking about changing the fundamental way they govern, and some worry that they've gotten themselves into micromanaging the CEO and company. There's a fair amount of turmoil and collective soul searching going on."[11] A second and more positive reason for this interest is that evidence suggests that a well-functioning corporate governance and control system can create a competitive advantage for a firm.[12] For example, one governance mechanism—the board of directors—has been suggested to be rapidly evolving into a major strategic force in U.S. business firms.[13] Thus, in this chapter, we describe actions designed to implement strategies that focus on monitoring and controlling mechanisms, which can help to ensure that top-level managerial actions contribute to the firm's ability to create value and earn above-average returns.

Effective corporate governance is also of interest to nations.[14] As stated by one scholar, "Every country wants the firms that operate within its borders to flourish and grow in such ways as to provide employment, wealth, and satisfaction, not only to improve standards of living materially but also to enhance social cohesion. These aspirations cannot be met unless those firms are competitive internationally in a sustained way, and it is this medium- and long-term perspective that makes good corporate governance so vital."[15]

Corporate governance, then, reflects company standards, which in turn collectively reflect societal standards.[16] In many corporations, shareholders hold top-level managers accountable for their decisions and the results they generate. As with these firms and their boards, nations that effectively govern their corporations may gain a competitive advantage over rival countries. In a range of countries, but especially in the United States and the United Kingdom, the fundamental goal of business organizations is to maximize shareholder value.[17] Traditionally, shareholders are treated as the firm's key stakeholders because they are the company's legal owners. The firm's owners expect top-level managers and others influencing the corporation's actions (for example, the board of directors) to make decisions that will result in the maximization of the company's value and, hence, of the owners' wealth.[18]

In the first section of this chapter, we describe the relationship providing the foundation on which the corporation is built: that between owners and managers. The majority of this chapter is used to explain various mechanisms owners use to govern managers and to ensure that they comply with their responsibility to maximize shareholder value.

The modern corporation uses three internal governance mechanisms and a single external one (see Table 11.1). The three internal governance mechanisms we describe in this chapter are (1) ownership concentration, as represented by types of shareholders and their different incentives to monitor managers; (2) the board of directors; and (3) executive compensation. We then consider the external corporate governance mechanism: the market for corporate control. Essentially, this market is a set of potential owners seeking to acquire undervalued firms and earn above-average returns on their investments by replacing ineffective top-level management teams.[19] The chapter's focus then shifts to the issue of international corporate governance. We briefly describe governance approaches used in German and Japanese firms in which traditional governance structures are being affected by global competition. In part, this discussion suggests the possibility that the structures used to govern global companies in many different countries, including Germany, Japan, the United Kingdom, and the United States, are becoming more, rather than less, similar. Closing our analysis of corporate governance is a consideration of the need for these control mechanisms to encourage and support ethical behavior in organizations.

Importantly, the mechanisms discussed in this chapter can positively influence the governance of the corporation, which has placed significant responsibility and authority in the hands of top-level managers. The most effective managers understand their accountability for the firm's performance and respond positively to corporate governance mechanisms.[20] In addition, the firm's owners should not expect any single mechanism to remain effective over time. Rather, the use of several mechanisms allows owners to govern the corporation in ways that maximize value creation and increase the financial value of their firm.[21] With multiple governance mechanisms operating simultaneously, however, it

**Table 11.1: Corporate Governance Mechanisms**

**Internal Governance Mechanisms**

**Ownership Concentration**
- Relative amounts of stock owned by individual shareholders and institutional investors

**Board of Directors**
- Individuals responsible for representing the firm's owners by monitoring top-level managers' strategic decisions

**Executive Compensation**
- Use of salary, bonuses, and long-term incentives to align managers' decisions with shareholders' interests

**External Governance Mechanism**

**Market for Corporate Control**
- The purchase of a company that is underperforming relative to industry rivals in order to improve the firm's strategic competitiveness

is also possible for some of the mechanisms to conflict.[22] Later, we review how these conflicts can occur.

## Separation of Ownership and Managerial Control

Historically, founder-owners and their descendants managed U.S. firms. In these cases, corporate ownership and control resided in the same people. As firms grew larger, "the managerial revolution led to a separation of ownership and control in most large corporations, where control of the firm shifted from entrepreneurs to professional managers while ownership became dispersed among thousands of unorganized stockholders who were removed from the day-to-day management of the firm."[23] These changes created the modern public corporation, which is based on the efficient separation of ownership and managerial control. Supporting the separation is a basic legal premise suggesting that the primary objective of a firm's activities is to increase the corporation's profit and thereby the financial gains of the owners (the shareholders).[24]

The separation of ownership and managerial control allows shareholders to purchase stock, which entitles them to income (residual returns) from the firm's operations after paying expenses. This right, however, requires that they also take a risk that the firm's expenses may exceed its revenues. To manage this investment risk, shareholders maintain a diversified portfolio by investing in several companies to reduce their overall risk.[25] As shareholders diversify their investments over a number of corporations, their risk declines. The poor performance or failure of any one firm in which they invest has less overall effect. Thus, shareholders specialize in managing their investment risk.

In small firms, managers often are high-percentage owners, so there is less separation between ownership and managerial control. In fact, ownership and managerial control are not separated in a large number of family-owned firms. In the United States, at least one-third of Standard and Poor's top 500 firms have substantial family ownership, holding on average about 18 percent of the outstanding equity. And family-owned firms perform better when a member of the family is the CEO than when the CEO is an outsider.[26] In many countries outside the United States, such as in Latin America, Asia, and some European countries, family-owned firms represent the dominant business organization form.[27] The primary purpose of most of these firms is to increase the family's wealth, which explains why a family CEO often is better than an outside CEO.[28] There are at least two critical issues for family-controlled firms as they grow. First, owner-managers may not have access to all of the skills needed to effectively manage the growing firm and maximize its returns for the family. Thus, they may need outsiders to help improve management of the firm. Second, they may need to seek outside capital and thus give up some of the ownership control. In these cases, protection of the minority owners' rights becomes important.[29] To avoid these potential problems, when these firms grow and become more complex, their owner-managers may contract with managerial specialists. These managers oversee decision making in the owner's firm and are compensated on the basis of their decision-making skills and the outcomes of those decisions. As decision-making specialists, managers are agents of the firm's owners and are expected to use their decision-making skills to operate the owners' firm in ways that will maximize the return on the owners' investment.[30]

Without owner (shareholder) specialization in bearing risk and management specialization in making decisions, a firm probably would be limited by the abilities of its owners to manage and make effective strategic decisions. Thus, the separation and specialization of ownership (risk bearing) and managerial control (decision making) should produce the highest returns for the firm's owners.

## Agency Relationships

The separation between owners and managers creates an agency relationship. An **agency relationship** exists when one or more people (the *principal* or principals) hire another person or people (the *agent* or agents) as decision-making specialists to perform a service.[31] Thus, an agency relationship exists when one party delegates decision-making responsibility to a second party for compensation (see Figure 11.1).[32] In addition to shareholders and top executives, other examples of agency relationships are consultants and clients and insured and insurer. Moreover, within organizations, an agency relationship exists between managers and their employees, as well as between top executives and the firm's owners.[33] In the modern corporation, managers must understand the links between these relationships and the firm's effectiveness.[34] Although the agency relationship between managers and their employees is important, in this chapter we focus on the agency relationship between the firm's owners (the principals) and top-level managers (the principals' agents) because this relationship is related directly to how the firm's strategies are implemented.

The separation between ownership and managerial control can be problematic. Research evidence documents a variety of agency problems in the modern corporation.[35] Problems can surface because the principal and the agent have different interests and goals, or because shareholders lack direct control of large publicly traded corporations. Problems also arise when an agent makes decisions that result in the pursuit of goals that conflict with

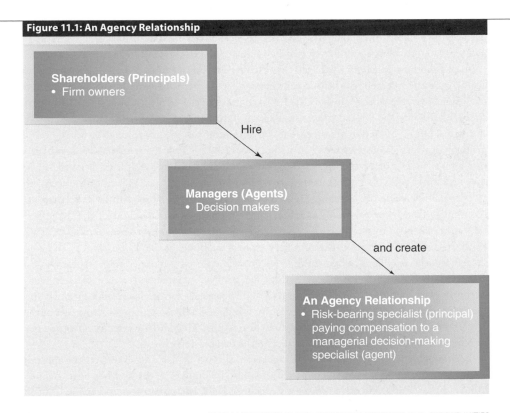

**Figure 11.1: An Agency Relationship**

**Shareholders (Principals)**
• Firm owners

Hire

**Managers (Agents)**
• Decision makers

and create

**An Agency Relationship**
• Risk-bearing specialist (principal) paying compensation to a managerial decision-making specialist (agent)

PART 4 / MONITORING AND CREATING ENTREPRENEURIAL OPPORTUNITIES those of the principals. Thus, the separation of ownership and control potentially allows divergent interests (between principals and agents) to surface, which can lead to managerial opportunism.

**Managerial opportunism** is the seeking of self-interest with guile (i.e., cunning or deceit).[36] Opportunism is both an attitude (e.g., an inclination) and a set of behaviors (i.e., specific acts of self-interest).[37] It is not possible for principals to know beforehand which agents will or will not act opportunistically. The reputations of top executives are an imperfect predictor, and opportunistic behavior is usually known only after it has occurred. Thus, principals establish governance and control mechanisms to prevent agents from acting opportunistically, even though only a few are likely to do so.[38] Any time that principals delegate decision-making responsibilities to agents, the opportunity for conflicts of interest exist. Top executives, for example, may make strategic decisions that maximize their personal welfare and minimize their personal risk.[39] Decisions such as these prevent the maximization of shareholder wealth. Decisions regarding product diversification demonstrate these possibilities.

## Product Diversification as an Example of an Agency Problem

As explained in Chapter 8, a corporate-level strategy to diversify the firm's product lines can enhance a firm's value creation and increase its returns, both of which serve the interests of shareholders and top executives. However, product diversification can result in two benefits to managers that shareholders do not enjoy, so top executives may prefer more product diversification than do shareholders.[40] First, diversification usually increases the size of a firm, and size is positively related to executive compensation. Also, diversification increases the complexity of managing a firm and its network of businesses and may therefore require more pay because of this complexity.[41] Thus, increased product diversification provides an opportunity for top executives to increase their compensation.[42]

Second, product diversification and the resulting diversification of the firm's portfolio of businesses can reduce top executives' employment risk.[43] Managerial employment risk includes the risk of managers losing their jobs, compensation, or reputations.[44] These risks are reduced with increased diversification because a firm and its upper-level managers are less vulnerable to the reduction in demand associated with a single or limited number of product lines or businesses.

Another concern that may represent an agency problem is a firm's free cash flows over which top executives have control. *Free cash flows* are resources remaining after the firm has invested in all projects that have positive net present values within its current businesses.[45] In anticipation of positive returns, managers may decide to invest these funds in products that are not associated with the firm's current lines of business to increase the firm's level of diversification. The managerial decision to use free cash flows to overdiversify the firm is an example of self-serving and opportunistic managerial behavior. Shareholders, for instance, may prefer that free cash flows be distributed to them as dividends, so they can control how the cash is invested.[46]

Curve S in Figure 11.2 depicts the shareholders' optimal level of diversification. Owners seek the level of diversification that reduces the risk of the firm's failure while simultaneously increasing the company's value through the development of economies of scale and scope (see Chapter 8). Of the four corporate-level diversification strategies shown in Figure 11.2, shareholders likely prefer the diversified position noted by point A on curve S— a position that is located between the dominant business and related-constrained diversification strategies. Of course, the optimal level of diversification owners seek varies from firm to firm.[47] Factors that affect shareholders' preferences include the firm's primary industry, the intensity of rivalry among competitors in that industry, and the top management team's experience with implementing diversification strategies.

Upper-level executives—as agents—also seek an optimal level of diversification. Declining performance resulting from too much product diversification increases the probability that corporate control of the firm will be acquired in the market. After a firm is acquired, the employment risk for the firm's top executives increases substantially. Furthermore, a manager's employment opportunities in the external managerial labor market (discussed in Chapter 2) are affected negatively by a firm's poor performance. Therefore, top executives prefer diversification, but not to a point at which it increases their employment risk and reduces their employment opportunities.[48] Curve M in Figure 11.2 shows that executives prefer higher levels of product diversification than shareholders. Top executives might prefer the level of diversification shown by point B on curve M.

In general, shareholders prefer riskier strategies and more focused diversification. They reduce their risk through holding a diversified portfolio of equity investments. Alternatively, managers obviously cannot balance their employment risk by working for a diverse portfolio of firms. Therefore, top executives may prefer a level of diversification that maximizes firm size and their compensation and that reduces their employment risk. Product diversification, therefore, is a potential agency problem that could result in principals incurring costs to control their agents' behaviors.

## Agency Costs and Governance Mechanisms

The potential conflict illustrated by Figure 11.2, coupled with the fact that principals do not know which managers might act opportunistically, demonstrates why principals establish governance mechanisms. However, such mechanisms incur costs. **Agency costs** are the

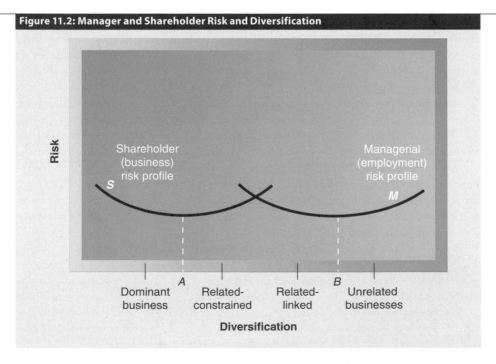

Figure 11.2: Manager and Shareholder Risk and Diversification

sum of incentive costs, monitoring costs, enforcement costs, and individual financial losses incurred by principals, because governance mechanisms cannot guarantee total compliance by the agent. If a firm is diversified, governance costs increase because it is more difficult to monitor actions inside the firm.[49]

In general, managerial interests are more likely to prevail when governance mechanisms are weak because managers have a significant amount of autonomy to make strategic decisions. If, however, the board of directors does not allow much managerial autonomy, or if other strong governance mechanisms are used, the firm's strategies should better reflect the interests of the shareholders. More recently, governance observers have been concerned about more egregious behavior that goes far beyond simply pursuing a suboptimal corporate-level strategy. Because of fraudulent behavior such as that found in the Enron and WorldCom cases, concerns regarding corporate governance have been increasing. In particular, it became evident that the external auditor in these cases, Arthur Andersen, had been co-opted into fraudulent behaviors regarding the accuracy of financial statements due to their significant consulting businesses with these two clients. In 2002, Congress enacted the Sarbanes—Oxley Act (SOX), which extended the regulatory powers of the U.S. Securities and Exchange Commission (SEC) regarding corporate governance procedures. SOX provides new requirements to ensure the independence of auditors, restricts firms that provide accounting services from either auditing or consulting services, creates rules requiring creation and disclosure of effective financial controls, requires that business records be retained for at least five years, and requires that financial reports be personally certified by the CEO and the chief financial officer of a firm.[50]

Research suggests that more intensive application of governance mechanisms may produce significant changes in strategies. William Donaldson, then chairman of the SEC, argued that collapse of investor confidence after the Enron and other scandals suggests that corporate America needs more intense governance in order for continued investment in the stock market to facilitate growth. "The short-term costs of compliance," Donaldson said, "particularly efforts to improve internal control and corporate governance over financial reporting, should be viewed as an investment. In the long term, the reforms realized from SOX will result in more sound corporate practices and more reliable financial reporting."[51]

However, others argue that the indirect costs of SOX—the effects on strategy formulation and implementation—are even more influential.[52] That is, because of more intense governance, firms may make fewer risky decisions and thus decrease potential shareholder wealth significantly.[53] In addition, "Some executives and accountants are concerned that the reporting requirements of SOX are an overreaction to the wrongdoings of a handful of companies and are suppressing the growth of small businesses, particularly those that would consider transitioning from a private entity to a public company through an Initial Public Offering."[54] This is because becoming a public company comes with the new SOX requirements, which can be very costly to implement. One observer noted: "Many boards have been vigilant in their oversight role in regard to corporate value. However, CEOs and directors have been distracted from more important strategic issues in order to meet detailed compliance deadlines provided by the Sarbanes—Oxley Act. Boards need to refocus on three critical strategic processes: strategic planning, risk assessment and renewal, which includes succession planning."[55] As this debate demonstrates, the longer-term effects of SOX have yet to be determined.

We now turn to the effects of different governance mechanisms on the decisions managers make and on the use of the firm's strategies.

# Ownership Concentration

**Ownership concentration** is defined by both the number of large-block shareholders and the total percentage of shares they own. **Large-block shareholders** typically own at least 5 percent of a corporation's issued shares. Ownership concentration as a governance mechanism has received considerable interest because large-block shareholders are increasingly active in their demands that corporations adopt effective governance mechanisms to control managerial decisions.[56]

In general, diffuse ownership (a large number of shareholders with small holdings and few, if any, large-block shareholders) produces weak monitoring of managers' decisions. Among other problems, diffuse ownership makes it difficult for owners to effectively coordinate their actions. Diversification of the firm's product lines beyond the shareholders' optimal level might result from weak monitoring of managers' decisions. Higher levels of monitoring could encourage managers to avoid strategic decisions that do not increase shareholder value. In fact, research evidence shows that ownership concentration is associated with lower levels of firm product diversification.[57] Thus, with high degrees of ownership concentration, the probability is greater that managers' strategic decisions will increase shareholder value.

As noted, such concentration of ownership influences strategies and firm value. Interestingly, research in Spain showed a curvilinear relationship between shareholder concentration and firm value. At moderate levels of shareholder concentration, firm value increased; at high levels of concentration, firm value decreased for shareholders, especially minority shareholders.[58] When large shareholders have a high degree of wealth, they have power relative to minority shareholders in extracting wealth from the firm, especially when they are in managerial positions. In the United States, the importance of boards of directors in mitigating expropriation of minority shareholders' value has been found to be relative to strong family ownership, where the family owners have incentives to appropriate shareholder wealth.[59] Such expropriation is often found in countries such as Korea where minority shareholder rights are not as protected as they are in the United States.[60] However, in the United States much of this concentration has come from increasing equity ownership by institutional investors.

## Institutional Owners

A classic work published in the 1930s argued that the "modern" corporation had become characterized by a separation of ownership and control.[61] This change occurred primarily because growth prevented founder-owners from maintaining their dual positions in their increasingly complex companies. More recently, another shift has occurred: ownership of many modern corporations is now concentrated in the hands of institutional investors rather than individual shareholders.[62]

**Institutional owners** are financial institutions such as stock mutual funds and pension funds that control large-block shareholder positions. Because of their prominent ownership positions, institutional owners, as large-block shareholders, are a powerful governance mechanism. Institutions of these types now own more than 50 percent of the stock in large U.S. corporations, and of the top 1,000 corporations, they own, on average, 56 percent of the stock. Pension funds alone control at least one-half of corporate equity.[63]

These ownership percentages suggest that as investors, institutional owners have both the size and the incentive to discipline ineffective top-level managers and can significantly influence a firm's choice of strategies and overall strategic decisions.[64] Research evidence indicates that institutional and other large-block shareholders are becoming more active in their efforts to influence a corporation's strategic decisions. Initially, these shareholder activists and institutional investors concentrated on the performance and accountability of CEOs and contributed to the ouster of a number of them. They are now targeting what they believe are ineffective boards of directors.[65]

For example, the California Public Employees' Retirement System (CalPERS) provides retirement and health coverage to approximately 1.5 million current and retired public employees.[66] One of the largest public employee pension funds in the United States, CalPERS acts aggressively to promote decisions and actions that it believes will enhance shareholder value in companies in which it invests. According to CalPERS: "Shareowners collectively have the power to direct the course of corporations. The potential impact of this power is staggering. Through shareowner action, economic wealth can either be created or destroyed. In CalPERS' view, the responsibility that results from this power must be exercised responsibly."[67] CalPERS has well-developed initiatives to influence corporate governance in targeted companies and to communicate with other investors. One of its initiatives includes an executive compensation program specifically designed to "raise the level of accountability of Boards and Compensation Committees to shareowners, to improve compensation disclosure, and to develop a stronger alignment of pay and performance in the market place."[68] The largest institutional investor, the Teachers Insurance and Annuity Association—College Retirement Equities Fund (TIAA-CREF), has taken actions similar to those of CalPERS, but with a less publicly aggressive stance. To date, research suggests that the activism of these institutions may not directly affect firm performance, but it may have indirect influences through its effects on important strategic decisions, such as those concerned with innovation.[69]

## Shareholder Activism

The SEC has issued several rulings that support shareholder involvement and control of managerial decisions. For example, the SEC eased its rule regarding communications among shareholders. Historically, shareholders could communicate only through a cumbersome and expensive filing process. Now, with a simple notification to the SEC of an upcoming meeting, shareholders can convene to discuss a corporation's strategic direction. If a consensus on an issue exists, shareholders can vote as a block.[70]

Shareholder activism has been increasing dramatically in recent years. It tends to be led either by a dissident shareholder with a large stake in the company, such as an institutional investor, or an "activist" firm that specializes in selecting targets that it believes are being managed below their potential and have governance vulnerabilities that increase the probability that shareholder actions will lead to positive changes (such as the ability to call special meetings or act by written consent).[71] Activist firms acquire significant ownership stakes and open communications with other investors to determine their levels of interest in taking action. The types of actions taken include threatening or initiating a proxy battle to unseat the current board of directors, organizing press conferences, threatening a takeover bid, or creating shareholder "proposals" for the board of directors to address at the next board meeting.

Activists have had many successes. For example, during the two-year period ending in 2006, several events occurred as a direct result of investor activism. Among them, Formation Capital forced the sale of Beverly Enterprises and then bid for the company itself. Also, Pershing Square pressured McDonald's to spin off Chipotle Mexican Grill and Wendy's Restaurants to spin off Tim Horton's Donuts. Carl Icahn's bid for Fairmont Hotels and

Resorts pushed the company to sell itself in an auction. Icahn also threatened a proxy fight at Time Warner, which led to several changes in finance and governance. In addition, he used a threat to secure multiple board seats at ImClone Systems. During the same period, Knightspoint successfully influenced Sharper Image to replace three directors with its own nominees. And, Legg Mason funds put pressure on Knight Ridder, which led to its sale to the McClatchy Company.[72]

# Board of Directors

Typically, shareholders monitor the managerial decisions and actions of a firm through the board of directors. The **board of directors** is a group of shareholder-elected individuals whose primary responsibility is to act in the owners' interests by formally monitoring and controlling the corporation's top-level executives.[73] Boards of directors can positively influence both managers and the companies they serve.[74] Furthermore, research indicates that the composition of the board of directors is particularly important during crisis situations, such as bankruptcies or takeovers.[75] Thus, an effective board of directors can be a source of competitive advantage.[76]

Those who are elected to the board of directors are expected to oversee managers and to ensure that the corporation is operated in ways that will maximize its shareholders' wealth. Even with large institutional investors having major equity ownership in U.S. firms, diffuse ownership still continues to exist in most firms, which means that monitoring and control of managers by individual shareholders is limited in large corporations. Furthermore, large financial institutions, such as banks, are prevented from directly owning stock in firms and from having representatives on companies' boards of directors, although this is not the case in Europe and elsewhere.[77] These conditions highlight the importance of the board of directors for corporate governance. Unfortunately, over time, some boards of directors have not been highly effective in monitoring and controlling top management's actions.[78]

Boards have power to direct the affairs of the organization, punish and reward managers, and protect shareholders' rights and interests.[79] Thus, an appropriately structured and effective board of directors protects owners from managerial opportunism. Board members are seen as stewards of their company's resources, and the way they carry out these responsibilities affects the society in which their firm operates.[80]

## Board Independence

Generally, board members (often called *directors*) are classified into one of three groups based on their relationship to the firm (see Table 11.2). *Insiders* are active top-level managers in the corporation who are elected to the board because they are a source of information about the firm's day-to-day operations.[81] *Related outsiders* have some relationship with the firm, contractual or otherwise, that may create questions about their independence, but these individuals are not involved with the corporation's day-to-day activities. *Outsiders* provide independent counsel to the firm and may hold top-level managerial positions in other companies or may have been elected to the board before the beginning of the current CEO's tenure.[82]

Historically, boards of directors were primarily dominated by inside managers, although boards have become more independent (more outsiders) in recent years.[83] A widely accepted view is that a board with a significant percentage of its membership drawn from the firm's top executives tends to provide relatively weak monitoring and control of managerial decisions.[84] Managers have been suspected of using their power to select and compensate directors in order to exploit their personal ties with them. In response, some companies have voluntarily established rules governing the nature of relationships between management and directors. For instance, BP, the British-based international oil company, has the following requirement: "The qualification for board membership includes a requirement that all our non-executive directors be free from any relationship with the executive management of the company that could materially interfere with the exercise of their independent judgment."[85]

In the early 1980s the SEC proposed that board committees responsible for firm audits be made up of outside directors. In 1984 the New York Stock Exchange, possibly to preempt formal legislation, implemented an audit committee rule requiring important board committees such as the compensation and nomination committees to be headed by independent outside directors.[86] These requirements were instituted more generally after SOX was passed, and policies of the New York Stock Exchange as well as the American Stock Exchange now require that boards be composed primarily of outsiders and that audit committees are fully independent. Thus one can clearly see that corporate governance is becoming more intense through the board of directors mechanism.

The trend toward including a higher percentage of outside directors on the board also creates some difficulties. Outsiders do not have contact with the firm's day-to-day operations and typically do not have easy access to the level of information about managers and their skills required to effectively evaluate managerial decisions and initiatives.[87] Insiders possess such information by virtue of their organizational positions. Thus, boards with a sufficient number of insiders typically are better informed about intended strategic initiatives, the reasons for the initiatives, and the outcomes expected from them.[88] Without this type of information, outsider-dominated boards may emphasize the use of financial, as opposed to strategic, controls to gather information to evaluate the performance of managers and business units. A virtually exclusive reliance on financial evaluations shifts risk to top-level managers, who, in turn, may make decisions to maximize their own interests and reduce their employment risk. Reductions in R&D investments, additional diversification of the firm, and the pursuit of greater levels of compensation are some of the results of managers' actions to achieve financial goals set by outsider-dominated boards.[89]

## Board Effectiveness

Because of the importance of boards of directors in corporate governance and as a result of increased scrutiny from shareholders—in particular, large institutional investors—the performance of individual board members and of entire boards is being evaluated more formally and with greater intensity.[90] Given the demand for greater accountability and improved performance, many boards have initiated voluntary changes in addition to the changes required by SOX. Trends among boards include (1) increases in the diversity of the backgrounds of board members (for example, a greater number of directors from public service, academic, and scientific settings; a greater percentage on boards of ethnic minorities and women; and members from different countries on boards of U.S. firms); (2) the establishment and consistent use of formal processes to evaluate the board's performance; (3) the creation of a "lead director" role that has strong powers with regard to the setting of the board's agenda and oversight of the activities of nonmanagement board members; (4) modifications of the compensation of directors, especially reducing or eliminating stock options as a part of the package; and (5) requirements that directors own significant stakes in the company in order to keep them focused on shareholder interests.[91]

In addition to monitoring the behavior of the CEO and other top managers, outside directors can provide social network ties that act as linkages to external stakeholders.[92] In addition, they can advise managers regarding strategies and the strategic direction of the firm. Consequently, boards composed of highly successful executives from a wide variety of industries will be able to provide a broader perspective to top management. Research shows that diverse boards help firms make more effective strategic decisions and perform better over time.[93] Furthermore, boards that work collaboratively make higher-quality strategic decisions, and they make them faster.[94] Once appointed, an outside director should seek effectiveness through three linked sets of behaviors: the nonexecutive director should (1) become engaged in the firm, but not try to micromanage it; (2) challenge the reasoning behind decisions, but still support them when they are made; and (3) provide an independent perspective on important decisions.[95]

## Executive Compensation

The compensation of top-level managers, and especially of CEOs, generates a great deal of interest and strongly held opinions.[96] Warren Buffett, CEO of Berkshire Hathaway and a well-known investor, recently expressed concern over what he sees as the excessive compensation of some executives: "Too often, executive compensation in the United States is ridiculously out of line with performance. The upshot is that a mediocre-or-worse CEO—aided by his handpicked V.P. of human relations and a consultant from the ever-accommodating firm of Ratchet, Ratchet & Bingo—all too often receives gobs of money from an ill-designed compensation arrangement."[97]

One reason for the widespread interest in executive compensation is the natural curiosity about extremes and excesses. For instance, William McGuire, CEO of UnitedHealth Group, has amassed options worth $1.6 billion, according to the firm's proxy statement.[98] Shareholders, angry about excessive executive pay, have increasingly sought a voice in regard to executive compensation. In 2007, activist investors submitted proposals to this effect to the boards of directors of a large number of firms for consideration during their annual meetings. Among the targeted companies were Citigroup, Wells Fargo, and Northrop Grumman. American Family Life Assurance Company (AFLAC) has granted shareholders an advisory vote beginning in 2009.[99]

Another reason for interest in executive compensation stems from a more substantive view that CEO pay is tied, in an indirect but very tangible way, to the fundamental governance processes in large corporations.[100] From this perspective, **executive compensation** is a governance mechanism that seeks to align the interests of top managers and owners through salaries, bonuses, and long-term incentive compensation, such as stock awards and stock options.[101] Research suggests that firms with a smaller pay gap between the CEO and other top executives perform better, especially when collaboration among top management team members is more important.[102] The performance improvement is attributed to better cooperation among top management team members.

Increasingly, long-term incentive plans are becoming a critical part of compensation packages in U.S. firms. The use of longer-term pay helps firms cope with or avoid potential agency problems by linking managerial wealth to the wealth of common shareholders.[103] Because of this, the stock market generally reacts positively to the introduction of a long-range incentive plan for top executives.[104] Nevertheless, sometimes the use of a long-term incentive plan prevents major stockholders (e.g., institutional investors) from pressing for changes in the composition of the board of directors because they assume that the long-term incentives will ensure that top executives will act in shareholders' best interests. Alternatively, stockholders largely assume that top-executive pay and the performance of a firm are more closely aligned when firms have boards that are dominated by outside members.[105]

Effectively using executive compensation as a governance mechanism is particularly challenging to firms implementing international strategies. For example, the interests of owners of multinational corporations may be best served when there is less uniformity among the compensation plans of the firm's foreign subsidiaries.[106] Developing an array of unique compensation plans requires additional monitoring and increases the firm's agency costs. Importantly, pay levels vary by regions of the world. For example, managers receive the highest compensation in the United States, while managerial pay is much lower in Asia. Compensation is lower in India partly because many of the largest firms are owned and controlled by families.[107] As corporations acquire firms in other countries, the managerial compensation puzzle becomes more complex and may cause additional executive turnover due to dissatisfaction with pay consideration.[108]

## A Complicated Governance Mechanism

For several reasons, executive compensation—especially long-term incentive compensation—is complicated. First, the strategic decisions that top-level managers make are typically complex and nonroutine, so it is difficult to evaluate the quality of those decisions. As a result the board of directors often links the compensation of top-level managers to measurable outcomes, such as the firm's financial performance. Second, an executive's decision often affects a firm's financial outcomes over an extended period, making it difficult to assess the effect of current decisions on the corporation's performance. In fact, strategic decisions are more likely to have long-term rather than short-term effects on a company's strategic outcomes. Third, a number of other factors affect a firm's performance besides top-level managerial decisions and behavior. Unpredictable economic, social, or legal changes (see Chapter 3) make it difficult to discern the effects of strategic decisions. Thus, although performance-based compensation may provide incentives to top management teams to make decisions that best serve shareholders' interests,[109] such compensation plans alone are imperfect in their ability to monitor and control managers.[110] Still, incentive compensation represents a significant portion of many executives' total pay.

Even incentive compensation plans that are intended to increase the value of a firm in line with shareholder expectations are subject to managerial manipulation. For instance, annual bonuses may provide incentives for managers to pursue short-run objectives at the expense of the firm's long-term interests. Supporting this conclusion, some research has found that bonuses based on annual performance were negatively related to R&D investments when the firm was highly diversified, which may affect the firm's long-term strategic competitiveness.[111] However, research has found a positive relationship between R&D investments and long-term compensation in nonfamily firms.[112]

Although long-term performance-based incentives may reduce the temptation to underinvest in the short run, they increase executive exposure to risks associated with uncontrollable events, such as market fluctuations and industry decline. The longer the focus of incentive compensation, the greater are the long-term risks top-level managers bear. Also, because long-term incentives tie a manager's overall wealth to the firm in a way that is inflexible, such incentives and ownership may not be valued as highly by a manager as by outside investors who have the opportunity to diversify their wealth in a number of other financial investments.[113] Thus, firms may have to overcompensate managers using long-term incentives.

## The Effectiveness of Executive Compensation

The primary reason for compensating executives in stock is that the practice affords them with an incentive to keep the stock price high and hence aligns the interests of managers and shareholders. Consequently, institutional investors prefer compensation schemes that link pay with performance.[114] However, there may be some unintended consequences. Managers who own greater than 1 percent of their firm's stock are less likely to be forced out of their jobs, even when the firm is performing poorly.[115] Furthermore, a review of the research suggests that over time, firm size has accounted for more than half of the variance in total CEO pay, while firm performance has accounted for less than 5 percent of the variance.[116] Thus, the effectiveness of pay plans as a governance mechanism is suspect.

By the turn of the 20th century and into the early part of the 21st, stock options became highly popular as a means of compensating top executives and linking pay and performance. Nevertheless, they have also become controversial.[117] Although some stock option–based compensation plans are well-designed, with option strike prices (the prices at which the options become attractive) substantially higher than current stock prices, too many have been designed simply to give executives more wealth that will not immediately show up on the balance sheet. Furthermore, stock option *repricing*, in which the strike price value of the option is lowered from its original position, is very common. Research suggests that repricing occurs more frequently in high-risk situations.[118] However, it also happens when firm performance is poor, to restore the incentive effect for the option. Evidence also suggests that organizational politics are often involved in repricing decisions.[119]

Option awards became a means of providing large compensation packages, and the options awarded did not seem to relate to the firm's performance, particularly when boards showed a propensity to reprice options at a lower strike price when stock prices fell dramatically.[120] Because of the large number of options granted in recent years and the increasingly common practice of repricing them, public pressure increased to adjust accounting rules so that the actual value given to executives was reflected in accounting statements. A new rule issued by the Financial Accounting Standards Board (FASB) required the firm to record stock options as an expense beginning in July 2005. Although some firms are finding ways around the new rule, the popularity of options has declined.[121]

Another practice that has caused a great deal of controversy is *backdating*, in which an options grant is dated earlier than it was actually drawn up to ensure an attractive exercise price for managers holding the options. An article in *Business Week* pointed out, "Companies from Apple Computer to UnitedHealth Group to McAfee have played games with stock option grants in recent years, often to the detriment of shareholders."[122] Backdating and other related practices in the United States led to a massive criminal investigation involving more than 100 firms, including Apple, Broadcom, KB Home (the fifth-largest U.S. homebuilder), and McAfee.[123] There is also evidence that some executives changed their own exercise dates in order to reduce taxes.[124] In early 2007, a U.S. federal court in Delaware ruled that directors who approved stock option backdating could be sued for breach of fiduciary duty.[125]

## Market for Corporate Control

Practices such as options repricing and backdating are evidence that internal governance mechanisms are an imperfect means of ensuring that the interests of top-level managers are aligned with the interests of the shareholders. When weak internal governance leads to suboptimal firm performance, sometimes external corporate governance mechanisms are needed. Primary among these is the market for corporate control.

The **market for corporate control** is an external governance mechanism that becomes active when a firm's internal controls fail.[126] It is composed of individuals and firms that buy ownership positions in or take over potentially undervalued corporations so they can form new divisions in established diversified companies or merge two previously separate firms. Because the undervalued firm's executives are assumed to be responsible for formulating and implementing the strategy that produced the poor performance, that team is usually replaced. Thus, when the market for corporate control operates effectively, it ensures that managers who are ineffective or act opportunistically are disciplined.[127]

The market for corporate control was very active in the 1980s. Then, because of government legislation to discourage hostile takeovers and the collapse of the high-yield (junk) bond market in 1990, takeovers became less popular. However, there is a resurgence of activity in the United States and elsewhere: "The current market for corporate control shares many characteristics with that of the 1980s. Once again, credit is plentiful and lenders are willing to finance deals with high debt to equity ratios. At the same time, there has been a resurgence of aggressive stock accumulation strategies, efforts to put companies 'in play' and unsolicited bids for control by financial buyers."[128]

The market for corporate control is often viewed as a "court of last resort."[129] This suggests that the takeover market as a source of external discipline is used only when internal governance mechanisms are relatively weak and have proved to be ineffective. Alternatively, other research suggests that the rationale for takeovers as a corporate governance strategy is not as strong as the rationale for takeovers as an ownership investment in target candidates that are performing well.[130] In support of this view, a study of active corporate raiders in the 1980s showed that takeover attempts often were focused on firms with above-average performance in their industries.[131] Consequently, although some takeovers are best explained in terms of their investment potential, others are indicative of external market discipline.

The market for corporate control as a governance mechanism should be triggered by a firm's poor performance relative to industry competitors. A firm's poor performance, often demonstrated by earning below-average returns, is an indicator that internal governance mechanisms have failed; that is, they did not result in managerial decisions that maximized shareholder value. This market has been active for some time. As noted in Chapter 9, the 1990s produced a surge in the number and value of mergers and acquisitions. During the short lull in merger and acquisition activity during the economic downturn of 2001–2002, unsolicited takeover bids increased, an indication that during a recession, poorly managed firms are more easily identified.[132] As of 2007, the number and size of deals were increasing again.[133] Furthermore, takeovers and even hostile takeovers involving firms from two countries are increasing.[134] In Europe, boards have much less influence regarding takeover bids than in the United States. In fact, typically in Europe all bids must be subjected to a shareholder vote. In the United States, boards are given much greater freedom to act on behalf of the shareholders. Consequently, the European market for corporate control may actually be more efficient than in the United States.[135]

Most hostile takeover attempts are due to the target firm's poor performance.[136] Therefore, target firm managers and members of the board of directors are highly sensitive about hostile takeover bids because they frequently mean that managers and directors have not managed the company effectively. If they accept the offer, they are likely to lose their jobs because the acquiring firm will appoint its own management. Even if they fend off the takeover attempt, they must improve the performance of the firm or risk losing their jobs anyway.[137] We now turn to the methods managers use to defend their companies against takeovers.

## Managerial Defense Tactics

Firms targeted for hostile takeovers may use multiple defense tactics to fend off the takeover attempt (see Table 11.3). Historically, the increased use of the market for corporate control as a governance mechanism has enhanced the sophistication and variety of such defense tactics.[138] The market for corporate control tends to increase risk for managers. As a result, managerial pay is often augmented indirectly through *golden parachutes*, wherein a CEO can receive up to three years' salary if his or her firm is taken over. Among other outcomes, takeover defenses increase the costs of making the acquisition, causing the incumbent management to become entrenched, while reducing the chances of introducing a new management team.[139] Some defense tactics require asset restructuring, created by divesting one or more divisions in the diversified firm's portfolio. Others necessitate changes in only the financial structure of the firm, such as repurchasing shares of the firm's outstanding stock.[140] Some tactics, such as reincorporation of the firm in another state, require shareholder approval. On the other hand, the *greenmail tactic*, wherein money is used to repurchase stock from a corporate raider to avoid the takeover of the firm, requires no approval. Defensive tactics are controversial, and the research on their effects is inconclusive. However, most institutional investors oppose the use of defense tactics.[141]

A potential problem with the market for corporate control is that it may not be entirely efficient. A study of several of the most active corporate raiders in the 1980s showed that approximately 50 percent of their takeover attempts targeted firms with above-average performance in their industry—corporations that were neither undervalued nor poorly managed.[142] The targeting of high-performance businesses may lead to acquisitions at premium prices and to decisions by managers of the targeted firm to establish costly takeover defense tactics to protect their corporate positions.[143]

Although the market for corporate control lacks the precision of internal governance mechanisms, the fear of acquisition and influence by corporate raiders is an effective constraint on the managerial-growth motive.[144] The market for corporate control has been responsible for significant changes in many firms' strategies and, when used appropriately, has served shareholders' interests.[145] But this market and other means of corporate governance vary by region of the world and by country. Accordingly, we next address the topic of international corporate governance.

## Table 11.3: Examples of Hostile Takeover Defense Tactics

| Defense Tactic | Category | Popularity among Firms | Effectiveness as a Defense | Stockholder Wealth |
|---|---|---|---|---|
| **Poison Pill** Preferred stock in the merged firm offered to shareholders at a highly attractive rate of exchange. | Preventive | High | High | Positive |
| **Corporate Charter Amendment** An amendment to stagger the elections of members to the board of directors of the attacked firm so that all are not elected during the same year, which prevents a bidder from installing a completely new board in the same year. | Preventive | Medium | Very low | Negative |
| **Golden Parachute** Lump-sum payments of cash that are distributed to a select group of senior executives when the firm is acquired in a takeover bid. | Preventive | Medium | Low | Negligible |
| **Litigation** Lawsuits that help a target company stall hostile attacks; areas may include antitrust, fraud, inadequate disclosure. | Reactive | Medium | Low | Positive |
| **Greenmail** The repurchase of shares of stock that have been acquired by the aggressor at a premium in exchange for an agreement that the aggressor will no longer target the company for takeover. | Reactive | Very low | Medium | Negative |
| **Standstill Agreement** Contract between the parties in which the pursuer agrees not to acquire any more stock of the target firm for a specified period of time in exchange for the firm paying the pursuer a fee. | Reactive | Low | Low | Negative |
| **Capital Structure Change** Dilution of stock, making it more costly for a bidder to acquire; may include employee stock option plans (ESOPs), recapitalization, new debt, stock selling, share buybacks. | Reactive | Medium | Medium | Inconclusive |

SOURCE: This article was published in *Business Horizons*, Volume 47(7), 2004, J. A. Pearce II & R. B. Robinson, Jr., Hostile takeover defenses that maximize shareholder wealth, pp. 15–24, Copyright Elsevier 2004.

# International Corporate Governance

This chapter has focused on governance structures found in the United States, which are similar to those found in the United Kingdom. However, understanding the corporate governance structures only in these countries is inadequate for a multinational firm in today's global economy.[146] Although the similarities among governance structures in industrialized nations is increasing, there are differences, and firms using an international strategy must understand these differences in order to operate effectively in different international markets.[147]

This section discusses some of the essential features associated with governance structures in Germany and Japan. Although the stability associated with German and Japanese governance structures historically has been viewed as an asset, the governance systems in these countries is changing, as it is changing in other parts of the world.[148] These changes are partially the result of multinational firms operating in many different countries and attempting to develop a more global governance system.[149]

## Corporate Governance in Germany

In many private German firms, the owner and manager may still be the same individual. In these instances, there is no agency problem.[150] Even in publicly traded German corporations, there is often a dominant shareholder. Thus, the concentration of ownership is an important means of corporate governance in Germany, as it is in the United States.[151]

Historically, banks have been at the center of the German corporate governance structure, as is also the case in many other European countries, such as Italy and France. As lenders, banks become major shareholders when companies they finance seek funding on the stock market or default on loans. Although the stakes are usually less than 10 percent, the only legal limit on how much of a firm's stock banks can hold is that a single ownership position cannot exceed 15 percent of the bank's capital. Through their shareholdings, and by casting proxy votes for individual shareholders who retain their shares with the banks, three banks in particular—Deutsche Bank, Dresdner Bank, and Commerzbank—exercise significant power. Although shareholders can tell the banks how to vote their ownership position, they generally do not do so. A combination of their own holdings and their proxies results in majority positions for these three banks in many German companies. These banks, along with others, monitor and control managers, both as lenders and as shareholders, by electing representatives to supervisory boards. Interestingly, research suggests that CEO compensation often depends on demographic and social similarities between CEOs and board chairs.[152]

German firms with more than 2,000 employees are required to have a two-tiered board structure that places the responsibility for monitoring and controlling managerial (or supervisory) decisions and actions in the hands of a separate group.[153] While all the functions of direction and management are the responsibility of the management board (the *Vorstand*), appointment to the Vorstand is the responsibility of the supervisory tier (the *Aufsichtsrat*). In large public companies, the supervisory board must contain an equal number of employee-elected and shareholder-elected representatives.[154]

Proponents of the German structure suggest that it helps prevent corporate wrongdoings and rash decisions by "dictatorial CEOs." However, critics maintain that it slows decision making and often ties a CEO's hands. In Germany the power sharing may have gone too far because it includes representation from the community as well as unions. Accordingly, the framework of corporate governance in Germany has made it difficult for companies to be restructured as quickly as they can be in the United States when their performance suffers.[155]

Because of the role of local government (through the board structure) and the power of banks in Germany's corporate governance structure, private shareholders rarely have major ownership positions in German firms. Large institutional investors, such as pension funds and insurance companies, are also relatively insignificant owners of corporate stock. Thus, at least historically, German executives generally have not been dedicated to the maximization of shareholder wealth, as they are in many other countries.[156]

Corporate governance in Germany is changing, at least partly, because of the increasing globalization of business. Many German firms are beginning to gravitate toward the U.S. system. Recent research suggests that the traditional system produced some agency costs because of a lack of external ownership power. Alternatively, firms with stronger external ownership power were less likely to undertake governance reforms. Firms that adopted governance reforms often divested poorly performing units and achieved higher levels of market performance.[157]

## Corporate Governance in Japan

Attitudes toward corporate governance in Japan are affected by the cultural concepts of obligation, family, and consensus.[158] In Japan, an obligation "may be to return a service for one rendered or it may derive from a more general relationship, for example, to one's family or old alumni, or one's company (or Ministry), or the country. This sense of particular obligation is common elsewhere but it feels stronger in Japan."[159] As part of a company family, individuals are members of a unit that envelops their lives; families command the attention and allegiance of parties throughout corporations. Moreover, a *keiretsu* (a group of firms tied together by cross-shareholdings) is more than an economic concept; it, too, is a family. A keiretsu firm usually owns less than 2 percent of any other member firm; however, each company typically has a stake in every firm in the keiretsu. As a result, somewhere between 30 and 90 percent of a firm is owned by other members of the keiretsu. Cross-shareholding is a manifestation of the close relationships that exist among a company and its primary stakeholders, including affiliates, suppliers, and customers. These close relationships "can decrease economic efficiency by preventing companies from doing business with the optimal suppliers or customers."[160] Cross-shareholding rates in Japan have been falling in recent years.

Consensus, an important influence in Japanese corporate governance, calls for the expenditure of significant amounts of energy to win the hearts and minds of people whenever possible, as opposed to top executives issuing edicts.[161] Consensus is highly valued, even when it results in a slow and cumbersome decision-making process. This system of governance places more importance on satisfying the needs of the group of stakeholders than of the shareholders. However, there are calls for changes in this system and attempts to achieve more balance in satisfying the stakeholders and increasing shareholder value.[162]

As in Germany, banks in Japan play an important role in financing and monitoring large public firms. The main bank—the one owning the largest share of stocks and the largest amount of debt—has the closest relationship with the company's top executives. It provides financial advice to the firm and also closely monitors managers. Thus, Japan's corporate governance structure is bank-based, whereas that in the United States is market-based.[163] Aside from lending money, a Japanese bank can hold up to 5 percent of a firm's total stock; a group of related financial institutions can hold up to 40 percent. In many cases, main-bank relationships are part of a horizontal keiretsu.

As is the case in Germany, Japan's structure of corporate governance is changing. For example, because of their continuing development as economic organizations, the role of banks in the monitoring and control of managerial behavior and firm outcomes is less significant than in the past.[164] The Asian economic crisis in the latter part of the 1990s made the governance problems in Japanese corporations apparent. The problems were readily evidenced in the large and once-powerful Mitsubishi keiretsu. Many of its core members lost substantial amounts of money in the late 1990s.[165]

Still another change in Japan's governance system has occurred in the market for corporate control, which was largely nonexistent in past years.[166] Corporate takeovers in Japan have generally been thought unacceptable, as indicated by two of the words used to describe them: *miurisuru*, to sell one's body, and *nottori*, or hijack.[167] Nevertheless, a bidding war between the British telecommunications group C&W and Japan's Nippon Telegraph & Telephone Corp. to control Japan's International Telegraph & Telephone Corp. erupted into what many analysts described as Japan's first hostile takeover battle.[168] Then in 2005 another takeover battle between the Internet service provider Livedoor and Fuji Television Network to control Nippon Broadcasting System (NBS) was described as a "milestone in the history of Japanese corporate governance" because it attracted a lot of media attention, it "demonstrated that the threat of hostile takeovers has become a reality in Japan," and it "provided an opportunity for Japanese to rethink the relationship between companies and their shareholders."[169]

One of the factors that could be driving this market for corporate control is the string of economic recessions that has plagued Japan since the 1990s. As mentioned previously, economic recessions make poorly performing firms easier to identify. Merger activity has been increasing recently in Japan, as have takeover defense strategies. Data collected by Nomura Securities demonstrated that "a surge in mergers and acquisitions in Japan is leaving corporate managers increasingly worried about unsolicited takeover bids."[170]

Interestingly, research suggests that the Japanese stewardship-management approach, historically dominated by inside managers, produces greater investments in long-term R&D projects than does the more financially oriented system in the United States.[171] As the potential for a stronger takeover market increases, some Japanese firms are considering delisting and taking their firms private in order to maintain long-term "strategic flexibility."[172] In fact, research suggests that private equity firms are beginning to pursue buyout strategies in Japan.[173]

## Global Corporate Governance

The 21st-century competitive landscape is fostering the creation of a relatively uniform governance structure that firms will use in developed economies throughout the world.[174] Even in Asia, as markets become more global and customer demands more similar, shareholders are becoming the focus of managers' efforts.[175] Furthermore, investors are becoming more and more active throughout the world.

Changes in governance are evident in many countries and are moving the governance models closer to that of the United States.[176] Firms in Europe, especially in France and the United Kingdom, are developing boards of directors with more independent members. Similar actions are occurring in Japan, where the boards are being reduced in size and foreign members added.[177] Even in transition economies, such as those of China and Russia, changes in corporate governance are occurring.[178] However, changes are implemented much more slowly in these economies. Chinese firms have found it helpful to use stock-based compensation plans, thereby providing an incentive for foreign companies to invest in China.[179] Because Russia has reduced its controls on the economy and on business activity much more quickly than China has, the country needs more effective governance systems to control its managerial activities. In fact, research suggests that ownership concentration leads to lower performance in Russia, primarily because minority shareholder rights are not well-protected through adequate governance controls.[180]

## Governance Mechanisms, Stakeholder Management, and Ethical Behavior

The governance mechanisms described in this chapter are designed to ensure that the agents of the firm's owners—the corporation's top executives—make strategic decisions that best serve the interests of the entire group of stakeholders, as described in Chapters 1 and 2. In the United States, governance mechanisms focus on the control of managerial decisions to ensure that shareholders' interests will be served, but product market stakeholders (e.g., customers, suppliers, and host communities) and organizational stakeholders (e.g., managerial and nonmanagerial employees) are important as well.[181]

As discussed in Chapters 1 and 2, excellent stakeholder relationships based on trust and mutual satisfaction of goals can enhance firm competitiveness by allowing the firm to obtain superior knowledge upon which to base strategic decisions[182] and by enhancing implementation of strategies due to higher levels of commitment among stakeholders.[183] Firms with trustworthy reputations also draw customers, suppliers, and business partners to them, thus enhancing strategic opportunities.[184] Dissatisfied stakeholders may withdraw their support from one firm and provide it to another. For example, dissatisfied customers are likely to purchase products from a supplier offering an acceptable substitute. Furthermore, neglect of stakeholders can lead to negative outcomes such as adverse regulation, legal suits and penalties, consumer retaliation, strikes, walkouts, and bad press.[185] Consequently, a firm creates more value when its governance mechanisms take into consideration the interests of all stakeholders.[186]

Companies that design and use governance mechanisms intended to encourage serving the interests of all stakeholders are also less likely to find themselves in situations in which their actions are considered unethical. The Enron, WorldCom, HealthSouth, and Tyco International scandals illustrate the devastating effect of poor ethical behavior not only on a firm's stakeholders, but also on other firms. These crises have influenced governance not only in the United States, but in other countries as well.[187]

The decisions and actions of a corporation's board of directors can be effective deterrents to unethical behavior and encourage socially responsible behavior. For example, research has found that firms with a CEO pay structure that has a long-term focus are more socially responsible than firms with a short-term pay focus.[188] Some believe that the most effective boards actively work to set boundaries for their firms' business ethics and values.[189] Once formulated, the board's expectations regarding ethical decisions and actions of all of the firm's stakeholders must be clearly communicated to its top-level managers. Moreover, as shareholders' agents, these managers must understand that the board will hold them fully accountable for the development and support of an organizational culture that results in ethical decisions and behaviors. As explained in Chapter 2, CEOs can be positive role models for ethical behavior.

Ethical behavior on the part of top executives is important, and effective governance systems are required to monitor it.[190] However, if the governance systems become too strong, they may eliminate the flexibility managers need to be creative, produce innovations, and respond quickly to changes in the firm's competitive environment. So, while too little or weak governance produces an internal environment whereby managerial opportunism can flourish, too much or overly strong governance may significantly reduce or eliminate managerial risk taking and the ability to adapt to changing environmental conditions.[191] Firms need to have effective governance mechanisms and simultaneously be able to be entrepreneurial.

## Summary

- Corporate governance is a relationship among stakeholders that is used to determine a firm's direction and control its performance. How firms monitor and control top-level managers' decisions and actions affects how they formulate and implement strategies. Effective governance that aligns managers' decisions with shareholders' interests can contribute to a competitive advantage.

- There are three internal governance mechanisms in the modern corporation: ownership concentration, the board of directors, and executive compensation. The market for corporate control is the single external governance mechanism influencing managers' decisions and the outcomes resulting from them.

- Ownership is separated from control in the modern corporation. Owners (principals) hire managers (agents) to make decisions that maximize the firm's value. As risk-bearing specialists, owners diversify their risk by investing in multiple corporations with different risk profiles. As decision-making specialists, owners expect their agents (the firm's top-level managers) to make decisions that lead to maximizing the firm's value. Thus, modern corporations are characterized by an agency relationship that is created when one party (the firm's owners) hires and pays another party (top-level managers) to use its decision-making skills.

- Separation of ownership and control creates an agency problem when an agent pursues goals that conflict with principals' goals. Principals establish and use governance mechanisms to control this potential problem.

- Ownership concentration is based on the number of large-block shareholders and the percentage of shares they own. With significant ownership percentages, such as those held by large mutual funds and pension funds, institutional investors often are able to influence top executives' strategic decisions and actions. Thus, unlike diffuse ownership, which often results in relatively weak monitoring and control of managerial decisions, concentrated ownership produces more active and effective monitoring. An increasingly powerful force in the United States and, to a lesser degree, the United Kingdom, institutional investors actively use their positions of concentrated ownership to force managers and boards of directors to make decisions that maximize a firm's value.

- In the United States and the United Kingdom, a firm's board of directors, composed of insiders, related outsiders, and outsiders, is a governance mechanism that shareholders expect to represent their collective interests. The percentage of outside directors on many boards now exceeds the percentage of inside directors. Outsiders are expected to be more independent of a firm's top-level managers compared with those selected from inside the firm.

■ Executive compensation is a highly visible and often criticized governance mechanism. Salary, bonuses, and long-term incentives are used to strengthen the alignment between managers' and shareholders' interests. A firm's board of directors is responsible for determining the effectiveness of the firm's executive compensation system. An effective system elicits managerial decisions that are in shareholders' best interests.

■ In general, evidence suggests that shareholders and boards of directors have become more vigilant in their control of managerial decisions. Nonetheless, these mechanisms are insufficient to govern managerial behavior in many large companies. Therefore, the market for corporate control is an important governance mechanism. Although it, too, is imperfect, the market for corporate control has been effective in combating inefficient corporate diversification and causing managers to implement more effective strategic decisions.

■ Corporate governance structures used in Germany and Japan differ from each other and from that used in the United States. Historically, the U.S. governance structure has emphasized maximizing shareholder value. In Germany, employees, as a stakeholder group, have a more prominent role in governance. By contrast, until recently, Japanese shareholders played virtually no role in the monitoring and control of top-level managers. However, all of these systems are becoming increasingly similar, as are many governance systems in developed countries, such as France and Italy, and transitional economies, such as Russia and China.

■ Effective governance mechanisms ensure that the interests of all stakeholders are served. Thus, long-term strategic success results when firms are governed in ways that foster the satisfaction of capital market stakeholders (e.g., shareholders), product market stakeholders (e.g., customers and suppliers), and organizational stakeholders (managerial and nonmanagerial employees). Moreover, effective governance encourages ethical behavior in the formulation and implementation of strategies.

## Ethics Questions

1. Do managers have an ethical responsibility to push aside their own values with regard to how certain stakeholders are treated (i.e., special interest groups) in order to maximize shareholder returns?
2. What are the ethical implications associated with owners assuming that managers will act in their own self-interest?
3. What ethical issues surround executive compensation? How can we determine whether top executives are paid too much?
4. Is it ethical for firms involved in the market for corporate control to target companies performing at levels exceeding the industry average? Why or why not?
5. What ethical issues, if any, do top executives face when asking their firm to provide them with a golden parachute?
6. How can governance mechanisms be designed to ensure against managerial opportunism, ineffectiveness, and unethical behaviors?

# Notes

1. K. Hendry & G. C. Kiel, 2004, The role of the board in firm strategy: Integrating agency and organisational control perspectives, *Corporate Governance*,12(4): 500–520; M. Carpenter & J. Westphal, 2001, Strategic context of external network ties: Examining the impact of director appointments on board involvement in strategic decision making, *Academy of Management Journal*, 44: 639–660.

2. N. Byrnes & J. Sasseen, 2007, Board of hard knocks; Activist shareholders, tougher rules and anger over CEO pay have put directors on the hot seat, *Business Week*, January 22, 37.

3. S. Werner, H. L. Tosi, & L. Gomez-Mejia, 2005, Organizational governance and employee pay: How ownership structure affects the firm's compensation strategy, *Strategic Management Journal*,26: 377–384; F. Elloumi & J.-P. Gueyie, 2001, CEO compensation, IOS and the role of corporate governance, *Corporate Governance*, 1(2): 23–33; J. E. Core, R. W. Holthausen, & D. F. Larcker, 1999, Corporate governance, chief executive officer compensation, and firm performance, *Journal of Financial Economics*, 51: 371–406.

4. M. A. Chen, 2004, Executive option repricing, incentives, and retention, *Journal of Finance*, 59: 1167–1199.

5. K. Allison & B. Masters, 2007, Ex-McAfee lawyer charged with fraud, *Financial Times*, February 28, 30.

6. M. D. Lynall, B. R. Golden, & A. J. Hillman, 2003, Board composition from adolescence to maturity: A multitheoretic view, *Academy of Management Review*, 28: 416–431; A. J. Hillman, G. D. Keim, & R. A. Luce, 2001, Board composition and stakeholder performance: Do stakeholder directors make a difference? *Business and Society*, 40: 295–314; R. K. Mitchell, B. R. Agle, & D. J. Wood, 1997, Toward a theory of stakeholder identification and salience: Defining the principle of who and what really counts, *Academy of Management Review*, 22: 853–886.

7. A. Desai, M. Kroll, & P. Wright, 2005, Outside board monitoring and the economic outcomes of acquisitions: A test of the substitution hypothesis, *Journal of Business Research*, 58: 926–934; C. M. Daily, D. R. Dalton, & A. A. Cannella, 2003, Corporate governance: Decades of dialogue and data, *Academy of Management Review*, 28: 371–382; P. Stiles, 2001, The impact of the board on strategy: An empirical examination, *Journal of Management Studies*, 38: 627–650; J. H. Davis, F. D. Schoorman, & L. Donaldson, 1997, Toward a stewardship theory of management, *Academy of Management Review*, 22: 20–47.

8. M.S. Schwartz, T. W. Dunfee, & M. J. Kline, 2005, Tone at the top: An ethics code for directors? *Journal of Business Ethics*, 58: 79–100; D. Finegold, E. E. Lawler III, & J. Conger, 2001, Building a better board, *Journal of Business Strategy*, 22(6): 33–37.

9. E. F. Fama & M. C. Jensen, 1983, Separation of ownership and control, *Journal of Law and Economics*, 26: 301–325.

10. M. Arndt, W. Zellner, & M. McNamee, 2002, Restoring trust in corporate America, *Business Week*, June 24, 30–35.

11. C. Hymowitz, 2004, Corporate governance (a special report)—Experiments in corporate governance: Finding the right way to improve board oversight isn't easy; but plenty of companies are trying, *Wall Street Journal*, June 21, R1.

12. M. Carney, 2005, Corporate governance and competitive advantage in family-controlled firms, *Entrepreneurship Theory and Practice*, 29: 249–265; R. Charan, 1998, *How Corporate Boards Create Competitive Advantage*, San Francisco: Jossey-Bass.

13. G. J. Nicholson & G. C. Kiel, 2004, Breakthrough board performance: How to harness your board's intellectual capital, *Corporate Governance*, 4(1): 5–23; A. Cannella Jr., A. Pettigrew, & D. Hambrick, 2001, Upper echelons: Donald Hambrick on executives and strategy, *Academy of Management Executive*, 15(3): 36–52; J. D. Westphal & E. J. Zajac, 1997, Defections from the inner circle: Social exchange, reciprocity and diffusion of board independence in U.S. corporations, *Administrative Science Quarterly*, 42: 161–212.

14. X. Wu, 2005, Corporate governance and corruption: A cross-country analysis, *Governance*, 18(2): 151–170; J. McGuire & S. Dow, 2002, The Japanese keiretsu system: An empirical analysis, *Journal of Business Research*, 55: 33–40.

15. J. Charkham, 1994, *Keeping Good Company: A Study of Corporate Governance in Five Countries*, New York: Oxford University Press, 1.

16. R. E. Hoskisson, D. Yiu, & H. Kim, 2004, Corporate governance systems: Effects of capital and labor market congruency on corporate innovation and global competitiveness, *Journal of High Technology Management Research*, 15: 293–315; A. Cadbury, 1999, The future of governance: The rules of the game, *Journal of General Management*, 24: 1–14.

17. R. Aguilera & G. Jackson, 2003, The cross-national diversity of corporate governance: Dimensions and determinants, *Academy of Management Review*, 28: 447–465; Cadbury Committee, 1992, *Report of the Cadbury Committee on the Financial Aspects of Corporate Governance*, London: Gee.

18. R. P. Wright, 2004, Top managers' strategic cognitions of the strategy making process: Differences between high and low performing firms, *Journal of General Management*, 30(1): 61–78; C. K. Prahalad & J. P. Oosterveld, 1999, Transforming internal governance: The challenge for multinationals, *Sloan Management Review*, 40(3): 31–39.

19. T. Moeller, 2005, Let's make a deal! How shareholder control impacts merger payoffs, *Journal of Financial Economics*, 76(1): 167–190; M. A. Hitt, R. E. Hoskisson, R. A. Johnson, & D. D. Moesel, 1996, The market for corporate control and firm innovation, *Academy of Management Journal*, 39: 1084–1119; J. P. Walsh & R. Kosnik, 1993, Corporate raiders and their disciplinary role in the market for corporate control, *Academy of Management Journal*, 36: 671–700.

20. B. B. Burr, 2005, Good governance rewarded, *Pensions and Investments*, 33(2): 20; K. Ramaswamy, M. Li, & R.Veliyath, 2002, Variations in ownership behavior and propensity to diversify: A study of the Indian context, *Strategic Management Journal*, 23: 345–358; Davis, Schoorman, & Donaldson, Toward a stewardship theory.

21. R. C. Anderson, T. W. Bates, J. M. Bizjak, & M. L. Lemmon, 2000, Corporate governance and firm diversification, *Financial Management*, 29(1): 5–22; C. Sundaramurthy, J. M. Mahoney, & J. T. Mahoney,

1997, Board structure, antitakeover provisions, and stockholder wealth, *Strategic Management Journal*, 18: 231–246; K. J. Rediker & A. Seth, 1995, Boards of directors and substitution effects of alternative governance mechanisms, *Strategic Management Journal*, 16: 85–99.

22  R. E. Hoskisson, M. A. Hitt, R. A. Johnson, & W. Grossman, 2002, Conflicting voices: The effects of ownership heterogeneity and internal governance on corporate strategy, *Academy of Management Journal*, 45: 697–716.

23  G. E. Davis & T. A. Thompson, 1994, A social movement perspective on corporate control, *Administrative Science Quarterly*, 39: 141–173.

24  R. Bricker & N. Chandar, 2000, Where Berle and Means went wrong: A reassessment of capital market agency and financial reporting, *Accounting, Organizations and Society*, 25: 529–554; M. A. Eisenberg, 1989, The structure of corporation law, *Columbia Law Review*, 89(7): 1461, as cited in R. A. G. Monks & N. Minow, 1995, *Corporate Governance*, Cambridge, MA: Blackwell Business, 7.

25  R. M. Wiseman & L. R. Gomez-Mejia, 1999, A behavioral agency model of managerial risk taking, *Academy of Management Review*, 23: 133–153.

26  R. C. Anderson & D. M. Reeb, 2004, Board composition: Balancing family influence in S&P 500 firms, *Administrative Science Quarterly*, 49: 209–237.

27  Carney, Corporate governance and competitive advantage; N. Athanassiou, W. F. Crittenden, L. M. Kelly, & P. Marquez, 2002, Founder centrality effects on the Mexican family firm's top management group: Firm culture, strategic vision and goals and firm performance, *Journal of World Business*, 37: 139–150.

28  G. Redding, 2002, The capitalist business system of China and its rationale, *Asia Pacific Journal of Management*, 19: 221–249.

29  T.-S. Lee & Y.-H. Yeh, 2004, Corporate governance and financial distress: Evidence from Taiwan, *Corporate Governance*, 12(3): 378–388; M. Carney & E. Gedajlovic, 2003, Strategic innovation and the administrative heritage of East Asian family business groups, *Asia Pacific Journal of Management*, 20: 5–26; D. Miller & I. Le Breton-Miller, 2003, Challenge versus advantage in family business, *Strategic Organization*, 1: 127–134.

30  E. F. Fama, 1980, Agency problems and the theory of the firm, *Journal of Political Economy*, 88: 288–307.

31  D. Dalton, C. Daily, T. Certo, & R. Roengpitya, 2003, Meta-analyses of financial performance and equity: Fusion or confusion? *Academy of Management Journal*, 46: 13–26; M. Jensen & W. Meckling, 1976, Theory of the firm: Managerial behavior, agency costs, and ownership structure, *Journal of Financial Economics*, 11: 305–360.

32  D. C. Hambrick, S. Finkelstein, & A. C. Mooney, 2005, Executive job demands: New insights for explaining strategic decisions and leader behaviors, *Academy of Management Review*, 30: 472–491; L. R. Gomez-Mejia, M. Nunez-Nickel, & I. Gutierrez, 2001, The role of family ties in agency contracts, *Academy of Management Journal*, 44: 81–95; H. L. Tosi, J. Katz, & L. R. Gomez-Mejia, 1997, Disaggregating the agency contract: The effects of monitoring, incentive alignment, and term in office on agent decision making, *Academy of Management Journal*, 40: 584–602.

33  M. G. Jacobides & D. C. Croson, 2001, Information policy: Shaping the value of agency relationships, *Academy of Management Review*, 26: 202–223.

34  H. E. Ryan Jr. & R. A. Wiggins III, 2004, Who is in whose pocket? Director compensation, board independence, and barriers to effective monitoring, *Journal of Financial Economics*, 73: 497–524; R. Mangel & M. Useem, 2001, The strategic role of gainsharing, *Journal of Labor Research*, 2: 327–343; T. M. Welbourne & L. R. Gomez-Mejia, 1995, Gainsharing: A critical review and a future research agenda, *Journal of Management*, 21: 577.

35  M. W. Peng, 2004, Outside directors and firm performance during institutional transitions, *Strategic Management Journal*, 25: 453–471; A. J. Hillman & T. Dalziel, 2003, Boards of directors and firm performance: Integrating agency and resource dependence perspectives, *Academy of Management Review*, 28: 383–396.

36  Hoskisson, Hitt, Johnson, & Grossman, Conflicting voices; O. E. Williamson, 1996, *The Mechanisms of Governance*, New York: Oxford University Press, 6; O. E. Williamson, 1993, Opportunism and its critics, *Managerial and Decision Economics*, 14: 97–107.

37  R. W. Coff & P. M. Lee, 2003, Insider trading as a vehicle to appropriate rent from R&D, *Strategic Management Journal*, 24: 183–190; C. C. Chen, M. W. Peng, & P. A. Saparito, 2002, Individualism, collectivism, and opportunism: A cultural perspective on transaction cost economics, *Journal of Management*, 28: 567–583; S. Ghoshal & P. Moran, 1996, Bad for practice: A critique of the transaction cost theory, *Academy of Management Review*, 21: 13–47.

38  K. H. Wathne & J. B. Heide, 2000, Opportunism in interfirm relationships: Forms, outcomes, and solutions, *Journal of Marketing*, 64(4): 36–51.

39  T. Yoshikawa, P. H. Phan, & J. Linton, 2004, The relationship between governance structure and risk management approaches in Japanese venture capital firms, *Journal of Business Venturing*, 19: 831–849; L. Tihanyi, R. A. Johnson, R. E. Hoskisson, & M. A. Hitt, 2003, Institutional ownership differences and international diversification: The effects of boards of directors and technological opportunity, *Academy of Management Journal*, 46: 195–211; Y. Amihud & B. Lev, 1981, Risk reduction as a managerial motive for conglomerate mergers, *Bell Journal of Economics*, 12: 605–617.

40  Anderson, Bates, Bizjak, & Lemmon, Corporate governance and firm diversification; R. E. Hoskisson & T. A. Turk, 1990, Corporate restructuring: Governance and control limits of the internal market, *Academy of Management Review*, 15: 459–477.

41  R. Bushman, Q. Chen, E. Engel, & A. Smith, 2004, Financial accounting information, organizational complexity and corporate governance systems, *Journal of Accounting and Economics*, 7: 167–201; M. A. Geletkanycz, B. K. Boyd, & S. Finkelstein, 2001, The strategic value of CEO external directorate networks: Implications for CEO compensation, *Strategic Management Journal*, 9: 889–898.

42  Y. Grinstein & P. Hribar, 2004, CEO compensation and incentives: Evidence from M&A bonuses, *Journal of Financial Economics*, 73: 119–143; A. Seth, K. P. Song, & R. R. Pettit, 2002, Value creation and destruction in cross-border acquisitions: An empirical analysis of foreign acquisitions of U.S. firms, *Strategic Management Journal*, 23: 921–940; P. Wright, M. Kroll, & D. Elenkov, 2002, Acquisition returns, increase in firm size and chief executive officer compensation: The moderating role of monitoring, *Academy of Management Journal*,

45: 599–608; S. Finkelstein & D. C. Hambrick, 1989, Chief executive compensation: A study of the intersection of markets and political processes, *Strategic Management Journal*, 16: 221, 239.

43 M. Goranova, T. M. Alessandri, P. Brandes, & R. Dharwadkar, 2007, Managerial ownership and corporate diversification: A longitudinal view, *Strategic Management Journal*, 28: 211–225.

44 Gomez-Mejia, Nunez-Nickel, & Gutierrez, The role of family ties in agency contracts.

45 M. C. Jensen, 1986, Agency costs of free cash flow, corporate finance, and takeovers, *American Economic Review*, 76: 323–329.

46 M. Jensen & E. Zajac, 2004, Corporate elites and corporate strategy: How demographic preferences and structural position shape the scope of the firm, *Strategic Management Journal*, 25: 507–524; T. H. Brush, P. Bromiley, & M. Hendrickx, 2000, The free cash flow hypothesis for sales growth and firm performance, *Strategic Management Journal*, 21: 455–472; H. DeAngelo & L. DeAngelo, 2000, Controlling stockholders and the disciplinary role of corporate payout policy: A study of the Times Mirror Company, *Journal of Financial Economics*, 56: 153–207.

47 K. Ramaswamy, M. Li, & B. S. P. Petitt, 2004, Who drives unrelated diversification? A study of Indian manufacturing firms, *Asia Pacific Journal of Management*, 21: 403–423; K. Ramaswamy, M. Li, & R. Veliyath, 2002, Variations in ownership behavior and propensity to diversify: A study of the Indian corporate context, *Strategic Management Journal*, 23: 345–358.

48 A. Desai, M. Kroll, & P. Wright, 2005, Outside board monitoring and the economic outcomes of acquisitions: A test of the substitution hypothesis, *Journal of Business Research*, 58: 926–934; P. Wright, M. Kroll, A. Lado, & B. Van Ness, 2002, The structure of ownership and corporate acquisition strategies, *Strategic Management Journal*, 23: 41–53.

49 T. K. Mukherjee, H. Kiymaz, & H. K. Baker, 2004, Merger motives and target valuation: A survey of evidence from CFOs, *Journal of Applied Finance*, 14(2): 7–24; R. Rajan, H. Servaes, & L. Zingales, 2001, The cost of diversity: The diversification discount and inefficient investment, *Journal of Finance*, 55: 35–79; A. Sharma, 1997, Professional as agent: Knowledge asymmetry in agency exchange, *Academy of Management Review*, 22: 758–798.

50 M. Osheroff, 2006, SOX as opportunity, *Strategic Finance*, April, 19–20; D. R. Dalton & C. M. Dalton, Sarbanes–Oxley legislation and the private company: If not a marriage, then certainly an engagement, *Journal of Business Strategy*, 26(2): 7–8; A. Borrus, L. Lavelle, D. Brady, M. Arndt, & J. Weber, 2005, Death, taxes and Sarbanes–Oxley? Executives may be frustrated with the law's burdens, but corporate performance is here to stay, *Business Week*, January 17, 28–31.

51 R. Marden & R. Edwards, 2005, The Sarbanes–Oxley axe, *CPA Journal*, April, 6–10.

52 J. Fox, 2005, Calling off the dogs, *Fortune*, June 27, 27–29.

53 J. McTague, 2005, Corporate tangle, *Barron's*, April 4, 19.

54 L. Stephens & R.G. Schwartz, 2006, The chilling effect of Sarbanes–Oxley: Myth or reality? *CPA Journal*, June, 14–19.

55 W. J. Hass & S. G. Pryor IV, 2005, The board's role in corporate renewal, *Journal of Private Equity*, 8(2): 12.

56 A. de Miguel, J. Pindado, & C. de la Torre, 2004, Ownership structure and firm value: New evidence from Spain, *Strategic Management Journal*, 25: 1199–1207; J. Coles, N. Sen, & V. McWilliams, 2001, An examination of the relationship of governance mechanisms to performance, *Journal of Management*, 27: 23–50.

57 M. Singh, I. Mathur, & K. C. Gleason, 2004, Governance and performance implications of diversification strategies: Evidence from large U. S. firms, *Financial Review*, 39: 489–526; S.-S. Chen & K. W. Ho, 2000, Corporate diversification, ownership structure, and firm value: The Singapore evidence, *International Review of Financial Analysis*, 9: 315–326; R. E. Hoskisson, R. A. Johnson, & D. D. Moesel, 1994, Corporate divestiture intensity in restructuring firms: Effects of governance, strategy, and performance, *Academy of Management Journal*, 37: 1207–1251.

58 De Miguel, Pindado, & de la Torre, Ownership structure and firm value.

59 R. C. Anderson & D. M. Reeb, 2004, Board composition: Balancing family influence in S&P 500 firms, *Administrative Science Quarterly*, 49: 209–237.

60 S. J. Chang, 2003, Ownership structure, expropriation and performance of group-affiliated companies in Korea, *Academy of Management Journal*, 46: 238–253.

61 A. Berle & G. Means, 1932, *The Modern Corporation and Private Property*, New York: Macmillan.

62 B. Ajinkya, S. Bhojraj, & P. Sengupta, 2005, The association between outside directors, institutional investors and the properties of management earnings forecasts, *Journal of Accounting Research*, 43: 343–376; P. A. Gompers & A. Metrick, 2001, Institutional investors and equity prices, *Quarterly Journal of Economics*, 116: 229–259; M. P. Smith, 1996, Shareholder activism by institutional investors: Evidence from CalPERS, *Journal of Finance*, 51: 227–252.

63 Hoskisson, Hitt, Johnson, & Grossman, Conflicting voices; C. M. Daily, 1996, Governance patterns in bankruptcy reorganizations, *Strategic Management Journal*, 17: 355–375.

64 Hoskisson, Hitt, Johnson, & Grossman, Conflicting voices; M. Useem, 1998, Corporate leadership in a globalizing equity market, *Academy of Management Executive*, 12(3): 43–59; R. E. Hoskisson & M. A. Hitt, 1994, *Downscoping: How to Tame the Diversified Firm*, New York: Oxford University Press.

65 K. Rebeiz, 2001, Corporate governance effectiveness in American corporations: A survey, *International Management Journal*, 18(1): 74–80.

66 2007, CalPERS, Facts at a glance, http://www.calpers.com, March 1.

67 2007, CalPERS shareowner forum, Shareowner action, http://www.calpers-governance.org, March 1.

68 Ibid.

69 Tihanyi, Hoskisson, Johnson, & Hitt, Institutional ownership difference; Hoskisson, Hitt, Johnson, & Grossman, Conflicting voices; P. David, M. A. Hitt, & J. Gimeno, 2001, The role of institutional investors in influencing R&D, *Academy of Management Journal*, 44: 144–157; B. J. Bushee, 2001, Do institutional investors prefer near-term earnings over long-run value? *Contemporary Accounting Research*, 18: 207–246.

70 2001, Shareholder activism is rising, *Investor Relations Business*, August 6, 8.

71 W. S. de Wied, 2006, The age of activism, *Corporate Governance Advisor*, 14(6): 1–7.

72  Ibid.

73  Rebeiz, Corporate governance effectiveness; J. K. Seward & J. P Walsh, 1996, The governance and control of voluntary corporate spinoffs, *Strategic Management Journal*, 17: 25–39.

74  Y. Y. Kor, 2006, Direct and interaction effects of top management team and board compositions on R&D investment strategy, *Strategic Management Journal*, 27: 1081–1099; A. Dehaene, V. De Vuyst, & H. Ooghe, 2001, Corporate performance and board structure in Belgian companies, *Long Range Planning*, 34(3): 383–398.

75  S. Chatterjee, J. S. Harrison, & D. D. Bergh, 2003, Failed takeover attempts, organizational governance and refocusing, *Strategic Management Journal*, 24: 87–96; S. Chatterjee & J. S. Harrison, 2001, Corporate governance, in M. A. Hitt, R. E. Freeman, & J. S. Harrison (eds.), *Blackwell Handbook of Strategic Management*, Oxford, UK: Blackwell Publishers, 543–563.

76  S. Finkelstein & A. C. Mooney, 2003, Not the usual suspects: How to use board process to make boards better, *Academy of Management Executive*, 17: 101–113.

77  S. Thomsen & T. Pedersen, 2000, Ownership structure and economic performance in the largest European companies, *Strategic Management Journal*, 21: 689–705.

78  R. V. Aguilera, 2005, Corporate governance and director accountability: An institutional comparative perspective, *British Journal of Management*, 16(S1): 539–553; E. H. Fram, 2004, Governance reform: It's only just begun, *Business Horizons*, 47(6): 10–14; D. R. Dalton, C. M. Daily, A. E. Ellstrand, & J. L. Johnson, 1998, Meta-analytic reviews of board composition, leadership structure, and financial performance, *Strategic Management Journal*, 19: 269–290; M. Huse, 1998, Researching the dynamics of board-stakeholder relations, *Long Range Planning*, 31: 218–226.

79  S. Young, 2000, The increasing use of non-executive directors: Its impact on UK board structure and governance arrangements, *Journal of Business Finance and Accounting*, 27(9/10): 1311–1342; P. Mallette & R. L. Hogler, 1995, Board composition, stock ownership, and the exemption of directors from liability, *Journal of Management*, 21: 861–878.

80  C. Caldwell & R. Karri, 2005, Organizational governance and ethical systems: A covenantal approach to building trust, *Journal of Business Ethics*, 58: 249–259; J. Chidley, 2001, Why boards matter, *Canadian Business*, October 29, 6; D. P. Forbes & F. J. Milliken, 1999, Cognition and corporate governance: Understanding boards of directors as strategic decision-making groups, *Academy of Management Review*, 24: 489–505.

81  Hoskisson, Hitt, Johnson, & Grossman, Conflicting voices; B. D. Baysinger & R. E. Hoskisson, 1990, The composition of boards of directors and strategic control: Effects on corporate strategy, *Academy of Management Review*, 15: 72–87.

82  Carpenter & Westphal, Strategic context of external network ties; E. J. Zajac & J. D. Westphal, 1996, Director reputation, CEO-board power, and the dynamics of board interlocks, *Administrative Science Quarterly*, 41: 507–529.

83  M. J. Canyon, 2006, Executive compensation and incentives, *Academy of Management Perspectives*, 20(1): 25–44.

84  J. Westphal & L. Milton, 2000, How experience and network ties affect the influence of demographic minorities on corporate boards, *Administrative Science Quarterly*, June, 45(2): 366–398.

85  2006, BP, Board independence, http://www.bp.com, August 8.

86  S. T. Petra, 2005, Do outside independent directors strengthen corporate boards? *Corporate Governance*, 5(1): 55–65.

87  J. Roberts, T. McNulty, & P. Stiles, 2005, Beyond agency conceptions of the work of the non-executive director: Creating accountability in the boardroom, *British Journal of Management*, 16(S1): S1–S4.

88  J. Coles & W. Hesterly, 2000, Independence of the chairman and board composition: Firm choices and shareholder value, *Journal of Management*, 26: 195–214; S. Zahra, 1996, Governance, ownership and corporate entrepreneurship among the Fortune 500: The moderating impact of industry technological opportunity, *Academy of Management Journal*, 39: 1713–1735.

89  Hoskisson, Hitt, Johnson, & Grossman, Conflicting voices.

90  E. E. Lawler III & D. L. Finegold, 2005, The changing face of corporate boards, *MIT Sloan Management Review*, 46(2): 67–70; A. Conger, E. E. Lawler, & D. L. Finegold, 2001, *Corporate Boards: New Strategies for Adding Value at the Top*, San Francisco: Jossey-Bass; J. A. Conger, D. Finegold, & E. E. Lawler III, 1998, Appraising boardroom performance, *Harvard Business Review*, 76(1): 136–148.

91  W. Shen, 2005, Improve board effectiveness: The need for incentives, *British Journal of Management*, 16(S1): 581–589; M. Gerety, C. Hoi, & A. Robin, 2001, Do shareholders benefit from the adoption of incentive pay for directors? *Financial Management*, 30: 45–61; J. Marshall, 2001, As boards shrink, responsibilities grow, *Financial Executive*, 17(4): 36–39; D. C. Hambrick & E. M. Jackson, 2000, Outside directors with a stake: The linchpin in improving governance, *California Management Review*, 42(4): 108–127.

92  Carpenter & Westphal, The strategic context of external network ties.

93  I. Filatotchev & S. Toms, 2003, Corporate governance, strategy and survival in a declining industry: A study of UK cotton textile companies, *Journal of Management Studies*, 40: 895–920; W. Q. Judge Jr. & C. Zeithaml, 1992, Institutional and strategic choice perspectives on board involvement in the strategic decision process, *Academy of Management Journal*, 35: 766–794.

94  C. A. Simmers, 2000, Executive/board politics in strategic decision making, *Journal of Business and Economic Studies*, 4: 37–56.

95  Roberts, McNulty, & Stiles, Beyond agency conceptions.

96  W. E. Gillis & J. G. Combs, 2006, How much is too much? Board of director response to shareholder concerns about CEO stock options, *Academy of Management Perspectives*, 20(2): 70–72; K. J. Martin & R. S. Thomas, 2005, When is enough, enough? Market reaction to highly dilutive stock option plans and the subsequent impact on CEO compensation, *Journal of Corporate Finance*, 11: 61–83.

97  G. Morgensen, 2006, Outside advice on boss's pay may not be so independent, *New York Times*, http://www .nytimes.com, April 10.

98  G. Anders, 2006, As patients, doctors feel pinch, insurer's CEO makes a billion, *Wall Street Journal*, April 18, A1.

99. E. White & A. O. Patrick, 2007, Shareholders push for vote on executive pay, *Wall Street Journal*, February 26, B1.

100. L. A. Bebchuk & J. M. Fried, 2004, *Pay without Performance: The Unfulfilled Promise of Executive Compensation*, Cambridge, MA: Harvard University Press; D. C. Hambrick & S. Finkelstein, 1995, The effects of ownership structure on conditions at the top: The case of CEO pay raises, *Strategic Management Journal*, 16: 175.

101. M. Makri, P. J. Lane, & L. R. Gomez-Mejia, 2006, CEO incentives, innovation, and performance in technology-intensive firms: A reconciliation of outcome and behavior-based incentive schemes, *Strategic Management Journal*, 27: 1057–1080; J. S. Miller, R. M. Wiseman, & L. R. Gomez-Mejia, 2002, The fit between CEO compensation design and firm risk, *Academy of Management Journal*, 45: 745–756; L. Gomez-Mejia & R. M. Wiseman, 1997, Reframing executive compensation: An assessment and outlook, *Journal of Management*, 23: 291–374.

102. A. Henderson & J. Fredrickson, 2001, Top management team coordination needs and the CEO pay gap: A competitive test of economic and behavioral views, *Academy of Management Journal*, 44: 96–117.

103. J. McGuire & E. Matta, 2003, CEO stock options: The silent dimension of ownership, *Academy of Management Journal*, 46: 255–265; W. G. Sanders & M. A. Carpenter, 1998, Internationalization and firm governance: The roles of CEO compensation, top team composition and board structure, *Academy of Management Journal*, 41: 158–178.

104. N. T. Hill & K. T. Stevens, 2001, Structuring compensation to achieve better financial results, *Strategic Finance*, 9: 48–51; J. D. Westphal & E. J. Zajac, 1999, The symbolic management of stockholders: Corporate governance reform and shareholder reactions, *Administrative Science Quarterly*, 43: 127–153.

105. L. Gomez-Mejia, M. Larraza-Kintana, & M. Makri, 2003, The determinants of executive compensation in family-controlled public corporations, *Academy of Management Journal*, 46: 226–237; Elloumi & Gueyie, CEO compensation, IOS and the role of corporate governance; M. J. Conyon & S. I. Peck, 1998, Board control, remuneration committees, and top management compensation, *Academy of Management Journal*, 41: 146–157; Westphal & Zajac, The symbolic management of stockholders.

106. S. O'Donnell, 2000, Managing foreign subsidiaries: Agents of headquarters, or an interdependent network? *Strategic Management Journal*, 21: 521–548; K. Roth & S. O'Donnell, 1996, Foreign subsidiary compensation: An agency theory perspective, *Academy of Management Journal*, 39: 678–703.

107. K. Ramaswamy, R. Veliyath, & L. Gomes, 2000, A study of the determinants of CEO compensation in India, *Management International Review*, 40(2): 167–191.

108. J. Krug & W. Hegarty, 2001, Predicting who stays and leaves after an acquisition: A study of top managers in multinational firms, *Strategic Management Journal*, 22: 185–196.

109. M. A. Carpenter & W. G. Sanders, 2002, Top management team compensation: The missing link between CEO pay and firm performance, *Strategic Management Journal*, 23: 367–375.

110. Werner, Tosi, & Gomez-Mejia, Organizational governance and employee pay; S. Bryan, L. Hwang, &

S. Lilien, 2000, CEO stock-based compensation: An empirical analysis of incentive-intensity, relative mix, and economic determinants, *Journal of Business*, 73: 661–693.

111. R. E. Hoskisson, M. A. Hitt, & C. W. L. Hill, 1993, Managerial incentives and investment in R&D in large multiproduct firms, *Organization Science*, 4: 325–341.

112. Gomez-Mejia, Larraza-Kintana, & Makri, The determinants of executive compensation.

113. L. K. Meulbroek, 2001, The efficiency of equity-linked compensation: Understanding the full cost of awarding executive stock options, *Financial Management*, 30(2): 5–44.

114. J. C. Hartzell & L. T. Starks, 2003, Institutional investors and executive compensation, *Journal of Finance*, 58: 2351–2374.

115. J. Dahya, A. A. Lonie, & D. A. Power, 1998, Ownership structure, firm performance and top executive change: An analysis of UK firms, *Journal of Business Finance and Accounting*, 25: 1089–1118.

116. L. Gomez-Mejia, 2003, What should be done about CEO pay? *Academy of Management Issues Forum*, July; H. Tosi, S. Werner, J. Katz, & L. Gomez-Mejia, 2000, How much does performance matter? A meta-analysis of CEO pay studies, *Journal of Management*, 26: 301–339.

117. P. T. Chingos, 2004, *Responsible Executive Compensation for a New Era of Accountability*, Hoboken, NJ: Wiley.

118. J. C. Bettis, J. M. Bizjak, & M. L. Lemmon, 2005, Exercise behavior, valuation and the incentive effects of employee stock options, *Journal of Financial Economics*, 76: 445–470.

119. T. G. Pollock, H. M. Fischer, & J. B. Wade, 2002, The role of politics in repricing executive options, *Academy of Management Journal*, 45: 1172–1182; M. E. Carter & L. J. Lynch, 2001, An examination of executive stock option repricing, *Journal of Financial Economics*, 59: 207–225; D. Chance, R. Kumar, & R. Todd, 2001, The "repricing" of executive stock options, *Journal of Financial Economics*, 59: 129–154.

120. M. A. Chen, 2004, Executive option repricing, incentives, and retention, *Journal of Finance*, 59: 1167–1199; P. Brandes, R. Dharwadkar, & G. V. Lemesis, 2003, Effective stock option design: Reconciling stakeholder, strategic and motivational factors, *Academy of Management Executive*, 17(1): 77–93.

121. L. Lavelle, 2005, A payday for performance, *Business Week*, April 28, 78; E. MacDonald, 2005, Optional end run, *Forbes*, June 20, 62.

122. J. Sasseen, 2006, Master of the options universe, *Business Week*, October 23, 38.

123. Allison & Masters, Ex-McAfee lawyer charged with fraud.

124. B. Chai, 2006, New twists to the scandal over options backdating, *Wall Street Journal*, December 12.

125. H. Maurer, 2007, The Feds weigh in, *Business Week*, February 26, 36.

126. Moeller, Let's make a deal!; R. Coff, 2003, Bidding wars over R&D intensive firms: Knowledge, opportunism and the market for corporate control, *Academy of Management Journal* 46: 74–85; Hitt, Hoskisson, Johnson, & Moesel, The market for corporate control and firm innovation; Walsh & Kosnik, Corporate raiders.

127. R. Sinha, 2004, The role of hostile takeovers in corporate governance, *Applied Financial Economics*, 14: 1291–1305; D. Goldstein, 2000, Hostile takeovers as corporate

governance? Evidence from the 1980s, *Review of Political Economy*, 12: 381–402.

128 De Wied, The age of activism.

129 O. Kini, W. Kracaw, & S. Mian, 2004, The nature of discipline by corporate takeovers, *Journal of Finance*, 59: 1511–1551.

130 Sinha, The role of hostile takeovers.

131 Walsh & Kosnik, Corporate raiders.

132 E. Thorton, F. Keenan, C. Palmeri, & L. Himelstein, 2002, It sure is getting hostile, *Business Week*, January 14, 28–30.

133 J. Weber, 2007, An irresistible urge to merge, *Business Week*, January 1, 72–73.

134 H. Sender, 2007, New predator in takeovers, *Wall Street Journal*, February 26, C1; K. Shimizu, M. A. Hitt, D. Vaidyanath, & P. Vincenzo, 2004, Theoretical foundations of cross-border mergers and acquisitions: A review of current research and recommendations for the future, *Journal of International Management*, 10: 307–353; M. A. Hitt & V. Pisano, 2003, The cross border merger and acquisition strategy, *Management Research*, 1: 133–144.

135 Sender, New predator in takeovers.

136 Sinha, The role of hostile takeovers; J. Anand & A. Delios, 2002, Absolute and relative resources as determinants of international acquisitions, *Strategic Management Journal*, 23: 119–134.

137 S. Chatterjee, J. S. Harrison, & D. D. Bergh, 2003, Failed takeover attempts, corporate governance and refocusing, *Strategic Management Journal*, 24: 87–96; J. Harford, 2003, Takeover bids and target directors' incentives: The impact of a bid on directors' wealth and board seats, *Journal of Financial Economics*, 69: 51–83.

138 J. Nelson, 2005, Corporate governance practices, CEO characteristics, and firm performance, *Journal of Corporate Finance*, 11: 197–228.

139 L. C. Field & J. M. Karpoff, 2002, Takeover defenses of IPO firms, *Journal of Finance*, 57: 1857–1889; Sundaramurthy, Mahoney, & Mahoney, Board structure, antitakeover provisions, and stockholder wealth.

140 W. G. Sanders & M. A. Carpenter, 2003, Strategic satisficing? A behavioral agency theory perspective on stock repurchase program announcements, *Academy of Management Journal*, 46: 160–178; J. Westphal & E. Zajac, 2001, Decoupling policy from practice: The case of stock repurchase programs, *Administrative Science Quarterly*, 46: 202–228.

141 J. A. Byrne, 1999, Poison pills: Let shareholders decide, *Business Week*, May 17, 104.

142 Walsh & Kosnik, Corporate raiders.

143 A. Chakraborty & R. Arnott, 2001, Takeover defenses and dilution: A welfare analysis, *Journal of Financial and Quantitative Analysis*, 36: 311–334.

144 A. Portlono, 2000, The decision to adopt defensive tactics in Italy, *International Review of Law and Economics*, 20: 425–452.

145 C. Sundaramurthy, 2000, Antitakeover provisions and shareholder value implications: A review and a contingency framework, *Journal of Management*, 26: 1005–1030.

146 C. C. J. M. Millar, T. I. Eldomiaty, C. J. Choi, & B. Hilton, 2005, Corporate governance and institutional transparency in emerging markets, *Journal of Business Ethics*, 59: 163–174; B. Kogut, G. Walker, & J. Anand, 2002, Agency and institutions: National divergence in diversification behavior, *Organization Science*, 13: 162–178; D. Norburn, B. K. Boyd, M. Fox, & M. Muth, 2000, International corporate governance reform, *European Business Journal*, 12(3): 116–133; Useem, Corporate leadership in a globalizing equity market.

147 A. Inkpen & K. Ramaswamy, 2006, *Global Strategy: Creating and Sustaining Advantage across Borders*, New York: Oxford University Press; Aguilera & Jackson, The cross-national diversity of corporate governance.

148 S. M. Jacoby, 2004, *The Embedded Corporation: Corporate Governance and Employment Relations in Japan and the United States*, Princeton, NJ: Princeton University Press; T. Yoshikawa & P. H. Phan, 2001, Alternative corporate governance systems in Japanese firms: Implications for a shift to stockholder-centered corporate governance, *Asia Pacific Journal of Management*, 18: 183–205; Y. Yafeh, 2000, Corporate governance in Japan: Past performance and future prospects, *Oxford Review of Economic Policy*, 16(2): 74–84.

149 P. Witt, 2004, The competition of international corporate governance systems: A German perspective, *Management International Review*, 44: 309–333; L. Nanchum, 2003, Does nationality of ownership make any difference and if so, under what circumstances? Professional service MNEs in global competition, *Journal of International Management*, 9: 1–32.

150 Carney, Corporate governance and competitive advantage; S. Klein, 2000, Family businesses in Germany: Significance and structure, *Family Business Review*, 13: 157–181.

151 A. Tuschke & W. G. Sanders, 2003, Antecedents and consequences of corporate governance reform: The case of Germany, *Strategic Management Journal*, 24: 631–649; J. Edwards & M. Nibler, 2000, Corporate governance in Germany: The role of banks and ownership concentration, *Economic Policy*, 31: 237–268; E. R. Gedajlovic & D. M. Shapiro, 1998, Management and ownership effects: Evidence from five countries, *Strategic Management Journal*, 19: 533–553.

152 P. C. Fiss, 2006. Social influence effects and managerial compensation evidence from Germany, *Strategic Management Journal*, 27: 1013–1031.

153 Inkpen & Ramaswamy, *Global Strategy*; S. Douma, 1997, The two-tier system of corporate governance, *Long Range Planning*, 30(4): 612–615.

154 Inkpen & Ramaswamy, *Global Strategy*.

155 M. Karnitschnig, 2005, Too many chiefs at Siemens? German consensus culture may hamper forward-looking CEO, *Wall Street Journal*, January 20, A12.

156 P. C. Fiss & E. J. Zajac, 2004, The diffusion of ideas over contested terrain: The (non) adoption of a shareholder value orientation among German firms, *Administrative Science Quarterly*, 49: 501–534.

157 Tuschke & Sanders, Antecedents and consequences of corporate governance reform.

158 T. Hoshi, A. K. Kashyap, & S. Fischer, 2001, *Corporate Financing and Governance in Japan*, Boston: MIT Press.

159 Charkham, *Keeping Good Company*, 70.

160 Inkpen & Ramaswamy, *Global Strategy*, 188.

161 M. A. Hitt, H. Lee, & E. Yucel, 2002, The importance of social capital to the management of multinational enterprises: Relational networks among Asian and Western Firms, *Asia Pacific Journal of Management*, 19: 353–372.

162 Yoshikawa & Phan, Alternative corporate governance systems in Japanese firms.

163 Inkpen & Ramaswamy, *Global Strategy*; Jacoby, *The Embedded Corporation*; P. M. Lee & H. M. O'Neill, 2003, Ownership structures and R&D investments of U.S. and Japanese firms: Agency and stewardship perspectives, *Academy of Management Journal*, 46: 212–225; R. E. Hoskisson, R. A. Johnson, D. Yiu & W. P. Wan, 2001, Restructuring strategies of diversified business groups: Differences associated with country institutional environments, in M. A. Hitt, R. E. Freeman, & J. S. Harrison, eds. *Blackwell Handbook of Strategic Management*, Oxford, UK: Blackwell Publishers, 433–463.

164 A. Kawaura, 2004, Deregulation and governance: Plight of Japanese banks in the 1990s, *Applied Economics*, 36: 479–484; B. Bremner, 2001, Cleaning up the banks—finally, *Business Week*, December 17, 86; 2000, Business: Japan's corporate-governance u-turn, *Economist*, November 18, 73.

165 B. Bremner, E. Thornton, & I. M. Kunii, 1999, Fall of a keiretsu, *Business Week*, March 15, 87–92.

166 C. L. Ahmadjian & G. E. Robbins, 2005, A clash of capitalisms: Foreign shareholders and corporate restructuring in 1990s Japan, *American Sociological Review*, 70:451–471.

167 Inkpen & Ramaswamy, *Global Strategy*, 188.

168 S. Moffett, 1999, A hostile takeover—in Japan? *Business Week*, http://www.businessweek.com, May 24.

169 T. Kotaro, 2007, RIETI: Research Institute of Economy, Trade and Industry, How to cope with the threat of hostile takeovers: Japanese corporate governance at a crossroads, http://www.rieti.go.jp, February 28.

170 2007, Nearly 200 Japanese firms introduce takeover defense measures, Jiji Press English News Service, February 23, 1.

171 P. M. Lee, 2004, A comparison of ownership structures and innovations of U.S. and Japanese firms, *Managerial and Decision Economics*, 26(1): 39–50; Lee & O'Neill, Ownership structures and R&D investments.

172 Y. Hayashi, 2005, Japan firms ponder private life, *Wall Street Journal*, August 1, C14.

173 M. Wright, M. Kitamura, & R. E. Hoskisson, 2003, Management buyouts and restructuring Japanese corporations, *Long Range Planning*, 36(4): 355–373.

174 J. B. White, 2000, The company we'll keep, *Wall Street Journal* online, http://www.wsj.com, January 17.

175 J.-S. Baek, J.-K. Kang, & K. S. Park, 2004, Corporate governance and firm value: Evidence from the Korean financial crisis, *Journal of Financial Economics*, 71: 265–313; Lee & Yeh, Corporate governance.

176 T. Edwards, 2004, Corporate governance, industrial relations and trends in company-level restructuring in Europe: Convergence towards the Anglo-American model? *Industrial Relations Journal*, 35: 518–535.

177 Inkpen & Ramaswamy, *Global Strategy*.

178 N. Boubarkri, J.-C. Cosset, & O. Guedhami, 2004, Postprivatization corporate governance: The role of ownership structure and investor protection, *Journal of Financial Economics*, 76: 369–399; K. Uhlenbruck, K. E. Meyer, & M. A. Hitt, 2003, Organizational transformation in transition economies: Resource-based and organizational learning perspectives, *Journal of Management Studies*, 40: 257–282; P. Mar & M. Young, 2001, Corporate governance in transition economies: A case study of 2 Chinese airlines, *Journal of World Business*, 36(3): 280–302; M. W. Peng, 2000, *Business Strategies in Transition Economies*, Thousand Oaks, CA: Sage.

179 J. Li, K. Lam, & J. W. Moy, 2005, Ownership reform among state firms in China and its implications, *Management Decision*, 43: 568–588; L. Chang, 1999, Chinese firms find incentive to use stock-compensation plans, *Wall Street Journal*, November 1, A2; T. Clarke & Y. Du, 1998, Corporate governance in China: Explosive growth and new patterns of ownership, *Long Range Planning*, 31(2): 239–251.

180 M. A. Hitt, D. Ahlstrom, M. T. Dacin, E. Levitas, & L. Svobodina, 2004, The institutional effects on strategic alliance partner selection in transition economies: China versus Russia, *Organization Science*, 15: 173–185; I. Filatotchev, M. Wright, K. Uhlenbruck, L. Tihanyi, & R. E. Hoskisson, 2003, Governance, organizational capabilities, and restructuring in transition economies, *Journal of World Business*, 38: 331–347; I. Filatotchev, R. Kapelyushnikov, N. Dyomina, & S. Aukutsionek, 2001, The effects of ownership concentration on investment and performance in privatized firms in Russia, *Managerial and Decision Economics*, 22(6): 299–313; E. Perotti & S. Gelfer, 2001, Red barons or robber barons? Governance and investment in Russian financial-industrial groups, *European Economic Review*, 45(9): 1601–1617; T Buck, I. Filatotchev, & M. Wright, 1998, Agents, stakeholders and corporate governance in Russian firms, *Journal of Management Studies*, 35: 81–104.

181 S. Sharma & I. Henriques, 2005, Stakeholder influences on sustainability practices in the Canadian forest products industry, *Strategic Management Journal*, 26: 159–180; Hillman, Keim, & Luce, Board composition and stakeholder performance; R. Oliver, 2000, The board's role: Driver's seat or rubber stamp? *Journal of Business Strategy*, 21: 7–9.

182 P. A. Argenti, R. A. Howell, & K. A. Beck, 2005, The strategic communication imperative, *MIT Sloan Management Review*, 46(3): 83–89; S. L. Hart & S. Sharma, 2004, Engaging fringe stakeholders for competitive imagination, *Academy of Management Executive*, 18(1): 7–18; P. Nutt, 2004, Expanding the search for alternatives during strategic decision-making, *Academy of Management Executive*, 18(4): 13–28.

183 F. Stinglhamber, D. De Cremer, & L. F. Mercken, 2006, Support as a mediator of the relationship between justice and trust, *Group and Organization Management*, 31: 442–468; K. A. Hegtvedt, 2005, Doing justice to the group: Examining the roles of the group in justice research, *Annual Review of Sociology*, 31: 25–45; C. C. Chen, Y.-R. Chen, & K. Xin, 2004, Guanxi practices and trust in management: A procedural justice perspective, *Organization Science*, 15: 200–209.

184 V. P. Rindova, I. O. Williamson, A. P. Petkova & J. M. Sever, 2005, Being good or being known: An empirical examination of the dimensions, antecedents, and consequences of organizational reputation, *Academy of Management Journal*, 48: 1033–1049; C. J. Fombrun, 2001, Corporate reputations as economic assets, in M. A. Hitt, R. E. Freeman, & J. S. Harrison, *Handbook of Strategic Management*, Oxford, UK: Blackwell Publishers, 289–312; B. R. Barringer & J. S. Harrison, 2000, Walking a tightrope: Creating value through interorganizational relationships, *Journal of Management*, 26: 367–403.

185 N. A. Gardberg, 2006, Corporate citizenship: Creating intangible assets across institutional environments, *Academy of Management Review*, 31: 329–346; J. S. Harrison & C. H. St. John, 1996, Managing and partnering with external stakeholders, *Academy of Management Executive*, 10(2): 46–60; B. Cornell &

A. C. Shapiro, 1987, Corporate stakeholders and corporate finance, *Financial Management*, 16: 5–14.

[186] A Kaufman & E. Englander, 2005, A team production model of corporate governance, *Academy of Management Executive*, 19(3): 9–22.

[187] N. Demise, 2005, Business ethics and corporate governance in Japan, *Business and Society*, 44: 211–217.

[188] J. R. Deckop, K. K. Merriman, & S. Gupta, 2006, The effects of CEO pay structure on corporate social performance, *Journal of Management*, 32: 329–342.

[189] Caldwell & Karri, Organizational governance and ethical systems; A. Felo, 2001, Ethics programs, board involvement, and potential conflicts of interest in corporate governance, *Journal of Business Ethics*, 32: 205–218.

[190] J. P. O'Connor Jr., R. L. Priem, J. E. Coombs, & K. M. Guilley, 2006, Do stock options prevent or promote fraudulent financial reporting? *Academy of Management Journal*, 49: 483–500.

[191] H. Kim & R. E. Hoskisson, 1996, Japanese governance systems: A critical review, in S. B. Prasad (ed.), *Advances in International Comparative Management*, Greenwich, CT: JAI, 165–189.

# CHAPTER 12

# Strategic Entrepreneurship

## KNOWLEDGE OBJECTIVES

*Studying this chapter should provide you with the strategic management knowledge needed to:*

1. Define and explain strategic entrepreneurship.
2. Explain the importance of entrepreneurial opportunities, innovation, and capabilities.
3. Discuss the importance of international entrepreneurship and describe why it is increasing.
4. Describe incremental and radical innovations and the firm characteristics and actions that foster them.
5. Discuss how cooperative strategies such as strategic alliances are used to develop innovation.
6. Explain how firms use acquisitions to increase their innovations and enrich their innovative capabilities.
7. Explain how the practice of strategic entrepreneurship creates value for customers and shareholders of all types of firms, large and small, new and established.

All firms exist in a highly complex and dynamic competitive environment. Such an environment produces considerable uncertainty, and important pressures often constrain the ability of firms to adapt to the environment. One of those pressures is a natural human tendency for inertia and resistance to change.[1] In addition, the emphasis on corporate governance and control explored in Chapter 11 increases the pressure for conformity and reduces the flexibility of executives to respond to changes in the environment. In the 21st-century competitive landscape, firm survival and success increasingly are a function of the firm's ability to continuously find new opportunities and quickly produce innovations to pursue them.[2] Consequently, top executives must ensure that innovation is appropriately emphasized in their firms to offset forces that would otherwise hurt the firm's flexibility.

This chapter explores how strategic entrepreneurship is important to firms so that they remain flexible in order to buffer against or respond to a dynamic competitive environment.[3] **Strategic entrepreneurship** occurs as firms seek opportunities in the external environment that they can exploit through innovations.[4] In the global competitive landscape, the long-term success of new ventures and established firms is a function of their ability to meld entrepreneurship with strategic management.[5] Innovative activity is essential to firms' efforts to differentiate their goods or services from competitors and create additional or new value for customers, which are critical to achieving competitive advantage.[6]

To describe how firms produce and manage innovation, we examine several topics in this chapter. To set the stage, we examine entrepreneurship and innovation in a strategic context. We then describe international entrepreneurship, a phenomenon reflecting the increased use of entrepreneurship in countries throughout the world. Next we examine the primary means firms use to innovate. Internally, they innovate through either autonomous or induced strategic behavior; however, they may also innovate through cooperative strategies or by acquiring firms to take advantage of their innovations and innovative capabilities. The focus of this chapter is on **corporate entrepreneurship,** which is the use or application of entrepreneurship within an established firm.[7]

## Strategic Entrepreneurship and Innovation

Joseph Schumpeter viewed entrepreneurship as a process of "creative destruction," through which existing products or methods of production are destroyed and replaced with new ones.[8] Thus, **entrepreneurship** is the process by which individuals or groups identify and pursue entrepreneurial opportunities without the immediate constraint of the resources they currently control.[9] Entrepreneurial activity is an important mechanism for creating changes and for helping firms adapt to changes created by others.[10] Firms that encourage entrepreneurship are risk takers, are committed to innovation, and are proactive—that is, they try to create opportunities rather than waiting to respond to opportunities that others create, identify, and/or exploit.[11]

**Entrepreneurial opportunities** represent conditions in which new products or services can satisfy a need in the market. These opportunities exist because of competitive imperfections in markets and among factors of production used to produce them,[12] and when information about these imperfections is distributed unevenly among individuals.[13] In other words, some people know about an opportunity to create value through satisfying an unmet need or by combining resources in a new way while others are unaware of the opportunity. For example, a firm may discover an opportunity to design and sell a new product, sell an existing product in a new market, or create a product with a more efficient technology.[14]

Recently, Amazon.com announced an entrepreneurial venture that provides significant diversification away from its retail core. As a *Business Week* reporter wrote: CEO Jeffrey Bezos "wants Amazon to run your business, or at least the messy technical and logistical parts of it, using those same technologies and operations that power his $10 billion online store. In the process, Bezos aims to transform Amazon into a kind of 21st century digital utility. It's as if Wal-Mart Stores Inc. had decided to turn itself inside out, offering its industry-supply chain and logistics systems to any and all outsiders, even retailers."[15] There is definitely an entrepreneurial spirit at Amazon.com. In a venture called "Elastic Compute Cloud," the company is selling part of its raw computing power. Amazon also rents space in its 10 million square feet of warehouses worldwide.

In this book, we examine the entrepreneurship of the individual firm; however, evidence suggests that entrepreneurship is the economic engine driving the economies of many nations in the global competitive landscape.[16] Entrepreneurship promotes economic growth, increases productivity, and creates jobs.[17] Thus, entrepreneurship, and the innovation it spawns, is important for companies competing in the global economy and for countries seeking to stimulate economic climates with the potential to enhance the living standards of their citizens.[18]

### Innovation

Author Peter Drucker defined *innovation* as "the means by which the entrepreneur either creates new wealth-producing resources or endows existing resources with enhanced potential for creating wealth." He then argued that "innovation is the specific function of entrepreneurship, whether in an existing business, a public service institution, or a new venture started by a lone individual."[19] Thus, innovation and entrepreneurship are vital for young and old, large and small, and service and manufacturing firms, as well as for high-technology ventures.[20]

Innovation is a key outcome that firms seek through entrepreneurial activity and is often the source of competitive success, especially in turbulent, highly competitive environments.[21] For example, research shows that firms competing in global industries investing more in innovation also achieve the highest returns.[22] In fact, investors often react positively to the introduction of a new product, thereby increasing the price of a firm's stock. Innovation, then, is an essential characteristic of high-performance firms.[23] Furthermore, "innovation may be required to maintain or achieve competitive parity, much less a competitive advantage in many global markets."[24] The most innovative firms understand that financial slack should be available at all times to support the pursuit of entrepreneurial opportunities.[25]

In his classic work, Schumpeter argued that firms engage in three types of innovative activity: invention, innovation, and imitation.[26] **Invention** is the act of creating or developing a new product or process. **Innovation** is the process of creating a commercial product from an invention. Innovation begins after an invention is chosen for development.[27] Thus, an invention brings something new into *being*, and an innovation brings something new into *use*. Accordingly, technical criteria are used to determine the success of an invention, and commercial criteria are used to determine the success of an innovation.[28] Entrepreneurship is critical to innovative activity because it turns inventions into innovations.[29] Finally, **imitation** is the adoption of an innovation by similar firms. Imitation usually leads to product or process standardization, and products based on imitation often are offered at lower prices, but without as many features.

In the United States, innovation is the most critical of these three types of innovative activity. Many companies are able to create ideas that lead to inventions, but commercializing those inventions has at times proved difficult. This difficulty is suggested by the fact that approximately 80 percent of R&D occurs in large firms, but these same firms produce fewer than 50 percent of patents.[30] Patents are a strategic asset, and the ability to regularly produce them can be an important source of competitive advantage, especially for firms competing in knowledge-intensive industries, such as pharmaceuticals.[31]

The process of creating an innovative product or service is entrepreneurial, but individual products or services are unlikely to lead to sustainable competitive advantage because they can be imitated. Remember from Chapter 4 that resources that lead to sustainable competitive advantage must be valuable, rare, difficult to imitate, and nonsubstitutable.[32] If a resource does not possess these characteristics, success will be only temporary.[33] However, the ability to continuously create new innovations can be a source of sustainable competitive advantage. This ability is embedded in the entrepreneurial nature of the people in the organization as well as in the systems and processes the firm uses to foster entrepreneurship.

## Entrepreneurs

**Entrepreneurs** are individuals, acting independently or as part of an organization, who create a new venture or develop an innovation and take risks by introducing them into the marketplace.[34] Entrepreneurs are found throughout an organization—from top-level managers to those producing the company's goods or services. For instance, entrepreneurs are found throughout W. L. Gore & Associates, where associates are encouraged to use approximately 10 percent of their time to develop innovations.[35] Entrepreneurs tend to demonstrate several characteristics, including optimism, high motivation, willingness to take responsibility for projects, and courage.[36] They also tend to be passionate and emotional about the value and importance of their innovation-based ideas.[37]

Evidence suggests that successful entrepreneurs have an **entrepreneurial mind-set,** which values uncertainty in the marketplace and seeks to continuously identify opportunities with the potential to lead to important innovations.[38] A firm that has many individuals with an entrepreneurial mind-set can enjoy a competitive advantage because of the potential for continuous innovation.[39] Firms need employees who think entrepreneurially.[40] Consequently, top-level managers should try to establish an entrepreneurial culture that inspires individuals and groups to engage in corporate entrepreneurship.[41] Importantly, entrepreneurs or entrepreneurial managers must be able to identify opportunities others don't perceive. Steve Jobs, CEO of Apple Computer, is committed to fostering innovation in the company, believing that one of his key responsibilities is to help Apple become more entrepreneurial. Apple has introduced products with innovative designs, such as its recent iPhone, which combines the technology of a cellular phone, a widescreen iPod, and an Internet communications device.[42]

Having people with intellectual talent is only part of the firm's challenge to be entrepreneurial. The talent must be well-managed so that its potential can be realized.[43] Because "innovation is an application of knowledge to produce new knowledge,"[44] effective management of knowledge within the firm is critical to strategic entrepreneurship. For instance, research has shown that business units within existing firms are more innovative when they have access to new knowledge.[45] Transferring knowledge, however, can be difficult because the person receiving it must have the capacity to understand it.[46] The ability to understand new knowledge is increased if it is linked to existing knowledge. Thus, managers need to help members of the firm develop a strong knowledge base in addition to expanding that knowledge base in order to foster entrepreneurship.[47] Information systems, training programs, and cross-functional teams (described later in this chapter) can help facilitate these objectives.

## International Entrepreneurship

**International entrepreneurship** is a process in which firms creatively discover and exploit opportunities that are outside their domestic markets in order to develop a competitive advantage.[48] Entrepreneurship is a global phenomenon.[49] One reason it is so popular is that, in general, internationalization leads to improved firm performance.[50] Nevertheless, decision makers should consider some of the risks associated with internationalization that are particularly relevant to entrepreneurship, such as unstable foreign currencies, inefficient markets, insufficient infrastructures to support businesses, and limitations on market size and growth.[51] Thus, the decision to engage in international entrepreneurship should be a product of careful analysis.[52]

Because of its positive benefits, entrepreneurship is at the top of public policy agendas in many of the world's countries, including Finland, Germany, Israel, and Ireland. Some argue that placing entrepreneurship on these agendas may be appropriate in that regulation hindering innovation and entrepreneurship is the root cause of Europe's productivity problems.[53] To support entrepreneurship, the Irish government established the Irish Development Authority (IDA), a state agency charged with attracting and growing foreign multinational businesses in Ireland. A second state agency called Enterprise Ireland is focused on "transforming Irish industry." In 2006, Enterprise Ireland established a venture with IBM to create a Dublin-based European Venture Capital Centre. From IBM's perspective, "Ireland offers a well established ecosystem which sees strong collaboration between the venture capital community, entrepreneurs, academia and government."[54] According to Claudia Fan Munce, managing director of the IBM Venture Capital Group, "This strategic relationship will strengthen the innovative culture and capability of Irish firms and further embed IBM's operations in Ireland."[55]

Some believe that "entrepreneurship is flourishing in New Zealand, a trend having a positive effect on the productivity of the nation's economy."[56] International entrepreneurship has also been an important factor in the economic development of Asia. China is now second only to the United States in total annual R&D investments.[57] Also, private companies owned by Chinese families outside of China compose the fourth largest economic power in the world. Significant learning from their international ventures occurs in these businesses, and this learning enhances their success with future ventures.[58] Learning contributes to a firm's knowledge of operating in international markets.[59]

Entrepreneurship is a global phenomenon, but there are differences in the rate of entrepreneurship across countries. A study of 29 countries found that the percentage of adults involved in entrepreneurial activity ranged from a high of more than 20 percent in Mexico to a low of approximately 5 percent in Belgium. The United States had a rate of about 13 percent. This study also found a strong positive relationship between the rate of entrepreneurial activity and economic development in a country.[60]

National culture contributes to the differences in rates of entrepreneurship across countries. For example, the tension between individualism and collectivism can affect entrepreneurship. Research has shown that entrepreneurship declines as collectivism is emphasized. However, research also suggests that exceptionally high levels of individualism can be dysfunctional for entrepreneurship—people might not combine the ideas of others with their own to create unique goods or services. These results appear to call for a balance between individual initiative and a spirit of cooperation and group ownership of innovation. For firms to be entrepreneurial, they must provide appropriate autonomy and incentives for individual initiative to surface, but they also must promote cooperation and group ownership of an innovation if it is to be implemented successfully. Thus, entrepreneurship often requires teams of people with unique skills and resources, especially in cultures where collectivism is a valued historical norm.[61]

Another important dimension of international entrepreneurship is the level of investment outside of the home country made by new ventures. In fact, with increasing globalization, a greater number of new ventures have been "born global."[62] It has been noted that "talent and ideas are flourishing everywhere—from Bangalore to Shanghai to Kiev—and no company, regardless of geography, can hesitate to go wherever those ideas are."[63] Research has shown that new ventures that enter international markets learn more new technological knowledge and thereby enhance their performance.[64] Because of these outcomes, the amount of international entrepreneurship has been increasing in recent years.[65]

The probability of entering international markets increases when the firm has top executives with international experience.[66] Furthermore, the firm has a higher likelihood of successfully competing in international markets when its top executives have such experience.[67] Because of the learning and economies of scale and scope afforded by operating in international markets, both young and established internationally diversified firms often are stronger competitors in their domestic markets as well. Additionally, research has shown that internationally diversified firms generally are more innovative.[68]

We now focus on the methods firms use to innovate, including internal innovation, cooperative ventures, and purchase of innovation through acquisitions. The method firms use to innovate can be influenced by their governance mechanisms. For example, research has shown that inside board members with equity positions favor internal innovation while outside directors with equity positions prefer acquisitions.[69]

---

## Internal Innovation

In established organizations, most corporate innovation is developed through R&D. Larger, established firms use R&D to create the new technology and products that make the old technologies and products obsolete.[70] Thus, some believe that the most competitively successful firms reinvent their industry or develop a completely new one across time as they engage in competition with current and future rivals.[71] In this sense, strategic entrepreneurship is about producing the innovation that creates tomorrow's businesses.[72] *Internal corporate venturing* is the set of activities firms use to develop internal inventions and innovations.[73]

3M has an impressive record of successful internal innovations. The company developed the first cellulose tape, Scotch Tape, in 1930, and it is still popular today. Since that time, some of the company's most famous innovations have included Post-It Notes, Scotchgard fabric protector, and Filtrete air-cleaning filters. 3M's attitude about entrepreneurship is reflected in the company's statement: "Our inspiration comes from listening to customers and creating new products and solutions for the challenges and opportunities you face."[74]

### Incremental Innovations

Firms produce two types of internal innovations—incremental and radical—when using their R&D activities. Most innovations are *incremental*—that is, they build on existing knowledge bases and provide small improvements in well-defined current product lines.[75] Incremental innovations are evolutionary and linear in nature, with the underlying production technologies emphasizing efficiency. Consequently, profit margins tend to be lower and competition is often based primarily on price.[76] Adding a different kind of whitening agent to a soap detergent is an example of an incremental innovation, as are improvements in televisions over the past few decades (black-and-white to color to stereo to digital to flat-screen).

The process through which incremental innovations typically are produced might be called induced strategic behavior. *Induced strategic behavior* is a top-down process whereby the firm's current strategy and structure foster product innovations that are closely associated with that strategy and structure. In this form of venturing, the strategy in place is filtered through the firm's existing structural hierarchy. In essence, induced strategic behavior results in internal innovations that do not alter the firm's current strategy. Often, firms that are market pioneers continue their innovation by using an induced approach, providing only incremental innovations to their existing products.[77]

### Radical Innovations

In contrast to incremental innovations, *radical innovations* usually provide significant technological breakthroughs and create new knowledge.[78] These types of innovations have become increasingly important to achieve and sustain a competitive advantage in many industries.[79] The microprocessing chip, the handheld calculator, the personal computer, and the cellular phone are examples of radical innovations. Although both incremental and radical innovations have the potential to lead to growth in revenues and profits, the potential is greater with radical innovations because they establish new functionalities for users.[80]

Despite potential returns, radical innovations are rare because of the difficulty and risk involved in developing them.[81] The value of the technology and the market opportunities are highly uncertain.[82] Because radical innovation creates new knowledge and uses only some or little of a firm's current product or technological knowledge, creativity is required. However, creativity does not create something from nothing. Rather, it discovers, combines, or synthesizes current knowledge, often from diverse areas.[83] This knowledge is then integrated into the development of new products or services that a firm can use in an entrepreneurial manner to move into new markets, capture new customers, or gain access to new resources.[84] Such innovations are often developed in separate units that start internal ventures.[85]

*Autonomous strategic behavior* is a bottom-up process in which product champions pursue new ideas, often through a political process, to develop and coordinate the commercialization of a new good or service. A *product champion* is an individual with an entrepreneurial vision of a new good or service who seeks to create support in the organization for its commercialization.[86] Product champions play critical roles in moving innovations forward.[87] In many corporations, "champions are widely acknowledged as pivotal to innovation speed and success."[88] Commonly, product champions use their social capital to develop informal networks within the firm. As progress is made, these networks become more formalized as a means of pushing an innovation to the point of successful commercialization.[89] Internal innovations springing from autonomous strategic behavior tend to diverge from the firm's current strategy, taking it into new markets and perhaps new ways of creating value for customers and other stakeholders.

Autonomous strategic behavior is based on a firm's wellsprings of knowledge and resources that are the sources of the firm's innovation. Thus, a firm's technological capabilities and competencies are the basis for new products and processes.[90] General Electric regularly depends on autonomous strategic behavior to produce innovations.[91] Essentially, "the search for marketable services can start in any of GE's myriad businesses. [For example], an operating unit seeks out appropriate technology to better do what it already does. Having mastered the technology, it then incorporates it into a service it can sell to others."[92]

To be effective, an autonomous process for developing new products requires that new knowledge be continuously diffused throughout the firm. In particular, the diffusion of tacit knowledge (which is difficult to convey in writing) is important for developing more effective new products.[93] Interestingly, some of the processes important for the promotion of behaviors conducive to autonomous new product development vary by the environment and country in which a firm operates. For example, the Japanese culture is high on uncertainty avoidance; thus, research has found that Japanese firms are more likely to engage in autonomous behaviors under conditions of low uncertainty.[94]

Internally developed innovations result from deliberate efforts. A larger number of radical innovations spring from autonomous strategic behavior, while the greatest percentage of incremental innovations come from induced strategic behavior. Most successful firms develop both radical and incremental innovations over time. Although critical to long-term competitiveness, the outcomes of investments in innovative activities are uncertain and often not achieved in the short term,[95] meaning that patience is required as firms evaluate the outcomes of their R&D efforts.

## Implementing Internal Innovation

As mentioned previously, an entrepreneurial mind-set is necessary for developing successful internal innovation. This mind-set embraces uncertainty and opportunities that come from changes in the environment. Those with an entrepreneurial mind-set are able to help firms create new products and new markets. However, they also emphasize execution as they "engage the energies of everyone in their domain," both inside and outside the organization.[96] Table 12.1 shows some of the factors that encourage and discourage innovation in established firms.

Established firms that are successful at innovation encourage people to discuss new ideas and take risks.[97] They not only tolerate failures, but encourage organizational members to learn from them. Rewards systems that encourage innovation—such as pay raises, promotions, awards, perquisites, and public and private recognition—are also important.[98] The people who are the lifeblood of innovation in organizations should be rewarded adequately so that they do not feel compelled to leave the organization in order to receive the rewards they deserve.

As important as the rewards for entrepreneurial behavior being high, the downside penalties for failure should be minimal. According to William McKnight, the former CEO of 3M who is credited with being the catalyst for the company's unique entrepreneurial culture: "Mistakes will be made. But if a person is essentially right, the mistakes he or she makes are not as serious in the long run as the mistakes management will make if it undertakes to tell those in authority exactly how they must do their jobs. Management that is destructively critical when mistakes are made kills initiative. And, it's essential that we have many people with initiative if we are to continue to grow."[99]

Having processes and structures in place through which a firm can successfully implement the outcomes of internal corporate ventures and commercialize innovations is critical. The successful introduction of innovations into the marketplace reflects implementation effectiveness.[100] In the context of internal corporate ventures, processes are the "patterns of interaction, coordination, communication, and decision making employees use" to convert the innovations resulting from either autonomous or induced strategic behaviors into successful market entries.[101]

Effective integration of the various functions involved in innovation processes—from engineering to manufacturing and, ultimately, market distribution—is required to make

## Table 12.1: Factors Encouraging and Discouraging Innovation in Established Firms

| Factors Encouraging Innovation | Factors Discouraging Innovation |
|---|---|
| • Vision and culture that support innovation, personal growth, and risk taking | • Rigid bureaucracy and conservative decision making |
| • Top management support and organizational champions | • Absence of management support or champions |
| • Teamwork and collaboration: a flat management hierarchy | • Authoritarian leadership and traditional hierarchy |
| • Decentralized approval process | • Difficult approval process |
| • Valuing the ideas of every employee | • Attention given to the ideas of only certain people (researchers or managers) |
| • Excellent communications | • Closed-door offices |
| • Innovation grants and time off to pursue projects | • Inadequate resources devoted to entrepreneurial activities |
| • Large rewards for successful entrepreneurs | • Harsh penalties for failure |
| • Focus on learning | • Exclusive emphasis on measurable outcomes |

SOURCE: J. S. Harrison, 2003, *Strategic Management of Resources and Relationships,* New York: John Wiley & Sons, 198.

effective use of the innovations that result from internal corporate ventures.[102] Increasingly, product development teams are being used to integrate the activities associated with different organizational functions. Product development teams are commonly used to produce cross-functional integration. Such coordination involves coordinating and applying the knowledge and skills of different functional areas in order to maximize innovation.[103] Effective product development teams can also help a firm dismantle projects once they are determined to be unsuccessful.[104]

## Cross-Functional Product Development Teams

Cross-functional teams facilitate efforts to integrate activities associated with different organizational functions, such as design, manufacturing, and marketing.[105] In addition, new product development processes can be completed more quickly and the products more easily commercialized when cross-functional teams work effectively.[106] Using cross-functional teams, product development stages are grouped into parallel or overlapping processes to allow the firm to tailor its product development efforts to its unique core competencies and to the needs of the market.

Horizontal organizational structures support the use of cross-functional teams in their efforts to integrate innovation-based activities across organizational functions.[107] Therefore, instead of being built around vertical hierarchical functions or departments, the organization is built around core horizontal processes that are used to produce and manage innovations. Some of the core horizontal processes that are critical to innovation efforts are formal; they may be defined and documented as procedures and practices. More commonly, however, these processes are informal: "They are routines or ways of working that evolve over time."[108] Often invisible, informal processes are critical to successful product innovations and are supported properly through horizontal organizational structures more so than through vertical organizational structures.

One of the primary barriers that may prevent the successful use of cross-functional teams as a means of integrating organizational functions is the independent frames of reference of team members.[109] Team members working within a distinct specialization (i.e., a particular organizational function) may have an independent frame of reference typically based on common backgrounds and experiences within that specialization. They are likely to use the same decision criteria to evaluate issues such as product development efforts as they use within their functional units. Research suggests that functional departments vary along four dimensions: time orientation, interpersonal orientation, goal orientation, and formality of structure.[110] Thus, individuals from separate functional departments who have different orientations on these dimensions can be expected to emphasize unique priorities in product development activities. For example, a design engineer may consider the characteristics that make a product functional and workable to be the most important of the product's characteristics. Alternatively, a person from the marketing function may hold characteristics that satisfy customer needs most important. These different orientations can create barriers to effective communication across functions.[111]

Organizational politics is a second potential barrier to effective integration in cross-functional teams.[112] In some organizations, considerable political activity may center on allocating resources to different functions. Interunit conflict may result from aggressive competition for resources among those representing different organizational functions. This dysfunctional conflict between functions creates a barrier to their integration.[113] Methods must be found to achieve cross-functional integration without excessive political conflict and without changing the basic structural characteristics necessary for task specialization and efficiency.

## Facilitating Integration and Implementation

Shared values and effective leadership are important to achieve cross-functional integration and to effectively implement innovation.[114] Highly effective shared values are framed around the firm's strategic intent and mission and become the glue that promotes integration between functional units. Thus, the firm's culture promotes unity and internal innovation.[115]

W. L. Gore & Associates is a highly innovative company. It uses fluoropolymer technology and manufacturing to produce a wide variety of fabrics, medical implants, industrial sealants, filters, and signal transmission and consumer products. Supporting innovation is a unique culture within the organization:

> How we work sets us apart. We encourage hands on innovation, involving those closest to a project in decision making. Teams organize around opportunities and leaders emerge. Our founder, Bill Gore created a flat lattice organization. There are no chains of command nor pre-determined channels of communication. Instead, we communicate directly with each other and are accountable to fellow members of our multi-disciplined teams. How does all this happen? Associates (not employees) are hired for general work areas. With the guidance of their sponsors (not bosses) and a growing understanding of opportunities and team objectives, associates commit to projects that match their skills. All of this takes place in an environment that combines freedom with cooperation and autonomy with synergy.[116]

As demonstrated by the example of Bill Gore, strategic leadership is also highly important for achieving cross-functional integration and promoting innovation. Leaders set the goals and allocate resources.[117] The goals include integrated development and commercialization of new goods and services. Effective strategic leaders remind organizational members continuously of the value of product innovations. In the most desirable situations, this value-creating potential becomes the basis for the integration and management of functional department activities. Effective strategic leaders also ensure a high-quality communication system to facilitate cross-functional integration. A critical benefit of effective communication is the sharing of knowledge among team members.[118] Effective communication thus helps create synergy and gains team members' commitment to an innovation throughout the organization. Shared values and leadership practices shape the communication systems that are formed to support the development and commercialization of new products.[119]

## Creating Value from Internal Innovation

Figure 12.1 shows how the firm can create value from the internal processes it uses to develop and commercialize new goods and services. An *entrepreneurial mind-set* is necessary so that managers and employees consistently try to identify entrepreneurial opportunities that the firm can pursue by developing new goods and services and new markets. *Cross-functional product development teams* are important to promote integrated new product design ideas and commitment to their implementation thereafter. *Effective leadership* and *shared values* promote integration and vision for innovation and commitment to it. The end result for the firm is the *creation of value* for the customers and shareholders through development and commercialization of new products.[120]

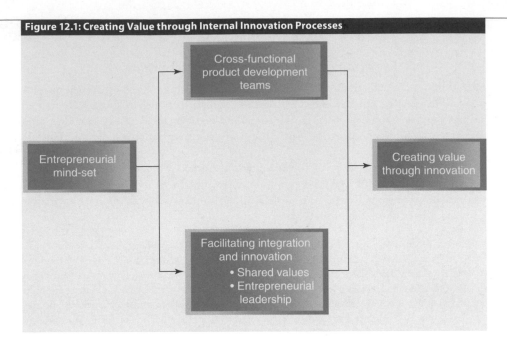

**Figure 12.1: Creating Value through Internal Innovation Processes**

We now turn to the other ways firms innovate—by using cooperative strategies and by acquiring companies.

## Innovation through Cooperative Strategies

Most firms lack the breadth and depth of internal resources and knowledge to produce the level of continuous innovation necessary to sustain competitive advantage in dynamic competitive markets.[121] With increasing frequency, alliances are used to acquire the resources needed to produce or manage innovations.[122] To innovate through a cooperative relationship, firms share their knowledge, skills, and other resources.[123]

For example, Intel and Micron Technology integrated their resources in a joint venture to manufacture NAND flash memory chips. The newly formed company, called IM Flash, is owned 51 percent by Micron and 49 percent by Intel. By combining their manufacturing technologies and expertise, the two companies were quickly able to produce the chips through manufacturing facilities in Idaho, Virginia, and Utah. In fact, the first products came out in less than a year! In 2006 IM Flash announced it would start manufacturing NAND flash memories in Singapore. Brian Harrison, general manager of Intel's flash memory group, says that given the progress the company has made in such a short time, it fully expects "to become one of the top manufacturers of NAND flash memory."[124]

Both entrepreneurial ventures and established firms use cooperative strategies, such as strategic alliances or joint ventures, to innovate. An entrepreneurial venture, for example, may seek investment capital along with an established firm's distribution capabilities to successfully introduce one of its products to the market.[125] Alternatively, more established companies may need new technological knowledge and can gain access to it through alliances with newer entrepreneurial firms.[126] Alliances between large pharmaceutical firms and biotechnology companies have become increasingly common to integrate the knowledge and resources of both to develop new products and bring them to market.[127]

Some companies specialize in matching large companies with small research companies and inventors and integrating their outputs. For example, UTEK is a "technology matchmaker" that gives small researchers an outlet for their ideas and larger companies a way to outsource innovation "by providing access to a database of more than 35,000 discoveries that would otherwise go unnoticed." As CEO Clifford M. Gross suggested: "To have a robust product pipeline, you have to spend an inordinate amount of capital. There are very few companies that can do that."[128]

Because of the importance of alliances, particularly in the development of new technology and in commercializing innovations, firms are beginning to build networks of alliances that represent a form of social capital to them.[129] This social capital in the form of relationships with other firms helps them to obtain the knowledge and other resources they need to develop innovations.[130] Knowledge from these alliances helps firms develop new capabilities.[131] Some firms now even allow external firms to participate in their internal new product development processes. It is not uncommon for firms to have supplier representatives on their cross-functional innovation teams because of the importance of the suppliers' input to ensure quality materials for any new product developed.[132]

However, alliances formed for the purpose of innovation are not without risks. In addition to the conflict that is natural when firms try to work together to reach a mutual goal,[133] participants in a cooperative activity also take a risk that a partner will appropriate the firm's technology or knowledge and use it to enhance its own competitive abilities.[134] To prevent or at least to minimize this risk, firms, particularly new ventures, need to select their partners carefully. The ideal partnership is one in which the firms have complementary skills and compatible strategic goals.[135] However, because companies are operating in a network of firms and thus may be participating in multiple alliances simultaneously, they encounter challenges in managing the alliances.[136] Research has shown that firms can become involved in too many alliances, which can harm rather than help their innovation capabilities.[137] Thus, effectively managing the cooperative relationships to produce innovation is critical.

## Innovation through Acquisitions

Firms sometimes acquire companies to gain access to their innovations and innovative capabilities. One reason for this is that the capital market values growth. Acquisitions provide a means to rapidly extend one or more product lines and increase the firm's revenues. Acquisitions pursued for this reason should, nonetheless, have a strategic rationale. When the Internet-service provider Cognos acquired Celequest, another Internet company, Rob Rose, chief strategy officer at Cognos, commented on how "complementary" the acquisition was for Cognos: "Celequest's innovation in self service dashboard creation and real-time information monitoring extends our vision for operational BI [business intelligence] and enhances our market-leading performance management solutions. Celequest's operational dashboards are immediately interoperable with Cognos 8 BI, delivering a more complete view of enterprise information for better overall performance management."[138]

Similar to internal corporate venturing and strategic alliances, acquisitions are not a risk-free approach to innovating. A key risk is that a firm may substitute an ability to buy innovations for an ability to produce innovations internally. Research shows that firms engaging in acquisitions may introduce fewer new products into the market.[139] This substitution may occur because firms lose strategic control and focus instead on financial control of their original and especially of their acquired business units.

We note in Chapter 9 that firms can also gain new capabilities to produce innovation from firms they acquire. For example, when Logitech announced it was acquiring Slim Devices, Guerrino De Luca, Logitech's CEO, noted that that Slim Devices brought to Logitech "expertise in both network-based music delivery and high-quality audio, and a committed community of developers."[140] Firms that emphasize innovation and carefully select companies for acquisition that also emphasize innovation are likely to remain innovative.[141]

## Creating Value through Strategic Entrepreneurship

Newer entrepreneurial firms often are more effective than larger firms in identifying opportunities.[142] As a consequence, it seems that entrepreneurial ventures produce more radical innovations than do their larger, more established counterparts. The strategic flexibility and willingness of such ventures to take risks may account for their ability to spot opportunities and then develop radical innovations to pursue them.

Alternatively, larger and well-established firms often have more resources and capabilities to exploit identified opportunities.[143] Younger, entrepreneurial firms are generally opportunity seeking, while more established firms are advantage seeking. Both orientations are essential to sustaining competitive advantage in the 21st-century competitive landscape.[144] Thus, newer entrepreneurial firms must learn how to gain a competitive advantage, and older, more established firms must relearn how to identify entrepreneurial opportunities.[145] The concept of strategic entrepreneurship suggests that firms can be simultaneously entrepreneurial and strategic regardless of their size and age.

As emphasized throughout this chapter, to be entrepreneurial, firms must develop an entrepreneurial mind-set among their managers and employees. Managers must emphasize the development of their resources, particularly human and social capital.[146] The importance of knowledge to identify and exploit opportunities as well as to gain and sustain a competitive advantage suggests that firms must have strong human capital.[147] Social capital is critical for access to complementary resources from partners in order to compete effectively in domestic and international markets.[148] Firms that seek knowledge from a broad group of external stakeholders can use that knowledge to sustain innovation.[149]

Many entrepreneurial opportunities continue to surface in international markets, a reality that is contributing to firms' willingness to engage in international entrepreneurship. By entering global markets that are new to them, firms can learn new technologies and management practices and diffuse this knowledge throughout the entire firm. Furthermore, the knowledge that firms gain can contribute to their innovations. As noted earlier in this chapter, firms operating in international markets tend to be more innovative.[150] Entrepreneurial ventures and large firms are now regularly moving into international markets. Both types of firms must also be innovative to compete effectively. Thus, by developing resources (human and social capital), taking advantage of opportunities in domestic and international markets, and using the resources and knowledge gained in these markets to be innovative, firms achieve competitive advantages.[151] In so doing, they create value for their customers and shareholders.

Firms that practice strategic entrepreneurship contribute to a country's economic development. In fact, some countries, such as Ireland, discussed at the beginning of the chapter, have made dramatic economic progress by changing the institutional rules for businesses operating in the country and by establishing government agencies to facilitate both domestic and international entrepreneurship.[152] This could be construed as a form of institutional entrepreneurship.[153] Likewise, firms that seek to establish their technology as a standard, also representing institutional entrepreneurship, are engaging in strategic entrepreneurship because creating a standard produces a sustainable competitive advantage for the firm.[154]

Research shows that because of its economic importance and individual motives, entrepreneurial activity is increasing across the globe. In particular, more women are becoming entrepreneurs because of the economic opportunity entrepreneurship provides and the individual independence it affords.[155] In the United States, for example, women are the nation's fastest-growing group of entrepreneurs.[156] In the future, entrepreneurial activity may increase the wealth of less-affluent countries and continue to contribute to the economic development of more-affluent countries. Regardless, the companies that practice strategic entrepreneurship are likely to be the winners in the 21st century.[157]

# Summary

- Strategic entrepreneurship means taking entrepreneurial actions using a strategic perspective. More specifically, it involves seeking entrepreneurial opportunities and competitive advantage simultaneously to design and implement entrepreneurial strategies to create wealth.

- The concepts of entrepreneurial opportunity, innovation, and capabilities are important to firms. Entrepreneurial opportunities represent conditions in which new products or services can satisfy a need in the market. The essence of entrepreneurship is to identify and exploit these opportunities. Innovation is the process of commercializing the products or processes developed through invention. Entrepreneurial capabilities include building an entrepreneurial culture, having a passion for the business, and taking measured risk.

- Entrepreneurship is being practiced in many countries and is strongly related to a nation's economic growth. This relationship is a primary reason for the increasing incidence of entrepreneurship and corporate entrepreneurship in countries throughout the global economy.

- Three basic approaches are used to produce and manage innovation: internal corporate venturing, strategic alliances, and acquisitions. Internal innovations can be classified as incremental or radical.

- Incremental innovations build on existing knowledge bases and provide small improvements in current product lines. Incremental innovations typically are produced through a process called induced strategic behavior, whereby the firm's current strategy and structure foster product innovations that are closely associated with that strategy and structure.

- Radical innovations provide significant technological breakthroughs and create new knowledge. These types of innovations are supported by autonomous strategic behavior, a bottom-up process in which product champions pursue new ideas to develop and coordinate the commercialization of a new good or service.

- Cross-functional integration is vital to a firm's efforts to develop and implement internal corporate venturing activities and to commercialize the resulting innovation.

Additionally, a firm can facilitate integration and innovation by developing shared values and practicing entrepreneurial leadership.

- It is difficult for an individual firm to possess all the knowledge needed to innovate consistently and effectively. To gain access to the kind of specialized knowledge that often is required to innovate, firms may form cooperative relationships such as strategic alliances with other firms, which may sometimes include competitors.

- Innovation can also be acquired through direct acquisition, or firms can learn new capabilities from an acquisition, thereby enriching their internal innovation processes.

- The practice of strategic entrepreneurship by all types of firms, large and small, new and more established, creates value for all stakeholders, especially for shareholders and customers. Strategic entrepreneurship also contributes to the economic development of nations. Thus, entrepreneurial activity has become important throughout the world.

# Ethics Questions

1. Do managers have an ethical obligation to any of their stakeholders to ensure that their firms remain innovative? If so, to which stakeholders and why?
2. What types of ethical issues do firms encounter when they use internal corporate-venturing processes to produce and manage innovation?
3. Firms that are partners in a strategic alliance may legitimately seek to gain knowledge from each other. At what point does it become unethical for a firm to gain additional and competitively relevant knowledge from its partner? Is this point different when a firm partners with a domestic firm as opposed to a foreign firm? Why or why not?
4. Discuss the ethical implications associated with quickly bringing a new product to market.
5. Small firms often have innovative products. When is it appropriate for a large firm to buy a small firm for its product innovations and new product ideas?

# Notes

1. D. Dobosz-Bourne & A. D. Jankowicz, 2006, Reframing resistance to change, *International Journal of Human Resource Management*, 17: 2021–2040; J. Jermias, 2006, The influence of accountability on overconfidence and resistance to change: A research framework and experimental evidence, *Management Accounting Research*, 17: 370–390.

2. D. A. Shepherd & D. R. DeTienne, 2005, Prior knowledge, potential financial reward, and opportunity identification, *Entrepreneurship Theory and Practice*, 29(1): 91–112; W. J. Baumol, 2004, Entrepreneurial cultures and countercultures, *Academy of Management Learning & Education*, 3(3): 316–326; R. D. Ireland & M. A. Hitt, 1999, Achieving and maintaining strategic competitiveness in the 21st century: The role of strategic leadership, *Academy of Management Executive*, 13(1): 43–57.

3. G. T. Lumpkin & B. B. Lichtenstein, 2005, The role of organizational learning in the opportunity-recognition process, *Entrepreneurship Theory and Practice*, 29: 451–472.

4. M. A. Hitt, R. D. Ireland, S. M. Camp, & D. L. Sexton, 2002, Strategic entrepreneurship: Integrating entrepreneurial and strategic management perspectives, in M. A. Hitt, R. D. Ireland, S. M. Camp, & D. L. Sexton (eds.), *Strategic Entrepreneurship: Creating a New Mindset*, Oxford, UK: Blackwell Publishers, 1–16; M. A. Hitt, R. D. Ireland, S. M. Camp, & D. L. Sexton, 2001, Strategic entrepreneurship: Entrepreneurial strategies for wealth creation, *Strategic Management Journal*, 22(special issue): 479–491; R. D. Ireland, M. A. Hitt, S. M. Camp, & D.L. Sexton, 2001, Integrating entrepreneurship and strategic management actions to create firm wealth, *Academy of Management Executive*, 15(1): 49–63.

5. R. D. Ireland, M. A. Hitt, & D. G. Sirmon, 2003, A model of strategic entrepreneurship: The construct and its dimensions, *Journal of Management*, 29: 963–989.

[6] R. Amit, C. Lucier, M. A. Hitt, & R. D. Nixon, 2002, Strategies for the entrepreneurial millennium, in M. A. Hitt, R. Amit, C. Lucier, & R. Nixon (eds.), *Creating Value: Winners in the New Business Environment*, Oxford, UK: Blackwell Publishers, 1–12; M. A. Hitt, R. D. Nixon, P. G. Clifford, & K. P. Coyne, 1999, The development and use of strategic resources, in M. A. Hitt, P. G. Clifford, R. D. Nixon, & K. P. Coyne (eds.), *Dynamic Strategic Resources: Development, Diffusion and Integration*, Chichester, UK: Wiley, 1–14.

[7] B. R. Barringer & R. D. Ireland, 2008, *Entrepreneurship: Successfully Launching New Ventures*, Upper Saddle River, NJ: Pearson Prentice Hall; G. G. Dess, R. D. Ireland, S. A. Zahra, S. W. Floyd, J. J. Janney, & P. J. Lane, 2003, Emerging issues in corporate entrepreneurship, *Journal of Management*, 29: 351–378.

[8] J. Schumpeter, 1934, *The Theory of Economic Development*, Cambridge, MA: Harvard University Press.

[9] Barringer & Ireland, *Entrepreneurship*; H. H. Stevenson & J. C. Jarillo, 1990, A paradigm for entrepreneurship: Entrepreneurial management, *Strategic Management Journal*, 16(special issue): 17–27.

[10] D. Lavie, 2006, Capability reconfiguration: An analysis of incumbent responses to technological change, *Academy of Management Review*, 31: 153–174; S. Shane & S. Venkataraman, 2000, The promise of entrepreneurship as a field of research, *Academy of Management Review*, 25: 217–226.

[11] R. Baron, 2006, Opportunity recognition as pattern recognition: How entrepreneurs "connect the dots" to identify new business opportunities, *Academy of Management Perspectives*, 20(1): 104–119; B. R. Barringer & A. C. Bluedorn, 1999, The relationship between corporate entrepreneurship and strategic management, *Strategic Management Journal*, 20: 421–444.

[12] S. A. Alvarez & J. B. Barney, 2005, Organizing rent generation and appropriation: Toward a theory of the entrepreneurial firm, *Journal of Business Venturing*, 19: 621–635.

[13] M. Minniti, 2005, Entrepreneurial alertness and asymmetric information in a spin-glass model, *Journal of Business Venturing*, 19: 637–658.

[14] W. Kuemmerle, 2005, The entrepreneur's path to global expansion, *MIT Sloan Management Review*, 46(2): 42–49.

[15] R. D. Hof, 2006, Jeff Bezos' risky bet, *Business Week*, November 13, 54.

[16] K. Karnik, 2005, Innovation's importance: Powering economic growth, NASSCOM, National Association of Software and Service Companies, http://www.nasscom. org, January 24; R. G. Holcombe, 2003, The origins of entrepreneurial opportunities, *Review of Austrian Economics*, 16: 25–54; C. M. Daily, P. P. McDougall, J. G. Covin, & D. R. Dalton, 2002, Governance and strategic leadership in entrepreneurial firms, *Journal of Management*, 28: 387–412.

[17] P. D. Reynolds, M. Hay, & S. M. Camp, 1999, *Global Entrepreneurship Monitor, 1999 Executive Report*, Babson Park, MA: Babson College.

[18] R. D. Ireland, J. W. Webb, & J. E. Coombs, 2005, Theory and methodology in entrepreneurship research, in D. J. Ketchen Jr. & D. D. Bergh (eds.), *Research Methodology in Strategy and Management*, Vol. 2, San Diego, CA: Elsevier, 111–141; S. D. Sarasvathy, 2005, The questions we ask and the questions we care about: Reformulating some problems in entrepreneurship research, *Journal of Business Venturing*, 19: 707–717.

[19] P. F. Drucker, 1998, The discipline of innovation, *Harvard Business Review*, 76(6): 149–157.

[20] K. G. Smith, C. J. Collins, & K. D. Clark, 2005, Existing knowledge, knowledge creation capability, and the rate of new product introduction in high technology firms, *Academy of Management Journal*, 48: 346–357; T. W. Y. Man, T. Lau, & K. F. Chan, 2002, The competitiveness of small and medium enterprises: A conceptualization with focus on entrepreneurial competencies, *Journal of Business Venturing*, 17: 123–142.

[21] J. E. Perry-Smith & C. E. Shalley, 2003, The social side of creativity: A static and dynamic social network perspective, *Academy of Management Review*, 28: 89–106.

[22] G. Hamel, 2000, *Leading the Revolution*, Boston: Harvard Business School Press; R. Price, 1996, Technology and strategic advantage, *California Management Review*, 38(3): 38–56; L. G. Franko, 1989, Global corporate competition: Who's winning, who's losing and the R&D factor as one reason why, *Strategic Management Journal*, 10: 449–474.

[23] J. W. Spencer, 2003, Firms' knowledge-sharing strategies in the global innovation system: Empirical evidence from the flat panel display industry, *Strategic Management Journal*, 24: 217–233; G. T. Lumpkin & G. G. Dess, 1996, Clarifying the entrepreneurial orientation construct and linking it to performance, *Academy of Management Review*, 21: 135–172; K. M. Kelm, V. K. Narayanan, & G. E. Pinches, 1995, Shareholder value creation during R&D innovation and commercialization stages, *Academy of Management Journal*, 38: 770–786.

[24] M. A. Hitt, R. D. Nixon, R. E. Hoskisson, & R. Kochhar, 1999, Corporate entrepreneurship and cross-functional fertilization: Activation, process and disintegration of a new product design team, *Entrepreneurship: Theory and Practice*, 23(3): 145–167.

[25] J. P. O'Brien, 2003, The capital structure implications of pursuing a strategy of innovation, *Strategic Management Journal*, 24: 415–431.

[26] Schumpeter, *The Theory of Economic Development*.

[27] R. Katila & S. Shane, 2005, When does lack of resources make new firms innovative? *Academy of Management Journal*, 48: 814–829.

[28] P. Sharma & J. L. Chrisman, 1999, Toward a reconciliation of the definitional issues in the field of corporate entrepreneurship, *Entrepreneurship: Theory and Practice*, 23(3): 11–27; R. A. Burgelman & L. R. Sayles, 1986, *Inside Corporate Innovation: Strategy, Structure, and Managerial Skills*, New York: The Free Press.

[29] D. K. Dutta & M. M. Crossan, 2005, The nature of entrepreneurial opportunities: Understanding the process using the 41 organizational learning framework, *Entrepreneurship: Theory and Practice* 29: 425–449.

[30] R. E. Hoskisson & L. W. Busenitz, 2002, Market uncertainty and learning distance in corporate entrepreneurship entry mode choice, in M. A. Hitt, R. D. Ireland, S. M. Camp, & D. L. Sexton (eds.), *Strategic Entrepreneurship: Creating a New Mindset*, Oxford, UK: Blackwell Publishers, 151–172.

[31] D. Somaya, 2003, Strategic determinants of decisions not to settle patent litigation, *Strategic Management Journal*, 24: 17–38.

[32] J. B. Barney, 1995, Looking inside for competitive advantage, *Academy of Management Executive*, 9(4):

59–60; J. B. Barney, 1991, Firm resources and sustained competitive advantage, *Journal of Management*, 17: 99–120.

33 J. B. Barney, 1999, How a firm's capabilities affect boundary decisions, *Sloan Management Review*, 40(3): 137–145.

34 S. D. Sarasvathy, 2004, Making it happen: Beyond theories of the firm to theories of firm design, *Entrepreneurship: Theory and Practice*, 28: 519–531.

35 2005, Gore & Associates, Gore cited as America's most innovative company, http://www.gore.com, July 11.

36 D. Duffy, 2004, Corporate entrepreneurship: Entrepreneurial skills for personal and corporate success, The Center for Organizational and Personal Excellence, http://www.centerforexcellence.net, June 14.

37 M. S. Cardon, C. Zietsma, P. Saparito, B. P. Matheren, & C. Davis, 2005, A tale of passion: New insights into entrepreneurship from a parenthood metaphor, *Journal of Business Venturing*, 19: 23–45.

38 R. G. McGrath & I. MacMillan, 2000, *The Entrepreneurial Mindset*, Boston: Harvard Business School Press.

39 R. D. Ireland, M. A. Hitt, & J. W. Webb, 2005, Entrepreneurial alliances and networks, in O. Shenkar and J. J. Reuer (eds.), *Handbook of Strategic Alliances*, Thousand Oaks, CA: Sage, 333–352; T. M. Begley & D. P. Boyd, 2003, The need for a corporate global mindset, *MIT Sloan Management Review*, 44(2): 25–32.

40 J. C. Hayton & D. J. Kelley, 2006, A competency-based framework for promoting corporate entrepreneurship, *Human Resource Management*, 45: 407–415.

41 M. B. Sarkar, R. Echambadi, R. Agrawal, & B. Sen, 2006, The effect of innovative environment on exit in entrepreneurial firms, *Strategic Management Journal*, 27: 519–539; D. F. Kuratko, R. D. Ireland, & J. S. Hornsby, 2001, Improving firm performance through entrepreneurial actions: Acordia's corporate entrepreneurship strategy, *Academy of Management Executive*, 15(4): 60–71; J. Birkinshaw, 1999, The determinants and consequences of subsidiary initiative in multinational corporations, *Entrepreneurship: Theory and Practice*, 24(1): 9–36.

42 2007, Introducing iPhone, http://www.apple.com/iphone, March 1.

43 T. W. Brailsford, 2001, Building a knowledge community at Hallmark Cards, *Research Technology Management*, 44(5): 18–25.

44 H.-J. Cho & V. Pucik, 2005, Relationship between innovativeness, quality, growth, profitability, and market value, *Strategic Management Journal*, 26: 555–575.

45 W. Tsai, 2001, Knowledge transfer in intraorganizational networks: Effects of network position and absorptive capacity on business unit innovation and performance, *Academy of Management Journal*, 44: 996–1004.

46 S. A. Zahra & G. George, 2002, Absorptive capacity: A review, reconceptualization, and extension, *Academy of Management Review*, 27: 185–203.

47 M. A. Hitt, L. Bierman, K. Shimizu, & R. Kochhar, 2001, Direct and moderating effects of human capital on strategy and performance in professional service firms, *Academy of Management Journal*, 44: 13–28.

48 Zahra & George, Absorptive capacity.

49 T. M. Begley, W.-L. Tan, & H. Schoch, 2005, Politico-economic factors associated with interest in starting a business: A multi-country study, *Entrepreneurship:*

*Theory and Practice*, 29: 35–52; J. W. Lu & P. W. Beamish, 2001, The internationalization and performance of SMEs, *Strategic Management Journal*, 22(special issue): 565–585.

50 L. Tihanyi, R. A. Johnson, R. E. Hoskisson, & M. A. Hitt, 2003, Institutional ownership differences and international diversification: The effects of boards of directors and technological opportunity, *Academy of Management Journal*, 46: 195–211.

51 R. D. Ireland & J. W. Webb, 2006, International entrepreneurship in emerging economies: A resource-based perspective, in S. Alvarez, A. Carrera, L. Mesquita, & R. Vassolo (eds.), *Entrepreneurship and Innovation in Emerging Economies*, Oxford, UK: Blackwell Publishers, 47–69; A. E. Ellstrand, L. Tihanyi, & J. L. Johnson, 2002, Board structure and international political risk, *Academy of Management Journal*, 45: 769–777.

52 S. Andersson, 2004, Internationalization in different industrial contexts, *Journal of Business Venturing*, 19: 851–875.

53 D. Farrell, H. Fassbender, T. Kneip, S. Kriesel, & E. Labaye, 2003, Reviving French and German productivity, *McKinsey Quarterly*, No. 1: 40–53.

54 2006, IBM, IBM collaborates with Irish Government to help local business innovate and grow, http://www.ibm.com/news, September 29.

55 Ibid.

56 J. McMillan, 2005, Creative destruction thrives, *New Zealand Herald*, January 13, C2.

57 2007, Is China really no. 2 in R&D? *Business Week*, January 1, 18.

58 E. W. K. Tsang, 2002, Learning from overseas venturing experience: The case of Chinese family businesses, *Journal of Business Venturing*, 17: 21–40.

59 M. A. Hitt, L. Bierman, K. Uhlenbruck, & K. Shimizu, 2006, The importance of resources in the internationalization of professional service firms: The good, the bad and the ugly, *Academy of Management Journal*, 49: 1137–1157; W. Kuemmerle, 2002, Home base and knowledge management in international ventures, *Journal of Business Venturing*, 17: 99–122.

60 A. L. Zacharachis, H. M. Neck, W. D. Bygrave, & L. W. Cox, 2002, Global Entrepreneurship Monitor, Kauffman Center for Entrepreneurial Leadership, Ewing Marion Kauffman Foundation.

61 M. H. Morris, 1998, *Entrepreneurial Intensity: Sustainable Advantages for Individuals, Organizations, and Societies*, Westport, CT: Quorum Books, 85–86; M. H. Morris, D. L. Davis, & J. W. Allen, 1994, Fostering corporate entrepreneurship: Cross-cultural comparisons of the importance of individualism versus collectivism, *Journal of International Business Studies*, 25: 65–89.

62 N. Nummeia, S. Saarenketo, & K. Puumalainen, 2005, Rapidly with a rifle or more slowly with a shotgun? Stretching the company boundaries of internationalizing ICT firms, *Journal of International Entrepreneurship*, 2: 275–288; S. A. Zahra & G. George, 2002, International entrepreneurship: The status of the field and future research agenda, in M. A. Hitt, R. D. Ireland, S. M. Camp, & D. L. Sexton (eds.), *Strategic Entrepreneurship: Creating a New Mindset*, Oxford, UK: Blackwell Publishers, 255–288.

63 R. Underwood, 2005, Walking the talk? *Fast Company*, March, 25–26.

64 S. A. Zahra, R. D. Ireland, & M. A. Hitt, 2000, International expansion by new venture firms:

International diversity, mode of market entry, technological learning and performance, *Academy of Management Journal*, 43: 925–950.

65 P. P. McDougall & B. M. Oviatt, 2000, International entrepreneurship: The intersection of two paths, *Academy of Management Journal*, 43: 902–908.

66 A. Van, G. Zhu, & D. T. Hall, 2002, International assignments for career building: A model of agency relationships and psychological contracts, *Academy of Management Review*, 27: 373–391.

67 H. Barkema & O. Chvyrkov, 2002, What sort of top management team is needed at the helm of internationally diversified firms? in M. A. Hitt, R. D. Ireland, S. M. Camp, & D. L. Sexton (eds.), *Strategic Entrepreneurship: Creating a New Mindset*, Oxford, UK: Blackwell Publishers, 290–305.

68 T. S. Frost, 2001, The geographic sources of foreign subsidiaries' innovations, *Strategic Management Journal*, 22: 101–122; M. A. Hitt, R. E. Hoskisson, & H. Kim, 1997, International diversification: Effects on innovation and firm performance in product diversified firms, *Academy of Management Journal*, 40: 767–798.

69 R. E. Hoskisson, M. A. Hitt, R. A. Johnson, & W. Grossman, 2002, Conflicting voices: The effects of institutional ownership heterogeneity and internal governance on corporate innovation strategies, *Academy of Management Journal*, 45: 697–716.

70 J. Battelle, 2005, Turning the page, *Business 2.0*, July, 98–100.

71 H. W. Chesbrough, 2002, Making sense of corporate venture capital, *Harvard Business Review*, 80(3): 90–99; G. Hamel, 1997, Killer strategies that make shareholders rich, *Fortune*, June 23: 70–88.

72 S. Michael, D. Storey, & H. Thomas, 2002, Discovery and coordination in strategic management and entrepreneurship, in M. A. Hitt, R. D. Ireland, S. M. Camp, & D. L. Sexton (eds.), *Strategic Entrepreneurship: Creating a New Mindset*, Oxford, UK: Blackwell Publishers, 45–65.

73 R. A. Burgelman, 1995, *Strategic Management of Technology and Innovation*, Boston: Irwin.

74 2007, 3M Worldwide, Products and services, http://solutions.3m.com, March 2.

75 W. C. Kim & R. Mauborgne, 2005, Navigating toward blue oceans, *Optimize*, February, 44–52.

76 2005, Strategies 2 Innovate, Radical and incremental innovation styles, http://www.strategies2innovate.com, July 12.

77 W. T. Robinson & J. Chiang, 2002, Product development strategies for established market pioneers, early followers and late entrants, *Strategic Management Journal*, 23: 855–866.

78 G. Ahuja & C. M. Lampert, 2001, Entrepreneurship in the large corporation: A longitudinal study of how established firms create breakthrough inventions, *Strategic Management Journal*, 22(special issue): 521–543.

79 J. Santos, Y. Doz, & P. Williamson, 2004, Is your innovation process global? *MIT Sloan Management Review*, 45(4): 31–37; R. Leifer, G. Colarelli, & M. Rice, 2001, Implementing radical innovation in mature firms: The role of hubs, *Academy of Management Executive*, 15(3): 102–113.

80 J. E. Ashton, F. X. Cook Jr., & P. Schmitz, 2003, Uncovering hidden value in a midsize manufacturing company, *Harvard Business Review*, 81(6): 111–119;

L. Fleming & O. Sorenson, 2003, Navigating the technology landscape of innovation, *MIT Sloan Management Review*, 44(2): 15–23; 2005, Getting an edge on innovation, *Business Week*, March 21, 124.

81 J. Goldenberg, R. Horowitz, A. Levav, & D. Mazursky, 2003, Finding your innovation sweet spot, *Harvard Business Review*, 81(3): 120–129.

82 G. C. O'Connor, R. Hendricks, & M. P. Rice, 2002, Assessing transition readiness for radical innovation, *Research Technology Management*, 45(6): 50–56.

83 A. Phene, K. Fladmoe-Lindquist, & L. Marsh, 2006, Breakthrough innovations in the U.S. biotechnology industry: The effects of technology space and geographic origin, *Strategic Management Journal*, 27: 369–388; R. I. Sutton, 2002, Weird ideas that spark innovation, *MIT Sloan Management Review*, 43(2): 83–87.

84 K. G. Smith & D. Di Gregorio, 2002, Bisociation, discovery, and the role of entrepreneurial action, in M. A. Hitt, R. D. Ireland, S. M. Camp, & D. L. Sexton (eds.), *Strategic Entrepreneurship: Creating a New Mindset*, Oxford, UK: Blackwell Publishers, 129–150.

85 Hoskisson & Busenitz, Market uncertainty and learning distance.

86 T. H. Davenport, L. Prusak, & H. J. Wilson, 2003, Who's bringing you hot ideas and how are you responding? *Harvard Business Review*, 81(2): 58–64.

87 S. K. Markham, 2002, Moving technologies from lab to market, *Research Technology Management*, 45(6): 31–42; R. Leifer & M. Rice, 1999, Unnatural acts: Building the mature firm's capability for breakthrough innovation, in M. A. Hitt, P. G. Clifford, R. D. Nixon, & K. P. Coyne (eds.), *Dynamic Strategic Resources: Development, Diffusion and Integration*, Chichester, UK: Wiley, 433–453.

88 J. M. Howell, 2005, The right stuff: Identifying and developing effective champions of innovation, *Academy of Management Executive*, 19(2): 108–119.

89 M. D. Hutt & T. W. Seph, 2004, *Business Marketing Management*, 8th ed., Cincinnati, OH: Thomson/South-Western.

90 M. A. Hitt, R. D. Ireland, & H. Lee, 2000, Technological learning, knowledge management, firm growth and performance, *Journal of Engineering and Technology Management*, 17: 231–246; D. Leonard-Barton, 1995, *Wellsprings of Knowledge: Building and Sustaining the Sources of Innovation*, Cambridge, MA: Harvard Business School Press.

91 A. Taylor III, 2005, Billion-dollar bets, *Fortune*, June 27, 139–154.

92 S. S. Rao, 2000, General Electric, software vendor, *Forbes*, January 24, 144–146.

93 M. Subramaniam & N. Venkatraman, 2001, Determinants of transnational new product development capability: Testing the influence of transferring and deploying tacit overseas knowledge, *Strategic Management Journal*, 22: 359–378.

94 M. Song & M. M. Montoya-Weiss, 2001, The effect of perceived technological uncertainty on Japanese new product development, *Academy of Management Journal*, 44: 61–80.

95 J. A. Fraser, 2004, A return to basics at Kellogg, *MIT Sloan Management Review*, 45(4): 27–30; P. M. Lee & H. M. O'Neill, 2003, Ownership structures and R&D investments of U.S. and Japanese firms: Agency and stewardship perspectives, *Academy of Management Journal*, 46: 212–225.

96  McGrath & MacMillan, *The Entrepreneurial Mindset*.

97  A. H. Lassen, F. Gertsen, & J. O. Riis, 2006, The nexus of corporate entrepreneurship and radical innovation, *Creativity and Innovation Management*, 15: 359–370.

98  J. S. Harrison, 2003, *Strategic Management of Resources and Relationships*, New York: Wiley; J. Chen, 2005, Weaving the threads of creativity, innovation and entrepreneurship into a Technicolor Dreamcoat, *British Journal of Management*, December, 22–23.

99  2007, 3M Worldwide, William L. McKnight management principles created 3M's corporate culture, http://solutions.3m.com, March 2.

100  2002, Building scientific networks for effective innovation, *MIT Sloan Management Review*, 43(3): 14.

101  C. M. Christensen & M. Overdorf, 2000, Meeting the challenge of disruptive change, *Harvard Business Review*, 78(2): 66–77.

102  L. Yu, 2002, Marketers and engineers: Why can't we just get along? *MIT Sloan Management Review*, 43(1): 13.

103  P. S. Adler, 1995, Interdepartmental interdependence and coordination: The case of the design/manufacturing interface, *Organization Science*, 6: 147–167.

104  I. Royer, 2003, Why bad projects are so hard to kill, *Harvard Business Review*, 81(2): 48–56.

105  P. Evans & B. Wolf, 2005, Collaboration rules, *Harvard Business Review*, 83(7): 96–104.

106  B. Fischer & A. Boynton, 2005, Virtuoso teams, *Harvard Business Review*, 83(7): 116–123; B. L. Kirkman & B. Rosen, 1999, Beyond self-management: Antecedents and consequences of team empowerment, *Academy of Management Journal*, 42: 58–74; A. R. Jassawalla & H. C. Sashittal, 1999, Building collaborative cross-functional new product teams, *Academy of Management Executive*, 13(3): 50–63.

107  Hitt, Nixon, Hoskisson, & Kochhar, Corporate entrepreneurship.

108  Christensen & Overdorf, Meeting the challenge of disruptive change.

109  Hitt, Nixon, Hoskisson, & Kochhar, Corporate entrepreneurship.

110  A. C. Amason, 1996, Distinguishing the effects of functional and dysfunctional conflict on strategic decision making: Resolving a paradox for top management teams, *Academy of Management Journal*, 39: 123–148; P. R. Lawrence & J. W. Lorsch, 1969, *Organization and Environment*, Homewood, IL: Irwin.

111  D. Dougherty, L. Borrelli, K. Muncir, & A. O'Sullivan, 2000, Systems of organizational sensemaking for sustained product innovation, *Journal of Engineering and Technology Management*, 17: 321–355; D. Dougherty, 1992, Interpretive barriers to successful product innovation in large firms, *Organization Science*, 3: 179–202.

112  Hitt, Nixon, Hoskisson, & Kochhar, Corporate entrepreneurship.

113  Ibid.

114  D. A. Garvin, & L. C. Levesque, 2006, Meeting the challenge of corporate entrepreneurship, *Harvard Business Review*, 84(10): 102–110; E. C. Wenger & W. M. Snyder, 2000, Communities of practice: The organizational frontier, *Harvard Business Review*, 78(1): 139–144.

115  C. Zehir & M. S. Eren, 2007, Field research on impacts of some organizational factors on corporate entrepreneurship and business performance in the Turkish automotive industry, *Journal of the American Academy of Business*, 10: 170–176; Hamel, *Leading the Revolution*.

116  2007, Gore & Associates, Corporate culture, http://www.gore.com, March 2.

117  M. A. Hitt & R. D. Ireland, 2002, The essence of strategic leadership: Managing human and social capital, *Journal of Leadership and Organizational Studies*, 9: 3–14.

118  McGrath & MacMillan, *The Entrepreneurial Mindset*.

119  Q. M. Roberson & J. A. Colquitt, 2005, Shared and configural justice: A social network model of justice in teams, *Academy of Management Review*, 30: 595–607.

120  Hitt, Ireland, Camp, & Sexton, Strategic entrepreneurship; S. W. Fowler, A. W. King, S. J. Marsh, & B. Victor, 2000, Beyond products: New strategic imperatives for developing competencies in dynamic environments, Journal of Engineering and Technology Management, 17: 357–377.

121  B.-S. Teng, 2007, Corporate entrepreneurship activities through strategic alliances: A resource-based approach toward competitive advantage, *Journal of Management Studies*, 44: 119–130; R. K. Kazanjian, R. Drazin, & M. A. Glynn, 2002, Implementing strategies for corporate entrepreneurship: A knowledge-based perspective, in M. A. Hitt, R. D. Ireland, S. M. Camp, & D. L. Sexton (eds.), *Strategic Entrepreneurship: Creating a New Mindset*, Oxford, UK: Blackwell Publishers, 173–199.

122  F. T. Rothaermel & D. L. Deeds, 2004, Exploration and exploitation alliances in biotechnology: A system of new product development, *Strategic Management Journal*, 25: 201–221; A. C. Cooper, 2002, Networks, alliances and entrepreneurship, in M. A. Hitt, R. D. Ireland, S. M. Camp, & D. L. Sexton (eds.), *Strategic Entrepreneurship: Creating a New Mindset*, Oxford, UK: Blackwell Publishers, 204–222.

123  P. Kale, H. Singh, & H. Perlmutter, 2000, Learning and protection of proprietary assets in strategic alliances: Building relational capital, *Strategic Management Journal*, 21: 217–237.

124  2006, neowin.net, Intel, Micron select Singapore for NAND Flash fab, http://www.neowin.net, November 6; C. Martens, 2005, Intel, Micron team up on NAND memory manufacture, InfoWorld, http://www.infoworld.com, November 21.

125  Cooper, Networks, alliances and entrepreneurship.

126  L. Y. Chen & F. B. Barnes, 2006, Leadership behaviors and knowledge sharing in professional service firms engaged in strategic alliances, *Journal of Applied Management and Entrepreneurship*, 11(2): 51–70; S. A. Alvarez & J. B. Barney, 2001, How entrepreneurial firms can benefit from alliances with large partners, *Academy of Management Executive*, 15(1): 139–148; F. T. Rothaermel, 2001, Incumbent's advantage through exploiting complementary assets via interfirm cooperation, *Strategic Management Journal*, 22(special issue): 687–699.

127  J. Hagedoorn & N. Roijakkers, 2002, Small entrepreneurial firms and large companies in interfirm R&D networks—the international biotechnology industry, in M. A. Hitt, R. D. Ireland, S. M. Camp, & D. L. Sexton (eds.), *Strategic Entrepreneurship: Creating a New Mindset*, Oxford, UK: Blackwell Publishers, 223–252.

128  L. Lavelle, 2007, A matchmaker for inventors, *Business Week*, February 26, 100.

129  D. Kline, 2003, Sharing the corporate crown jewels, *MIT Sloan Management Review*, 44(3): 89–93; B. R.

Koka & J. E. Prescott, 2002, Strategic alliances as social capital: A multidimensional view, *Strategic Management Journal*, 23: 795–816.

[130] H. Yli-Renko, E. Autio, & H. J. Sapienza, 2001, Social capital, knowledge acquisition and knowledge exploitation in young technology-based firms, *Strategic Management Journal*, 22(special issue): 587–613.

[131] C. Lee, K. Lee, & J. M. Pennings, 2001, Internal capabilities, external networks and performance: A study of technology-based ventures, *Strategic Management Journal*, 22(special issue): 615–640.

[132] A. Takeishi, 2001, Bridging inter- and intra-firm boundaries: Management of supplier involvement in automobile product development, *Strategic Management Journal*, 22: 403–433.

[133] J. Weiss & J. Hughes, 2005, Want collaboration? Accept—and actively manage—conflict, *Harvard Business Review*, 83(3): 92–101.

[134] R. D. Ireland, M. A. Hitt, & D. Vaidyanath, 2002, Strategic alliances as a pathway to competitive success, *Journal of Management*, 28: 413–446.

[135] M. A. Hitt, M. T. Dacin, E. Levitas, J. L. Arregle, & A. Borza, 2000, Partner selection in emerging and developed market contexts: Resource-based and organizational learning perspectives, *Academy of Management Journal*, 43: 449–467.

[136] J. J. Reuer, M. Zollo, & H. Singh, 2002, Post-formation dynamics in strategic alliances, *Strategic Management Journal*, 23: 135–151.

[137] F. Rothaermel & D. Deeds, 2002, More good things are not always necessarily better: An empirical study of strategic alliances, experience effects, and new product development in high-technology start-ups, in M. A. Hitt, R. Amit, C. Lucier, & R. Nixon (eds.), *Creating Value: Winners in the New Business Environment*, Oxford, UK: Blackwell Publishers, 85–103.

[138] 2007, Cognos acquires Celequest, *Al Bawaba*, January 28, 1.

[139] M. A. Hitt, R. E. Hoskisson, R. A. Johnson, & D. D. Moesel, 1996, The market for corporate control and firm innovation, *Academy of Management Journal*, 39: 1084–1119.

[140] J. Laponsky, 2006, Logitech acquires Slim Devices in $20M deal, *Twice*, October 23, 72.

[141] M. A. Hitt, J. S. Harrison, & R. D. Ireland, 2001, *Mergers and Acquisitions: A Guide to Creating Value for Stakeholders*, New York: Oxford University Press.

[142] Ireland, Hitt, & Sirmon, A model of strategic entrepreneurship.

[143] Amit, Lucier, Hitt, & Nixon, Strategies for the entrepreneurial millennium.

[144] Hitt, Ireland, Camp, & Sexton, Strategic entrepreneurship.

[145] Lavie, Capability reconfiguration.

[146] D. G. Sirmon, M. A. Hitt, & R. D. Ireland, 2007, Managing firm resources in dynamic environments to create value: Looking inside the black box, *Academy of Management Review*, 32: 273–292.

[147] Hitt, Bierman, Shimizu, & Kochhar, Direct and moderating effects of human capital.

[148] M. A. Hitt, H. Lee, & E. Yucel, 2002, The importance of social capital to the management of multinational enterprises: Relational networks among Asian and Western firms, *Asia Pacific Journal of Management*, 19: 353–372.

[149] K. Laursen & A. Salter, 2006, Open for innovation: The role of openness in explaining innovation performance among U.K. manufacturing firms, *Strategic Management Journal*, 27: 131–150.

[150] Hitt, Hoskisson, & Kim, International diversification.

[151] M. A. Hitt & R. D. Ireland, 2002, The essence of strategic leadership: Managing human and social capital, *Journal of Leadership and Organization Studies*, 9(1): 3–14.

[152] 2006, IBM collaborates with Irish Government.

[153] 2006, Institutional entrepreneurship: The importance of choice, *International Journal of Entrepreneurship & Innovation*, 7: 269–270.

[154] R. Garud, S. Jain, & A. Kumaraswamy, 2002, Institutional entrepreneurship in the sponsorship of common technological standards: The case of Sun Microsystems and JAVA, *Academy of Management Journal*, 45: 196–214.

[155] Zacharachis, Neck, Bygrave, & Cox, Global Entrepreneurship Monitor.

[156] J. D. Jardins, 2005, I am woman (I think), *Fast Company*, May, 25–26.

[157] Hitt, Ireland, Camp, & Sexton, Strategic entrepreneurship; Amit, Lucier, Hitt, & Nixon, Strategies for the entrepreneurial millennium.

# CHAPTER 13

# Strategic Flexibility and Real Options Analysis

## KNOWLEDGE OBJECTIVES

*Studying this chapter should provide you with the strategic management knowledge needed to:*

1. Define real options and contrast them with other types of strategic investments by firms.

2. Describe the different types of real options that exist and in what strategic circumstances they are important.

3. Explain the purposes and importance of real options analysis.

4. Describe the value drivers underlying real options.

5. Value simple real options using two techniques: (1) the Black–Scholes and the Black–Scholes approximation method; and (2) the binomial lattices and risk-neutral method.

6. Explain some of the most important assumptions underlying real options valuation methods.

Several years ago Sony opened in San Francisco The Metreon—a novel retail complex that consists of stylish restaurants and one-of-a-kind stores, an IMAX theater, and interactive exhibits for children.[1] When making the choice to launch this complex, Sony had to make a number of related decisions: With how many complexes should the firm proceed? Should they open the outlets all at once or roll them out in sequence? How should decisions concerning locations and formats be made over time as the firm receives new information on the success or failure of individual locations? The fundamental structure surrounding the process and timing of Sony's investment decision can be found in many types of strategic decisions, including whether or how to develop a new technology or product platform, whether to invest in a new region of the world or in a new product market, how to undertake an R&D program, and how to manage production outsourcing decisions in new ventures.[2]

One of the key points that the preceding chapters have underscored is that strategic decisions are complex and ambiguous. They often touch upon multiple functional areas of the firm, involve sizable resource commitments that may or may not prompt reactions by rivals, and are difficult to analyze because they include many qualitative inputs that can be difficult to integrate. Strategic decisions also typically are made in the context of considerable uncertainty, which further complicates analyses of investment choices and strategic courses of action for organizations. All indications are that such uncertainties—whether due to economic risks, technological developments, industry convergence and creative destruction, geopolitical crises, the global integration of industries, and so forth—are becoming increasingly important for many organizations and are likely to continue to be so.[3]

In response to this uncertainty, firms seek to craft strategies that enhance their **strategic flexibility**.[4] A strategy can be said to be flexible when it allows a firm to react to changing uncertainties by quickly changing course or, better still, allows the firm to position itself to take advantage of the resolution of uncertainty.[5] In the aftermath of September 11, 2001, airlines took a number of actions to reduce their costs while simultaneously enticing customers to return to air travel. All U.S. airlines except Southwest Airlines reduced the number of flights and personnel, and some eliminated routes as well. Southwest had substantial cash on hand because of a conscious strategy by the firm to have cash available for operations during an emergency or crisis situation. This decision provided Southwest with strategic flexibility.[6]

Strategic flexibility might be enhanced by organizational structures, systems, or other internal resources that augment the responsiveness of an organization.[7] Strategic flexibility might also be advanced by the particular design of investments and operations by incorporating staging opportunities (i.e., investing sequentially in a project as milestones are reached), by switching opportunities (i.e., shifting inputs or outputs across machines, geographic markets), and by articulating the follow-on opportunities embedded in strategic choices (i.e., other prospective investments opened up by initial resource commitments).[8] Entrepreneurial activities also enhance strategic flexibility. As firms make decisions to invest in new ventures, they are also opening a number of future opportunities. For instance, a firm that decides to open a small hotel on a large property could, at a later date, decide to enlarge the hotel, add a restaurant, or convert the hotel to condominiums. Consequently, firms that are entrepreneurial tend to have greater strategic flexibility (see Chapter 12).

The preceding chapters have introduced several of the tools for dealing with uncertainty in strategic decision making. For example, environmental analysis (see Chapter 3) can be used as an input to scenario planning, which aims to collapse the many uncertainties confronting a firm into a small number of internally consistent scenarios of the future.[9] Also, the analysis of competitive rivalry and competitive dynamics (see Chapter 6) helps firms understand how the effectiveness of their strategies can hinge upon the simultaneous decisions or subsequent reactions of rivals. A firm does not need to accept rivals' actions and their consequences passively, and in fact it can shape them through its own investments and strategies, which in turn figure into rivals' own decisions.[10]

Real options analysis is also a tool that helps firms deal with uncertainty and increase strategic flexibility. In the past few years, real options analysis has received increased attention as a tool for strategic decision making.[11] It has attracted interest because it offers a means of quantitatively evaluating the role of uncertainty in firms' investment decisions; it changes the ways in which strategists think about particular investments and the ways in which they can deliver value to firms; and it offers the promise of beginning to reconcile strategic and financial analyses in organizations. It can do this by simultaneously injecting strategic reality into traditional financial valuation models while rigorously bringing the discipline of financial markets into strategic analyses.[12]

We examine several topics in this chapter concerning real options, beginning with a precise definition of the term. We then discuss various types of real options and explain some of the primary purposes of real options analysis. We consider why real options are of practical importance for firms and include in this discussion ways in which real options analysis provides a disciplined approach for bringing strategic considerations into capital budgeting processes. Accordingly, this chapter contains a brief introduction to some of the ways that real options can be valued, both for firms as a whole and for individual strategic investments. An appendix provides detailed instructions for two of the most common valuation approaches. Even if individual investments are not valued using some of the formal techniques of real options analysis, an understanding of the value drivers underlying real options and their implications can be useful in the design and implementation of strategic investments (e.g., acquisitions, supply contracts, alliances, foreign direct investment) and working constructively with uncertainty in strategic decision making.

# Real Options Analysis

A definition of **real options** must explain both why the options are real and why they are options.[13] Precision is needed to distinguish the term *option* from related concepts in order for the analysis of real options to offer something that is distinctive to executives, consultants, and analysts. For example, it is true that options provide strategic alternatives, yet alternatives are not necessarily options per se as the latter have a particular structure to them as well as a set of additional criteria that must be met for firms to actually obtain option value. Real options are real because the immediate underlying asset, unlike in the case of financial options, is a real asset rather than a financial security.

An analogy with financial options helps us to clarify the definition of real options. Suppose an individual purchases a financial call and pays some amount of money, say $5 per share, to obtain the right, but not the obligation, to purchase 10 shares of a company's stock for $100 per share in the future. If the firm's share price collapses, the individual does nothing and has lost only the original option purchase price of $50 (i.e., $5 per share times 10 shares). He or she is not compelled to make the second stage investment. However, if the individual discovers through monitoring the company's stock price that the price surges above $100 to $120 because of a change in demand for the company's products, technological improvement, or some other development, the individual can exercise his or her option to purchase the shares at $100 each, and in the process makes $20 per share (or $200 total) on the terminal purchase. By way of analogy, for Sony executives, rather than committing to five retail outlets initially, they might go forward with only one small outlet; determine how the uncertain demand for such retail complexes evolves with macroeconomic, industry, or other conditions; and then decide whether to expand the outlet or increase their number of locations on the basis of the new information.

This comparison yields five criteria for an option to exist. An option provides a firm (1) with the right, (2) but not the obligation, (3) to take some future specified action, (4) enabling the firm to reduce its downside risk (5) while accessing upside opportunities. Each of these criteria deserves attention when considering whether options are embedded in a firm's investments or its operational practices. To say that an option provides a right and that it confers access to upside opportunities means that it gives the firm some preferential claim to a follow-on investment opportunity.[14] In the case of financial options, this right is to claim the shares for $100 each, and this right costs $50 total at the outset. In the case of real options, this means that other firms cannot obtain the same investment on the same terms in the second stage, and the potential second-stage investment is conditional upon the first. In the case of the financial call, this right accounts for the difference between the $100 purchase price and $120 market price, as the former is set contractually and the latter is set by the stock market. It is equally important that the firm *not* have an *obligation* to make the second-stage investment. If the firm is compelled to make a follow-on investment, there is no flexibility and an option does not exist because a commitment has already been made.

The asymmetry between having the *right but not the obligation* gives rise to a parallel asymmetry in outcomes: options help firms *reduce downside risk while accessing upside opportunities*.[15] In the case of the financial option, the individual's initial $50 investment is entirely sunk, and he or she purchases the shares only if it makes economic sense to do so; if not, the individual obtains a terminal payoff of zero. In the case of Sony, by going forward with a single small outlet initially, it can reduce its downside risk in the event that the complex is not successful; and although it is not compelled to expand, it is able to do so if demand turns out to be unexpectedly favorable for this new retail format in other geographic locations.

## Types of Real Options

Just as strategic commitments come in many varieties (e.g., acquisitions to achieve market power, staking out competitive positions, etc.), a wide range of real options can be seen in firms' investments and their operations.[16] Table 13.1 shows examples of different types of options and the contexts in which they are often relevant.

**Growth Options. Growth options** represent investments that enable the firm to expand the investment in the future, if that action turns out to be valuable. The Sony example discussed above would be such an option. A decision made by Nucor, the mini-mill steel manufacturer, is another example of this type of option. Nucor has produced various metal products directly from scrap metal rather than through the traditional process of heating and reheating inputs in large batches. The company was evaluating the establishment of a plant reliant on a new technology of thin-slab casting, which would enable it to produce sheet metals that would directly take on integrated players in the industry. When evaluating this decision and the uncertainties it presented, the firm was betting on its key capabilities of opening new plants and transferring best practices. These capabilities suggest that if the plant were successful, it would likely create opportunities for additional plants throughout the country.[17]

Another example of a growth option is an *equity joint venture*, which involves firms establishing a business with joint ownership, such as a 50/50 ownership split.[18] A pharmaceutical firm can invest in a biotechnology joint venture rather than by simply acquiring the firm to obtain its technology. By doing so, the pharmaceutical firm potentially reduces its downside risk by limiting its initial outlay relative to what would be required if it purchased the biotechnology firm outright. If the technology proves to be unattractive or the market for the biotech firm's products doesn't materialize, the pharmaceutical firm is not compelled

## Table 13.1: Types of Real Options

| Option | Description | Typical Contexts |
|--------|-------------|------------------|
| Growth | An early investment opens future expansion opportunities. | • Infrastructure investments<br>• Investments in products with multiple generations |
| Abandonment | The presence of resale markets allows the firm to realize value from exiting markets with deteriorating conditions. | • New product introductions<br>• Capital-intensive industries |
| Switching | Product flexibility allows shifts in output mix; process flexibility permits shifts in inputs. | • Consumer goods susceptible to volatile demand<br>• Tapered vertical integration |
| Defer | A lease or option to buy land allows the firm to wait to see whether output prices justify investment. | • Natural-resource extraction industries<br>• Real estate development |
| Compound | Investments conferring multiple options of the types listed above. | • Any of the above |

SOURCE: Adapted from Lenos Trigeorgis, *Real Options: Managerial Flexibility and Strategy in Resource Allocation*, © 1996 Lenos Trigeorgis, published by The MIT Press.

to expand; but if the technology or products prove to be favorable, the pharmaceutical firm can expand by buying out the biotech firm from the venture.[19] Of course, the question is at what price this acquisition of additional equity occurs for this strategy to make sense. Although only a limited number of firms take the time to negotiate an option clause directly into joint venture contracts,[20] Siemens has claimed that this contractual provision was the most important element of its collaborative agreement with Allis-Chalmers.[21]

**Abandonment Options.** If growth options are akin to financial calls, then **abandonment options** are akin to financial puts. Abandonment options provide firms flexibility by allowing them to reverse course and exit deteriorating competitive situations. For instance, in high-tech start-ups, it might be possible for firms to sell technologies, capital equipment, or other assets through a resale market. Such options might also be negotiated in individual contracts between firms. In a highly publicized and contentious collaborative relationship between Fiat and General Motors, Fiat had negotiated the ability to sell its shares to GM at an agreed-upon price that ultimately became quite unattractive to GM with the worsening of Fiat's financial condition and other problems.[22]

**Switching Options.** **Switching options** combine the features of the options just discussed by allowing firms to change the mix of outputs or inputs. For instance, flexible manufacturing systems allow firms to shift output across two or more products at a relatively low switching cost. For firms producing different products that have highly variable demands, this option can be attractive because it enables firms to alter production decisions on the basis of the conditions of the market conditions for the firm's products. A second example of a switching option is the network of generating units in the electric utility industry.[23] Within a given day, the profitability of a given unit is based on its "spark gap," or the price it can charge less the cost of production, which can vary on the basis of environmental and operational contingencies. To meet demand at a given time, a utility seeks to bring online the units with the highest spark gap. By contrast, units with the lowest spark gaps are brought offline first. A final example of switching options is provided by firms' foreign direct investment, or ownership of assets in multiple countries. As currency rates or other environmental conditions change over time, firms can reallocate production or other activities throughout their network of operations to reduce their cost structure relative to rivals that have operations in only one country and are therefore subject to the currency and other risks associated with that particular country.[24]

**Option to Defer.** The **option to defer** is present when there is value in waiting. Some students might find graduate school valuable not only because of the knowledge they obtain, but also because of an option to defer other commitments, such as marriage or full-time work. For executives, the option to defer comes into existence because uncertainty surrounds a strategic investment, and the commitment to that investment is irreversible. The combination of irreversibility and uncertainty makes such options valuable because of the gains from waiting. For this reason, executives judging investment projects may require the net present value (NPV) to be significantly greater than zero to compensate for the value of deferral options that are lost when the firm makes a strategic commitment.[25] Options to defer can be found in natural resource–based industries, in decisions such as whether to harvest timber or extract natural resources such as copper or oil.[26] Deferral options can also figure into real estate development decisions.

**Compound Options.** In formal analyses that value real options, analysts, consultants, or others will often simplify an investment decision to capture a single option. In most real-life investment projects or operations, however, multiple options are often present. **Compound options** refer to investments that confer multiple options that are built upon one another. Another way to understand compound options is to consider that the underlying asset is not a real asset, but another option. For instance, in R&D activities, a number of stages proceed from basic research to applied research, and then development work, proto-typing, and commercialization, which together amount to a series of options on options. Treating such compound options as simple options will understate the flexibility available to the firm holding such options and therefore their value, yet such treatment can yield important insights concerning an investment decision. Moreover, simply understanding the direction of this bias can be sufficient for making a strategic investment decision.

## Purpose and Importance of Real Options Analysis

We now turn to the purpose of real options analysis and the question of how important real options are in strategic management.[27] Real options and the analyses of these invest-ments are important because they have recast motives for a variety of strategic decisions, have opened new opportunities to bridge strategic and financial analyses, and have shown how managers need to alter their investment thresholds. They are also important because they are practically relevant, as they can represent an important source and share of firm value.

**Challenging Received Wisdom on Motives for Strategic Investments.** Real op-tions analysis changes the way managers think about strategic investments and the ben-efits that accrue from them.[28] Consider the example above of switching options offered by foreign direct investment and contrast this view of multinational strategy with the tradi-tional perspective. Before the advent of real options theory, the received view was that mul-tinational firms largely make foreign direct investments involving the ownership of foreign affiliates in order to maintain control over their intangible assets such as brands or tech-nologies.[29] Not only are such assets difficult to value for potential licensees, but they are difficult to monitor and control appropriately without the parent firm's ownership and con-trol. In contrast to this perspective emphasizing the efficiencies associated with ownership, the real options perspective instead focuses attention on the dynamic gains that firms can obtain by shifting their value chain activities across country borders in response to changes in environmental conditions (e.g., currencies, wages, demand, etc.). The central focus is op-erational *flexibility* rather than operational *control*. During the Asian financial crisis in the late 1990s, for instance, companies such as ABB and General Electric were able to reallo-cate production flexibly to locations in Asia with relatively lower production costs to reduce their global cost structure.[30]

A second example demonstrates how real options directly challenges a conventional perspective on strategic investment and the benefits it provides a company. Traditionally, joint ventures were routinely compared to marriages or interpersonal relationships, and the objectives of the investing firm were therefore thought to be making such collaborations as long-lasting and harmonious as possible.[31] Under the real options lens, however, termina-tion no longer has the negative connotations of "divorce," and in fact firms can obtain value at the termination stage just as they can by forming joint ventures.[32]

For example, suppose $\alpha$ is the firm's ownership stake in a joint venture that has a value of $v$, which can change over time. The value of the part of the joint venture the firm owns is therefore $\alpha v$. Assume that the firm can buy out the equity held by its partner for a price of $p$. Thus, if the value of the part of the joint venture the firm does *not* own falls short of this price, that is, $(1 - \alpha)v < p$, the firm does nothing and holds the option open. In the event of some positive demand change, however, it might be the case that this value exceeds the purchase price and the firm can buy out its partner and therefore gain $(1 - \alpha)v - p$. With the development of real options theory, joint ventures and minority investments have come to be seen as stepping stones or transitional investments providing companies with flexibility rather than as marriages or investments meant to last forever.[33] For instance, Cisco Systems is widely known to have an acquisition-led strategy, yet the company relies on small equity investments as stepping stones for approximately 25 percent of its acquisitions.[34]

**Reconciling Strategic Analysis and Financial Analysis.** The power of real options analysis can be further illustrated with a very simple question: Would you invest in a project with a negative NPV? Presented with this question, some managers and students respond that strategic considerations need to be taken into proper account. Presumably, negative-NPV projects might be acceptable, provided that they are "strategic." But what does this really mean? On the basis of finance theory, others respond that such decisions are not in the interest of shareholders and therefore should definitely be rejected. As a variant on this answer, someone who is uncomfortable with qualitative analyses might suggest that if strategic considerations do matter, they should be reflected in firms' cash flow forecasts such that the NPV should be positive for the firm to proceed.

Resolution of this dilemma comes in part from an understanding of the histories of strategic analysis and capital budgeting.[35] It can be argued that both blossomed in parallel after World War II and that both are inherently interested in the allocation of a firm's resources to achieve value for shareholders. The key strength of capital budgeting lies in its ability to handle tangible cash flows as well as its explicit decision criterion for corporate investment (i.e., NPV > 0). Its chief weakness is that the tools are designed to value passive investments without flexibility. On the side of strategic analysis, it is intrinsically interested in active management and follow-on opportunities, yet it lacks the type of tight decision criterion to make resource allocation decisions. Ideally, a tool could bridge corporate finance and strategy by injecting strategic reality (e.g., uncertainty, follow-on opportunities, active management) into financial models of investment while also incorporating the discipline of financial markets and mathematical rigor into strategic analyses. At the broadest level, this is the promise and potential contribution of real options analysis.

To see the importance of real options analysis, consider why traditional valuation techniques are flawed for many strategic investments as well as how the presence of embedded options moves firms' investment thresholds away from the NPV > 0 standard. Suppose a firm is investing in a high-tech project that has two equally likely outcomes, yielding a payoff of $V^+ = \$180$ million under "good" market conditions and $V^- = \$60$ million under "poor" market conditions one year hence.[36] Assume that the risk-adjusted discount rate is 20 percent and the risk-free rate is 8 percent. The present value (PV) of the project is the expected value of the payoff, discounted to time zero at the risk-adjusted rate. Thus, PV = $(1 + 0.20)^{-1}[0.5(180) + 0.5(60)] = \$100$ million.

Now suppose the firm is able to write a contract with another company, which is able to take over the technology in one year's time and is willing to commit to paying $180 million at that time. The question is, what should the firm be willing to pay for such a contract? Using the above formula and subtracting the $100 million value yields $(1.2)^{-1}[0.5(180) + 0.5(180)] - 100 = \$50$ million. However, given that the firm obtains $180 million under all conditions, it is inappropriate to use the same discount rate for a 100 percent chance of getting $180 million as for a 50/50 chance of getting $180 million versus $60 million. Since the former payoff is riskless, it should be discounted by the risk-free rate of 8 percent. This means that the correct value for this abandonment option is $(1.08)^{-1}[0.5(180) + 0.5(180)] - 100 = \$67$ million, which is 34 percent higher than the value previously calculated. Of course, this simple example works because the risk-free rate can be used since the future payouts are made certain. In real-life situations, it is necessary to use option valuation methods since this discount rate cannot be obtained so easily. An important lesson of this example is that traditional financial valuation methods will undervalue projects with flexibility and overvalue commitment-intensive projects, which means that firms are likely to underinvest in projects with embedded options and overinvest in inflexible projects.

**Shifting Investment Thresholds.** Another implication of the example above is that the presence of real options changes firms' investment thresholds. For instance, suppose a potential start-up is considering offering synthetic mats for construction sites, and these mats are superior to wooden mats, as the latter suffer from drawbacks, such as lack of durability, cumbersome transportation and storage, and risks of damage to heavy equipment.[37] Previous efforts to develop synthetic mats ran into difficulties, such as excessive "memory" from prior loads and electrostatic properties that are problematic for usage in industries such as oil and gas exploration. Initial analyses estimated the initial investment to proceed with commercialization of the new patent to be $6.5 million for a plant and working capital for a post-test start-up period, and the estimated NPV was −$1.1 million. Traditional valuation approaches would suggest that the new venture not be launched because the expected cash flows are inadequate in relation to the investment required (i.e., NPV < 0). However, the entrepreneur was convinced that if the project was successful, it would pave the way for additional applications for the synthetic technology. Algebraically stated, it is economically sensible for the entrepreneur to launch the business if the "package" of the value attached to any such growth options and the value attached to the first-stage investment is greater than zero, or $NPV_1 + C_2 > 0$, where $NPV_1$ is the NPV just described (−$1.1 million) and $C_2$ is the call option value of the growth options obtained from the first-stage investment. In other words, the value of the call option $(C_2)$ must be worth at least $1.1 million for the firm to proceed with the launch (i.e., for −$1.1 million + $C_2 > 0$). If not, the business should not be started, unless other valuable options can be identified.

Whereas the previous example illustrates the point that a firm might invest in a project even if its NPV is negative, if embedded growth options are sufficiently valuable, the reverse side of the coin also holds: it can make sense for a firm *not* to sell assets or exit a business even if an NPV of doing so is *positive*. Consider Eli Lilly or other firms in pharmaceuticals or high-tech fields as an example. Such firms hold a wide range of patents and need to decide how best to manage the intellectual property they possess. For any given patent, the firm might proceed with commercialization, license the technology out to another firm, donate the patent to a university to obtain a tax write-off, or hold onto the technology. At first, it might appear irrational that these firms are holding on to many patents that are seemingly unrelated to their current businesses. Such investment choices might make sense rather than commercialization, but why not simply donate the patent to obtain tax benefits (or license it for royalties)? Suppose that $NPV_{d,p}$ is the NPV from donating patent $p$, and $NPV_{d,p} < 0$. Given uncertainty surrounding the value of the technology and other circumstances, this patent can have a call option value (i.e., $C_p$) because the firm has the right but not the obligation to commercialize the underlying technology in the future.

Donating (or licensing) the patent today implies giving up the value of these embedded options. Thus, while $NPV_{d,p} > 0$, it might be the case that $NPV_{d,p} - C_p < 0$. It makes sense to donate if the package value, $NPV_{d,p} - C_p$, clear is greater than zero or, in other words, if the NPV obtained from donating is greater than the call value from holding onto the patent (i.e., $NPV_{d,p} > C_p$).[38] Thus, it is important that managers account for embedded options whether they are on the buy side (e.g., expanding, acquiring, or launching businesses) or on the sell side (e.g., selling or exiting businesses) of strategic investment decisions. The presence of real options suggests that it might make economic sense for firms to take on negative-NPV investments or to avoid positive-NPV investments not simply because these investments are "strategic," but because valuable options are embedded in such investments.

**Driving Actual Firm Value.** From a conceptual standpoint, real options are therefore important in providing a bridge between strategic analyses and capital budgeting, and they are important when a firm makes important strategic investment decisions because they can alter the firm's investment thresholds as opposed to using the standard criterion of $NPV > 0$.

The importance of options to the projects firms pursue and the overall value of companies can be demonstrated with actual data from actual firms. A simple way to do this is to consider that the value of a firm can be expressed in terms of the value of its assets in place, or the value derived from assets in their present use, plus the value of the firm's growth opportunities. The present value of a firm's growth opportunities has been defined as its *value of growth options* because growth in economic profits reflects discretionary future investments by the firm.[39] This leads to the formula $V = V_{AIP} + V_{GO}$, where $V$ is the value of the firm, $V_{AIP}$ is the value of assets in place, and $V_{GO}$ is the value of the firm's growth options. If we divide $V_{GO}$ by the value of the firm, this yields an expression that can be labeled "growth option value," or GOV, which represents the proportion of firm value attributable to growth options (i.e., $GOV = V_{GO}/V$).[40]

The technical details of how to estimate these values are beyond the scope of this chapter, but a few illustrations using data patterns can illustrate the importance of growth options across industries as well as across firms within industries. Data on firms' economic profits, discount rates, and capital invested were obtained from Stern Stewart & Co. to arrive at estimates of GOV.[41] Figure 13.1 illustrates how the proportion of firm value attributable to growth options varies across industries. For example, in the electrical and electronics equipment industry, on average 54 percent of firm value is due to growth options. In the chemicals industry, this proportion is also high at 48 percent. At the opposite end of the spectrum, firms in industries such as stone, clay, glass, and concrete derive little of their value from growth options (i.e., 12 percent), and similar patterns exist in industries such as furniture and fixtures (i.e., 20 percent).[42]

Despite these general tendencies across industries, the degree to which growth options matter within industries varies greatly. For example, within the electrical and electronics equipment industry (see Figure 13.2), the average growth option value is 0.54. Yet some firms obtain most of their value from growth options, and others, such as Rockwell, have more modest value attributable to growth options (18 percent). Likewise, even in an industry such as stone, clay, glass, and concrete, in which firms tend to derive very little of their value from growth options, firms exist that obtain more than a quarter (i.e., 26 percent) of their value from growth options. The value of a firm's growth options will therefore be driven not only by its industry, but by its own strategic investments and capabilities. When investing in a new industry or when benchmarking a firm vis-à-vis rivals, it can be useful to

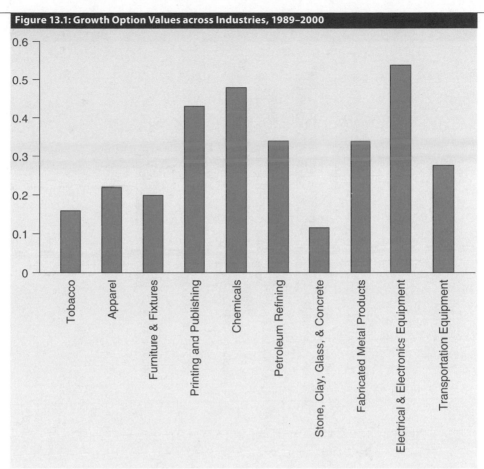

**Figure 13.1: Growth Option Values across Industries, 1989–2000**

determine when value is due to growth options or to reliance on assets in their present uses to understand firms' competitive positions and future prospects.[43]

These patterns indicate that real options analysis is important not only as a tool that can begin to reconcile strategic considerations and capital budgeting, and as a method for evaluating "go–no go" decisions for individual strategic investments, but also because real options are an important source of value for many firms. As such, companies need to obtain, exercise, and manage options appropriately. The objective of the firm is not to maximize option value per se, but to obtain the option value from the investments they undertake specifically for their flexibility benefits. Managers therefore need to understand what drives option value and how specific options can be valued.

## Value Drivers for Real Options

Once a particular type of option has been identified as being embedded in a strategic investment decision, the next task for decision makers is to determine how particular aspects of the investment correspond to the value drivers for real options. The value of real options is driven by five factors, as shown in Table 13.2.[44] For simplicity, we will focus on call options, though the value of put options can also be described in terms of the same five

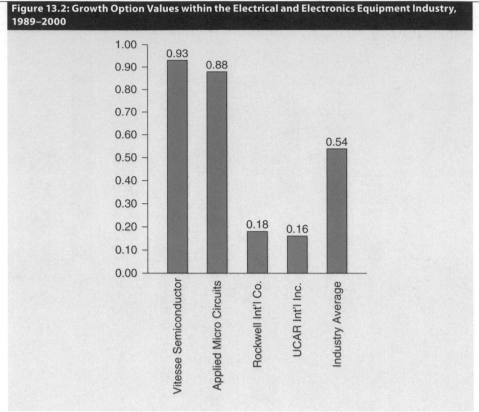

**Figure 13.2: Growth Option Values within the Electrical and Electronics Equipment Industry, 1989–2000**

variables. Furthermore, each of these factors is analogous to the individual value drivers for financial calls.

First, the current value of the underlying asset ($S$) is akin to the current price of a stock. For real options, the current value of the underlying asset is equivalent to the present value of the estimated cash flows associated with the underlying asset, or second-stage investment. This value sets the starting point for potential variations in the value of the second-stage investment in the future. For example, if a firm builds a scaleable plant in Stage I, the value of the underlying asset is equal to the present value of the cash flow attributable to expansion of the plant in Stage II, say, three years in the future. The higher this present value, the greater the likelihood that it will ultimately finish higher than the cost of exercising the option, $X$. The exercise price is therefore equal to the amount that must be paid three years in the future to expand the plant. In this particular example, $X$ amounts to capital expenditures that the firm must make to expand the facility. As such, option value increases in $S$ and decreases in $X$, just as the NPV of any investment increases in the cash flows generated in the future and decreases in the initial investment required.

However, in the case of an option, the commitment is made in the future rather than at time zero. This future commitment, or exercise price, is therefore discounted at the risk-free rate of return ($r_f$) because it is assumed to be fixed and known with certainty at the time the option is purchased. Increases in the risk-free rate therefore discount the exercise

**Table 13.2: Drivers of Call Option Value**

| Parameter | Definition | Effect of Increase in Parameter | Logic |
|---|---|---|---|
| $S$ | Value of the underlying asset | ↑ Value of option | The higher the value is today, the better the chance the option has to finish in the money, or be worth more than its exercise price. |
| $X$ | Cost of exercise | ↓ Value of option | Increasing the cost to exercise decreases the opportunity for a positive payout. |
| $r_f$ | Risk-free rate | ↑ Value of option | The exercise price is discounted at the risk-free rate. Increases in the risk-free rate therefore decrease the cost of investment ($X$). |
| $t$ | Time to investment | ↑ Value of option | Additional time increases the likelihood for the option to finish in the money. |
| $\sigma$ | Volatility | ↑ Value of option | Volatility creates both additional upside and downside potential. Since options allow firms to access upside opportunities while limiting downside risk, higher volatility increases option value. |

price more substantially, which implies that the option value increases. It is also the case that the ability to delay this decision for a longer period of time enhances the firm's discretion and flexibility, so with everything else held constant, the value of the option also increases in the time to investment ($t$). In the simple example just discussed, the option value of building a second-stage plant after four years will be greater than for a similar project after three years, with everything else held constant.

Finally, whereas uncertainty is considered a liability for typical investment projects, in the case of call options, uncertainty relates *positively* to option value. This is because of the inherent properties of options: the firm has the right but not the obligation to take some future specified action. In the presence of uncertainty, this means that the firm is able to limit its downside risk and access upside opportunities. Given these two asymmetries between right versus obligation and upside opportunities versus downside risk, this implies that increases in uncertainty enhance, rather than detract from, option value. In the worst-case scenario, the firm is compelled to do nothing, but if uncertainty leads to very favorable outcomes, the firm is positioned to act on them. In other words, with options the firm is more exposed to positive developments and not exposed to negative developments.[45] The uncertainty dimension is represented by the parameter *volatility* ($\sigma$) in Table 13.2.

The five parameters can be summarized by two values that fully capture the value of real options.[46] First, the value of the underlying asset ($S$) can be divided by the present value (PV) of the exercise price $[PV(X) = X/(1 + r_f)^t]$ to yield $NPV_q = S/PV(X)$. This expression is called $NPV_q$ because the value attached to the future cash flows relative to the exercise price is stated in quotient form. This expression provides an indication of how far the value of the underlying asset is above or below the present value of the exercise price of the option. When $NPV_q > 1$, the option is "in the money," in that the value of the underlying asset is worth more than the present value of the cost of obtaining it. Conversely, when $NPV_q < 1$, the option is "out of the money," or the value of the underlying asset falls short of the present value of the cost to acquire it. The greater the value of $NPV_q$, the greater the value of the option, as depicted in Figure 13.3.

Second, the volatility and time to investment parameters can similarly be combined into a single variable driving option value. In this case, the variable is referred to as *cumula-*

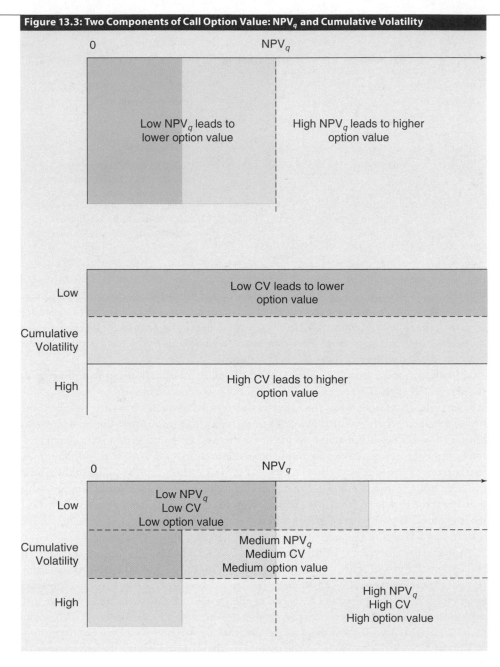

**Figure 13.3: Two Components of Call Option Value: $NPV_q$ and Cumulative Volatility**

0          $NPV_q$

Low $NPV_q$ leads to lower option value

High $NPV_q$ leads to higher option value

Low

Low CV leads to lower option value

Cumulative Volatility

High

High CV leads to higher option value

0          $NPV_q$

Low

Low $NPV_q$
Low CV
Low option value

Cumulative Volatility

Medium $NPV_q$
Medium CV
Medium option value

High

High $NPV_q$
High CV
High option value

*tive volatility* and is defined as: Cumulative Volatility (CV) = $\sigma\sqrt{t}$. Sigma, $\sigma$, is equal to the standard deviation in annual returns to the underlying asset, and *t* is equal to the number of years until exercise. This expression indicates that it is the combination of volatility per period and the time until exercise that drives option value. As Figure 13.3 indicates, holding $NPV_q$ constant, the higher the value of cumulative volatility, the higher the value of the call option. As will be discussed in the next section, once $NPV_q$ and $\sigma\sqrt{t}$ are determined, it is possible to use a table to look up the value of an option.

## Valuation of Real Options

Many different techniques are used to value real options, and the purpose of this chapter is not to present these approaches in an exhaustive manner nor to delve into the technical complexities of valuing real options in practice. Rather, the objective is to illustrate the application of two different approaches commonly used in the valuation of real options and to offer a brief introduction to real option valuation. We recommend that readers refer to the appendix for an overview of real options valuation techniques as well as application guidelines. In large-scale projects for which real option valuation is appropriate, financial experts and others may be engaged in developing very sophisticated and customized valuation models. However, even relatively straightforward models such as those presented in the appendix can yield important insights over applications of traditional financial theory, and such insights can assist managers in reconciling strategic analyses and capital budgeting processes.

## Implementation Requirements of Real Options

While current thinking on real options has focused primarily on identifying the options that firms obtain from various investments and operational practices, considerably less has been considered or written on the side of organization and the implementation requirements presented by real options. At the broadest level, it seems intuitive to suggest that firms seeking value from real options require organizations and systems that enable them to implement flexible strategies effectively; however, details on how real options or strategic flexibility ought to be implemented best require more development.

When implementation requirements are being considered, it is important as a first broad-brush distinction to differentiate the *analysis* of real options from real option investments *per se*. Regarding the former, the above discussion of how real options analyses might be used in strategic decision-making processes suggests a variety of approaches, ranging from the qualitative to the very formal.[47] For some firms, real options can be as much a way of thinking or an organizational process in itself as a formal analytical tool. However, critics of real options analysis sometimes suggest that it is overly technical and beyond the mathematical competence of many managers. It is true that many of the firms that have adopted real options analysis, often without appropriate procedures to evaluate options,[48] have abandoned this technique, and many express concerns about its complexity.[49] While these concerns are often well-placed and tend to deal with violation of assumptions and difficulties associated with valuation models, sometimes they are merely a result of communication problems rather than more substantive ones.[50] The fact that this technique became popular during the time when Internet stocks became highly overvalued (and subsequently lost most of their value) didn't help its cause.[51] Nor did the fact help that Enron and other companies caught up in scandals were among its early adopters.

Nevertheless, as the illustrations found in this chapter and appendix suggest, considerable insights can be gained from relatively simple extensions of existing techniques such as discounted cash flow models and decision tree analysis. Firms will also likely benefit from establishing ground rules for the use of this technique and targeting its application to large projects for which the NPV is uncertain. The adoption of real options analysis in some ways might resemble the replacement of other valuation methods (e.g., payback criteria, valuation multiples, etc.) by currently used financial valuation approaches. Suggestions for beginning this transition in firms include conducting one or more experimental pilot projects, getting support from top managers and those involved in the project, codifying the real options technique through an expert group and training materials, and institutionalizing real options analysis as a way of thinking as well as an analytical tool.[52]

Turning attention to the real options themselves, the question of implementation requirements in essence boils down to whether and how executives of business units that depend on real options should be managed any differently from other units. If much of the value that such managers add to, or detract from, the firm is due to their option formation and exercise decisions, the use of financial metrics geared to assessing current operational performance can be problematic. As one example, if managers are punished for "failures" that arise on the basis of the state of the world that is actually realized, this approach to performance assessment misses the more important point that the manager might have faced a wide range of possible outcomes at the time of investment and appropriately structured an investment to minimize downside risk while positioning the firm to capture upside opportunities had external conditions turned out differently.[53] Such problems might be avoided by examining a portfolio of projects under the control of management, distinguishing uncertainties that are partially under the control and beyond the control of managers, and relying on additional information to judge management performance and provide incentives for appropriate behavior.

# Summary

■  A real option provides a firm with the right, but not the obligation, to take some future specified action. This enables the firm to reduce its downside risk while accessing upside opportunities. Types of real options include growth, abandonment, switching, deferral, and compound options. Each of these types is relevant in different strategic contexts.

■  Real options challenge received wisdom on firms' motives and payoffs from strategic investments. For example, joint ventures are seen as stepping stones rather than marriages. The benefits of foreign direct investment include not only operational control, but also operational flexibility.

■  Real options help reconcile strategic analysis and financial analysis. Real options inject strategic reality (active management and follow-on opportunities) into traditional financial theory (discounted cash flow analyses and net present value), while bringing the discipline of the financial markets and the rigor of quantitative investment criteria into strategic analyses.

■  Real options shift firms' investment thresholds. Firms might economically invest in projects that have negative net present values if the value of embedded options is sufficiently high such that the value of the first-stage investment plus the value of embedded options is greater than zero. Conversely, firms might avoid investment decisions with positive net present values if such decisions require them to give up valuable options. In such cases, the net present value of the investment has to not only be greater than zero, but also greater than the value of options that are sacrificed. Managers intuitively incorporate the value of forgone deferral options into their investment decisions by requiring net present values to be substantially positive.

- Options can represent a substantial portion of firm value. The economic importance of real options differs across industries as well as across firms within industries.

- The value of an option is driven by five parameters: the underlying asset, the exercise price, the risk-free rate of return, the time to exercise, and uncertainty (volatility). These can be collapsed into two summary parameters: $NPV_q$ and cumulative volatility. Quantitative assessment of options can be conducted, and options can be compared, using these parameters.

- Real options have unique implementation requirements, so businesses that depend on real options must use appropriate monitoring, control, and incentive systems to address potential biases in managers' option purchase and exercise decisions. Firms using real options analyses as a part of their strategic resource allocation process must also institute appropriate systems for this tool for evaluating investment projects.

- Adoption of real options analysis might be facilitated by pilot projects, endorsement by top managers, codification efforts, and institutionalizing both the strategic thinking and more formal aspects of real options analysis.

- The appendix shows that option values can be calculated using the Black-Scholes approach, the Black-Scholes approximation technique, and binomial lattices. Each of these methods requires different input data and assumptions. In instances in which assumptions are violated, more sophisticated option valuation models can be used, or simple valuation models can be implemented based on knowledge of the expected direction of bias.

- In Black-Scholes valuation models, the uncertainty parameter is often the one that is most difficult to obtain. Sigma can be estimated from historical returns data and from benchmark, pure-play companies, yet sensitivity analyses that calculate option value for a range of uncertainty values are useful.

## Ethics Questions

1. What are the ethical implications of making an investment that appears to be a money loser in the short term on the basis that there will be options to make money from the opportunities that the investment provides in the longer term? For instance, as a shareholder, would you be comfortable with a management team that routinely makes these types of decisions?

2. How can a firm include human issues (such as the well-being of employees, or human risk factors) in a real options analysis?

3. Can real options analysis be used to justify poor decisions? If so, what are the agency implications? What are the legal implications?

4. How can a board of directors ensure that real options analysis does not result in management decisions that hurt shareholders and other important stakeholders?

# Appendix: Detailed Valuation Guidelines

Here we provide detailed guidelines for using the Black-Scholes valuation method, as well as an alternative to the Black-Scholes method called *binomial lattices*. We conclude with a discussion of several practical application issues.

## Black-Scholes Valuation

The **Black-Scholes option pricing formula** for a European financial call option is often used to value real options. A European option can be exercised only on the date of the option's maturity. Finance textbooks present the details of this technique, and we will only summarize the essentials for application to real option valuation. The Black-Scholes formula is:

$$\text{Call Option Value} = [S \times N(d_1)] - [\text{PV}(X) \times N(d_2)],$$

where $S$ = current value of the underlying asset, $\text{PV}(X)$ = present value of the exercise price, $N(\cdot)$ = standard normal cumulative distribution function, $d_1 = [\log(S/X) + (r_f + 0.5\sigma^2)t]/[\sigma\sqrt{t}]$, $d_2 = d_1 - \sigma\sqrt{t}$, $\sigma$ = standard deviation of returns, and $t$ = years to maturity.

Notice that in addition to a table for the normal distribution, the five parameters just discussed are sufficient to calculate option values using the Black-Scholes formula. There are four steps to calculating a call option's value using this approach:

1. Calculate the value of the underlying asset and the present value of the exercise price, $\text{PV}(X)$.
2. Determine $d_1$ and $d_2$ using these two values as well as $\sigma$ and $t$.
3. Use the normal distribution table to find $N(d_1)$ and $N(d_2)$.
4. Use the Black-Scholes formula to compute the option value.

An example will help to clarify this approach. Upon graduation, an MBA student takes a position as the vice president of purchasing for a small firm in Wisconsin, an airline called Dairy Air. She is trying to complete negotiations with a French aircraft manufacturer for a new plane. Given her firm's current financial condition, she does not seek to acquire a new plane for operations today. In fact, the French firm is demanding a price of $100 million, but she determines that it would only be worth $90 million given the current industry environment. However, for planning purposes she would like to be able to lock in a price and potentially add a new aircraft to the firm's fleet in the next few years if demand for travel improves. She assumes that $\sigma = 0.50$ and the risk-free rate of return is 5 percent. The French company is requesting a payment of $25 million for an option to purchase the plane for $100 million in three years, and the question is whether Dairy Air should secure this option at a price of $25 million.

*Step 1: Calculate the value of the underlying asset and the present value of the exercise price,* $\text{PV}(X)$. The student has already estimated the value of the underlying asset to be $90 million. The present value of the exercise price, $\text{PV}(X)$, is given by $\$100e^{-0.05(3)} = \$86.07$ million. This latter expression reflects continuous compounding at 5 percent for three years. (If annual compounding were used as a simplification, the present value of the exercise price would be $86.38 million.)

*Step 2: Determine $d_1$ and $d_2$ using these two values as well as $\sigma$ and $t$.*

$$d_1 = [\log(S/X) + (r_f + 0.5\sigma^2)t]/[\sigma\sqrt{t}]$$
$$= [\log(90/100) + (0.05 + 0.5(0.5)^2)3]/[0.5\sqrt{3}] = 0.4846;$$
$$d_2 = d_1 - \sigma\sqrt{t} = 0.4846 - 0.5\sqrt{3} = -0.3815.$$

*Step 3: Use the normal distribution table to find $N(d_1)$ and $N(d_2)$.* Using a table for the standard normal cumulative distribution function yields $N(d_1) = N(0.4846) = 0.6860$ and $N(d_2) = N(-0.3815) = 0.3514$.

*Step 4: Use the Black-Scholes formula to compute the option value.* By this formula, the call option value = $[S \times N(d_1)] - [PV(X) \times N(d_2)] = 90(0.6860) - 86.07(0.3514) =$ $31.49 million.

Given that this value exceeds the price the aircraft manufacturer is asking for the option on the plane, $25 million, Dairy Air should proceed with the option purchase.

This example simplified the calculation in a number of ways. First, the value of the underlying asset was given. When this value is not available, it can be estimated by pro forma statements of cash flows and by addressing two complications. These cash flows include both the cost of exercising the option and the cash flows enjoyed by the firm after it exercises the option. Hence, the costs associated with the commitment to the project (e.g., the capital expenditure) need to be separated from the cash flows and counted as part of $X$. Other cash flows, including routine capital expenditures, become part of the cash flows used to calculate $S$. The cash flows attached to $S$ will be discounted by the risk-adjusted discount rate to reflect the riskiness of these cash flows. By contrast, cash flows making up $X$ are discounted at the risk-free rate to reflect the fact that the cost of exercise is assumed by the Black-Scholes approach to be fixed and known with certainty at time zero.

Second, the volatility parameter was also given. Obtaining a measure of the investment's volatility can also be a challenging task. Obtaining an estimate for this parameter can be accomplished by gathering historical data, using industry standards as a benchmark, or taking an educated guess based on similar projects or experience. Sensitivity analysis therefore becomes important when estimating volatility, and it is recommended that a range of volatilities and their corresponding option values be computed. For example, if call option values are calculated for a range of sigmas ($\sigma$), a chart like Figure 13.4 can be constructed to determine the break-even value for the volatility parameter for the firm to go forward with the purchase of the option. The horizontal dashed line represents the payment of $25 million for the option, and the graph indicates that as long as the volatility parameter is clearly greater than 0.40, it makes sense for Dairy Air to purchase the option. If uncertainty is lower than this value, the value of the option drops below its purchase price, and the firm should not go forward with the contract with its present terms. Additional application issues and guidelines are mentioned below.

## Black-Scholes Approximation

As noted earlier in the chapter, the five parameters making up the value drivers for options can be reduced to two summary parameters: (1) $NPV_q$, and (2) cumulative volatility. Once these two values are known, the value of an option can be approximated by looking up a value in a table instead of using the Black-Scholes formula above. Even when values can readily be obtained by the Black-Scholes approach, this approximation technique is useful because it is intuitively appealing, requires less mathematical background, and is easier to

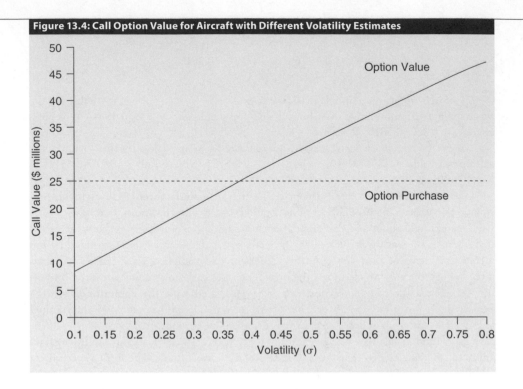

**Figure 13.4: Call Option Value for Aircraft with Different Volatility Estimates**

communicate to others involved in evaluating a project. This method involves the following four steps:

1. Calculate NPV$_q$.
2. Calculate cumulative volatility.
3. Look up the table value expressing the value of the option as a percentage of the value of the underlying asset (see Table 13.3).
4. Multiply the table value by the value of the underlying asset in order to calculate the option value.

This approach can be applied to the option contract for the aircraft just discussed:

*Step 1: Calculate NPV$_q$.* NPV$_q$ = S/PV(X), and for simplicity we will use annual compounding to discount the exercise price. Hence, NPV$_q$ = $S/[X/(1 + r_f)^t)] = 90/[100/(1.05)^3]$ = 1.04.

*Step 2: Calculate cumulative volatility.* Cumulative volatility = $\sigma\sqrt{t} = 0.5\sqrt{3} = 0.87$.

*Step 3: Look up the table value expressing the value of the option as a percentage of the value of the underlying asset.* On Table 13.3, NPV$_q$ is found moving from top to bottom along the left side of the chart, and cumulative volatility is found moving from left to right along the top of the chart. NPV$_q$ = 1.04 is found along the left side and the closest cumulative volatility of 0.85 is found on the other axis; the table value equals 34.2 percent for this pair. Interpolation yields 34.92 percent for the cumulative volatility of 0.87.

*Step 4: Multiply the table value by the value of the underlying asset to calculate the option value.* The value of the call option equals 34.92 percent of the value of the underlying asset,

**Table 13.3 : Black-Scholes European Call Option Pricing Table (% of underlying asset value)**

| NPV$_q$ | Cumulative Volatility | | | | | | | | | | | | | | | | | | | |
|---|---|---|---|---|---|---|---|---|---|---|---|---|---|---|---|---|---|---|---|---|
| | 0.05 | 0.10 | 0.15 | 0.20 | 0.25 | 0.30 | 0.35 | 0.40 | 0.45 | 0.50 | 0.55 | 0.60 | 0.65 | 0.70 | 0.75 | 0.80 | 0.85 | 0.90 | 0.95 | 1.00 |
| 0.50 | 0.0 | 0.0 | 0.0 | 0.0 | 0.0 | 0.2 | 0.4 | 0.9 | 1.7 | 2.6 | 3.3 | 5.1 | 6.5 | 8.1 | 9.8 | 11.5 | 13.3 | 15.2 | 17.1 | 19.1 |
| 0.60 | 0.0 | 0.0 | 0.0 | 0.0 | 0.2 | 0.7 | 1.4 | 2.4 | 3.7 | 5.1 | 6.6 | 8.3 | 10.0 | 11.9 | 13.7 | 15.7 | 17.6 | 19.6 | 21.6 | 23.6 |
| 0.70 | 0.0 | 0.0 | 0.1 | 0.4 | 1.0 | 2.0 | 3.3 | 4.8 | 6.5 | 8.2 | 10.0 | 11.9 | 13.8 | 15.8 | 17.3 | 19.8 | 21.8 | 23.8 | 25.8 | 27.7 |
| 0.75 | 0.0 | 0.0 | 0.2 | 0.8 | 1.8 | 3.1 | 4.6 | 6.3 | 8.1 | 10.0 | 11.9 | 13.8 | 15.8 | 17.8 | 19.3 | 21.8 | 23.8 | 25.8 | 27.7 | 29.7 |
| 0.80 | 0.0 | 0.1 | 0.5 | 1.5 | 2.8 | 4.4 | 6.2 | 8.0 | 9.9 | 11.8 | 13.8 | 15.8 | 17.8 | 19.8 | 21.8 | 23.7 | 25.7 | 27.7 | 29.6 | 31.6 |
| 0.82 | 0.0 | 0.1 | 0.7 | 1.9 | 3.3 | 5.0 | 6.8 | 8.7 | 10.6 | 12.6 | 14.6 | 16.6 | 18.6 | 20.6 | 22.5 | 24.5 | 26.5 | 28.4 | 30.4 | 32.3 |
| 0.84 | 0.0 | 0.2 | 1.0 | 2.3 | 3.9 | 5.7 | 7.5 | 9.4 | 11.4 | 13.4 | 15.4 | 17.4 | 19.4 | 21.3 | 23.3 | 25.3 | 27.2 | 29.2 | 31.1 | 33.0 |
| 0.86 | 0.0 | 0.3 | 1.3 | 2.8 | 4.5 | 6.3 | 8.2 | 10.2 | 12.2 | 14.2 | 16.1 | 18.1 | 20.1 | 22.1 | 24.1 | 26.0 | 28.0 | 29.9 | 31.8 | 33.7 |
| 0.88 | 0.0 | 0.5 | 1.8 | 3.4 | 5.2 | 7.1 | 9.0 | 11.0 | 13.0 | 14.9 | 16.9 | 18.9 | 20.9 | 22.9 | 24.8 | 26.8 | 28.7 | 30.6 | 32.5 | 34.4 |
| 0.90 | 0.0 | 0.8 | 2.3 | 4.0 | 5.9 | 7.8 | 9.8 | 11.8 | 13.7 | 15.7 | 17.7 | 19.7 | 21.7 | 23.6 | 25.6 | 27.5 | 29.4 | 31.3 | 33.2 | 35.1 |
| 0.92 | 0.1 | 1.2 | 2.8 | 4.7 | 6.6 | 8.6 | 10.6 | 12.6 | 14.5 | 16.5 | 18.5 | 20.5 | 22.5 | 24.4 | 26.3 | 28.3 | 30.2 | 32.0 | 33.9 | 35.1 |
| 0.94 | 0.3 | 1.7 | 3.5 | 5.4 | 7.4 | 9.4 | 11.4 | 13.4 | 15.4 | 17.3 | 19.3 | 21.3 | 23.2 | 25.2 | 27.1 | 29.0 | 30.9 | 32.7 | 34.6 | 36.4 |
| 0.96 | 0.6 | 2.3 | 4.2 | 6.2 | 8.2 | 10.2 | 12.2 | 14.2 | 16.2 | 18.1 | 20.1 | 22.0 | 24.0 | 25.9 | 27.8 | 29.7 | 31.6 | 33.4 | 35.2 | 37.0 |
| 0.98 | 1.2 | 3.1 | 5.1 | 7.1 | 9.1 | 11.1 | 13.0 | 15.0 | 17.0 | 18.9 | 20.9 | 22.8 | 24.7 | 26.6 | 28.5 | 30.4 | 32.2 | 34.1 | 35.9 | 37.7 |
| 1.00 | 2.0 | 4.0 | 6.0 | 8.0 | 10.0 | 11.9 | 13.9 | 15.9 | 17.8 | 19.7 | 21.7 | 23.6 | 25.5 | 27.4 | 29.2 | 31.1 | 32.9 | 34.7 | 36.5 | 38.3 |
| 1.02 | 3.1 | 5.0 | 7.0 | 8.9 | 10.9 | 12.8 | 14.8 | 16.7 | 18.6 | 20.5 | 22.5 | 24.3 | 26.2 | 28.1 | 29.9 | 31.8 | 33.6 | 35.4 | 37.2 | 38.9 |
| 1.04 | 4.5 | 6.1 | 8.0 | 9.9 | 11.8 | 13.7 | 15.6 | 17.5 | 19.5 | 21.3 | 23.2 | 25.1 | 27.0 | 28.8 | 30.6 | 32.4 | 34.2 | 36.0 | 37.8 | 38.9 |
| 1.06 | 6.0 | 7.3 | 9.1 | 10.5 | 12.8 | 14.6 | 16.5 | 18.4 | 20.3 | 22.1 | 24.0 | 25.9 | 27.7 | 29.5 | 31.3 | 33.1 | 34.9 | 36.6 | 38.4 | 40.1 |
| 1.08 | 7.5 | 8.6 | 10.2 | 11.5 | 13.7 | 15.6 | 17.4 | 19.3 | 21.1 | 22.9 | 24.8 | 26.6 | 28.4 | 30.2 | 32.0 | 33.8 | 35.5 | 37.3 | 39.0 | 40.7 |
| 1.10 | 9.1 | 10.0 | 11.4 | 13.0 | 14.7 | 16.5 | 18.3 | 20.1 | 21.9 | 23.7 | 25.5 | 27.3 | 29.1 | 30.9 | 32.7 | 34.4 | 36.2 | 37.9 | 39.6 | 41.3 |
| 1.12 | 10.7 | 11.3 | 12.6 | 14.1 | 15.7 | 17.4 | 19.2 | 21.0 | 22.7 | 24.5 | 26.3 | 28.1 | 29.8 | 31.6 | 33.3 | 35.1 | 36.8 | 38.5 | 40.2 | 41.8 |
| 1.14 | 12.3 | 12.7 | 13.8 | 15.2 | 16.7 | 18.4 | 20.1 | 21.8 | 23.5 | 25.3 | 27.0 | 28.8 | 30.5 | 32.3 | 34.0 | 35.7 | 37.4 | 39.1 | 40.7 | 42.4 |
| 1.16 | 13.8 | 14.1 | 15.0 | 16.3 | 17.7 | 19.3 | 21.0 | 22.6 | 24.4 | 26.1 | 27.8 | 29.5 | 31.2 | 32.9 | 34.6 | 36.3 | 38.0 | 39.6 | 41.3 | 42.9 |
| 1.18 | 15.3 | 15.4 | 16.2 | 17.4 | 18.7 | 20.3 | 21.9 | 23.5 | 25.2 | 26.8 | 28.5 | 30.2 | 31.9 | 33.6 | 35.3 | 36.9 | 38.6 | 40.2 | 41.8 | 43.4 |
| 1.20 | 16.7 | 16.8 | 17.4 | 18.5 | 19.8 | 21.2 | 22.7 | 24.3 | 26.0 | 27.6 | 29.3 | 30.9 | 32.6 | 34.2 | 35.9 | 37.2 | 39.2 | 40.8 | 42.4 | 44.0 |
| 1.25 | 20.0 | 20.0 | 20.4 | 21.2 | 22.3 | 23.5 | 24.9 | 26.4 | 27.9 | 29.5 | 31.0 | 32.6 | 34.2 | 35.8 | 37.4 | 39.0 | 40.6 | 42.1 | 43.7 | 45.2 |
| 1.30 | 23.1 | 23.1 | 23.3 | 23.9 | 24.7 | 25.8 | 27.1 | 28.4 | 29.8 | 31.3 | 32.8 | 34.3 | 35.8 | 37.4 | 38.9 | 40.4 | 41.9 | 43.5 | 45.0 | 46.5 |
| 1.35 | 25.9 | 25.9 | 26.0 | 26.4 | 27.1 | 28.1 | 29.2 | 30.4 | 31.7 | 33.1 | 34.5 | 35.9 | 37.4 | 38.8 | 40.3 | 41.8 | 43.3 | 44.7 | 46.2 | 47.7 |

(continued)

**Table 13.3** (*continued*)

| NPV$_q$ | | | | | | | | | Cumulative Volatility | | | | | | | | | | | |
|---|---|---|---|---|---|---|---|---|---|---|---|---|---|---|---|---|---|---|---|---|
| | 0.05 | 0.10 | 0.15 | 0.20 | 0.25 | 0.30 | 0.35 | 0.40 | 0.45 | 0.50 | 0.55 | 0.60 | 0.65 | 0.70 | 0.75 | 0.80 | 0.85 | 0.90 | 0.95 | 1.00 |
| 1.40 | 28.6 | 28.6 | 28.6 | 28.9 | 29.9 | 30.2 | 31.2 | 32.3 | 33.5 | 34.8 | 36.1 | 37.5 | 38.9 | 40.3 | 41.7 | 43.1 | 44.5 | 46.0 | 47.4 | 48.8 |
| 1.45 | 31.0 | 31.0 | 31.1 | 31.2 | 31.7 | 32.3 | 33.2 | 34.2 | 35.3 | 36.5 | 37.7 | 39.0 | 40.3 | 41.7 | 43.0 | 44.4 | 45.8 | 47.1 | 48.5 | 49.9 |
| 1.50 | 33.3 | 33.3 | 33.4 | 33.5 | 33.8 | 34.3 | 35.1 | 36.0 | 37.0 | 38.1 | 39.2 | 40.4 | 41.7 | 43.0 | 44.3 | 45.6 | 46.9 | 48.3 | 49.6 | 50.9 |
| 1.75 | 42.9 | 42.9 | 42.9 | 42.9 | 42.9 | 43.1 | 43.5 | 44.0 | 44.6 | 45.3 | 46.1 | 47.0 | 48.0 | 49.0 | 50.1 | 51.1 | 52.2 | 53.3 | 54.5 | 55.6 |
| 2.00 | 50.0 | 50.0 | 50.0 | 50.0 | 50.0 | 50.1 | 50.2 | 50.5 | 50.8 | 51.3 | 51.9 | 55.5 | 53.3 | 54.0 | 54.9 | 55.8 | 56.7 | 57.6 | 58.6 | 59.5 |
| 2.50 | 60.0 | 60.0 | 60.0 | 60.0 | 60.0 | 60.0 | 60.0 | 60.1 | 60.2 | 60.4 | 60.7 | 61.0 | 61.4 | 61.9 | 62.4 | 63.0 | 63.6 | 64.3 | 65.0 | 65.7 |

and the value of the underlying asset is $90 million. Therefore, the value of the option is (34.92 percent)($90 million) = $31.42 million.

The result of $31.42 million compares favorably with the $31.49 million calculated earlier.

## Binomial Lattices

An alternative to the Black-Scholes methods described above that is also intuitively appealing and mathematically straightforward relies upon the construction of lattices, also known as *decision trees*.[54] These lattices are referred to as *binomial lattices* because the value of an asset can assume two values based on an "up" or "down" movement in value each period; and following a succession of such up and down movements, the possible values for the underlying asset follow a binomial distribution. In the Black-Scholes example above, this stochastic process was reflected in the uncertainty parameter sigma instead, but as the number of nodes in a lattice increases, the distributions approach one another, as do the valuations obtained from the two methods.

These up and down movements are represented by two parameters, $u$ and $d$, respectively. For instance, suppose that $u = 1.1$ and $d = 0.9091$. If these parameters are known, along with the value of the underlying asset at time zero, then the entire stochastic process for the asset over time can be modeled by constructing an event tree. For example, if the value of the underlying asset begins at $V_0 = \$100$, then after one period, the value of the asset will be either $V_u = 1.1(100) = 110$ or $V_d = 0.9091(100) = 90.91$. Suppose that these values occur with equal probability. In the second period, the asset will be worth $V_{uu} = (1.1)^2(100) = 121$ if an up movement was followed by another up movement. At the opposite extreme, following two down movements, the asset will be valued at $V_{dd} = (0.9091)^2(100) = 82.64$. If the asset experiences an up movement followed by a down movement in the lattice, it will take on a value of $V_{ud} = (1.1)(0.9091)(100) = 100$, which is equivalent to $V_{du} = (0.9091)(1.1)(100) = 100$. Note that these values equal the initial value of the asset, $V_0 = 100$, because $u = 1/d$. Figure 13.5 gives the event tree for this asset. The first step in valuing options using binomial lattices is to construct such an event tree.

The next step is to convert the event tree to a decision tree. While an event tree portrays how the value of the underlying asset moves over time, a decision tree depicts how managers make decisions within this tree in order to maximize the value of the option. For illustration, suppose that a manager has the right to acquire the above asset initially worth $100 for an exercise price of $115. The question is how much such an option is worth. If we

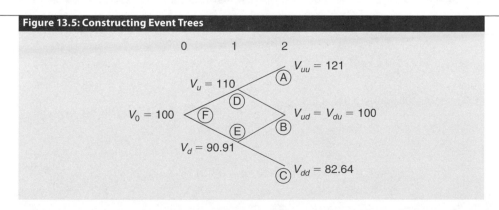

**Figure 13.5: Constructing Event Trees**

define $C_0$ to be the value of this option at time zero, we can similarly define the value of the option at various nodes in the lattice. For example, after a single up movement, the value of the call option is $C_u$, the value of the call option after an up and down movement is $C_{ud}$, and so forth. The nodes on the event tree in Figure 13.5 have been labeled A–F to describe particular positions in the lattice.

The key to constructing the decision tree is to work backwards in the event tree to calculate the value of the option at each node. Starting at node A (see Figure 13.6), the manager has the decision to do nothing and earn zero, or to exercise the call option and obtain the value of the asset, $V_{uu}$, less the exercise price of 115. The value of the option at this node can therefore be written as $C_{uu} = \max(V_{uu} - 115, 0)$. Since $V_{uu} = 121$, this formula can be rewritten as $\max(121 - 115, 0)$. The manager therefore chooses to exercise the option to get \$6, rather than do nothing and get zero. $C_{uu}$ therefore equals 6. At node B, the same calculation is made. Here, $C_{ud} = \max(V_{ud} - 115, 0) = \max(100 - 115, 0)$. Here, exercising the option would lead the firm to obtain $-\$5$, while the manager could do nothing and obtain zero; so the option is not exercised. Thus, $C_{ud} = 0$. Similarly at node C, the value of the underlying asset falls short of the exercise price; the option would not be exercised, and $C_{dd} = 0$.

At this time, the last column in the tree is complete, and the intermediate nodes that occur at the end of one year, nodes D and E, can be analyzed. At node D, the manager's choice is to exercise the option and claim the value of the underlying asset or to leave the option open for potential exercise in the future. In order to calculate this latter value, we need to be able to determine a present value for $C_{uu}$ and $C_{ud}$ by discounting these values for one period of time. The problem noted earlier is that we cannot simply use the risk-adjusted rate to calculate present values for option payouts.

The solution to this problem lies in using a technique called the *risk-neutral method*. Under typical applications of using discounted cash flow analysis to calculate present values, estimated cash flows are discounted at a risk-adjusted rate. For instance, in our particular illustration, given that there is an equal probability (0.5) of an up or down movement in the lattice, these objective probabilities can be used to calculate an expected payout in a successive period. This approach incorporates risk into the present value calculation by "punishing" the cash flows through a higher denominator, which incorporates the risk-adjusted discount rate. An alternative, less-known technique is to adjust the cash flows in

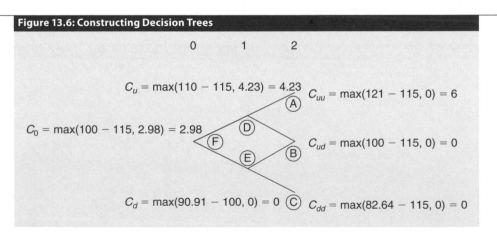

**Figure 13.6: Constructing Decision Trees**

PART 4 / MONITORING AND CREATING ENTREPRENEURIAL OPPORTUNITIES the numerator in such a way that these cash flows can simply be discounted at the risk-free rate instead. In the valuation of real options, this approach is particularly helpful because the risk of the project changes throughout the lattice, yet a single, simple discount rate can be employed by using the risk-neutral method (i.e., the risk-free rate). The technical details of the risk-free method are beyond the scope of this chapter, but for our purposes it is sufficient to introduce a single formula to permit such calculations of present values in decision trees.

The solution lies in converting the objective probabilities ($q = 0.50$ and $1 - q = 0.50$ in our case) to "risk-neutral" probabilities that can be used to weight payouts from different nodes in the lattice. The formula for the risk-neutral probability for the up movement is simply $p_u = [(1 + r_f) - d] \div (u - d)$ and $p_d = 1 - p_u$. If the risk-free rate of return is 5 percent, then $p_u = (1.05 - 0.9091) \div (1.1 - 0.9091) = 0.74$, and $p_d = 1 - 0.74 = 0.26$. We can now calculate the value of holding the option open at node D (see Figure 13.6) by weighting the option payouts at the two successive nodes in this "nest" by the risk-neutral probabilities and by discounting one period at the risk-free rate. Specifically, this value is $(p_u C_{uu} + p_d C_{ud}) \div (1 + r_f) = [0.74(6) + 0.26(0)] \div (1.05) = 4.23$. Thus, at node D, the value of the option is $C_u = \max(110 - 115, 4.23)$. In this case, the firm would obtain $110 - 115 = -5$ from exercising the option, and this option is worth 4.23 if a manager continues to hold it; so it is optimal to hold it rather than exercise it.

Moving to node E, the above calculations become considerably easier. We noted earlier that managers will not exercise the option at successive nodes B and C because the value of the underlying asset is less than the exercise price in both cases. Since there is certainty that the option will not be exercised regardless of the state of nature, the value of holding the option open at node E is also zero. Thus, the value of the option at node E can be written as $C_d = \max(90.91 - 115, 0)$. Even though the value of holding the option open at this node has no value, the manager will not exercise it because doing so yields a value of $90.91 - 115 = -24.09$. This suggests that the manager will simply allow the option to expire and ultimately obtain a value of zero.

Since we now know the value of the option at nodes D and E, we can fold back the calculations a final time to obtain the value of the option at time zero, $C_0$, which is the objective of the exercise. The firm can exercise the option at time zero, but it will not do so because the value of the asset (i.e., 100) is less than the exercise price (i.e., 115). The value of holding the option open is 4.23 at node D and 0 at node E. The value of holding the option open at time zero can be obtained by weighting these two values by the appropriate risk-neutral probabilities and discounting one period at the risk-free rate. That is, $C_0 = (p_u C_u + p_d C_d) \div (1 + r_f) = [0.74(4.23) + 0.26(0)] \div (1.05) = 2.98$.

The completed decision tree of Figure 13.6 can be used to draw several conclusions from this problem. First, as long as it costs no more than 2.98 to purchase this option, it is valuable for the firm to do so. Second, the option will not be exercised after one year because it is more valuable to hold the option rather than obtain the underlying asset at a price of 115. Third, in the final year, the option will be exercised only at node A, which means that the best-case scenario of two up movements in the asset's value has transpired.

This example illustrates that the risk-neutral method consists of five steps: (1) estimate the value of the underlying asset at time zero as well as the up and down parameters, $u$ and $d$; (2) construct an event tree that depicts how the value of the underlying asset increases or decreases over time; (3) calculate the value of the risk-neutral probabilities used in weighting values in the lattice for discounting purposes; (4) construct a decision tree that shows how the decision maker chooses to hold open or exercise the option at various nodes in the event tree; (5) work backwards in the lattice to value the option at all of the nodes. During this final step, the value of holding the option will be obtained by weighting the value of the option in the two successive nodes in the corresponding "nest" in the lattice and discounting at the risk-free rate. This technique can also be applied to put options, using a real-life example that was briefly mentioned above.[55]

An entrepreneur is considering starting up a firm to commercialize a new technology for producing synthetic mats to be used at construction sites to enable the transportation of heavy equipment around sites that often have poor soil conditions. Most firms use wooden mats to create temporary roads, staging areas, and support around the site, but such mats are quite heavy and bulky and therefore difficult to store and move. Firms had previously tried to produce mats of synthetic materials, but these initial products had serious drawbacks: they often maintained a "memory" of prior traffic of equipment and vehicles, and, even more problematic for use around hazardous materials, they exhibited electrostatic properties that created sparking conditions. The entrepreneur believes that the new technology solves these problems and represents a potential breakthrough product for construction sites.

Initial analysis indicated that $6.5 million would be needed in capital expenditures and working capital to start up this business, yet discounted cash flow analysis placed the NPV at −$1.112 million. This initial calculation suggests that the business idea should not be pursued, but the entrepreneur also believes that the initial plant could be sold for $4 million in three years and converted for the production of molded synthetics products if the initial business does not develop favorably. The entrepreneur wonders whether this embedded put option is sufficiently valuable to make the launch of the business sensible despite the negative NPV.

*Step 1: Estimate the value of the underlying asset at time zero as well as the up and down parameters, u and d.* To value the put option and draw a conclusion on this question, a number of inputs are needed. First, assume that the value of the underlying asset can increase by 64.9 percent or decrease by 39.3 percent each year, which corresponds to up and down parameters of 1.649 and 0.607, respectively. Also assume that the risk-free rate stands at 5.5 percent. We also need to obtain the starting value of the underlying asset in order to develop an event tree. This value can be inferred from the $6.5 million initial expenditure and the −$1.112 million NPV, which together indicate that the present value of the business's cash flows stands at $5.388 million.

*Step 2: Construct an event tree that depicts how the value of the underlying asset increases or decreases over time.* Based on the information provided, $V_0 = \$5.388$, and in this case we have a three-year problem, so we need to calculate $V_{uuu} = (1.649)^3(5.388) = 24.157$, $V_{uud} = (1.649)^2(0.607)(5.388) = 8.884$, $V_{udd} = 1.649(0.607)^2(5.388) = 3.270$, $V_{ddd} = (0.607)^3(5.388) = 1.205$, and the values in all intermediate years. Figure 13.7 shows the event tree for this problem.

*Step 3: Calculate the value of the risk-neutral probabilities used in weighting values in the lattice for discounting purposes.* The formula for the risk-neutral probability for the up movement is simply $p_u = [(1 + r_f) - d] \div (u - d)$, and $p_d = 1 - p_u$. For this particular problem, the inputs are as follows: the risk-free rate, $r_f$, is 5.5 percent; $u = 1.649$; and $d = 0.607$. Thus, $p_u = (1.055 - 0.607) \div (1.649 - 0.607) = 0.43$, and $p_d = 1 - p_u = 1 - 0.43 = 0.57$.

*Steps 4 and 5: (4) Construct a decision tree that shows how the decision maker chooses to hold open or exercise the option at various nodes in the event tree; and (5) work backwards in the lattice to value the option at all of the nodes.*

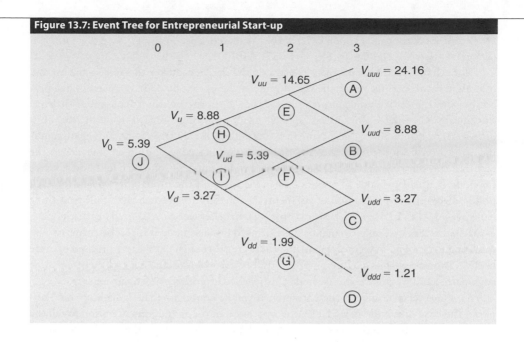

**Figure 13.7: Event Tree for Entrepreneurial Start-up**

|  | 0 | 1 | 2 | 3 |
|--|---|---|---|---|

$V_{uuu} = 24.16$  (A)

$V_{uu} = 14.65$  (E)

$V_u = 8.88$  (H)

$V_{uud} = 8.88$  (B)

$V_0 = 5.39$  (J)

$V_{ud} = 5.39$  (I)

$V_d = 3.27$  (F)

$V_{udd} = 3.27$  (C)

$V_{dd} = 1.99$  (G)

$V_{ddd} = 1.21$  (D)

In this problem, the decision maker has the right but not the obligation to sell the underlying asset for $4 million. Examining nodes A and B, the value of the underlying asset is considerably greater than $4 million, so the put option is not exercised and is allowed to expire, yielding a payout of zero. These facts, combined with the observation that the value of the underlying asset is worth more than 4 at node E also implies that the option is worth zero at this node as well.

The firm will exercise the abandonment, or put, option at nodes C and D. At node C we have $C_{udd} = \max(4 - 3.27, 0) = 0.73$. Notice for this problem that the value of the underlying asset is subtracted from the exercise price of the option in this case because the firm is *selling* the underlying asset because this is a put option. Similarly, at node D, $C_{ddd} = \max(4 - 1.21, 0) = 2.79$. Using this information from nodes C and D, we can work back to determine the value of the option at node G. The value to holding the option at node G is obtained by using the risk-neutral probabilities to weight the option values at nodes C and D, and then discounting this weighted value back one year at the risk-free rate. Thus, $C_{dd} = (p_u C_{udd} + p_d C_{ddd}) \div (1 + r_f) = [0.43(0.73) + 0.57(2.79)] \div (1.055) = 1.81$. The problem was set up such that the entrepreneur could only sell the equipment after three years, making the put option a European option, or one that could be exercised only at maturity. However, note in this case that if the entrepreneur could sell the equipment early, or an American option was involved, the entrepreneur would sell the equipment at this node and obtain $4 - 1.99 = 2.01$, which is greater than the value of holding onto the option (i.e., 1.81).

A similar approach is used to calculate the value of the option at node F. Here, $C_{ud} = (p_u C_{uud} + p_d C_{udd}) \div (1 + r_f) = [0.43(0) + 0.57(0.73)] \div (1.055) = 0.39$. Likewise, now that the value of the option at nodes E (i.e., 0), F (i.e., 0.39), and G (i.e., 1.81) are known, the values at H and I can be quickly obtained. At node H, $C_u = (p_u C_{uu} + p_d C_{ud}) \div (1 + r_f) = [0.43(0) + 0.57(0.39)] \div (1.055) = 0.21$. At node I, $C_d = (p_u C_{ud} + p_d C_{dd}) = (1 + r_f) =$

$[0.43(0.39) + 0.57(1.81)] \div (1.055) = 1.14$. Finally, now that the values at nodes H and I are determined, the value at node J, $C_0$, can be calculated. Specifically, $C_0 = (p_u C_u + p_d C_d) \div (1 + r_f) = [0.43(0.21) + 0.57(1.14)] \div (1.055) = 0.70$.

Note that because the problem constrains the decision maker to exercise the option, if at all, only after three years, the initial value of the option could have been obtained directly from the option values present at nodes A–D in the rightmost column of the tree. Specifically, $C_0 = (p_u^3 C_{uuu} + 3p_u^2 p_d C_{uud} + 3p_u p_d^2 C_{udd} + p_d^3 C_{ddd}) \div (1 + r_f) = [(0.43)^3(0) + 3(0.43)^2(0.57)(0) + 3(0.43)(0.57)^2(0.73) + (0.57)^3(2.79)] \div (1.055)^3 = 0.70$. The discounting is for three periods in this case, and the more complicated weighting scheme reflects the fact that there are eight potential paths to the final four nodes—one path for node A, three for node B, three for node C, and one for node D—and the probability weight for each node reflects the multiplication of risk-neutral probabilities to reach that node over three time periods (i.e., $p_u^3 + 3p_u^2 p_d + 3p_u p_d^2 + p_d^3 = 1$). In other words, $p_u^3$ is used because node A is reached after three up movements; $3p_u^2 p_d$ is used because node B is reached after two up movements and one down movement, and there are three such paths; $3p_u p_d^2$ is used because node C is reached after one up movement and two down movements, and there are three such paths; and $p_d^3$ is used because node D is reached after three down movements.

So what decision should the entrepreneur make concerning the launch of this business? The base case NPV is $-\$1.112$. Incorporation of the abandonment option to sell the plant and equipment in three years brings $0.70 million in additional value, but this value is not sufficient to go forward (i.e., $-1.112 + 0.70 = -0.412 < 0$). Absent some other embedded option and source of flexibility, the business should not be started.

## Application Issues and Guidelines

We conclude with a few practical application issues concerning option valuation models, emphasizing the Black-Scholes approach because it rests on several important assumptions, all of which have the potential to create problems for analysts and decision makers and which deserve sensitivity when the approaches discussed above are used.

**European versus American Options.** As mentioned previously, Black-Scholes assumes that all options are European, meaning that the option can be exercised only on the date of the option's maturity. In reality, real options are often more like American options, which can be exercised early. The main reason to exercise a financial option early would be to realize a dividend payment, which Black-Scholes assumes to be zero. Since dividend payments go to those who hold the underlying asset, one holding open an option does not benefit from these payments. In the case of real options, there might not be dividend payments as such, but analysts might be able to identify dividend-like features to the options they hold, including competitor preemption, loss of required skills, and so forth, that may lead the firm to want to exercise the option early rather than wait.

**Known and Fixed Exercise Price.** Black-Scholes also assumes that the exercise price is known and constant, just like it would be in a financial option contract. For many projects, this assumption is not valid because of the changing nature of the external environment. In many instances, the same economic factors that influence the value of the underlying asset also affect the cost of investment. Assuming that the cost of investment is fixed, especially when a contract is not in place, can be overly simplistic and may cause a disconnect between the calculated value and the actual value of the option. When the exercise price is not fixed, the decision maker ideally needs to account for the joint distribution of the exercise price and value of the underlying asset, which requires modeling approaches more technical than those described here.

**Single Source of Uncertainty.** Many real-world investment decisions are affected by several different sources of uncertainty. The Black-Scholes method assumes that there is a single source of uncertainty, simplifying a complex set of factors into one measure. The complex nature of estimating multiple sources of risk, and the relationship between these sources of uncertainty, is beyond the scope of this chapter. For example, Monte Carlo simulation techniques can be used to deal with multiple sources of uncertainty affecting option value.

**Simple versus Compound Options.** Besides having multiple sources of risk, many real options are compound options, meaning that the value of the original real option is affected by follow-on options. For instance, option A's value may be affected by subsequent options B and C. A simple way to obtain a conservative estimate of option A's value is to treat all follow-on options as commitments made at the time of A's exercise. The valuation exercise is then amenable to the Black-Scholes and NPV $q$ techniques presented above because a compound option is converted to a simple option. By neglecting flexibility in future estimates, however, the value of option A is understated.

**Distribution of the Underlying Asset's Value.** For the Black-Scholes and approximation approaches, one assumes that the underlying asset's value follows a lognormal distribution with a constant level of volatility. The returns to the underlying asset are assumed to be normally distributed. For some applications, the distribution of the underlying asset's value does not become wider over time as depicted by the lognormal distribution. Other option pricing models have been developed for projects requiring different distributional assumptions.

**Value of the Underlying Asset.** Using Black-Scholes to compute real option values means that the user has to estimate the components required by the formula. Although the market sets the current price for a financial asset ($S$), there is often no such market estimation for the value of underlying assets in a real option calculation. Real option theory adds significantly to the valuation of uncertain investments, but it does not address management concerns about the accuracy of cash flow projections or the appropriate discount rate. Practitioners have accepted the imperfections of discounted cash flow analysis as it relates to cash flow projections, and the estimation of the value of the underlying asset using this methodology will therefore not be a significant obstacle.

**Different Values of $t$.** The specification of the years to maturity, $t$, would appear to be straightforward. In some projects, however, the cost of investment can occur at a point after the resolution of the uncertainty associated with the project. For this reason, different values of $t$ may need to be used for discounting the exercise price and calculating cumulative volatility. For example, consider an option to purchase a piece of property three years from today. The value of this property is highly uncertain because of the possibility of a new highway system being built near the land. Public disclosure of the coordinates of the new highway will be made in one year, resolving the uncertainty of the land value. While the option contract to buy the property is three years out, the uncertainty surrounding the property value will be known in one year. In this case, the exercise price is discounted $t = 3$ years, but $t = 1$ is used in estimating cumulative volatility.

# Notes

1. R. Gertner & A. Rosenfield, 2000, How real options lead to better decisions, *Financial Times Mastering Strategy Series*, London: FT Prentice Hall.

2. T. Luehrman, 1998, Strategy as a portfolio of real options, *Harvard Business Review*, 76: 89–100; D. Kim & B. Kogut, 1996, Technological platforms and diversification, *Organization Science*, 7: 283–301; B. Kogut & S. J. Chang, 1996, Platform investments and volatile exchange rates: Direct investment in the U.S. by Japanese electronic companies, *Review of Economics and Statistics*, 78: 221–231; G. R. Mitchell & W. F. Hamilton, 1988, Managing R&D as a strategic option, *Research Technology Management*, 27: 789–798; G. P. Pisano, Nucleon, 1991, Harvard Business School Case 9-692-041, http://harvardbusinessonline.hbsp.harvard.edu/b01/en/cases/cases_home.jhtml; D. Spar & A. Young, 1993, Gerber Products Company: Investing in the New Poland, Harvard Business School Case 9-793-069, http://harvardbusinessonline.hbsp.harvard.edu/b01/en/cases/cases_home.jhtml.

3. H. Courtney, J. Kirkland, & P. Viguerie, 1997, Strategy under uncertainty, *Harvard Business Review* (November–December): 67–79.

4. M. A. Hitt, 1998, Presidential address: Twenty-first-century organizations: Business firms, business schools, and the academy, *Academy of Management Review*, 23: 218–224.

5. R. D'Aveni, 1994, *Hypercompetition*, New York: The Free Press.

6. H. Lee & M. A. Hitt, 2002, Top management team composition and characteristics as predictors of strategic flexibility, working paper, University of Connecticut; A. Edgecliffe-Johnson, 2001, Southwest braced to weather trouble, *Financial Times*, http://www.ft.com, October 2; L. Zuckerman, 2001, With seats empty, airlines cut fares to bargain levels, *New York Times*, http://www.nytimes.com, December 18.

7. R. Sanchez, 1993, Strategic flexibility, firm organization, and managerial work in dynamic markets: A strategic-options perspective, in P. Shrivastava, A. Huff, & J. Dutton (eds.), *Advances in Strategic Management*, Vol. 9, Greenwich, CT: JAI, 251–291.

8. B. Kogut & N. Kulatilaka, 1994, Options thinking and platform investments: Investing in opportunity, *California Management Review*, 36: 52–71.

9. K. Van der Heijden, 1996, *Scenarios: The Art of Strategic Conversation*, New York: Wiley.

10. P. Ghemawat, 2000, *Games Businesses Play: Cases and Models*, Cambridge. MA: MIT Press.

11. R. G. McGrath & I. MacMillan, 2000, *The Entrepreneurial Mindset*, Boston: Harvard Business School Press; M. Amram, 2002, *Value Sweep: Mapping Corporate Growth Opportunities*, Boston: Harvard Business School Press; T. Copeland & P. Tufano, 2004, A real-world way to manage real options, *Harvard Business Review*, 82: 90–99.

12. M. Amram & N. Kulatilaka, 1999, Disciplined decisions: Aligning strategy with the financial markets, *Harvard Business Review*, 77(1): 95–104.

13. S. C. Myers, 1977, Determinants of corporate borrowing, *Journal of Financial Economics*, 5: 147–175.

14. J. J. Reuer & M. J. Leiblein, 2001, Real options: Let the buyer beware, in J. Pickford (ed.), *Financial Times Mastering Risk*, Vol. 1, London: FT Prentice Hall, 79–85.

15. J. J. Reuer & M. J. Leiblein, 2000, Downside risk implications of multinationality and international joint ventures, *Academy of Management Journal*, 43: 203–214.

16. L. Trigeorgis, 1993, Real options and interactions with financial flexibility, *Financial Management* (autumn): 202–224; L. Trigeorgis, 1997, *Real Options*, Cambridge, MA: MIT Press.

17. P. Ghemawat & H. J. Stander III, 1992, Nucor at a Crossroads, Harvard Business School Case 9-793-039, http://harvardbusinessonline.hbsp.harvard.edu/b01/en/cases/cases_home.jhtml.

18. B. Kogut, 1991, Joint ventures and the option to expand and acquire, *Management Science*, 37: 19–33.

19. T. B. Folta & K. D. Miller, 2002, Real options and equity partnerships, *Strategic Management Journal*, 23: 77–88.

20. J. J. Reuer, J. J. Tong, & T. Tong, 2005, Real options in international joint ventures, *Journal of Management*, 31: 403–423.

21. J. Bleeke & D. Ernst, 1995, Is your strategic alliance really a sale? *Harvard Business Review*, 73: 97–105.

22. 2005, Valentine's day divorce, *Economist*, February 19, 59.

23. 2002, Real Options at Polaris Energy Corporation (A): The Spectrum Alliance, European Case Clearing House 302-093-1, http://www.ecch.com/casesearch/.

24. B. Kogut & N. Kulatilaka, 1994, Operating flexibility, global manufacturing, and the option value of a multinational network, *Management Science*, 40: 123–139.

25. A. K. Dixit & R. S. Pindyck, 1994, *Investment under Uncertainty*, Princeton, NJ: Princeton University Press.

26. M. J. Brennan & E. Schwartz, 1985, Evaluating natural resource investments, *Journal of Business*, 58: 135–157.

27. E. Bowman & D. Hurry, 1993, Strategy through the options lens, *Academy of Management Review*, 18: 760–782.

28. M. J. Leiblein, 2003, The choice of organizational governance form and performance: Predictions from transaction cost, resource-based, and real options theories, *Journal of Management*, 29: 937–961; R. G. McGrath, 1999, Falling forward: Real options reasoning and entrepreneurial failure, *Academy of Management Review*, 24: 13–30; R. G. McGrath, 1997, A real options logic for initiating technology positioning investments, *Academy of Management Review*, 22: 974–996.

29. R. E. Caves, 1996, *Multinational Enterprise and Economic Analysis*, 2nd ed., New York: Cambridge University Press.

30. C. Fleming, 1998, ABB's net profit for 1997 declined 54% on provisions for Asian financial crisis, *Wall Street Journal Europe*, February 27–28, 3; K. D. Miller & J. J. Reuer, 1998, Firm strategy and economic exposure to foreign exchange rate movements, *Journal of International Business Studies*, 29: 493–514; S. Rangan, 1998, Do multinationals operate flexibly? Theory and evidence, *Journal of International Business Studies*, 29: 217–237.

31. G. Hamel, 1991, Competition for competence and interpartner learning within international strategic alliances, *Strategic Management Journal*, 12: 83–103.

32  J. J. Reuer, 2000, Parent firm performance across international joint venture life-cycle stages, *Journal of International Business Studies*, 31: 1–20.

33  T. Chi, 2000, Option to acquire or divest a joint venture, *Strategic Management Journal*, 21: 665–687.

34  J. H. Dyer, P. Kale, & H. Singh, 2004, When to ally and when to acquire, *Harvard Business Review*, 82: 109–115.

35  S. C. Myers, 1984, Finance theory and financial strategy, *Interfaces*, 14: 126–137.

36  T. Copeland & V. Antikarov, 2001, *Real Options*, New York: Texere.

37  2004, Wellington Synthetics, European Case Clearing House 804-014-1, http://www.ecch.com/casesearch/.

38  2004, Innovis Technology: Capturing the Value of Intellectual Property, European Case Clearing House 304-066-1, http://www.ecch.com/casesearch/.

39  S. C. Myers, 1977, Determinants of corporate borrowing, *Journal of Financial Economics*, 5: 147–175.

40  W. C. Kester, 1984, Today's options for tomorrow's growth, *Harvard Business Review*, 62: 153–160.

41  G. B. Stewart, 1991, *The Quest for Value: A Guide for Senior Managers*, New York: Harper; S. D. Young & S. F. O'Byrne, 2001, *EVA and Value-Based Management*, New York: McGraw-Hill.

42  J. J. Reuer & T. W. Tong, 2007, Corporate investments and growth options, *Managerial and Decision Economics*, forthcoming.

43  P. J. Strebel, 1983, The stock market and competitive analysis, *Strategic Management Journal*, 4: 279–291.

44  R. Black & M. Scholes, 1973, The pricing of options and corporate liabilities, *Journal of Political Economy*, 81: 637–659.

45  For an application to economic exposure to currency movements, see K. D. Miller & J. J. Reuer, 1998, Asymmetric corporate exposures to foreign exchange rate changes, *Strategic Management Journal*, 19: 1183–1191.

46  T. Luehrman, 1998, Investment opportunities as real options: Getting started on the numbers, *Harvard Business Review*, 26: 51–67.

47  R. G. McGrath, W. J. Ferrier, & A. L. Mendelow, 2004, Real options as engines of choice and heterogeneity, *Academy of Management Review*, 29: 86–101.

48  J. S. Busby & C. G. C. Pitts, 1997, Real options in practice: An exploratory survey of how finance officers deal with flexibility in capital appraisal, *Management Accounting Research*, 8: 169–186.

49  1999, Keeping all options open, *Economist*, August 14, 62.

50  E. H. Bowman & G. T. Moskowitz, 2001, Real options analysis and strategic decision making, *Organization Science*, 12: 772–777.

51  E. S. Schwartz & M. Moon, 2000, Rational pricing of internet companies, *Financial Analysts Journal*, 56: 62–75.

52  A. Triantis & A. Borison, 2001, Real options: State of the practice, *Journal of Applied Corporate Finance*, 14: 8–24.

53  McGrath, Falling forward.

54  Copeland & Tufano, A real-world way to manage real options; Copeland & Antikarov, *Real Options*.

55  Wellington Synthetics.

# Name Index

Garg, V. K., 92n21
Garland, S. B., 208n95
Garnham, P., 93n57
Garrette, B., 206n61, 207n72
Garten, J. E., 179n18, 298n159
Garud, R., 353n154
Garvin, D. A., 169, 352n114
Gary, M. S., 238n45
Gates, Bill, 36, 37
Gatignon, H., 263n51
Gavetti, G., 122nn20, 27, 123n57, 154n1
Gawer, A. 58n44, 125n97
Gedajlovic, E. R., 327n29, 331n151
Geiger, S. W., 181n64
Geletkanycz, M. A., 154n12, 241n144, 327n41
Gelfer, S., 332n180
Genesove, D., 239n73
George, G., 296n103, 350nn46, 48, 62
Gepp, A., 24n17
Geppert, M., 295n71
Gerchak, Y., 238n49
Gerety, M., 329n91
Geringer, J. M., 294n44, 298n164, 299n189
Gerstenhaber, M., 208n113
Gerstner, Louis, 40
Gertner, R., 382n1
Gertsen, F., 352n97
Geyskens, I., 239n77
Ghemawat, P., 156n99, 209n127, 292n9, 294n60, 382n10, 382n17
Ghoshal, S., 26n56, 61nn137, 142, 145, 93n70, 261n1, 295nn65, 70, 83, 327n37
Gibbert, M., 25n52, 92n10
Gibson, C., 295n79
Gibson, H. D., 265n116
Gilbert, C., 25n39
Gile, C., 125n94
Gillin, L. M., 209n155
Gillis, W. E., 329n96
Gilson, R., 240n126
Gimeno, J., 91n3, 179n7, 180nn33, 37, 38, 39, 181n69, 207n93, 239n73, 296n95, 328n69
Gingrich, J. A., 263n44
Gittell, J. H., 63n195
Glader, P., 207n81, 262n9
Gleason, K. C., 328n57
Glick, W. H., 25n48, 57n18, 58n57, 59n93, 91n2, 262n17

Glynn, M. A., 299n193, 352n121
Gnyawali, D. R., 180n21
Goerzen, A., 209n130
Goffee, R., 61n155, 62n173
Golden, B. R., 59n62, 208n94, 326n6
Goldenberg, J., 351n81
Goldsborough, R., 92n24
Goldstein, D., 330n127
Goldstein, H. R., 156n82
Goll, I., 58n42, 92n92
Gomes, L., 330n107
Gomez, J., 179n15, 180n33, 205n27
Gomez-Mejia, L. R., 241nn131, 145, 326n3, 327nn25, 32, 34, 328n44, 330 nn101, 105, 110, 112, 116
Gompers, P. A., 328n62
Gong, Y., 297n132
Gonzalez, I. S., 95n117
Gonzalez, M., 205n21
Goold, M., 236n7
Goranova, M., 241n147, 328n43
Gordon, R. A., 26n59, 27n96
Gore, William, 343
Gorman, P., 122n23
Gove, S., 60n99
Govindarajan, V., 24nn25, 26, 57nn14, 15, 61nn144, 145, 125n88, 292nn4, 5
Graffin, S. D., 58n37
Grant, L., 155n68
Grant, R. M., 103, 104, 241n129
Gratton, L., 26n56, 61n131
Graves, Michael, 148
Graves, S. B., 27n124, 28n130, 28n142
Gray, S. R., 241n145
Greco, J., 56n4, 155n57, 237n31
Green, J., 58n45, 60n113, 181n84
Green, S., 56n5
Greene, J., 182n101
Greene, P. G., 122n4
Greening, D. W., 28n138, 124n61
Greiner, L., 59n91
Greve, H. R., 95nn113, 118, 181n71
Grewal, R., 181n73
Griffin, D. A., 239n80
Griffith, D. A., 294n47
Griffith, R. W., 124n60
Grimm, C. M., 57n16, 91n3, 179nn4, 5, 10, 13, 19, 180nn22, 23, 31, 36, 50, 52, 181nn69, 75, 90, 95, 182n97
Grinstein, Y., 327n42

Grinyer, P., 122n24
Grohmann, B., 208n106
Gross, Clifford M., 345
Grosse, R., 299nn183, 193
Grossman, W., 241n144, 263n50, 327nn22, 36, 328n63, 64, 69, 329nn81, 89, 351n69
Grundei, J., 182n109
Gudridge, K., 240n122
Guedhami, O., 332n178
Gueyie, J.-P., 326n3, 330n105
Guilley, R. M., 333n190
Guirguis, H. S., 208n96
Gulati, R., 210n159, 239n77
Gunkel, J. D., 63n203
Gunz, H. P., 58n41
Gupta, A. K., 24nn25, 26, 57n15, 61nn144, 145, 125nn88, 93, 154n6, 156n101, 292nn4, 5
Gupta, S., 333n188
Guth, W. D., 8, 63nn63, 64, 122n24
Guthrie, J. P., 58n48
Gutierrez, I., 205n29, 327n32, 328n44
Gwynne, P., 265n123

Haahti, A., 296n110
Hachigian, Kirk S., 246
Hackman, J. R., 157n123
Hadjimarcou, J., 154n24
Hafeez, K., 124n72, 125n102
Hafner, K., 181nn60, 62
Hagedoorn, J., 208n122, 265n120, 298n158, 352n127
Hair, J. F., Jr., 154n34
Haleblian, J., 265nn106, 107, 125
Halevy, T., 206n40
Haliinan, J. T., 94n104
Hall, D. T., 61n132, 351n66
Hall, R. H., 104, 155n70, 156n71
Hall, Terence, 284
Hall, W. K., 156n100
Hallaq, J. H., 95n127
Halligan, A., 181n81
Hambrick, D. C., 34, 43, 57nn13, 17, 58nn36, 49, 56, 59n86, 60nn98, 101, 106, 107, 93n48, 154n9, 181n73, 207n79, 209n133, 236n2, 237n13, 241n144, 263n67, 265n110, 297n133, 300n198, 326n13, 327n32, 328n42, 329n91, 330n100
Hamel, G., 28nn145, 146, 154, 60n105, 124n72, 125n102, 154nn10, 14, 179n3, 181n59,

Hamel, G. (*continued*)
298n169, 349n22, 351n71, 382n31
Hamilton, W. F., 382n2
Hamm, S., 241n132
Hammonds, K. H., 25nn35, 37
Handfield, R. B., 293n28
Handfield-Jones, H., 61n155
Hanlon, S. C., 205n11, 208n97
Hannan, M., 125n112
Hansen, M. H., 28nn134, 139, 209nn150, 151, 210n158
Hansen, M. T., 124n69
Hanvanich, S., 91n7, 182n110
Harback, H. E., 58n43
Harbison, J. R., 205n7, 264n80
Hardee, C., 28n147
Harder, J., 125n107
Harford, J., 331n137
Harlan, C., 95n124
Harper, N. W. C., 241n134
Harrigan, K. R., 26n55, 205n8, 207n87, 239n84
Harris, C., 24n17
Harris, D., 60n96
Harris, I. C., 59n72
Harris, M., 239n95
Harris, R., 266n147
Harrison, A. E., 298n167
Harrison, Brian, 344
Harrison, D. A., 62n175, 125n117
Harrison, J. S., 26n80, 28nn136, 141, 143, 150, 60n100, 62n165, 63n192, 94n107, 124n77, 125n119, 157n125, 179n16, 180n40, 205n13, 14, 206nn54, 64, 207nn82, 87, 238nn41, 51, 240nn115, 121, 128, 261nn1, 5, 262n11, 263nn45, 51, 56, 61, 64, 264nn74, 77, 89, 100, 265nn105, 115, 118, 119, 125, 129, 296n123, 297n141, 300n196, 329n75, 331n137, 332nn184, 185, 341, 352n98, 353n141
Harryson, S., 207n71
Hart, Clare, 88
Hart, M. M., 122n4
Hart, S. L., 28n132, 292nn9, 12, 332n182
Hartel, C. E. J., 60n94
Hartzell, J. C., 330n114
Harvey, M. G., 61n136, 294n47
Harzing, A.-W., 206n41, 237n12, 295nn65, 72, 297n146
Haspeslagh, P., 262n30

Hass, W. J., 328n55
Hassan, F., 56n5
Hassan, S. S., 155n35
Hatch, N. W., 124n60, 207n66, 209n144
Haveman, H. A., 179n14, 239n76
Hawawini, G., 27n113, 123n39
Hay, M., 349n17
Hayashi, Y., 332n172
Hayes, C., 264n77
Hayes, E., 61n155
Hayton, J. C., 296n102, 350n40
Hayward, M. L. A., 58n38, 264n72, 265nn110, 113
Hebert, L., 297n148
Heeley, M. B., 155n47
Hegarty, H., 206n54, 264n83
Hegarty, W., 330n108
Hegtvedt, K. A., 28n140, 332n183
Heide, J. B., 327n38
Hejazi, W., 292n9
Helfat, C. E., 26n83, 58n41, 60n96, 123n58, 154nn7, 12, 236nn4, 9, 263n63
Hemphill, T. A., 205n1
Henderson, A., 330n102
Henderson, R., 26n93
Hendricks, R., 351n82
Hendrickx, M., 236n8, 328n46
Hendry, K., 326n1
Henisz, W. J., 299nn177, 194
Hennart, J. F., 125n93, 154n6, 156n101, 208n104
Henriksson, K., 209n140
Henriques, I., 27n117, 332n181
Henry, D., 266n146
Henry, N., 180n45
Herbert, T. T., 295n71
Hesterly, W. S., 59n69, 209n129, 329n88
Hill, C. W. L., 25n36, 57n26, 93n74, 123n42, 125n93, 154n6, 155n40, 156n101, 205n10, 206n44, 237n35, 238n59, 239n92, 240nn110, 111, 264n102, 266n147, 292n8, 296n105, 330n111
Hill, N. T., 330n104
Hill, W. L., 27n127
Hiller, N. J., 58n36
Hillman, A. J., 27nn120, 130, 93nn59, 61, 299n194, 326n6, 327n35, 332n181
Hilton, B., 331n146
Himelstein, L., 331n132
Hindo, B., 123n36

Hines, A., 92n38
Hitt, M. A., 24nn1, 3, 7, 25nn34, 46, 26nn57, 60, 27nn95, 108, 120, 28n147, 29n159, 56n6, 57nn13, 26, 58n43, 61, 59n76, 60nn98, 99, 121, 122, 127, 61n139, 62nn169, 172, 63n207, 91nn1, 6, 92nn9, 17, 93nn61, 76, 77, 94n79, 94nn82, 90, 91, 96, 95n120, 123nn39, 52, 56, 124nn59, 70, 154nn5, 12, 205nn3, 16, 29, 206nn38, 54, 207n83, 208nn118, 121, 209nn134, 138, 141, 234, 236n4, 237n16, 238nn43, 44, 59, 239nn78, 79, 95, 240nn110, 111, 128, 241n140, 261nn1, 5, 262n11, 263nn45, 50–52, 55, 56, 61, 64, 69, 72, 264nn74, 77, 81, 89, 92, 99, 100, 103, 265nn105, 108, 109, 115, 117–119, 125, 129, 132, 266nn137, 141, 155, 292nn3, 5, 6, 293n31, 296n114, 123, 124, 297nn129, 133, 141, 142, 298nn161, 165, 166, 171, 175, 299nn189, 191, 300n200, 326n19, 327nn22, 36, 39, 328nn63, 64, 69, 329nn81, 89, 330nn111, 126, 331nn134, 161, 332nn178, 180, 348nn2, 4, 5, 349nn6, 24, 350nn39, 47, 50, 59, 64, 351nn68, 69, 90, 352nn107, 109, 112, 113, 117, 120, 353nn134, 135, 139, 141–144, 146–148, 150, 151, 157, 382nn4, 6
Ho, K. W., 328n57
Hoang, H., 206n45
Hochwarter, W. A., 62n172
Hodges, J., 95n125
Hodgetts, R. M., 62n167, 295n62
Hodgkinson, G. P., 180n45
Hoetker, G., 156n105, 207n85
Hof, B., 181n61
Hof, R. D., 25n44, 349n15
Hofer, C. W., 9, 26nn58, 75, 76, 89, 155n51
Hoffmann, W. H., 297n139
Hogarth, R. M., 57n22
Hogler, R. L., 329n79
Hoi, C., 329n91
Hoiweg, M., 181n73
Holbein, G. F., 266n143

Holcomb, T. R., 298n166
Holcombe, R. G., 349n16
Holden, N., 124n65
Hollenbeck, G. P., 61nn134, 138
Holm, U., 298n166
Holmes, R. M., 93n77, 299n191
Holmes, S., 60n115
Holthausen, R. W., 326n3
Hom, P. W., 124n60
Homberg, C., 264n78
Homqvist, M., 242n156, 296n122
Hong, J., 155n44, 237n23, 298n159
Hood, N., 295n66
Hoopes, D. G., 124n59
Hopkins, H. D., 179n11, 295n75
Hornsby, J. S., 25n49, 61nn141, 146, 155, 124n69, 206n40, 238n40, 350n41
Horowitz, R., 351n81
Hoshi, T., 331n158
Hoskisson, R. E., 26n60, 28nn134, 139, 57nn18, 26, 58n61, 59nn76, 84, 63n207, 91n3, 93n77, 94n79, 122n30, 155n44, 181n69, 205n30, 206n54, 207n69, 208n121, 209nn150, 151, 234, 236nn3, 4, 237nn16, 22, 26, 29, 35, 238nn43, 44, 59, 240nn105, 110, 111, 115, 241nn144, 148, 153, 242n153, 261n1, 263nn50, 52, 55, 56, 61, 69, 264nn74, 89, 92, 102, 103, 265nn105, 108, 109, 119, 128, 266nn137, 141, 142, 149, 150, 159, 292nn3, 4, 12, 293n12, 294nn44, 46, 296nn95, 123, 298nn159, 171, 299n189, 300n200, 326nn16, 19, 327nn22, 36, 39, 40, 328nn57, 63, 64, 69, 329nn81, 89, 330nn111, 126, 332nn163, 173, 180, 333n191, 349nn24, 30, 350n50, 351nn68, 69, 85, 352nn107, 109, 112, 113, 353nn139, 150
Hough, J. R., 92n21
Houghton, K. A., 296n111
House, R. J., 59n81, 294n41
Howell, J. E., 26n59, 27n96
Howell, J. M., 351n88
Howell, R. A., 28n132, 332n182
Hrebiniak, L. G., 26n77, 63n190, 124n70

Hribar, P., 327n42
Hsieh, L.-F., 263n52
Hsu, C. C., 299n190
Huang, C.-H., 236n5
Hubbard, T. N., 264n85
Huber, G. P., 57n18, 91n2, 262n17
Huey, J., 124n84
Huff, A. S., 95n114
Huff, L., 297n135
Hughes, J. P., 265n108, 353n133
Hulland, J., 241n141
Hult, G. T. M., 94n94
Hunt, M. S., 95n112
Hurry, D., 382n27
Huse, M., 329n78
Huselid, M. A., 63n199
Hussey, D., 155n44
Hutt, M. D., 205n4, 209n154, 351n89
Hutzschenreuter, T., 29n159
Huy, Q. N., 265n125
Huyghebaert, N., 181n92
Hwang, L., 330n110
Hymowitz, C., 326n11

Iacocca, Lee, 4
Iaquito, A. L., 58n40
Icahn, Carl, 311–312
Ihlwan, M., 180n54, 181n85
Immelt, J., 40, 44, 56n5, 257, 266n139
Incandela, D., 238n42
Ingram, P., 124n65
Inkpen, A. C., 25n46, 205nn6, 9, 206n50, 208n105, 293n30, 295nn68, 82, 86, 88, 92, 299n185, 331nn147, 153, 154, 160, 332nn163, 167, 177
Insinga, R. C., 125n108
Irarvani, S. M., 156n114
Ireland, R. D., 24n1, 25n49, 26n81, 27nn95, 108, 29n159, 60nn98, 121, 61n146, 62nn169, 172, 91n1, 92nn9, 17, 93n76, 94n82, 95n120, 123n52, 124n59, 69, 70, 154nn5, 13, 205n3, 16, 29, 206nn38, 40, 54, 207n83, 209nn134, 141, 237n16, 238nn40, 43, 240n128, 261nn1, 5, 262n11, 263nn45, 51, 52, 56, 61, 64, 264nn74, 77, 89, 100, 265nn105, 109, 115, 118, 119, 125, 129, 292n6, 296nn114, 123, 297n141, 298n165, 299n189,

348nn2, 4, 5, 349nn7, 9, 18, 350nn39, 41, 51, 64, 351n90, 352nn117, 120, 353nn134, 141, 142, 144, 146, 151, 157
Irwin, N., 154n26
Isaac, S., 156n116
Isaak, R., 296n105
Isobe, T., 292n1
Ito, K., 293n35
Itoh, H., 237n32
Ivy, R. L., 206n64
Izushi, H., 296n99

Jackson, E. M., 329n91
Jackson, G., 326n17
Jackson, S. E., 25n46, 57n16, 58n53, 60n122
Jacob, R., 295n94
Jacobides, M. G., 239n83, 327n33
Jacoby, M., 93n60
Jacoby, S. M., 331n148
Jacque, L. L., 299n182
Jagersma, P. K., 297n133
Jain, S. C., 132, 155n34, 353n154
Jalland, R. M., 58n41
Jammine, A. P., 241n129
Jankowicz, A. D., 348n1
Janne, O. E. M., 293n31, 298n176
Janney, J. J., 154n13, 241n148, 349n7
Jardins, J. D., 353n156
Jarillo, J. C., 349n9
Jarvenpaa, S., 125n101
Jassawalla, A. R., 352n106
Javidan, M., 292n5
Jawahar, I. M., 92n28
Jayachandran, S., 179n7, 180n38, 207n93
Jenkins, M., 180n45
Jennings, D. F., 209n155
Jensen, M.
Jensen, M. C., 9, 26n72, 27n115, 126n129, 240n125, 262n21, 264n97, 326n9, 327n31, 328nn45, 46
Jenster, P., 155n44
Jeong, E., 265n132
Jermias, J., 348n1
Jevnaker, B. H., 125n102
Jiang, F., 293n25
Joachimsthaler, E., 122n19
Jobe, L. A., 239nn78, 79
Jobs, Steve, 337
Johaansson, J. K., 295n75
Johnson, G., 180n45
Johnson, J. L., 208n106, 329n78, 350n51

Johnson, M., 205n23, 296n118
Johnson, M. E., 239n84
Johnson, M. W., 25n39
Johnson, R. A., 58n61, 59n75,
63n207, 94n79, 236n3,
237nn22, 26, 240n105,
241n152, 263nn50, 52, 55,
264nn92, 103, 265nn105,
108, 127, 128, 131,
266nn141, 142, 294n46,
298n171, 326n19, 327nn22,
36, 39, 328nn57, 63, 64,
69, 329nn81, 89, 330n126,
332n163, 350n50, 351n69,
353n139
Jonacas, H., 205n5
Jones, C., 209n129
Jones, G., 61n155, 62n173
Jones, R., 181n86
Jones, S., 125n99
Jones, T. M., 27nn116, 127, 130,
28n131, 205n10
Joshi, M., 62n182
Joshi, S., 261n4
Joyce, W. F., 26n77, 63n190
Judge, W.
Judge, W. Q., Jr., 58–59n61,
61n148, 300n198, 329n93
Junttila, M. A., 123n47, 238n47

Kaeufer, K., 126n127
Kahan, M., 241n149
Kahn, R. L., 26n68
Kahneman, D., 57nn20, 21, 32
Kakabadse, A., 59n82
Kakabadse, N., 59n82
Kale, P., 25n48, 60n119,
206nn39, 40, 208n104,
209n143, 263n58, 297n139,
352n123, 383n34
Kallendar, P., 156n81, 182n96
Kalnins, A., 94n107, 182n103
Kandemir, D., 207n79
Kang, J.-K., 332n175
Kang, S.-H., 265n114
Kanter, R. M., 25n45, 91n5
Kapelyushnikov, R., 332n180
Kaplan, R. S., 63nn198, 200–
202, 154n4, 156n121,
181n79
Kaplan, S., 62n161
Karim, S., 237n33
Karlgaard, R., 25n38
Karnani, A., 182n99
Karnik, K., 349n16
Karnitschnig, M., 262n27,
266n135, 331n155

Karpoff, J. M., 331n139
Karri, R., 125n116, 329n80,
333n189
Kashuk, Sonia, 148
Kashyap, A. K., 331n158
Kassinis, G., 59n62, 62n170,
126n131
Katila, R., 123n41, 263n52,
349n27
Kato, Y., 63n196
Katz, D., 26n68
Katz, J., 327n32, 330n116
Katz, M., 125n109
Kaufman, A., 333n186
Kaufmann, P. J., 208nn112, 114
Kawaura, A., 332n164
Kay, I. T., 264n82
Kay, N. M., 241n136
Kayworth, T. K., 25n49
Kazanjian, R. K., 239n91,
352n121
Keats, B. W., 25n34, 58n43,
61n139, 92n9, 155nn45,
49, 53
Kedia, B. L., 292n7
Kedia, S., 239n97
Keeble, D., 208n122
Keels, J. K., 266n158
Keenan, F., 331n132
Keil, M., 122n18
Keim, G. D., 27n130, 93n59,
326n6, 332n181
Keister, L. A., 237n23
Keith, T., 298n157
Keller, S. B., 155nn63, 69
Kelley, D. J., 350n40
Kelley, L., 297n135
Kelly, L. M., 327n27
Kelly, M. J., 205n5
Kelm, K. M., 349n23
Kendrick, John, 103
Kennedy, Aaron, 197
Kern, D., 62n161
Kerr, S., 62n172
Kerwin, K., 180n54, 181n85
Kesner, I. F., 181n57
Kessler, E. H., 206nn45, 47
Kester, W. C., 383n40
Ketchen, D. J., Jr., 29n160, 94n94,
154n5, 205n3, 206n38,
208n109
Kets de Vries, M. F. R., 60n123
Keuslein, W., 241n140
Khanna, T., 25n29, 237n23,
240nn102, 103, 292n9
Khermouch, G., 155n42
Kidder, D. L., 60n95

Kiel, G. C., 326n1, 326n13
Killman, S., 239n82
Kim, C., 236n11
Kim, D., 382n2
Kim, G. M., 207n68
Kim, H., 59n84, 155n44,
207n69, 208n121, 236n4,
237n35, 240n110, 242n153,
292n4, 298n159, 299n189,
300n200, 326n16, 333n191,
351n68, 353n150
Kim, J., 296n108
Kim, J.-J., 265nn106, 107, 125
Kim, L., 156n102
Kim, S., 236n11
Kim, W. C., 351n75
Kim, Y. J., 296n117
Kindler, Jeffrey B., 257
King, A. W., 124n87, 155n40,
352n120
King, D. R., 206n54
Kini, O., 331n129
Kirkland, J., 382n3
Kirkman, B. L., 352n106
Kirkpatrick, S. A., 62n168
Kirsch, D. A., 155n44
Kirsch, L. J., 63n195
Kisfalvi, V., 242n156
Kitamura, M., 332n173
Kiymaz, H., 328n49
Klaas, B. S., 125n98
Klein, S., 331n150
Kleindienst, I., 29n159
Kleinfeld, Klaus, 51
Kleinman, M., 123n55
Kline, D. M., 123n41, 296n114,
352n129
Kline, J. P., 240n122
Kline, M. J., 326n8
Kneip, T., 350n53
Knell, M. J., 205n34
Knight, D., 57n11, 58n47
Knight, G. A., 297n138
Knoedler, J. T., 240n118
Knolt, A. M., 241n142
Knott, A. M., 122n4, 123n44
Koberstein, W., 58n59
Kochhar, R., 60n127, 124n59,
239n95, 241n140, 264n81,
349n24, 350n47, 352nn107,
109, 112, 113, 353n147
Kogut, B., 331n146, 382nn2, 8,
18, 24
Koka, B. R., 352–353n129
Koller, T., 266n138
Kono, T., 238n56
Konopaske, R., 296n104

Williamson, I. O., 28n136, 332n184
Williamson, O. E., 9, 26n73, 62n164, 155n55, 237nn34, 37, 239nn81, 94, 264n91, 327n36
Williamson, P. J., 25n53, 236n6, 238n59, 295n84, 351n79
Willis, Randall L., 189
Wilson, D. T., 239n87
Wilson, G., 179n8
Wilson, H. J., 351n86
Wind, J., 181n73
Winfrey, Oprah, 140
Wingfield, N., 93n75
Winklhofer, H., 296n111
Winter, S., 27n105
Wise, R., 94n100, 154n34
Wiseman, R. M., 207n83, 236n3, 241n131, 294n46, 327n25, 330n101
Witt, P., 331n149
Wolf, B., 29n161, 352n105
Wolf, J., 123n37
Wolfe, Sid, 173
Wolff, J. A., 60n126
Wolfson, M., 240n126
Wolfson, P. J., 60n96
Wolpert, J. D., 25n51
Wonacott, P., 92n12, 94nn81, 87, 262n28, 292n1
Woo, C. Y., 180nn33, 39, 239n73, 241n152
Wood, D. J., 126n123, 326n6
Woodward, J., 155n43
Wooldridge, B., 123n38
Woyke, E., 181n76
Wright, M., 57n18, 93n77, 122n14, 205n30, 241n153, 266nn147, 149, 150, 156, 159, 292nn3, 12, 293n12, 296n112, 332nn173, 180
Wright, P., 27n107, 61n148, 236n6, 262n31, 300n198, 326n7, 327n42, 328n48
Wright, P. M., 27n108, 61n130, 122n14, 154n23, 292n7
Wright, R. P., 326n18
Wright, T., 262n25
Wrigley, L., 237n14

Wu, L., 208n115
Wu, P. C. S., 293n24
Wu, X., 326n14
Wujin, C., 209n153, 210n159
Wurst, J., 154n34

Xin, K., 28n140, 207n79, 209n133, 297n133, 332n183
Xin, K. R., 93n49
Xu, D., 294nn41, 42, 55

Yafeh, Y., 331n148
Yago, G., 264n96
Yan, A., 61n132
Yang, B., 58n44, 125n97
Yang, X., 122n21
Yaprak, A., 295n77
Yavas, U., 296n110
Yeh, R. S., 293n31
Yeh, Y.-H., 327n29, 332n175
Yeoh, P. L., 122n7
Yeung, G., 181n83, 292n7
Yeung, V. W. S., 157n124
Yip, G. S., 93n76, 121n1, 295n75
Yip, P., 92n26
Yiu, D., 26n60, 59n84, 63n207, 236n3, 240n105, 265n128, 266n142, 294n46, 326n16, 332n163
Yli-Renko, H., 92n30, 353n130
Yoffie, D. B., 180n51
Yoshikawa, T., 263n58, 327n39, 331nn148, 162
Youndt, M. A., 60n128
Young, A., 382n2
Young, G. J., 92n16, 179nn10, 13, 19, 180nn22, 23, 31, 36, 181n75, 207n75
Young, M., 332n178
Young, S. D., 261n7, 297n145, 329n79, 383n41
Young, T., 156n82
Young-Ybarra, C., 208n106
Yu, L., 25n52, 352n102
Yucel, E., 61n139, 123n56, 331n161, 353n148

Zacharachis, A. L., 350n60, 353n155
Zack, M. H., 92n30

Zaheer, A., 94n95, 209n156, 294n57
Zaheer, S., 94n95, 294nn56, 57
Zahra, S. A., 59n61, 61n155, 123n45, 205n29, 264n87, 292n6, 296nn102, 103, 298n165, 329n88, 349n7, 350nn46, 48, 62, 64
Zajac, E.
Zajac, E. J., 38, 59nn62, 64, 73, 326n13, 328n46, 329n82, 330nn104, 105, 331nn140, 156
Zalewski, D. A., 240n122
Zamiska, N., 93n62, 296n116
Zander, I., 298n170
Zehir, C., 352n115
Zeisel, S., 180n29, 261n6
Zeithaml, C. P., 59n61, 124n87, 155n40, 329n93
Zelleke, A. S., 59n71, 241n148
Zellmer-Bruhn, M., 295n79
Zellner, W., 62n177, 326n10
Zelner, B. A., 299n194
Zeng, M., 262n43
Zhang, H., 238n53
Zhang, Y. B., 124n72, 125n102
Zhao, H., 296n104
Zhao, J., 265n133
Zhao, N. B., 298n174
Zhao, Z., 206n63
Zhou, D., 180n47
Zhou, H., 237n32
Zhou, Z., 29n157
Zhu, G., 61n132, 351n66
Zietsma, C, 350n37
Zineldin, M., 24n15
Zingales, L., 239n97, 328n49
Zolli, R., 28n155
Zollo, M., 205n4, 209n142, 263n70, 264nn77, 79, 297n137, 353n136
Zook, C., 293n32, 296n119
Zott, C., 25n43, 124n71, 125n96
Zuckerman, L., 382n6
Zuniga-Vicente, J. A., 91n2, 95n117
Zweig, P. L., 240n122

# Company Index

# Subject Index

Strategic thinking
  characteristics of, 18–20
  encouragement of, 3, 20
  strategic leadership and, 41, 43
  strategic management process
    and, 20, *21*
Structures
  business-level strategy and,
    129, 133–134
  cooperative form, 219–221,
    225
  cross-functional development
    teams and, 342–343
  firm performance and, 18
  functional structure, 134,
    138–139, *139*, 143–144,
    *144*, 147
  strategic flexibility and, 149,
    355
  strategic management process
    and, 22
  worldwide combination struc-
    ture, 277–278
  worldwide geographic area
    structure, 275, *275*
  worldwide product divisional
    structure, 276, *277*
Substitute products, threat of,
  83–84
Suburban growth, 76
Suppliers
  bargaining power of, 82–83,
    137–138, 143
  firm performance and, 120
  transaction costs economics
    and, 9
Support activities, in value chain,
  110, 111, *112*, 113, 129–130,
  135
Sustainable competitive advantage
  criteria of, 107–110, *108*
  defined, 2
  internal analysis and, *100*, 101
  outcomes from combinations of
    criteria, 110, *110*
  *See also* Competitive advantage
Sustainable development
  defined, 119
  firm performance and,
    119–120
  strategic direction and, 50
Switching costs, 81, 85
Switching options, 358
Synergy, 231–232, 251–252, 255,
  287
Systems perspective, 8, 15, 18, 19

Tacit collusion, 195
Tacit knowledge, 187, 232
Tactical actions, 166, 171
Tactical responses, 166
Takeovers
  defined, 245
  hostile takeovers, 245, 255,
    318, *319*
  in Japan, 322
  organizational size and, 254
Tangible resources, 13, 102–103,
  *103*, 232, 234
Taper integration, 223
Tax laws, 230–231
Tax Reform Act of 1986,
  230–231
Technological segment, of general
  environment, 68, 76–77
Technology
  in automobile industry, 4
  competition and, 5–7
  cooperative strategies and, 184
  external environment and, 66
  fast-cycle markets and, 174,
    186
  firm performance and, 18
  innovation and, 339–340,
    346–347
  integrated cost-leadership/
    differentiation strategy,
    147
  international strategy and, 270
  resource-based model and,
    13–14
  strategic center firms and, 192
  strategic management and, 6, 7
Terrorism, economic effect of,
  289
Terrorist attacks of September
  11, 2001, 67, 355
Threat
  business-level strategies and,
    131
  defined, 69
  of new entrants, 80–82
  of substitute products, 83–84
Top management teams
  acquisitions and, 254
  CEO's role, 38–39
  corporate governance and,
    303–304, 323–324
  defined, 36
  diversification and, 233, 308
  entrepreneurial culture and,
    337, 341
  ethical behavior of, 323–324

  executive compensation and,
    315
  executive succession processes
    and, 39–41, *41*
  heterogeneity in, 36–37
  international entrepreneurship
    and, 338
  international strategies and,
    289–290
  and managerial opportun-
    ism, 307
  product diversification and,
    212
  strategic thinking and, 18
Total quality management
  (TQM), 101, 150–151
Trade groups, 188
Transaction costs, 251–252
Transaction costs economics, 9,
  10, 17
Transformational leadership, 31
Transnational strategy, 277–279
Trust
  cooperative strategies and,
    202–203
  intangible resources and, 102
  strategic alliances and, 284

Uncertain future cash flows, 231
Uncertainty, 99, *99*, 340, 354–
  355, 368, 381
Uncertainty-reducing alliances,
  193, 194
Unique historical conditions, 109
United States
  corporate governance and,
    303, 320
  population size, 72
  retirement trends in, 70
Unrelated diversification strategy,
  214, *216*, 217, 225–229, *228*,
  249, 253

Valuable capabilities, 107–108
Valuable resources, 13
Valuation
  Black-Scholes valuation, 370–
    371, *372*, 380–381
  real option valuation guide-
    lines, 370–381
Value, defined, 101
  *See also* Value creation
Value chain, 110–111, *111*, *112*,
  113, 129–130, 135
Value chain analysis, 110–114,
  135, 141